CASES AND MATERIALS ON IRISH COMPANY LAW

Second Edition

D1649955

AUSTRALIA

LBC Information Services
Sydney

CANADA AND THE USA

Carswell

NEW ZEALAND
Brooker's
Auckland

SINGAPORE AND MALAYSIA
Thompson Information (S.E. Asia)
Singapore

Cases and Materials
on
Irish Company Law

2nd edition

MICHAEL FORDE, S.C.

B.A. (Mod.) and LL.B. (Dublin),
LL.M. (Brussels),
Ph.D. (Cantab.)
of King's Inns and Middle Temple
Barrister-at-Law

ROUND HALL SWEET & MAXWELL
1998

Published in 1998 by
Round Hall Sweet & Maxwell
Brehon House, 4 Upper Ormond Quay,
Dublin 7.

Typeset by
Gilbert Gough Typesetting, Dublin.

Printed by
MPG Books Ltd., Cornwall.

ISBN 1–899738–47–9

A catalogue record for this book
is available from the British Library.

Contents

Foreword

(to the first edition)

Those involved in commercial affairs today, be it as managers of businesses or as professional advisors, need to have a knowledge of Company Law.

It is a complex subject and until recently there were no books dealing with Irish Company Law.

Within the last two years, however, several excellent books on the subject have been published, including Dr Forde's *Company Law in Ireland* (1985, The Mercier Press), for which I had the pleasure of writing the Foreword.

Dr Forde has not rested on his laurels but has applied his wealth of knowledge and industry to writing this book, *Cases on Irish Company Law*, which should prove an invaluable complement to his earlier book.

Exhaustive as are the Companies Acts, there are many important areas of company law which are governed primarily by case law, either because there are no statutory provisions relating thereto or because the relevant statute gives the Courts a wide discretion.

As this book *Cases on Irish Company Law* so ably demonstrates, there is a wealth of cases on Company Law and this case book illustrates the major contribution made by the Irish Judiciary to the development of Company Law in this country.

Dr Forde's case book is a very welcome addition to Irish legal literature, providing as it does, in one volume, all the relevant cases.

He and his publishers, The Mercier Press, are to be congratulated for their combined efforts, which have resulted in this excellent production.

Liam Hamilton
President of the High Court

October 1986

Acknowledgements

I wish to thank the following for generously allowing me to reproduce copyright material: The Stationery Office for *The Statutes*; The Incorporated Council of Law Reporting for Ireland for *The Irish Reports*; The Round Hall Press for the *Irish Law Reports Monthly*; the Incorporated Council of Law Reporting for England and Wales for the *Law Reports*; Butterworth & Co. Ltd. for the *All England Law Reports* and the *British Company Law Cases*; the Scottish Council of Law Reporting and Messrs. T. & T. Clark for the *Session Cases*; Butterworih & Co. (N.Z.) Ltd. for the *New Zealand Law Reports*.

Preface

This book is simply a collection of the major cases on Irish Company Law, which it is hoped will prove useful to the student of the subject and to commercial law practitioners The law regarding registered companies is governed principally by the Companies Act 1963, and by the Amendment Acts of 1977, 1982, 1983, 1986 and 1990. Nevertheless, much of the law is contained in the cases. Indeed, on many of the most important aspects of the subject there are no directly relevant legislative provisions but there is an abundance of cases. Thus, mastering the cases is essential in order to understand Company Law

Since Company Law in this country was originally United Kingdom Law, and because the Companies Acts 1963–1986 are identical in numerous respects to U.K. law, the U.K. cases are highly relevant to the law here. Of the 138 cases reproduced in this book, 57 are decisions of the Irish Courts and the remainder are decisions of the English and Scottish courts, and also of the Australian and New Zealand courts.

In this second edition of the book, I have chosen to include some of the most important of the statutory provisions and also the provisions of Table A. Important as the case law may be, one risks getting the wrong overall picture unless the statutory framework is kept in mind. I have not included any cases on examinership or on liquidation; constraints of space made it impossible to publish a representative number of cases on corporate insolvency. Perhaps as an act of extravagant self-indulgence, I have included the contents of the written submissions made in one of the cases in which I appeared as counsel (p. 87), and perhaps more audaciously, I have added a criticism of the Supreme Court's judgment in another case in which I appeared (p. 131). This book can perhaps be best used in conjunction with my *Company Law* (2nd edition, 1992). The cases are set out in accordance with the sequence of that book; and the reader should consult that book to see if the law as stated in some of the cases has been changed by legislation or in the light of other cases.

I wish to thank Catherine, Patrick and Peter for their patience while I assembled this book, and also Therese Carrick of Round Hall Sweet & Maxwell and Gilbert Gough for their persistence and assistance in getting it completed Once again I wish to thank the Honourable Mr Justice Liam Hamilton (who is currently the Chief Justice) for his most gracious forward.

Michael Forde
Halloween 1998

Table of Cases

Ireland

Other jurisdictions
(England, Australia, New Zealand, United States of America)

Other Tables

Irish Constitution 1937

Acts of Great Brtiain, Ireland and the United Kingdom pre–1922

Ireland post 1922

New Zealand

Table of Statutory Instruments

European Treaties

CHAPTER 1

Introductory

CHARTERED AND STATUTORY CORPORATIONS

See *Company Law*, pp 4-7.

The Bank of Ireland is a chartered corporation which is quoted on the Stock Exchange and is one of the two principal banks in the State, and also has an extensive branch network in the U.K. and, via a wholly-owned subsidiary, in the U.S.A. The Bank's affairs are managed in accordance with its charter, which has been amended on several occasions.

Act for Establishing the Bank of Ireland
21 & 22 Geo. Ill, c. 16, 1781-82

WHEREAS it will tend to the advancement of publick credit in this kingdom, and to the extension of its trade and commerce if a bank with publick security, shall be established therein; be it enacted by the King's most excellent Majesty by and with the advice and consent of the lords spiritual and temporal and commons in this present Parliament assembled, and by the authority of the same, That it shall and may be lawful to and for your Majesty, your heirs and successors, by commission under the great seal of Ireland, to authorize and appoint any number of persons, at any time after the first day of August next, to take and receive all such voluntary subscriptions as shall be made on or before the first day of January which shall be in the year of our Lord one thousand seven hundred and eighty four by any person or persons, natives or foreigners, bodies politick or corporate, for and towards the raising and paying into the receipt of your Majesty's treasury in this kingdom the sum of six hundred thousand pounds sterling, to be paid in money or by debentures which have been or shall be issued from your Majesty's treasury, by virtue of any act or acts of Parliament heretofore, and in this present session made in this kingdom, bearing an interest at the rate of four pounds per centum per annum, which debentures shall be taken at par from such subscriber or subscribers, and be considered as money by the persons to whom the same shall be paid; for which sums so to be subscribed, a sum, by way of annuity, equal in amount to the interest upon said debentures, at the rate of four pounds per centum per annum, shall be paid at your Majesty's treasury in manner herein after mentioned.

II. And be it enacted by the authority aforesaid, That if from competition for a preference amongst the persons desiring to subscribe, they shall be willing to pay or advance any sum or sums, by way of premium for obtaining such preference or permission to subscribe; in that case the amount of such sum so advanced and paid, over and above the said sum of six hundred thousand pounds to the said commissioners impowered to receive such subscriptions, and premiums for such preference or permission, shall be applied towards any purposes for the beginning or better carrying on the business of the said bank, and also towards the erecting a proper building and convenient accommodation for the same, pursuant to such plan as shall be furnished by said commissioners; which plan and situation for such building, shall be subject to the approbation of the lord lieutenant, or other chief governor or governors of this kingdom for the time being.

III. And be it further enacted by the authority aforesaid, That it shall and may be lawful to and for your Majesty, your heirs and successors, by letters patent under the great seal of Ireland, to limit, direct, and appoint, how and in what manner and proportions, and under what rules and directions the said sum of six hundred thousand pounds sterling, and every or any part or proportion thereof, may be assignable or transferable, assigned or transferred to such person or persons only as shall freely and voluntarily accept of the same, and not otherwise, and to incorporate all and every such subscribers and contributors, their executors, administrators, successors, or assigns, to be one body politick and corporate, by the name of the Governor and Company of the Bank of Ireland; and by the same name of the Governor and Company of the Bank of Ireland, to have perpetual succession, and a common seal; and that they and their successors, by the name aforesaid, shall be able and capable in law, to have, purchase, receive, possess, enjoy, and retain to them, and their successors, lands, rents, tenements and hereditaments of what kind, nature or quality soever, and also to sell, grant, alien, demise, or dispose of the same; and by the same name to sue and implead, and be sued and impleaded, answer and be answered in courts of record, or any other places whatsoever, and to do and execute all and singular other matters and things by the name aforesaid, that to them shall or may appertain to do, subject nevertheless, to the proviso or condition of redemption herein after mentioned. Etc. Etc.

[This Act, has twenty-five sections in all]

The Bank's Acts

Acts of the Parliament of Ireland

Session and Chapter	Title or Short Title
21 & 22 Geo III. c. 16.	An Act for establishing a Bank by the name of the Governor and Company of the Bank of Ireland.
31 Geo. III. c. 22.	An Act to extend the provisions of an Act, passed in

	the 21st and 22nd years of His Majesty's reign entitled An Act, for establishing a Bank by the Name of the Governor and Company of the Bank of Ireland.
37 Geo. III. c. 50.	An Act for further extending the provisions of an Act, passed in the 21st and 22nd years of His Majesty's reign entitled An Act, for establishing a Bank by the name of the Governor and Company of the Bank of Ireland.

Acts of the United Kingdom Parliament

48 Geo. III. c. 103.	The Bank of Ireland Act, 1808.
1 & 2 Geo. W. c. 72.	The Bank of Ireland Act, 1821.
1 Will. IV. c. 32.	An Act, to explain two Acts of His present Majesty for establishing an agreement with the Governor and Company of the Bank of Ireland, for advancing the sum of £500,000 Irish currency and for the better regulation of co-partnerships of certain bankers in Ireland.
8 & 9 Vic. c. 37.	The Bankers (Ireland) Act, 1845.
23 & 24 Vic. c. 31.	The Bank of Ireland Act, 1860.
27 & 28 Vic. c. 78.	The Bank Notes (Ireland) Act, 1864.
35 & 36 Vic. c. 5.	The Bank of Ireland Charter Amendment Act, 1872.

Acts of the Oireachtas

Year and Number

1929 no. 4 (Private)	The Bank of Ireland Act, 1929 (infra).
1935 no. 1 (Private)	The Bank of Ireland Act, 1935 (infra).

Bank of Ireland Act 1929

(1) Notwithstanding anything to the contrary contained in the Charter or in the Bank's Acts.

    (a) no banking company registered outside Saorstát Éireann or banking corporation trust or other company carrying on its principal business outside Saorstát Éireann shall be qualified to vote or capable of voting at any general court or otherwise through a trustee nominee or other person or otherwise in any matter relating to the affairs or government of the Bank, and

    (b) the members of the Bank duly assembled in a general court may from time to time by resolution reduce or increase as they think fit the number of the Directors (exclusive of the Governor and the Deputy Governor) of the Bank and fix the amount of capital stock of the Bank which must be held as their qualifications by the Governor Deputy Governor and Directors respectively and may from time to time fix the quorum of Directors necessary for the transaction of business, and

(c) the Governor and Deputy Governor and at least three fourths of the other directors shall be domiciled and resident in Saorstát Éireann, and

(d) all members of the Bank holding the amount of the capital stock of the Bank necessary to qualify them to vote shall have the same rights of voting at general courts whether the capital stock of the Bank of which they are the registered holders or any part thereof is held by them in their own right or in trust for any other person or persons or for any company or corporation not disqualified to vote by paragraph (a) of this sub-section: Provided that where capital stock in the Bank is held in trust for the same company corporation person or persons by different members of the Bank not more than one of such members of the Bank shall be entitled to vote at any general court, and

(e) where capital stock of the bank is registered in the names of two or more persons as joint holders thereof any one of such persons shall have the same right to vote at any general court as if he were solely entitled thereto and if more than one of such joint holders be present at any general court that one of the said persons so present whose name stands first on the register in respect of such capital stock shall alone be entitled to vote, and

(f) any company or corporation holding the amount of the capital stock of the Bank necessary to entitle members to vote for the period prescribed by the Charter and not being disqualified to vote by paragraph (a) of this sub-section may by resolution of its directors or governing body appoint any person to vote at any general court and the person so appointed shall have the same right of voting at such general court on behalf of the company or corporation by which he shall have been appointed as if he were a member of the Bank: Provided that a duly authenticated copy of such resolution shall in every case be sent or delivered to the Secretary of the Bank at least seven days before the holding of the general court or courts at which such person is to be entitled to vote on behalf of such company or corporation, and

(g) at any general court a poll of the members of the Bank qualified to vote at general courts may be demanded by the Chairman presiding at such general court or by at least nine other persons qualified to vote and personally present and if a poll is duly demanded it shall be taken in such manner and at such time and place as the Chairman shall direct and the result of the poll shall be deemed to be the resolution of the general court at which the poll was demanded, and

(h) any member of the Bank holding the amount of the capital stock of the Bank necessary to qualify members to vote may be required by the Directors to declare by statutory declaration whether he is entitled to the capital stock of which he is the registered holder in his own right or otherwise and if the whole or any part of such capital stock is held by him otherwise than in his own right to disclose and specify every company corporation person or persons in trust for whom or on whose behalf he holds the same and where any member has been required to make such declaration as aforesaid the making by him of such declaration shall be a condition precedent to the right of such member to vote at any general court, and

(i) the Bank shall not absorb any other bank without the consent in writing of the Minister for Finance previously obtained, and

(j) the Bank shall not be absorbed by any other bank corporation trust or other company whatsoever, and

(k) notwithstanding any notice of any trust the Bank so far as not restrained by Order or Rules of Court shall pay the dividends on the capital stock of the Bank for the time being to the members of the Bank appearing from the Register to be the owners thereof and shall allow such members to sell and transfer such capital stock, and

(l) the members of the Bank may by bye-laws duly made under the Charter determine the number of general courts to be held in every year and may for that purpose reduce or increase as they think fit the number of such general courts as fixed by the Charter or by such bye-laws, but so that no less than one general court shall be held in every year, and

(m) the members of the Bank may by bye-laws duly made under the Charter appoint the days on which general courts shall be held, and

(n) whenever the number of general courts is fixed or the dates for holding general courts are appointed by such bye-laws, general courts shall be summoned in accordance with such bye-laws and not otherwise.

(2) Nothing in this section shall prejudice or affect the summoning at any time in accordance with the Charter of a general court on the demand of nine or more members of the Bank qualified as mentioned in the Charter.

Bank of Ireland Act, 1935, §2

Notwithstanding anything contained in the Act of the Irish Parliament passed in the 21st and 22nd years of the reign of His late Majesty King George the Third and entitled 'An Act for establishing a bank by the name of the Governors and Company of the Bank of Ireland' or contained in the Charter or Letters Patent under the Great Seal of Ireland [on] the 10th day of May, 1783 and granted by His said late Majesty in pursuance of the said Act, by which a Bank was established and a Company was incorporated by the name of the Governor and Company of the Bank of Ireland hereinafter called the Bank or contained in the Acts amending the same or any of them, no past or present member of the Bank shall, in the event of a winding up, be liable to contribute towards the debts or liabilities of the Bank to an amount exceeding the amount, if any, unpaid on the stock of the Bank held by him at the date of the commencement of the winding up or within the period of twelve months prior to that date. . . .

Several of the State-owned enterprises are statutory corporations, which have been established by special Acts of the Oireachtas, *e.g.* the Voluntary Health Insurance Board.

Voluntary Health Insurance Act 1957

Establishment of the Board

3.—(1) There shall, by virtue of this section, be established on the establishment day a board to be styled and known as the Voluntary Health Insurance Board to fulfil the functions assigned to it by this Act.

(2) The Board shall be a body corporate with perpetual succession and power to sue and be sued in its corporate name and to acquire, hold and dispose of land.

Several other State-owned enterprises are companies registered under the Companies Acts but having special features which are provided for in particular Acts of the Oireachtas, *e.g.* An Post and Bord Telecom Éireann.

Postal and Telecommunications Services Act 1983

Formation of companies

9.—(1) The Minister after consultation with the Minister for Finance, shall cause two limited companies conforming to the conditions laid down in this Act to be formed and registered under the Companies Acts.

(2) The Minister shall by order appoint a day to be the vesting day for each

of the two companies as soon as practicable after the companies have been registered.

Names and capital formation of companies

10.—(1) The names of the companies shall be, respectively–

(a) An Post or, in the English language, The Post Office, and

(b) Bord Telecom Éireann or, in the English language, The Irish Telecommunications Board.

(2) Each company shall be exempt from the requirement of section 6(1)(a) of the Companies Act, 1963, to include the word "limited" or "teoranta" in its title.

(3) (a) Subject to *paragraph* (c), the authorised share capital of An Post shall be an amount not exceeding the total of the following–
  (i) the value of the property to be transferred to the company on the vesting day under *sections 40* and *41*,
  (ii) the amount of money which may be made available to the company under *section 29(1)* to finance capital works, and
  (iii) the amount of working capital to be made available to the company under *section 31*,
divided into shares of one pound each.

(b) Subject to *paragraph* (c), the authorised share capital of Bord Telecom Éireann shall be an amount not exceeding the total of the following–
  (i) the value of the proverty to be transferred to the company on the vesting day under *sections 40* and *41*, less the amount by which sums issued by the Minister for Finance under the Telecommunications Capital Acts, 1924 to 1981, which have not been repaid before that day exceed the sum of £355,000,000 plus the amount of the outstanding liability of the Minister to Irish Telecommunications Investments Limited immediately before the vesting day, and
  (ii) the amount of working capital to be made available to the company under *section 31*,
divided into shares of one pound each.

(c) The totals obtained under *paragraphs* (a) and (b) shall, if required. be rounded upwards to the nearest £500,000 or £1,000,000, as the case may be.

(d) Each company may, with the consent of the Minister and the Minister for Finance, divide the shares in its share capital into several classes and attach thereto respectively any preferential, deferred, qualified or special rights. privileges or conditions.

Form of memorandum of association

11.—The memorandum of association of each company shall be in such form consistent with this Act as may be approved of by the Minister with the consent of the Minister for Finance.

Principal objects of postal company

12.—(1) The principal objects of the postal company shall be stated in its memorandum of association to be–

(*a*) to provide a national postal service within the State and between the State and places outside the State,

(*b*) to meet the industrial, commercial, social and household needs of the State for comprehensive and efficient postal services and, so far as the company considers reasonably practicable, to satisfy all reasonable demands for such services throughout the State,

(*c*) to provide services by which money may be remitted (whether by means of money orders, postal orders or otherwise) as the company thinks fit,

(*d*) to provide counter services for the company's own and Government business and, provided that they are compatible with those services and with the other principal objects set out in this subsection, for others as the company thinks fit, and

(*e*) to provide such consultancy, advisory, training and contract services inside and outside the State as the company thinks fit.

(2) Nothing in this section shall prevent or restrict the inclusion among the objects of the company as stated in its memorandum of association of all such objects and powers as are reasonably necessary or proper for or incidental or ancillary to the due attainment of the principal objects aforesaid and are not inconsistent with this Act.

(3) The company shall have power to do anything which appears to it to be requisite, advantageous or incidental to, or which appears to it to facilitate, either directly or indirectly, the performance by it of its functions as specified in this Act or in its memorandum of association and is not inconsistent with any enactment for the time being in force.

General duty of postal company

13.—(1) It shall be the general duty of the postal company to conduct the company's affairs so as to ensure that–

    (*a*) charges for services are kept at the minimum rates consistent with meeting approved financial targets, and

    (*b*) revenues of the company are not less than sufficient to-

        (i) meet all charges properly chargeable to revenue account (including depreciation of assets and proper allocation to general reserve) taking one year with another,

        (ii) generate a reasonable proportion of capital needs, and

        (iii) remunerate capital and repay borrowings.

(2) Nothing in *section 12* or this section shall imposing on the company, either directly or indirectly duty or liability enforceable by proceedings before any court to which it would not otherwise be subject.

Principal objects of telecommunications company

    14.—(similar to section 12).

General duty of telecommunications company

    15.—(similar to section 13).

Articles of association

    16.—(1) The articles of association of each company shall be in such form consistent with this Act as may be approved of by the Minister with the consent of the Minister for Finance and, where appropriate, the consent of the Minister for the Public Service.

    (2) The articles of association of each company shall provide that–

    (*a*) the number of directors (including the chairman) shall be at least 12 or such greater number as the Minister with the consent of the Minister for Finance may determine from time to time;

    (*b*) the chairman and other directors shall be appointed and may be removed from office by the Minister with the consent of the Minister for Finance;

    (*c*) the remuneration of the chairman and other directors shall be determined by the Minister with the consent of the Minister for the Public Service;

    (*d*) no person shall be appointed as auditor of the company without the approval of the Minister given with the consent of the Minister for Finance;

(*e*) the company shall, in consultation and agreement with recognised trade unions and staff associations, set up machinery for the purposes of negotiations concerned with the pay and conditions of service of its staff;

(*f*) the company shall not invest in any other undertaking without the approval of the Minister given with the consent of the Minister for Finance.

(3) The articles of association of the postal company shall provide that the company shall, in consultation and agreement with recognised unions and associations, set up machinery for the purposes of negotiations concerning the remuneration and other contractual conditions of postmasters.

Restriction no alteration of memorandum or articles of association

17.—Notwithstanding anything contained in the Companies Acts, memorandum or no alteration in the memorandum of association or articles of association of either company shall be valid or effectual unless made with the prior approval of the Minister given with the consent of the Minister for Finance and, where appropriate, the consent of the Minister for the Public Service. Any proposed alteration shall be notified by the company to recognised trade unions and staff associations and recognised unions and associations.

Index to 1983 Act's other sections

HARMONISATION OF COMPANY LAW

See *Company Law*, pp.27–33.

The European Communities have been most influential in the field of Company Law and the EC Council has issued a considerable number of Directives on the subject, some of which have been implemented in Ireland by Acts of the Oireachtas and many others by way of statutory instrument. Until they have been so implemented, E.C. Directives do not create legally enforceable rights and obligations as between private individuals and organisations. But public bodies and agencies are bound by and have legally enforceable obligations arising from those Directives. Notwithstanding that formal steps have not been taken to fully implement them into Irish law, public bodies or agencies are in a sense estopped from relying on the E.C. Directive in question not being so implemented. Additionally, the provision in question in the Directive must be unconditional and sufficiently precise to be capable of imposing enforceable obligations. There has been very little reported case law at the European Court level regarding the Company Law Directives, other than on Directive 69/335 concerning Capital Duties.

Ministere Public v. Blanguernon
Case C38/89 [1991] B.C.L.C. 635

Blanguernon was the financial director of a private limited liability company, governed by French law, and a member of a group which specialised in packing. That group has to face competition from foreign manufacturers, in particular German and Italian producers.

On instructions Blanguernon did not lodge group annual accounts at the Registry of the Tribunal de Commerce, within one month of their approval by the shareholders in general meeting. As a result of that failure, a prosecution was brought against him.

At the hearing, he claimed that the Law of 30 April 1983 and the Decree of 29 November 1983, enacted for the purpose of bringing French internal law into line with the Fourth Council Company Law Directive were prejudicial to French companies. French companies are required to publish their accounts, while German and Italian companies are under no such obligation. Italy and of Germany had not adopted measures similar to the French Law and Decree in implementation of the directive.

[640] 11 January 1990. THE COURT OF JUSTICE delivered the following judgment.

1. By judgment dated 30 June 1988, which was received at the court on 16 February 1989, the Tribunal de Police, Aix-les-Bains, referred to the court for a preliminary ruling under art 177 of the EEC Treaty a question on the interpretation of art 54(3) (9) of the EEC Treaty and the Fourth Council Directive (78/660/EEC) Of 25 July 1978 on the annual accounts of certain types of companies.

2. That question was raised in the course of criminal proceedings against Mr Blanguernon, the financial director of PAKEM, a private limited liability company, who is charged with failing to lodge the annual accounts of that company at the Registry of the Tribunal de Commerce [Commercial Court], Chambéry, within the month following their approval by the general meeting of shareholders.

3. A failure of that kind is punishable under the French legislation laying down accounting requirements for traders and certain companies. The purpose of that legislation is to transpose into French law the provisions of the Fourth Directive, which is based on art 54(3)(g) of the Treaty. That article provides for the adoption of directives co-ordinating to the necessary extent the safeguards which, for the protection of the interests of members and others, are required by member states of the companies or firms referred to in the second paragraph of art 58 of the Treaty with a view to making such safeguards equivalent throughout the Community.

4. Before the national court, Mr Blanguernon claimed that the application of the French legislation concerning accounting requirements was prejudicial to French companies in as much as they were obliged to publish their accounts while their competitors in other member states were under no such obligation. [641] Certain member states had not adopted measures to implement the Fourth Directive.

5. In view of that argument the Tribunal de police, Aix-les-Bains, decided to stay the proceedings and seek a preliminary ruling from the court on the

following question:

> 'Is it in accordance with the wording and spirit of art 54(3)(g) of the EEC Treaty and the Fourth Council Directive of 25 July 1978 for national laws enacted pursuant thereto to enter into force individually so long as not all the member states have adopted equivalent legislation, which is a necessary condition for the simultaneous co-ordination required by the Fourth Directive?'

6. Reference is made to the report for the hearing for a fuller account of the facts of the case in the main proceedings, the course of the procedure and the observations submitted to the court, which are mentioned or discussed hereinafter only in so far as is necessary for the reasoning of the court.

7. It must first of all be pointed out that, as the court has consistently held, a member state may not rely on the fact that other member states have also failed to perform their obligations in order to justify its own failure to fulfil its obligations under the Treaty (see, in particular, the judgment of 26 February 1976 in *EC Commission v. Italy* Case 52/75 [1976] ECR 277). In the legal order established by the Treaty, the implementation of Community law by the member states cannot be made subject to a condition of reciprocity. Articles 169 and 170 of the Treaty provide the appropriate remedies in cases where member states fail to fulfil their obligations under the Treaty.

8. It follows that the national law of a member state giving effect to a Community directive must have full force, even if the directive in question has not yet been transposed and implemented in the legislation of other member states.

9. This also applies to national legislation giving effect to the Fourth Directive based on art. 54(3)(g) of the Treaty. That directive and that article refer to the equivalence of the safeguards required by member states for the protection of the interests of members and others only in order to specify the degree of harmonisation to be achieved. It cannot, therefore, be inferred from that aim that the applicability of measures implementing the Fourth Directive in a member state is conditional upon the adoption of equivalent measures in all the other member states.

10. The answer to the national court's question must therefore be that art. 54(3)(g) of the Treaty and the Fourth Council Directive (78/660/EEC) of 25 July 1978 on the annual accounts of certain types of companies must be interpreted as meaning that the legislation of member states intended to implement that directive must be brought into force and applied even if other member states have not yet adopted measures to implement the directive.

11. The costs incurred by the French government and the Commission, which have submitted observations to the court, are not recoverable. Since these proceedings are, in so far as the parties to the main proceedings are concerned, in the nature of a step in the proceedings pending before the national court, the decision on costs is a matter for that court.

On those grounds, the court (Fourth Chamber), in answer to the question submitted to it by the Tribunal de Police, Aix-les-Bains, by judgment of 30 June 1988, hereby rules: art 54(3)(9) of the EEC Treaty and the Fourth Council Directive (78/660/EEC) of 25 July 1978 on the annual accounts of certain types of companies must be interpreted as meaning that the legislation of member states intended to implement that directive must be brought into force and applied even if other member states have not yet adopted measures to implement the directive.

CHAPTER 2

Company Formation

A most convenient way of setting up business as a registered company is to buy an already-formed company from one of those firms of solicitors or accountants that specialise in selling companies 'off-the-shelf'. The purchasers would then make whatever alterations to that company they deem necessary, such as changing its name, the address of its registered office, directors, capital structure, articles of association and the like. Alternatively, they may decide to form a new company themselves, which in any event is not a particularly onerous or complex task. Essentially all that is needed is two founders and a signed memorandum and articles of association; these documents must be accompanied by a statutory declaration and a cheque for capital tax, and be registered with the registrar of companies. A number of additional formalities must be complied with before some companies can commence doing business.

THE PRINCIPAL KINDS OF REGISTERED COMPANIES

See *Company Law*, pp. 34–38.

Single Member Private Limited Companies. In 1994 the 12th Council Directive on Company Law, Directive 89/667 on Single Member Private Limited Companies, was implemented by S.I. No. 275 of 1994.

MEMORANDUM OF ASSOCIATION

See *Company Law*, pp. 38–41

Companies Act 1963 Act, section 5

Way of forming incorporated company

5.—(1) Any seven or more persons or, where the company to be formed will be a private company, any two or more persons, associated for any lawful purpose may, by subscribing their names to a memorandum of association and otherwise complying with the requirements of this Act relating to registration, form an incorporated company, with or without limited liability.

TABLE B
FORM OF MEMORANDUM OF ASSOCIATION OF A COMPANY LIMITED BY SHARES

1. The name of the company is "The Western Mining Company, Limited".

2. The objects for which the company is established are the mining of minerals of all kinds and the doing of all such other things as are incidental or conducive to the attainment of the above object.

3. The liability of the members is limited.

4. The share capital of the company is £200,000, divided into 200,000 shares of £1 each.

We, the several persons whose names and addresses are subscribed, wish to be formed into a company in pursuance of this memorandum of association, and we agree to take the number of shares in the capital of the company set opposite our respective names.

Names, Addresses and Descriptions of Subscribers	Number (of Shares taken by each Subscriber

1.   James Walsh of ....
        in the County of ....
        Solicitor.
	50

2.   John Murphy of ....
        in the County of ....
        Engineer.
	2,700

3.   Patrick Ryan of ....
        in the County of ....
        Geologist.
	1,250

4.   Thomas O'Connell of ....
        in the County of ....
        Engineer.
	500

5.   Daniel Clarke of ....
        in the County of ....
        Geologist ....
	50

6.   Patrick Byrne of ....
        in the County of ....
        Accountant
	300

7.   John Collins of ....
        in the County of ....
        Solicitor.
	150

Total Shares taken	5,000

Dated the .... day of ...., 19......

Witness to the above Signatures:

Name:
Address:

ARTICLES BY ASSOCIATION

See *Company Law*, pp. 41–42.

Companies Act 1963 Act, sections 11 and 13(1) and (2)

Articles prescribing regulations for companies

11.—There may, in the case of a company limited by shares, and there shall, in the case of a company limited by guarantee or unlimited, be registered with the memorandum articles of association signed by the subscribers to the memorandum and prescribing regulations for the company.

Adoption and application of Table A or Tábla A

13.—(1) Articles of association may adopt all or any of the regulations contained in Table A, or of the equivalent regulations in the Irish language contained in Tábla A.

(2) In the case of a company limited by shares and registered after the operative date, if articles are not registered or, if articles are registered, in so far as the articles do not exclude or modify the regulations contained in Table A, those regulations shall, so far as applicable, be the regulations of the company in the same manner and to the same extent as if they were contained in duly registered articles.

TABLE A.

PART 1.

REGUULATIONS FOR MANAGEMENT OF A COMPANY LIMITED BY SHARES NOT BEING A PRIVATE COMPANY

Interpretation

1. In these regulations:

"the Act" means the Companies Act, 1963 (No. 33 of 1963);

"the directors" means the directors for the time being of the company or the directors present at a meeting of the board of directors and includes any person occupying the position of director by whatever name called;

"the register" means the register of members to be kept as required by section 116 of the Act;

"secretary" means any person appointed to perform the duties of the secretary of the company;

"the office" means the registered office for the time being of the company;

"the seal" means the common seal of the company.

Expressions referring to writing shall, unless the contrary intention appears, be construed as including references to printing, lithography, photography, and any other modes of representing or reproducing words in a visible form.

Unless the contrary intention appears, words or expressions contained in these regulations shall bear the same meaning as in the Act or in any statutory modification thereof in force at the date at which these regulations become binding, on the company.

Index to Articles

Bratton Seymour Service Co. Ltd. v. Oxborough
[1992] B.C.L.C. 693

The defendant bought land and a substantial house from a company that had been set up to develop that land and surrounding property. The deed of conveyance said nothing about certain common areas, notably tennis courts, a swimming pool and gardens. As was envisaged, the plaintiff company was incorporated as a management company, which would hold certain common parts of the estate; its members would be residents of the various residential units that had been built. The common areas referred to above were conveyed to the company. The members/residents contended that the defendant, who resided in one of the flats and was a shareholder, must contribute towards the upkeep of those areas because such obligation was implicit in the company's articles of

DILLON L.J. [696]: It is the submission of the company, which the learned judge upheld, that by necessary implication and in order to give business efficacy to the scheme which the promoters of the company had in mind in relation to the management of the Bratton House estate, there is to be implied into the articles of association of the company the obligation, which the judge declared, to contribute 'such reasonable contribution, determined by the Company, towards the expenses reasonably incurred of maintaining both the utility and the amenity areas of the Bratton House development'. The judge limited the contribution in relation to the utilities because of the covenants which I have mentioned which Mr Oxborough and other purchasers entered into, and the benefit of those covenants was assigned by the development company to the present plaintiff company.

I see insuperable difficulties in the way of any such implication into the articles of association of the company. It is said, 'Oh, the articles constitute a contract between the company and its members, and so you can imply any term into such a contract as you can imply any term into any other contract in order to give business efficacy'. But the articles of association of a company differ very considerably from a normal contract. They are a document which has statutory force. If a company, limited by shares, chooses to have articles of association instead of merely relying on Table A, then those articles have to be registered. These articles were registered when the company was incorporated. The articles thus registered are one of the statutory documents of the company open for inspection by anyone minded to deal with the company or to take shares in the company. It is thus a consequence, as was held by this court in *Scott v. Frank F. Scott (London) Ltd* [1940] Ch. 794, that the court has no jurisdiction to rectify the articles of association of a company, even if those articles do not accord with what is proved to have been the concurrent intention of the signatories of the memorandum at the moment of signature.

It is because of the statutory force of the articles, when registered, that that conclusion was reached. The articles, if not in accordance with the intention of the subscribers, have to be altered by the statutory procedure of a special resolution if the appropriate majority of the members agree to such an alteration. There is the further restriction that the company cannot, by an alteration of its articles, impose an extra burden of contribution on a member who does not [697] vote in favour of the alteration. That was introduced into company law by way of clarification in the Companies Act, 1928 and is now to be found in s.16(2) of the Companies Act 1985 [s.27 of the 1963 Act] . Of course, Mr Asprey, appearing for the company in this court, does not seek to rely on alteration of the articles. He says that he can get round that difficulty by implication into the original articles at the time the company was incorporated. But there is nothing in the articles to give any hint of any contribution by the members to the maintenance of the utilities or the amenity areas or anything else. He has to reach his implication by taking into account surrounding circumstances not apparent from the articles themselves or from the memorandum.

On the facts, what was in issue in *Scott v. Scott Ltd* was whether the executor of a deceased member of a company was bound to offer the deceased member's shares in the company to the other members at par. It was said that the common intention of the subscribers was that if one of the subscribers died the others should be entitled to acquire his shares at par. When one died his widow and sole executrix claimed, by virtue not of any special provision in the articles but of her ownership of the shares in the absence of any provision to the contrary in the articles, to be registered in the share register of the company as the owner of her deceased husband's shares in the company. This court held that she was so entitled, and held also, affirming in this respect the decision of the judge at first instance, that the court had no jurisdiction to rectify the articles of association, even if they did not accord with what was proved to have been the concurrent intention of the signatories at the moment of signature.

The argument advanced in the present case of an implied term necessary to give business efficacy to the scheme which the subscribers had formed would, it would seem, have been open to the respondents in *Scott v. Frank F. Scott (London) Ltd* but their counsel, Mr Charles Harman KC, and Mr Winterbotham, apparently did not think of that easy way round their difficulties and they argued instead for the court's right to rectify the articles to bring in a provision obliging the executrix to offer the deceased's shares to the other shareholders at par. I do not need to quote specifically from the judgment of the court delivered by Luxmore L.J. To my mind it is wholly inconsistent with that judgment that there should be any such power in the court to imply a term into the articles of association, such as Mr Asprey has contended for, which arises from the surrounding circumstances not apparent from the terms of the memorandum and articles themselves. In particular, it does not in the least appear from the memorandum and articles themselves that the purchasers of the various parts of the property are going to enter into covenants to contribute to the cost of the utilities but not covenants to contribute to the maintenance of the amenity areas: nor does it appear from the memorandum and articles that there was no intention to form some members' club to run the amenity areas for the benefit of those residents and others who wished to take advantage of the tennis courts and swimming pools.

There is the further point in relation to Mr Oxborough that his conveyance came subsequent to the incorporation of the company, and so at the time of the incorporation of the company it would have been perfectly possible that terms might have been negotiated in his conveyance which did put a contractual obligation on him to contribute to the development company a due proportion, whatever it may have been, of the cost of maintaining the amenity areas. The percentages also that are fixed for contribution to the upkeep of the utilities [698] must make it highly doubtful whether contribution to the upkeep of the amenities was intended to be per shareholding in the company rather than by some other means related to user.

REGISTRATION

See *Company Law*, pp.43–45.

Companies Act 1963 Act, sections 17 and 18(1)

Registration of memorandum and articles

17.—The memorandum and the articles, if any, shall be delivered to the registrar of companies, and he shall retain and register them.

Effect of registration

18.—(1) On the registration of the memorandum of a company the registrar shall certify under his hand that the company is incorporated and, in the case of a limited company, that the company is limited.

Irish Permanent Building Society v. Cauldwell
[1981] I.L.R.M. 242

The Irish Life Building Society (the second named defendant) was registered as a building society by the registrar of Building Societies (the first named defendant) in 1979. The initial capital was provided by the Irish Life Assurance Co. (the third named defendant) which continued to retain an absolute controlling interest in the society's share capital. The major shareholder in Irish Life Building Society was the Minister for Finance, who directed the Irish Life Assurance Co. to provide funds by way of mortgages for house purchase. The board of directors of the Assurance Co. (the fourth named defendant) agreed to do so and founded the Irish Life Building Society. The executives of the Assurance Co. were invited to become founding members of the building society and each individual member acknowledged that he held his share on trust for the Assurance Co. and undertook to use his shares to vote as it would direct. The plaintiffs sought a number of declarations against the defendants. The issue revolved around whether a building society having such close connections with a major financial institution, such as the Irish Life Assurance Co., was registrable under the Building Societies Act, 1976. The plaintiffs submitted that the society was not registrable because it was not an autonomous co-operative society but the subsidiary of another body, the Irish Life Assurance Co.

BARRINGTON J.: . . . [259] I accept that the society is, in all respects, the creature of the Irish Assurance Company Limited. That company decided to set it up; provided its deposit at the Central Bank; assigned employees to be the founding members and the Board of Directors of the society; provided the founding members with their share capital on their undertaking to hold these shares in trust for the company and to use them to vote as directed by it; arranged the share capital so that its nominees could control the constitution of the society and outvote any opposition for the foreseeable future and generally provided the finance to set the society in business. . . .

[261] The real issue in the present case is whether the law permits the kind of relationship which exists between the Irish Life Assurance Company and the [262] Irish Life Building Society. If such a relationship is permissible in law it is permissible and this abstract issue cannot be determined by whether a particular relationship does or does not give rise to possibilities of abuse. If abuses exist they are to be dealt with by the agencies set up to control the activities of Building Societies and Insurance Companies.

The defendants submit that the plaintiffs have failed to grasp the significance of the fact that a building society, under the 1976 Act, is an incorporated body and that certain incidents attach to the fact of incorporation. They submit that it is quite unreal for a great financial institution like the Irish Permanent Building Society to compare itself with the small unincorporated budding societies contemplated by the 1836 Act. When, they say, s.9 of the Building Societies Act, 1874 provided for the incorporation of building societies it opened the way to the formation of a society such as the Irish Life Building Society.

The defendants submit that the plaintiffs have missed the significance of the concept of incorporation, and to illustrate their point, they refer to the judgment of the Court of Appeal in *Salomons Case* (1895) 2 Ch. D. 323.

In that case Salomon caused a limited liability company to be incorporated and the seven subscribers of the memorandum of association consisted of Mr Salomon, his wife, his daughter and his four sons. Twenty thousand shares were issued to Mr Salomon and one share only to each of the other six subscribers to the memorandum of association. Mr Salomon transferred his business to the company, took a floating charge over the company, became managing director and carried on his business as before. The other members of the company were merely his nominees.

Lopes LJ (at page 340 of the report) commented on this situation and his comments are interesting as they almost exactly reproduce the submissions made on behalf of the plaintiffs in the present case. He said:

'The incorporation of the company was perfect – the machinery by which it was framed was in every respect perfect, every detail had been observed; but notwithstanding, the business was, in truth and in fact the business of Aron Salomon; he had the beneficial interest in it; the company was a mere nominis umbra, under cover of which he carried on his business as before, securing himself against loss by a limited liability of £1 per share, all of which shares he practically possessed, and obtaining a priority over unsecured creditors of the company by the debentures of which he had constituted himself the holder. It would be lamentable if a scheme like this could not be defeated. If we were to permit it to succeed, we would be authorising a perversion of the Joint Stock Companies Act. We would be giving vitality to that which is a myth and a fiction. The transaction is a device to apply the machinery of the Joint Stock Companies Act, to a state of things never contemplated by that Act – an ingenious device to obtain the protection of that Act in a way and for objects not authorised by that Act, and in my judgment in a way inconsistent with and opposed to its policy and provisions. It never was intended that the company to be constituted should consist of one substantial person and six mere dummies, the nominees of that person, without any real interest in the company. The Act contemplated the incorporation of seven independent bona fide members, who had a mind and a will of their own, and were not the mere puppets of an individual who, adopting the machinery of the Act, carried on his old business in the same way as before, when he was a sole trader. To legalise such a transaction would be a scandal.'

[263] The significance of these comments for the purposes of the present case is that they were totally rejected by the House of Lords (see post p. 59) as revealing a failure to understand what was involved in the incorporation of a limited liability company under the Companies Act. . . .

The defendants submit that the Oireachtas, in the 1976 Act, by providing that a building society must have at least ten founding members and that it must make a deposit of not less than £20,000 with the Central Bank, has accepted that building societies have changed greatly from the small associations of working men contemplated by the 1836 Act. Likewise, they say the Minister by providing, in effect, by S.I. No. 119 of 1977 that the share qualification of directors must be £10,000 each has recognised the financial importance of building societies and has sought to protect the public by having them run by men of substance. Moreover the defendants say that shortly before the enactment of the 1976 Act, the Norwich Union Insurance Group caused to be formed the Norwich Irish Building Society and the legislature could have been expected to intervene had it considered such a close relationship between an insurance company and a building society to be undesirable.

It therefore appears to me that I should approach this case on the basis that the incidents of incorporation attach to building societies as they do to limited liability companies except in so far as they are affected by the differing provisions of the Companies Act and the Building Societies Act.

The plaintiffs submit that there are relevant distinctions between the Companies Act of 1963 and the Building Societies Act 1976 concerning the formation of a company or building society. Section 5 of the 1963 Act, provides that any seven or more persons, or in the case of a private company, any two or more persons 'associated for any lawful purpose' may by 'subscribing their names' to a memorandum of association form an incorporated company. Section 8 of the 1976 Act, on the other hand provides that any ten or more persons not disqualified by law may form a building society by 'agreeing on rules'.

The plaintiffs submit that an 'agreement' of ten persons contemplates ten individual wills converging on a particular course but, they submit, there can be no [264] agreement if all of the ten persons are nominees of the same person and each is expressing not his own will but the will of the person who nominated him. For the same reason they submit that there can be no delivery of 'agreed' rules under s. 11 of the Building Societies Act as there had in fact been no agreement.

This submission appears to me to be answered in part by the extract from the speech of Lord Herschell in *Salomon's* case (see *post*, p. 60). As a matter of fact I am satisfied that each of the ten founder members of the building society was pleased to act in the formation of the building society and that each of them accepted the rules. In these circumstances I reject the plaintiffs' submission on this score as being based on too fine and metaphysical a distinction to be useful in dealing with practical affairs.

Rex v. Registrar of Companies, ex p. Moore
[1931] 2 K.B. 197

It was sought to register in England a company, the principal object of which was to sell Irish Hospital Sweepstake tickets there.

SLESSER L.J.: [201] It is clear that a company cannot be formed whose proposed constitution necessarily involves an offence against the general law. That was assumed in *Rex v. Registrar of Companies. Ex parte Bowen* [1914] 3 K.B. 1161 and in [202] *Bowman v. Secular Society* [1917] A.C. 406. Mr Beyfus seeks to obtain a rule for a writ of mandamus requiring the Registrar of Companies to register a company, the object of which the Registrar has said is to carry out something which is contrary to law, because of s. 41 of the Lotteries Act, 1823. That section repeats the language of earlier Acts, making it illegal for a person to sell any ticket 'in any lottery or lotteries except such as are or shall be authorised by this or some other Act, of Parliament.' It is not suggested that the lottery which is now being promoted in the Irish Free State is authorised by the Act of 1823, and therefore Mr Beyfus has to find some other Act of Parliament which authorises lottery tickets to be sold in England. He says that it is now lawful to sell these tickets in England, because since the passing of the Irish Free State Constitution Act, 1922, the Irish Free State has power to legislate in that State: see art. 2 of Sch. I. A constitution has been set up for the Irish Free State, and its Parliament in 1930 passed an Act which enables the Minister to sanction schemes for lotteries in Ireland notwithstanding anything to the contrary in any other Act. It still, however, remains for Mr Beyfus to satisfy the Court that the prohibition in s. 41 of the Lotteries Act, 1823, which forbids the selling of lottery tickets in England, has been in any way affected. I cannot accept the contention that the Irish Act is itself an Act of Parliament within the meaning of the exception in s. 41 of the Lotteries Act, 1823. The distinction is made clear throughout the history of the legislation. Thus, it appears that by a statute of George I (6 Geo. I, c. 5) it was enacted by the British Parliament that 'the said kingdom of Ireland hath been, is, and of right ought to be subordinate unto and dependent upon the Imperial Crown of Great Britain, as being inseparably united and annexed thereunto; and that the King's Majesty, by and with the advice and consent of the Lords spiritual and temporal, and Commons of Great Britain in Parliament assembled, had, hath, and of right ought to have full power and authority to [203] make laws and statutes of sufficient force and validity, to bind the Kingdom and people of Ireland.' The position thus stated was altered by 23 Geo. 3, c. 28, which provided (inter alia): 'that the said right claimed by the people of Ireland to be bound only by laws enacted by His Majesty and the Parliament of that Kingdom, in all cases whatever, . . . shall be, and it is hereby declared to be established and ascertained for ever, and shall, at no time hereafter, be questioned or questionable.' So after that date the Irish Parliament had power to pass Acts of Parliament, but only for Ireland. In 1800, by the Act of Union (39 & 40 Geo. 3, c. 67), the two Parliaments were united, and thereafter the words 'some Act of Parliament' mean an Act of Parliament of the United Kingdom. Now looking at the Lotteries Act, 1823, it is clear to me that the words 'some Act, of Parliament', mean some Act of the Imperial Parliament. Although it is true that in 1922 an Act of the United Kingdom set up a Legislature for Ireland, that has not altered the meaning of the expression, 'Act of Parliament' in the Act, of 1823, and it is impossible to say that an Act passed by the Irish legislature is an 'Act of Parliament' within the meaning of s. 41. The Irish Free State Constitution Act, 1922, by Article 2 of the First Schedule provided that 'all authority legislative . . . shall be exercised in the Irish Free State . . . through the organisations established by or under, and in accord with,' the Constitution. It follows that there has been no Act of Parliament within the meaning to be attributed to that expression in s. 41, which authorises the sale of lottery tickets in England. Permission to sell those tickets in Ireland is limited to Ireland, and therefore the sale in England of tickets in connection with the Irish lottery is as illegal now as it was before the Act of 1922.

Note: In *R. v. Registrar of Companies, ex p. Attorney General* [1991] B.C.L.C. 476, the court quashed the registration of a company which was engaged in an unlawful business, *viz.* prostitution. In *Re Senator Hanseatische Verwaltungsgesellschaft mbH* [1996] 2 B.C.L.C. 563 the court ordered the winding up of a German-incorporated company and of a partnership under German law because they were engaged in an unlawful business in England, *viz.* the 'Titan' pyramid scheme, which was held to be a lottery.

CHAPTER 3

Corporate Personality

The principal attraction that the registered company offers over other legal forms of business organisation is that the company has a separate legal personality from that of its owners. When it is said that an individual or thing possesses legal personality what is meant is that he, she or it enjoys rights and is subject to duties under a given legal system. That is to say, within that legal system he, she or it has a distinctive identity and autonomy in that they or it can acquire rights and incur liabilities in respect of themselves or itself, and not merely vicariously on behalf of others. Thus in Ireland neither trees nor dogs possess legal personality, although the law lays down certain rights and obligations that individuals possess and are subject to regarding trees and dogs. In many slave-owning societies, slaves are regarded as not possessing legal personality. Prior to the Married Women's Status Act 1957, married women did not have quite the same legal capacity to act as their spouses. And it has been a matter of considerable political as well as legal controversy whether the human foetus is a legal person, and if it is, to what extent and with what effect. Adult citizens of sound mind, by contrast, possess as complete a legal personality as can exist in Irish law.

THE CONCEPT OF CORPORATE PERSONALITY

See *Company Law*, pp.47-50.

Companies Act 1963, section 18(2)

Effect of registration

(2) From the date of incorporation mentioned in the certificate of incorporation, the subscribers of the memorandum, together with such other persons as may from time to time become members of the company, shall be a body corporate with the name contained in the memorandum, capable forthwith of exercising all the functions of an incorporated company, and having perpetual succession and a common seal, but with such liability on the part of the members to contribute to the assets of the company in the event of its being wound up as is mentioned in this Act.

THE SCOPE OF LEGAL CAPACITY

Tort and Regulatory Liability

See *Company Law*, pp. 65–66.

Meridian Global Funds Management Asia Ltd. v. Securities Commission
[1995] 2 A.C. 500

The chief investment officer of an investment management company and its senior portfolio manager, with the company's authority but unknown to the board of directors and managing director, used funds managed by the company to acquire shares in a public issuer. The company thus became for a short period a substantial security holder in that public issuer, but the company did not give notice thereof as required by section 20(3) of the Securities Amendment Act 1988. The Securities Commission instituted proceedings against the company for failing to comply with that section.

LORD HOFFMANN: [504] Stockmarket regulators have found that one way to help boards and investors to resist such raids is to require immediate disclosure to the target company and the stock exchange of the identity of anyone acquiring a substantial interest of any kind in the company's shares. This enables the board and the investors to know who is behind the respectable nominees. Part 11 of the New Zealand Securities Amendment Act, 1988 was intended, among other things, to introduce such transparency into dealings in publicly quoted securities. The relevant duties of disclosure are contained in section 20(3) and (4):

> "(3) Every person who, after the commencement of this section, becomes a substantial security holder in a public issuer shall give notice that the person is a substantial security holder in the public issuer to-(a) the public issuer; and (b) any stock exchange on which the securities of the public issuer are listed.

> (4) Every notice under subsection (3) of this section shall-(a) be in the prescribed form; and (b) contain the prescribed information; and (c) be accompanied by, or have annexed, such documents, certificates, and statements as may be prescribed; and (d) be given in the prescribed manner; and (e) be given as soon as the person knows, or ought to know, that the person is a substantial security holder in the public issuer."

A "public issuer" means a company listed on the New Zealand Stock Exchange and "substantial security holder" means a person who has a relevant interest" in five *per* cent or more of the voting securities in the public issuer. The definition of "relevant interest" in section 5 is both complicated and comprehensive, but there is no need to examine its terms [505] because, although the matter was disputed in the courts below, Meridian has accepted before their Lordships' Board that the effect of the transaction was to give Meridian a relevant interest in the 49 *per* cent holding in E.N.C. between 9 November 1990, when its money was used to buy it, and 10 December 1990 when the scheme was unwound. It gave no notice under section 20(3).

Section 30 of the Act provides that where them are "reasonable grounds to suspect" that a substantial security holder has not complied with, among other provisions, section 20, the court may, on the application of the Securities Commission, make one or more of a number of orders mentioned in section 32. These range from ordering the substantial security holder to comply with the Act to forfeiting the shares in which he has an interest. After holding its own inquiry in March 1991, the commission applied for orders against various participants in the scheme. Meridian was not among the original defendants but was joined a few days before the trial began.

Heron J. held that Meridian knew on 9 November that it was a "substantial security holder" in E.N.C. for the purposes of section 20(4)(e). He arrived at this conclusion by attributing to Meridian the knowledge of Koo and Ng, who undoubtedly knew all the relevant facts. He did not go into the juridical basis for this attribution in any detail. . . .

The Court of Appeal [1994] 2 N.Z.L.R. 291 affirmed the decision of Heron J. on somewhat different grounds. It decided that Koo's knowledge should be attributed to Meridian because he was the "directing mind and will" of the company. The Court of Appeal received some evidence about how Meridian functioned. The members of the board lived partly in Hong Kong and partly in Australia and met only once a year, for the formal business before the annual general meeting. Other matters which required a board resolution were circulated by post. Koo used to be managing director but was replaced by a Mr. Armour on 1 August 1990. Although Koo thereafter in theory reported to Mr. Armour, in the matter of buying and selling securities he went on in the same way as before. The E.N.C. purchases and sales were openly recorded in the books but Koo did not specifically report them to Mr. Armour, who only found out about them after Koo had left. Nor did Koo report anything else and there was no evidence that Mr. Armour or the other members of the board tried to supervise what he was doing. By leave of the Court of Appeal, Meridian now appeals to their Lordships' Board. It says that its only directing mind and will was that of its board, or possibly of Mr. Armour, but not Koo, whom the Court of Appeal, at p. 301, correctly described as "under Mr. Armour" in the corporate hierarchy.

[506] The phrase "directing mind and will" comes of course from the celebrated speech of Viscount Haldane L.C. in *Lennard's Carrying Co. Ltd v.*

Asiatic Petroleum Co. Ltd. [1915] A.C. 705, 713. But their Lordships think that there has been some misunderstanding of the true principle upon which that case was decided. It may be helpful to start by stating the nature of the problem in a case like this and then come back to *Lennard's* case later.

Any proposition about a company necessarily involves a reference to a set of rules. A company exists because there is a rule (usually in a statute) which says that a *persona ficta* shall be deemed to exist and to have certain of the powers, rights and duties of a natural person. But there would be little sense in deeming such a *persona ficta* to exist unless there were also rules to tell one what acts were to count as acts of the company. It is therefore a necessary part of corporate personality that there should be rules by which acts are attributed to the company. These may be called "the rules of attribution."

The company's primary rules of attribution will generally be found in its constitution, typically the articles of association, and will say things such as "for the purpose of appointing members of the board, a majority vote of the shareholders shall be a decision of the company" or "the decisions of the board in managing the company's business shall be the decisions of the company." There are also primary rules of attribution which are not expressly stated in the articles but implied by company law, such as:

> "the unanimous decision of all the shareholders in a solvent company about anything which the company under its memorandum of association has power to do shall be the decision of the company:" see *Multinational Gas and Petrochemical Co. v. Multinational Gas and Petrochemical Services Ltd.* [1983] Ch. 258.

These primary rules of attribution are obviously not enough to enable a company to go out into the world and do business. Not every act on behalf of the company could be expected to be the subject of a resolution of the board, or a unanimous decision of the shareholders. The company therefore builds upon the primary rules of attribution by using general rules of attribution which are equally available to natural persons, namely, the principles of agency. It will appoint servants and agents whose acts, by a combination of the general principles of agency and the company's primary rules of attribution, count as the acts of the company. And having done so, it will also make itself subject to the general rules by which liability for the acts of others can be attributed to natural persons, such as estoppel or ostensible authority in contract and vicarious liability in tort.

It is worth pausing at this stage to make what may seem an obvious point. Any statement about what a company has or has not done, or can or cannot do, is necessarily a reference to the rules of attribution (primary and general) as they apply to that company. Judges sometimes say that a company "as such" cannot do anything; it must act by servants or agents. This may seem an unexceptionable, even banal remark. And of course the meaning is usually perfectly clear. But a reference to a company "as such" might suggest that there is something out there called the company of [507] which one can meaningfully say that it can or cannot do something. There is in fact no such thing as the company as such, no ding an sich, only the applicable rules. To say that a company cannot do something means only that there is no one whose doing of that act would, under the applicable rules of attribution, count as an act of the company.

The company's primary rules of attribution together with the general principles of agency, vicarious liability and so forth are usually sufficient to enable one to determine its rights and obligations. In exceptional cases, however, they will not provide an answer. This will be the case when a rule of law, either expressly or by implication, excludes attribution on the basis of the general principles of agency or vicarious liability. For example, a rule may be stated in language primarily applicable to a natural person and require some act or state of mind on the part of that person "himself," as opposed to his servants or agents. This is generally true of rules of the criminal law, which ordinarily impose liability only for the actus reus and *mens rea* of the defendant himself. How is such a rule to be applied to a company?

One possibility is that the court may come to the conclusion that the rule was not intended to apply to companies at all; for example, a law which created an offence for which the only penalty was community service. Another possibility is that the court might interpret the law as meaning that it could apply to a company only on the basis of its primary rules of attribution, i.e. if the act giving rise to liability was specifically authorised by a resolution of the board or a unanimous agreement of the shareholders. But there will be many cases in which neither of these solutions is satisfactory; in which the court considers that the law was intended to apply to companies and that, although it excludes ordinary vicarious liability, insistence on the primary rules of attribution would in practice defeat that intention. In such a case, the court must fashion a special rule of attribution for the particular substantive rule. This is always a matter of interpretation: given that it was intended to apply to a company, how was it intended to apply? Whose act (or knowledge, or state of mind) was for this purpose intended to count as the act etc. of the company? One finds the answer to this question by applying the usual canons of interpretation, taking into account the language of the rule (if it is a statute) and its content and policy.

The fact that the rule of attribution is a matter of interpretation or construction of the relevant substantive rule is shown by the contrast between two decisions of the House of Lords, *Tesco Supermarkets Ltd. v. Nattrass* [1972] A.C. 153 (see *infra* p. 53) and *In re Supply of Ready Mixed Concrete (No. 2)* [1995] 1 A.C. 456. In the *Tesco* case [1972] A.C. 153 the question involved the construction of a provision of the Trade Descriptions Act 1968. Tesco were prosecuted under section 11(2) for displaying a notice that goods were being "offered at a price less than that at which they were in fact being offered. . . ." Its supermarket in Norwich had advertised that it was selling certain packets of washing powder at the reduced price of 2s.11d., but a customer who asked for one was told he would have to pay the normal price of 3s.11d. This happened because the shop manager had negligently failed to notice that he had run out of the specially marked low-price packets. Section 24(1) provided a defence for a shopowner [508] who could prove that the commission of the offence was caused by "another person" and that: "he took all reasonable precautions and exercised a due diligence to avoid the commission of such an offence by himself or any person under his control." The company was able to show that it owned hundreds of shops and that the board had instituted systems of supervision and training which amounted, on its part, to taking reasonable precautions and exercising all due diligence to avoid the commission of such offences in its shops. The question was: whose precautions counted as those of the company? If it was the board, then the defence was made out. If they had to include those of the manager, then it failed.

The House of Lords held that the precautions taken by the board were sufficient for the purposes of section 24(1) to count as precautions taken by the company and that the manager's negligence was not attributable to the company. It did so by examining the purpose of section 24(1) in providing a defence to what would otherwise have been an absolute offence: it was intended to give effect to "a policy of consumer protection which does have a rational and moral justification:" *per* Lord Diplock, at pp. 194-195. This led to the conclusion that the acts and defaults of the manager were not intended to be attributed to the company. . . .

On the other hand, in *In re Supply of Ready Mixed Concrete (No. 2)* [1995] 1 A.C. 456, a restrictive arrangement in breach of an undertaking by a company to the Restrictive Practices Court was made by executives of the company acting within the scope of their employment. The board knew nothing of the arrangement; it had in fact given instructions to the company's employees that they were not to make such arrangements. But the House of Lords held that, for the purposes of deciding whether the company was in contempt, the act and state of mind of an employee who entered into an arrangement in the course of his employment should be attributed to the company. This attribution rule was derived from a construction of the undertaking against the background of the Restrictive Trade Practices Act 1976: such undertakings by corporations would be worth little if the company could avoid liability for what its employees had actually done on the ground that the board did not know about it. As Lord Templeman said, at p. 465, an uncritical transposition of the construction in *Tesco Supermarkets Ltd. v. Nattrass* [1972] A.C. 153:

"would allow a company to enjoy the benefit of restrictions outlawed by Parliament and the benefit of arrangements prohibited by the [509] courts provided that the restrictions were accepted and implemented and the arrangements were negotiated by one or more employees who had been forbidden to do so by some superior employee identified in argument as a member of the 'higher management' of the company or by one or more directors of the company identified in argument as 'the guiding will' of the company."

Against this background of general principle, their Lordships can return to Viscount Haldane L.C. in *Lennard's Carrying Co. Ltd v. Asiatic Petroleum Co. Ltd* [1915] A.C. 705. The substantive provision for which an attribution rule had to be devised was section 502 of the Merchant Shipping Act 1894 , which provided a shipowner with a defence to a claim for the loss of cargo put on board his ship if he could show that the casualty happened "without his actual fault or privity." The cargo had been destroyed by a fire caused by the unseaworthy condition of the ship's boilers. The language of section 502 excludes vicarious liability; it is clear that in the case of an individual owner, only his own fault or privity can defeat the statutory protection. How is this rule to be applied to a company? Viscount Haldane L.C. rejected the possibility that it did not apply to companies at all or (which would have come to the same thing) that it required fault or privity attributable under the company's primary rules. Instead, guided by the language and purpose of the section, he looked for the person whose functions in the company, in relation to the cause of the casualty, were the same as those to be expected of the individual shipowner to whom the language primarily applied. Who in the company was responsible for monitoring the condition of the ship, receiving the reports of the master and ship's agents, authorising repairs etc.? This person was Mr. Lennard, whom Viscount Haldane L.C., at pp. 713–714, described as the "directing mind and will" of the company. It was therefore his fault or privity which section 502 attributed to the company.

Because Lennard's Carrying Co. Ltd. does not seem to have done anything except own ships, there was no need to distinguish between the person who fulfilled the function of running the company's business in general and the person whose functions corresponded, in relation to the cause of the casualty, to those of an individual owner of a ship. They were one and the same person. It was this coincidence which left Viscount Haldane L.C.'s speech open to the interpretation that he was expounding a general metaphysic of companies. In *H. L Bolton (Engineering) Co. Ltd. v. T.J. Graham & Sons Ltd.* [1957] 1 Q.B. 159 Denning L.J. certainly regarded it as a generalisation about companies "as such" when, in an equally well known passage, at p. 172, he likened a company to a human body: "It has a brain and nerve centre which controls what it does. It also has hands which hold the tools and act in accordance with directions from the centre."

But this anthropomorphism, by the very power of the image, distracts attention from the purpose for which Viscount Haldane L.C. said, at p. 713, he was using the notion of directing mind and will, namely to apply the attribution rule derived from section 502 to the particular defendant in the case:

> "For if Mr. Lennard was the directing mind of the company, then his action must, unless a corporation is not to be liable at all, have been [510] an action which was the action of the company itself *within the meaning of section 502*." (Emphasis supplied.)

The true nature of the exercise became much clearer, however, in later cases on the Merchant Shipping Act 1894. In *Admiralty v. Owners of the Steamship Divina (The Truculent)* [1952] P. 1, an action to limit liability for damage caused by collision under section 503, which also required the owner of the ship which caused the collision to show that the casualty happened without his "actual fault or privity," the offending ship was a Royal Navy submarine. Her collision with a fishing vessel had been caused by the inadequate system of navigation lights then carried by submarines. Willmer J. held that for this purpose the "directing mind and will" of the Crown, which owned the submarine, was the Third Sea Lord, to whom the Board of Admiralty had entrusted the function of supervising such matters as the systems of navigation lights carried by warships. That function was one which an individual owner of a ship would be expected to fulfil. In *The Lady Gwendolen* [1965] P. 294 the owners of the ship were Arthur Guinness, Son & Co. (Dublin) Ltd. The collision occurred because the master, in accordance with his custom, had taken his vessel laden with stout up the Mersey Channel to Liverpool at full speed in dense fog without more than the odd casual glance at his radar. Owning ships was a very subsidiary part of the company's activities. It had a traffic department which managed the ships under the general supervision of a member of the board who was a brewer and took no interest in the safety of their navigation. The manager of the traffic department knew about railways but took equally little interest in ships. The marine superintendent, one beneath him in the hierarchy, failed to observe that the master of *The Lady Gwendolen* was given to dangerous navigation although, as Willmer L.J. said, at p. 338:

> "It would not have required any very detailed examination of the engine room records in order to ascertain that *The Lady Gwendolen* was frequently proceeding at full speed at times when the deck log was recording dense fog."

In applying section 503 of the Merchant Shipping Act 1894, Sellers L.J. said of the company, at p. 333:

> "In their capacity as shipowners they must be judged by the standard of conduct of the ordinary reasonable shipowner in the management and control of a vessel or of a fleet of vessels."

The court found that a reasonable shipowner would have realised what was happening and given the master proper instruction in the use of radar. None of the people in the company's hierarchy had done so.

It is difficult to see how, on any reasonable construction of section 503, these findings would not involve the actual fault or privity of Guinness. So far as anyone in the hierarchy had functions corresponding to those to be expected of an individual owner, his failure to discharge them was attributable to the company. So far as there was no such person, the superior management was at fault in failing to ensure that there was. In either case, the fault was attributable to the company. But the Court of Appeal found it necessary to identify a "directing mind and will" of the [511] company and lodged it in the responsible member of the board or (in the case of Willmer L.J.) the railway expert who manage the traffic department.

Some commentators have not been altogether comfortable with the idea of the Third Sea Lord being the directing mind and will of the Crown or the traffic manager being the directing mind and will of Guinness. Their Lordships would agree that the phrase does not fit the facts of *The Truculent* [1952] P. 1 or *The Lady Gwendolen* [1965] P. 294 as happily as it did those of *Lennard's* case [1915] A.C. 705. They think, however, that the difficulty has been caused by concentration on that particular phrase rather than the purpose for which Viscount Haidane L.C. was using it. It will often be the most appropriate description of the person designated by the relevant attribution rule, but it might be better to acknowledge that not every such rule has to be forced into the same formula.

Once it is appreciated that the question is one of construction rather than metaphysics, the answer in this case seems to their Lordships to be as straightforward as it did to Heron J. The policy of section 20 of the Securities Amendment Act 1988 is to compel, in fast-moving markets, the immediate disclosure of the identity of persons who become substantial security holders in public issuers. Notice must be given as soon as that person knows that he has become a substantial security holder. In the case of a corporate security holder, what rule should be implied as to the person whose knowledge for this purpose is to count as the knowledge of the company? Surely the person who, with the authority of the company, acquired the relevant interest. Otherwise the policy of the Act would be defeated. Companies would be able to allow employees to acquire interests on their behalf which made them substantial security holders but would not have to report them until the board or someone else in senior management got to know about it. This would put a premium on the board paying as little attention as possible to what its investment managers were doing. Their Lordships would therefore hold that upon the true construction of section 20(4)(*e*), the company knows that it has become a substantial security holder when that is known to the person who had authority to do the deal. It is then obliged to give notice under section 20(3). The fact that Koo did the deal for a corrupt purpose and did not give such notice because he did not want his employers to find out cannot in their Lordships' view affect the attribution of knowledge and the consequent duty to notify.

It was therefore not necessary in this case to inquire into whether Koo could have been described in some more general sense as the "directing mind and will" of the company. But their Lordships would wish to guard themselves against being understood to mean that whenever a servant of a company has authority to do an act on its behalf, knowledge of that act will for all purposes be attributed to the company. It is a question of construction in each case as to whether the particular rule requires that the knowledge that an act has been done, or the state of mind with which it was done, should be attributed to the company. Sometimes, as in *In re Supply of Ready Mixed Concrete (No. 2)* [1995] 1 A.C. 456 and this case, it will be appropriate. Likewise in a case in which a company was required to make a return for revenue purposes and the statute made it an offence [512] to make a false return with intent to deceive, the Divisional Court held that the *mens rea* of the servant authorised to discharge the duty to make the return should be attributed to the company: see *Moore v. I. Bresler Ltd.* [1944] 2 All E.R. 515. On the other hand, the fact that a company's employee is authorised to drive a lorry does not in itself lead to the conclusion that if he kills someone by reckless driving, the company will be guilty of manslaughter. There is no inconsistency. Each is an example of an attribution rule for a particular purpose, tailored as it always must be to the terms and policies of the substantive rule.

The commission in their printed case put forward an alternative argument based upon section 35 of the Act of 1988, which creates a presumption of knowledge:

> "In any proceedings under this Part of this Act, it shall be presumed in the absence of proof to the contrary, that a person knew, at a material time, of the existence of a relevant interest in voting securities in a public issuer or of a fact or matter concerning the existence of a relevant interest in the securities if, at that time, an employee or agent of that person knew in his or her capacity as employee or agent of the existence of the relevant interest or of a fact or matter concerning the existence of it."

Their Lordships did not find it necessary to call upon counsel for the commission on this or any other point and have therefore heard no oral submissions in support of the commission's alternative argument. But they find it difficult to see how, on the facts of this case, section 35 can advance the matter. There is no doubt that the knowledge of Koo and Ng would have activated the presumption. But the presumption may be rebutted by "proof to the contrary." Proof of what? Proof, presumably, that in fact none of the persons whose knowledge counted as the knowledge of the company did know about the relevant interest. But the section gives no guidance as to who those persons are. That is left to the process of construction of section 20(4)(*e*) which their Lordships have undertaken. If, as they think, Koo's knowledge was attributable to the company, the evidence made reliance on the presumption unnecessary. And if only the knowledge of Mr. Armour or the board was so attributable, then the evidence showed clearly that they did not know and the presumption was rebutted. Either way, it would have had no effect on the outcome of the case.

Wedick v. Osmond & Son (Dublin) Ltd.
[1935] I.R. 820

The matter in question here was whether the reference to "a person or persons"' in a regulatory measure included a registered company.

SULLIVAN P.: [833] James Wedick, the complainant in this case, is an Inspector of the Pharmaceutical Society of Ireland. The defendants are a Limited Company. . . . By the summonses the complainant charged the defendants with [several] offences. . . . [834] On the facts . . . found the District Justice convicted the defendants of the offences charged in the said summonses and on the application of the defendants stated a case for the opinion of this Court whether, having regard to the facts so found by him, he was right in law in so convicting.
[838] The third summons charges an offence under sect. 17 of the Pharmacy Act, (Ireland), 1875, Amendment Act, 1890. That section provides:

> "Any person or persons lawfully keeping open shop for selling, retailing, or mixing poisons shall personally manage and conduct such shop and the retailing and mixing of poisons therein, or shall employ for the purposes aforesaid, as an assistant or manager in such shop, a duly registered chemist and druggist, or registered druggist, or pharmaceutical chemist or licentiate apothecary, and such person or persons lawfully keeping open shop as aforesaid shall, for the purposes of this Act and of the principal Act, be held to be the retailer and compounder of poisons aforesaid therein; . . . and any person or persons acting in contravention of this enactment shall for every such offence be liable to pay a penalty not exceeding five pounds."

It was argued by counsel for the defendants that the conviction on this third summons was wrong, on the ground that the words 'person or persons' in that section do not include a Limited Company. In support of that argument counsel relied on the decisions in *Pharmaceutical Society v. London and Provincial Supply Association* (5 A.C. 857) and *Pharmaceutical Society of Ireland v. Boyd & Co.* [1896] 2 I.R. 344.
In *Pharmaceutical Society v. London and Provincial Supply Association* the question to be determined was whether the word 'person' in the first and

fifteenth sections of the Pharmacy Act, 1868 (31 & 32 Vict. c. 121), applied to an incorporated company. The first section of that Act enacts that it shall be unlawful for any person to sell, or keep open shop for retailing, dispensing, or compounding poisons, or to assume, or use the title 'Chemist and Druggist', or Chemist or Druggist, or Pharmacist, or Dispensing Chemist or Druggist, unless such person shall be a Pharmaceutical Chemist or a Chemist and Druggist within the meaning of the Act and be registered under the Act and conform to such regulations as to the keeping, dispensing, and selling of such poisons as may from time [839] to time be prescribed. The fifteenth section enacts that any person who shall sell, or keep an open shop, for the retailing, dispensing, or compounding poisons, or who shall take, use or exhibit the name or title of Chemist and Druggist, or Chemist or Druggist, not being a duly registered Pharmaceutical Chemist or Chemist and Druggist, or who shall take, use, or exhibit the name or title Pharmaceutical Chemist, Parmaceutist, or Pharmacist, not being a Pharmaceutical Chemist, or shall fail to conform with any regulation as to the keeping or selling of poisons made in pursuance of the Act, or who shall compound any medicine of the British Pharmacopeia except according to the formularies of the said Pharmacopeia shall for every such offence be liable to pay a penalty or sum of £5. It was held by the Court of Appeal and by the House of Lords, that the word 'person' in these sections did not include a corporation. In the House of Lords, Lord Selborne L.C. stated (p. 86l): 'There can be no question that the word "person" may, and I should be disposed myself to say *prima facie* does, in a public statute, include a person in law: that is a corporation, as well as a natural person,' but he accepted the principle that 'if a statute provided that no person shall do a particular act except on a particular condition, it is, *prima facie*, natural and reasonable (unless there be something in the context or in the manifest object of the statute, or in the nature of the subject-matter, to exclude that construction) to understand the Legislature as intending such persons, as, by the use of proper means, may be able to fulfil the condition; and not those who, though called "persons" in law, have no capacity to do so at any time, by any means, or under any circumstances, whatsoever.' He held that *prima facie* the first section contemplates persons such as may, or may not, be pharmaceutical chemists or chemists and druggists within the meaning of the Act and be registered under the Act, and that as it was clear that a corporation could not be a Pharmaceutical Chemist or a Chemist and Druggist, and be registered under the Act the word 'person' did not include a corporation, in the absence of anything in the context or object of the Act to require that it should. Lords Blackburn and Watson were of the same opinion. In *The Pharmaceutical Society of Ireland v. Boyd & Co.* [1896] 2 I.R. 344 the same question arose on the construction of sect. 30 of the Pharmacy (Ireland) Act, 1875 (37 & 38 Vict. c. 57) which is practically identical in its terms with sects. 1 and 15 of the Pharmacy Act, [840] 1868. The Court of Queen's Bench in Ireland (O'Brien, Johnson and Holmes JJ.) following the decision in *The Pharmaceutical Society v. London and Provin-*

cial Supply Association upon the construction of corresponding sections of the Pharmacy Act, 1868, held that the word 'person' in sect. 30 of the Pharmacy (Ireland) Act, 1875 did not include a body corporate. The principles stated by the House of Lords in *The Pharmaceutical Society v. London and Provincial Supply Association* were also accepted and applied in this country in *O'Duffy v. Jaffe* [1904] 2 I.R. 27 and *R (King) v. Antrim JJ* [1906] 2 I.R. 298. In the latter case Palles C.B. at 327, having quoted from the opinion of Lord Blackburn the following passage: 'I am quite clear about this, that whenever you can see that the object of the Act requires that the word "person" shall have the more extended or the less extended sense, then, whichever sense it requires, you should apply the word in that sense and construe the Act accordingly,' proceeds: 'Of course this principle is applicable only when the words are capable of being used in the extended sense. Therefore, if the special description in the statute of the person within it is one which cannot be answered by a body corporate, or if the Act contemplated or prohibited, be one which a body corporate is incapable of committing, then the limited construction must prevail. The *Pharmaceutical Company's* Case and that of *O'Duffy v. Jaffe* are instances of the first class of limitation. Offences in which either intent or *mens rea* is an essential ingredient are illustrations of the other.' In that case the Court had to consider the question whether the word 'person' in sect. 80 of the Fisheries (Ireland) Act, 1842 (5 & 6 Vict. c. 106), included a corporation. The Court held that it did. Palles C.B. in the course of his judgment (at 326), having referred to the Interpretation Act, 1889, sect. 2, subsect. 1, which provides that, in the construction of every enactment relating to an offence punishable on summary conviction, 'person' shall, unless the contrary intention appears, include a body corporate, said: 'In determining this question, although the Act as a whole, cannot be disregarded, the ultimate decision must be on the particular section itself. Of the various sections of the Act there are many in which a contrary intention does appear, such as those which constitute offences of which intent is a material part. 1, therefore, restrict my consideration to sect. 80 alone.'

[841] These words of the Chief Baron are singularly applicable to the present case. Mr Fitzgerald pointed out that in several sections of the Pharmacy Act, (Ireland), 1875, Amendment Act, 1890, the word 'person' or the word 'persons' obviously means a natural person or persons and does not include a corporation; see sects. 5, 8, 10, 12, 13, 15. But when we consider the terms of sect. 17, upon which the third summons in this case was based, I think the word 'person' or 'persons' must receive a different interpretation. There is an obvious and very material difference between that section and sects. 1 and 15 of the Pharmacy Act, 1868, which were under consideration in *The Pharmaceutical Society v. London and Provincial Supply Association* and *The Pharmaceutical Society of Ireland v. Boyd & Co*. It was admitted by the defendants' counsel that a corporation can lawfully keep open shop for the sale of poisons, and it is obvious that a corporation can comply with the con-

ditions imposed by sect. 17 on persons lawfully keeping open shop for selling, retailing, or mixing poisons, for though it cannot 'personally manage and conduct such shop' it can 'employ for the purpose aforesaid as an Assistant or Manager in such shop a duly registered chemist and druggist, or registered druggist, or pharmaceutical chemist, or licentiate apothecary.' There is, therefore, nothing in the special description in the section of the persons within it that cannot be answered by a corporation, and I can see nothing in the apparent object of the section to require that the word 'persons' should be so construed as to exclude corporations. I am, therefore, of the opinion that a corporation is a 'person' within the meaning of sect. 17 of 53 & 54 Vict. c. 48.

McMahon v. Murtagh Properties Ltd.
[1982] I.L.R.M. 342

The defendant company was prosecuted for breach of the Licensing Acts in a public house that it owned. Among the questions raised in a case stated by way of appeal was the position of registered companies with regard to holding liquor licenses.

BARRINGTON J.: . . . [344] [This case] raises . . . issues of practical importance concerning the right of a limited liability company to hold an intoxicating liquor licence, and the practice of such companies holding their licences through nominees, and the complications which this practice may create in the prosecution of offenders against the licensing code and in the administration of Part 3 of the Intoxicating Liquor Act, 1927.

It was at one time thought that an incorporated company could not itself hold an intoxicating liquor licence, and that it required a nominee to hold the licence on its behalf. It is hard to find the logical basis for this theory.

On incorporation, a limited liability company becomes a body corporate capable of exercising all the functions of an incorporated company and having [345] a perpetual succession and a Common Seal. (See s. 18 of the Companies Act, 1963) If the powers contained in the memorandum of association include power to carry on the business of selling intoxicating liquor by retail for consumption on or off the premises, the company has power to carry on that business on obtaining the appropriate licence and complying with other relevant legal requirements. One of these requirements is that the company should own an appropriate estate in premises in which to carry on the business, but it is well established that there is no property or goodwill in a licence itself apart from the ownership of the premises to which the licence is attached. (See *Kelly v. Montague*, 16 LRI 424). It would appear to follow logically from this, that the property and the licence should both be held by the same person.

However, notwithstanding this, the practice has grown up in Ireland of appointing nominees to hold licences for limited liability companies engaged in the intoxicating liquor trade. This practice has even secured Statutory recognition, and it is probably too late now to say that it is wrong.

The learned District Justice himself referred to s. 28 of the Intoxicating Liquor Act, 1960, which reads as follows:

> "A licence held by a nominee of a body corporate in respect of premises in which the lowest estate or tenancy is held by the body corporate may, on the application by the body corporate to the court at any sitting thereof for the court area within which the premises are situate, be transferred, by indorsement made by the court on the licence or, if the licence is not available, on a copy thereof, to such other person as the body corporate may nominate."

It is quite clear, however, that such a nominee has himself, no beneficial interest whatsoever in the licence, and that he must comply with all lawful directions of the body corporate in relation to it. While the Statute acknowledges that he holds the licence, he holds it only for the body corporate which is the beneficial and, indeed, the real holder of the licence, just as it is the real holder of the premises in which the business is carried on.

The present practice of companies holding their licence through nominees probably goes back to a time when the implications of incorporation were not fully understood. It has, however, the authority of a passage in O'Connor's *The Licensing Laws of Ireland* which appears at page 86 of that book and which reads as follows: 'The provisions of the licensing code go to show that a licence cannot be granted to a limited company, but the application may be made in the name of the secretary or other servant or nominee.'

The cases cited for this proposition are: *R v. Lyon* (1898), 14, TLR 357; 62 JP, 357 and *R v. Jones* (1895) 59 JP 87.

In the first case, the Court of Appeal in England held that a notice of application for a licence, brought by the secretary of a company on behalf of a company was not necessarily bad on its face because brought in the name of the secretary as secretary of the company. The court accordingly issued an order of mandamus directing the justices to hear and determine the application. In the course of the argument in the case it was apparently conceded that the company itself could not hold the licence.

[346] In the second case (*R v. Jones*) the Queens Bench division for England and Wales refused to issue an order of mandamus to justices directing them to hear and determine an application by a branch manager of a company for an 'off' licence to sell spirits. Under the relevant statutory provision a licensed dealer in spirits might take an additional retail spirits licence for the sale of spirits not consumed on the premises. The branch manager was not such a dealer. The company was, but it held its 'on' licence in the name of three of its directors as nominees.

Neither case therefore appears to be strong authority for the proposition in support of which it is cited in O'Connor (*supra*).

However, two years after the publication of O'Connor's *Licensing Laws*, the matter was fully discussed in the case of *The King (Cottingham) v. Justices of County Cork* [1906] 2 IR 415.

In his judgment in that case, the Chief Baron Palles emphasised that a body corporate was a 'person' and that it could therefore have a 'character' or reputation and nailed the fallacy that a body corporate could not apply for a licence because it could not satisfy the justices that it had a 'good character'. At page 419 he goes so far as to say:

> "I am aware that much difference of practice, and as I believe, much irregularity, exists as to the names in which licences are taken out, even when the real trader is a natural person and not a company – still the questions will some day arise, IS A LICENCE RIGHTLY ISSUED TO THE MANAGER OF A COMPANY? CAN THE INCORPORATED COMPANY LAWFULLY SELL BEER UNDER SUCH A LICENCE? I am inclined to hold that each of these questions should be answered in the negative."

As I said earlier, it is probably too late now, to hold that the practice of companies holding licences through nominees is wrong. But Chief Baron Palles had no difficulty whatsoever in holding that a body corporate was a 'persons' capable of applying for and obtaining an intoxicating liquor licence and that it was capable of having a good character. He goes on to say:

> "I cannot see why a public company cannot have a character. No doubt it has no soul; but it can act by others, and through others do acts which in the case of a natural person would affect conscience, and be a foundation of that reputation which the law knows as 'character', be it good or bad. It can be guilty of fraud, or malice, and of various criminal offences, some of commission, others of omission; some punishable summarily, others by indictment. 'Character' as used in the section means 'reputation'. Reputation is acquired by conduct. The conduct of the authorised agents, of a company is its conduct. Why should not that conduct give rise to a reputation as to this character, good, bad or indifferent. An unincorporated company of seven persons can acquire a reputation for fair dealing, for truth in their representations, for close supervision of their business, for carrying on their business in an orderly and peaceable manner. But this reputation is not that of an individual. It is, or may be, something different from the reputation of each. It may be a reputation acquired by the aggregation of the seven; as the reputation of an unincorporated bank for solvency. Why cannot those seven persons acquire a similar reputation by their action in aggregation, although that aggregation has assumed the more intimate form of incorporation?" [347]

Johnson J. agreed with the Chief Baron's reasoning. He said:

"The second ground raises the question whether this company is a 'person' within the meaning of The Beerhouses (Ireland) Acts and the Licensing Act, 1874. The contention for the prosecutor is, as I understand it, that ihe whole scope of these Acts as ascertained from the language of the legislature in the Acts *ex visceribus actus* (C. Co. Litt, 381b), points to the individual and personal responsibility of the applicant for a licence or transfer of a licence, and that it is in this sense his character must be 'good'; and that in as much as 'Beamish & Crawford Ltd' is merely an impersonal incorporated legal entity, it cannot in the nature of things obtain from the justices a certificate of good character, and therefore cannot have a wholesale beerdealers' licence. But though this company is of such impersonal character, it is competent to employ and act, and practically must employ and act, by and through such individuals as by its constitution it is competent to engage, and engages, for its purposes, and by whose conduct within the scope of their employment, the 'company' is bound. A limited liability company is capable of suing, and liable to be sued, in almost every kind of action in the nature of tort or contract. It may be made criminally responsible for most offences which are not punishable solely by imprisonment or corporal punishment. It may be enjoined, and its property may be sequestrated for payment of its debts or fines imposed for offences. Good or bad character is a matter of local or public reputation and the widest discretion is given by Statute to justices in respect of their certificate. In *Leader v. Yell* (16.CB)(NS) 584, where this matter is discussed, Erle, C.J. at 593, suggests how the words 'good character' came to be introduced into the Beer Acts. I think if the house is conducted in a disorderly way, if convictions are had for breaches of the Licensing Acts, if improper characters were allowed to resort there for improper purposes, or public feeling is outraged by lewd or improper acts knowingly committed, this 'company' would, through their agent or manager, who they put in charge of, or whose omissions or acts they are liable for, have an evil reputation and a bad character; but if, on the contrary, the house is conducted in an orderly and decent manner, the provisions of the Licensing Acts observed, and perhaps I may venture to add, reasonably good and wholesome beer supplied, the local and public reputation of this company, through their agent or manager whom this company places in charge and for whom they are responsible, would be good, and this company would be, as the justices have certified them to be, of good character." (at 426)

The case of *The King (Cottingham) v. Justices of Cork* went to the Court of Appeal where the decision of the Divisional Court was upheld, but on a different point, and the *dicta* quoted are, therefore, in a certain sense *obiter*. Nevertheless they are of high authority and it is surprising that they appear to have had so little effect on practice.

The matter came up for discussion before the modern Supreme Court in the case of *The State (John Hennessy and Chatior Inns Ltd) v. Superintendent J. Commons* [1976] IR 238. Again, the decision in the case turned upon a different point, but in his judgment, Kenny J. went out of his way to cite with approval the judgments of Johnson J. and the Chief Baron in *The King (Cottingham) v. Justices of County Cork*, and referred to the 'myth' widely accepted by 'both branches of the legal profession' that a company incorporated under the Companies Acts cannot be granted a licence to sell intoxicating drink and that when it seeks to be licensed in respect of premises, or when it acquires licensed premises, the licence must be granted to its nominee.

From this discussion I drew three conclusions. First the present practice of [348] companies holding their licences through nominees has no basis in sound logic. Second the practice has however received statutory recognition so that it is now too late to say that it is wrong. Third the practice, not being based on sound logic, will necessarily give rise to difficulties in administering the licencing code so that one can sympathise with the position in which the learned District Justice found himself. Nevertheless I drew the following practical conclusions. First, a limited liability company is entitled itself to hold its licence without resorting to the device of having a nominee.

Secondly, it is not incorrect to refer to the nominee as being the 'holder' of the licence as long as it is remembered that the company is the beneficial and as previously indicated, the real holder of the licence. The nominee must comply with all legal instructions of the company in relation to the licence, and he is, in effect, no more than a peg on which the company finds it convenient to hang its licence. This being so, if the company, through its agents, breaks the law in the running of the business, it is at all times liable as the holder of the licence. The nominee, provided he does no more than hold the licence, commits no offence, but if the nominee is also the manager of the business or if he assists in the commission of the offence then he may be liable for aiding and abetting the company as holder of the licence, notwithstanding that he is a nominal 'holder' himself.

CRIMINAL LIABILITY

See *Company Law*, pp. 71-74.

Dean v. John Menzies (Holdings) Ltd.
(1981) S.C. 23

The issue to be determined here was whether it is ever possible for a registered company to commit the criminal offence in question. The defendant company was charged in the Sheriff Court of North Strathclyde at Dumbarton on a complaint at the instance of Ian Dean, Procurator-fiscal, which set forth that 'On 30th January 1979 at the premises occupied by you at 50 High Street, Dumbarton, you did conduct yourself in a shamelessly indecent manner in respect that you did sell, expose for sale and have for sale 64 indecent and obscene magazines as specified in the Schedule annexed hereto, which magazines were likely to deprave and corrupt the morals of the lieges and to create in their minds inordinate and lustful desires.' The accused company stated pleas to both the competency and the relevancy of the libel and the Sheriff (Jardine), sustaining the plea to competency, dismissed the complaint. At the request of the Procurator-fiscal, the Sheriff stated a case for the opinion of the High Court of Justiciary.

LORD CAMERON (dissenting): . . . [24] The issue of competency as presented in argument is short, substantial but not simple: it is whether by the law of Scotland a fictional person can be guilty of the common law offence libelled. It is of course a matter of necessary concession and of everyday practice, that such persons can be guilty of statutory offences even of those offences where proof of knowledge or even intention on the part of the accused is an essential element in proof of guilt.

Before I come to deal with the arguments which were presented by counsel I think it is desirable to set out in the simplest form what it is that the respondents are alleged to have done – it is the sale or exposure for sale as a transaction of commerce, presumably in shop premises occupied by them for the purpose of their business, of certain specified magazines. It is the alleged quality of these particular magazines and their consequent effects or potential effects on the minds of the purchaser and reader which constitute the criminal character of what would otherwise be a very ordinary everyday commercial transaction. Such prosecutions in the case of individual shopkeepers are not uncommon and the recent case of *Robertson v. Smith* 1980 J.C. 1 makes it clear that sale to the public or exposure for sale of such literature constitutes a criminal offence in the common law of Scotland.

One obvious consequence of the Sheriff's decision would be that if an individual shopkeeper were to transfer the control of such a business as was conducted by the appellant in *Robertson v. Smith* from himself as an individual to a limited company controlled by him he could escape the penal consequences of his action. I make this observation because, while the present appeal is concerned with the affairs of a large company, with, as is well known, many trading outlets, the issue is equally applicable to a 'one-man company' operating in a back street in Glasgow.

[25] The submissions for the appellant were presented by the Advocate-Depute in a careful and able argument in which his broad submission was that those directing and controlling the activities of a limited company, being its

responsible officers, are persons capable of supplying the 'will' of the company sufficient for the company to be able to possess the *mens rea* required for a common law offence and in particular the offence with which this company is charged in this complaint.

In elaboration of this submission the Advocate-Depute drew attention to the nature of the offence here charged as that has been identified in *Watt v. Annan* (1978) J.C. 84 and *Robertson v. Smith* (1980) J.C. 1. The general question of the capacity of a corporate entity or fictional person to exercise a will and to form and carry into effect an intent had for long been settled in Scotland as in England. In *Gordon v. British & Foreign Metaline Co.* (1886) 14 R. 75 the capacity of such a 'person' to act with malice was affirmed, and the classic authority *of Lennard's Carrying Co. Ltd v. Asiatic Petroleum Co. Ltd.* [1915] A.C. 705 left no room for doubt as to how the law would approach the question of a company's capacity to commit a common law offence and therefore to form the necessary wicked intent. A company's capacity to be guilty of malicious defamation was also recognised in English law: cf. *Triplex Safety Glass v. Lancegaye Safety Glass (1934) Ltd.* [1939] 2 K.B. 395, *per* du Parcq L.J. at 408, while the case of *D.P.P. v. Kent and Sussex Contractors* [1944] K.B. 146 showed that in England a company could be convicted of making statements which they knew to be false 'with intent to deceive'. This was a case of breach of regulation but that did not affect the principle.

There was ample authority in Scotland for the proposition for which he contended. . . .

[26] The broad proposition which Mr Kerrigan advanced was that as there was no reported case which decided that a limited company could be liable to a charge of criminal conduct at common law; the corollary of that proposition was that so to charge a limited company was by clear inference incompetent. The remedy lay not with the Court but with the legislature. For this Court to decide that a common law charge would lie against a limited company would be to make new law and in effect to create a whole catalogue of new offences; this was beyond the competence of the Court.

If what the Crown is seeking in this case to do were, as Mr Kerrigan argued, to induce the Court to create a new offence or offences which were previously unknown to the law then I would think there was great force in his argument, but the absence of direct authority affirming the Crown's submissions as to the competency of this charge is not by itself authority for the contrary; in any event the offence here libelled is not new: it is well known and has been the subject of more than one prosecution.

The question therefore is not one of the creation of new offences but the application of the existing law to a corporate body as that law applies to an individual. The width of Mr Kerrigan's argument is such that logically applied it would, in Scotland, apply equally to a partnership as to a limited company. But Mr Kerrigan's argument went much further. He drew a distinction between those *mala prohibita* the commission of which admittedly may involve the formation of a deliberate intent, but only in those areas or fields identified by Parliament, and *mala in se*; fictional persons as such could not be guilty of acts of moral turpitude, and it is that quality which is involved in the concept of the malum in se, and it is because of the nature of a company that the limits of its criminal liability require to be drawn by its creator *i.e.* Parliament. The nature of the offence here requires proof of dole, which while in substance the same as *mens rea* (cf. *Hume on Crimes*, Vol. 1, 25) differs in that dole infers a degree of moral obliquity. A company could not be [27] charged with culpable homicide, though it might be guilty of libel or even of criminal libel in England. In any event this was an offence in a 'subjective area' and there was no precedent for such a charge being brought against a company where the essence of the charge was of moral delinquency. Further, it was impossible to fasten the label of 'shameless conduct' to a limited company. The capacity for a sensation of shame was not within the necessary category of those senses which could be credited to a company. Therefore it could not (in the absence of expressed parliamentary enactment to the contrary) be guilty of shameless conduct, it being incapable of any sense of shame. This was a matter which should be left to the consideration and decision of Parliament. . . .

In considering the arguments addressed to the competency of the charge in this case it is necessary to have its precise terms in mind; it is a charge of an offence against public decency as specified in the complaint and is a charge at common law. The arguments presented against the competency of the proceedings were not directed to the nature of the charge as being one unknown to the common law if committed by an individual, but solely to the competency of charging a limited company, being a fictional person, with a common law offence. The argument proceeded in three steps (1) that a fictional person could not be charged with a common law offence, that being a matter for Parliament; (2) that in any case the particular offence charged, being one involving subjective considerations, could not be competently charged, and (3) that, as it was impossible for a company to have or feel a sense of shame, this offence in which subjective shamelessness was an essential ingredient could not be competently libelled against the respondents.

While the arguments were presented in general terms on both sides of the bar, I think it is necessary to isolate the precise issue which arises on the competency of the present complaint. It is whether a limited company, acting within its statutory powers and in pursuit of its objects as prescribed by its articles, can be competently charged with an offence at common law. The case is not concerned directly with any wider question, but solely with whether a limited company acting in course of its ordinary and legitimate business can be prosecuted for a common law offence, where its action in its specific facts would in the case of an individual render him liable to prosecution for a contravention of the common law. I think it is particularly important to limit the field of decision in this case to such action as falls within the powers of the corporation. This complaint and the issues arising upon it [28] are not concerned with actions which are *ultra vires* or in excess of the powers conferred on the corporation by its incorporating statutes or instruments or articles of association. The assumption here is that the sale or exposure was in course of the respondents' business.

The criminal law has long recognised that a corporate body may be guilty of breaches of statute and incur a penalty, and therefore be susceptible to prosecution as a person recognised in the eyes of the law. Further, the law has also recognised that an incorporation may be guilty of statutory offences the commission of which is the result of intended or deliberate action or inaction. It was not Parliament which specifically provided that corporate bodies such as limited companies should be subject to prosecution: the various statutes assumed that no distinction in capacity to offend should exist between natural and other persons recognised by law as legal entities with capacity to discharge certain functions and perform certain actions. The responsibility of both for breaches of statute is the same, and the individuals and the company alike can be cited and charged in their own names. . . .

[T]his is not a case of creating or declaring a new crime or offence which never existed before, nor of extending the boundaries of criminal responsibility to a group of legal persons on whose shoulders criminal responsibility had not been rested before. If therefore a limited company has the capacity to form an intention, to decide on a course of action, to act in accordance with that deliberate intent within the scope and limits of its articles, it is difficult to see on what general principle it should not be susceptible to [29] prosecution where that action offends against the common law. It must no doubt be conceded that this principle could not be applied to a crime where the law prescribes only one and that a custodial penalty; but the fact that *lex non cogit ad impossibilia* in a particular instance does not imply that as a consequence it follows that *lex non cogit ad possibilia* in other instances where penalties for breaches of the common law can be effectively imposed. It has long been settled in our civil law that a company can be guilty of malice: malice implies a harmful intention deliberately directed against another person or persons. The parallel between malice in the field of defamation and the essense of this *mens rea* which is essential to criminal liability at common law appears to me close. What then is criminal intent? While it is of course true that the 'wicked intent' – (which is *mens rea*) is a matter of proof in which the burden of proof lies upon the Crown, 'the wicked intent is an inference to be drawn from the circumstances of the deed, as well as from any explanations by the man. Although a man considers his deed meritorious, the law may hold him to have acted wickedly and feloniously. Whenever a person does what is criminal, the presumption is that he does so wilfully': *MacDonald* 5th edition p. 1. Further it was put by Hume in writing on the nature of dole thus 'It is not material to the notion of guilt, that the offender have himself been fully conscious of the wickedness of what he did': *Hume on Crimes*, Vol. 1, 25. No distinction is drawn by Hume between the concept of 'dole' and that of *mens rea*: dole being defined as 'that corrupt and evil intention, which is essential . . . to the guilt of any crime' op. cit. Vol. 1, 21. These are general principles applicable to all common law crimes and offences and therefore it follows that the presumption of law is precisely the same in all cases – whatever the degree of moral obliquity involved in the commission of the offence. Therefore the bald submission that a company cannot in Scotland in any circumstances be guilty of a common law offence does not commend itself to me as sound in principle. It is without any authority and if it be argued that a company cannot possess the capacity to exhibit *mens rea* it can be sufficiently answered that *mens rea* is no more than that 'wicked intent' which is the presumed element in all acts which are criminal at common law. It is trite law also that a company is legally capable of many deliberate actions within the limits of its powers as set out in its Articles of Association, these powers being exercised by those who are the 'directing mind' or 'will' of the company. In the case of *Lennards' Carrying Co. Ltd. v. Asiatic Petroleum Co. Ltd.* [1915] A.C. 705 at p. 713 Lord Chancellor Haldane, with whom his colleagues, including Lord Dunedin, concurred, at p. 713, in analysing the elements which taken together demonstrate the basis on which a company can be held responsible as an entity for deliberate acts or omissions where these acts or omissions are those at least in the field of civil liability, said: 'A corporation is an abstraction. It has no mind of its own any more than it has a body of its own; its active and directing will must consequently be sought in the person of somebody who for some purposes may be called an agent, but who is really the directing mind and will of the corporation, the very ego and centre of the personality of the corporation. That person may be under the direction of the shareholders in general meeting; that person may be the board of directors itself, or it may be, and in some companies it is so, that that person has an authority co-ordinate [30] with the board of directors given to him under the articles of association, and is appointed by the general meeting of the company, and can only be removed by the general meeting of the company.' This may well indicate that difficulties of proof will arise when a charge of criminal conduct at common law is brought against a limited company, but does nothing to suggest that such a charge may not be competently brought, and that without the necessity in all cases of specifying in the complaint or indictment which particular officer or employee of the company was in fact responsible for the act or omission charged. The argument put forward by Mr Kerrigan, who cast aside any support which he might get from *Miles v. Finlay* and the passage in Green's Encyclopaedia founded on by the Sheriff, that there is no reported authority in Scotland supporting the Crown's contention on competency does not seem to me to carry the matter very far: stood on its head the argument on the absence of direct authority is equally potent – that the absence of authority indicates that the matter is beyond argument. But the authorities demonstrate that a company can be guilty *of mala prohibita* even where the offence involves knowledge, intentional action of permission. Further, in the field of civil liability a company can be held liable in reparation for defamation where malice has to be established, while in England there is authority for the proposition that a company may be guilty of criminal libel. If a company can by law – by legal fiction, if you will – be endowed with a mind and will exerciseable by natural persons acting within the confines of the company's legal competence, and be held responsible for actings in pursuance of the exercise of that mind and will, then if those actings are contrary to the common criminal law, I find it difficult to see upon what basis of principle it can be said that the company is free of criminal liability, however this may be enforced. The wicked intent in all common law crimes is the intent to perform the criminal act. The motive or moral depravity of the actor is alike irrelevant to the quality of that act in the eye of the law. Therefore if the act is intentional, the criminal intent is presumed whatever the motive which inspired the actor.

The rules of law as to a company's capacity to exercise a conscious mind and will enunciated in the case of *Lennard's Carrying Company* have been further illustrated in the recent and important case of *Tesco Ltd. v. Nattrass* [1972] A.C. 153 (post p. 53). No doubt the decision is concerned with a statutory charge and with the defences open to a company charged with a contravention of that statute, but in my view its importance lies in the extent to which the House of Lords held that a company could be susceptible to criminal proceedings whether under statute or at common law. In that case Lord Reid at page 171, after citing the passage I have quoted from the speech of Lord Haldane, went on to refer to a passage from the judgment of Lord Denning in *H.L. Bolton (Engineering) Co. Ltd. v. T.J. Graham & Sons Ltd.* [1957] Q.B. 159 where he said at page 172 'A company may in many ways be likened to a human body. It has a brain and nerve centre which controls what it does. It also has hands which hold tools and act in accordance with directions from the centre. Some of the people in the company are mere servants and agents who are nothing more than hands to do the work and cannot be said to represent the mind or will. Others are directors and managers who represent the directing mind and will of the company, and [31] control what it does. The state of mind of these managers is the state of mind of the company and is treated by the law as such.' Having quoted that passage Lord Reid went on to say 'In that case the directors of the company only met once a year: they left the management of the business to others, and it was the intention of those managers which was imputed to the company. I think that was right.' I draw particular attention to the word 'intention'. Later in his speech Lord Reid referred to the case of *D.P.P. v. Kent and Sussex Contractors* cited by the Advocate-Depute and also *R. v. I.C.R. Haulage Ltd.* [1944] K.B. 551 where it was held that a company can be guilty of common law conspiracy. Lord Reid added in relation to this latter case at page 173 'I think that the true view is that the judge must direct the jury that if they find certain facts proved then as a matter of law they must find that the criminal act of the officer, servant or agent including his state of mind, intention, knowledge or belief is the act of the company. I have already dealt with the considerations to be applied in deciding when such a person can and when he cannot be identified with the company. I do not see how the nature of the charge can make any difference.'

No doubt the decision in the case of *Tesco* is one concerned with English criminal law, but the statute under which the prosecution was brought is a United Kingdom statute effective in Scotland and the judgment and opinions in the case, if technically not binding in this country, are necessarily to be treated with the highest respect. One thing may be taken as clear, that in England a charge of common law crime may be competently laid against a company, and while I agree that there is no reason why the criminal jurisprudence of the two countries should necessarily fall into line, at the same time I see no reason in principle why a different rule of law should operate in Scotland, the same statute governing the structure, powers and functioning of limited companies in both countries. In both countries the rules and principles governing the civil liabilities of companies are the same: in both countries the rules and principles governing criminal liability in respect of statutory offences are the same and it is therefore not easy to see upon what principle of Scots criminal law a company created by statute should not be amenable to the common law in matters criminal – the only authority for the contrary view which appealed to the Sheriff was thrown overboard by Mr Kerrigan and in my opinion rightly – particularly as in both countries the capacity of a company to form an intent, to carry it into effect, to exercise a will and to make a conscious choice of courses of action or inaction is undoubted and is precisely the same. In my opinion the competency of the present charge is not open to successful challenge on the broad general principle that a company cannot in Scots law be guilty of a common law offence.

This however is not the end of the matter. It must necessarily be conceded that certain criminal conduct cannot be ascribed to a company. Thus, where the only penalty prescribed or permitted by law is custodial or personally physical, it may be presumed that no charge will lie, but no such objection could be levelled here and that is a question that does not arise in the present case. The narrower question is whether this charge can be brought against a limited company, and it is to this particular aspect of the matter that Mr [32] Kerrigan's subsidiary argument was directed. Whatever might be the general liability of a limited company, this charge, it was submitted, was not one which could be competently brought. Mr Kerrigan's argument in brief was that as this charge involved as a critical element an accusation of 'shamelessness' it went far beyond any acceptable limits. His argument could be put in very simple form. He said that 'shame' or a 'sense of shame' was something which could not be attributed to a fictional person. Therefore a fictional person could not possess the capacity to act 'shamelessly'. But the charge was one of 'shameless' conduct. The accused was a fictional person, therefore the charge lacked its essential content because no fictional person could have a sense of shame. The simplicity of the argument thus presented is attractive. But the 'shameless' quality of the conduct here libelled is essentially an objective and not a subjective quality. It is of the essence of this offence that the conduct be directed towards some person or persons with an intention or in the knowledge that it should corrupt, or be calculated or be liable to corrupt or deprave in the manner libelled, those towards whom the conduct is directed. It is this which determines the shameless quality of the act, with which the moral obliquity of the actor – if any – has nothing to do. In the present case the qualification of the conduct is that the exposure for sale or sale to persons, members of the public, was done with the knowledge or intention of the company – knowledge of the calculated consequences or those liable to follow or intention that such consequences should follow. Now the respondents here are primarily a commercial company concerned in the sale of *inter alia* magazines. It may be presumed that the selection of stock is not a matter of accident but at least dictated to some extent by commercial considerations and in the hope and expectation that the articles exposed will be attractive and saleable and that the selection is at the will and intention of the seller. The transactions under consideration therefore represent conduct which is directed and deliberately directed to members of the public to influence them to purchase articles for sale. In these circumstances I do not see why that conduct directed, as it admittedly would be, towards members of the public as potential purchasers, should not be capable of bearing the qualitative description which the Crown seeks to put upon it. In effect, the test of criminality is objective and not subjective and it is here that Mr Kerrigan's subsidiary or 'subjective' argument appears to me unsound , because it is ill-founded. The question is not whether a company is an entity which is endowed with a conscience to be appeased or a capacity for moral sensation or an absence of a sense of shame or even a capacity to overcome a sense of shame by the prospect of financial profit. It may well be that the offence libelled is one which falls within the category of offences against public morals, but in order to commit it the offender does not require to be possessed of capacity to feel a sense of personal shame or even to lack it. What however is of the essence of the offence is that the action itself of an indecent character should be directed towards a person or persons with certain intentions or knowledge of the consequences or likely consequences to that person or those persons – the intention or knowledge that it should corrupt or be calculated or liable to corrupt or deprave those towards whom the conduct is directed. If these matters can be established by relevant and sufficient evidence then the [33] qualification and therefore the criminal character of the actions themselves are also proved.

In my opinion therefore Mr Kerrigan's two main attacks on the competency of this charge as directed against the respondents fail. By libelling this offence against the respondents it cannot be said the prosecutor is seeking to create a new offence. The offence is one known to the common law, as Mr Kerrigan conceded. Further I do not think that he succeeded in demonstrating that a company cannot possess a capacity in law to intend its actions and therefore be incapable of forming the wilful intent essential to the commission of a common law offence, and as I have already indicated, I think his argument on 'shamelessness' of conduct was misconceived. I do not intend to imply however that a limited company is in law to be regarded as capable of the commission of any and every common law offence, other than those for which the only penalty is custodial, or of offences – such as rape – which are obviously and necessarily physical acts of a natural person. In my opinion, and as at present advised, so to hold would go much further than is necessary for a decision as to the competency of libelling this offence against a limited company. Having considered the arguments presented in this case I am of opinion that a company may competently be charged with an offence at common law, where that offence consists of action purposely taken by the company within its statutory powers and in pursuance of its objects as defined and set out in its articles, and where such action if taken by a natural person would constitute a common law offence.

Tesco Supermarkets Ltd. v. Nattrass
[1972] A.C. 153

This case concerned the attribution of criminal responsibility to companies, a matter touched on in the *Meridian Global Funds* case [1995] 2 A.C. 501 (*supra*, p. 28). The defendant (Tesco) owned a large chain of supermarkets, and from time to time it sold products at prices considerably lower than their normal price. On one occasion there was advertised in a Tesco store a washing power as selling for 2*s*. 11d., when the normal selling price was 3*s*. 11d. A customer, relying on the advertisement, sought washing powder in the store at the advertised price, but could only find it at 3*s*. 11d. Tesco Ltd. were prosecuted for contravening s.11(2) of the Trade Descriptions Act, 1968. According to s.11(2):

> "If any person offering to supply any goods, by whatever means, any indication likely to be taken as an indication that the goods are offered at a price less than that at which they are in fact being offered he shall, subject to the provisions of this Act, be guilty of an offence."

It was not disputed that that section applied to this case. Tesco Ltd. relied on section 24(1) which provides:

> "In any proceedings for an offence under this Act it shall, subject to subsection (2) of this section, be a defence for the person charged to prove – (a) that the commission of the offence was due to a mistake or to reliance on information supplied to him or to the act or default of another person, an accident or some other cause beyond his control; and (b) that he took all reasonable precautions and exercised all due dili-

gence to avoid the commission of such an offence by himself or any person under his control."

LORD REID: . . . [168] The relevant facts as found by the magistrates were that on the previous evening a shop assistant, Miss Rogers, whose duty it was to put out fresh stock found that there were no more of the specially marked packs in stock. There were a number of packs marked with the ordinary price so she put them out. She ought to have told the shop manager, Mr Clement, about this, but she failed to do so. Mr Clement was responsible for seeing that the proper packs were on sale, but he failed to see to this although he marked his daily return 'all special offers O.K.' The magistrates found that if he had known about this he would either have removed the poster advertising the reduced price or given instructions that only 2s. 11d. was to be charged for the packs marked 3s. 11d.

Section 24(2) requires notice to be given to the prosecutor if the accused is blaming another person and such notice was duly given naming Mr Clement.

In order to avoid conviction the appellants had to prove facts sufficient to satisfy both parts of section 24(1) of the Act of 1968. The magistrates held that they had exercised all due diligence in devising a proper system for the operation of the said store and by securing so far as was reasonably practicable that it was fully implemented and thus had fulfilled the requirements of section 24(1)(b).

But they convicted the appellants because in their view the requirements of sections 24(1)(a) had not been fulfilled: they held that Clement was not 'another person' within the meaning of that provision.

[169] The Divisional Court held that the magistrates were wrong in holding that Clement was not 'another person'. The respondent did not challenge this finding of the Divisional Court so I need say no more about it than that I think that on this matter the Divisional Court was plainly right. But that court sustained the conviction on the ground that the magistrates had applied the wrong test in deciding that the requirements of section 24(1)(b) had been fulfilled. In effect that court held that the words 'he took all reasonable precautions . . .' do not mean what they say: 'he' does not mean the accused, it means the accused and all his servants who were acting in a managerial or supervisory capacity. I think that earlier authorities virtually compelled the Divisional Court to reach this strange construction. So the real question in this appeal is whether these earlier authorities were rightly decided.

But before examining those earlier cases I think it necessary to make some general observations.

Over a century ago the courts invented the idea of an absolute offence. The accepted doctrines of the common law put them in a difficulty. There was a presumption that when Parliament makes the commission of certain acts an offence it intends that *mens rea* shall be a constituent of that offence whether or not there is any reference to the knowledge or state of mind of the accused.

And it was and is held to be an invariable rule that where *mens rea* is a constituent of any offence the burden of proving *mens rea* is on the prosecution. Some day this House may have to re-examine that rule, but that is another matter. For the protection of purchasers or consumers Parliament in many cases made it an offence for a trader to do certain things. Normally those things were done on his behalf by his servants and cases arose where the doing of the forbidden thing was solely the fault of a servant, the master having done all he could to prevent it and being entirely ignorant of its having been done. The just course would have been to hold that, once the facts constituting the offence had been proved, *mens rea* would be presumed unless the accused proved that he was blameless. The courts could not, or thought they could not, take that course. But they could and did hold in many such cases on a construction of the statutory provision that Parliament must be deemed to have intended to depart from the general rule and to make the offence absolute in the sense that *mens rea* was not to be a constituent of the offence.

This has led to great difficulties. If the offence is not held to be absolute the requirement that the prosecutor must prove *mens rea* makes it impossible to enforce the enactment in very many cases. If the offence is held to be absolute that leads to the conviction of persons who are entirely blameless: an injustice which brings the law into disrepute. So Parliament has found it necessary to devise a method of avoiding this difficulty. But instead of passing a general enactment that it shall always be a defence for the accused to prove that he was no party to the offence and had done all he could to prevent it, Parliament has chosen to deal with the problem piecemeal, and has in an increasing number of cases enacted in various forms with regard to particular offences that it shall be a defence to prove various exculpatory circumstances.

In my judgment the main object of these provisions must have been to distinguish between those who are in some degree blameworthy and those [170] who are not, and to enable the latter to escape from conviction if they can show that they were in no way to blame. I find it almost impossible to suppose that Parliament or any reasonable body of men would as a matter of policy think it right to make employers criminally liable for the acts of some of their servants but not for those of others and I find it incredible that a draftsman, aware of that intention, would fail to insert any words to express it. But in several cases the courts, for reasons which it is not easy to discover, have given a restricted meaning to such provisions. It has been held that such provisions afford a defence if the master proves that the servant at fault was the person who himself did the prohibited act, but that they afford no defence if the servant at fault was one who failed in his duty of supervision to see that his subordinates did not commit the prohibited act. Why Parliament should be thought to have intended this distinction or how as a matter of construction these provisions can reasonably be held to have that meaning is not apparent.

In some of these cases the employer charged with the offence was a limited company. But in others the employer was an individual and still it was held that he, though personally entirely blameless, could not rely on these provisions if the fault which led to the commission of the offence was the fault of a servant in failing to carry out his duty to instruct or supervise his subordinates.

Where a limited company is the employer difficult questions do arise in a wide variety of circumstances in deciding which of its officers or servants is to be identified with the company so that his guilt is the guilt of the company.

I must start by considering the nature of the personality which by a fiction the law attributes to a corporation. A living person has a mind which can have knowledge or intention or be negligent and he has hands to carry out his intentions. A corporation has none of these: it must act through living persons, though not always one or the same person. Then the person who acts is not speaking or acting for the company. He is acting as the company and his mind which directs his acts is the mind of the company. There is no question of the company being vicariously liable. He is not acting as a servant, representative, agent or delegate. He is an embodiment of the company or, one could say, he hears and speaks through the persona of the company, within his appropriate sphere, and his mind is the mind of the company. If it is a guilty mind then that guilt is the guilt of the company. It must be a question of law whether, once the facts have been ascertained, a person in doing particular things is to be regarded as the company or merely as the company's servant or agent. In that case any liability of the company can only be a statutory or vicarious liability.

In *Lennard's Carrying Co. Ltd. v. Asiatic Petroleum Co. Ltd.* [1915] A.C. 705 the question was whether damage had occurred without the 'actual fault or privity' of the owner of a ship. The owners were a company. The fault was that of the registered managing owner who managed the ship on behalf of the owners and it was held that the company could not dissociate itself from him so as to say that there was no actual fault or privity on the part of the company. Viscount Haldane L.C. said, at pp. 713, 714:

> [171] "For if Mr Lennard was the directing mind of the company, then his action must, unless a corporation is not to be liable at all, have been an action which was the action of the company itself within the meaning of section 502. . . . It must be upon the true construction of that section in such a case as the present one that the fault or privity is the fault or privity of somebody who is not merely a servant or agent for whom the company is liable upon the footing respondent superior, but somebody for whom the company is liable because his action is the very action of the company itself."

Reference is frequently made to the judgment of Denning L.J. *in H.L. Bolton (Engineering) Co. Ltd. v. T.F. Graham & Sons Ltd.* [1957] 1 Q.B. 159. He said, at p. 172:

"A company may in many ways be likened to a human body. It has a brain and nerve centre which controls what it does. It also has hands which hold the tools and acts in accordance with directions from the centre. Some of the people in the company are mere servants and agents who are nothing more than hands to do the work and cannot be said to represent the mind or will. Others are directors and managers who represent the directing mind and will of the company, and control what it does. The state of mind of these managers is the state of mind of the company and is treated by the law as such."

In that case the directors of the company only met once a year: they left the management of the business to others, and it was the intention of those managers which was imputed to the company. I think that was right. There have been attempts to apply Lord Denning's words to all servants of a company whose work is brain work, or who exercise some managerial discretion under the direction of superior officers of the company. I do not think that Lord Denning intended to refer to them. He only referred to those who 'represent the directing mind and will of the company, and control what it does'.

I think that is right for this reason. Normally the board of directors, the managing director and perhaps other superior officers of a company carry out the functions of management and speak and act as the company. Their subordinates do not. They carry out orders from above and it can make no difference that they are given some measure of discretion. But the board of directors may delegate full discretion to act independently of instructions from them. I see no difficulty in holding that they have thereby put such a delegate in their place so that within the scope of the delegation he can act as the company. It may not always be easy to draw the line but there are cases in which the line must be drawn. *Lennard's* case [1915] A.C. 705 was one of them.

In some cases the phrase alter ego has been used. I think it is misleading. When dealing with a company the word alter is I think misleading. The person who speaks and acts as the company is not alter. He is identified with the company. And when dealing with an individual no other individual can be his alter ego. The other individual can be a servant, agent, delegate or representative but I know of neither principle [172] nor authority which warrants the confusion (in the literal or original sense) of two separate individuals. . . .

[173] In the next two cases a company was accused and it was held liable for the fault of a superior officer. In *Director of Public Prosecutions v. Kent and Sussex Contractors Ltd.* [1944] K.B. 146 he was the transport manager. In *Rex v. I.C.R. Haulage Ltd.* [1944] K.B. 551 it was held that a company can be guilty of common law conspiracy. The act of the managing director was held to be the act of the company. I think that a passage in the judgment is too widely stated, at p. 559:

"Where in any particular case there is evidence to go to a jury that the criminal act of an agent, including his state of mind, intention, knowledge or belief is the act of the company, and, in cases where the presiding judge so rules, whether the jury are satisfied that it has been proved, must depend on the nature of the charge, the relative position of the officer or agent, and the other relevant facts and circumstances of the case."

This may have been influenced by the erroneous views expressed in the two *Hammett* cases. I think that the true view is that the judge must direct the jury that if they find certain facts proved then as a matter of law they must find that the criminal act of the officer, servant or agent including his state of mind, intention, knowledge or belief is the act of the company. I have already dealt with the considerations to be applied in deciding when such a person can and when he cannot be identified with the company. I do not see how the nature of the charge can make any difference. If the guilty man was in law identifiable with the company then whether his offence was serious or venial his act was the act of the company but if he was not so identifiable then no act of his, serious or otherwise, was the act of the company itself.

In *John Henshall (Quarries) Ltd. v. Harvey* [1965] 2 Q.B. 233 a company was held not criminally responsible for the negligence of a servant in charge of a weighbridge. In *Magna Plant v. Mitchell* (unreported) April 27, 1966, the fault was that of a depot engineer and again the company was held not criminally responsible. I think these decisions were right. In the *Magna Plant* case Lord Parker C.J. said:

"... knowledge of a servant cannot be imputed to the company unless he is a servant for whose actions the company are criminally responsible, and as the cases show, that only arises in the case of a company where one is considering the acts of responsible officers forming the brain, or in the case of an individual, a person to whom delegation in the true sense of the delegation of management has been passed."

I agree with what he said with regard to a company. But delegation by an individual is another matter. It has been recognised in licensing cases but that is in my view anomalous (see *Vane v. Yiannopoullos* [1965] A.C. 486).

The latest important authority is *Series v. Poole* [1969] 1 Q.B. 676. That was an appeal against the dismissal of an information that the holder of a carrier's licence had failed to keep or cause to be kept records required by the Road Traffic Act, 1960 with regard to the driver of a vehicle. That was [174] an absolute offence but that was amended by the Road Traffic Act, 1962 which provided by section 20 that it should 'be a defence to prove that he used all due diligence to secure compliance with those provisions.' The respondent proved that he had given proper instructions to the driver, that he employed a secretary to check the driver's records and had to begin with supervised her work, but that thereafter she failed to make the proper checks. The justices held, possibly wrongly, that the accused had used all due diligence as required by the Act. The court accepted that finding but nevertheless sent the case back with a direction to convict.

Lord Parker C.J. dealt with the case on the basis that the accused had done everything that was reasonable. He said, at p. 684:

> "He may . . . acting perfectly reasonably appoint somebody else to perform his duty, his alter ego, and in that case it seems to me if the alter ego fails in his duty the employer is liable. Equally, if the employer seeks to rely on the defence under section 20, he must show that the alter ego has observed due diligence."

I have already said that the phrase alter ego is misleading. In my judgment this case was wrongly decided and should be overruled. When the second statute introduced a defence if the accused proved that 'he used all due diligence' I think that it meant what it said. As a matter of construction I can see no ground for reading in 'he and all persons to whom he had delegated responsibility.' And if I look to the purpose and apparent intention of Parliament in enacting this defence I think that it was plainly intended to make a just and reasonable distinction between the employer who is wholly blameless and ought to be acquitted and the employer who was in some way at fault, leaving it to the employer to prove that he was in no way to blame.

What good purpose could be served by making an employer criminally responsible for the misdeeds of some of his servants but not for those of others? It is sometimes argued – it was argued in the present case – that making an employer criminally responsible, even when he has done all that he could to prevent an offence, affords some additional protection to the public because this will induce him to do more. But if he has done all he can how can he do more? I think that what lies behind this argument is a suspicion that magistrates too readily accept evidence that an employer has done all he can to prevent offences. But if magistrates were to accept as sufficient a paper scheme and perfunctory efforts to enforce it they would not be doing their duty – that would not be 'due diligence' on the part of the employer.

Then it is said that this would involve discrimination in favour of a large employer like the appellants against a small shopkeeper. But that is not so. Mr Clement was the 'opposite number' of the small shopkeeper and he was liable to prosecution in this case. The purpose of this Act must have been to penalise those at fault, not those who were in no way to blame.

The Divisional Court decided this case on a theory of delegation. In that they were following some earlier authorities. But they gave far too wide a meaning to delegation. I have said that a board of directors can delegate part of their functions of management so as to make their delegate an [175] embodiment of the company within the sphere of the delegation. But here the board never delegated any part of their functions. They set up a chain of command through regional and district supervisors, but they remained in control. The shop managers had to obey their general directions and also take orders from their superiors. The acts or omissions of shop managers were not the acts of the company itself.

SEGREGATION FROM OWNERS

See *Company Law*, pp. 51–63.

The overriding consequence of incorporation of a company is that the company is legally distinct from its owners and, if it is a limited company, the liability of its members to company creditors is limited in the manner provided for, *i.e.* either what remains unpaid on the issued share capital or, in the case of guarantee companies, the sum so guaranteed.

Salomon v. Salomon & Co. Ltd.
[1897] A.C. 22

Mr Salomon (the vendor) sold a solvent business to a limited company with a nominal capital of 40,000 shares of £1 each, the company consisting only of the vendor, his wife, a daughter and four sons, who subscribed for one share each, all the terms of sale being known to and approved by the shareholders. In part payment of the purchase-money, debentures forming a floating security were issued to the vendor. Twenty thousand shares were also issued to him and were paid for out of the purchase-money. These shares gave the vendor the power of outvoting the six other shareholders. No shares other than these 20,007 were ever issued. All the requirements of the Companies Act, 1862 were complied with. The vendor was appointed managing director, bad times came, the company was wound up, but, after satisfying the debentures, there was not enough to pay the ordinary creditors.

LORD HALSBURY L.C.: [29] [T]he important question in this case, I am not certain it is not the only question, is whether the respondent company was a company at all – whether in truth that artificial creation of the Legislature had been validly constituted in this instance; and in order to determine that question it is necessary to look at what the statute itself had determined in that respect. I have no right to add to the requirements of the statute, nor to take from the requirements thus enacted. The sole guide must be the statute itself.

Now, that there were seven actual living persons who held shares in the company has not been doubted. As to the proportionate amounts held by each I will deal presently; but it is important to observe that this first condition of the statute is satisfied, and it follows as a consequence that it would not [30] be competent to any one – and certainly not to these persons themselves – to deny that they were shareholders.

I must pause here to point out that the statute enacts nothing as to the extent or degree of interest which may be held by each of the seven, or as to the proportion of interest or influence possessed by one or the majority of the shareholders over the others. One share in enough. Still less is it possible to contend that the motive of becoming shareholders or of making them share-holders is a field of inquiry which the statute itself recognises as legitimate. If they are shareholders, they are shareholders for all purposes; and even if the statute was silent as to the recognition of trusts, I should be prepared to hold that if six of them were the cestuis que trust of the seventh, whatever might be their rights inter se, the statute would have made them shareholders to all intents and purposes with their respective rights and liabilities, and, dealing with them in their relation to the company, the only relations which I believe the law would sanction would be that they were corporators of the corporate body.

I am simply here dealing with the provisions of the statute, and it seems to me to be essential to the artificial creation that the law should recognise only that artificial existence – quite apart from the motives or conduct of individual corporators. In saying this, I do not at all mean to suggest that if it could be established that this provision of the statute to which I am adverting had not been complied with, you could not go behind the certificate of incorporation to shew that a fraud had been committed upon the officer entrusted with the duty of giving the certificate, and that by some proceeding in the nature of scire facias you could not prove the fact that the company had no real legal existence. But short of such proof it seems to me impossible to dispute that once the company is legally incorporated it must be treated like any other independent person with its rights and liabilities appropriate to itself, and that the motives of those who took part in the promotion of the company are abso-lutely irrelevant in discussing what those rights and liabilities are.

I will for the sake of argument assume the proposition that [31] the Court of Appeal lays down – that the formation of the company was a mere scheme to enable Aron Salomon to carry on business in the name of the company. I am wholly unable to follow the proposition that this was contrary to the true intent and meaning of the Companies Act. I can only find true intent and meaning of the Act from the Act itself; and the Act appears to me to give a company a legal existence with, as I have said, rights and liabilities of its own, whatever may have been the ideas or schemes of those who brought it into existence.

I observe that the learned judge (Vaughan Williams J.) held that the busi-ness was Mr Salomon's business, and no one else's, and that he chose to em-ploy as agent a limited company; and he proceeded to argue that he was employing that limited company as agent, and that he was bound to indemnify that agent (the company). I confess it seems to me that that very learned judge becomes involved by this argument in a very singular contradiction. Either the limited company was a legal entity or it was not. If it was, the business belonged to it and not to Mr Salomon. If it was not, there was no person and no thing to be an agent at all; and it is impossible to say at the same time that there is a company and there is not.

Lindley L.J., on the other hand, affirms that there were seven members of the company; but he says it is manifest that six of them were members simply in order to enable the seventh himself to carry on business with limited liability. The object of the whole arrangement is to do the very thing which the Legislature intended not to be done.

It is obvious to inquire where is that intention of the Legislature manifested in the statute. Even if we were at liberty to insert words to manifest that intention, I should have great difficulty in ascertaining what the exact intention thus imputed to the Legislature is, or was. In this particular case it is the members of one family that represent all the shares; but if the supposed intention is not limited to so narrow a proposition as this, that the seven shareholders must not be members of one family, to what extent may influence or authority or intentional purchase of a majority among the shareholders be carried so as [32] to bring it within the supposed prohibition? It is, of course, easy to say that it was contrary to the intention of the Legislature – a proposition which, by reason of its generality, it is difficult to bring to the test; but when one seeks to put as an affirmative proposition what the thing is which the Legislature has prohibited, there is, as it appears to me, an insuperable difficulty in the way of those who seek to insert by construction such a prohibition into the statute.

As one mode of testing the proposition, it would be pertinent to ask whether two or three, or indeed all seven, may constitute the whole of the shareholders? Whether they must be all independent of each other in the sense of each having an independent beneficial interest? And this is a question that cannot be answered by the reply that it is a matter of degree. If the legislature intended to prohibit something, you ought to know what that something is. All it has said is that one share is sufficient to constitute a shareholder, though the shares may be 100,000 in number. Where am I to get from the statute itself a limitation of that provision that that shareholder must be an independent and beneficially interested person? . . .

[33] Vaughan Williams J. appears to me to have disposed of the argument that the company (which for this purpose he assumed to be a legal entity) was defrauded into the purchase of Aron Salomon's business because, assuming that the price paid for the business was an exorbitant one, as to which I am myself not satisfied, but assuming that it was, the learned judge most cogently observes that when all the shareholders are perfectly cognisant of the conditions under which the company is formed and the conditions of the purchase, it is impossible to contend that the company is being defrauded. . . .

My Lords, the truth is that the learned judges have never allowed in their own minds the proposition that the company [34] has a real existence. They have been struck by what they have considered the inexpediency of permitting one man to be in influence and authority (over) the whole company; and, assuming that such a thing could not have been intended by the Legislature, they have sought various grounds upon which they might insert into the Act some prohibition of such a result. Whether such a result be right or wrong, politic or impolitic, I say, with the utmost deference to the learned judges, that we have nothing to do with that question if this company has been duly constituted by law; and, whatever may be the motives of those who constitute it, I must decline to insert into that Act of Parliament limitations which are not to be found there.

LORD MACNAGHTEN: . . . [50] [The liquidator] disputed the validity of the debentures on the ground of fraud. On the same ground he claimed rescission of the agreement for the transfer of the business, cancellation of the debentures, and repayment by Mr Salomon of the balance of the purchase-money. In the alternative, he claimed payment of £20,000 on Mr Salomon's shares, alleging that nothing had been paid on them. When the trial came on. . . it was not disputed that the 20,000 shares were fully paid up. The case presented by the liquidator broke down completely; but the learned judge suggested that the company had a right of indemnity against Mr Salomon. The signatories of the memorandum of association were, he said, mere nominees of Mr Salomon – mere dummies. The company was Mr Salomon in another form. He used the name of the company as an alias. He employed the company as his agent; so the company, he thought, was entitled to indemnity against its principal. The counter-claim was accordingly amended to raise this point; and on the amendment being made the learned judge pronounced an order in accordance with the view he had expressed.

The order of the learned judge appears to me to be founded on a misconception of the scope and effect of the Companies Act, 1862. In order to form a company limited by shares, the Act requires that a memorandum of association should be signed by seven persons, who are each to take one share at least. If those conditions are complied with, what can it matter whether the signatories are relations or strangers? There is nothing in the Act requiring that the subscribers to the memorandum should be independent or unconnected, or [51] that they or any one of them should take a substantial interest in the undertaking, or that they should have a mind and will of their own, as one of the learned Lord Justices seems to think, or that there should be anything like a balance of power in the constitution of the company. In almost every company that is formed the statutory number is eked out by clerks or friends, who sign their names at the request of the promoter or promoters without intending to take any further part or interest in the matter.

When the memorandum is duly signed and registered, though there be only seven shares taken, the subscribers are a body corporate 'capable forthwith, to use the words of the enactment', 'of exercising all the functions of an incorporated company.' Those are strong words. The company attains maturity on its birth. There is no period of minority – no interval of incapacity. I cannot understand how a body corporate thus made 'capable' by statute can lose its individuality by issuing the bulk of its capital to one person, whether he be a subscriber to the memorandum or not. The company is at law a different person altogether from the subscribers to the memorandum; and, though it may be that after incorporation the business is precisely the same as it was before, and the same persons are managers, and the same hands receive the profits, the company is not in law the agent of the subscribers or trustee for them. Nor are the subscribers as members liable, in any shape or form, except to the extent and in the manner provided by the Act. That is, I think, the declared intention of the enactment. If the view of the learned judge were sound, it would follow that no common law partnership could register as a company limited by shares without remaining subject to unlimited liability. . . .

[52] Among the principal reasons which induce persons to form private companies, as is stated very clearly by Mr Palmer in his treatise on the subject, are the desire to avoid the risk of bankruptcy, and the increased facility afforded for borrowing money. By means of a private company, as Mr Palmer observes, a trade can be carried on with limited liability, and without exposing the persons interested in it in the event of failure to the harsh provisions of the bankruptcy law. A company, too, can raise money on debentures, which an ordinary trader cannot do. Any member of a company, acting in good faith is as much entitled to take and hold the company's debentures as any outside creditor. Every creditor is entitled to get and to hold the best security the law allows him to take. . . .

[53] The unsecured creditors of A. Salomon and Company, Limited, may be entitled to sympathy, but they have only themselves to blame for their misfortunes. They trusted the company, I suppose, because they had long dealt with Mr Salomon, and he had always paid his way; but they had full notice that they were no longer dealing with an individual, and they must be taken to have been cognisant of the memorandum and of the articles of association. For such a catastrophe as has occurred in this case some would blame the law that allows the creation of a floating charge. But a floating charge is too convenient a form of security to be tightly abolished. I have long thought, and I believe some of your Lordships also think, that the ordinary trade creditors of a trading company ought to have a preferential claim on the assets in liquidation in respect of debts incurred within a certain limited time before the winding-up. But that is not the law at present. Everybody knows that when there is a winding-up debenture-holders generally step in and sweep off everything; and a great scandal it is.

It has become the fashion to call companies of this class 'one man companies'. That is a taking nickname, but it does not help one much in the way of argument. If it is intended to convey the meaning that a company which is under the absolute control of one person is not a company legally incorporated, although the requirements of the Act of 1862 may have been complied with, it is inaccurate and misleading: if it merely means that there is a predominant partner possessing an overwhelming influence and entitled practically to the whole of the profits, there is nothing in that that I can see contrary to the true intention of the Act, of 1862, or against public policy, or detrimental to the interests of creditors. If the shares are fully paid up, it cannot matter whether they are in the hands of one or many. If the shares are not fully paid, it is as easy to gauge the solvency of an individual as to estimate the financial ability of a crowd.

Roundabout Ltd. v. Beirne
[1959] I.R. 423

The net issue was whether, because the defendants had previously been employed by the lessor of a public house, they should be regarded as ex-employees of the lessee company for the purposes of the Trade Disputes Act 1916. The owners of a pub, having closed the premises in circumstances giving rise to a trade dispute with the defendants, leased the premises with an option to purchase to the plaintiff company, the directors of which were those same owners, their accountant and three barmen. When the premises were subsequently re-opened for business by the company, the entire work there was carried out by the directors themselves, no person being employed by them. The barmen directors were paid a fixed yearly sum by way of directors' remuneration, which was paid at such irregular intervals and in such irregular proportions as was found convenient. The defendants, who had been picketing the premises throughout the period that they were closed, continued to picket there subsequent to their re-opening. The plaintiff brought an action for, *inter alia*, an injunction to restrain the defendants from watching, besetting or picketing the plaintiffs' premises.

DIXON J.: . . . [426] There is no doubt that a trade dispute was raised and existed between the trade union and some of its members on the one hand and the Marian Park Inn Company on the other hand. [427]

That company has ceased to carry on business in these premises, and the only question in this case is whether the trade dispute survives as against the new company which has been formed and which has taken a lease of the premises from the Marian Park Inn Company. The trade dispute still exists with what I may call the old company, and the question is whether the Union can avail itself of that dispute for the purpose of picketing the premises which are now occupied, and in which business is now carried on, by the new company.

The new company is in law a distinct entity, as is the old company. Each company is what is known as a legal person. I have to regard the two companies as distinct in the same way as I would regard two distinct individuals. I must therefore proceed on the basis that a new and different person is now in occupation of the premises and carrying on business there.

It has been suggested – and there is some basis for the suggestion – that the new company was formed for the purpose of getting rid of the trade dispute and also of enabling the employment of Union staff to be dispensed with. There is considerable substance in that suggestion. I think that it is quite permissible to describe the formation of the new company as a subterfuge – a legal subterfuge – to put an end to the trade dispute and enable the business to be carried on without the inconvenience of being subject to the picket. To this description there are two qualifications: first, that even though the formation of the new company may be a subterfuge, the question I have to decide is not ruled by that; the question which I must determine is whether it is a successful subterfuge, capable of effectually achieving its purpose. The second qualification is that I do not think that the sole, or possibly even the primary, purpose of the formation of the new company was to get rid of the trade dispute. I think that there was a genuine idea of getting new blood into the business and a genuine idea of the business eventually being taken over in some way by which the Morans would cease to have a substantial interest, and might possibly cease to have any interest in the premises or business. At the moment, indeed, the Morans are in control, constituting the three permanent directors of the new company. The other directors of the new company are at their mercy in a sense – in the sense that if the permanent directors see fit to remove the other directors, they can require them to transfer their entire shares or interest in the company. The new directors, however, are satisfied with that position: they are satisfied to rely on the Morans, and to trust to the [428] Morans that the new directors will not, as it were, be thrown out, and that, to put it colloquially, there will eventually be something in it for them.

While this new arrangement contains a considerable element of subterfuge, as a scheme designed to get rid, if legally possible, of the existing trade dispute, that is not the whole end and object of the arrangement. I must regard the new company as what it is, a distinct legal entity, and approach the position from the same point of view as if some individual or company totally unconnected with the old company had taken a lease of these premises similar to the lease taken here. The question then is whether a picket can be placed on the premises of the new owner by reason of a trade dispute with the previous owner. In the only case decided in this country on that matter, *Ferguson v. O'Gorman and Others* [1937] I.R. 620, Meredith J. held that, in the circumstances of that case, the existing trade dispute did attach to the premises when purchased by the new company, but there are distinctions between the facts of that case and those of the present case, which, I think, render the decision in that case inapplicable to the present case. In that case a company was formed which purchased the premises and took over the business of a partnership as a going concern, so that a new owner of the premises was substituted for the old, and the legal effect was the same as if the partnership had converted itself into a company.

In the present case, that is not the legal position. The old company still has not merely an interest in, but the ownership of, the premises. The new company has taken a lease of the premises from the old company; it has not taken over the business as a going concern.

Another distinction between the two cases is that, in the present case, the new company are not 'employers' in the sense that would bring them within the terms of the Trade Disputes Act, 1906. To make picketing lawful within that Act, it must be conducted 'in contemplation of furtherance of a trade dispute' and a 'trade dispute' is defined, in s. 5, sub-s. 3, of the Act as being (so far as material here) a 'dispute between employers and workmen . . .' There is no doubt that 'workmen,' within the definition thereof in the Trade Disputes Act, 1906, are involved in this dispute, but there must, on the other side, be employers. 'Workmen' are defined, in s. 5, sub-s. 3, of the Act as 'all persons employed in trade or industry, whether or not in the employment of the employer with whom a trade dispute arises.' The practical effect of that definition is that, if a [429] trade dispute arises between workmen and employers in one premises, it might, and in most cases would, be permissible for the workmen or for other members of their trade union to picket entirely different premises owned or occupied by a totally different employer. It is an everyday feature of trade disputes that the dispute does not exist with the particular employer who is being picketed; the object of that provision of the Trade Disputes Act is to legalise sympathetic or consequential picketing. Before such picketing can be legalised the person whose premises are being picketed must first be an employer, for the obvious reason that the object of the picketing must be to act by influence or persuasion on employees. The distinction is perhaps a fine one, but where there is no trade dispute with the individual owner or occupier of the premises which are being picketed, such picketing can be justified only if such owner or occupier is in fact an employer.

The new company here is not an employer. It is true that it is a potential employer in the sense that it may well in the future be compelled by circumstances to take on staff, but at present it is not, and never has been, an employer in the sense in which that term is used in the Trade Disputes Act, 1906. It is true that the directors of the company do work in the licensed premises, but a distinction must be observed between directors who do work for a company and workmen who are employed by the company. The former cannot be regarded as working in pursuance of any contract of employment, and, therefore, cannot be regarded as workmen of the company. The fact that the company may at some future time be an employer is not sufficient to entitle me to hold that it is at present an employer, so as to entitle the defendants to claim the protection of the Trades Disputes Act, 1906.

The onus of establishing the existence of a trade dispute lies on the persons alleging its existence; in my view no trade dispute has been shown to exist between the plaintiffs, Roundabout Ltd., and the defendants, and accordingly the plaintiffs are entitled to have the interim injunction continued in a more permanent form. I propose, however, to grant the perpetual injunction only against the four named defendants.

Note: The legal position there would now be affected by the European Communities (Safeguarding of Employees' Rights on Transfer of Undertakings) Regulations, 1980 (S.I. No. 306), giving effect to the E.C. Council Directive 77/187, OJ. No. L61/26 (1977); see *Westman Holdings Ltd v. McCormack* [1992] 1 I.R. 151.

Lee v. Lee's Air Farming Ltd
[1961] A.C. 12

The issue here was whether, for the purposes of workers' compensation, a person who beneficially owns all the shares in a company, has complete control over its affairs and is also its managing director can at the same time be its employee. The plaintiff's husband formed a company for carrying on the business of aerial top-dressing. He was the controlling shareholder and was, by its articles of association, appointed governing director and employed at a salary as its chief pilot. In his capacity as governing director and controlling shareholder he exercised full and unrestricted control over all the operations of the company. Pursuant to its statutory obligations the company had insured itself against liability to pay compensation in the case of accident to him. While piloting an aircraft belonging to the company in the course of aerial top-dressing operations, the aircraft crashed and he was killed. His widow claimed against the company for compensation, alleging that at the time of the accident her husband was a "worker" employed by the respondent company within the meaning of the Workers' Compensation Act, 1922.

LORD MORRIS OF BORTH-Y-GEST: [24] The New Zealand Court of Appeal recognised that a director of a company may properly enter into a service agreement with his company but they considered that, in the present case, inasmuch as the deceased was the governing director in whom was vested the full government and control of the company he could not also be a servant of the company. After referring in his judgment to the delegation to the deceased of substantially all the powers of the company, North J. said [1959] N.Z.L.R. 393: These powers were moreover delegated to him for life and there remained with the company no power of management whatsoever. One of his first acts was to appoint himself the only pilot of the company, for, although article 33 foreshadowed this appointment, yet a contract could only spring into existence after the company had been incorporated. Therefore, he became in effect both employer and worker. True, the contract of employment was between himself and the company: see *Booth v. Helliwell* [1914] 3 K.B. 252 but on him lay the duty both of giving orders and obeying them. In our view, the two offices are clearly incompatible. There could exist no power of control and therefore the relationship of master-servant was not created.

The substantial question which arises is, as their Lordships think, whether the deceased was a "worker" within the meaning of the Workers' Compensation Act, 1922, and its amendments. Was he a person who had entered into or worked under a contract of service with an employer? The Court of Appeal thought that his special position as governing director precluded him from being a servant of the company. On this view it is difficult to know what his status and position was when he was performing the arduous and skilful duties of piloting an aeroplane [25] which belonged to the company and when he was carrying out the operation of top-dressing farm lands from the air. He was paid wages for so doing. The company kept a wages book in which these were recorded. The work that was being done was being done at the request of farmers whose contractual rights and obligations were with the company alone. It cannot be suggested that when engaged in the activities above referred to the deceased was discharging his duties as governing director. Their Lordships find it impossible to resist the conclusion that the active aerial operations were performed because the deceased was in some contractual relationship with the company. That relationship came about because the deceased as one legal person was willing to work for and to make a contract with the company which was another legal entity. A contractual relationship could only exist on the basis that there was consensus between two contracting parties. It was never suggested (nor in their Lordships' view could it reasonably have been suggested) that the company was a sham or a mere simulacrum. It is well established that the mere fact that someone is a director of a company is no impediment to his entering into a contract to serve the company. If, then, it be accepted that the respondent company was a legal entity their Lordships see no reason to challenge the validity of any contractual obligations which were created between the company and the deceased. In this connection reference may be made to a passage in the speech of Lord Halsbury L.C. in *Salomon v. Salomon & Co.* [1897] A.C. 22, 33:

> "My Lords, the learned judges appear to me not to-have been absolutely certain in their own minds whether to treat the company as a real thing or not. If it was a real thing; if it had a legal existence, and if consequently the law attributed to it certain rights and liabilities in its constitution as a company, it appears to me to follow as a consequence that it is impossible to deny the validity of the transactions into which it has entered."

A similar approach was evidenced in the speech of Lord MacNaghten when he said [1897] A.C. 22, 53:

"It has become the fashion to call companies of this class 'one man companies.' That is a taking nickname, but it does not help one much in the way of argument. If it is intended to convey the meaning that a company which is under the absolute control of one person is not a company legally incorporated, although the requirements of the Act, of 1862 may have [26] been complied with, it is inaccurate and misleading: if it merely means that there is a predominant partner possessing an overwhelming influence and entitled practically to the whole of the profits, there is nothing in that that I can see contrary to the true intention of the Act of 1862, or against public policy, or detrimental to the interests of creditors."

Nor in their Lordships' view were any contractual obligations invalidated by the circumstance that the deceased was sole governing director in whom was vested the full government and control of the company. Always assuming that the company was not a sham then the capacity of the company to make a contract with the deceased could not be impugned merely because the deceased was the agent of the company in its negotiation. The deceased might have made a firm contract to serve the company for a fixed period of years. If within such period he had retired from the office of governing director and other directors had been appointed his contract would not have been affected. The circumstance that in his capacity as a shareholder he could control the course of events would not in itself affect the validity of his contractual relationship with the company. When, therefore, it is said that "one of his first acts was to appoint himself the only pilot of the company," it must be recognised that the appointment was made by the company, and that it was none the less a valid appointment because it was the deceased himself who acted as the agent of the company in arranging it. In their Lordships' view it is a logical consequence of the decision in *Salomon's* case that one person may function in dual capacities. There is no reason, therefore, to deny the possibility of a contractual relationship being created as between the deceased and the company. If this stage is reached then their lordships see no reason why the range of possible contractual relationships should not include a contract for services, and if the deceased as agent for the company could negotiate a contract for services as between the company and himself there is no reason why a contract of service could not also be negotiated. It is said that therein lies the difficulty, because it is said that the deceased could not both be under the duty of giving orders and also be under the duty of obeying them. But this approach does not give effect to the circumstance that it would be the company and not the deceased that would be giving the orders. Control would remain with the company whoever might be the agent of the company [27] to exercise it. The fact that so long as the deceased continued to be governing director, with amplitude of powers, it would be for him to act as the agent of the company to give the orders does not alter the fact that the company and the deceased were two separate and distinct legal persons. If the deceased had a contract of service with the company then the company had a right of control. The manner of its exercise would not affect or diminish the right to its exercise. But the existence of a right to control cannot be denied if once the reality of the legal existence of the company is recognised. Just as the company and the deceased were separate legal entities so as to permit of contractual relations being established between them, so also were they separate legal entities so as to enable the company to give an order to the deceased.

An illustration of the validity of transactions entered into between a company comparable to the respondent company and its sole governing director is found in the case of *Inland Revenue Commissioners v. Sansom* [1921] 2 K.B. 492. Sansom sold his business as a going concern to a private company, John Sansom Ltd. He became the sole governing director of the company, and the whole direction, control and management of the business and affairs of the company were in his hands. The company made large profit but no dividends were ever declared. He was the only director. The capital of the company was £25,000 divided into 2,500 shares of £10 each. Sansom held 2,499 shares and had given one share to someone who had previously been employed by him. By its memorandum the company had power to lend money to such persons and on such terms as it should think fit. The company made what were described in the balance sheets as loans or "advances" to Sansom. They were made without interest and without any security. Sansom was assessed to super-tax on the loans; he was so assessed on the basis that the amounts received by him were in fact not "loans or advances" but constituted an income received by him from the company. Sansom appealed to the commissioners. They found that the company was a properly constituted legal entity: that it had power to make loans to such persons and upon such terms as it should think fit: that it did make such loans to Sansom, and that such loans did not form part of Sansom's income for the purposes of super-tax. On appeal by the Crown on a case stated the judge made an order remitting the case to the commissioners to find whether in point [28] and in fact the company did carry on, the business or Sansom really carried it on to the exclusion of the company: whether if the company did carry on the business it carried it on as agent for Sansom who was to be regarded as a principal standing outside the company: whether the company carried on the business on its own behalf and for the benefit of the corporators. On appeal to the Court of Appeal it was held that the findings of the commissioners being on questions of fact were conclusive and involved the negativing of the questions which the judge had directed to be put to them: accordingly, the order remitting the case to the commissioners was discharged. In his judgment Younger L.J. said: "It is conceded that the entire property in this business was bought and paid for by the company, that it passed to the company nearly ten years ago, that every transaction thereafter was carried out by and the company's name, and has now been carried to completion in a liquidation regularly constituted. In those circumstances unless the company's legal status is to be denied to it – and this is expressly disclaimed by the learned judge-there appears to me to be no room on this case as stated for directing any such inquiry." He further said: In my judgment so long as such a company as this was is recognised by the legislature there can be no reason why the contracts and the engagements made in its name or entered into on its behalf, and themselves ex facie regular, should not everywhere until the contrary is alleged and proved be regarded as the company's. . ."

An illustration of circumstances in which a person may possess dual roles is seen in *Fowler v. Commercial Timber Co. Ltd* [1930] 2 K.B. 1. In that case the plaintiff was appointed managing director of the defendant company (which was not a so-called "one man company" for a period of years. The company did not prosper and the time came when it became clear' that if it were not voluntarily wound up it would be compulsorily wound up. The directors, including the plaintiff, resolved that it was desirable to wind up the company voluntarily. An extraordinary general meeting was called at which the plaintiff was present and it was unanimously resolved to wind up the company voluntarily. The liquidators gave the plaintiff notice that his agreement was terminated and that his services were no longer required. He claimed damages for wrongful dismissal, and it was held that [29] there was no implied term in his agreement that he should lose his right to recover damages for breach of his agreement if the company went into voluntary liquidation with his assent or approval. Scrutton L.J. said: "Such a complicated term cannot be implied for this reason: the two positions of the plaintiff (1) as managing director, who claims damages for breach of the contract of employment, and (2) as a director and shareholder of the company who thinks that in its own interests the company ought to stop business are quite consistent."

In the present case their Lordships see no reason to doubt that a valid contractual relationship could be created between the respondent company and the deceased even though the deceased would act as the agent of the company in its creation. If such relationship could be established their Lordships see no reason why it should not take the form of a master and servant relationship. The facts of the present case lend no support for the contention that if a contract existed it was a contract for services. Article 33, recited above, shows that what was designed and contemplated was that after its incorporation the respondent company would, as a master, employ the deceased, as a servant, in the capacity of chief pilot of the company. All the facts and all the evidence as to what was actually done point to the conclusion that what purported to be a contract of service was entered into and was operated. Unless this was an impossibility in law, then the deceased was a worker within the statutory definition as referred to above. It is said that the deceased could not both give orders and obey them and that no power of control over the deceased was in existence. It is true that an inquiry as to whether a person is or is not employed upon the terms that he will, within the scope of his employment, obey his master's orders may constitute an important inquiry if it is being tested in a particular case whether there is a contract of service as opposed to a contract for services: see *Simmons v. Heath Laundry Co.* [1910] 1 K.B. 543 and *Short v. J. & W. Henderson Ltd* [1946] S.C. (H.L.) 24. But in the present case their Lordships can find nothing to support the contention that there was or may have been a contract for services but not a contract of service.

Ex facie there was a contract of service. Their Lordships conclude, therefore, that the real issue in the case is whether the [30] position of the deceased as sole governing director made it impossible for him to be the servant of the company in the capacity of chief pilot of the company. In their Lordships' view, for the reasons which have been indicated, there was no such impossibility. There appears to be no greater difficulty in holding that a man acting in, one capacity can give orders to himself in another capacity than there is in holding that a man acting in one capacity can make a contract with himself in another capacity. The company and the deceased were separate legal entities. The company had the right to decide what contracts for aerial top-dressing it would enter into. The deceased was the agent of the company in making the necessary decisions. Any profits earned would belong to the company and not to the deceased. If the company entered into a contract with a farmer, then it lay within its right and power to direct its chief pilot to perform certain operations. The right to control existed even though it would be for the deceased in his capacity as agent for the company to decide what orders to give. The right to control existed in the company, and an application of the principles of *Salomon's* case demonstrates that the company was distinct from the deceased. As pointed out above, there might have come a time when the deceased would remain bound contractually to serve the company as chief pilot though he had retired from the office of sole governing director. Their Lordships consider, therefore, that the deceased was a worker and that the question posed in the case stated should be answered in the affirmative.

Macaura v. Northern Assurance Co.
[1925] A.C. 619

What was called for decision here was whether the owner of a 'one-man' company, who also was an unsecured creditor of the company, has an insurable interest in the company's assets. The plaintiff/appellant had transferred his business into a company but the insurance policy on the assets transferred remained in his name.

LORD BUCKMASTER: . . . [623] [T]he appellant is the owner of the Killymoon estate in the county of Tyrone. The respondents are five insurance companies with whom at various dates in January and February of 1922, the appellant effected insurance against fire on timber and wood goods in the open situate on the Killymoon domain not within a hundred yards of any saw mill or any building [624] in which wood working by power other than wind or water was carried on. Neither the amounts not the exact language of the policies are material for the purposes of the present appeal, nor is the fact that the policies were really effected in the name of the appellant and the Governor and the Company of the Bank of Ireland, for the real questions that arise for determination are these:

1. Whether the appellant had any insurable interest in the goods the subject of the policies, and

2. Whether the respondents were, in the circumstances, at liberty to raise the contention that he had no such interest in the manner in which it was raised in the course of these proceedings.

The history of the matter can be stated in a few sentences. The appellant upon whose estate the timber in question was originally standing on December 30, 1919, assigned the whole of it to a company known as the Irish Canadian Saw Mills, Ltd., the amount to be paid for the timber felled and unfelled being £27,000, while a further £15,000 was to be paid for the cost incurred by the appellant in felling the timber that was then down. The total price paid was therefore £42,000, satisfied by the allotment to the appellant or his nominees of £42,000 fully paid £1 shares in the company; no further shares than these were ever issued. The company proceeded with the operations of cutting the timber, and by the end of August, 1921, it had all been felled and sawn up in the saw mills. In the course of these operations the appellant had become the creditor of the company for £19,000, and beyond this it is stated that the debts of the company were trifling in amount. The timber when cut remained lying on the appellant's land, and on February 22, 1922 the greater part of it was destroyed by fire. The appellant accordingly claimed against the companies upon the policies and, on May 30, 1922, in an answer sent on behalf of all the companies, it was stated that the companies must decline to accept liability for the loss of any timber within a hundred yards of the saw mill. The appellant and the Bank of Ireland accordingly instituted [625] proceedings by issuing writs against each of the respondent companies, and each of the statements of claim delivered contained the following allegation: '3. The plaintiffs were at the date of the effecting of the said policy of insurance and at the time of the loss and damage hereinafter mentioned interested in the said timber to the amount so insured thereon as aforesaid.' . . .

[626] Turning now to his position as shareholder, this must be independent of the extent of his share interest. If he were entitled to insure holding all the shares in the company, each shareholder would be equally entitled, if the shares were all in separate hands. Now, no shareholder has any right to any item of property owned by the company, for he has no legal or equitable interest therein. He is entitled to a share in the profits while the company continues to carry on business and a share in the distribution of the surplus [627] assets when the company is wound up. If he were at liberty to effect an insurance against loss

by fire of any item of the company's property, the extent of his insurable interest could only be measured by determining the extent to which his share in the ultimate distribution would be diminished by the loss of the asset – a calculation almost impossible to make. There is no means by which such an interest can be definitely measured and no standard which can be fixed of the loss against which the contract of insurance could be regarded as an indemnity. This difficulty was realized by counsel for the appellant, who really based his case upon the contention that such a claim was recognized by authority and depended upon the proper application of the definition of insurable interest given by Lawrence J. in *Lucena v. Craufurd* (2 Bos. & P.N.R. 269, 302). I agree with the comment of Andrews L.J. upon this case. I find equally with him a difficulty in understanding how a moral certainty can be so defined as to render it an essential part of a definite legal proposition. In the present case, though it might be regarded as a moral certainty that the appellant would suffer loss if the timber which constituted the sole asset of the company were destroyed by fire, this moral certainty becomes dissipated and lost if the asset be regarded as only one in an innumerable number of items in a company's assets and the shareholding interest be spread over a large number of individual shareholders. The authorities which have the closest relation to the present are those of *Peterson v. Harris* (I.B. & S. 336) and *Wilson v. Jones* (L.R. 1 Ex. 193; L.R. 2 Ex. 139). In the first of these cases a shareholder in a company that was established for the purpose of laying down a submarine cable between the United Kingdom and America, effected an insurance upon his interest in the cable. The shareholder's insurable interest in the cable does not appear to have been disputed and the real question, therefore, was never argued. In the case of *Wilson v. Jones*, where another policy was effected by a shareholder in the same company, it was distinctly held that the policy was not upon [628] the cable but upon the shareholder's interest in the adventure of the cable being successfully laid. It was attempted by the underwriters to limit the insurance to an interest in the cable itself, which would have lessened the risk, but it was held that this was not the true construction of the policy. It was not argued that, if it were, the shareholder had no interest to insure, but both Martin B. in the Court of Exchequer and Willes J. in the Exchequer Chamber, stated that the plaintiff had no direct interest in the cable as a shareholder in the company, and, so far as I can see, this consideration it was that assisted the Court in determining that the insurance was upon the adventure in which the shareholder had an interest, and not upon the cable in which he had none. There are no other cases that even approximately approach the present case, and, properly regarded, I think the case of *Wilson v. Jones* is against and not in favour of the appellant's contention. Upon the merits of this dispute, therefore, the appellant must fail. Neither a simple creditor nor a shareholder in a company has any insurable interest in a particular asset which the company holds.

Nor can his claim to insure be supported on the ground that he was a bailee of the timber, for in fact he owed no duty whatever to the company in respect of the safe custody of the goods; he had merely permitted their remaining upon his land.

Note: The Canadian Supreme Court has declined to follow *Macaura* on the question of what is an insurable interest and held that a substantial share-holder in a company has an insurable interest in its assets: *Constitution Insurance Co. of Canada v. Kosmopoulos*, 304 D.L.R. 4d 208 (1983). Cf. *Verdame v. Commercial Union Assur. Co. plc.* [1992] B.C.L.C. 793 – unsuccessful claim by directors/shareholders against insurance brokers for negligence, for not obtaining cover in the company's own name

In addition to the many statutory provisions that permit or require the courts to disregard the segregation between companies and their owners, there are circumstances where the courts will 'pierce the corporate veil' and disregard that distinction, *e.g.* where the company is being used for fraudulent purposes or it is merely an agent of its owners and has no independent existence what-soever.

Fraud

Jones v. Lipman
[1962] 1 All E.R. 442

The issue here was in what circumstances, if any, persons can use companies in order to avoid their contractual obligations. Here, the first defendant sought to do this, in order to reap the benefit of rapidly rising house prices and thereby 'gazump' the plaintiffs. He agreed to sell freehold land with registered tide to them for £5,250. Pending completion, he sold and transferred the land to the defendent company (having a capital of £100), which he acquired and of which he and a clerk of his solicitors were sole shareholders and directors, for £3,000, of which £1,564 was borrowed by the company from a bank and the rest re-mained owing to the first defendant.

RUSSELL J.: . . . [444] The affidavit evidence by the first defendant made it plain (i) that the defendant company was, and at all material times had been, under the complete control of the first defendant, and (ii) that the acquisition of the defendant company by the first defendant and the transfer to it of the real property comprised in the contract with the plaintiffs (for the chattels remained in the ownership of the first defendant) was carried through solely for the purpose of defeating the plaintiff's rights to specific performance and in order to leave them to claim such damages, if any, as they might establish. So much was, quite rightly, admitted by counsel for the defendants.

For the plaintiffs the argument was twofold. First: that specific perform-ance would be ordered against a party to a contract who has it in his power to compel another person to convey the property in question; and that admittedly the first defendant had this power over the defendant company. Second: that specific performance would also, in circumstances such as the present, be ordered against the defendant company. For the first proposition reference was made to *Elliott v. Pierson* [1948] Ch. 452. In that case resistance to specific performance at the suit of a vendor was grounded on the fact that the property was vested in a limited company and not in the vendor. The company, however, was wholly owned and controlled by the vendor, who could compel it to transfer the property, and on this ground the defence to the claim for specific performance failed. It seems to me, not only from dicta of the learned judge but also on principle, that it necessarily follows that specific performance cannot be resisted by a vendor who, by his absolute ownership and control of a limited company in which the property is vested, is in a position to cause the contract to be completed.

For the second proposition reference was made to *Gilford Motor Co., Ltd. v. Horne* [1933] Ch. 935. In that case the individual defendant had entered into covenants restricting his trading activities. It caused the defendant company in that case to be formed. This company was under his control and did things which, if they had been done by him, would have been a breach of the covenants. An injunction was granted not only against him but also against the company. In that case Lord Hanworth M.R., after referring to *Smith v. Hancock* [1894] 2 Ch. 377 said:

> "Lindley L.J., indicated the rule which ought to be followed by the court. 'If the evidence admitted of the conclusion that what was being done was a mere cloak or sham, and that in truth the business was being carried on by the wife and Kerr for the defendant, or by the defendant through his wife for Kerr, I certainly should not hesitate to draw that conclusion, and to grant the plaintiff relief accordingly.'
>
> I do draw that conclusion. I do hold that the company was 'a mere cloak or sham'; I do hold that it was a mere device for enabling Mr. E. B. Horne to continue to commit breaches of [the covenant], and in those circumstances the injunction must go against both defendants. . . ."

Lawrence L.J., in his judgment, said:

> [385] ". . . I agree with the finding by the learned judge that the defendant company was a mere channel used by the defendant Horne for the purpose of enabling him, for his own benefit, to obtain the advantage of the customers of the plaintiff company, and that therefore the defendant company ought to be restrained as well as the defendant Horne."

Similarly, Romer L.J., said:

> "In my opinion, Farwell J., was perfectly right in the conclusion to which

he came . . . that this defendant company was formed and was carrying on business merely as a cloak or sham for the purpose of enabling the defendant Home to commit the breach of the covenant that he entered into deliberately with the plaintiffs on the occasion of and as consideration for his employment as managing director. For this reason, in addition to the reasons given by my Lords, I agree that the appeal must be allowed with the consequences which have been indicated by the Master of the Rolls.

Those comments on the relationship between the individual and the company apply even more forcibly to the present case. The defendant company is the creature of the first defendant, a device and a sham, a mask which he holds before his face in an attempt to avoid recognition by the eye of equity. The case cited illustrates that an equitable remedy is rightly to be granted directly against the creature in such circumstances. . . ."

The proper order to make is an order on both the defendants specifically to perform the agreement between the plaintiffs and the first defendant, but excepting from the order against the defendant company that part of the agreement which involved the chattels. Accordingly, the court will declare that the contract dated February 27, 1961, mentioned in the writ of summons, ought to be specifically performed as to both the realty and personalty comprised therein by the first defendant and as to the realty comprised therein of the second defendant.

Note: In *Creasey v. Breachwood Motors Ltd* [1993] B.C.L.C. 480 where the assets of a business were deliberately transferred out of one company to the other, leaving the transferor insolvent, in breach of the company's owners/directors' duties to the company as well as to its creditors, the court held the transferee liable for the transferor's unpaid liabilities.

In *Re H.* [1996] 2 B.C.L.C. 501, where a *prima facie* case was made out that a family company had been used for the fraudulent evasion of excise duty on an large scale, the court was justified in treating the company's assets as belonging to the defendants, who owned its entire issued share capital.

Agency

Power Supermarkets Ltd. v. Crumlin Investments Ltd.
Costello J., June 22, 1981

The issue here was in what circumstances may a company be regarded as the agent or *alter ego* of its owner. The first defendant, a company that was later acquired by the Dunnes Stores group, leased a unit in a shopping centre to the plaintiff. In the lease the defendant covenanted not to allow any extra-large supermarket to be operated in the centre; specifically, not to 'grant a lease for or to sell or permit or suffer the sale of any of its tenants or. . . any sub or under tenants' of groceries in a unit greater than 3,000 square feet. Subsequently, the Dunnes group decided to open a 3,000 square feet-plus supermarket in the unit. To that end, it incorporated a new company, the second defendant, and the first defendant conveyed to it the fee simple in the unit. All the evidence showed that the Dunnes companies involved were merely vehicles for carrying out the wishes of the controlling family, and that their wishes prevailed in respect of each company in the group. The first defendant was the wholly-owned subsidiary of Cornelscourt Shopping Centre Ltd., which was a wholly-owned subsidiary of Dunnes Holding Co., which was an unlimited company whose shareholders were trustees of a discretionary trust for the Dunne family. Through another chain of subsidiaries, the second defendant's ownership could be traced back to Dunnes Holding Co. Since they were incorporated, there had been no meeting as such of either defendants' shareholders or board of directors. Instead, they were managed and controlled by members of the Dunne family meeting informally. Costello J. instanced the conveyance of the unit to highlight the reality of the relationship between the companies. The consideration was only £100, it contained none of the usual easements, and it was not registered.

COSTELLO J.: . . . [7] The plaintiffs submit that I should pierce the corporate veil and look to the realities in this case and hold, notwithstanding the fact that Crumlin Investments and Dunnes Stores (Crumlin) are two separate corporate entities, that the business in the unit is being carried on by a single entity. I was referred to *Smith Stone and Knight Ltd v. Birmingham Corporation* [1939] 4 All E.R. 116, a case in which a parent company was held entitled to compensation in respect of a business carried on by its subsidiary on the basis that the subsidiary was in reality carrying it on on behalf of the parent company, and to *D.H.N. Ltd v. Tower Hamlets London Borough Council* [1976] 1 W.L.R. 852 a case also dealing with the payment of compensation for the compulsory acquisition of property. The claimants in that case were a group of three companies associated in a wholesale grocery business. The Court of Appeal held that it should pierce the corporate veil, and that it should not regard the companies as separate legal entities but treat the group as a single economic entity for the purpose of awarding compensation. I need not refer to the facts of the case; however, the reasons which prompted [8] the court's approach are very material for the resolution of the issues in the present case. Lord Denning pointed out (at page 860) that the group of companies was virtually the same as a partnership in which all three were partners; that they should not be treated separately so as to defeat the claim to compensation on a technical point; that they should not be deprived of the compensation which should be justly payable for disturbance. So, he decided that the three companies should be treated as one. Lord Justice Shaw (at page 867) pointed out that if each member of the group of companies was to be regarded as a company in isolation that nobody at all could claim compensation 'in a case which plainly calls for it', and he said that the true relationship should not be ignored because to do so would amount to a denial of justice. He too considered that the group should be regarded as a single entity.

It seems to me to be well established from these as well as from other authorities (See *Harold Holdsworth & Co. Ltd. v. Caddies* [1955] 1 W.L.R. 353; *Scottish Co-operative Wholesale Society Ltd. v. Meyer* [1959] A.C. 324 (see post, p. 471)) that a Court may, if the justice of the case so requires, treat two or more related companies as a single entity so that the business notionally carried on by one will be regarded as the business of the group, or another member of the group, if this conforms to the economic and commercial realities of the situation. It would in my [9] view, be very hard to find a clearer case than the present one for the application of this principle. I appreciate that Crumlin Investments is a property-owning not a trading company but it is clear that the creation of the new company and the conveyance to it of the freehold interest in a unit in the shopping centre were means for carrying out the commercial plans of the Dunne family in the centre. The enterprise had a two-fold aspect (a) the creation of a new retail outlet for the Dunnes Stores'Group in the shopping centre and (b) the enhancement of the rents in the centre as a whole which the creation of such an outlet would hopefully produce. To treat the two companies as a single economic entity seems to me to accord fully with the realities of the situation. Not to do so could involve considerable injustice to the plaintiffs as their rights under the covenant might be defeated by the mere technical device of the creation of a company with a £2 issued capital which had no real independent life of its own. If it is established that the covenant is breached there should in my opinion be an injunction against both defendants.

Company Groups

See *Company Law*, pp. 465–471.

Re Polly Peck International plc (In Administration) (No. 3)
[1996] 1 B.C.L.C. 428

The question to be determined here too was when may a company within a corporate group to be treated as the agent or *alter ego* of one or more companies in that group, or was it a complete sham which could be disregarded. The company (PPI) was a holding company for a group of companies. It acquired financing through a wholly-owned subsidiary (PPIF), a Cayman Island company; the reasons for using this vehicle as that there would be no need to comply with the listing rules of the London Stock Exchange and there would also be tax advantages. The manner in which the funds were raised was broadly as follows. PPIF would issue bonds to a group of financing banks and PPI would guarantee the obligation of PPIF to repay the loan. The money received by PPIF was 'on-loaned' to PPI. The bond issues also contained a clause whereby in certain circumstances PPI could be substituted for PPIF. PPI went into administration. Under a scheme of arrangement creditors were to be paid in the same manner as if PPI had gone into notional liquidation. Banks lodged a claim under the PPI guarantee and PPIF also lodged a claim with respect to the moneys that it had on-loaned to PPI. The administrators sought directions under the, scheme as to whether or not PPIF were entitled to prove in the scheme in the light of the fact that the court may pierce the corporate veil of PPIF so that PPIF would be prevented from lodging a claim separate from that of the banks. [438]

WALKER J.: – [438] Mr Kosmin contend[ed] that the bond issues by PPIF (guaranteed by PPI) and PPIF's on-lending to PPI were so closely connected as to result in the bondholders' claim against PPI as guarantor and PPIF's claim against PPI as principal creditor being 'in substance, claims for payment of the same debt twice over'. Mr Kosmin developed his argument in various ways which naturally involved some overlap; but I hope I can fairly summarise the way he put his case as follows:

(1) That on a correct view of the facts, PPIF was in effecting the bond issues (a) an agent of nominee for PPI or alternatively (b) a cipher or facade for PPI; (2) that even if PPIF acted as an independent principal, the on-lending within [439] the Polly Peck group was still so much a part of the same composite transaction as not to rank, in substance, as a separate debt. Mr Kosmin accepted that there is no authority illustrating the application of the rule against double proof in this sort of situation (that is, indebtedness within a group of companies) but called in aid the words of Kerr L.J. in *Barclays Bank Ltd v. TOSG Trust Fund Ltd* [1984] A.C. 626 at 652:

> ". . . sometimes, in new situations, the court has to find a just solution which stems simply from the nature of the transaction, the relationship between the parties and their presumed common intention."

Mr Moss for his part says, rightly, that this sort of transaction of guaranteed borrowing and on-lending by a special-purpose financial vehicle is a commonplace occurrence in capital markets (this point is borne out by the letter from the Cayman attorneys, which seems to be giving fairly standard advice in a fairly standard situation). Mr Moss goes on to submit that the double proof point, if sound, would introduce a new and alarming element of uncertainty into capital markets. I think this argument in terrorem may be a bit overstated.

since investors in unsecured bonds issued in this way must be relying on the credit rating of the guarantor, and not on some calculation of the chances of a 'double-dip' against the guarantor and the financial subsidiary in the event of default. Nevertheless the point raised is a novel point of some commercial importance.

Before I examine more closely the different ways in which Mr Kosmin puts his case it may be helpful to make some preliminary points. First, as to substance. In *Welsh Development Agency v. Export Finance Co Ltd* [1992] B.C.L.C. 148 at 185 Staughton L.J. said (in the context of deciding whether a commercial document effected a sale or a charge):

> "The problem is not made any easier by the variety of language that has been used: substance, truth, reality, genuine are good words; disguise, cloak, mask, colourable device, label, form, artificial, sham, stratagem and pretence are "bad names", to adopt the phrase quoted by Dixon J. in *Palette Shoes Pty Ltd v. Krohn* (1937) 58 C.L.R. 1 at 28. It is necessary to discover, if one can, the ideas which these words are intended to convey. One can start from the position that statute law in this country, when it enacts rules to be applied to particular transactions, is in general referring to the legal nature of a transaction and not to its economic effect. The leading authority on this point, albeit in a case from Malaya, is the advice of Lord Devlin in *Chow Yoong Hong v. Choong Fab Rubber Manufactory Ltd* [1962] A.C. 209 at 216:
>
> > 'There are many ways of raising cash besides borrowing. . . . If in form it is not a loan, it is not to the point to say that its object was to raise money for one of them or that the parties could have produced the same result more conveniently by borrowing and lending money'."

Those were statutory contexts (registration of charges and regulation of moneylending) but I think they also support the general proposition that when the law is looking for the substance of a matter, it is normally looking for its legal substance, not its economic substance (if different). As Robert Goff [440] LJ put it in *Bank of Tokyo Ltd v. Karoon* [1987] A.C. 45 at 64, we are concerned not with economics but with law.

Second, the House of Lords' affirmation in *Salomon & Co. Ltd v. Salomon* [1897] A.C. 22 of the separate legal personality of even a 'one-man' company does not of course mean that registered companies have all the characteristics of, and no characteristics not shared by, natural persons. One aspect of this has recently been explained by Lord Hoffmann in giving the opinion of the Privy Council in *Meridian Global Funds Management Asia Ltd v. Securities Commission* [1995] 2 A.C. 500 (see ante, p. 28). Another aspect is that whereas natural persons do not (since the abolition of slavery and the passing of the Married Women's Property Acts) own the persons or property of other human beings, commercial companies do have owners. Their shareholders have an economic interest in their commercial success. Although the shareholders do not own their company's assets, a wrong to the company (if uncompensated) may cause them economic loss. But in general the shareholders will have no direct right of action in respect of such loss (see *Prudential Assurance Co. Ltd v. Newman Industries Ltd (No. 2)* [1982] Ch. 204 at 223 (see *post*, p. 455)). This point was mentioned in argument, being neither controversial nor directly relevant; but I think it worth mentioning both in order to identify and distinguish another corporate 'double recovery' problem which does not arise here, and because it leads on to the topic of intra-group indebtedness, which is directly relevant in this case.

The third point is that where there is a group of companies and they are all solvent, a claim by one group company against another, even though sound in law, is likely to have only marginal economic effects (it may have some, for instance in connection with taxation). But as soon as both companies go into insolvent liquidation, any claim between them assumes much greater importance (unless by an extraordinary coincidence both have identical creditors with identical claims, which is certainly not the case here). That is, I think, the point that Lord Wilberforce must have had in mind when he said in *Ford Carter Ltd v. Midland Bank Ltd* (1979) 129 NQ 543 at 544: "When creditors become involved, as they do in the present case, the separate legal existence of the constituent companies of the group has to be respected".

This important effect of group insolvency needs to be underlined because it has sometimes been suggested (for instance by Oliver L.J. in *Barclays Bank Ltd v. TOSG Trust Fund Ltd* [1984] A.C. 626 at 636-637) that it is useful to test a disputed case of double proof by reference to the situation as it would be if all parties were solvent. In circumstances of all-round group insolvency that may not be a wholly reliable test. It is not now open to PPI's administrators to pay off the bondholders in full and, by doing so, to discharge its obligation to PPIF (and, simultaneously, PPIFs obligation to the bondholders).

Issue 1(a): Was PPIF an agent or nominee?
[441] In *Salomon v. Salomon & Co.* the House of Lords roundly rejected the conclusion of the lower courts that Salomon & Co. was a 'mere nominee or agent' of Mr Aron Salomon, or his 'alias', or that his fellow shareholders were 'dummies' (see [1897] A.C. 22 at 35, 42, 43). There are of course many cases in which it has been held, on the facts, that a company has acted as an agent or nominee, either for its principal shareholder or for some other party, and several of them were cited to me (for instance *Canada Rice Mills Ltd v. R.* [1939] 3 All E.R. 991 and *Firestone Tyre and Rubber Co. Ltd v. Lewellin (Inspector of Taxes)* [1957] 1 W.L.R. 464). But neither agency nor nomineeship – nor, still less, sham or something akin to sham – is to be inferred simply because a subsidiary company has a small paid-up capital and has a board of directors all or most of whom are also directors or senior executives of its holding com-

pany.

Mr Kosmin does not, as I understand his submissions, contend that the arrangements between PPI, PPIF and the lead mangers were a sham (I will return below to 'cipher' and 'facade'). He does contend that a variety of factors lead to an inference of agency or nomineeship. . . .

In short, Mr Kosmin submits that PPIF had only a nominal role in the arrangements. and that as a matter of substance PPI should be recognised as having borrowed direct from the original bondholders, so depriving the on-loan of any legal significance (or indeed existence). To come to that conclusion I would have to find that that was the effect, not merely of what was informally arranged in the boardroom at 42 Berkeley Square. but also of the format legal documents which were entered into on the occasion of each bond issue. . . . All these documents made clear that the bond issue was to be made by PPIF and that PPIFs obligations, were to be guaranteed by PPI subject to the provision for substitution which I have already mentioned. The documentation on the later loans was essentially similar, subject to small variations (already mentioned) on the DM issue.

[442] In the face of these documents I find it impossible to conclude that the factors that Mr Kosmin relies on establish a relationship of agency or nomineeship. Mr Moss referred me to some passages from the speeches in *McEntire v. Crossley Bros. Ltd* [1895] A.C. 457, quoted by Dillon LJ in *Welsh Development Agency v. Export Finance Co. Ltd* [1992] M.C.L.C. 148 at 160-161. Lord Herschell LC said ([1895] A.C. 457 at 463):

> ". . . there is no such as seems to have been argued here, as looking at the substance, apart from looking at the language which the parties have used. It is only by a study of the whole of the language that the substance can be ascertained."

Similarly Lord Watson said ([1895] A.C. 457 at 467):

> "The substance of the agreement must ultimately be found in the language of the contract itself. The duty of the court is to examine every part of the agreement, every stipulation which it contains, and to consider their mutual bearing upon each other; but it is entirely beyond the function of a court to discard the plain meaning of any term in the agreement unless there can he found within its four corners other language and other stipulations which necessarily deprive such term of its primary significance."

(It is interesting to note that less than three weeks after judgment was given in *McEntire v. Crossley Bros.*, Lord Herschell LC said almost exactly the same thing in another well-known case, *Helby v. Matthews* [1895] A.C. 471 at 475; and it was his observations in the latter case that were cited to and discussed by the House of Lords in the leading tax case on the substance of a transaction, *I.R.C v. Duke of Westminster* [1936] A.C. 1 at 20. The on-loan in this case might he thought to have at least a passing resemblance to the on-transfer that was considered by the House of Lords in another leading tax case, *Furniss (Inspector of Taxes) v. Dawson* [1984] A.C. 474. But neither counsel suggested that I could get any guidance from that specialised and difficult area of authority, and probably they were right not to do so.)

Some of the factors on which Mr Kosmin relies do tend to show that the Polly Peck personnel who were concerned with the matter at 42 Berkeley Square were (to say the least) less than meticulous in their administrative procedures. I make no specific finding about that. But even blatant and reprehensible 'cutting of corners' (if it occurred) could not, it seems to retroactively alter the character of the transactions embodied in the formal documents by which the bond issues were effected. The factors which Mr Kosmin relies on cannot and do not in my judgment establish PPIF's role as that of agency or nomineeship, and so they do not eliminate the on-loan as significant part of the composite transaction.

Issue 1(b): Sham, pretence cipher, facade
My conclusion that there was no conventional relationship of agency or nomineeship is not conclusive of the case, because Mr Kosmin had further [443] submissions. On what I have called his point (1)(b) and his point (2) I was referred to quite a lot of authority touching on what is sometimes called lifting (or piercing) the corporate veil. That is a vivid but imprecise metaphor which has possible application in several different contexts, some far removed from this case. The most relevant, it seems to me, is where corporate personality is (in the words of Lord Keith in *Woolfson v. Strathclyde Regional Council* 1978 SLT 159 at 161) used as 'a mere facade concealing the facts'.

Sham, pretence, cipher and facade are all (as was said by Dixon J. in the passage already quoted) 'bad names' implying a value judgment of disapprobation. 'Sham' was at least half way to becoming a term of art (requiring an intention common to all parties) but has now, it seems, been supplanted (at least in the context of licence or tenancy) by 'pretence' (see *Aslan v. Murphy (Nos. 1 and 2), Duke v. Wynne* [1990] 1 W.L.R. 766 at 770 and *AG Securities v. Vaughan, Antoniades v. Villiers* [1990] 1 A.C. 417 at 462-465). Mr Kosmin did not rely on sham or pretence. He did submit (orally) that PPIF was a 'cipher' and (in his skeleton argument) that it was a 'facade'. I think that his use of 'cipher' was to add colour and force to his submission on agency or nomineeship (which I have already considered). 'Facade' (or 'cloak' or 'mask') is perhaps most aptly used where one person (individual or corporate) uses a company either in an unconscionable attempt to evade existing obligations (*Gilford Motor Co. Ltd v. Horne* [1933] Ch. 935, *Jones v. Lipman* [1962] 1 W.L.R. 832 (see supra, p. 76)) or to practice some other deception (a sort of unilateral sham, since the corporate facade has no independent mind). In *Adams v. Cape Industries plc* [1990] Ch. 433 the establishment and interposition of the Liechtenstein corporation referred to as AMC was a facade in this sense, and 'no more than a corporate name' (see [1990] Ch. 433 at 479 in the judgment of Scott J., and [1990] Ch. 433 at 543 in the judgment of the Court of Appeal), though the new Illinois corporation, CPC, was not. But the notion that regular sales of large volumes of South African asbestos to an United States purchaser were being effected through a lawyer's office in Vaduz is to my mind of a quite different order of artificiality from the function of PPIF as a single-purpose financial vehicle (I am not overlooking the two other isolated transactions entered into by PPIF; but they add little to its independent reality). In my judgment PPIF was more than a mere facade.

Issue (2): Single economic unit
It is on this part of the case that I have found Mr Kosmin's submissions most persuasive, though I am not ultimately persuaded by them. The arguments for considering a closely-integrated group of companies as a single economic unit were fully considered (principally in the context of corporate presence as founding jurisdiction) in *Adams v. Cape Industries plc* [1990] Ch. 433 [444] at 476-477, both of Scott J. and, with a full citation of authority, in the judgment of the Court of Appeal (see [1990] Ch. 433 [444] at 532-537). Both passages merit careful study. The Court of Appeal concluded that: "save in cases which turn on the wording of particular statutes or contracts, the court is not free to disregard the principle of *Salomon v. Salomon & Co.* merely because it considers that justice so requires [1990] Ch. 433 at 536."

Mr Kosmin seeks to add to these exceptions (turning on particular statutes or contracts) a further exception where a rule of law founded in public policy (the rule against double proof) would be frustrated by ignoring the economic reality of the single group. In that submission Mr Kosmin can and does call in aid the words of Oliver LJ in *Barclays Bank Ltd v. TOSG Trust Fund Ltd* [1984] A.C. 626 at 636 that the test is 'a much broader one which transcends a close jurisprudential analysis of the persons by and to whom the duties are owed'.

Nevertheless I am not persuaded by the argument. I can accept that as a matter of economic reality the bondholders (whose presumed intentions may be material) must have intended to rely on the credit-rating and covenant of PPI, whether as guarantor or (after substitution) as principal obligor. It is doubtful whether even the most far-sighted of them can have calculated that in the event of a crash, PPIF might have fewer unsecured creditors than PPI, and a claim against PPI under an on-loan. It was perfectly possible, consistently with each prospectus, that the proceeds of some or all of the bond issues would be loaned on, not to PPI, but to other group subsidiaries. It is also possible, though less likely, to imagine a situation in which PPIF lent on to another subsidiary, with PPI guaranteeing that borrowing also, and the second subsidiary then lending on to PPI. Each of those sequences of events would be likely to produce a different result in the event of a crash of the whole group, whether or not the rule against double proof has any application. The possibility of there being subsidiaries which were not wholly-owned subsidiaries adds to the range of imaginable variations.

Were I to accede to Mr Kosmin's submission it would create a new exception unrecognised by the Court of Appeal in *Adams v. Cape Industries plc* and that is not open to me. Moreover I think that Mr Kosmin is in one sense assuming what he seeks to prove, since the unjust or inequitable result which he asserts does not occur unless the group is recognised as being in substance a single economic entity, whose constituent members' internal rights and obligations are to be disregarded. But the authorities to which I have already referred show that substance means legal substance, not economic substance (if different), and that (as Lord Wilberforce said *in Ford & Carter Ltd v. Midland Bank Ltd*) the separate legal existence of group companies is particularly important when creditors become involved. Injustice may be in the eye of the beholder, but I do not perceive any obvious injustice – certainly not such as the court can remedy – in the unpredictable consequences that may follow from the unforeseen insolvency of a large international group of companies such as the Polly Peck group.

Involuntary Creditors

See *Company Law*, pp. 62–63.

Sweeney v. Duggan
[1997] 2 I.R. 531

It was contended by the plaintiff here that the owner/manager of a 'one man' company can owe a duty of care to its employees in respect of tertian financial loss; that the *Salomon & Co.* principle does not apply to a company's tort creditors. The plaintiff, a former employee of a quarrying company, had been injured whilst operating a drill in the company's quarry and, in separate proceedings, was awarded damages against the company. At the time of the award the company was in voluntary liquidation and was unable to pay even its preferential creditors in full. The defendant was the managing director and effectively the only shareholder of the quarrying company. He also held the post of quarry manager and as such was, by virtue of s. 23 of the Mines and Quarries Act 1965, under a duty to ensure that the Act's provisions concerning the safety, health and physical welfare of persons in quarrying operations were observed. The plaintiff instituted proceedings against the defendant claiming that he personally had a duty to ensure that the company, as the plaintiff's employer, procure employer's liability insurance to meet any claims for damages for personal injuries, or alternatively, to ensure that the company warned the plaintiff that no such policy of insurance was in existence. The plaintiff submitted (the submissions are set out at infra p. 92) that such a duty derived from the exceptionally dangerous nature of the business of quarrying, the precarious state of the company's finances at the time of the accident and the fact that he had insured himself to a small extent against loss in connection with injuries sustained in the course of his employment.

MURPHY J.: [538] There are at least two situations where the courts will, independently of statutory requirement, imply a term which has not been expressly agreed by the parties to a contract. The first of these situations was identified in the well-known *Moorcock* case (1889) 14 PD 64 where a term not expressly agreed upon by the parties was inferred on the basis of the presumed intention of the parties. The basis for such a presumption was explained by MacKinnon L.J. in *Shirlaw v. Southern Foundries* (1926) *Ltd* [1939] 2 K.B. 206 at p. 227 in an expression, equally memorable, in the following terms:
Prima facie that which in any contract is left to be implied and need not be expressed is something so obvious that it goes without saying; so that, if while the parties were making their bargain, an officious bystander were to suggest some express provision for it in their agreement, they would testily suppress him with a common, 'Oh, of course'.
In addition there are a variety of cases in which a contractual term has been implied on the basis, not of the intention of the parties to the contract but deriving from the nature of the contract itself. Indeed in analysing the different types of case in which a term will be implied Lord Wilberforce in *Liverpool City Council v. Irwin* [1977] A.C. 239 preferred to describe the different categories which he identified as no more than shades on a continuous spectrum.
[539] The relevance of the presumed intention of the parties differs in different cases. . . .
[540] Clearly the plaintiff in the present case would have little difficulty in appreciating the general concept of employer's liability insurance but so far from an immediate acquiescence to any proposals in relation to such insurance I think it is reasonable to anticipate that a debate would have arisen as to the value of such insurance to the employee seeing that such insurance is primarily for the benefit of the employer and, if it were explained how it might also benefit the employee, further and useful discussion might well follow as to whether the interests of the plaintiff would not be better secured by some other arrangement which would be of immediate and direct benefit to the plaintiff. The parties to the negotiations might recognise (as did their counsel) that a contractual obligation by [541] the company to insure would add little protection to the plaintiff as default by the company would merely duplicate the plaintiff's right to recover a judgment against the company with no greater

prospect of recovering thereon. I would reject the contention that the term for which the plaintiff contends could be implied on the basis of the *Moorcock* doctrine.

Both parties referred to the decision of the Court of Appeal in England in two cases, namely, *Reid v. Rush & Tompkins Group plc* [1990] 1 W.L.R. 212 and *Van Oppen & Clarke v. Bedford Charity Trustees* [1990] 1 W.L.R. 235 on the issue as to whether the disputed provision with regard to insurance should be implied as a legal incident to the plaintiffs contract of employment. Each of these cases has a similarity to the other and a relevance to the existing matter in as much as it was alleged (unsuccessfully) that the defendants in each case were under an obligation or duty to take out and maintain some form of insurance for the benefit of the plaintiff or at any rate to advise him in relation to such insurance.

In the *Reid* case the plaintiff was employed by the defendant to travel to Ethiopia as a quarry foreman. While in that country the plaintiff was injured in a motor car accident caused by the negligence of a third party whose identity was never discovered. In Ethiopia there was not, at the time, any compulsory third party motor insurance nor any scheme for compensating persons injured in accidents caused by the negligence of uninsured or untraced drivers. In those circumstances the plaintiff brought an action against his employer – the defendant – for damages in respect of the economic loss which he had suffered in being unable to recover such compensation. He alleged that the defendant was in breach of an implied term of his contract of employment to the effect that it would take out appropriate indemnity insurance cover for the plaintiff or, alternatively, [219] that it would, prior to his departure for Ethiopia, advise him of any special risks so that he could obtain such insurance cover for himself. Alternatively, the plaintiff argued, that the defendant was negligent in failing to discharge its duty of care as an employer to protect the plaintiffs economic welfare by providing the appropriate insurance cover. Ralph Gibson L.J. delivering the main judgment of the Court of Appeal declined to imply the term for which the plaintiff contended. He analysed the facts of the case and went on (at pp. 227-8) to state as follows:

> "It is, however, impossible, in my judgment, to imply in this case a term as a matter of law in the form contended for, namely, a specific [542] duty to advise the plaintiff to obtain specific insurance cover. Such a duty seems to me inappropriate for incorporation by law into all contracts of employment in the circumstances alleged. The length of time during which the servant will work abroad and the nature of his work may vary greatly between one job and another and hence the extent to which the servant would be exposed to the special risk. Further, having regard to the many different ways in which a servant working abroad may run the risk of uncompensated injury caused by the wrong doing of a third party, apart from a traffic accident, it seems to me impossible to

formulate the detailed terms in which the law could incorporate into the general relationship of master and servant a contractual obligation to the effect necessary to cover the plaintiff's claim."

Again having referred to the judgment of Lord Scarman in *Tai Hing Cotton Mill Ltd v. Liu Chong Hing Bank Ltd* [1986] A.C. 80 (to which I will refer again) he expressed his conclusion with regard to the allegation based on tort (at p. 232) in the following terms:

"It therefore seems to me that, on the facts alleged, it is not open to this Court to extend the duty of care owed by this defendant to the plaintiff by imposing a duty in tort which, if I am right, is not contained in any express or implied term of the contract."

The judgment of the Court of Appeal in *Van Oppen v. Bedford Charity Trustees* (above) does not significantly advance the matter either way. It was a case in which the defendant trustees, who owned and managed a school, were advised by a competent association of the desirability of taking out. accident insurance for all of their pupils who played rugby. The school informed the parents of the advice which they had received in this regard but before any action was taken on the proposals the plaintiff suffered serious injuries to his cervical spine while playing rugby. In those circumstances the pupil claimed damages against the defendants for negligence alleging that they had failed to take reasonable care for his safety on the rugby field and failed to advise his father of the risk of serious injury and the consequent need for personal accident insurance. It may be sufficient to say that Balcombe L.J. in delivering the main judgment of the court endorsed substantially the judgment of Ralph Gibson L.J. [220] in *Reid v. Rush & Tompkins Group plc*. It is, however, notable that the insurance in the *Van Oppen* case and the *Reid* case would have had the effect of providing the plaintiff with a positive economic benefit and not merely security for the discharge by the employer of a pre-existing liability.

[543] It seems to me that the decision of the House of Lords in *Scally v. Southern Health and Social Services Board* [1992] 1 A.C. 294 and in particular the speech of Lord Bridge of Harwich provides even more persuasive authority for the proposition that a term such as that for which the plaintiff contends cannot in circumstances such as the present be found by reference to the law of tort. It is helpful also as to the circumstances in which a term will be implied as a matter of law independently of the intention of the parties. In the *Scally* case the plaintiffs were employees of the Northern Ireland Health Board whose contracts of employment had been negotiated by representatives of their professional bodies. The terms of their employment provided for certain pension benefits. By virtue of certain legislative provisions, the plaintiffs were given the right to purchase particular 'additional years' on advantageous terms but that right was required to be exercised within a specified time from the

date on which the legislative regulations came into operation.

Lord Bridge dealing with the claim based in contract expressed his views (at p. 302) in the following terms:

">. . . it seems to me that the plaintiffs' common law claims can only succeed if the duty allegedly owed to them by their employers arose out of the contract of employment. If a duty of the kind in question was not inherent in the contractual relationship, I do not see how it could possibly be derived from the tort of negligence. . . ."

[544] In his judgment with which all of their Lordships were in agreement, Lord Bridge in fact concluded that the term for which the plaintiffs contended should be implied in the contract between them and their employers. His analysis of the circumstances in which the term was implied is to be found at p. 306 in the following terms:

">. . . Here there is no doubt whatever that the terms of the superannuation scheme as laid down in the regulations in force from time to time were embodied in the terms of the contract of employment of each plaintiff. Since the relevant board was in each case the employer upon whom, although acting as agent for the department, all liabilities were imposed by paragraph 2 of schedule I to the Order of 1972, it seems to me beyond question that the legal obligation, if there was one, to notify the plaintiffs of their rights in relation to the purchase of added years rested in each case on the board, not on the department.

Will the law then imply a term in the contract of employment imposing such an obligation on the employer? The implication cannot, of course, be justified as necessary to give business efficacy to the contract of employment as a whole. I think there is force in the submission, that since the employee's entitlement to enhance his pension rights by the purchase of added years is of no effect [545] unless he is aware of it and since he cannot be expected to become aware of it unless it is drawn to his attention, it is necessary to imply an obligation on the employer to bring it to his attention to render efficacious the very benefit which the contractual right to purchase added years was intended to confer."

I agree that a term may be implied independently of the intention of the parties where it is necessary as a matter of law and logic to enable the provisions of the agreement to have operative effect. No such necessity exists in the present case. The decision is also relevant in setting out the principles, with which I fully agree, which establish that the obligation as between the employer and employee in a case such as the present are to be found in contract and not in tort.

Accordingly, as to the first and crucial argument submitted on behalf of the plaintiff, I am satisfied that there is no basis for the implication in the contract of employment between the company and the plaintiff of a term that the employer should in any circumstances extract risk insurance cover or otherwise make special provision to ensure the payment of compensation to the plaintiff in the event of injury or to warn the plaintiff of the absence of such policy or such arrangement. Likewise I am satisfied that no such obligation or duty can be identified by reference to the law of tort. If the company has no liability in contract to the plaintiff then neither has Mr Duggan. The piercing of the corporate veil bestowed upon the company by law, or even its complete removal, cannot impose on Mr Duggan or the other shareholder in the company an obligation in contract to which the company itself was not subject.

That Mr Duggan may have had a variety of duties to the plaintiff in tort is hardly open to dispute. In so far as Mr Duggan was a fellow workman of the plaintiff he was of course bound to exercise reasonable care in the exercise of his duties as an employee not to cause injury to Mr Sweeney. Again in his capacity as quarry manager Mr Duggan had wide ranging statutory obligations the breach of which might well have given rise to a liability on his part to the plaintiff. However the neglect of such duties has not been alleged nor would the breach of any of them provide the remedy which the plaintiff seeks to assert in these proceedings.

I find it difficult to accept that a director or shareholder as such has the necessary relationship with an employee of his company to give rise to any duty on the part of the director/shareholder for the economic welfare [546] of the employee. I find it inconceivable that any such duty on the part of a corporator, if it did exist, could be more extensive than that of the corporation itself.

I would of course recognise that the case put forward on behalf of the plaintiff was that the company did have the particular obligations in contract so that the argument for liability on the part of Mr Duggan was essentially his failure to ensure that 'his' company failed to fulfil its obligations. To find a duty in Mr Duggan to protect the economic welfare of the plaintiff in a manner which is [223] not sustained by the terms of employment of the plaintiff, express or implied, is in my view unstateable.

Appellant's Case

(*i.e.* Counsels' written submissions summarising Mr Sweeney's argument):

1. At the relevant time, the plaintiff was an unskilled labourer employed by Kenmare Lime Works Ltd. ("the Company") in its quarry at Caher, Kenmare, Co. Kerry. The defendant and his wife were the sole directors and shareholders of the Company, and the defendant managed the business and was the designated manager of the quarry under the Mines and Quarries Act 1965. In February, 1984, the plaintiff was injured in an accident at the quarry in the

course of his employment. He sued and obtained judgment against the Company in October, 1987, but, by that time, the Company was in a creditors' voluntary liquidation and was insolvent. He now seeks some compensation for being deprived of the value of his judgment against the defendant.

2. A summary of the evidence has been agreed by Counsel. Matters on which the plaintiff places special emphasis include:

(i) the Company's business, quarrying, is an exceptionally dangerous business;

(ii) at the time of the accident, the Company's finances were precarious and it was in a "Section 40" situation;

(iii) the plaintiff had himself insured to a small extent;

(iv) the plaintiff believed and was assured by a co-employee that the Company had employers' liability insurance.

It will be submitted that there was an implied term in the contract of employment with the Company that there would be employers' liability insurance or at least the employee would be warned if there were no insurance cover.

3. The plaintiff's case, in summary, is that, by virtue of (i) – (iv) above and in the light of that implied term, under the law of negligence the defendant owed him a duty of care, either to:

(a) ensure that the Company was not under-capitalised or was adequately, insured, or;

(b) at least to warn the plaintiff that there was no employers' liability insurance in the circumstances.

If the plaintiff was one of the Company's trade creditors, the defendant may be entitled to rely on the "public policy" defence to claims in respect of economic loss, on the basis of *Salomon v. Salomon & Co.* [1897] A.C. 22. But that defence is not open where the plaintiff is a non-unionised and unskilled labourer suing the owner-manager of an insolvent one-person company in tort for an injury he received working in its quarry. The defendant ought not to be permitted to hide behind the shield of separate legal personality. The plaintiff does not contend that, at common law, *all* owners/directors of businesses have a duty to insure or else to warn their employees that there is no liability insurance.

Implied term of contract

4. There was an implied term in the contract of employment that the Company would warn or insure, arising from:

(i) the uniquely dangerous nature of quarrying;

(ii) the statutory matrix for quarrying: Mines and Quarries Act 1965, and regulations thereunder – *Siney v. Dublin Corporation* [1980] I.R. 400;

(iii) s. 40 Companies Act 1983, was applicable but not complied with; the "sinking ship" analogy applies and the captain should have taken the appropriate precautions to either warn that no insurance or else to take out insurance.

R.J. Friel, *The Law of Contract* (1995) 160-164; distinguish *Reid v. Rush & Tompkins plc.* [1990] 1 W.L.R 212 at pp. 227-228. However, a contract to take out insurance cover for oneself is most peculiar in that it can never be enforced after the risk in question occurs; if the contracting party is in funds, he can pay the compensation to the other party but if he is not in funds, he is in no position to pay any damages that might be awarded for breach of his contract to insure. This presumably explains the dearth of authority and no extended discussion of the question.

5. A duty to insure has already been recognised in several contexts, *e.g.* *Semtex v. Gladstone* [1954] 1 W.L.R. 945 – there is an implied term in the contract of employment that the employer will comply with the provisions of the Road Traffic Acts and he will be liable to an employee who suffers any loss as a result of the vehicle not being insured. *British School of Motoring Ltd v. Simms* [1971] 1 All E.R. 317 – there is an implied term in the contract between a driving school and its pupil that the car used for the lessons will be insured so as to cover it while being driven by the pupil.

Economic loss

6. The Common Law world is divided on the scope of liability for negligently inflicted economic or financial loss. In the U. K. governing principles were laid down by the House of Lords in *Anns v. London Merton B.C.* [1978] A.C. 728 but the Courts there have since resiled from the *Anns* position, *e.g.* *Murphy v. Brentwood D.C.* [1991] 1 A.C. 398. In the U.K. moreover all employers are obliged by law to take out appropriate employers' liability insurance: Employers' Liability (Compulsory Insurance) Act, 1969, which explains why the matter at issue here has not been canvassed in the U.K. courts.

7. Most of the Common Law world has endorsed the *Anns* position for determining whether the requisite duty of care exists, *e.g. Invercargill City Council v. Hamlin* [1996] 2 W.L.R. 367 (N. Zealand), *Norsk Pacific S.S. Co. v. Canadian National Railway* [1992] 91 D.L.R. 4th 289 (Canada), *Caltex Oil (Australia) Pty Ltd v. The Dredge "Willemstad"* (1976) 136 C.L.R. 129 (Australia). The Irish case law is in much the same vein, *e.g. Ward v. McMaster* [1988] I.R. 337. Apart from cases similar to *Hedley Byrne* [1964] A.C. 465, there seems to be no equivalent Irish case where the defendant was not a public sector body.

8. The matters that are material, as indicated in *Ward v. McMaster* [1988] I.R. 337 include:

(i) The "verbally attractive proposition of incremental growth in this branch of the law" was rejected because otherwise 'rights should be determined by the accident of birth'.

(ii) The central test is that in *Anns, viz.* whether 'there is a sufficient relationship of proximity or neighbourhood so that, in the reasonable contemplation of the former, carelessness on his part maybe likely to cause damage to the latter – in which case a *prima facie* duty of care arises'. There was an exceptionally close relationship of proximity between the plaintiff and defendant here, equivalent to that in *Junior Books Ltd. v. Veitchi Co. Ltd* [1983] 1 A.C. 547; their relationship was virtually one of contract. And to quote McCarthy J. in *Ward* at p. 351, it does not require much imagination for the defendant to contemplate that if a serious accident occurred in the quarry and there was no employers' liability insurance, the plaintiff would never receive compensation for his injury'.

(iii) The 'absence of any compelling exemption based on public policy' (p. 349). What compelling public policy (other than the arguable *Salomon & Co.* [1897] A.C. 22 principle) justifies the court not imposing liability on the defendant?

(iv) The comparative indigence and social disadvantage of the plaintiff *vis-à-vis* the defendant (p. 342). Employers of unskilled non-union labour have a paternal obligation to ensure that their employees' welfare is reasonably safeguarded, equivalent to the duty this court held local authorities were under in relation to defective public housing, *e.g. Siney* and *Ward*.

9. The defendant had a duty to warn the plaintiff that there was no liability insurance cover: *Phillips v. Dorgan* [1991] I.L.R.M. 321, *Banque Keyser Ulman S.A. v. Skandia (UK) Insurance Ltd.* [1990] 1 Q.B. 665 and McMahon & Binchy, *Irish Law of Torts* (2nd ed., 1990) Ch. 8.

10. In the alternative, the defendant had a duty to ensure that the plaintiff was sufficiently covered by employers' liability insurance. A duty to insure has been accepted in some U.K. cases, *e.g. Semtex v. Gladstone* [1954] 1 W.L.R. 945 and *British School of Motoring Ltd v. Simms* [1971] 1 All E.R. 317. Although there is no reported authority squarely on point:

(i) the existence of compulsory employers' liability insurance in the U. K. for many years may explain why the common law there has not developed in this regard;

(ii) the common law has demonstrated a healthy capacity to adapt, innovate and rectify clear injustices, *e.g. White v. Jones* [1995] 2 A.C. 207. Is not the plaintiff's loss here as deserving of compensation as the loss of the disappointed legatees?

11. The U. K. cases in which a duty to insure was rejected are distinguishable because they reject the *Anns* [1978] A.C. 728 overall approach and, additionally, on their own special facts/circumstances. *Reid v. Rush & Tompkins Group plc* [1990] 1 W.L.R. 212 – but there the parties' financial arrangements were the subject of detailed contractual terms; also it is wrong to say (at pp. 220-221) that there are no U.K. cases where employers were held obliged to safeguard their employees' financial interests – *Spring v. Guardian Royal Exchange Ass. Co.* [1995] 2 A.C. 296 being the most obvious example (negligence in contents of reference). *Van Oppen v. Bedford Charity Trustees* [1990] 1 W.L.R. 235 – but that was in a non-economic/quasi-charitable context: also the plaintiffs' parents had been notified in writing that there was no insurance at the time and the accident there would not have resulted in the school's vicarious liability. *Richardson v. Pitt-Stanley* [1995] 1 All E.R. 460 – but the issue there was whether the 1969 English Act conferred an implied right of action; none of the leading negligence/economic loss cases were relied on.

12. The parties were in a relationship, of sufficient proximity to give rise to a duty of care to either warn or to insure – that proximity arose from *inter alia*:

(i)   smallness of the workplace;
(ii) defendant being for all practical purposes the owner as well as the sole manager/director of the business;
(iii) plaintiff and defendant were in each other's presence almost every day and defendant ought to have appreciated the risks he was exposing the plaintiff to. Accordingly, almost on all fours with *Junior Books* [1983] 1 A.C. 547.

13. In many of the instances where public policy was held to preclude a duty of care, the defendant was some public sector body carrying out public functions and the existence of such duty was regarded as an unacceptable interference with those functions, *e.g. Hill v. Chief Constable* [1989] A.C. 53 ('Yorkshire ripper') and *Swinney v. Chief Constable* [1996] 3 W.L.R. 968 (police informers). P. Cane, *Tort Law and Economic Interests* (2nd ed., 1996) pp. 238-246. However, the public policy that has the first claim under the loyalty of the law is that wrongs should be remedied; very potent counter considerations are required to override that policy – *X. (Minors) v. Bedfordshire C.C.* [1995] 2 A.C. 633 at pp. 663 C-D and 749 G.

Statutory provisions
14. Barron J. held that no such duty could arise because of *prima facie* contradictory statutory provisions.

(1)   That the Mines and Quarries Act 1965, and the Safety in Industry Acts 1955-1980 contain no such obligation is neither here nor there,

as is illustrated by *inter alia Donoghue v. Stevenson* [1932] A.C. 562, *Kirby v. Burke* [1944] I.R. 207 and *Re Frederick Inns Ltd* [1991] 1 I.L.R.M. 582 (where a transaction at undervalue principle was imported into Company Law via equity when not in the Companies Act 1990, although in U.K. legislation and in the Bankruptcy Act 1988).

  (ii) Section 285(2)(g) of the Companies Act 1963. That a preference is given to victims of accidents is not inconsistent with a court granting redress where there are no funds that can be the subject of the preference.

Imposing a duty to warn/insure in appropriate cases is not a matter solely for the Oireachtas. Otherwise the tort of negligence would never have developed since 1932, *e.g.* cases on occupiers' liability where eventually the Oireachtas intervened to curb judicial developments – Occupiers Liability Act 1995.

Piercing the veil

15. The only plausible such public policy in the present instance is that of the limited liability of members of registered companies as expounded in *Salomon & Co.* [1897] A.C. 22.

16. However,

  (i) The defendant is not being sued exclusively in his capacity as a company member; account must also be taken of his role as managing director and designated manager of the quarry, as well as his constant presence in the quarry: *Trevor Ivory v. Anderson* [1992] 2 N.Z.L.R. 517.

  (ii) He has not shown that the Company sufficiently complied with the Companies Acts to warrant him obtaining all the privileges of a duly registered company, especially s. 40 of the Companies Act, 1983.

  (iii) *Salomon & Co.* [1897] A.C. 22 was concerned with the position of contract creditors, persons who had chosen to sell goods or services to a company or to lend it money. Public policy does not warrant extending that case to tort or 'involuntary' creditors, at least in the context of the present case: *Briggs v. James Hardie & Co.* (1989) 16 N.S.W.L.R. 49; Halpern et al., 'An Economic Analysis of Limited Liability *30 U. Toronto L.J.* 117 (1980) at pp. 145-147; Hackney & Benson, 'Shareholder Liability for Inadequate Capital', 43 *U. Pittsburgh L. Rev.* 837 at pp. 863–865 and 867–869; Hansmann & Kraakman, 'Toward Unlimited Shareholder Liability for Corporate Torts', 100 *Yale L.J.* 1879. Cf. Civil Liability Act, 1961. s. 61(1), *Walkovsky v. Carlton* (1966) 223 N.E. 2d 6 (which on its facts is distinguishable) and *Jablonski v. Klemm* (1985) 377 NW 2d 560.

  (iv) *Salomon & Co.* [1897] A.C. 22 assumed that there was transparency of information and the creditors were in an equal bargaining position and were able to deal at arms length with the company [1897] A.C. at pp. 40, 45, 46, 53. The same cannot be said of an unskilled labourer with only very basic education and no trade union to represent his interests to his employer. In *Ward v. McMaster* [1988] I.R. 333 and again in *Siney v. Dublin Corp.* [1980] I.R. 400 this Court demonstrated solicitude for economically and educationally disadvantaged plaintiffs, neither of whom had been victims of serious personal injuries.

(v) Because the Respondent would today be regarded as having an insurable interest in the Company's own assets, notwithstanding its separate legal personality, *Constitution Insurance Co. of Canada v. Kosmopoulos* (1983) 149 D.L.R. 3rd 775 (see McGillivray & Parkington, *Insurance Law* (8th ed., 1988) pp. 26-27 and 48-49), there is no fundamental inconsistency with him having some duty to take out employers' liability insurance for the Company's unskilled and non-union employees, given the state of the Company's finances at the time the plaintiffs injuries occurred.

17. Section 297A of the Companies Act 1963 (as amended) is not a sufficient remedy because:-

(i) the circumstances may not come within the concept of 'reckless trading'.

(ii) any damages recovered must be shared out among all the creditors, possibly even among the secured creditors too.

(iii) the accident here happened in 1984; s. 297A did not become law until 1990.

18. If s. 5 (1) of the Companies Act 1963, is to be interpreted to prevent the plaintiff obtaining redress, it is unconstitutional, contravening Article 40.3, i-ii and the right to bodily integrity: *Byrne v. Ireland* [1972] I.R. 241. Otherwise there could be a Bhopal in Kenmare and the victims of the catastrophe would have no redress in law.

Note: the author, along with Peter Somers B.L. and James McGowan B.L., were the plaintiff's counsel.

Constitutional rights

See *Company Law*, pp. 68–71.

Iarnród Éireann v. Ireland
[1996] 3 I.R. 321

Iarnród Éireann, the state-owned railway transport company, challenged the constitutionality of certain provisions of the Civil Liability Act 1961, regarding the liability of joint tortfeasors. A preliminary issue to be determined was whether the company had the requisite *locus standi* to mount a challenge of that nature.

KEANE J.: [338] Iarnród Éireann and Mr Dowling rely primarily for the relief claimed in these proceedings on the provisions of Article 40.3 of the Constitution which are as follows:

> [339] "1° The State guarantees in its laws to respect, and, as far as practicable, by its laws to defend and vindicate the personal rights of the citizen.

> 2° The State shall, in particular, by its laws protect as best it may from unjust attack and, in the case of injustice done, vindicate the life, good name and property rights of every citizen."

The ability of corporate bodies to rely on the guarantees contained in these provisions does not appear to have been questioned in decisions prior to 1969 in which the constitutionality of legislation was challenged by such bodies in reliance on those provisions: see *Attorney General v. Southern Industrial Trust Ltd; Educational Company of Ireland Ltd v. Fitzpatrick* [1961] IR 345. In that year, however, the question was adverted to by O'Keeffe P. in *East Donegal Co-Operative Livestock Marts Ltd v. Attorney General* [1970] IR 317. He observed (at p. 333) that: "Artificial persons may possibly not be entitled to rely on the constitutional guarantees (although they have been held to be so entitled in the United States). . . ."

The Supreme Court expressed no view on the question in that case.

In *Private Motorists Provident Society Ltd v. Attorney General*, the first named plaintiff challenged the constitutionality of certain provisions of the Industrial and Provident Societies (Amendment) Act 1978 which it claimed were invalid having regard to the provisions of Article 40, already cited, guaranteeing the property rights of every citizen and provisions of Article 43. . . .

[340] The second plaintiff in the action was a shareholder in the first named plaintiff and an Irish citizen. The defendants contested the rights of the plaintiffs to rely on these provisions of the Constitution. Carroll J dealt with this contention [179] as follows (at p. 349):

> "The first issue to be determined is whether the society, as such, can claim that its constitutional rights under Article 40.3 and under Article

43 of the Constitution have been infringed. The property rights which are guaranteed by Article 40.3, are those stated in Article 43, see p. 176 of the report of *Attorney General v. Southern Industrial Trust Ltd.* In Article 43.1.1°, the State acknowledges that man, in virtue of his rational being, has the natural right, antecedent to positive law, to the private ownership of external goods. The remainder of Article 43 flows from that statement. In Article 43.1.2°, the word 'accordingly' shows a reference back to s. 1.1, of that article. Article 43.2.1° specifically refers to the rights mentioned in the foregoing provisions of the article and s. 2.2, of the article refers to 'the said rights'. In my opinion the provisions of Article 43.1.1°, cannot be construed as acknowledging or conferring a constitutional right on a corporate body – itself a creature of positive law. The right protected by Article 43 is the right of a human person."

Therefore, in so far as a claim is made by the society that its constitutional rights under Article 40.3 and Article 43 have been infringed by the Act, the claim is unsustainable as the society does not have such rights. This view is in accord with the view expressed, in respect of Article 40. 1, by the Supreme Court at p. 14 of the report of *Quinn's Supermarket v. Attorney General* [1972] IR 1.

However, Mr Moore is a shareholder in the society. He invested his money with other shareholders in a society incorporated under the law which is entitled to carry on business *intra vires*. If the business of the society is affected by the Act, of 1978 in such a way that the property rights of Mr Moore as a shareholder are affected, then he is entitled, *prima facie*, to make a claim that his constitutional rights that are protected by Article 40.3 and Article 43 have been infringed. Ownership of shares is one of the bundle of rights which constitute ownership of private property; *per* Kenny J. at p. 84 of the report of *Central Dublin Development Association v. Attorney General* (1969) 109 ILTR 69."

In *Quinn's Supermarket Ltd v. Attorney General* to which Carroll J referred in this passage, neither Article 40.3 nor Article 43 [341] were under consideration. The plaintiff, however, did rely on Article 40.1 which provides that:

"All citizens shall, *as human persons*, be held equal before the law. This shall not be held to mean that the State shall not in its enactments have due regard to differences of capacity, physical and moral, and of social function". [Emphasis added]

Speaking for the Supreme Court in that case, Walsh J said of this provision (at p. 14):

"Furthermore, it need scarcely be pointed out that under no possible construction of the constitutional guarantee could a body corporate or any entity but a human being be considered to be a human person for the purposes of this provision. In my view this provision has no bearing whatsoever upon the point to be considered in the present case, as no question of human equality or inequality arises."

It will be observed that the word 'citizen' in the provisions under consideration, in this case is not qualified by the addition of the words 'as human persons' or similar words.

The plaintiffs, having failed on the substantive issue in the *PMPS* case in the High Court, appealed to the Supreme Court. Their appeal was disallowed, but no opinion was expressed as to the *locus standi* of the first named plaintiff. Having pointed out that the plaintiffs' challenge in that case was based, not only on Article 40.3, but also on Article 40.6.1°iii guaranteeing freedom of association, O'Higgins CJ, delivering the judgment of the court, said (at p. 358):

> "The rights which are alleged to have been infringed are among the personal rights which the Constitution guarantees to citizens. The society is a creature of statute law and it is argued that, as such, it does not enjoy that constitutional protection. However, Mr Moore, as a citizen, is entitled to complain if the impugned legislation interferes with any of his personal rights. This he does in the claim that both his property rights and his freedom of association have been violated. In the circumstances, it is unnecessary to decide the question of the society's rights. Therefore, the court does not express any opinion on this question."

Having referred to the submission on behalf of the Attorney General in that case that the second named plaintiff had no property rights as a shareholder in the assets or business of the first named plaintiff but merely contractual rights in and against that body, O'Higgins CJ went on (at p. 359):

> [342] "In the opinion of the court it is sufficient that, as a shareholder and to the extent rights of his investment, Mr Moore has an interest in the society and contractual arising therefrom. This interest and these contractual rights are property rights which belong to Mr Moore and they are capable of being harmed by injury done to the society. The court, therefore, rejects the submission made on behalf of the Attorney General that, as a shareholder in the society, Mr Moore has no property rights capable of being invoked for the purposes of Article 40.3 of the Constitution. The court's acceptance of the argument put forward by Mr Moore on this point is in accordance with the judgment of Kenny J in *Central Dublin Development Association v. Attorney General* and with the judgments of O'Keeffe P and of this Court in *East Donegal Co-Operative Livestock Marts Ltd v. Attorney General*. Therefore, the court will con-

sider the question of the validity of the impugned legislation having regard to its effect on Mr Moore's property rights as a shareholder in the society."

As already noted, the capacity of bodies corporate to invoke the provisions of the Constitution now under consideration does not seem to have been questioned in cases decided by the Supreme Court in which they wore plaintiffs prior to the *PMPS* case, and the issue does not appear to have been specifically addressed by that court in any decisions subsequent to that case. It arose directly for consideration, however, in this Court in *Chestvale Properties Ltd v. Glackin* [1993] 3 IR 35; [1992] ILRM 221.

In that case, the applicant companies contended that the power claimed by the first named respondent, an inspector appointed to investigate the affairs of those companies under the relevant provision of the Companies Act 1990, was invalid having regard to the provisions of Article 40.3 as being an unjust attack on their property rights. It is relevant to note that the particular enquiry being conducted by the first named respondent was as to the identity of the persons effectively in control of the applicant companies and that none of the shareholders in either of the companies was joined as a plaintiff. Murphy J. dealt as follows (at p. 46) with the contention advanced on behalf of the respondents that the applicant companies had no *locus standi*.

> "As the rights guaranteed by [Article 40.3] are the personal and property rights of citizens, the respondent and the Attorney General contended that an argument based on this subsection was not available to the corporate applicants.
>
> This objection is supported by the decision of Carroll J in *Private Motorists Provident Society Ltd v.* [343] *Attorney General*. Ordinarily when this problem arises it is overcome by joining as a plaintiff a shareholder of the corporate plaintiff who is an Irish citizen (as was done in the *PMPS* case). This solution was consciously rejected by counsel on behalf of the applicants in the present case.
>
> Whilst I accept that the court should be astute to protect the rights of citizens, even when they are attacked only indirectly through particular corporate structures, it does seem to me that in the particular circumstances of this case, the absence of an individual Irish citizen asserting his own constitutional rights is fatal to the argument based on the constitutionality of the 1990 legislation. However as the matter was argued in full before me it is proper that I should express a view on it."

Murphy J went on to reject the contention that, assuming the applicants were entitled to rely on the provisions of Article 40.3, the purported exercise by the first named respondent of the relevant powers would be invalid having regard to those provisions, holding that, to the extent that they interfered with the property rights of the applicants, they were justified under the terms of Article 43 as a means of reconciling the exercise of such rights with the exigencies of the common good.

It is an important feature of the decision of Carroll J in the *PMPS* case that it was expressly based on the premise that the rights on which the plaintiff sought to rely derived from Article 43. The learned judge laid particular emphasis on the acknowledgement by the State in the opening words of that article that 'man, in virtue of his rational being' is entitled to rights of private property and that the remainder of the article flows from that statement. She concluded, in the result, that the right protected by Article 43 is 'the right of a human person'.

However, subsequent to the decision in *PMPS*, the relationship of Articles 40.3 and Article 43 was further elucidated in the judgment of the Supreme Court in *Blake v. Attorney General* [1982] IR 117. In that case, certain provisions of the Rent Restrictions Act 1960, were challenged as being invalid having regard to the provisions of Articles 40 and 43. Giving the judgment of the court, O'Higgins CJ said of Article 43. . . .

"Article 43 does not state what the rights of property are. It recognises private property as an institution and forbids its abolition. The rights in respect of particular items of property are protected by Article 40.3.2°, by which the State undertakes by its laws to protect from unjust attack and, in the case of injustice done, to vindicate the property rights of every citizen."

The learned Chief Justice went on to cite with approval the following statement by Davitt P at first instance in *Attorney General v. Southern Industrial Trust Ltd*: "Article 40.3 seems to me to be the only provision in the Constitution which protects the individual's rights to the property which he does own."

It is, accordingly, clear that the rationale on which Carroll J based her rejection of the *locus standi* of the corporate plaintiff in the *PMPS* case can no longer be supported. In contrast to Article 40.1 and Article 43, Article 40.3.2°, [345] in enumerating the rights which are thereby guaranteed, refers simply to 'the property rights of every citizen'. If the decision in *PMPS* is to be supported, it must be on the ground that the 'property rights of every citizen' thereby guaranteed are confined to rights enjoyed by the citizens as human persons.

Undoubtedly, some at least of the rights enumerated in Article 40.3.2° – the rights to life and liberty – are of no relevance to corporate bodies and other artificial legal entities. Property rights are, however, in a different category. Not only are corporate bodies themselves capable in law of owning property, whether moveable or immoveable, tangible or intangible. The 'property' referred to clearly includes shares in companies formed under the relevant companies' legislation which was already a settled feature of the legal and commercial life of this country at the time of the enactment of the Constitution. There would accordingly be a spectacular deficiency in the guarantee to every citizen that his or her property rights will be protected against 'unjust attack', if such bodies were incapable in law of being regarded as 'citizens', at least for the purposes of this article, and if it was essential for the shareholders to abandon the protection of limited liability to which they are entitled by law in order to protect, not merely their own rights as shareholders, but also the property rights of the corporate entity itself, which are in law distinct from the rights of its members.

Article 43 undoubtedly treats the general right of private property, the abolition of which in its entirety is expressly prohibited, as one inhering in 'man in virtue of his rational being' and, in that sense, as being 'antecedent to positive law', including the Constitution itself. But it does not necessarily follow that the property rights of the individual citizens which are protected against 'unjust attack' by Article 40.3 are confined to rights enjoyed by human persons. Had the framers of the Constitution wished to confine the comprehensive guarantee in Article 40.3 in that manner, there was nothing to prevent them including a similar qualification to that contained in Article 40. 1.

The present case demonstrates that the restriction on the property rights of the citizen which would logically result from confining the protection of Article 40.3 to individual citizens would not necessarily be eased in every case by joining the shareholders as plaintiffs in the proceedings. If this case were to depend on the *locus standi* of Mr Dowling it would appear that his property rights as an individual arising out of his ownership of one share in Iarnród Éireann are of so nominal a nature as not to afford him any such *locus standi*. It is unnecessary at this [346] point to consider how many other corporate bodies would be in a similarly impotent state, although they would clearly include some in the private sector, such as companies limited by guarantee. It is sufficient to say that, although the strategy adopted in the *PMPS* case of joining the shareholder as a plaintiff was accepted by the Supreme Court as obviating any constitutional difficulty that might have arisen in that case, it is of critical importance that the court expressly refrained from holding that the corporate plaintiff had no *locus standi*. In the result, I consider that I am not bound to hold that where, as here, it is not possible to make effective use of such a strategy, the claim of a corporate plaintiff must necessarily fail.

I am satisfied that the expression 'every citizen' is not confined in Article 40.3.2° to citizens in their individual capacity as human persons and that artificial legal entities must also be protected by the laws of the State against unjust attacks on their property rights. In the case of injustice done, it is peculiarly the role of the courts to vindicate the property fights of such entities in accordance with Article 40.3.2°. No doubt such a conclusion might not be reached if one were to adopt a strictly literal approach to these provisions, but as Henchy J observed in *People (DPP) v. O'Shea* [1982] IR 384 at p. 426: "It may be said of a Constitution, more than of any other legal instrument, that 'the letter killeth, but the spirit giveth life'."

The submission on behalf of the State, that even if corporate bodies had any *locus standi* to invoke the relevant provisions of the Constitution, this did not apply to Iarnród Éireann, having regard to the statutory provisions under which it was incorporated, must next be considered. . . .

[347] Iarnród Éireann is, accordingly, what is usually referred to as a 'semi-state body', i.e. a body incorporated by statute to carry out defined public objectives and which is normally accountable, through a specified minister, to the government and, through the government, to the Oireachtas. Their legal structures take different forms: thus, in the present instance, Iarnród Éireann is required by statute to be a company limited by shares formed under the Companies Acts 1963 to 1990. Its parent body, however, Córas Iompair Éireann, which, as has been already noted, owns virtually the entire share capital of Iarnród Éireann, is a board incorporated by statute (the Transport Act 1950).

Bodies of this nature are endowed by law with the capacity, inter alia, to own property and institute proceedings. However, if the submissions on behalf of the State are well-founded, they also suffer from a disadvantage peculiar to them. It is argued that, since they derive their legal existence exclusively from legislation, it would be in some sense anomalous for them to litigate the constitutionality of legislation purportedly enacted by the Oireachtas. Since the Oireachtas has brought them into being, the argument runs, it can equally impose whatever disability it wishes on them and cannot be held to account, as it were, by the courts.

It is, of course, within the competence of the Oireachtas to provide for the establishment of bodies which do not have the normal *indicia* of corporate bodies, including the capacity to own property and sue and be sued. Where, however, the Oireachtas has decided, as it manifestly has in the present instance, that a semi-state body charged with the achievement of statutory objectives of a public nature should take the form of a body corporate enjoying the usual powers of such bodies, I see no reason for [348] attributing to the Oireachtas the intention that its powers should be emasculated in the manner suggested. The requirement that Iarnród Éireann should be formed and registered as a company under the Companies Acts 1963 to 1990, was presumably because the Oireachtas considered that this was the form of organisation best calculated to facilitate the achievement of its statutory objectives. It was clearly envisaged that, although Iarnród Éireann was to enjoy a statutory monopoly in the provision of certain services, it was also to operate as a commercial body. To that end, it needed powers, *inter alia*, to own property and institute proceedings. I see no reason to suppose that the Oireachtas intended that, unlike other commercial companies formed for purely private profit, Iarnród Éireann was precluded from invoking the protection of the Constitution when those rights were under unjust attack, whether from the Oireachtas, the executive or any other quarter. I am, accordingly, satisfied that this submission is not well-founded.

As already noted, it was submitted on behalf of Iarnród Éireann that, even if the rights of private property and fair procedures on which it relied were not vested in it because it was a body corporate and Mr Dowling's shareholding was of too nominal a nature to afford him *locus standi*, it was nevertheless entitled to institute the present proceedings since, if its arguments on the substantive issue were well-founded, it would be unarguably seriously affected by the unconstitutional provisions of the 1961 Act. Although this issue does not now arise, I think that since it was fully argued I shall state my conclusions.

ULTRA VIRES CONTRACTS AND TRANSACTIONS

Crédit Suisse v. Allerdale B.C. (CA)
[1996] 3 W.L.R. 894

This extract from Neill L.J.'s judgment is an excellent summary of how the doctrine of *ultra vires* has evolved in the last two hundred years or so. With a view to putting a swimming pool in its area, the defendant, a local authority, set up a company which would develop a site and build a leisure centre along with time share units. That company borrowed from the plaintiff bank on the security of inter alia a guarantee given by the defendant council. It was held at first instance and on appeal that this guarantee was *ultra vires* the council's powers.

NEILL L.J.: [919] In the light of the conclusion which I have reached on the issue of the statutory power of the council these submissions are no longer of direct relevance to the outcome of this appeal. Nevertheless I have decided that I should express some opinion on the questions which were raised. I propose to consider these questions as shortly as possible under four headings: (1) the development of the doctrine of *ultra vires*; (2) the doctrine of *ultra vires* in relation to limited companies; (3) the doctrine of *ultra vires* in public law; (4) the present case.

(1) The development of the doctrine of ultra vires
Since the abolition of the Court of Star Chamber the Court of King's Bench and subsequently the High Court have played a supervisory role in relation to decisions made by local administrative bodies. It is not necessary, however, in this judgment to consider the nature or the extent of this control in so far as it affected municipal corporations or other bodies established otherwise than by statute. Blackburn J. may or may not have been right when in his judgment in the Exchequer Chamber in *Riche v. Ashbury Railway Carriage and Iron Co. Ltd.* (1874) L.R. 9 Ex. 224, 263 when, after referring to *Sutton's Hospital Case* (1612) 10 Co. Rep. 1, he said, at p. 263:

"This seems to me an express authority that at common law it is an incident to a corporation to use its common seal for the purpose of binding itself to anything to which a natural person could bind himself, and to deal with its property as a natural person might deal with his own. And further, that an attempt to forbid this on the part of the King, even by express negative words, does not bind at law. Nor am I aware of any authority in conflict with this case."

The incorporation of some municipalities by statute dates from the Municipal Corporations Act 1835 (5 & 6 Will. 4, c. 76). In this case we are concerned with a local authority which is a body corporate within the meaning of section 2(3) of the Act of 1972.

[920] It seems, however, that the origins of the modern doctrine of *ultra vires* are to be found not so much in the cases where the courts sought to exercise control over local administrative bodies allegedly acting in excess of jurisdiction by, for example, passing impermissible byelaws, but in cases where consideration was given to the powers of trading companies, and in particular of railway companies, incorporated by statute towards the end of the first half of the 19th century. The courts found themselves in unfamiliar territory. In *Colman v. Eastern Counties Railway Co.* (1846) 10 Beav. 1, 13 Lord Langdale M.R. referred to some of the recently established railway companies and said:

"I think it right to observe, that companies of this kind, possessing most extensive powers, have so recently been introduced to this country, that neither the legislature nor courts of justice have been yet able to understand all the different lights in which their transactions ought properly to be viewed. We must, however, adhere to ancient general and settled principles, so far as they can be applied to great combinations and companies of this kind."

A little later, at p. 14, he expressed the view that a railway company had to be scrutinised more closely than a partnership. He added:

". . . I am clearly of opinion, that the powers which are given by an Act of Parliament, like that now in question, extend no farther than is expressly stated in the Act or is necessarily and properly required for carrying into effect the undertaking and works which the Act has expressly sanctioned."

Thereafter the courts progressed cautiously until the position was clarified by the important decisions in *Riche v. Ashbury Railway Carriage and Iron Co. Ltd.* (1875) L.R. 7 H.L. 653, *Attorney General v. Great Eastern Railway Co.*, 5 App.Cas. 473 and *Small v. Smith* (1884) 10 App.Cas. 119.

In the last 100 years, and particularly in the last 50, the doctrine of *ultra vires* has become a potent force in many areas of the law. In public law it has been used as the foundation for the intervention by the courts in judicial review proceedings. In private law it has been used as a method of confining the lawful activities of limited companies to those which are authorised by the memorandum of association.

But, despite the great importance which the doctrine of *ultra vires* has assumed in the field of public law and, until recently, in relation to the activities of limited companies, the doctrine still gives rise to conceptual and practical difficulties. It is easy to state that if a body with limited powers makes a decision which it has no power to make the decision is void and of no legal effect. But such a statement may not accord with the reality of the situation.

The problem is well illustrated by the well known dictum of Lord Radcliffe in *Smith v. East Elloe Rural District Council* [1956] A.C. 736, 769-770 where he said:

> "An order, even if not made in good faith, is still an act capable of legal consequences. It bears no brand of invalidity upon its forehead. Unless the necessary proceedings are taken at law to establish the cause of invalidity and to get it quashed or otherwise upset, it will remain as effective for its ostensible purpose as the most impeccable of orders."

Moreover, even an order which is manifestly bad can be effective until its invalidity has been exposed in court. The counterfeit is as good as the genuine article until it has been weighed.

[921] It is no doubt because it has been difficult to find an appropriate epithet to describe the quality of an *ultra vires* decision in the period before it has been pronounced ineffective ab initio that judges have deprecated the use of the word void. By way of example one can take a passage in the speech of Lord Diplock in *Hoffmann-La Roche & Co. A.G. v. Secretary of State for Trade and Industry* [1975] A.C. 295, 366 where he said:

> "I think it leads to confusion to use such terms as 'voidable,'voidable ab initio,' 'void' or 'a nullity' as descriptive of the legal status of subordinate legislation alleged to be *ultra vires* for patent or for latent defects, before its validity has been pronounced on by a court of competent jurisdiction."

The problem, however, is not merely one of terminology. Even after an order or decision has been declared to be void or a nullity or has been quashed it may return as a ghost to show that it was once very much alive. The law has not yet found a way to deal satisfactorily with the simulacrum of a decision.

I turn next to the application of the doctrine in relation to limited companies.

(2) The doctrine of ultra vires in relation to limited companies
I referred earlier to the fact that the courts have drawn a distinction between the effect of acts which are *ultra vires* a company and of acts which are beyond the powers of the directors. This matter was discussed together with the various uses of the words "*ultra vires*" by Browne Wilkinson L.J. in his important judgment in *Rolled Steel Products (Holdings) Ltd. v. British Steel Corporation* [1986] Ch. 246, 302–304 (see *infra*, p. 110) where he said, in a case decided before the Companies Act 1985:

> "In my judgment, much of the confusion that has crept into the law flows from the use of the phrase *'ultra vires'* in different senses in different contexts. The reconciliation of the authorities can only be achieved if one first defines the sense in which one is using the words *'ultra vires.'* Because the literal translation of the words is 'beyond the powers,' there are many cases in which the words have been applied to transactions which, although within the capacity of the company, are carried out otherwise than through the correct exercise of the powers of the company by its officers; indeed, that is the sense in which the judge seems to have used the words in this case. For reasons which will appear, in my judgment, the use of the phrase *'ultra vires'* should be restricted to those cases where the transaction is beyond the capacity of the company and therefore wholly void. A company, being an artificial person, has no capacity to do anything outside the objects specified in its memorandum of association. If the transaction is outside the objects, in law it is wholly void. But the object of a company and the powers conferred on a company to carry out those objects are two different things. . . . If the concept that a company cannot do anything which is not authorised by law had been pursued with ruthless logic, the result might have been reached that a company could not (*i.e.*, had no capacity) to do anything otherwise than in due exercise of its powers. But such ruthless logic has not been pursued and it is clear that a transaction falling within the objects of the company is capable of conferring rights on third parties even though the transaction was an abuse of the powers of the company [922]: see, for example, *In re David Payne & Co. Ltd.* [1904] 2 Ch. 608. It is therefore established that a company has capacity to carry out a transaction which falls within its objects even though carried out by the wrongful exercise of its powers. . . . If the transaction is beyond the capacity of the company it is in any event a nullity and wholly void: whether or not the third party had notice of the invalidity, property transferred or money paid under such a transaction will be recoverable from the third party. If, on the other hand, the transaction (although in excess or abuse of powers) is within the capacity of the company, the position of the third party depends on whether or not he had notice that the transaction was in excess or abuse of the powers of the company."

It may be noted that this distinction between the capacity of a company and the powers of directors in relation to the rights of a third party must have been in the mind of Lord Campbell C.J. in *Mayor of Norwich v. Norfolk Railway Co.* (1855) 4 E. & B. 397, 443 when he suggested that the purchase of a large quantity of iron rails by the directors of a railway company for the purposes of a private speculation would be treated differently from a similar purchase of a thousand gross of green spectacles.

In the last two decades, however, the doctrine of *ultra vires* in its application to ordinary limited companies has been fundamentally changed by legislation.

Section 35 of the Companies Act 1985 (which resembles s. 8(1) of the 1963 Act – see *post*, p. 578) was enacted as part of a number of measures introduced in order to bring United Kingdom law into conformity with European Community law, as contained in the First Company Law Directive (68/151/E.E.C.)(as amended). By section 108(1) of the Companies Act 1989, however, a new section 35 was substituted. The substitution was brought into force on 4 February 1991. The Act of 1989 also introduced provisions relating to charitable companies.

At the relevant time the U.K. Company Law had not been amended to give effect to the 1st E.E.C. Directive.

Note: The main issues in recent case law concern gratuitous disbursements made by companies which do not in any way benefit them. These disbursements can be either to third parties (*e.g.* the guarantee given in the *Rolled Steel* case, infra, and the *Northern Bank* case, *infra*, p. 126) to the Revenue Commissioners (*e.g.* to payments made in the *Frederick Inns* case, *infra*, p. 130) or to all or some of the company's own members (*e.g.* the sale of the property in the *Aveling Barford* case, *infra*, p. 123) and the payments considered in the *Greendale* case, *infra*, p. 131). Section 8(1) of the 1963 Act, which is similar to section 35 of the British Companies Act, 1985 (as amended) referred to above in the *Credit Suisse* case, was relied on by the defendants in both the *Northern Bank* case and in the *Frederick Inns* case but it is more convenient to deal with section 8(1) separately in chap. 13 on company contracts (*post*, p. 578).

Rolled Steel Products (Holdings) Ltd. v. British Steel Corp.
[1986] 1 Ch. 246

The company guaranteed the very substantial liabilities of one of is directors, who also was its principle shareholder. It was contended, *inter alia*, that the guarantee was *ultra vires* the company and, accordingly, was not binding on it. Among the objects in its memorandum of association were the following:

"(A) To carry on business as exporters and importers of, and manufacturers of, and dealers in, and buying and selling agents for, iron, steel, copper, bronze, aluminium, lead, tin, zinc, antimony and other metal goods of all descriptions and home and foreign and dominion and colonial goods, merchandise and produce of all descriptions. . . .

(K) To lend and advance money or give credit to such persons, firms, or companies and on such terms as may seem expedient, and in particular to customers of and others having dealings with the company, and to give guarantees or become security for any such persons, firms, or companies.

(L) To borrow or raise money in such manner as the company shall think fit, and in particular by the issue of debentures or debenture stock (perpetual or otherwise), and to secure the repayment of any money borrowed, raised, or owing, by mortgage, charge, or lien upon the whole or any part of the company's property or assets (whether present or future), including its uncalled capital, and also by a similar mortgage, charge, or lien to secure and guarantee the performance by the company of any obligation or liability it may undertake."

The objects clause ended with the words:

"It is hereby expressly declared that each sub-clause of this clause shall be construed independently of the other sub-clauses hereof, and that none of the objects mentioned in any sub-clause shall be deemed to be merely subsidiary to the objects mentioned in any other sub-clause."

The articles of association contained, inter alia, the following provisions:

"17. Provided that a director declares his interest in a contract or arrangement or proposed contract or arrangement with the company in manner provided by section 199 of the Act he shall be counted in the quorum at any meeting of directors at which the same is considered and shall be entitled to vote as a director in respect thereof.

"18 (a) The quorum necessary for the transaction of the business of the directors may be fixed by the directors, and unless so fixed, shall, be two."

SLADE L.J.: [286] For many years the phrase "*ultra vires*", has from time to time been used by company lawyers in two senses. Primarily it is used to describe [287] acts which are beyond the capacity of a company. As is pointed out by the editors of *Gore-Browne on Companies*, 43rd ed. (1977), para. 3-1, the phrase is also sometimes used to describe acts which are not beyond the capacity of the company but simply beyond the authority of either the board of directors or a majority of the shareholders.

In many instances the sense in which the phrase is being used is far from clear. However, I think it plain that paragraphs 11 and 13 of the statement of claim in this case, in alleging that each of the guarantee and the debenture were "*ultra vires* and void," were intended to allege that their execution was beyond the *corporate capacity* of the plaintiff on the grounds that they were executed not for the purposes or benefit of the plaintiff but for the purposes or benefit of Mr. Shenkman.

Subject to a point relating to the true construction of the words "as may seem expedient in clause 3(K) of the memorandum of association, there is no doubt that these two transactions fell within the letter of clause 3(K) and (L) of the memorandum. Accordingly, two important points of principle which arise in the present context may be expressed thus: Is a transaction which falls within the letter of the powers conferred on a company incorporated under the Companies Acts but is effected for a purpose not authorised by its memorandum of association properly to be regarded as being beyond the corporate capacity of the company? Apart from section 9(1) of the European Communities Act 1972, is such a transaction capable of conferring rights on a third party dealing with the company and, if so, in what circumstances?

The legal personality of a company incorporated under the Companies Acts exists only for the purpose of its incorporation, as defined in the objects clause, which have to be set out in its memorandum of association as required by section 2(1)(c) of the Companies Act 1948. It does not, however, follow that any act is beyond its capacity unless expressly authorised by its objects clause. Any such company is treated as having implied powers to do any act which is reasonably incidental to the attainment or pursuit of any of its express objects, unless such act is expressly prohibited by the memorandum: see *In re Horsley & Weight Ltd.* [1982] Ch. 442, 448 *per* Buckley L.J. Strictly, therefore, it is not essential for the memorandum to insert any reference at all to mere powers as distinct from objects. Indeed, in *Cotman v. Brougham* [1918] A.C. 514, 522-523 Lord Wrenbury deprecated the widespread practice of introducing what should properly be called mere powers in memoranda, as opposed to articles of association, though he confessed that, when a junior at the Bar, he himself had had to yield to it after "a vain struggle."

The statutory requirement that the objects of a company shall be specified in the memorandum marks one important difference between objects and powers. In my judgment, however, whether a particular transaction, carried out in purported exercise of an express or implied power contained in a company's memorandum of association, is within the capacity of the company must still depend on the true construction of that memorandum.

Correctly, therefore, in my opinion, Mr. Heyman's argument has focused attention in the present context on the wording of the [288] memorandum of the plaintiff. His first submission has been that the guarantee was *intra vires* the plaintiff as a matter of corporate capacity because the provisions of clause 3(K) of the plaintiff's memorandum, read together with the closing words of that clause, set out a separate independent object which the plaintiff was capable of carrying on as such, and that the execution of the guarantee fell within that provision.

If this submission as to the construction of clause 3(K) were well-founded, I think the suggested conclusion would follow and that, while the relevant transactions might have involved breaches of duty on the part of the directors of the plaintiff, there would be no possible question of their having been beyond its corporate capacity. For the recent decision of this court in *In re Horsley & Weight Ltd*. [1982] Ch. 442 has made clear, if this was not clear before: "the doing of an act which is expressed" – by the company's memorandum – to be, and is capable of being, an independent object of the company cannot be *ultra vires*, for it is by definition something which the company is formed to do and so must be *intra vires*.

See *per* Buckley L.J. at p. 449, and also *per* Cumming-Bruce L.J. at p. 454 and *per* Templeman L.J. at p. 455. Furthermore, I think this decision also shows that this same principle applies whether or not the transaction in question is of a gratuitous nature:

"The objects of a company do not need to be commercial; they can be charitable or philanthropic; indeed, they can be whatever the original incorporators wish, provided that they are legal. Nor is there any reason why a company should not part with its funds gratuitously or for noncommercial reasons if to do so is within its declared objects."

See *per* Buckley L.J. at p. 450.

In the light of the observations of Buckley L.J. in that case, at p. 452, of Pennycuick J. in *Charterbridge Corporation Ltd. v. Lloyds Bank Ltd* [1970] Ch. 62, 69–71 and of Oliver J. in *In re Halt Garage (1964) Ltd* [1982] 3 All E.R. 1016, 1028–1030 (see *post*, 228), the three tests of *ultra vires* suggested by Eve J. in an often cited passage in his judgment in *In re Lee, Behrens and Co. Ltd* [1932] 2 Ch. 46, 51, should, in my opinion, now be recognised as being of no assistance, and indeed positively misleading, when the relevant question is whether a particular gratuitous transaction is within a company's corporate capacity. To this extent the tests should, I think, be finally laid to rest, though they may well be helpful in considering whether or not in any given case directors have abused the powers vested in them by the company.

The question whether clause 3(K) of the plaintiffs memorandum contains a separate independent object of the company is purely one of construction of that memorandum. The decision of the House of Lords in *Cotman v. Brougham* [1918] A.C. 514 requires that, in answering it, full force must be given, so far as possible, to the provision at the end of clause 3 of the memorandum, which directs that each sub-clause shall be construed independently of the other sub-clauses. I accept Mr. Heyman's [289] submission that clause 3(K) must be treated as containing a substantive object unless either (i) the subject matter of this sub-clause is by its nature incapable of constituting a substantive object (as was the power to borrow in *Introductions Ltd. v. National Provincial Bank Ltd.* [1970] Ch. 199) or (ii) the wording of the memorandum shows expressly or by implication that the sub-clause was intended merely to constitute an ancillary power only: see, for example, the observations of Buckley J. in the latter case at first instance [1968] 2 All E.R. 1221, 1224.

Mr. Heyman has submitted, and I agree, that there is no reason in principle why a company should not be formed for the specific purpose, inter alia, of giving guarantees whether gratuitous or otherwise, rather unusual though such an object might be.

Attention, however, has to be directed to the particular wording of clause 3(K). The authority to give guarantees and become security conferred by the second limb of the sub-clause is not an unrestricted authority. It is merely an authority to give guarantees or become security for "any such persons, firms or companies." The six words just quoted echo the words of the first limb of the sub-clause, which authorise the company to "lend and advance money or give credit to such persons, firms, or companies and on such terms as may seem expedient, and in particular to customers of and others having dealings with the company."

The phrase "as may seem expedient" necessarily implies that there is some criterion by which expediency is to be tested. The only possible criterion, in my opinion, can only mean "as may seem expedient for the furtherance of the objects of the company." The references in clause 3(K) to the giving of credit and to customers of and persons having dealings with the company make it additionally clear that the sub-clause in its context was intended to comprise merely a series of ancillary powers. It follows that, in my opinion, the powers to give guarantees and become security, which are the relevant powers in the present case, are not to be construed as independent objects of the plaintiff and the judge was right in so holding. Correspondingly, I think he was right to reject the defendants' argument that the relevant transactions were *intra vires* the plaintiff, in so far as that argument was based on the hypothesis that the powers conferred by clause 3(K) were independent objects of the plaintiff.

What, then, is the position if, as I have concluded, the power to give guar-antees and to become security are to be regarded as mere powers ancillary to the objects of the plaintiff? Even on this footing, the plaintiff in executing the guarantee and the debenture was performing acts of a nature which, at least seemingly, it was expressly authorised by clause 3(K) and (L) of its memoran-dum to perform. The particular exercises of these powers were, on the face of them, well capable of falling within the objects of the plaintiff.

The judge, as I have read his judgment, accepted that these transactions were capable of failing within the scope of the wording of the powers con-ferred on the plaintiff by its memorandum. Nevertheless, [290] he considered that there is a general principle of company law that a transaction, which ostensibly falls within the scope of the wording of a company's memorandum but is in fact entered into for some purpose not authorised by that memorandum, will be *ultra vires* the company in what he called the "wider sense" and will confer rights on another party only if he can show that he dealt with the company in good faith and did not have notice that the transaction was entered into for an unauthorised purpose [1982] Ch. 478, 499. It was primarily on the basis of this principle that the judge ultimately held the defendants in the present case liable to restore the moneys which they had received.

As Lord Selborne said in *Ashbury Railway Carriage and Iron Co. Ltd. v. Riche* (1875) L.R. 7 H.L. 653, 693: "a statutory corporation, created by Act of Parliament for a particular purpose, is limited, as to all its powers, by the purposes of its incorporation as defined in that Act."

Strict logic might therefore appear to require that any act purported to be done by a company in purported exercise of powers ancillary to its objects conferred on it by its memorandum of association, whether express or implied, (*e.g.*, a power to borrow) would necessarily and in every case be beyond its capacity and therefore wholly void if such act was in fact performed for purposes other than those of its incorporation. However, the practical difficulties resulting from such a conclusion for persons dealing with a company carrying on a business authorised by its memorandum would be intolerable. As Buckley J. put it, in regard to a power to borrow, in *In re David Payne & Co. Ltd.* [1904] 2 Ch. 608, 613:

> "A corporation, every time it wants to borrow, cannot be called upon by the lender to expose all its affairs, so that the lender can say, 'Before I lend you anything, I must investigate how you carry on your business, and I must know why you want the money, and how you apply it, and when you do have it I must see you apply it in the right way.' It is perfectly impossible to work out such a principle."

The *David Payne* decision, in my opinion, indicates the proper alternative approach. In that case, the company concerned had express power under its memorandum of association "to borrow and raise money for the purposes of the company's business." It borrowed money and issued a debenture to secure the loan. Its liquidator claimed that the debenture was *ultra vires* and void because there was evidence that the borrowing had not in fact been made for the purposes of the company's business. Buckley J. in his judgment considered the force of the phrase "for the purposes of the company's business." He asked the question, at 612:

> "is it a condition attached to the exercise of the power that the money should be borrowed for the purposes of the business, or is that a matter to be determined as between the sharcholders and the dircctors?"

In the course of answering this question he said, at p. 612:

[291] "A corporation cannot do anything except for the purposes of its business, borrowing or anything else; everything else is beyond its power, and is *ultra vires*. So that the words 'for the purposes of the company's business' are a mere expression of that which would be involved if there were no such words."

This passage has been frequently echoed in later cases and, perhaps not surprisingly, has on occasions been read as referring to the capacity of the company. However, I think that in using the phrase *'ultra vires'* in this particular context Buckley J. can only have meant *"ultra vires* the directors." This, in my opinion, is made clear by what followed. He accepted that, if the phrase "for the purpose of the company's business" was a condition attached to the exercise of the power, a loan would be *ultra vires* and void if the condition had not been complied with. He did not, however, regard it as such a condition: in his view it did no more than state the obvious. In these circumstances, his conclusion was, at p. 613:

"If this borrowing was made, as it appears to me at present it was made, for a purpose illegitimate so far as the borrowing company was concerned, that may very well be a matter on which rights may arise as between the shareholders and directors of that company. It may have been a wrongful act on the part of the directors. But I do not think that a person who lends to the company is by any words such as these required to investigate whether the money borrowed is borrowed for a proper purpose or an improper purpose. The borrowing being effected, and the money passing to the company, the subsequent application of the money is a matter in which the directors may have acted wrongly; but that does not affect the principal act, which is the borrowing of the money."

In these circumstances, he held, at p. 614, that the defendants: "who have paid this money and taken this debenture without notice that the money was going to be applied as it was, are not affected by anything arising in regard to that."

The most relevant passages in the judgments of the Court of Appeal in the *David Payne* case [1904] 2 Ch. 608 are cited in Vinelott J.'s judgment [1982] Ch. 478, 498 and I will not repeat them. Vaughan Williams and Cozens-Hardy L.JJ. expressly approved the manner in which Buckley J. had approached the problem. Vaughan Williams L.J. expressly, at p. 615, and the other members of the court implicitly rejected the borrower's first argument that, since the debenture was not issued to raise money for the purposes of the company, it was *ultra vires* altogether "in such a sense that nothing could make it right." All three members of the court considered that the plaintiff company could succeed if, but only if, it showed that, at the time of the loan, the lending company knew that the money was going to be applied by the borrowers for an improper purpose and that this had not been proved.

The one crucially important point to which Buckley J. and the Court of Appeal in *David Payne* did not expressly advert is the basis upon which the lenders would have lost their security if they had known of [292] the improper purpose for which the moneys lent were going to be applied. The basis is, in my opinion, this. The directors of the borrowing company in fact had no authority from the company to take the loan and grant the debenture because these transactions were not effected for the purposes of the company. Nevertheless, as a general rule, a company incorporated under the Companies Acts holds out its directors as having ostensible authority to do on its behalf anything which its memorandum of association expressly or by implication gives the company the capacity to do. In *David Payne* the company's memorandum gave it the capacity to borrow. As a matter of construction of the company's memorandum, the court was not prepared to construe the words "for the purposes of the company's business" as limiting its corporate capacity but construed them simply as limiting the authority of the directors. In the absence of notice to the contrary, the lenders would thus have been entitled to assume, on the authority of the principle in *Turquand's* case, 6 E. & B. 327 and on more general principles of the law of agency, that the directors of the borrowing company were acting properly and regularly in the internal management of its affairs and were borrowing for the purposes of the company's business: see, for example, *In re Hampshire Land Co.* [1896] 2 Ch. 743, a decision of Vaughan Williams J. which was cited in the *David Payne* case [1904] 2 Ch. 608, and *Bowstead on Agency*, 14th ed. (1976), pp. 241-242 and the cases there cited. However, a party dealing with a company cannot rely on the ostensible authority of its directors to enter into a particular transaction if it knows they in fact have no such authority because it is being entered into for improper purposes. Neither the rule in *Turquand's* case nor more general principles of the law of agency will avail him in such circumstances: see *Bowstead on Agency*, 14th ed., p. 243. The various passages in the judgments in both courts in the *David Payne* case which refer to the extent of the lender's obligation, if any, to inquire as to the purposes for which the loan is to be used, in my opinion, are not directed at all to the corporate capacity of the borrowing company; they are directed to the right of the lender to rely on the ostensible authority of the borrower's directors.

In *Introductions Ltd. v. National Provincial Bank Ltd.* [1970] Ch. 199 the Court of Appeal again had to consider the validity of debentures granted by a company as security for a loan. The company under its memorandum of association had a general ancillary power to borrow money and to issue debentures to secure its repayment. But this power was not an independent object of the company. As Harman L.J. put it, at p. 210, "borrowing is not an end in itself and must be for some purpose of the company." The power was not expressed in terms to be exercisable only "for the purposes of the company" but, following the reasoning of Buckley J. in *In re David Payne & Co. Ltd.* [1904] 2 Ch. 608, 612, the court held that the words necessarily had to be implied. The company had borrowed money from a bank and granted debentures to secure the loan. But the only business carried on by it was that of pig-breeding which was a purpose not authorised by its memorandum of association. On the liquidation of the company a question arose as to the validity of the debentures. Harman L.J., who gave the leading judgment, after deciding that the power to borrow conferred by the [293] memorandum was a mere ancillary power not an independent object, proceeded to cite, at p. 210, the following passage from the speech of Lord Parker of Waddington *in Cotman v. Brougham* [1918] A.C. 514, 521:

> "A person who deals with a company is entitled to assume that a company can do everything which it is expressly authorised to do by its memorandum of association, and need not investigate the equities between the company and its shareholders."

This passage, it will be seen, closely echoes some of the language used by Buckley J. in his judgment in the *David Payne* case [1904] 2 Ch. 608 and is, I think, an expression of the rule in *Turquand's* case, 6 E. & B. 327 and the more general principles of agency to which I have already referred. Harman L.J. went on to say [1970] Ch. 199, 210:

> "I would agree that, if the bank did not know what the purpose of the borrowing was, it need not inquire' – the emphasis is mine – "but it did know, and I can find nothing in *Cotman v. Brougham* to protect it notwithstanding that knowledge."

The words "it need not inquire," in my opinion, make it clear that Harman L.J. did not regard the borrowing as having been beyond the capacity of the company. However, he then went on to point out that the *David Payne* decision [1904] 2 Ch. 608 shows that the protection afforded by the principle stated by Lord Parker affords no protection to a lender who knows that the money is intended to be misapplied. The absence of any express provision in the company's memorandum of association requiring the loan to be applied for the purposes of the company, in his judgment, did not improve the bank's position, since such a provision would fall to be implied anyway. He concluded, at p. 211:

> This borrowing was not for a legitimate purpose of the company: the bank knew it, and, therefore, "-the emphasis is mine-"cannot rely on its debentures."

As I read his judgment, therefore, Harman L.J. reached his decision that the bank could not rely on the debentures following the ratio of the *David Payne* decision, that is to say, not because they had been granted by the company in excess of its corporate capacity, but because the bank knew that the directors of the company, in purporting to grant them, had exceeded the authority conferred on them by the company by entering into the transaction for purposes other than the company's corporate purpose.

Russell L.J. [1970] Ch. 199, 211, in a very short judgment, reached the same conclusion but by rather a different route from that of Harman L.J. As I read his judgment, his view was that the borrowing and execution of the debentures were *ultra vires* the company as a matter of corporate capacity because it was an implicit condition attached to the power to borrow contained in the company's memorandum that moneys should not be borrowed for use *in an undertaking ultra vires the company*. Since the sole undertaking of that company was the pig-breeding business, which was beyond the company's corporate capacity, [294] the loans taken for use in that business were likewise inevitably beyond its corporate capacity. I read Russell L.J.'s decision as being limited to the facts of that particular case and not in any way conflicting with my interpretation of the *David Payne* decision.

It follows that, in my opinion, the decisions of this court in *David Payne* [1904] 2 Ch. 608 and *Introductions Ltd.* [1970] Ch. 199, on their true analysis, lend no support to the plaintiffs submission that the relevant transactions in the present case were beyond the corporate capacity of the plaintiff simply because they were effected for improper purposes not authorised by its memorandum of association. Nor does this argument derive any support from the powerful judgment of Pennycuick J. in *Charterbridge Corporation Ltd. v. Lloyds Bank Ltd.* [1970] Ch. 62, where one finds the following statement of principle, at p. 69:

> "Apart from authority, I should feel little doubt that where a company is carrying out the purposes expressed in its memorandum, and does an act within the scope of a power expressed in its memorandum, that act is an act within the powers of the company. The memorandum of a company sets out its objects and proclaims them to persons dealing with the company and it would be contrary to the whole function of a memorandum that objects unequivocally set out in it should be subject to some implied limitation by reference to the state of mind of the parties concerned."

> "Where directors misapply the assets of their company, that may give rise to a claim based on breach of duty. Again, a claim may arise against the other party to the transaction, if he has notice that the transaction was effected in breach of duty. Further, in a proper case, the company concerned may be entitled to have the transaction set aside. But all that results from the ordinary law of agency and has not of itself anything to do with the corporate powers of the company."

Pennycuick J., having subsequently proceeded to review the authorities cited to him, apparently saw no reason to qualify this statement of the law and neither do I. I respectfully agree with it in its entirety and would regard the principles stated in the *David Payne* case [1904] 2 Ch. 608 as giving effect to the "ordinary law of agency."

I also respectfully agree with the following observations made by Oliver J., after an extensive review of the authorities, in *In re Halt Garage (1964) Ltd.* [1982] 3 All E.R. 1016, 1029-1030:

> "I cannot help thinking, if I may respectfully say so, that there has been a certain confusion between the requirements for a valid exercise of the fiduciary powers of directors (which have nothing to do with the capacity of the company but everything to do with the propriety of acts done within that capacity), the extent to which powers can be implied or limits be placed, as a matter of construction, on express powers, and the matters which the court will take into consideration at the suit of a minority shareholder in determining the extent to which his interests can be overridden by a majority vote. These three matters, as it seems to me, raise [295] questions which are logically quite distinct but which have sometimes been treated as if they demanded a single, universal answer leading to the conclusion that, because a power must not be abused, therefore, beyond the limit of propriety it does not exist."

My conclusions from these authorities on these questions of principle may be summarised as follows.

(1) The basic rule is that a company incorporated under the Companies Acts only has the capacity to do those acts which fall within its objects as set out in its memorandum of association or are reasonably incidental to the attainment or pursuit of those objects. Ultimately, therefore, the question whether a particular transaction is within or outside its capacity must depend on the true construction of the memorandum.

(2) Nevertheless, if a particular act (such as each of the transactions of 22 January 1969 in the present case) is of a category which, on the true construction of the company's memorandum, is *capable* of being performed as reasonably incidental to the attainment or pursuit of its objects, it will not be rendered *ultra vires* the company merely because in a particular instance its directors, in performing the act in its name, are in truth doing so for purposes other than those set out in its memorandum. Subject to any express restrictions on the relevant power which may be contained in the memorandum, the state of mind or knowledge of the persons managing the company's affairs or of the persons dealing with it is irrelevant in considering questions of corporate capacity.

(3) While due regard must be paid to any express conditions attached to or limitations on powers contained in a company's memorandum (*e.g.*, a power to borrow only up to a specified amount), the court will not ordinarily con-

strue a statement in a memorandum that a particular power is exercisable "for the purposes of the company" as a condition limiting the company's corporate capacity to exercise the power; it will regard it as simply imposing a limit on the authority of the directors: see the *David Payne* case [1904] 2 Ch. 608.

(4) At least in default of the unanimous consent of all the shareholders (as to which see below), the directors of a company will not have *actual* authority from the company to exercise any express or implied power other than for the purposes of the company as set out in its memorandum of association.

(5) A company holds out its directors as having *ostensible* authority to bind the company to any transaction which falls within the powers expressly or impliedly conferred on it by its memorandum of association. Unless he is put on notice to the contrary, a person dealing in good faith with a company which is carrying on an *intra vires* business is entitled to assume that its directors are properly exercising such powers for the purposes of the company as set out in its memorandum. Correspondingly, such a person in such circumstances can hold the company to any transaction of this nature.

(6) If, however, a person dealing with a company is on notice that the directors are exercising the relevant power for purposes other than the purposes of the company, he cannot rely on the ostensible authority [296] of the directors and, on ordinary principles of agency, cannot hold the company to the transaction.

In the present case I construe the words "as may seem expedient" in clause 3(K) of the plaintiffs memorandum not as limiting the corporate capacity of the plaintiff but as simply imposing a limit on the authority of its directors. To adapt the wording of Harman L.J. in the *Introductions Ltd.* case [1970] Ch. 199 following the *David Payne* decision [1904] 2 Ch. 608, the guarantee and pro tanto the debenture were not executed for a legitimate purpose of the plaintiff; Colvilles and British Steel Corporation knew it and, therefore, cannot rely on the guarantee and pro tanto the debenture. All this results from the ordinary law of agency, not from the corporate powers of the plaintiff. The relevant transactions in the present case, in my opinion, were not beyond its corporate capacity.

The judge [1982] Ch. 478, 499 explained that the reason why he regarded a transaction which is within the powers, express or implied, of a company but which is entered into for a purpose which is not authorised by its memorandum of association as equated with one which is *ultra vires* in the narrow sense is that "such a transaction like a transaction which is *ultra vires* in the narrow sense is incapable of being made binding on the company even by the assent of all the members." We have had the benefit of extensive argument as to the extent, if any, to which the assent of all the members of a company is capable of binding it to a transaction of this nature. Since the shareholders' consent point is not open to British Steel Corporation and Mr. Cooper on the facts of the present case, I wish to make only the following few, *obiter*, observations in the context of this argument.

First, if an act is beyond the corporate capacity of a company it is clear that it cannot be ratified. As against the company itself "an *ultra vires* agreement cannot become *intra vires* by means of estoppel, lapse of time, ratification, acquiescence, or delay": *York Corporation v. Henry Leetham and Sons Ltd.* [1924] 1 Ch. 557, 573 *per* Russell J. However, the clear general principle is that any act that falls within the corporate capacity of a company will bind it if it is done with the unanimous consents of all the shareholders or is subsequently ratified by such consents: see, for example, *Salomon v. A. Salomon & Co. Ltd.* [1897] A. C. 22, 57 *per* Lord Davey; *In re Horsley & Weight Ltd.* [1982] Ch. 442, 454 *per* Buckley L.J. and *Multinational Gas and Petrochemical Co. v. Multinational Gas and Petrochemical Services Ltd.* [1983] Ch. 258. This last-mentioned principle certainly is not an unqualified one. In particular, it will not enable the shareholders of a company to bind the company itself to a transaction which constitutes a fraud on its creditors: see, for example, *In re Halt Garage (1964) Ltd.* [1982] 3 All E.R. 1016, 1037, *per* Oliver J. But none of the authorities which have been cited to us have convinced me that a transaction which (i) falls within the letter of the express or implied powers of a company conferred by its memorandum, and (ii) does not involve a fraud on its creditors, and (iii) is assented to by all the shareholders, will not bind a fully solvent company merely because the intention of the directors, or the shareholders, is to effect a purpose not authorised by the memorandum. [297] The recent decision of this court in the *Multinational* case [1983] Ch. 258 seems to me to point to a contrary conclusion: see also *Attorney-General's Reference (No. 2 of 1982)* [1984] Q.B. 624, 640, *per* Kerr L.J. However, none of these matters relating to ratification, in my opinion, call for decision on this appeal. I have touched on them only because they weighed with the judge and have been covered fully in argument.

Whether or not in 1969 the consent or ratification of all the shareholders was incapable of rendering the transactions of 22 January 1969 binding the plaintiff, I myself think that the concept of *ultra vires* "in the wider sense" embodied by the judge in his judgment carries with it some risk of confusion. If confusion is to be avoided, it seems to me highly desirable that, as a matter of terminology, the phrase "*ultra vires*" in the context of company law should for the future be rigidly confined to describing acts which are beyond the corporate capacity of a company. Transactions entered into by a company such as those considered in the *David Payne* case [1904] 2 Ch. 608 and those under consideration in the present case cannot, in my opinion, be properly regarded as beyond its corporate capacity (and, therefore, *ex hypothesi* wholly void) if they are capable of conferring rights on a third party – albeit only on a third party who dealt with the company in good faith and without notice that they were being entered into in furtherance of improper purposes.

To sum up, my conclusions on the *ultra vires* point are these. The relevant transactions of 22 January 1969 were not beyond the corporate capacity of the plaintiff and thus were not *ultra vires* in the proper sense of that phrase. However, the entering into the guarantee and, to the extent of the sum guaranteed, the debenture was beyond the authority of the directors, because they were entered into in furtherance of purposes not authorised by the plaintiff's memorandum. Despite this lack of authority, they might have been capable of conferring rights on Colvilles if Colvilles had not known of this lack of authority. Colvilles, however, did have such knowledge and so acquired no rights under these transactions. Even if the no due authorisation point discussed earlier in this judgment were not open to the plaintiff, because Mr. Shenkman had duly declared his interest at the relevant board meeting, the plaintiff could disclaim these transactions, which its directors had carried out on its behalf, as being unauthorised, inasmuch as they were carried out for improper purposes. The practical relevance of the no due authorisation point discussed in an earlier section of this judgment is that it enables the plaintiff also to disclaim the borrowing of the £401,448 and the whole (as opposed to part only) of the security given by the debenture (as having been in each case entered into by the directors without its authority) and also to attack the validity of the receiver's appointment.

Aveling Barford Ltd. v. Perion Ltd.
[1989] B.C.L.C. 626

Under its balance sheet, a company's assets exceeded its liabilities but it had an accumulated deficit in its profits and loss account of £18m., thereby disentitling it to make any distributions to shareholders. L controlled the company and also controlled the defendant company. The company sold a property to the defendant for £350,000. That property had been independently valued at £650,000, the mortgage company which financed the purchase valued it at £1,150,000 and it was a term in the sale contract that, if the property were sold within the following 12 months for more than £800,000, the company would be paid a further £400,000. Within 12 months the property was sold for £1,526,000. Subsequently the company went into liquidation and proceedings were brought to recover the entire proceeds of the re-sold property.

HOFFMANN J.: [630] The general rule is that any act which falls within the express or implied [631] powers of a company conferred by its memorandum of association, whether or not a breach of duty on the part of the directors, will be binding on the company if it is approved or subsequently ratified by the shareholders: see *Rolled Steel Products (Holdings) Ltd v. British Steel Corp* [1986] Ch. 246 at 296. But this rule is subject to exceptions created by the general law and one such exception is that a company cannot without the leave of the court or the adoption of a special procedure return its capital to its shareholders. It follows that a transaction which amounts to an unauthorised return of capital is *ultra vires* and cannot be validated by shareholder ratification or approval. Whether or not the transaction is a distribution to shareholders does not depend exclusively on what the parties choose to call it. The court looks at the substance rather than the outward appearance. Thus in *Ridge Securities Ltd v. I.R.C.* [1964] 1 W.L.R. 479 Pennycuick J. was concerned with a tax avoidance scheme by a solvent company which involved the grant of a debenture to its parent under which very large and uncommercial sums were payable, purportedly as interest. He said that the 'interest' payments were *ultra vires* because they were dressed-up gifts of capital to the parent company [1964] 1 W.L.R. 479 at 495):

> "A company can only lawfully deal with its assets in furtherance of its objects. The corporators may take assets out of the company by way of dividend, or, with the leave of the court, by way of reduction of capital, or in a winding up. They may of course acquire them for full consideration. They cannot take assets out of the company by way of voluntary disposition, however described, and if they attempt to do so, the disposition is *ultra vires* the company."

That case was followed by Oliver J. in *Re Halt Garage (1964) Ltd.* [1982] 3 All E.R. 1016 (see post p. 228). In that case the liquidator of the company challenged payments of £30 a week purporting to be director's remuneration to a director and shareholder who had rendered no services to the company. Oliver J. decided that so far as the payments exceeded £10 a week, which he considered to be the maximum remuneration reasonably payable to someone who merely held the office of director, they were dressed-up returns of capital to a shareholder and therefore *ultra vires*. The test, said the learned judge, was:

> "whether the transaction in question was a genuine exercise of the power [to pay remuneration]. The motive is more important than the label. Those who deal with a limited company do so on the basis that its affairs will be conducted in accordance with its constitution, one of the express incidents of which is that the directors are entitled to be paid remuneration. Subject to that, they are entitled to have the capital kept intact. They have to accept the shareholders' assessment of the scale of that remuneration but they are entitled to assume that, whether liberal or illiberal, what is paid is genuinely remuneration and that the power is not used as a cloak for making payments out of capital to the shareholders as such."

[632] (See [1982] 3 All E.R. 1016 at 1039.) This did not mean that the payments have been made fraudulently or in bad faith: '*bona fides* (in the sense of absence of fraudulent intention) and genuineness are [not] necessarily the a same thing.' Applying his test, the learned judge said that no challenge could

be made to the payments made at a time when the company had enough distributable reserves to have made equivalent payments by way of dividend. But thereafter:

> "the sums paid to [the director] were so out of proportion to any possible value attributable to her holding of office that the court is entitled to treat them as not being genuine payments of remuneration at all but dressed-up dividends out of capital, like the dressed-up payments of 'interest' in the *Ridge Securities* case."

(See [1982] 3 All E.R. 1016 at 1042.) So it seems to me in this case that looking at the matter objectively, the sale to Perion was not a genuine exercise of the company's power under its memorandum to sell its assets. It was a sale at a gross undervalue for the purpose of enabling a profit to be realised by an entity controlled and put forward by its sole beneficial shareholder. This was as much a dressed-up distribution as the payment of excessive interest in *Ridge Securities* or excessive remuneration in *Halt Garage*. The company had at the time no distributable reserves and the sale was therefore *ultra vires* and incapable of validation by the approval or ratification of the shareholder. The fact that the distribution was to Perion rather than to Dr Lee or his other entities which actually held the shares in Aveling Barford is in my judgment irrelevant.

Counsel for the defendants relied on a passage in the judgment of Slade L.J. in *Rolled Steel Products (Holdings) Ltd v. British Corp* [1986] Ch. 246 at 296:

> ". . . if a particular act . . . is of a category which, on the true construction of the company's memorandum, is *capable* of being performed as reasonably incidental to the attainment or pursuit of its objects, it will not be rendered *ultra vires* the company merely because in a particular instance its directors, in performing the act in its name, are in truth doing so for purposes other than those set out in its memorandum. Subject to any express restrictions on the relevant power which may be contained in the memorandum, the state of mind or knowledge of the persons managing the company's affairs or of the persons dealing with it is irrelevant in considering questions of corporate capacity." (Slade L.J.'s emphasis.)

Counsel for the defendants says that this was an act within the terms of the memorandum. It may have been a sale at an undervalue, but it was certainly a sale: a conveyance in exchange for a payment in money. It was not a sham. The terms of the transaction were in no way different from those appearing on the face of the documents. The purpose for which it was done was therefore irrelevant. Counsel submits that the test for the genuineness of the transaction proposed by Oliver J. in *Re Halt Garage* admits by the back door all the questions about the motives, state of mind and knowledge of the company's directors which the Court of Appeal appeared to have expelled by the front door in the *Rolled Steel* case.

[633] It is clear however that Slade LJ excepted from his general principle cases which he described as involving a 'fraud on creditors' ([1986] Ch. 146 at 296). As an example of such a case, he cited *Re Halt Garage*. Counsel for the defendants said that frauds on creditors meant transactions entered into when the company was insolvent. In this case Aveling Barford was not at the relevant time insolvent. But I do not think that the phrase was intended to have such a narrow meaning. The rule that capital may not be returned to shareholders is a rule for the protection of creditors and the evasion of that rule falls within what I think Slade L.J. had in mind when he spoke of a fraud on creditors. There is certainly nothing in his judgment to suggest that he disapproved of the actual decisions in *Re Halt Garage* or *Ridge Securities*. As for the transaction not being a sham, I accept that it was in law a sale. The false dressing it wore was that of a sale at arms' length or at market value. It was the fact that it was known and intended to be a sale at an undervalue which made it an unlawful distribution.

Northern Bank Finance Corp. Ltd. v. Quinn
[1979] I.L.R.M. 221

An unlimited company, which was wholly owned beneficially by the first defendant, guaranteed bank loans made to him. When the bank sought to enforce that guarantee, it was contended that it was *ultra vires* the company and not binding on it.

KEANE J.: [224] It was submitted on behalf of the company that the execution of the guarantee was *ultra vires* the memorandum and articles of association and that, accordingly, both the guarantee and the mortgage (insofar as it comprised the company's property) were void. Counsel for the bank submitted that the guarantee was *intra vires* the memorandum and articles of association; but, that even if it were not, the bank were protected by the modification of the *ultra vires* rule effected by s. 8 of the Companies Act, 1963 (see post, p. 578). He further submitted that, since the memorandum had been subsequently altered by a resolution of the 18th May, 1974, so as to put beyond doubt the power of the company to execute guarantees, the guarantee of 30th November, 1973, was retrospectively validated and he relied in this connection on s. 10(1) of the Act (see post, p. 510). Counsel for the bank finally submitted that, in any event, the company were estopped from relying on the alleged lack of *vires*.

The company is an unlimited company having a share capital. Its objects are set out in paragraph 2 of the memorandum of association. The first of them, in truncated form, reads as follows :

> "To acquire and hold . . . shares and stocks of any class or description, debentures, debenture stock, bonds, bills, mortgages, obligations, investments and securities of all descriptions and of any kind issued or guaranteed by any company, corporation or undertaking . . . and investments, securities and property of all descriptions and of any kind. . . ."

[225] This, coupled with the fact that the company is an unlimited company, would suggest, so far as it is relevant, that the company was not intended to be a trading company in the ordinary sense but rather an investment company. Clause 2 (f) empowers the company:

> "Incidentally to the objects aforesaid, but not as a primary object, to sell, exchange, mortgage (with or without power of sale), assign, turn to account or otherwise dispose of and generally deal with the whole or any part of the property, shares, stocks, securities, estates, rights or undertakings of the company. . . ."

This clause was not relied on by counsel for the bank as empowering the transaction in question, but was relied on by counsel for the company as indicating that the company was empowered to mortgage its property only where the execution of the mortgage was incidental to one of the objects of the Company set out in sub-paragraphs (a) to (e). Sub-paragraph (k) empowers the company:

> "to raise or borrow or secure the payment of money in such manner and on such terms as the directors may deem expedient and in particular by the issue of bonds, debentures or debenture stock, perpetual or redeemable, or by mortgage, charge, lien or pledge upon the whole or any part of the undertaking, property, assets and rights of the company, present or future, including its uncalled capital and generally in any other manner as the directors shall from time to time determine and to guarantee the liabilities of the company and any debentures, debenture stock or other securities may be issued at a discount, premium or otherwise, and with any special privileges as to redemption, surrender, transfer, drawings, allotments of shares, attending and voting at general meetings of the company, appointment of directors and otherwise."

This sub-paragraph – and in particular the words 'secure the payment of money' – was relied on by counsel for the bank as authorising the execution of the guarantee. It was accepted that the words 'to guarantee the liabilities of the company' in this clause were meaningless as they stood; but counsel for the bank submitted that the clear intention was to enable the company to guarantee the liabilities of third parties and that these words in the sub-paragraph should be so read. Counsel for the company submitted that, insofar as the words could be given any meaning, they should be read as empowering the company to procure the guaranteeing of its own liabilities by third parties.

Sub-paragraph (t) empowered the company to do and carry out all such things as may be deemed by the company to be incidental or conducive to the attainment of the above objects or any of them or calculated to enhance the value of or render profitable any of the company's properties or rights.

It was submitted on behalf of the bank that this sub-paragraph was sufficiendy wide ranging in its terms to enable the company to execute the guarantee in question. It was submitted on behalf of the company that the sub-paragraph merely authorised the doing of such things as were incidental to the attainment of any of the preceding objects and that since it could not be shown that the execution of a guarantee was incidental or conducive to the attainment of any of the objects referred to in the preceding sub-paragraphs, of itself it could not render the transaction in question *intra vires*.

It is clear that sub-paragraph (f) did not authorise the execution of the guarantee [226] in question and that, insofar as it authorised the company to execute a mortgage, this could only be done incidentally to the objects set out in sub-paragraphs (a) to (e). Counsel for the bank did not indeed advance any submission to the contrary. He did, however, as I have already indicated rely on sub-paragraph (k). I have set out that sub-paragraph in full, because I think the wording used plainly indicates that it was essentially intended to confer a power of borrowing on the Company. Viewed in this context, the words 'secure the payment of money' could not reasonably be read, in my opinion, as conferring a power to execute guarantees. The words 'secure the payment of' are used disjunctively in apposition to 'raise' and 'borrow', clearly indicating that it was intended to confer on the company a power of obtaining money for its own purposes and not a power to guarantee advances made to other persons. Counsel also relied on the words 'to guarantee the liabilities of the company' and submitted that, as this phrase literally construed was meaningless, it should be construed as though, in place of the words 'the company', there appear the words 'other persons' or similar words. While I accept that the words, literally construed, are meaningless, since a company cannot guarantee its own liabilities, I see no warrant in the wording of sub-paragraph (k) as a whole for giving the expression in question the meaning contended for by Mr O'Neill SC. To give it such a meaning would not merely be to do violence to the actual language used but would also be inappropriate in any event in the context of a sub-paragraph which, as I have said, is essentially concerned with enabling the company, and not other persons, to borrow money. It seems more likely to me that it was intended by the use of this phrase to enable the company to secure the guaranteeing by third parties of its own liabilities.

Sub-paragraph (t) was also relied on by counsel for the bank; but, in my view, the execution of a guarantee could not reasonably be regarded as 'incidental or conducive to the attainment of, any of the objects set out in the preceding sub-paragraphs. The sole object of executing the guarantee was to facilitate the borrowing by Mr Quinn of the sum of £145,000.00 from the bank. Only the bank and Mr Quinn could possibly derive any benefit from this transaction; the bompany could derive no benefit from the advancing of money to Mr Quinn. The securing by means of a guarantee of a loan to Mr Quinn could not properly be regarded as being fairly incidental to the objects expressly authorised by the memorandum within the meaning of the well known rule laid down in *Attorney General v. Great Eastern Railway*, (5 App. Cas. 473). The effecting of such a transaction was not 'incidental or conducive to the attainment of' any of the expressly authorised objects within the meaning of sub-paragraph (t); nor was it 'calculated to enhance the value of or render profitable any of the company's properties or rights' within the meaning of that subparagraph.

It follows, in my view, that the memorandum conferred neither expressly nor by implication any power on the company to execute a guarantee for the purpose of securing the payment of a bank loan to Mr Quinn. In these circumstances, it is unnecessary to express any final opinion on a further submission advanced by Mr McCracken SC that, even were the Memorandum to be read as conferring an express power on the company to execute such a guarantee, the transaction would nonetheless be *ultra vires* since no conceivable benefit could result to the [227] company from it. The celebrated observations of Bowen L.J., in *Hutton v. West Cork Railway* (23 Ch. D. 654) that 'charity cannot sit at the boardroom table' and 'there are to be no cakes and ale except for the benefit of the company' may have been extended too far in *Re Lee, Behrens and Company* [1932] 2 Ch. 46); and while this latter decision might appear to afford support for Mr McCracken's proposition, its authority as a persuasive precedent would require reconsideration to-day in the light of the decision in *Charterbridge Corporation Limited v. Lloyds Bank* [1970] Ch. 62. Having regard, however, to the conclusion I have arrived at, it is unnecessary that I should say anything more on this aspect of the case.

Note: See post pp. 578 for a consideration of section 8(1) of the 1963 Act, which Keane J. held did not in the circumstances prevent the *ultra vires* principle from applying there. In the *Rolled Steel Products* case (supra p. 110) the Court of Appeal construed an almost identical objects clause as permitting an entirely gratuitous guarantee given by the company. That guarantee rendered the company insolvent and it was held to be unenforceable on other grounds, unrelated to *ultra vires*.

Question: In *Northern Bank* the company's shareholders were agreeable to it giving the guarantee and, further, the guarantee did not in any way prejudice the company's creditors; indeed it was an unlimited company. What useful purpose therefore was served by preventing the bank from enforcing the guarantee?

In the Matter of Frederick Inns Ltd
[1994] 1 I.L.R.M. 387 (SC)

Under the threat of being wound up by the Revenue Commissioners, a group of companies make a settlement of the outstanding tax liabilities of several companies in the group. Shortly afterwards those companies were would up and were heavily insolvent. The question was whether those payments to the Revenue were *intra vires* companies in the group which did not have any tax liabilities themselves.

BLAYNEY J.: [393] The first submission made on behalf of the Revenue Commissioners was that the memorandum of association of each of the four companies contained a power to make the relevant payments. A number of different clauses in the respective memoranda of association were relied upon, but most reliance was placed on the following two clauses which are to be found in the memorandum of association of each of the companies:

"1. To establish or promote or concur in establishing or promoting any other company whose objects shall include the acquisition and taking over of all or any of the assets and liabilities of, or the promotion of which shall be in any manner calculated to advance directly or indirectly the objects or interests of this company, and to acquire and hold, or dispose of shares, stock or securities of, and guarantee the payment of any securities issued by or any other obligation of any such company.

2. To purchase or otherwise acquire and undertake all or any part of the business, property, liabilities and transactions of any person, firm or company carrying on or proposing to carry on any business which this company is authorised to carry on, or possessed of property suitable for the purpose of the company or to promote any company or companies for the above purpose."

[394] In my opinion neither of these clauses gives the power to pay the debts of an associate company, which is what happened here. What the first clause gives is a power 'to establish or promote or concur in establishing or promoting' another company in certain circumstances. That could not be construed as a power to pay the debts of another company. And the second clause gives the power 'to purchase or otherwise acquire and undertake all or any part of the . . . liabilities . . . of any company etc.' The companies here were neither

'purchasing' nor 'acquiring and undertaking' the liabilities of the other companies. They were paying part of their debts. This clause did not give any power to do this.

It was also submitted that the power to lend money could be relied upon, such as the following power in the memorandum of association of Frederick Inns Ltd:

> "To advance and lend money from time to time either with or without mortgage or other security at such rates of interest and generally upon such terms and conditions and in such manner as may be thought expedient."

I reject this submission also. The four companies did not lend any monies to the other six. What they did was to pay part of their debts which was something very different.

I have read the other clauses in the four memoranda of association on which reliance was also placed and I am satisfied that none of them gave power to make the relevant payments. I find accordingly that the payments were *ultra vires*.

Note: See post, p. 582 for a consideration of section 8(1) of the 1963 Act, which the Supreme Court held did not prevent the *ultra vires* principle applying. The question which was then considered was whether any or all of the *ultra vires* payments could be recovered by the company; see *post*, p. 578. Compare, however, *Re PMPA Garage (Longmile) Ltd.* [1982] 1 I.R. 315 at 321–325, where Murphy J. held that it was not *ultra vires* for a company to guarantee the liabilities of other companies in the same group.

Re Greendale Developments Ltd
February 20, 1997

The company, which had three-shareholders (Mr. and Mrs. Fagan and Mr. Burgess), developed a site at Islandbridge. Differences arose between the Fagans and Mr. Burgess, who then commenced proceedings under section 205 of the 1963 Act for 'oppression'. The Fagans responded by petitioning to have the company wound up on 'just and equitable' grounds. Thereafter, the liquidator commenced 'misfeasance' proceedings against the Fagans, wherein it was alleged that the company had unlawfully made very substantial payments to them, approximately £430,000; orders were sought against *inter alia* Mr. Fagan to repay that money. Other issues arose in the case regarding the conduct of the trial before Costello P., which are not directly relevant to the Company law issues, namely, that the Fagans had been given only three working days notice of the trial commencing, at a time when they had neither solicitors nor counsel, and accordingly had insufficient time and opportunity to prepare their defence.

KEANE J. (Blayney and Murphy JJ. concurring): As to the new case now being made, Dr. Forde submitted that the evidence clearly established that all the payments made to Mr. or Mrs. Fagan or benefits obtained by them on which the liquidator relied as constituting an indebtedness by them to the company were made or obtained with the assent of all the shareholders. He submitted that this had two results. First, the proceedings under s.298 were misconceived, since the alleged misapplication of the company's assets was effected by Mr. and Mrs. Fagan in their capacity as shareholders, citing in support *Re S.M. Barker Ltd* [1950] I.R. 123. Secondly, since there was no evidence that the company was insolvent, it did not constitute any form of wrongdoing or breach of trust for which the shareholders could be made amenable. He relied, in support of this latter proposition, on *Re S.M. Barker Ltd, Buchanan Ltd v. McVey* [1954] I.R. 89 and *Multinational Fuel and Petrochemical Co. v. Multinational Fuel and Petrochemical Services Ltd* [1983] 1 Ch. 258. . . .

[19] In considering Dr. Forde's submissions that the appellants cannot be required to return these monies to the company because the transactions were assented to by all the shareholders, it is necessary to make three assumptions: [20] first, that the transactions would otherwise be invalid as not being for the benefit of the company, secondly, that the company was solvent at all material times and, thirdly, that the relevant transactions were assented to by the other shareholders *i.e.* Mrs. Fagan and Mr. Burgess.

As to the first of these assumptions, it is obvious that, if the payments in question were legally made by the company and, in particular, were for the benefit of the company, the appellants could not be required by the liquidator to repay them to the company. It should be borne in mind, however, that the order of the High Court requiring the repayment of the sums in question is challenged on other grounds and that in the event of this court rejecting Dr. Forde's submissions on this and the next issue, the question would remain as to whether the case should nonetheless be remitted to the High Court for a rehearing.

As to the second assumption, it might seem reasonable to suppose that the company was at the relevant time solvent, since the order for its winding-up was not made at the instance of a creditor on the ground that it was insolvent. However, it should also be borne in mind that the Statement of Affairs filed by Mr. Fagan and showing a surplus of assets over liabilities in the sum of £338,664, states one of the assets of the company to be outstanding legal claims by the company against the company's former legal and financial advisers [21] which are estimated to realise £3,571,000. The Statement also shows, in addition to trade creditors estimated at £64,330, a liability to the Revenue of £269,356.04 and a note to the latter sum says that the returns have not been submitted to the Revenue Commissioners to date. There are, in addition, the costs and expenses of the winding-up itself. Given the hazards attendant on all forms of litigation, the solvency of the company, in these circumstances, certainly cannot be taken for granted.

As to the legal principles applicable they were summarised by Kingsmill Moore J. in *Buchanan Ltd & Anor. v. McVey* [1954] I.R. 89 as follows:

> "If all the corporators agree to a certain course then, however informal the manner of their agreement, it is an act of the company and binds the company subject only to two pre-requisites: *In re Express Engineering Works Ltd* [1920] 1 Ch. 466, *Parker & Cooper Ltd v. Reading* [1926] 1 Ch. 975. The two necessary pre-requisites are:
>
> (1), that the transaction to which the corporators agree should be *intra vires* the company;
> [22] (2), that the transaction should be honest, *per* Astbury J. at pp. 984, 985."

That view of the law was, on appeal, unanimously upheld by the former Supreme Court.

Assuming, accordingly, that the consent of all the shareholders was given to the transactions in the present case, the question remains as to whether they were *intra vires* the company. Since *ex hypothesi* the company obtained no benefits whatever from the impugned payments, Dr. Forde's submission necessarily involved the proposition, which he did not shrink from asserting, that such payments are nevertheless *intra vires*.

It has been settled law since the decision in *Hutton v. West Cork Railway Co.* [1883] 23 Ch. D. 654 that a company cannot spend money or dispose of its property except for purposes which are reasonably incidental to the carrying on of the business of the company. In that case, a general meeting of the company had passed a resolution to pay compensation to officials for their loss of employment, although they were under no legal obligation in those days to do so. In a frequently cited passage, Bowen L.J. said:

> [23] "A company which always treated its employees with draconian severity, and never allowed them a single inch more than the strict letter of the bond, would soon find itself deserted – at all events, unless labour was very much more easy to obtain in the market than it often is. The law does not say that there are to be no cakes and ale, but that there are to be no cakes and ale except such as are required for the benefit of the company."

To the same effect are the decisions in *In re Lee, Behrens and Co.* [1932] 2 Ch. 46 and *Parke v. Daily News Ltd* [1962] Ch. 927. The principle was also applied by Carroll J. in *Roper v. Ward* [1981] I.L.R.M. 408.

No doubt if the transaction was expressly authorised by the memorandum and articles of association, different considerations might apply: see *Charterbridge Corporation Ltd v. Lloyds Bank Ltd* [1970] Ch. 62. No such provision in the memorandum and articles of the company was relied on in the present case. Dr. Forde did, however, rely strongly on the decision of Gavan Duffy P., in *Re: S M Barker Ltd* [1950] I.R. 123 as supporting his submissions.

[24] In that case, a company voluntarily released a number of debts due to it and arising out of certain transactions between three persons in their personal capacity and the company. The three persons concerned were, at the time, the sole directors of the company and the entire share capital was vested in them. They sold all their shares to another group and the purchase price as actually paid to them was the balance left after deducting from the agreed price the debts due by the company (after giving credit for debts due to the company). As a result of some credits and adjustments, the details of which are not material, this latter sum deducted from the purchase price exactly equalled the amount of the shareholders' forgiven debts. As part of the arrangements for the purchase of the shares, the purchasers paid to the company a sum equivalent to this latter sum which was then in due course used by the company, under the new management, for the discharge of the company's debts. The company, under the new management, having encountered difficulties and ultimately become insolvent, was compulsorily wound-up. The official liquidator then issued misfeasance proceedings under the corresponding provision of the Companies (Consolidation) Act 1908 claiming that the three former owners were liable to repay to the company the total of the forgiven debts, the company having received no consideration for their release.

[25] In the course of his judgment, Gavan Duffy P. made scathing comments on the unorthodox methods employed by the parties, but adds:

> "It cannot be stressed too emphatically that on the evidence the three Latchmans were in truth the owners of the entire share capital so they were at liberty to do virtually whatever they chose, short of acting dishonestly or *ultra vires*. The transaction was the honest result of negotiations between the Latchmans and an external group of businessmen, eager for their own ends to gain control of the company and its assets without paying an excessive price for the shares which carry control. And I discern no moral obliquity in the deeds and omissions of the Latchmans as directors in this transaction. . . .
>
> However improvident the resolution releasing the Latchmans' indebtedness and however regrettable the failures to observe the requirements and the formalities of company law, quite beyond their ken, I think, the outstanding fact is the fact that true owners of the property, acting with the full assent of their prospective assignees, all concurred at the two meetings and throughout in every step taken. Consequently, in my view, the company cannot through its liquidators make the Latchman [26] share-

holders liable in their capacity as directors for the value of the released debts, unless the liquidator can show some act done *ultra vires* of the company by the Latchmans as directors to have caused loss, or prove an improper pecuniary benefit acquired by the directors, for which they are accountable to the company."

Having gone on to point out that the propriety of the company having forgiven the debts for no consideration was at least questionable, but that the persons concerned had acted honestly and on what must have seemed competent advice, he added:

"Can such considerations as these be invoked to validate, as being *intra vires*, a costly indulgence, conceded at best for a small return, to an apparently solvent creditor at the expense of the corporation? And, if not, can the Latchmans, for their participation as directors, invoke s. 279 of the Act of 1908 and establish a claim that they ought fairly to be excused, having acted honestly and reasonably, if they did commit a breach of their trust?

[27] In my view of this motion for summary redress under s. 215, based on the alleged misfeasance of directors and on nothing else, those interesting points, though much discussed, call for no decision here. I am unable to find any single thing wrongfully done by the Messrs. Latchman as directors and causing damage, to justify the application of sanctions under s.215."

Re S.M. Barker Ltd is, accordingly, not authority for the proposition that a company may spend money or apply property for purposes which are *ultra vires* the company provided all the shareholders agree to the *ultra vires* transaction. The ratio of the decision is that shareholders in a company cannot be made amenable under misfeasance proceedings for profits made by them, not in their capacity as directors of the company, but as shareholders.

I am, accordingly, satisfied that Dr. Forde's submissions are unsupported by authority and contrary to legal principle. On the proved or admitted facts of this case, the impugned payments were made by the company to or for the benefit of the appellants in circumstances where the company derived no benefit in return. They were not expressly authorised by the memorandum or articles of association of the company. They were, accordingly, *ultra vires* the company and their fundamental illegality cannot be cured by the fact, if it be [28] the fact, that all the shareholders assented to each and every one of the payments in question.

Note: In the *Greendale* case, the question posed above had not been considered at all by the trial judge (Costello P.), who had insisted on the trial going ahead notwithstanding the fact that the defendants had only three working days notice of the trial and had no reasonable opportunity to fully instruct a solicitor and counsel in their defence.[1] The Supreme Court (Blayney, Keane and Murphy JJ.) decided to determine the question *de novo* but, without hearing argument from either side on this issue,[2] concluded that transactions of this nature are *ultra vires* and unlawful and that the assets disposed of in the circumstances were recoverable by the company. This decision would seem to be wrong for the following reasons.

(i)   The authorities relied on by Keane J. (for the Court) to support the conclusion were cases where either a minority shareholder was contesting a gratuitous disposition[3] or where the company was insolvent,[4] or it was a non-profit company.[5] It has never previously been held that all of the members of a solvent 'for profit' company cannot make a distribution of assets to such one or more of them as they choose, provided they do not thereby render the company insolvent.

(ii)   The *raison d'etre* of companies (other than 'non-profit' companies) is to distri bute surpluses to their members; companies' objects implicitly envisage substantial pay-outs to their members where surpluses over paid up capital and are not needed, except where there is an express prohibition to that effect (*e.g.* non-profit companies and companies holding charitable status).[6]

(iii)   How any surplus is to be shared among the members is exclusively a

---

1.   An adjournment was sought, which the liquidator did not oppose, but was refused by Costello P.; that decision is presently being challenged before the European Commission on Human Rights as a denial of a fair trial.
2.   Blayney J., who presided, directed at an early stage to deal first with questions in a motion concerning the mode of trial, adjournment and adducing additional evidence: he directed the Court would later hear argument on the *ultra vires* point if it ruled against the defendants on those other issues. In the event, the Court ruled against the first defendant on those issues and, at the same time, decided the *ultra vires* question without giving him (the author was counsel in the appeal) an opportunity to argue it in full. Within a few weeks, Blayney J. retired from the Court on the grounds of age.
3.   *Hutton v. West Cork Railway Co.* [1883] 23 Ch. D 654 and *Parke v. Daily News Ltd.* [1962] Ch. 927.
4.   *Re Lee Behrens & Co.* [1932] Ch. 46.
5.   *Roper v. Ward* [1981] I.L.R.M. 408, which concerned how the assets of the Dublin Gas Company Employees' Social and Sports Club Limited should be distributed in its liquidation; moreover, *all* the company's members had not supported the impugned mode of distribution.
6.   For a company to be recognised as charitable, or for a limited company not to have the word 'limited' in its name, it must *inter alia* stipulate in its memorandum of association that any profits it makes or surplus it has will not be divided among its members.

matter for them to decide and has nothing at all to do with the objects or capacity or *vires* of the company as such. Normally, the matter is dealt with in the articles of-association, which usually (as is the case in *Greendale*) confer a power on the company to pay dividends to its members, provided they are not paid out of capital.[7]

(iv) Where the articles of association stipulate one formula for dividing up a surplus (*e.g. pro rata*) the members acting unanimously may informally agree to an alternative formula (*e.g.* to one member only), which will be treated as amending the articles to that effect.[8] In any event, the company's articles in Greendale placed no restriction on how dividends were to be shared between the members or the times when or manner in which dividends should be distributed; the only restriction was that they should not come from capital.

(v) Further, even if the mode in which a surplus is to be divided up among a company's members indeed relates to the objects clause and corporate capacity, and not just powers, the members acting unanimously may informally agree to permit a large distribution to one of them, which will be treated as amending the objects clause to that effect.[9] Indeed, the companys articles in *Greendale* stated that the assent of all of the members is equivalent to a resolution to that effect duly passed by them.

(vi) Further still, the grounds on which one of the case that supports the lawfulness of such distributions, *Re S.M. Barker & Co.*[10] is distinguished are thin,[11] to say the least. Curiously, no attempt was made to distinguish the other case that suggests that such distributions are not *ultra vires*, *Peter Buchanan Ltd v. McVey*;[12] Keane J. relied on a dictum in it to find for the liquidator[13] but the relevant facts there are almost on all fours with

---

7. Article 116 of Table A (empowering the company in general meeting to declare dividends) and article 118 (no payments from capital).
8. *Cane v. Jones* [1980] 1 W.L.R. 1451; see post p. 174.
9. *Re Home Treat Ltd.* [1991] B.C.L.C. 705. Prior to 1963, the members could not alter the objects without the consent of the court, which explains why the 'informal unanimity' principle did not previously apply to such decisions.
10. [1950] I.R. 123.
11. In the *Barker* case, as in *Greendale*, the alleged wrongdoers were also directors (as well as members) of the company at the time the 'wrongs' occurred and were sactioned by them, which renders the two cases indistinguishable. Unlike in *Barker*, the members in *Greendale* did not pass a formal resolution approving the impugned distributions but, since *ultra vires* concerns capacity rather than abuse of a power that exists, the formal passing of a resolution can hardly be decisive when all the members are *ad idem*. Further, unlike in the *Barker* case, *Greendale* was not wound up on grounds of insolvency,nor was it shown to have since become insolvent.
12. [1954] I.R. 89.
13. *Id.* at p. 91.

Greendale, except that the massive distribution made in that case was done for an unlawful purpose (tax evasion) and it was designed to ensure that (and resulted in) the company not being able to pay its only creditor, (the Revenue) tax assessed at £370,000 (in 1945).

(vii) Where all the members of a 'for profit' company are agreeable to a particular mode of distributing company assets among themselves, then unless the memorandum of association contains an entrenched prohibition against that distribution, the true test of illegality is whether the provisions in the Companies (Amendment) Act 1983, on distributions from capital have been contravened.[14] Lord Hoffman has referred to, as a primary rule of attribution implied by company law, 'the unanimous decision of all the shareholders in a solvent company about anything which the company under its memorandum of association has power to do shall be the decision of the company.'[15]

(viii) The analysis set out here accords with the modern case law on *ultra vires*, which emphasises that the doctrine concerns the very capacity of a company to enter into a particular transaction, not the manner in which it executes transactions which it has intrinsic powers to conclude[16] (*e.g.* distribute surplus assets to one or more of its members).

(ix) If the decision in *Greendale* is correct, then as a matter of logic it would seem that, unless expressly allowed by their memoranda of association, all dividend payments by companies are *ultra vires*, since there is no reciprocal benefit for the company. Or does it matter that the dividend is quite big rather than comparatively small and, if yes, how is 'quite big' to be measured?

(x) In any event, the company's objects in *Greendale* expressly authorised paying 'gratuities' to officers and their dependents and, as well, distributing any assets among the members in such manner as they choose, which according to *Rolled Steel*[17] renders the contested payments *intra vires*. Those objects were not relied on in the appeal, which dealt with the matter *de novo*, because the presiding judge (Blaney J.) had ruled that other matters should first be considered but then the court gave a reserved judgment on them and also on *ultra vires* without affording either side an opportunity to make full submissions on that central point.

---

14. *Re Wellington Publishing Co.* [1973] 1 N.Z.L.R. 133 (see post, p. 549).
15. *Meridian Global Funds Management Asia Ltd v. Securities Commission* [1995] 2 A.C. 500 (see supra, p. 28). See too P. Davies, *Gower's Principles of Modern Company Law* (6th ed., 1997), pp. 177-176.
16. E.g. *Rolled Steel Products (Holdings) Ltd v. British Steel Corp.* [1986] Ch. 246 (see supra, p. 110).
17. *Ibid.*

CHAPTER 4

Governance

By governance in the context of company law is meant the way in which companies are organised and run by those who own and control them. It can be contrasted with management, which signifies how a company's ordinary business affairs are conducted, although the line between overall governance and day-to-day management is not watertight. Different companies possess different methods of governance, just as there is an enormous variety of management systems. The Companies Acts, however, lay down certain minimum ground rules for governance. Ultimate control over companies' destinies is consigned to their members or shareholders. Members' meetings must be convened at least once a year, and a significant minority of the membership may call such meetings at any time; various matters concerning the company must be decided at such meetings. It is for companies themselves to determine how votes are to be allocated among their shareholders and what particular powers should be entrusted to the directors. Companies can change their own regulations provided sufficient members support such a change.

COMPANY MEETINGS AND RESOLUTIONS

See *Company Law*, pp. 83–97.

Companies Act 1963, sections 134 and 141(1), (2)

General provisions as to meetings and votes

134.—The following provisions shall have effect in so far as articles of the company do not make other provision in that behalf–

(*a*) notice of the meeting of a company shall be served on every member of the company in the manner in which notices are required to be served by Table A and for the purpose of this paragraph "Table A" means that Table as for the time being in force;

(*b*) two or more members holding not less than one-tenth of the issued share capital or, if the company has not a share capital, not less than 5 per cent in number of all the members of the company may call a meeting;

(c) in the case of a private company two members, and in the case of any other company three members, personally present shall be a quorum (except, of course, in duly registered one-person companies);

(d) any member elected by the members present at a meeting may be chairman thereof;

(e) in the case of a company originally having a share capital, every member shall have one vote in respect of each share or each £10 of stock held by him, and in any other case, every member shall have one vote.

Resolutions

141.—(1) A resolution shall be a special resolution when it has passed by not less than three-fourths of the votes cast by such members as, being entitled so to do, vote in person or, where proxies are allowed, by proxy at a general meeting of which not less than 21 days' notice, specifying the intention to propose the resolution as a special resolution, has been duly given.

(2) A resolution may be proposed and passed as a special resolution at a meeting of which less than 21 days' notice has been given if it is so agreed by a majority in number of the members having the right to attend and vote at any such meeting, being a majority together holding not less than ninety per cent in nominal value of the shares giving that right or, in the case of a company not having a share capital, together representing not less than ninety per cent of the total voting rights at that meeting of all the members.

Table A articles 47–74 and Part II articles 4–6

General Meetings

47.—All general meetings of the company shall be held in the State.

48.—(1) Subject to paragraph (2) of this regulation, the company shall in each year hold a general meeting as its annual general meeting in addition to any other meeting in that year, and shall specify the meeting as such in the notices calling it; and not more than 15 months shall elapse between the date of one annual general meeting of the company and that of the next.

(2) So long as the company holds its first annual general meeting within 18 months of its incorporation, it need not hold it in the year of its incorporation or in the year following. Subject to regulation 47, the annual general meeting shall be held at such time and place as the directors shall appoint.

49.—All general meetings other than annual general meetings shall be called extraordinary general meetings.

50.—The directors may, whenever they think fit, convene an extraordinary general meeting, and extraordinary general meetings shall also be convened on such requisition, or in default, may be convened by such requisitionists, as provided by section 132 of the Act. If at any time there are not within the State sufficient directors capable of acting to form a quorum, any director or any 2 members of the company may convene an extraordinary general meeting in the same manner as nearly as possible as that in which meetings may be convened by the directors.

Notice of General Meetings

51.—Subject to sections 133 and 141 of the Act, an annual general meeting and a meeting called for the passing of a special resolution shall be called by 21 days' notice in writing at the least, and a meeting of the company (other than an annual general meeting or a meeting for the passing of a special resolution) shall be called by 14 days' notice in writing at the least. The notice shall be exclusive of the day on which it is served or deemed to be served and of the day for which it is given, and shall specify the place, the day and the hour of the meeting, and in the case of special business, the general nature of that business, and shall be given, in manner hereinafter mentioned, to such persons as are, under the regulations of the company, entitled to receive such notices from the company.

52.—The accidental omission to give notice of a meeting to, or the non-receipt of notice of a meeting by, any person entitled to receive notice shall not invalidate the proceedings at the meeting.

Proceedings at General Meetings

53.—All business shall be deemed special that is transacted at an extraordinary general meeting, and also all that is transacted at an annual general meeting, with the exception of declaring a dividened, the consideration of the accounts, balance sheets and the reports of the directors and auditors, the election of directors in the place of those retiring, the re-appointment of the retiring auditors and the fixing of the remuneration of the auditors.

54.—No business shall be transacted at any general meeting unless a quorum of members is present at the time when the meeting proceeds to business; save as herein otherwise provided, three members present in person shall be a quorum.

55.—If within half an hour from the time appointed for the meeting a quorum is not present, the meeting, if convened upon the requisition of members, shall be dissolved; in any other case it shall stand adjourned to the same day in the next week, at the same time and place or to such other day and at such other time and place as the directors may determine and if at the adjourned meeting a quorum is not present within hall an hour from the time appointed for the meeting, the members present shall be a quorum.

56.—The chairman, if any, of the board of directors shall preside as chairman at every general meeting of the company, or if there is no such chairman, or if he is not present within 15 minutes after the time appointed for the holding of the meeting or is unwilling to act, the directors present shall elect one of their number to be chairman of the meeting.

57.—If at any meeting no director is willing to act as chairman or if no director is present within 15 minutes after the time appointed for holding the meeting, the members present shall choose one of their number to be chairman of the meeting.

58.—The chairman may, with the consent of any meeting at which a quorum is present, and shall if so directed by the meeting, adjourn the meeting from time to time and from place to place, but no business shall be transacted at any adjourned meeting other than the business left unfinished at the meeting from which the adjournment took place. When a meeting is adjourned for 30 days or more, notice of the adjourned meeting shall be given as in the case of an original meeting. Save as aforesaid it shall not be necessary to give any notice of an adjournment or of the business to be transacted at an adjourned meeting.

59.—At any general meeting a resolution put to the vote of the meeting shall be decided on a show of hands unless a poll is (before or on the declaration of the result of the show of hands) demanded-

(a) by the chairman; or

(b) by at least three members present in person or by proxy;

or

(c) by any member or members present in person or by proxy and representing not less than one-tenth of the total voting rights of all the members having the right to vote at the meeting; or

(d) by a member or members holding shares in the company conferring the right to vote at the meeting being shares on which an aggregate sum has been paid up equal to not less than one-tenth of the total sum paid up on all the shares conferring that right.

Unless a poll is so demanded, a declaration by the chairman that a resolution has, on a show of hands, been carried or carried unanimously, or by a particular majority, or lost, and an entry to that effect in the book containing the minutes of the proceedings of the company shall be conclusive evidence of the fact without proof of the number or proportion of the votes recorded in favour of or against such resolution.

The demand for a poll may be withdrawn.

60.—Except as provided in regulation 62, if a poll is duly demanded it shall be taken in such manner as the chairman directs, and the result of the poll shall be deemed to be the resolution of the meeting at which the poll was demanded.

61.—Where there is an equality of votes, whether on a show of hands or on a poll, the chairman of the meeting at which the show of hands takes place or at which the poll is demanded, shall be entitled to a second or casting vote.

62.—A poll demanded on the election of a chairman or on a question of adjournment shall be taken forthwith. A poll demanded on any other question shall be taken at such time as the chairman of the meeting directs, and any business other than that on which a poll is demanded may be proceeded with pending the taking of the poll.

Votes of Members

63.—Subject to any rights or restrictions for the time being attached to any class or classes of shares, on a show of hands every member present in person and every proxy shall have one vote, so, however, that no individual shall have more than one vote, and on a poll every member shall have one vote for each share of which he is the holder.

64.—Where there are joint holders the vote of the senior who tenders a vote, whether in person or by proxy, shall he accepted to the exclusion of the votes of the other joint holders, and for this purpose, seniority shall be determined by the order in which the names stand in the register.

65.—A member of unsound mind, or in respect of whom an order has been made by any court having jurisdiction in lunacy, may vote, whether on a show of hands or on a poll, by his committee, receiver, guardian or other person appointed by that court, and any such committee, receiver, guardian or other person may vote by proxy on a show of hands or on a poll.

66.—No member shall be entitled to vote at any general meeting unless all calls or other sums immediately payable by him in respect of shares in the company have been paid.

67.—No objection shall be raised to the qualification of any voter except at the meeting or adjourned meeting at which the vote objected to is given or tendered, and every vote not disallowed at such meeting shall be valid for all purposes. Any such objection made in due time shall be referred to the chairman of the meeting, whose decision shall be final and conclusive.

68.—Votes may be given either personally or by proxy.

69.—The instrument appointing a proxy shall be in writing under the hand of the appointer or of his attorney duly authorised in writing, or, if the appointer is a body corporate, either under seal or under the hand of an officer or attorney duly authorised. A proxy need not be a member of the company.

70.—The instrument appointing a proxy and the power of attorney or other authority, if any, under which it is signed, or a notarially certified copy of that power or authority shall be deposited at the office or at such other plact, within the State as is specified for that purpose in the notice convening the meeting, not less than 48 hours before the time for holding the meeting or adjourned meeting at which the person named in the instrument proposes to vote, or, in the case of a poll, not less than 48 hours before the time appointed for the taking of the poll, and, in default, the instrument of proxy shall not be treated as valid.

71.—An instrument appointing a proxy shall be in the following form or a form as near thereto as circumstances permit-
"   Limited.
I/We of ....
in the County of ....
member/ members of the above-named company hereby appoint ....
....
of ....
or failing him ....
of ....
as my/our proxy to vote for me/us on my/our behalf at the (annual or extra-ordinary, as the case may be) general meeting of the company to be held on the .... day of ...., 19.................. and at any adjournment tehreof.

        Signed this ....day of ...., 19................

This form is to be used *in favour of the resolution.
                          against

Unless otherwise instructed the proxy will vote as he thinks fit.

*Strike out whichever is not desired."

72.—The instrument appointing a proxy shall be deemed to confer authority to demand or join in demanding a poll.

73.—A vote given in accordance with the terms of an instrument of proxy shall be valid notwithstanding the previous death or insanity of the principal or revocation of the proxy or of the authority under which the proxy was executed or the transfer of the share in respect of which the proxy is given, if no intimation in writing of such death, insanity, revocation or transfer as aforesaid is received by the company at the office before the commencement of the meeting or adjourned meeting at which the proxy is used.

Bodies Corporate acting by Representatives at Meetings

74.—Any body corporate which is a member of the company may, by resolution of its directors or other governing body, authorise such person as it thinks fit to act as its representative at any meeting of the company or of any class of members of the company, and the person so authorised shall he entitled to exercise the same powers on behalf of the body corporate which he represents as that body corporate could exercise if it were an individual member of the company.

PART II

4.—Subject to sections 133 and 141 of the Act, an annual general meeting and a meeting called for the passing of a special resolution shall be called by 21 days' notice in writing at the least and a meeting of the company (other than an annual general meeting or a meeting for the passing of a special resolution) shall be called by 7 days' notice in writing at the least. The notice shall be exclusive of the day on which it is served or deemed to be served and of the day for which it is given and shall specify the day, the place and the hour of the meeting and, in the case of special business, the general nature of that business and shall be given in manner authorised by these regulations to such persons as are under the regulations of the company entitled to receive such notices from the company.

5.—No business shall be transacted at any general meeting unless a quorum of members is present at the time when the meeting proceeds to business; save as herein otherwise provided, two members present in person or by proxy shall be a quorum.

6.—Subject to section 141 of the Act, a resolution in writing signed by all the members for the time being entitled to attend and vote on such resolution at a general meeting (or being bodies corporate by their duly authorised representatives) shall be as valid and effective for all purposes as if the resolution had been passed at a general meeting of the company duly convened and held, and if described as a special resolution shall be deemed to be a special resolution within the meaning of the Act.

Companies Act 1963, sections 132(1) and 135(1)

Convening of extraordinary general meeting on requisition

132.—(1) The directors of a company, notwithstanding anything in its articles, shall, on the requisition of members of the company holding at the date of the deposit of the requisition not less than one-tenth of such of the paid up capital of the company as at the date of the deposit carries the right of voting at general meetings of the company, or, in the case of a company not having a share capital, members of the company representing not less than one-tenth of the total voting rights of all the members having at the said date a right to vote at general meetings of the company, forthwith proceed duly to convene an extraordinary general meeting of the company.

Power of court to order a meeting

135.—(1) If for any reason it is impracticable to call a meeting of a company in any manner in which meetings of that company may be called or to conduct the meeting of the company in manner prescribed by the articles or this Act, the court may, either of its own motion or on the application of any director of the company or of any member of the company who would be entitled to vote at the meeting, order a meeting of the company to be called, held and conducted in such manner as the court thinks fit, and where any such order is made may give such ancillary or consequential directions as it thinks expedient; and is hereby declared that the directions that may be given under this subsection include a direction that one member of the company present in person or by proxy shall be deemed to constitute a meeting.

Note: Court orders were made relating to general meetings, under the equivalent of section 135 of the 1963 Act, in *e.g. Re Sticky Fingers Restaurant Ltd* [1992] B.C.L.C. 84 and in *Re Whitechurch Insurance Consultants Ltd.* [1993] B.C.L.C. 1359, notwithstanding that parties had instituted proceedings claiming 'oppression'. In *Re British Union for the Abolition of Vivisection* [1995] 2 B.C.L.C. 1, although the company's articles of association required votes to be cast in person, Rimer J. ordered that in the circumstances they could be cast by ballot. But in *Harman v. B.M.L. Group Ltd.* [1994] 1 W.L.R. 893, where there were A and B shareholders and the articles of association provided that a meeting could not be quorate unless a B shareholder attended, the Court of Appeal refused to order that a meeting could take place in the absence of a B shareholder, because to do so would be to vary their 'class rights'.

Re Moorgate Mercantile Holdings Ltd.
[1980] 1 All E.R. 40

The issue here was the extent to which the terms of a special resolution that has been passed may deviate from the terms or the description contained in the notice of the meeting convened to consider the proposed resolution. Notices were circulated of a proposed special resolution that the company's share premium account, standing at £1,356,900, be cancelled on the grounds that the entire amount was lost. Due to an oversight, the proposers did not make provisions for a premium of £321 that was obtained shortly before then. On discovering this amount, the chairman sought to amend the proposed resolution to a proposal to reduce the share premium account from £1,356,900 to £321.

SLADE J.: . . . [44] Section 141(1) the Companies Act 1948 defines an extraordinary resolution as follows:

> "A resolution shall be an extraordinary resolution when it has been passed by a majority of not less than three fourths of such members as, being entitled so to do, vote in person or, where proxies are allowed, by proxy, at a general meeting of which notice specifying the intention to propose the resolution as an extraordinary resolution has been duly given."

Section 141(2) of that Act, omitting an immaterial proviso, defines a 'special resolution' as follows:

> "A resolution shall be a special resolution when it has been passed by such a majority as is required for the passing of an extraordinary resolution and at a general meeting of which not less than twenty-one days' notice, specifying the intention to propose the resolution as a special resolution has been duly given. . . ."

Section 141(5) provides that for the purpose of the section – ". . . notice of a meeting shall be deemed to be duly given and the meeting to be duly held when the notice is given and the meeting held in manner provided by this Act or the articles".

[Compare section 140 of the 1963 Act.]

The company's articles, so far as I am aware, contain no provisions which are relevant to the question which I have to decide. The doubts as to the validity of the special resolution of 26th April 1979 arise solely from the provisions of section 141(2).

It will be seen that, under the terms of section 141(2), one of the conditions precedent to the validity of any special resolution is that'. . . not less than 21 days' notice specifying the intention to propose the resolution as a special resolution, has been duly given'. As counsel as amicus curiae has submitted, the phrase 'the resolution' in this context in my judgment manifestly means 'the aforesaid resolution', that is to say, the resolution which has been actually passed. This is a point of crucial importance in the present case.

The problem which now arises may be briefly summarised as follows. The notices dated 2nd April 1979 specified the intention to propose as a special resolution the resolution that 'the share premium account of the Company amounting to £1,356,900.48p be cancelled'. However, the resolution which was actually passed at the meeting of 26th April 1979 was a resolution that 'the share premium account of the Company amounting to £1,356,900.48p be reduced to £321.17p'. In these circumstances, did the notices of 2nd April 1979 give notice within the meaning of section 141(2), specifying the intention to propose the resolution which was in the event actually passed?

In the absence of authority, I would have thought that the answer to this short question of statutory construction was manifestly No. The notices of 2nd April 1979 specified the intention to propose one resolution; the resolution actually passed at the meeting of 26th April 1979 was another, different resolution. Furthermore, the difference was not one merely of form but also of substance, albeit of slight substance, inasmuch as one resolution provided for the entire cancellation of the company's share premium account, while the other provided merely for its reduction, albeit by almost the entirety thereof.

The terms of section 141(2), at least if read in isolation and in the absence of authority, would seem to me to require that, if a special resolution passed at a meeting of members is to be valid, it must be the same resolution as that which the requisite notice has specified the intention to propose. As I have already indicated, the phrase 'the resolution' appearing in the later words of the subsection clearly refers back to and echoes the phrase 'a resolution' appearing at the beginning of the subsection. I can see strong arguments for contending that a resolution passed at a meeting of members may properly be regarded as the resolution (that is, the same resolution as that) referred to in the preceding notice, if the only differences between the two are merely clerical or grammatical; I will revert [45] to this point later. If, however, there is any difference whatsoever of substance between the two I would not, in the absence of authority, have regarded the later resolution, which was actually passed, as having been preceded by proper notice for the purpose of section 141(2).

Do the authorities lead me to a different conclusion?. . . [53] I. . . find nothing in the authorities which precludes me from reaching the conclusion as to the construction of section 141(2) of the 1948 Act which I would have reached [54] in the absence of authority and indeed I think this conclusion derives strong support from the *MacConnell* decision [1916] 2 Ch. 57. In the light of this analysis of the authorities and of the wording of section 141(2), I shall now attempt to summarise what are in my judgment the relevant principles relating to notices of, and the subsequent amendment of, special resolutions:

(1) If a notice of the intention to propose a special resolution is to be a valid notice for the purpose of section 141(2), it must identify the intended resolution by specifying either the text or the entire substance of the resolution which it is intended to propose. In the case of a notice of intention to propose a special resolution, nothing is achieved by the addition of such words as 'with such amendments and alterations as shall be determined on at such meeting'.

(2) If a special resolution is to be validly passed in accordance with section 141(2), the resolution as passed must be the same resolution as that identified in the preceding notice; the phrase 'the resolution' in section 141(2) means 'the aforesaid resolution'.

(3) A resolution as passed can properly be regarded as 'the resolution' identified in a preceding notice, even though (i) it departs in some respects from the text of a resolution set out in such notice (for example by correcting those grammatical or clerical errors which can be corrected as a matter of construction, or by reducing the words to more formal language) or (ii) it is reduced into the form of a new text, which was not included in the notice, provided only that in either case there is no departure whatever from the substance.

(4) However, in deciding whether there is complete identity between the substance of a resolution as passed and the substance of an intended resolution as notified, there is no room for the court to apply the de minimis principle or a 'limit of tolerance'. The substance must be identical. Otherwise the condition precedent to the validity of a special resolution as passed, which is imposed by section 141(2), namely that notice has been given 'specifying the intention to propose the resolution as a special resolution' is not satisfied.

(5) It necessarily follows from the above propositions that an amendment to the previously circulated text of a special resolution can properly be put to and voted on at a meeting if, but only if, the amendment involves no departure from the substance of the circulated text, in the sense indicated in propositions (3) and (4) above.

(6) References to notices in the above propositions are intended to include references to circulars accompanying notices. In those cases where notices are so accompanied, the notices and circulars can and should, in my judgment, ordinarily be treated as one document.

(7) All the above propositions may be subject to modification where all the members, or a class of members, of a company unanimously agree to waive their rights to notice under section 141(2): see section 143(4)(d) of the 1948 Act, *Re Pearce, Duff & Co Ltd.* [1960] 3 All E.R. 222 and *Re Duomatic Ltd.* [1969] 2 Ch. 365.

I would emphasise that these propositions are directed solely to special resolutions. Very different considerations may apply in the case of ordinary resolutions, in relation to which the criteria of permissible amendments suggested by counsel for the company could well be very relevant: see, for example, *Betts & Co Ltd. v. Macnaghten* [1910] 1 Ch. 430. In relation to special resolutions, however, I think that my conclusions of principle accord not only with the wording of the 1948 Act and with the authorities, but also with the following considerations of public policy. The 1948 Act requires a special resolution only in about ten circumstances. Thus, for example, such a resolution is required by section 5 for the alteration of a company's memorandum, by section 10 for the alteration of its articles, by [55] section 18(1) for the change of its name, by section 66 for the reduction of its capital, by section 222(a) for a resolution that the company may be wound up by the court, and is also required for a resolution for voluntary winding-up passed under section 278(1)(b). It may, I think, fairly be said that all the situations in which special resolutions are required are special situations, where the resolutions in question are by their nature likely either to affect the company's constitution or to have an important effect on its future. Since the passing of the 1929 legislation, the shareholders of a company, when faced with the intention to propose a special resolution, no longer have the protection of a locus poenitentiae in the shape of a second confirmatory meeting, at which they can accept or reject a special resolution passed at the first meeting. It is therefore all the more important that each shareholder should now have clear and precise advance notice of the substance of any special resolution which it is intended to propose, so that he may decide whether he should attend the meeting or is content to absent himself and leave the decision to those who do; the provisions imposed by section 141(2) of the 1948 Act must be intended as much for the protection of the members who in the event decide to absent themselves as for those who decide to attend: see for example *Tiessen v. Henderson* [1899] 1 Ch. 861 *per* Kekewich J. If it were open to the members who did attend to propose and vote on a special resolution differing in substance (albeit slightly) from the resolution of which notice had been given, there would be a risk of unfair prejudice to those members who, after due consideration, had deliberately absented themselves. I do not think that their interests would be sufficiently protected by the safeguard suggested by counsel for the company, namely that an amendment could properly be put to and voted on by the meeting only if a member, who had formed a view or intention with regard to a resolution as circulated, could not reasonably adopt a different view on the amended version. Nor do I think that the alternative 'whittling down' criterion suggested by him would offer them adequate protection. In many circumstances, albeit not on the facts of the particular case, either test when applied in practice could involve serious uncertainties and difficult questions of degree. Furthermore, in many cases it would present substantial embarrassment both to the chairman of the meeting who had to apply it and to any persons holding 'two-way' proxies on behalf of absent members. The absent members would be correspondingly faced with unpredictable risks.

These considerations strengthen my conclusion that the strict interpretation which I have placed on section 141(2) is likely to represent the true intention of the legislature, as well as the grammatical meaning of the words used. There must be absolute identity, at least in substance, between the intended resolution referred to in the notice and the resolution actually passed.

I now turn to apply the seven propositions set out above to the facts of the present case. The qualifications referred to in the last of them are not relevant here, since not all members of the company entitled to vote thereat were present at the meeting of 26th April 1979. While I have no reason to doubt that the amendment to the resolution was put to the meeting in good faith and on legal advice, it was in my judgment improperly put and voted on. Counsel as amicus curiae accepted, and I accept, the correctness of the advice given to Mr Silman, on the facts, that no shareholder who had made up his mind how to vote on the resolution in its original form could reasonably have adopted a different view in regard to the amended form. For this reason I have a measure of sympathy with this petition. This point, however, in my judgment is irrelevant in law. In my judgment, the crucial point is that the resolution which the meeting of 26th April 1979 approved was not the same resolution, either in form or in substance, as that of which the text had been circulated to shareholders in the notices of 2nd April 1979. There is no room for the application of any 'de minimis' principle; a resolution to reduce the share premium account of a company to £321 could not even be deemed to be the same as a resolution to reduce it to £320.

[56] In the circumstances the resolution was not in my judgment validly passed in accordance with section 141(2) of the 1948 Act. The court, therefore, has no jurisdiction to confirm the reduction of the share premium account as asked for by this petition.

Jackson v. Munster Bank Ltd.
(1884) 13 L.R.Ir. 118

This case concerns directors circulating misleading information to shareholders, when seeking their support on matters that directly relate to those directors' wellbeing. The bank's articles of association provided inter alia that the directors' remuneration should be determined by the company in general meeting; and that the company should not make any advance or allow any credit to a director, or to any firm of which a director should be partner, on his or their personal guarantee or security only, or otherwise than on adequate security. Complaints were made by certain shareholders that these provisions of the articles had not been adhered to; and a report of the company's auditor as to directors' overdrafts stated that, in some instances, these were inadequately secured. A meeting of shareholders was held, at which they expressed their dissatisfaction; and on the 10th of January, 1884, a sub-committee was appointed at one of these meetings to require the directors to give full information as to advances to directors, and the securities held for same, and the directors declined. A circular was issued convening an extraordinary general meeting of the company at which resolutions were to be proposed altering the articles of association by authorising advances to directors on their personal security, subject to certain restrictions, and by increasing the remuneration of directors, and leaving to the discretion of the directors the-future remuneration of the chairman and vice-chairman, as well as the remuneration of the former for past services. Proxy forms, drawn in favour of two of the directors, accompanied the circulars.

CHATTERTON V.C.: . . . [134] I am of opinion that a misleading circular has been published convening the meeting, by which the great body of the shareholders may have been misled, and that statements are contained in it which are calculated to have the effect of obtaining proxies from the shareholders without having the information which would enable them to form a just judgment as to who are the proper persons to whom their votes should be entrusted. It is an unfortunate thing that this circular should have been issued under the hand of the person who, above all others, should not have been the party to have proposed or advocated either one or other of the two resolutions which are the main objects of contention before me now: for beyond all doubt – and this was not disputed on the part of the defendants – there was considerable objection made by a number of shareholders, to which the directors in part acceded, as to the permission to the chairman, Mr Shaw, to overdraw his account without having, as is alleged, supplied adequate security. It is, therefore, unfortunate that Mr Shaw should be the person to propose to the shareholders at large that the proxies should be signed in the name of his three nominees. But this is not the only point, though it is a material one, upon which I base my decision. Another point is this, that in reference to the special resolution E, which it was proposed either to rescind altogether or to alter by substituting for it clause C1, there has been, in my opinion, a statement which did not call the attention of the shareholders to the real operation that would be effected by such a change. It is alleged that the opinion of Mr Benjamin had been obtained about a year ago, he having been consulted on the question of the liability of the directors for having been parties to, or [135] privy to, or for not complaining of, breaches of trust on the part of their co-directors in reference to advances of loans to directors of the bank. That might be a reason for suggesting some alteration in the special resolution of 1866; but this falls very short of the clause which is now proposed to be substituted for that special resolution. One alternative put forward was that this special resolution E should be altogether rescinded. If the facts now known upon this motion could have been communicated to them, I do not think that the majority of the shareholders would have been disposed to authorise by their proxies or their votes the alteration proposed which is so manifestly contrary to their interests. That special resolution was passed, I suppose, because the occasion for it arose so far back as 1866, and it has been in force – whether acted upon or not I do not know or inquire – from that year to the present time. The first thing proposed to be done at this extraordinary meeting is to do away with that special resolution, which provides a wholesome and a very moderate check upon the directors in reference to granting loans to one another – namely, that they should not be allowed to lend money to each other upon 'personal guarantee or security alone, or otherwise than on adequate security.' Can anyone contend that it would be for the benefit of the shareholders of the company, or for the benefit of anyone but the directors themselves, that that provision should be rescinded? And yet this is one of the matters contemplated by the circular of the chairman. But when I come to consider what is to be substituted for that resolution, I doubt whether it does not make matters worse than if the resolution were simply rescinded. It is as follows: 'The company shall not make any advance or allow any credit to a director, or to any firm of which a director is a partner, on his or their personal guarantee or security only, or otherwise, unless the Board, without a division, by an entry in their minutes, sanction such advance or credit: that the applicant for such advance or credit shall not be present upon any motion respecting the loan or advance of money, or otherwise giving credit to himself or his partner or partners.' This in point of fact would authorise the lending of money belonging to the bank on the personal guarantee or security only of the director seeking to [136] borrow, provided his brother directors in his absence should come to the conclusion that he ought to have the advance. Can anyone say that this would be for the benefit of the company, or that it would be a *bona fide* exercise of their powers by the directors for the benefit of the shareholders? It is not for the purpose of guarding shareholders against *bona fide* acts of directors that restraining clauses are inserted in Articles of Association; it is for the purpose of guarding them against *mala fides* on the part of the directors, amongst whom A.B. might to-day vote a sum of money to C.D., and C.D. might next day vote a similar sum to A.B. I do not go into the question whether the passing of these resolutions will absolve the directors from liability for acts already done by them. The Defendants may be right in arguing that it cannot do so; but this is not the point. The question I have to consider is whether the shareholders have been fully and fairly informed and instructed upon what is to be done, and for the doing of which their proxies have now been probably obtained.

Then I come to another of the proposed resolutions, D1, 'That the ordinary directors shall for their services receive in future and be paid such sum as may amount to but not exceed £250 *per* annum for each director, to be divided between them in such manner as they may determine: and the directors shall and are hereby authorised to make such arrangement for the remuneration of the chairman for his past services as they shall deem right, and pay to him such sum as shall be agreed upon,' &c. How can it be for the benefit of the company that the directors should be invested with unlimited authority to pay an increased and uncovenanted remuneration to the chairman for his services rendered in the past? His past services he has rendered to the company as its chairman, for the remuneration he has received. But the circular in this respect is also misleading, because a clause exists – the 86th – in the Articles of Association, which is not adverted to, and in the very teeth of which this new resolution is brought forward; that clause providing that the remuneration of directors must be fixed by the shareholders. Without their attention, then, being called to the 86th Article, the shareholders are asked by this circular to forego this right, and to entrust it to [137] the last persons who ought to be entrusted with it. I think that the effect of the proposed resolution has not been fairly communicated to the shareholders; and I must add that, when a chairman of a company thinks proper to do an unnecessary act, namely, to make a commentary on the resolutions which the directors are about to bring forward – as Mr Shaw has done in this circular – it should be a fair and candid commentary; and in my opinion this circular is neither fair nor candid. Under these circumstances, and for these reasons, without disputing the proposition of law, which is well established, that no dissentient minority of shareholders has a right to come into Court for the purpose of interfering with the decision of the majority in reference to matters of internal management, in the absence of fraud or proceedings *ultra vires*, a rule of law which, in my opinion, does not affect this motion, I give my decision entirely upon what I consider to be the probable effect of this circular upon the general body of the shareholders. Bearing in mind the rule as to convenience affecting interlocutory injunctions, and not offering any opinion upon any facts that hereafter may be discussed, but simply being of opinion that this circular has a misleading tendency (whether intentional or unintentional it is unnecessary to consider), and that proxies have been obtained by the nominees of the chairman by means of it, I think that greater inconvenience would be caused if the meeting were to come to a decision under such circumstances, than if such decision were postponed – more particularly when the directors can call another meeting at any time to consider any resolutions they may think necessary. I do not say that these resolutions, when fully understood and fairly considered, may not hereafter be adopted and conclusively ratified, a matter as to which I offer no opinion. I think that under the circumstances which I have stated, they ought not to be brought forward at to-morrow's meeting, as the general body of the shareholders might thereby be seriously affected.

Byng v. London Life Association Ltd
[1990] Ch. 170

The issue here relates to the overall conduct of general meetings. An extraordinary general meet was to be held at 12 noon at a cinema in the Barbican for the purpose of amending the company's memorandum of association so that the company could finalise negotiations with another life assurance company to transfer its long-term insurance business. An agreement was conditional on the merger being approved by 31 March but it would have been more convenient if the transaction could be completed at the end of both companies' financial year on 31 January. Because of opposition to the merger, the company expected a large attendance at the meeting and therefore arranged for other rooms nearby and, the cinema foyer to be available with audio-visual links to the cinema and as an extra precaution, the Café Royal, seating 800 people, was booked. About 800 people attended the meeting but there were no audio-visual links functioning. Because of difficulties in members registering to vote, it was not until 12.30, that the president of the company purported as chairman to open the meeting. Members were still registering to vote and some members proposed that the meeting should be abandoned and others, including the plaintiff, that it should be adjourned sine die. At about 12.45, the chairman indicated that he was adjourning the meeting to 2.30 p.m. at the Café Royal, despite a number of members indicating that they would not be able to attend. The adjourned meeting at the Café Royal was attended by 600 people, including 335 of the 468 members who had registered to vote at the Barbican. The resolution was put to the meeting and, as there was an insufficient majority, the chairman demanded a poll, which gave a sufficient majority to pass the resolution.

BROWNE-WILKONSON V.-C.: [182] *Was there a meeting?* The first difficulty is to identify what, if anything, was the meeting. Was it the assembly of the members in the cinema alone (from which all those in the overflow rooms and foyer were excluded) or was it the conglomerate assembly of those in the cinema plus those in the overflow rooms and foyer?

Mr. Potts' first submission under this head was made with a view to showing that the conglomerate assembly in the cinema, the overflow rooms and the foyer could not constitute a meeting. He submitted that for there to be a meeting at all everyone must be in the same place, face to face. If this submission were correct, even if the audio-visual links had worked perfectly, there would still have been no meeting at the Barbican on 19 October since all the members attending would not have been face to face but scattered between different rooms. In support of was this submission Mr. Potts relied on the definition of the word "meet" in the Shorter *Oxford English Dictionary, viz.*: to come face to face with or into the company of [another person]." He also relies on the fact that the requirement in section 378 of the Companies Act 1985 (similar to s.141 of the 1963 Act) that an extraordinary resolution has to be passed at a general meeting has a long statutory history dating back to times long before the invention of [183] audio-visual links. This, he submits, shows that a meeting for the purpose of the Companies Act 1985 requires that everyone shall be physically present in the same room or space.

I do not accept this submission. The rationale behind the requirement for meetings in the Companies Act, 1985 is that the members shall be able to attend in person so as to debate and vote on matters affecting the company. Until recently this could only be achieved by everyone being physically present in the same room face to face. Given modern technological advances, the same result can now be achieved without all the members coming face to face: without being physically in the same room they can be electronically in each other's presence so as to hear and be heard and to see and be seen. The fact that such a meeting could not have been foreseen at the time the first statutory requirements for meetings were laid down, does not require us to hold that such a meeting is not within the meaning of the word "meeting" in the Act, of 1985. Thus, communication by telephone has been held to be a "telegraph" within the meaning of the Telegraph Acts 1863 and 1869, notwithstanding that the telephone had not been invented or contemplated when those Acts were passed: *Attorney-General v. Edison Telephone Co. Ltd.* (1880) 6 Q.B.D. 244.

I have no doubt therefore that, in cases where the original venue proves inadequate to accommodate all those wishing to attend, valid general meetings of a company can be properly held using overflow rooms provided. First, that all due steps are taken to direct to the overflow rooms those unable to get into the main meeting and, second, that there are adequate audio-visual links to enable those in all the rooms to see and hear what is going on in the other rooms. Were the law otherwise, with the present tendency towards companies with very large numbers of shareholders and corresponding uncertainty as to how many shareholders will attend meetings, the organisation of such meetings might prove to be impossible.

In the event, Mr. Oliver for the defendants did not contend that the conglomerate assembly was a meeting of the company. He submitted that the assembly in the cinema was the meeting. I accept this submission. If there was a meeting at all it was the assembly in the cinema, that being the venue specified in the notice convening the meeting. Such meeting was incapable of proceeding to business, since all those members unable to get into the cinema were excluded. For the reasons I have given, if proper overflow facilities had in fact been provided, those in the overflow rooms and the foyer would not have been excluded from that meeting but would, electronically, have been present at it. But since the audio-visual links did not work, those in the overflow rooms and foyer were excluded and the meeting in the cinema was incapable of transacting any business.

Does the fact that the assembly in the cinema was incapable of conducting any business necessarily mean that it was not a "meeting" at all? Mr. Potts submitted that it was an invalid meeting, a nullity. He says that, as in the case of a meeting of which proper notice has not been given or at which there is no quorum, where members are excluded from a meeting it is invalid and cannot be adjourned.

[184] In my judgment the phrase "invalid meeting," although useful as a shorthand description of a meeting at which no business can be validly transacted, is capable of giving rise to confusion. The fact that a meeting cannot pass a valid resolution in certain circumstances does not necessarily mean that there has been no meeting at all. Thus in many cases (including the present) the articles of a company provide that, in the event of there being no quorum present at a meeting, the meeting shall be adjourned for a fixed period. In such a case it is clear that the inquorate meeting was a meeting notwithstanding the fact that it could conduct no business.

In my judgment there is no absolute rule of law that a meeting from which members are wrongly excluded is a nullity. The meeting, as such, can conduct no business, but it is nevertheless a meeting. I can see no good reason why the law should shut its eyes to the reality that, in response to a notice convening them, certain members of the company have assembled together at what, in ordinary usage, would be called a meeting. What that meeting can validly do is quite another matter.

In the present case the sole question is whether Mr. Dawson was, within article 17, the chairman of a general meeting of London Life. The answer to that question must depend on the meaning of the word "meeting" in the articles of London Life. Article 15 provides: "no business shall be transacted at a general meeting unless a quorum is present when the meeting proceeds to business". Article 16 then provides:

> "If within half an hour from the time appointed for the meeting a quorum is not present, the meeting, if convened on the requisition of members, shall be dissolved. In any other case it shall stand adjourned to the same day in the next week, at the same time and place. . . ."

These two articles therefore proceed on the basis that an inquorate meeting incapable of conducting any business is still a "meeting" of London Life, capable of being adjourned. Similarly, under articles 40 and 41 of Table A to the Companies Acts an inquorate meeting is treated as a meeting capable of adjournment. Therefore, the draftsman of the London Life articles and Parliament both plainly envisaged that the word "meeting" covered an assembly which could conduct no business.

Mr. Potts relied on certain authorities to show that as a rule of law a meeting from which those entitled to be present were excluded is a nullity. In *Harben v. Phillips* (1883) 23 Ch.D. 14 four directors were wrongly excluded from a board meeting. The three directors present at the board meeting purported to adjourn it. The adjourned board meeting purported to take certain decisions. Chitty J., at p. 26, said that the first meeting was "an unlawful meeting, that it was not properly constituted, and that everything that was done at it is invalid." In consequence he held that the adjourned board meeting could not validly transact the business it purported to transact. In the Court of Appeal Cotton L.J., at p. 34, expressed very great doubt whether the first board meeting could be considered a proper meeting. The only question in [185] that case was whether the first board meeting had been validly adjourned. The purported adjournment was the act of the meeting itself (*i.e.* of the three directors present). Therefore in that case it was being contended that the meeting itself (as opposed to the chairman of the meeting) could conduct business, notwithstanding the exclusion of some members entitled to be there and to vote on the resolution. That, to my mind, is a wholly different case. In the present case the meeting at the cinema did not purport to transact business: the claim is that its ex officio chairman had power to adjourn it.

In *In re Portuguese Consolidated Copper Mines Ltd.* (1889) 42 Ch. D. 160 there was a board meeting of which inadequate notice was given. Only two directors attended. They resolved that two directors should be a quorum, purported to allot certain shares and adjourned the meeting. The adjourned meeting purported to ratify the allotment. The Court of Appeal held that, there having been no proper notice of the first meeting, it was "no valid meeting, and being an invalid meeting could not adjourn itself": *per* Lord Esher M.R., at p. 167. The position, therefore, was the same as in *Harben v. Phillips, viz.,* a meeting which had excluded (through lack of notice) persons entitled to attend. It therefore could not transact business and could not resolve to adjourn itself. Certainly the language used by Lord Esher goes wider than that, but it must be read in the light of the question he was there considering.

The Canadian case, *McLaren v. Fisken* (1881) 28 Gr.Ch.R. 352 is the same. An inquorate meeting of a board purported to do business by adjourning itself, there being no article permitting it so to do. It was held that the purported adjournment was a nullity and therefore no business could be validly transacted at the adjourned meeting. There again the question was not whether a meeting had been held but whether such meeting could validly adjourn itself.

On the other side there is one authority which lends some support to the view that there can be a general meeting even when that meeting is incapable of conducting business. In *Fletcher v. New Zealand Glue Co. Ltd.* (1911) 31 N.Z.L.R. 129, the company was bound to submit a return of the persons who were its members on the 14th day after its annual general meeting. The company duly convened an annual general meeting which proved to be inquorate. Under its articles, an inquorate meeting was automatically adjourned sine die. The company made a return of the members 14 days after the date of the inquorate meeting. It was held that the return was proper since there was a valid general meeting but valid only for the purposes of adjournment. Although the circumstances there under consideration were very different, the case is some authority for the proposition that there can be a meeting of a company even though such a meeting is incapable of conducting any business.

I can therefore see no reason why, as common sense suggests, the assembly at the cinema should not in law constitute a "meeting" within the meaning of that word in the Companies Act 1985 and the articles of London Life. It follows that I agree with Vinelott J. that under article 17 Mr. Dawson was the chairman of the meeting and had all the powers of the chairman.

Did the chairman have power to adjourn?

[186] Mr. Potts submits that since article 18 expressly provides that the chairman can only adjourn the meeting with its consent, Mr. Dawson could have no power in any circumstances to adjourn without such consent. Vinelott J. rejected this submission, to my mind rightly.

I will first consider the powers of a chairman at common law, there being no document expressly regulating powers of adjournment. A chairman has no general right to adjourn a meeting at his own will and pleasure, there being no circumstance preventing the effective continuation of the proceedings: *National Dwellings Society v. Sykes* [1894] 3 Ch. 159, 162. However, it is clearly established that a chairman has such power where unruly conduct prevents the continuation of business: *John v. Rees* [1970] Ch. 345, 379 et seq. In my judgment it is also established that when in an orderly meeting a poll is demanded on a motion to adjourn and such poll cannot be taken forthwith, the chairman has power to suspend the meeting with a view to its continuance at a later date after the result of the poll is known: *Jackson v. Hamlyn* [1953] Ch. 577. In that case Upjohn J. expressly held, at p. 588, that the chairman was not "adjourning" the meeting within the meaning of the article there in question. Even so, he held that the chairman had power to stand over the proceedings to another time, since some such power had to exist in order to give effect to the provisions as to polls in the articles. Therefore, although it may not have been an adjournment within the meaning of the articles there under consideration, he held that there was a residual power in the chairman to take such steps as would, in the ordinary usage of the word, amount to an adjournment.

In my judgment the position at common law is correctly set out in *John v. Rees* [1970] Ch. 345 and in the two following passages. The first quoted, at p. 380, is from *Reg. v. D'Oyly* (1840) 12 Ad. & El. 139, 159:

"Setting aside the inconvenience that might arise if a majority of the parishioners could determine the point of adjournment, we think that the person who presides at the meeting is the proper individual to decide this. It is on him that it devolves, both to preserve order in the meeting, and to regulate the proceedings *so as to give all persons entitled a reasonable opportunity of voting*. He is to do the acts necessary for these purposes on his own responsibility, and subject to being called upon to answer for his conduct if he has done anything improperly." (My emphasis.)

The second passage quoted, at p. 381, is from *A Practical Arrangement of Ecclesiastical Law* by F.N. Rogers Q.C. published in 1840. The passage says that a particular decision:

> "By no means interferes with the right which every chairman has to make a bona fide adjournment, whilst a poll or other business is proceeding, if circumstances of violent interruption make it unsafe, or seriously difficult for the voters to tender their votes; nor of adjourning the place of polling, if the ordinary place used for that purpose be insufficient or greatly inconvenient. In most of such cases, the question will turn upon the intention and effect of the adjournment, if the intention and effect were to interrupt and [187] procrastinate the business, such an adjournment would be illegal; if on the contrary, the intention and effect were to forward or facilitate it, *and no injurious effect were produced*, such an adjournment would, it is conceived, be generally supported." (My emphasis.)

In my judgment, were it not for article 18, Mr. Dawson would at common law have had power to adjourn the meeting at the cinema since the inadequacy of the space available rendered it impossible for all those entitled to attend to take part in the debate and to vote. A motion for adjournment could not be put to the meeting as many who would be entitled to vote on the motion were excluded. Therefore, at common law it would have been the chairman's duty to regulate the proceedings so as to give all persons entitled a reasonable opportunity of debating and voting. This would have required him either to abandon the meeting or to adjourn it to a time and a place where the members could have a reasonable opportunity to debate or vote. I see no reason to hold that in all circumstances the meeting must be abandoned: in my judgment the chairman can, in a suitable case, merely adjourn such meeting.

What then is the effect of article 18 which expressly confers on the chairman power to adjourn but only with the consent of a quorate meeting? Mr. Potts submits that the chairman's power to adjourn having been expressly laid down and expressly circumscribed, there is no room for the chairman to have any implied power at common law. He relies on the decision of the Privy Council in *Salisbury Gold Mining Co. v. Hathorn* [1897] A.C. 268. In that case the articles provided that the chairman could adjourn with the consent of the members: the articles did not provide (as does article 18 in the present case) that the chairman was bound to adjourn if so directed by the meeting. It was held that the chairman was not bound to put a motion for adjournment to the meeting but was entitled to insist on the meeting proceeding to business. Lord Herschell L.C. treated the express provision making it the chairman's decision whether or not to adjourn as ousting the general rule that a meeting can always adjourn itself. So, by analogy, Mr. Potts argues that the express provision in article 18 requiring the chairman to obtain the consent of the meeting as a precondition to the exercise of his power to adjourn precludes the existence of any power in the chairman to adjourn without such consent.

Like the judge, I reject this submission. In my judgment article 18 regulates the chairman's powers of adjournment to the extent that its machinery is effective to cover the contingencies which occur. Therefore if the circumstances are such that it is possible to discover whether or not the meeting agrees to an adjournment, article 18 lays down a comprehensive code. But if the circumstances are such that the wishes of the meeting cannot be validly ascertained, why should article 18 be read as impairing the fundamental common law duty of the chairman to regulate proceedings so as to enable those entitled to be present and to vote to be heard and to vote? In my judgment *Jackson v. Hamlyn* [1953] Ch. 577 is an authority in support of that view since in that case there was an article in much the same terms as article 18 in the present case.

[188] As the judge pointed out, the contrary result would produce manifest absurdities. Say that there was a disturbance in a meeting which precluded the taking of any vote on a motion to adjourn. Would this mean that the meeting had to be abandoned even though a short adjournment would have enabled peace to be restored and the meeting resumed? Again, say that in the present case the adjoining Barbican theatre had been available on 19 October so that a short adjournment to the theatre would have enabled an effective meeting of all members wishing to attend to be held that morning. Can it really be the law that because a valid resolution for such an adjournment could not be passed in the cinema (many members entitled to vote being excluded from the cinema) no such adjournment could take place?

I do not find that any principle of construction requires me to hold that an express provision regulating adjournment when the views of the meeting can be ascertained necessarily precludes the existence of implied powers when consent of the meeting cannot be obtained. The *Salisbury Gold Mining* case lays down no such proposition. Accordingly, I reach the conclusion that in any circumstances where there is a meeting at which the views of the majority cannot be validly ascertained, the chairman has a residual common law power to adjourn "so as to give all persons entitled a reasonable opportunity of voting" and, I would add, speaking at the meeting.

Was the power validly exercised?

Vinelott J. held that Mr. Dawson validly exercised the power to adjourn by adjourning the meeting to the Café Royal in the afternoon. This is the only point (though a decisive one) on which I differ from the judge. As I understand his judgment, he took the view that provided Mr. Dawson acted in good faith (which it is accepted that he did) his decision could not be impugned and in particular that it was irrelevant that the effect of the adjournment to the Café

Royal was that some 200 of those present in the morning did not attend the meeting at the Café Royal in the afternoon and that 133 people (being over 25 *per* cent. of the total) who had registered at the Barbican did not register at the Café Royal. I am unable to agree with this view.

The starting point is to consider the nature of the residual power to adjourn which in my judgment remains vested in the chairman. It was a residual power exercisable only when the machinery provided by the articles had broken down. This residual common law power is itself tightly circumscribed by reference to the objects for which it exists. I quote again from the passages which I have emphasised above in the quotations from *Reg. v. D'Oyly* and F. N. Rogers' book. The power is to regulate proceedings "so as to give all persons entitled a reasonable opportunity of voting." The chairman must "do the acts necessary for these purposes." The power to adjourn is only validly exercised if "no injurious affect were produced." I would add that at a company meeting a member is entitled not only to vote but also to hear and be heard in the debate. Therefore it is the very purpose of the power to facilitate the presence of those entitled to debate and vote on a resolution at a meeting where such debate and voting is possible. To my mind, this is [189] inconsistent with the view that the exercise of the power can only be impugned on the ground of lack of good faith. In my judgment the chairman's decision must also be taken reasonably with a view to facilitating the purpose for which the power exists. Accordingly the impact of the proposed adjournment on those seeking to attend the original meeting and the other members must be a central factor in considering the validity of the chairman's decision to adjourn.

The quotation from F. N. Rogers' book might suggest that if the chairman's decision proves in the event to have an adverse effect on the members, that will render the decision invalid. In my judgment that is not the correct test. The chairman's decision will not be declared invalid unless on the facts which he knew or ought to have known he failed to take into account all the relevant factors, took into account irrelevant factors or reached a conclusion which no reasonable chairman, properly directing himself as to his duties, could have reached, *i.e.* the test is the same as that applicable on judicial review in accordance with the principles of *Associated Provincial Picture Houses Ltd. v. Wednesbury Corporation* [1948] 1 K.B. 223. This was the approach adopted by Uthwatt J. in *Second Consolidated Trust v. Ceylon and Amalgamated Tea and Rubber Estates Ltd.* [1943] 2 All E.R. 567 where he held a chairman's decision invalid on the grounds that he had failed to take into account a relevant factor.

I turn then to consider the position confronting Mr. Dawson at the Barbican cinema on the morning of 19 October. The principal factors were as follows. . .

[190] In these circumstances, in my judgment, the chairman's decision to adjourn to the Café Royal on the same afternoon was not valid on the ground either that he failed to take into account relevant factors or that the decision

was *Wednesbury* unreasonable. The legal advice tendered was in my judgment erroneous, probably because it failed to take account of the very limited ambit of the chairman's residual power to adjourn. Since such power is only exercisable for the purpose of giving the members a proper opportunity to debate and vote on the resolution, there must in my judgment be very special circumstances to justify a decision to adjourn the meeting to a time and place where, to the knowledge of the chairman, it could not be attended by a number of the members who had taken the trouble to attend the original meeting and could not even lodge a proxy vote. To overlook this factor is to leave out of account a matter of central importance. True it is that those who were available for the afternoon meeting would have been inconvenienced by an adjournment to another date or the convening of a wholly new meeting since they would either have to have attended at the fresh meeting or to have lodged proxies. But in my judgment this could not outweigh the central point that the form of the adjournment was such as undoubtedly to preclude certain members from taking any part in the meeting either by way of debate or by way of vote.

If the time factor had been such that the merger proposal could not have been carried through at all unless there was an immediate decision on the resolution before the meeting (*i.e.* if the merger had to be approved within a period which rendered impossible the convening of a further meeting on 21 days notice or the adjournment of the original meeting for a sufficient period to allow proxies to be lodged) the matter might have been different. But in fact there was no compelling time factor in this case. True it is that expenditure would have to be incurred in calling a further meeting. But if, instead of adjourning to the detriment of certain members, the meeting at the Barbican had either been abandoned or adjourned sine die, 21 days notice could have been given of a fresh meeting to be held, say, a month later, well before even the date fixed for the hearing in court. If such fresh meeting had been called, all the members would have had an opportunity to be present either in person or by proxy. There is no sign that Mr. Dawson ever appreciated this factor or took it into account in reaching his decision.

Accordingly, although Mr. Dawson acted in complete good faith, his decision to adjourn to the Café Royal on the same date was not one which, in my judgment, he could reasonably have reached if he had properly apprehended the restricted nature and purpose of his powers. Therefore in my judgment his decision was invalid.

Note: In *Re Bradford Investments Ltd.* [1991] B.C.L.C. 224, Hoffman J. held that, where a dispute as to entitlement to vote arises at a time the chairman of the general meeting has to be elected, and a person assumes control as chairman, his ruling as to who was allowed to vote is not unchangeable by virtue of article 67 of Table A.

Barron v. Potter
[1914] 1 Ch. 895

To what extent can members be manoeuvred or tricked into attending meetings and can decisions be taken therein? Potter stated that Barron arrived at the office of the company with the object of attending the extraordinary general meeting called by him. Potter thereupon proposed to Barron that three persons should be appointed additional directors of the company, proposing each name separately. Barron disregarded the proposals and refused to vote thereon, whereupon Potter voted in favour of them and declared the persons named to be duly elected directors.

According to Barron's evidence, he attended at the registered office of the company at 3 o'clock p.m. to attend the extraordinary general meeting, and as he entered the inner room where the meeting was to be held Potter came after him and said, 'I propose Mrs Clara Rose Potter and (mentioning another name) as directors. Have you any amendments?' Barron answered laughingly, 'Yes, I have plenty of amendments which we shall discuss.' Here Potter interrupted him and said, 'Then I give my casting vote; they are elected.'

WARRINGTON J.: . . . [902] The question then arises, Was the resolution passed at the general meeting of the company a valid appointment? The argument against the validity of the appointment is that the articles of association of the company gave to the board of directors the power of appointing additional directors, that the company has accordingly surrendered the power, and that the directors alone can exercise it. It is true that the general point was so decided by Eve J. in *Blair Open Hearth Furnace Co. v. Reigart* (108 L.T. 665), and I am not concerned to say that in ordinary cases where there is a board ready and willing to act it would be competent for the company to override the power conferred on the directors by the articles except by way of special resolution for the purpose of altering the articles. But the case which I have to deal with is a different one. For practical purposes there is no board of directors at all. The only directors are two persons, one of whom refuses to act with the other, and the question is, What is to be done under these circumstances? On this point I think that I can usefully refer to the judgment of the Court of Appeal in *Isle of Wight Ry. Co. v. Tahourdin* (25 Ch. D. 320), not for the sake of the decision, which depended on the fact that it was a case under the Companies Clauses Consolidation Act, 1845, but for the sake of the observations of Cotton and Fry L.J. upon the effect of a deadlock such as arose in the present case. Cotton L.J. says: 'Then it is said that there is no power in the meeting of shareholders to elect new directors, for that under the 89th section the power would be in the remaining directors. The remaining directors would no doubt have that power if there was a quorum left. But suppose the meeting were to remove so many directors that a quorum was not left, what then follows? It has been argued that in that case, there being no board which could act, there would be no power of filling up the board so as to enable it to work. In my opinion that is utterly wrong. A power is given by the 89th section to the remaining directors 'if they think proper so to do' to elect persons to fill up the vacancies. I do not see how it is possible for a non-existent body to think proper [903] to fill up vacancies. In such a case a general meeting duly summoned for the purpose must have power to elect a new board so as not to let the business of the company be at a dead-lock.' Fry L.J. says this: 'Then with regard to the objection that a general meeting cannot elect directors to fill up vacancies, it appears to me that a general meeting would at any rate have that power in the event of all the directors being removed. In my judgment it is quite impossible to read the 89th section as the only section relating to the filling up of vacancies in the office of directors. That applies only where there are remaining directors, and those remaining directors think proper to exercise their power. That does not, in my judgment, deprive the general meeting of the power to elect directors, where there are no directors, or where the directors do not think fit to exercise their powers.' Those observations express a principle which seems to me to be as applicable to the case of a limited company incorporated under the Companies (Consolidation) Act, 1908. as to a case falling under the Companies Clauses Consolidation Act, 1845, and moreover to be a principle founded on plain common sense. If directors having certain powers are unable or unwilling to exercise them – are in fact a non-existent body for the purpose – there must be some power in the company to do itself that which under other circumstances would be otherwise done. The directors in the present case being unwilling to appoint additional directors under the power conferred on them by the articles, in my opinion, the company in general meeting has power to make the appointment. The company has passed a resolution for that purpose, and though a poll has been demanded no date or place has yet been fixed for taking it. The result therefore is that I must grant an injunction on the motion in Canon Barron's action and refuse the motion in Mr Potter's action.

THE CORPORATE FRANCHISE

Bushell v. Faith
[1970] A.C. 1099

The issue here was the extent to which, by appropriately drafting of the memorandum and articles of association, mandatory requirements of the Companies Acts can in substance be over ridden. The articles of association of a private company provided that, in the event of a resolution being proposed at a general meeting of the company for the removal of a director, any shares held by that director should carry three votes *per* share. The company had an issued capital of £300 in £1 shares, which were distributed equally between the plaintiff, the defendant (her brother) and B., their sister. The plaintiff and defendant were the only directors of the company. The two sisters, requisitioned a general meeting of the company for the purpose of passing a resolution removing him from office as a director. On a poll at the meeting they both voted for the resolution, and he voted against it. A dispute having arisen as to whether the resolution had been passed or defeated, the plaintiff contended that it had been passed by 200 votes, being those of herself and her sister, to 100, those of the defendant. The defendant contended that in accordance with article 9 his 100 shares carried 300 votes to 200. The plaintiff claimed a declaration that the resolution had been validly passed and an injunction restraining the defendant from acting as a director.

LORD UPJOHN: . . . [1107] [T]he whole question is whether special article 9 is valid and applicable, in which case the resolution was rejected by 300 votes to 200, or whether that article must be treated as overridden by section 184 and therefore void, in which case the resolution was passed by 200 votes to 100. So to test this matter the appellant began an action for a declaration that the respondent was removed from office as a director by the resolution of November 22, 1968, and moved the court for an interlocutory injunction restraining him from acting as a director. This motion comes by way of appeal before your Lordships.

The appellant argues that special article 9 is directed to frustrating the whole object and purpose of section 184 (same as section 182 of the 1963 Act) so that it can never operate where there is such a special article and the director in fact becomes irremovable. So she argues that, having regard to the clear words 'notwithstanding anything in its articles' in section 184, special article 9 must be rejected and treated as void. The learned judge, Ungoed-Thomas J., so held. He said: 'It would make a mockery of the law if the courts [1108] were to hold that in such a case a director was to be irremovable.' And later he concluded his judgment by saying: 'A resolution under article 9 is therefore not in my view an ordinary resolution within section 184. The plaintiff succeeds in the application.'

The brother appealed, and the Court of Appeal (Harman, Russell and Karminski L.JJ.) allowed the appeal. Harman L.J. did so on the simple ground that the Act of 1948 did not prevent certain shares or classes of shares having special voting rights attached to them and on certain occasions. He could find nothing in the Act of 1948 which prohibited the giving of special voting rights to the shares of a director who finds his position attacked. Russell L.J. in his judgment gave substantially the same reasons for allowing the appeal and he supported his judgment by reference to a number of recent precedents particularly those to be found in *Palmer's Company Precedents*, 17th ed. (1956), but, with all respect to the learned Lord Justice, I do not think these precedents which, so far as relevant, are comparatively new can be said to have the settled assent and approbation of the profession, so as to render them any real guide for the purposes of a judgment; especially when I note the much more cautious approach by the learned editors of the *Encyclopaedia of Forms and Precedents*, 4th ed. (1966), Vol. 5, p. 428, where in reference to a form somewhat similar to special article 9 they say in a footnote:

"The validity of such a provision as this in relation to a resolution to remove a director from office remains to be tested in the courts."

My Lords, when construing an Act of Parliament it is a canon of construction that its provisions must be construed in the light of the mischief which the Act was designed to meet. In this case the mischief was well known; it was a common practice, especially in the case of private companies, to provide in the articles that a director should be irremovable or only removable by an extraordinary resolution; in the former case the articles would have to be altered by special resolution before the director could be removed and of course in either case a three-quarters majority would be required. In many cases this would be impossible, so the Act provided that notwithstanding anything in the articles an ordinary resolution would suffice to remove a director. That was the mischief which the section set out to remedy; to make a director removable by virtue of an ordinary resolution instead of an extraordinary resolution or making it necessary to alter the articles.

An ordinary resolution is not defined nor used in the body of the Act of 1948 though the phrase occurs in some of the articles of Table A in the First Schedule to the Act. But its meaning is, in my opinion, clear. An ordinary resolution is in the first place passed by a bare majority on a show of hands by the members entitled to vote who are present personally or by proxy and on such a vote each member has one vote regardless of his shareholding. If a poll is demanded then for an ordinary resolution still only a bare majority of votes is required. But whether a share or class of shares has any vote upon the matter and, if so, what is its voting power upon the resolution in question depends [1109] entirely upon the voting rights attached to that share or class of shares by the articles of association.

I venture to think that Ungoed-Thomas J. overlooked the importance of article 2 of Table A which gives to the company a completely unfettered right to attach to any share or class of shares special voting rights upon a poll or to restrict those rights as the company may think fit. Thus, it is commonplace that a company may and frequently does preclude preference shareholders from voting unless their dividends are in arrears or their class rights are directly affected. It is equally commonplace that particular shares may be issued with specially loaded voting rights which ensure that in all resolutions put before the shareholders in general meeting the holder of those particular shares can always be sure of carrying the day, aye or no, as the holder pleases.

Mr Dillon, for the appellant, felt, quite rightly, constrained to admit that if an article provided that Mr Faith's shares should, on every occasion when a resolution was for consideration by a general meeting of the company, carry three votes such a provision would be valid on all such occasions including any occasion when the general meeting was considering a resolution for his removal under section 184.

My Lords, I cannot see any difference between that case and the present case where special voting rights are conferred only when there is a resolution for the removal of a director under section 184. Each case is an exercise of the unfettered right of the company under article 2 whereby any share in the company may be issued with such. . . special rights. . . in regard to. . . voting. . . as the company may from time to time by ordinary resolution determine.

Parliament has never sought to fetter the right of the company to issue a share with such rights or restrictions as it may think fit. There is no fetter which compels the company to make the voting rights or restrictions of general application and it seems to me clear that such rights or restrictions can be attached to special circumstances and to particular types of resolution. This makes no mockery of section 184; all that Parliament was seeking to do thereby was to make an ordinary resolution sufficient to remove a director. Had Parliament desired to go further and enact that every share entitled to vote should be deprived of its special rights under the articles it should have said so in plain terms by making the vote on a poll one vote one share. Then, what about shares which had no voting rights under the articles? Should not Parliament give them a vote when considering this completely artificial form of ordinary resolution? Suppose there had here been some preference shares in the name of Mr Faith's wife, which under the articles had in the circumstances no vote; why in justice should her voice be excluded from consideration in this artificial vote?

I only raise this purely hypothetical case to show the great difficulty of trying to do justice by legislation in a matter which has always been left to the corporators themselves to decide.

Note: A similar question was considered in *Russell v. Northern Bank Development Corp.* [1992] 1 W.L.R. 588 (see *infra*, p. 185) regarding provisions in shareholders' agreements.

Kinsella v. Alliance & Dublin Consumers Gas Co.
Barron J., October 5, 1982

What is called for consideration here is whether, through their control of a company's administration, the management may influence the outcome of a proposed resolution on a matter of vital concern. Under the Companies Clauses Consolidation Act, 1845, every member possessed one vote *per* share held, but no one shareholder could possess more than a limited number of votes regardless of how many shares he owned. In an attempt to wrest control of the company from its board of directors, the plaintiff and his supporters bought substantial blocks of shares in the company. Because many of the share transfers were not registered, their anti-directors resolutions were defeated. They sought to have the rejection of their resolutions set aside.

BARRON J.: This action challenges the validity of the proceedings at an extraordinary general meeting of the company held on the 10th September, 1982. At that meeting, voting was permitted only by stockholders whose names had been entered in the register of shareholders and only such stockholders were permitted to attend the meeting. Persons to whom stock had been transferred and in respect of which transfers had been received by the secretary of the company, but whose names had not been entered in the register of shareholders were not permitted to attend the meeting.

Before dealing with the legal issues raised I feel it necessary to refer to the facts to show how such a situation arose. The extraordinary general meeting was called upon the requisition of the plaintiffs and those who support them. The resolutions for consideration at the meeting were essentially to remove the existing board and to replace its members with nominees of the plaintiffs. In the ordinary way, this trial of strength would have been decided by the respective shareholdings of the members supporting each side. However, [2] in the case of the Gas Company the voting rights of its members are governed by the Company Clauses Consolidation Act, 1845. Under this Act, which in the main, comprises the constitution of the company, each member has one vote for each share held by him up to ten, one additional vote for every five shares beyond the first ten shares up to one hundred, and an additional vote for every ten shares held by him beyond the first hundred shares. The original shares were of a nominal value of £10 each and for many years had been converted into stock. Reference to a vote *per* share or number of shares is accordingly a reference to multiples of stock of £10 denomination.

It was seen by each side in the coming trial of strength that it was to their advantage to subdivide larger holdings in order to increase the voting power attributable to the stock comprising such holdings. Because of the need to build up voting strength not only by purchasing stock in the market place but also by subdivision of existing holdings, a very large number of transfers were required and these were delivered to the Secretary in the days preceding the date fixed for the meeting. While less than ten such transfers a week was the norm, three hundred and eighty eight transfers were lodged in the last week of August, three hundred and forty one transfers on the 2nd and 3rd September, ten hundred and fifty two transfers on the 6th September, four hundred and forty nine transfers on the 7th September, three hundred and eighty six [3] transfers on the 8th September and seventy six transfers on the 9th September.

It was the secretary's duty to register these transfers. As might be expected, the facilities available to the secretary to process such a large number of transfers were inadequate and it became necessary for him to call in registration staff from Craig Gardner & Company the company's auditors to assist him in this job. The secretary's task was further complicated by the need to process some four thousand proxies delivered to him in respect of the meeting. Here again he was obliged to rely upon the assistance of the registration staff of Craig Gardner & Company. . . .

[4] It became obvious to Mr Jackson, one of the two solicitors acting for the plaintiffs, that the weight of paper being delivered by him to the company both in the form of stock transfers and proxies was such that there was a serious doubt whether or not all the transfers could be registered in time for the meeting. He telephoned Mr Hogan his colleague acting for the company on Wednesday the 8th September and asked him whether or not unregistered stockholders would be allowed to vote. Mr Hogan said that he would consider the matter. Mr Jackson rang Mr Hogan again that evening and was told by Mr Hogan that he had no answer for him yet but that he was getting counsel's opinion the following morning. On the following day Thursday the 9th September Mr Jackson wrote to Mr Hogan as follows:

"Dear Mr Hogan,

Further to my telephone conversation of the 8th instant, I wish to confirm my telephone conversation with you on the 8th in connection with the Alliance and Dublin Consumers Gas Company. My client, Donal Kinsella, shall be claiming a right to vote on foot of proxies lodged in respect of transfers which have been duly delivered to the Secretary and accepted by him prior to 11 o'clock on Wednesday the [5] 8th September, 1982.

I particularly confirm that I referred you to Sections 61, 62 and 64, as well as Sections 14 to 20 inclusive of the Companies Clauses Consolidation Act, 1845. In addition, I referred you to Halsburys Statutes of England, third edition, volume 5 page 49 and thereabouts as well as the case of Nanney v. Morgan (1887) 37 Ch.D. 346.

My client's supporters through their proxy of my client will be claiming entitlement to vote on foot of those proxies lodged concerning any stocks that may remain unregistered (but having been duly delivered) at the time of the meeting.

I would also point out that there appears to be no regulation whereby the register of transfers can he closed and it would be my client's contention that registration in any event can be completed by the time of the meeting of those transfers as yet unregistered in view of the number that were registered on Monday, the 6th September, 1982.

I felt it best to put the basics of our conversation and my client's contentions in writing at this stage even though I realise that at the time of writing you are urgently considering the contents of my telephone call.

Yours sincerely."

[6] On the same day Mr Hogan's secretary rang Mr Jackson to say that he had as yet no answer for him. He got no answer that day nor was he able to contact Mr Hogan the following morning prior to the meeting. He attended the meeting and learned from the opening remarks of the chairman of the meeting that the attendance of unregistered stockholders was not being permitted.

The plaintiffs complain that the failure to register all the transfers submitted was as a result of a conscious decision to deprive the transferees affected of their rights as stockholders and that the failure of Mr Hogan to answer the question put to him was part of that conscious decision and deprived them of the opportunity to apply to the Court for an injunction to restrain the holding of the meeting.

The evidence adduced shows that no more work could have been done by the registration staff prior to the meeting . . . [7] I have no evidence that there was any conscious decision by the board of the company or any one acting on its behalf to leave these transfers unregistered. The evidence is all to the contrary as I have indicated. . . .

No reasonable explanation was given for the failure by Mr Hogan to reply to the question raised by Mr Jackson. . . .

[8] The basic question raised in these proceedings is the stage at which a transferee of shares in the company becomes entitled to exercise his or her voting rights in respect of such shares. The plaintiffs say it is when the transfer of such shares is acknowledged by the secretary of the company to have been received by him. The defendants say it is when the stockholder is actually registered as a stockholder in the register of shareholders.

In support of his submission counsel for the plaintiffs relies on the wording of Section 15 of the 1845 Act, and on a passage in the judgment of Cotton L.J. in *Nanney v. Morgan*, 37 Ch.D. 346. Section 15 of the 1845 Act in so far as it is material is as follows:

"The said deed of transfer (when duly executed) shall be delivered to the secretary, and be kept by him; and the secretary shall enter a memorial thereof in a book to be called the 'Register of Transfers', and shall endorse such entry on the deed of transfer, and shall, on demand, deliver a new certificate to the purchaser, . . . and on the request of the purchaser of any share an endorsement of such transfer shall be made on the certificate of such share, [9] instead of a new certificate being granted; and such endorsement being signed by the secretary, shall be considered in every respect the same as a new certificate, and until such transfer has been so delivered to the secretary as aforesaid the vendor of the share shall continue liable to the company for any calls that may be made upon such share, and the purchaser of the share shall not be entitled to receive any share of the profits of the undertaking, or to vote in respect of such share."

In *Nanney v. Morgan*, Cotton L.J. at page 353 cites Section 15 from the words 'and until such transfer has been so delivered' until the end of the section and continues:

> "that as regards the company provides that the deeds shall not have any effect, so as to put the transferees into the position of the transferor until it has been left with the Secretary, and it must be not only left, but accepted by him as properly left, because if the secretary finds that it does not comply with the provisions of the Act it is his duty to refuse to receive it."

Further on in the same paragraph the judge says:

> "I do not place any reliance on the transferee being entered on the register, because when a deed of transfer duly executed is left with the [10] secretary, it becomes the duty of the company to register the transferee as entitled to the shares, and the mere neglect of the company to do that, will not in my opinion affect the right of the transferee to be treated as the legal owner of the shares."

This was the view of the majority of the Court, although one member, Lopes L.J. regarded it as unnecessary to express an opinion on the point.

The defendants' reply to this submission is that it is well settled law that only shareholders are entitled to vote and that, for the purpose of ascertaining who are shareholders, the company, whether incorporated under the Companies Acts or a statutory corporation as in the present case, need look only to its register of shareholders. Counsel for the defendants relied so far as companies governed by the 1845 Act are concerned, upon a passage in the judgment of Linley L.J. in *Powell v. London and Provincial Bank* [1893] 2 Ch. 555. At page 560 Linley L.J. said:

> ". . . in order to acquire the legal title to stock or shares in companies governed by the Companies Clauses Consolidation Act, you must have a deed, executed by the transferor, and you must have that transfer registered. Until you have got both you have not got the legal title in the transferee."

Counsel for the defendants also referred to several sections in the 1845 [11] Act in support of his argument. He relied particularly upon Sections 3, 8, 9 and 75. These sections are as follows:

> "3. The following words and expressions both in this and the special Act shall have the several meanings hereby assigned to them, unless there be something in the subject or the context repugnant to such construction: the word 'shareholder' shall mean a shareholder, proprietor, or member

of the company; and in referring to any such shareholder, expressions properly applicable to a person shall be held to apply to a Corporation.

8. Every person who shall have subscribed the prescribed sum or upwards to the capital of the company, or shall otherwise have become entitled to a share in the company, and those whose name shall have been entered on the register of shareholders hereinafter mentioned, shall be deemed a shareholder of the company.

9. The company shall keep a book, to be called the 'register of shareholders'; and in such book shall be fairly and distinctly entered, from time to time, the names of the several corporators, and the names and additions of the several persons entitled to shares in the company, together with the number of shares to which such [12] shareholders shall be respectively entitled. . . .

75. At the general meetings of the company every shareholder shall be entitled to vote according to the prescribed scale of voting, and where no scale shall be prescribed every shareholder shall have one vote for every share up to ten, and he shall have an additional vote for every five shares beyond the first ten shares held by him up to one hundred, and an additional vote for every ten shares held by him beyond the first one hundred shares. . . ."

Counsel further submitted that similar sections in the Companies Act 1862 and later Acts had been construed as he suggested, and relied amongst other decisions upon *Pender v. Lushington* (1877) 6 Ch. D. 471.

The provisions of the 1845 Act like any other document must be construed as a whole. I am of the view that they are quite clear. Persons entitled to stock must be registered in the register of shareholders. Until they are, they are not entitled to vote. This is a well established principle and I would be wrong not to follow it.

I do not regard either section 15 of the 1845 Act or the decision in *Nanney v. Morgan* as being contrary to this view. *Nanney v. Morgan* was a case in which the issue for the Court was whether a settlor of stock in a railway company held such stock under a legal or an equitable tide at the date of the [13] settlement. If he had held under a legal tide, a settlement would have been invalid, whereas if he had held under an equitable tide it would have been good. The Court took the view that if a valid transfer had been accepted by the secretary at the date of the settlement, the settlor would have had the legal estate, but that the failure of the company to do what it had to do, *i.e.* register the transferee in the register of shareholders, could not have affected the transferees rights. Presumably, the Court was acting on the equitable maxim that it regards as having been done that which ought to have been done and was not prepared to permit failure by a company to determine whether the settlement was effective or ineffective.

There is nothing either in section 15 which provides that the right to vote acquired by the transferee shall be exercisable before registration of the name of the transferee in the Register of Shareholders. Having regard to the view expressed in *Nanney v. Morgan* and the express words of Section 15 of the Act, it may be that the true interpretation of that section is that the legal interest when completed by registration relates back to the date of receipt of a valid transfer.

Informal Unanimity

See *Company Law*, pp. 96–97.

Cane v. Jones
[1981] 1 All E.R. 533

What had to be determined here was whether the unanimous consent of a company's members about its internal affairs is the equivalent of a special resolution amending the articules of association in relation to the matter. All the members of a family company, the shares in which were split evenly between two factions, at one stage agreed in writing that the chairman should not possess a casting vote at directors' meetings. The plaintiff contended that this agreement had the effect of a special resolution altering the company's articles of association.

WHEELER Q.C.: . . . [537] Counsel for the plaintiff contends that it operated as an alteration of the articles on what was conveniently called in argument 'the Duomatic principle' based on *Re Duomatic Ltd.* [1969] 2 Ch. 365, and the principle is, I think, conveniently summarised in a short passage in the judgment of Buckley J. in that case where he says:

> ". . . I proceed on the basis that where it can be shown that all shareholders who have a right to attend and vote at a general meeting of the company assent to some matter which a general meeting of the company could carry into effect, that assent is as binding as a resolution in general meeting would be."

Applying that principle to the present case, counsel for the plaintiff says that the agreement of all the shareholders embodied in the 1967 agreement had the effect, so far as requisite, of overriding the articles. In other words, it operated to deprive the chairman for the time being of the right to use his casting vote except, perhaps, in so far as an independent chairman contemplated by cl. 1 might need to do. I should add here that it is quite clear that Percy, who was actually chairman of the company at the time, was well aware of the terms of the 1967 agreement.

For the first and third defendants, counsel has two answers to counsel's argument for the plaintiff. First, that on its true interpretation in relation to a special or extraordinary resolution the *Duomatic* principle only applies if there has been (i) a resolution and (ii) a meeting; and that here he says, with some truth, there was neither a resolution nor a meeting of the four shareholders; second, he stresses that the agreement does not in terms purport to alter the articles at all: it rests, he says, solely in contract and Gillian, not being a party, cannot take either the benefit or the burden of the agreement.

On the first of these two arguments, counsel for the first and third defendants helpfully reminded me of the line of cases in which the effect of the unanimous consent of the corporators had been considered, starting with *Baroness Wenlock v. River Dee Co* [1883] 36 Ch.D. 675. I do not propose to refer to all these cases in detail but, for the record, I will list them. The other cases are *Re George Newman & Co* [1895] 1 Ch. 674. [538] Then there is *Re Express Engineering Works Ltd.* [1920] 1 Ch. 466, *Re Oxted Motor Co Ltd.* [1921] 3 K.B. 32, *Parker and Cooper Ltd. v. Reading* [1926] Ch. 975, *Re Pearce Duff & Co Ltd.* [1960] 3 All E.R. 222, *Re Duomatic*, to which I have already referred and finally a decision of Slade J. in *Re Moorgate Mercantile Holdings Ltd.* [1980] 1 All E.R. 40 (ante p. 147).

Counsel for the first and third defendants pointed out, correctly, that of these cases only three were concerned with special or extraordinary resolutions, namely *Re Pearce Duff & Co Ltd*, and *Re Moorgate Mercantile Holdings Ltd.* (both of which were concerned with special resolutions) and *Re Oxted Motor Co. Ltd.* (which is concerned with an extraordinary resolution). All the rest were concerned with matters which, if capable of ratification at all, could have been validated by ordinary resolutions.

The starting point of counsel for the first and third defendants is section 10 of the Companies Act 1948 which provides for the alteration of articles by special resolution; and from that he goes on to section 141, mentioning sub-ss. (1) and (2) and including the particular proviso, laying down how special and extraordinary resolutions are to be passed. First of all section 10 (same as section 15 of the 1963 Act):

"(1) Subject to the provisions of this Act and to the conditions contained in its memorandum, a company may by special resolution alter or add to its articles.

(2) Any alteration or addition so made in the articles shall, subject to the provisions of this Act, be as valid as if originally contained therein, and be subject in like manner to alteration by special resolution."

Then section 141 (similar to section 141 of the 1963 Act):

"(1) A resolution shall be an extraordinary resolution when it has been passed by a majority of not less than three fourths of such members as, being entitled so to do, vote in person or, where proxies are allowed, by proxy, at a general meeting of which notice specifying the intention to propose the resolution as an extraordinary resolution has been duly given.

(2) A resolution shall be a special resolution when it has been passed by such a majority as is required for the passing of an extraordinary resolution and at a general meeting of which not less than twenty-one days' notice, specifying the intention to propose the resolution as a special resolution, has been duly given. Provided that, if it is so agreed by a majority in number of the members having the right to attend and vote at any such meeting, being a majority together holding not less than ninety-five *per* cent. in nominal value of the shares giving that right, or in the case of a company not having a share capital, together representing not less than ninety-five *per* cent. of the total voting rights at that meeting of all the members, a resolution may be proposed and passed as a special resolution at a meeting of which less than twenty-one days' notice has been given. . . . ."

Thus, says counsel for the first and third defendants, you can only alter the articles by special resolution. That is his first argument. Secondly, a special resolution must be passed at a meeting; thirdly, here there was neither a resolution nor a meeting. . . .

[539] The first of counsel's two arguments for the first and third defendants (namely that there must be a 'resolution' and a 'meeting') does not appear to have been raised in any of the three reported cases which were concerned with special or extraordinary resolutions. But it is not an argument to which I would readily accede because in my judgment it would create a wholly artificial and unnecessary distinction between those powers which can, and those which cannot, be validly exercised by all the corporators acting together.

For my part I venture to differ from counsel for the first and third defendants on the first limb of his argument, namely that articles can *only* be altered by special resolution. In my judgment, section 10 of the Act, is merely laying down a procedure whereby *some only* of the shareholders can validly alter the articles; and, if, as I believe to be the case, it is a basic principle of company law that all the corporators, acting together, can do anything which is intra vires the company, then I see nothing in section 10 to undermine this principle. I accept that the principle requires all the corporators to 'act together'; but with regard to this I respectfully adopt what Astbury J. said in *Parker and Cooper Ltd. v. Reading.*

Now the view I take of both these decisions [those were in *Re Express*

Engineering Works Ltd. and *Re George Newman & Co*] is that where the transaction is intra vires and honest, and especially if it is for the benefit of the
company, it cannot be upset if the assent of all the corporators is given to it. I
do not think it matters in the least whether that assent is given at different
times or simultaneously.

See also *per* Younger L.J. in *Re Express Engineering Works Ltd.* at 471
and [540] the passage from the judgment of Buckley J. in *Re Duomatic Ltd.*
which I have read earlier in this judgment. I should add that the evidence in
the case before me is that the 1967 agreement was signed by 'the two sides' (if
I may call them that) separately and that they did not meet together, however
informally, for the purpose of signing the document. But it is clear beyond
doubt that the agreement did represent a meeting of minds which is, after all,
the essence of a meeting and the passing of a resolution.

Some light is also, I think, thrown on the problem by section 143(4) of the
1948 Act. Section 143 deals with the forwarding to the Registrar of Companies of copies of every resolution or agreement to which the section applies
(see 1963 Act, section 143), and sub-s. (4) reads as follows:

> "This section shall apply to – (*a*) special resolutions; (*b*) extraordinary
> resolutions; (*c*) resolutions which have been agreed to by all members of
> a company, but which, if not so agreed to, would not have been effective
> for their purpose unless, as the case may be, they had been passed as
> special resolutions or as extraordinary resolutions; (*d*) resolutions or
> agreements which have been agreed to by all the members of some class
> of shareholders but which, if not so agreed to, would not have been ef-
> fective for their purpose unless they had been passed by some particular
> majority or otherwise in some particular manner, and all resolutions or
> agreements which effectively bind all the members of any class of share-
> holders though not agreed to by all those members. . . ."

Paragraph (c) thus appears to recognise that you can have a resolution, at
least, which has been agreed to by all the members and is as effective as a
special or extraordinary resolution would have been, but, as counsel for the
first and third defendants was quick to point out, para. (*c*) says nothing about
'agreements' in contrast to para. (*d*) which refers to resolutions or agreements
which have been agreed to by all members of some class of shareholders. I
should say in passing that I think the reference in para. (*d*) to 'resolutions or
agreements' stems directly from Reg 4 of Part 1 of the 1948 Table A (similar
to reg. 3 in 1963 Act's Table A), which, dealing with class meetings, provides
briefly as follows:

> "If at any time the share capital is divided into different classes of shares,
> the rights attached to any class (unless otherwise provided by the terms
> of issue of the shares of that class) may, whether or not the company is

> being wound up, be varied with the consent in writing of the holders of
> three-fourths of the issued shares of that class, or with the sanction of an
> extraordinary resolution passed at a separate general meeting of the hold-
> ers of the shares of the class, so that you have either a consent which
> might be termed an agreement or a resolution."

I cannot regard this difference in drafting between paras (*c*) and (*d*) of section
143(4) as fatal to the basic argument. It may be, as counsel for the plaintiff
suggested, that a document which is framed as an agreement can be treated as
a 'resolution' for the purposes of para. (*c*). (I should add in passing that a copy
of the 1967 agreement was never, as far as I am aware, sent to the Registrar of
Companies for registration.) It may be that there is a gap in the registration
requirements of section 143. But be that as it may, the fact that the 1967 agreement was drafted as an agreement and not as a resolution, and that the four
signatories did not sign in each other's presence does not in my view prevent
that agreement overriding pro tanto, and so far as necessary, the articles of the
company; in my judgment counsel for the first and third defendants' first argument fails and unless he can show that the 1967 agreement has been superseded, the chairman of the company has no casting vote at board or general
meetings.

Note: In *Re Home Treat Ltd.* [1991] B.C.L.C. 705, Harman J. held that the
unanimous assent of a companys' members to a course of conduct that would
be *ultra vires* is equivalent to them passing a special resolution amending the
objects cause and rendering that conduct *intra vires*

DIVISION OF POWERS BETWEEN THE MEMBERS AND THE DIRECTORS

See *Company Law*, pp.97–102.

Table A art. 80

80.—The business of the company shall be managed by the directors, who
may pay all expenses incurred in promoting and registering the company and
may exercise all such powers of the company as are not, by the Act or by these
regulations, required to be exercised by the company in general meeting, subject, nevertheless, to any of these regulations, to the provisions of the Act and
to such directions, being not inconsistent with the aforesaid regulations or
provisions, as may be given by the company in general meeting; but no direction given by the company in general meeting shall invalidate any prior act of
the directors which would have been valid if that direction had not been given.

Automatic Self-Cleansing Filter Syndicate Co. Ltd. v. Cuninghalme
[1906] 2 Ch. 34

The matter in issue here is the extent to which the directors of a company, with articles similar to Article 80 of Table A (*supra*) are legally bound to act in accordance with members' resolutions. The company had power under its memorandum of association to sell its undertaking to another company having similar objects, and by its articles of association the general management and control of the company were vested in the directors, subject to such regulations as might from time to time be made by extraordinary resolution, and, in particular, the directors were empowered to sell or otherwise deal with any property of the company on such terms as they might think fit. At a general meeting of the company a resolution was passed by a simple majority of the shareholders for the sale of the company's assets on certain terms to a new company formed for the purpose of acquiring them, and directing the directors to carry the sale into effect. The directors, being of opinion that a sale on those terms was not for the benefit of the company, declined to carry the sale into effect.

COLLINS M.R.: [41] At a meeting of the company a resolution was passed by a majority – I was going to say a bare majority, but it was a majority – in favour of a sale to a purchaser, and the directors, honestly believing, as Warrington J. thought, that it was most undesirable in the interests of the company that the agreement should be carried into effect, refused to affix the seal of the company to it, or to assist in carrying out a resolution which they disapproved of; and the question is whether under the memorandum and articles of association here the directors are bound to accept, in substitution of their own view, the views contained in the resolution of the company. Warrington J. held that the majority could not impose that obligation upon the directors, and that on the true construction of the articles the directors were the persons [42] authorized by the articles to effect this sale, and that unless the other powers given by the memorandum were invoked by a special resolution, it was impossible for a mere majority at a meeting to override the views of the directors. That depends, as Warrington J. put it, upon the construction of the articles. First of all there is no doubt that the company under its memorandum has the power in clause 3 (*k*) to sell the undertaking of the company or any part thereof. In this case there is some small exception, I believe, to that which is to be sold, but I do not think that that becomes material. We now come to clause 81 of the articles, which I think it is important to refer to in this connection. [His Lordship read the clause.] Then come the two clauses which are most material, 96 and 97, whereby the powers of the directors are defined. [His Lordship read clause 96 and clause 97 (1).] Therefore in the matters referred to in article 97 (1) the view of the directors as to the fitness of the matter is made the standard; and furthermore, by article 96 they are given in express terms the full powers which the company has, except so far as they 'are not hereby or by statute expressly directed or required to be exercised or done by the company,' so that the directors have absolute power to do all things other than those that are expressly required to be done by the company; and then comes the limitation on their general authority – 'subject to such regulations as may from time to time be made by extraordinary resolution.' Therefore, if it is desired to alter the powers of the directors that must be done, not by a resolution carried by a majority at an ordinary meeting of the company, but by an extraordinary resolution. In these circumstances it seems to me that it is not competent for the majority of the shareholders at an ordinary meeting to affect or alter the mandate originally given to the directors, by the articles of association. It has been suggested that this is a mere question of principal and agent, and that it would be an absurd thing if a principal in appointing an agent should in effect appoint a dictator who is to manage him instead of managing the agent. I think that that analogy does not strictly apply to this case. No doubt for some purposes directors are agents. For whom are they agents? You have, no doubt, in theory and law [43] one entity, the company, which might be a principal, but you have to go behind that when you look to the particular position of directors. It is by the consensus of all the individuals in the company that these directors become agents and hold their rights as agents. It is not fair to say that a majority at a meeting is for the purposes of this case the principal so as to alter the mandate of the agent. The minority also must be taken into account. There are provisions by which the minority may be over-borne, but that can only be done by special machinery in the shape of special resolutions. Short of that the mandate which must be obeyed is not that of the majority – it is that of the whole entity made up of all the shareholders. If the mandate of the directors is to be altered, it can only be under the machinery of the memorandum and articles themselves. I do not think I need say more.

One argument used by Warrington J. strongly supports that view. He says in effect: 'There is to be found in these articles a provision that a director can only be removed by special resolution. What is the use of that provision if the views of the directors can be overridden by a mere majority at an ordinary meeting? Practically you do not want any special power to remove directors if you can do without them and differ from their opinion and compel something other than their view to be carried into effect.' That argument appears to me to confirm the view taken by the learned judge.

COZENS-HARDY L.J.: . . . [44] [I]t seems to me that the shareholders by their express contract mutually stipulated that their common affairs should be managed by certain directors to be appointed by the shareholders in the manner described by other articles, such directors being liable to be removed only by special resolution. If you once get a stipulation of that kind in a contract made between the parties, what right is there to interfere with the contract, apart, of course, from any misconduct on the part of the directors? There is no such misconduct in the present case. Is there any analogy which supports the case of the plaintiffs? I think not. It seems to me the analogy is all the other way. Take the case of an ordinary partnership. If in an ordinary partnership there is a stipulation in the partnership deed that the partnership business shall be managed by one of the partners, it would be plain that in the absence of misconduct, or in the absence of circumstances involving the total dissolution of the partnership, the majority of the partners would have no right to apply to the Court to restrain him or to interfere with the management of the partnership business. I would refer to what is said in *Lindley on Partnership*, 7th ed. p. 574: 'Where, however, the partner complained of has by agreement been constituted the active managing partner, the Court will not interfere with him unless a strong case be made out against him' – that is to say, unless there is some case of fraud or misconduct to justify the interference of the Court. Nor is this doctrine limited to [45] a case of co-partners. It is not a peculiar incident of co-partnership: it applies equally to cases of co-ownership. I think in some of the earlier cases before Lord Eldon with reference to the co-owners of one of the theatres, he laid down the principle that when the co-owners had appointed a particular member as manager the Court would not, except in the case of misconduct, interfere with him. And why? Because it is a fallacy to say that the relation is that of simple principal and agent. The person who is managing is managing for himself as well as for the others. It is not in the least a case where you have a master on the one side and a mere servant on the other. You are dealing here, as in the case of a partnership, with parties having individual rights as to which there are mutual stipulations for their common benefit, and when you once get that, it seems to me that there is no ground for saying that the mere majority can put an end to the express stipulations contained in the bargain which they have made. Still less can that be so when you find in the contract itself provisions which shew an intention that the powers conferred upon the directors can only be varied by extraordinary resolution, that is to say, by a three-fourths majority at one meeting, and that the directors themselves when appointed shall only be removed by special resolution, that is to say, by three-fourths majority at one meeting and a simple majority at a confirmatory meeting. That being so, if you once get clear of the view that the directors are mere agents of the company, I cannot see anything in principle to justify the contention that the directors are bound to comply with the votes or the resolutions of a simple majority at an ordinary meeting of the shareholders. I do not think it true to say that the directors are agents. I think it is more nearly true to say that they are in the position of managing partners appointed to fill that post by a mutual arrangement between all the shareholders. So much for principle. On principle I agree entirely with what the Master of the Rolls has said, agreeing as he does with the conclusions of Warrington J.

Breckland v. London and Suffolk Properties
[1989] B.C.L.C. 100

This case concerns whether it is the directors or a majority of the members who are entitled to authorise that legal proceedings be instituted by the company. Breckland owned 49% and Crompton owned 51% of the shares of the company. A shareholders' agreement provided that Crompton was entitled to appoint two non-executive directors and that Breckland was entitled to appoint one director to the board: also that the institution of material legal proceedings by the company had to have the support of one Crompton and one Breckland director. Proceedings were commenced in the company's name against, *inter alios*, A, who was the principal shareholder in Breckland and also the managing director of the company. The action was commenced without any prior board resolution and was purportedly authorised by Crompton. A board meeting was summoned, at which a resolution was to be proposed to adopt and ratify the action. Breckland commenced proceedings for, inter alia, an injunction to restrain (i) Crompton and its principal shareholder from using the name of the company in the proceedings commenced on 8 July 1988 and (ii) the company from taking further steps in the action without leave of the court.

HARMAN J.: [104] The question whether articles of association in the form or Art. 80, which applies to this company, are such as to allow a general meeting to give directions to directors about the conduct of the business of a company has long been known to be a vexed subject. The decision of Jessel MR, one of the greatest of all equity judges, in *Pender v. Lushington* (1877) 6 Ch. D 70, is as always with that great judge, clear and to the point. He firmly holds that in that case he ought not, there being an action started without any proper authorisation on behalf of the company, to strike out the name of the company on the ground that the action was unauthorised, but he ought to stand the matter over to let a general meeting be called to decide whether the company's name was to be used or not. However, that matter does not appear to have turned on the terms of the articles of association there, and I cannot find in the citation of facts in the report of that case any reference to an article in terms anything like Art. 8o in this case.

There is then the well-known decision of Neville J. in *Marshall's Valve Gear Co. Ltd. v. Manning Wardle & Co Ltd.* [1909] 1 Ch. 267, where he purported to distinguish *Automatic Self-Cleansing Filter Syndicate Co Ltd. v. Cuninghame* [1906] 2 Ch. 34 (see *supra*, p. 179), and decided, in a case where there was an article in almost precisely the same terms as art 80, that the general meeting was entitled to decide what should be done about an action brought without due authority. That decision was reached in November 1908, and in December of that same year *Salmon v. Quin & Axtens Ltd.* [1909] 1 Ch. 311 (see *post*, p. 435) came before a two-judge Court of Appeal with distinguished members sitting, Cozens-Hardy MR and Farwell L.J. In that case the argument seeking to upset the decision below included a straight attack on the *Marshall's Valve Gear* case. It was said to be distinguishable because there was a matter of personal interest involved, but also that Neville J. had taken his view inconsistently with the principles in the *Automatic Self-Cleansing Filter* case. The judgment of Farwell L.J., who delivered the first judgment, sets the matter out very clearly, and particularly adopts the observations of Buckley L.J. in *Gramophone and* [105] *Typewriter Ltd. v. Stanley* [1908] 2 KB 89 at 105 (see [1909] 1 Ch. 311 at 319). Farwell L.J. held that the resolutions to be proposed to a general meeting were inconsistent with Art 80. It was an attempt to alter the terms of the contract constituted by the articles by a simple resolution instead of by a special resolution. Farwell L.J. went on to say that the case was entirely governed, if not by the decision, at any rate by the reasoning of the Lords Justices in the *Automatic Self-Cleansing* case, and he cited Buckley L.J. in *Gramophone and Typewriter Ltd. v. Stanley* [1908] 2 K.B. 89 at 105-106:

> ". . . even a resolution of a numerical majority at a general meeting of the company cannot impose its will upon the directors when the articles have confided to them the control of the company's affairs. The directors are not servants to obey directions given by the shareholders as individuals; they are not agents appointed by and bound to serve the shareholders as their principals. They are persons who may by the regulations be entrusted with the control of the business, and if so entrusted they call be dispossessed from that control only by the statutory majority which can alter the articles."

Farwell L.J. went on to say ([1909] 1 Ch. 311 at 319-320):

> "Any other construction might, I think, be disastrous, because it might lead to all interference by a bare majority very inimical to the interests of the minority who had come into a company on the footing that the business should be managed by the board of directors."

That sentence appears to me to be directly applicable to what has happened in this particular case. The decision in *Salmon v. Quin & Axtens Ltd.* was approved by the House of Lords *sub nom Quin & Axtens Ltd. v. Salmon* [1909] AC 442. without the respondents even being called on, and Lord Loreburn LC delivered an unreserved short judgment saying ([1909] AC 442 at 443):

> "The bargain made between the shareholders is contained in articles 75 and 80 of the articles of association, and it amounts for the purpose in hand to this, that the directors should manage the business; and the company, therefore, are not to manage the business unless there is provision to that effect."

Lord Macnaghten went so far as to say that he thought the judgment of the Court of Appeal was perfectly right (at 444). That encomium on Farwell L.J.'s judgment is one which many would have been glad to have had for themselves from such a source.

Thus one has in my view observations which are not stated to be expressly overruling Neville J.'s decision but are inevitably wholly in conflict with it. I would cite only briefly also the well-known decision in *John Shaw & Sons (Salford) Ltd. v. Shaw* [1935] 2 K.B. 113 at 134 where Greer L.J. observed:

> "A company is all entity distinct alike from its shareholders and its directors. Some of its powers may, according to its articles, be exercised by directors, certain other powers may be reserved for the shareholders in general meeting. If powers of management are vested in the directors, they and they alone can exercise these powers. The only way in which the general body of the shareholders call control the exercise of the powers vested by the articles in the directors is by altering their articles. . . ."

[106] That is entirely to the same effect and is of course a citation from high authority on the Queen's Bench side of the law.

Thus, as it seems to me, there is little doubt that the law is that, where a matters are confided by articles such as art 80 to the conduct of the business by the directors, it is not a matter where the general meeting can intervene. Counsel for the defendants sought to distinguish the cases by saying that in the cases which have been referred to the directors had come to one decision and the general meeting sought to overrule them and come to an opposite decision. In my belief that factor or distinction which undoubtedly exists is not a distinction which in law affects the principles which I have to try and apply. The principle, as I see it, is that art 80 confides the management of the business to the directors and in such a case it is not for the general meeting to interfere. It is a fortiori when the shareholders coming together have specifically resolved some matters be required to have their joint consent and have confided that matter particularly to the directors. That seems to me to reinforce the general proposition which I derive from the authorities cited.

Thus, as it seems to me, the action was, as is admitted, wrongly brought: it cannot at present be known whether the board will adopt it or ratify it on 3 August. If the board do not adopt it, a general meeting would have no power whatever to override that decision of the board and to adopt it for itself. Thus at the moment there can be no certainty whatever as to what would happen. It seems to me that in those circumstances I ought to restrain further steps in this action pending a decision whether the company will by its proper organ, that is the board, adopt it. It may do so. If so, it will be valid and ratified and adopted from its initiation.

In those circumstances as it seems to me I ought to say that until that matter is decided no further steps should be taken in action no 1951. I will not and

I should not strike it out at present. The matter of striking out must await later resolution. It could not be right at present when there is a pending board meeting. But it is right to say that an unauthorised action should not be pursued, particularly not at the cost of the company whose funds may be being wrongly misapplied. Further, in my judgment, a party should not obtain an advantage out of an action which is, by definition, wrongly constituted at present, over other parties by wrongfully, at present, taking the name of the company into his own hands and using it without authority. Thus, as it seems to me, a temporary stay on all further steps in action no 1951 ought to be imposed on the particular persons concerned, Crompton and Mr Holmes. The form of the order in the notice of motion in para 1, restraining them from continuing in the name of London and Suffolk to carry on the action seems to me a proper one which I ought to make.

An order restraining the company itself from purporting to take any further steps seems to me necessarily to follow. There is a relationship between the plaintiff and the company in that the plaintiff is a 49% shareholder of the company. It is plainly wrong that the company's affairs be conducted in a manner which is wholly unauthorised and a shareholder in my view has a right to bring an action to restrain the company from so conducting itself. I therefore make an order in the terms of para. 2 of the notice of motion also.

Note: In *Mitchell & Hobbs (U.K.) Ltd. v. Mills* [1996] 2 B.C.L.C. 102, proceedings brought by a company's managing director in the company's name were struck out because, under a variant of Article 80 of Table A, the management of the company was entrusted to the board of directors as a whole, unless the board delegated certain functions, and the authority to institute litigation had not been delegated to the managing director.

In *Fletcher Hunt (Bristol) Ltd.* [1989] B.C.L.C. 108 a claim that solicitors pay the costs of an action, on the grounds that it had not been properly authorised by the company, was dismissed by Knox J. because all of the shareholders had informally agreed to those proceedings being instituted, as had one director/shareholder.

Shareholders' Agreements

Russell v. Northern Bank Development Corp.
[1992] 1 W.L.R. 588

Shareholders' agreements are a common feature in private companies, especially so-called quasi-partnerships. A holding company was set up to effect a merger of two other companies. Of the original 1,000 £1 authorised share capital, 200 shares were allotted to the five original shareholders, the rest remained unallotted. The shareholders entered into an agreement, to which the company itself was also a party, "to regulate the relationship between them with regard to the management and control of the company as long as they remained shareholders". Clause 3 provided, *inter alia*, that "no further share capital shall be created or issued in the company . . . without written consent of each of the parties hereto." In 1988, an extraordinary general meeting was called to consider a proposal that the share capital of the company be increased (from £1,000 to £4,000,000) and allotted on a *pro rata* basis. The plaintiff, a shareholder, applied for an injunction restraining the defendants – the other four shareholders – from voting upon the resolution.

LORD JAUNCY OF TULLICHETTE: – [592] In March 1988 article 131 of the Companies (Northern Ireland) Order 1986 (S.I. 1986 No. 1032 (N.I. 6)) was in force and was in, inter alia. the following terms:

> "(1) A company limited by shares or a company limited by guarantee and having a share capital, if so authorised by its articles, may alter the conditions of its memorandum in any of the following ways. (2) The company may – (*a*) increase its share capital by new shares of such amount as it thinks expedient; . . ." (same as section 68(1)(1) of the 1963 Act).

Article 1 of the articles of association of T.B.L. incorporates the regulations contained in Part 11 of Table A in the first Schedule to the Companies Act (Northern Ireland) 1960 of which regulation 44 provides:

> "The company may from time to time by ordinary resolution increase the share capital by such sum, to be divided into shares of such amount, as the resolution shall prescribe."

It follows that of as the date of the proposed extraordinary general meeting T.B.L. had statutory power to increase its share capital.

The issue between the parties in this House was whether article 3 of the agreement constituted an unlawful and invalid fetter on the statutory power of T.B.L. to increase its share capital or whether it was no more than an agreement between the shareholders as to their manner of voting in a given situation. Both parties accepted the long established principle that "a company cannot forgo its right to alter its articles:" *Southern Foundries* (1926) *Ltd. v. Shirlaw* [1940] A.C. 701, 739, *per* Lord Porter. A principle that was earlier stated in *Allen v. Gold Reefs of West Africa Ltd.* [1900] 1 Ch. 656, 671 (see *post*, p. 506), *per* Lindley M.R.:

> "the company is empowered by the statute to alter the regulations contained in its articles from time to time by special resolutions (sections 50 and 51 of the Companies Act 1861); and any regulation or article purporting to deprive the company of this power is invalid on the ground

that it is contrary to the statute: *Walker v. London Tramways Co.* (1879) 12 Ch.D. 705".

Murray J. and MacDermott L.J. both considered that this principle applied also to the right of a company to alter its memorandum and I agree that this must be the case. Mr. McCartney for the plaintiff advanced a number of arguments to the effect that the agreement in no way contravened the above principle in as much as it was merely an agreement between shareholders outside the scope of company legislation [593] which in no way fettered the statutory power of T.B.L. to alter its memorandum and articles. Mr. Girvan, on the other hand, submitted that the agreement was not only a voting arrangement between shareholders inter se but was tantamount to an article of association which constituted a restriction on the power of T.B.L. to alter its share capital.

My Lords while a provision in a company's articles which restricts its statutory power to alter those articles is invalid an agreement dehors the articles between shareholders as to how they shall exercise their voting rights on a resolution to alter the articles is not necessarily so. In *Welton v. Saffery* [1897] A.C. 299, 331, which concerned an ultra vires provision in the articles of association authorising the company to issue shares at a discount, Lord Davey said:

> "Of course, individual shareholders may deal with their own interests by contract in such way as they may think fit. But such contracts, whether made by all or some only of the shareholders, would create personal obligations, or an *exceptio personalis* against themselves only, and would not become a regulation of the company, or be binding on the transferees of the parties to it, or upon new or non-assenting shareholders. There is no suggestion here of any such private agreement outside the machinery of the Companies Acts."

I understand Lord Davey there to be accepting that shareholders may lawfully agree inter se to exercise their voting rights in a manner which, if it were dictated by the articles, and were thereby binding on the company would be unlawful.

I turn to examine the agreement in more detail. It appears from the narrative clauses that the agreement was intended to regulate the relationship between the shareholders with regard to the management and control of T.B.L. Clause 1 provides that the terms of the agreement shall have precedence "*between the shareholders* over the articles of association" (the emphasis is mine). It further provides that where there is a conflict between the provisions of the agreement and the articles parties shall co-operate where necessary to have the articles amended to take account of the provisions of the agreement. It further provides that no further share capital shall be created or issued in T.B.L, without the written consent of the parties to the agreement. T.B.L. was incorporated under a previous name on 13 July 1979 and the agreement was executed on 14 December of that year. Since that date no attempt has been made to amend the articles for the purposes of clause 1 but I do not find that in any way surprising because clause 3 affects only existing shareholders and does not purport to bind other persons who may at some future date become shareholders in T.B.L. by allotment or transfer. Clause 3 at least so far as shareholders are concerned constitutes an agreement collateral to the provisions of regulation 44 of Table A and is, as MacDermott L.J. has concluded, neither in substitution for nor in conflict with that regulation.

However, it must be remembered that the agreement was executed not only by the shareholders but also by T.B.L. In *Bushell v. Faith* [1969] 5 Ch. 438 (see *supra*, p. 165) one of the articles of a private company provided that in the event of a resolution being proposed at a general meeting of the company for the removal of a director any share held by him should carry three votes *per* share. The issued capital of the company was [594] equally divided between three persons and an attempt by two shareholders to remove the third from the office of director failed because his 300 votes outnumbered the 200 of the two other shareholders. It was held that the article in question was not invalidated by section 184 of the Companies Act 1948 (same as section 182 of the 1963 Act) which empowered a company by ordinary resolution to remove a director. Russell L.J. said, at pp. 147-448:

> "Mr. Dillon argued by reference to section 10. and the well known proposition that a company cannot by its articles or otherwise deprive itself of the power by special resolution to alter its articles or any of them. But the point is the same one. An article purporting to do this is ineffective. But a provision as to voting rights which has the effect of making a special resolution incapable of being passed, if a particular shareholder or group of shareholders exercises his or their voting rights against a proposed alteration, is not such a provision. An article in terms providing that no alteration shall be made without the consent of X is contrary to section 10 and ineffective. But the provision as to voting rights that I have mentioned is wholly different, and it does not serve to say that it can have the same result."

Both parties sought to derive comfort from this dictum. Mr. McCartney relied on it as demonstrating that a provision as to the exercise of voting rights, even although it had the effect of preventing a resolution being passed, was nevertheless valid. Mr. Girvan argued that the effect of clause 3 was the same as that of an article containing a provision that "no alteration should be made without the consent of X."

I do not doubt that if clause 3 had been embodied in the articles of association so as to be binding on all persons who were or might become shareholders in T.B.L. it would have been invalid but it was, of course, not so embodied.

To my mind the significant part of this dictum for the purposes of this appeal is the words "articles or otherwise" occurring in the first sentence thereof. These words appear to recognise that it is not only fetters on the power to alter articles of association imposed by the statutory framework of a company which are obnoxious. Turning back to clause 3 of the agreement it appears to me that its purpose was twofold. The shareholders agreed only to exercise their voting powers in relation to the creation or issue of shares in T.B.L. if they and T.B.L. agreed in writing. This agreement is purely personal to the shareholders who executed it and as I have already remarked does not purport to bind future shareholders. It is, in my view, just such a private agreement as was envisaged by Lord Davey in *Welton v. Saffery* [1897] A.C. 299, 331. T.B.L. on the other hand agreed that its capital would not be increased without the consent of each of the shareholders. This was a clear undertaking by T.B.L. in a formal agreement not to exercise its statutory powers for a period which could, certainly on one view of construction, last for as long as any one of the parties to the agreement remained a shareholder and long after the control of T.B.L. had passed to shareholders who were not party to the agreement. As such an undertaking it is. in my view, as obnoxious as if it had been contained in the articles of association and therefore is unenforceable as being contrary to the provisions of article 131 of the Companies (Northern Ireland) Order 1986. T.B.L.'s undertaking is, however, independent of and severable from that of the shareholders and there is no reason why the latter should not he enforceable by the shareholders [595] *inter se* as a personal agreement which in no way fetters T.B.L. in the exercise of its statutory powers. I would therefore allow the appeal.

CHAPTER 5

Management and the Directors

By law, every company must have directors and a secretary, and various duties regarding the company's affairs are imposed on these officers. In a typical company, there will be a board of directors comprising a managing director, some salaried executive directors who work full time for the company, and some non-executive directors who have significant business interests elsewhere as well. Especially in large companies, various managerial functions will be assigned to management committees. Occasionally, companies delegate the running of their business to outsiders through what are known as management contracts. Ordinarily, it is the shareholders who select the directors; and directors can be removed by a simple majority vote of the shareholders. Directors must not be negligent in exercising their functions, and they owe their company extensive fiduciary duties. The Companies Acts have established an elaborate set of rules governing directors' remuneration and the disclosure of information about directors' affairs to the shareholders and to the general public.

THE SYSTEM OF MANAGEMENT

See *Company Law*, pp. 103–109.

Companies Act 1963, sections 174, 175(1) and 178

Directors

174.—Every company shall have at least two directors.

Secretary

175.—(1) Every company shall have a secretary, who may be one of the directors.

Validity of acts of directors

178.—The acts of a director shall be valid notwithstanding any defect which may afterwards be discovered in his appointment or qualification.

Table A articles 75, 88-89, 101–112

75. The number of the directors and the names of the first directors shall be determined in writing by the subscribers of the memorandum of association or a majority of them.

88. All cheques, promissory notes, drafts, bills of exchange and other negotiable instruments and all receipts for moneys paid to the company shall be signed, drawn, accepted, endorsed or otherwise executed, as the case may be, by such person or persons and in such manner as the directors shall from time to time by resolution determine.

89. The directors shall cause minutes to be made in books provided for the purpose–

(*a*) of all appointments of officers made by the directors;

(*b*) of the names of the directors present at each meeting of the directors and of any committee of the directors;

(*c*) of all resolutions and proceedings at all meetings of the company and of the directors and of committees of directors.

Proceedings of Directors

101. The directors may meet together for the despatch of business, adjourn and otherwise regulate their meetings as they think fit. Questions arising at any meeting shall be decided by a majority of votes. Where there is an equality of votes, the chairman shall have a second or casting vote. A director may, and the secretary on the requisition of a director shall, at any time summon a meeting of the directors. If the directors so resolve, it shall not be necessary to give notice of a meeting of directors to any director who, being resident in the State, is for the time being absent from the State.

102. The quorum necessary for the transaction of the business of the directors may be fixed by the directors, and unless so fixed shall be two.

103. The continuing directors may act notwithstanding any vacancy in their number but, if and so long as their number is reduced below the number fixed by or pursuant to the regulations of the company as the necessary quorum of directors, the continuing directors or director may act for the purpose of increasing the number of directors to that number or of summoning a general meeting of the company but for no other purpose.

104. The directors may elect a chairman of their meetings and determine the period for which he is to hold office, but if no such chairman is elected, or, if at any meeting the chairman is not present within five minutes after the time appointed for holding the same, the directors present may choose one of their number to be chairman of the meeting

105. The directors may delegate any of their powers to committees consisting of such member or members of the board as they think fit; any committee so formed shall, in the exercise of the powers so delegated, conform to any regulations that may be imposed on it by the directors.

106. A committee may elect a chairman of its meetings; if no such chairman is elected, or if at any the chairman is not present within five minutes after the time appointed for holding, the members present may choose one of their number to be chairman of the meeting.

107. A committee may meet and adjourn as it thinks proper. Questions arising at any meeting shall be determined by a majority of votes of the members present, and where there is an equality of votes, the chairman shall have a second or casting vote.

108. All acts done by any meeting of the directors or of a committee of directors or by any person acting as a director shall, notwithstanding that it be afterwards discovered that there was some defect in the appointment of any such director or person acting as aforesaid, or that they or any of them were disqualified, be as valid as if every such person had been duly appointed and was qualified to be a director.

109. A resolution in writing signed by all the directors for the time being entitled to receive notice of a meeting of the directors shall be as valid as if it had been passed at a meeting of the directors duly convened and held.

Managing Director

110. The directors may from time to time appoint one or more of themselves to the office of managing director for such period and on such terms as to remuneration and otherwise as they think fit, and, subject to the terms of any agreement entered into in any particular case, may revoke such appointment. A director so appointed shall not, whilst holding that office, be subject to retirement by rotation or be taken into account in determining the rotation of retirement of directors but (without prejudice to any claim he may have for damages for breach of any contract of service between him and the company), his appointment shall be automatically determined if he ceases from any cause to be a director.

111. A managing director shall receive such remuneration whether by way of salary, commission or participation in the profits, or partly in one way and partly in another, as the directors may determine.

112. The directors may entrust to and confer upon a managing director any of the powers exercisable by them upon such terms and conditions and with such restrictions as they may think fit, and either collaterally with or to the exclusion of their own powers, and may from time to time revoke, withdraw, alter or vary all or any of such powers.

Secretary

113. The secretary shall be appointed by the directors for such term, at such remuneration and upon such conditions as they may think fit; and any secretary so appointed may be removed by them.

114. A provision of the Act or these regulations requiring or authorising a thing to be done by or to a director and the secretary shall not be satisfied by its being done by or to the same person acting both as director and as, or in place of, the secretary.

Barron v. Potter
[1914] 1 Ch. 895

To what extent can directors be manoeuvred or tricked into attending meetings and can decisions be taken therein? See *supra*, p. 164 for one aspect of this case. Owing to the refusal of Barron to attend any board meeting the position of the affairs of the company was becoming so serious that Potter was advised in the interests of the company to meet Barron wherever he could be found and to use his casting vote as chairman in case Barron should refuse to agree to the appointment of additional directors. He met the train at Paddington by which he expected Barron to arrive, and seeing him alight from it walked by his side along the platform and said to him, 'I want to see you, please.' Barron replied, 'I have nothing to say to you.' Potter then said, 'I formally propose that we add the Reverend Charles Herbert, Mr William George Walter Barnard, and Mr John Tolehurst Musgrave as additional directors to the board of the British Seagumite Company, Limited. Do you agree or object?' Barron replied, 'I object and I object to say anything to you at all.' Potter then said, 'In my capacity as chairman I give my casting vote in their favour and declare them duly elected.' He continued to walk with Barron a few steps and then said, 'That is all I want to say; thank you. Good day.'

WARRINGTON J.: . . . [900] The question is whether certain additional directors appointed at a general meeting of the company were validly appointed or whether certain additional directors were validy appointed at a directors' meeting, in which case the resolution of the company in general meeting would be invalid. . . . [901] What then took place is said to have been a directors' meeting at which a valid appointment was made of the three additional directors proposed by Mr Potter. The answer, in my opinion, is that there was no directors' meeting at all for the reason that Canon Barron to the knowledge of Mr Potter insisted all along that he would not attend any directors' meeting with Mr Potter or discuss the affairs of the company with him, and it is not enough that one of two directors should say 'This is a directors' meeting' while the other says it is not. Of course if directors are willing to hold a meeting they may do so under any circumstances, but one of them cannot be made to attend the board or to convert a casual meeting into a board meeting, and in the present case I do not see how the meeting in question can be treated as a board meeting. In my opinion therefore the true conclusion is that there was no board meeting, but that Canon Barron came with the deliberate intention of not attending a board meeting. If he had received the notice sent to him by Mr Potter summoning him to a board meeting different considerations might have arisen, but he had not received it and came with the fixed intention of not attending any such meeting. There was therefore no board meeting at which Canon Barron was present. Mr Potter was alone present, so that there was no quorum, and I must hold that the three additional directors named by him were not validly appointed.

Clark v. Workman
[1920] 1 I.R. 107

Who, if anyone, is entitled to chair directors' meetings can be vital at times. This dispute concerned the take-over of a company (see *post*, p. 557). At a general meeting of the company held in March 1881, the following resolution was passed: 'That Mr John Workman and Mr Charles Workman be re-elected directors for the ensuing year, and Mr Frank Workman be elected chairman.' From that time on, Mr Frank Workman acted as chairman without objection on the part of the other directors.

ROSS J.: . . . [114] The first question that arises is whether Mr Frank Workman [is] lawfully chairman of.. the directors. . . . The articles dealing with this matter are 91, 92, and 93. Article 91 provides that questions arising at any meeting of directors shall be decided by a majority of votes of those present, and in case of an equality of votes the chairman of the meeting shall have a casting vote. Article 92 provides that the directors may appoint a chairman and vice-chairman of their meetings, and determine the period for which he or they shall hold office. There you have the precise contract with the shareholders, and it is [115] essential that the chairman should be elected by the machinery provided by that contract, and in no other way. The power of electing a chairman having a casting vote is of vital importance. The power having been delegated by the company to the directors, cannot be controlled or affected by the company, unless the contract is altered by a special resolution, but no such special resolution was passed. Article 93 provides that all meetings shall be presided over by the chairman of the directors (if any) if present. This article contemplates the possibility of the elected chairman's death or the expiration of his period of office as fixed by Article 92. In that case the directors are to choose one of their number to preside.

The defendant, Mr Frank Workman, was never appointed by the directors as chairman of their meetings. The defendants say that the resolution passed at the general meeting of shareholders held on the 21st March, 1881, was sufficient. . . . This is claimed to have the effect of conferring on Mr Frank Workman the chairmanship, not for the ensuing year only, but for life or until removal.

But the election of a chairman of directors is not the function of a general meeting. It can elect directors, but not the chairman of the directors. The minute does not state who attended. It is thirty-eight years ago since the meeting was held. But even assuming that nobody attended, it is not a meeting of directors. It is a general meeting, and all attended as shareholders, and in no other capacity.

Morris v. Kanssen
[1946] A.C. 459

To what extent do irregularities in convening and/or conducting directors' meetings invalidate decisions made there, in the light of section 178 of the 1963 Act (see *supra*, p. 190). Cromie and Kanssen were the only directors and the only shareholders in a company, holding one share each. C. and one Strelitz falsely claimed that at a meeting held at that time was duly appointed a director and a minute was concocted to record the alleged appointment. Two months later, C. and S. requested K. to resign his office and on April 12, they purported to hold a meeting of directors and to issue one share to S. and seven more shares to C. An extraordinary general meeting of the company was held at which G, K. and S. were present; C. moved and S. purported to second a resolution to confirm the appointment of S. as a director. C. voted in favour of the resolution and K. against it and S. having purported to vote in favour of it, it was treated as carried, so that S. thereafter purported to act as a director. Subsequently S. purported to hold a meeting of directors and thereat to appoint one M. a director; all three then purported to allot thirty-four shares to M.; thirty-two more shares to S., and twenty-four more shares to C. Subsequently S. transferred seventeen of his shares to M.

LORD SIMMONDS: . . . [470] Section 143 of the Companies Act, 1929, which is in the same terms as corresponding sections in previous Acts, provides that: 'The acts of a director or manager shall be valid notwithstanding any defect that may afterwards be discovered in his appointment or qualification.' (see section 178 of the 1963 Act). Article 88 of Table A (Article 108 of 1963 Act's Table A), which does not materially differ from similar articles in earlier Tables, provides that 'All acts done by any meeting of the directors or of a committee of directors, or by any person acting as a director, shall notwithstanding that it be afterwards discovered that there was some defect in the appointment of any such director or person acting as aforesaid, or that they or any of them were disqualified, be as valid as if every such person had been duly appointed and was qualified to be a director.' The section can be invoked only where there is a defect afterwards discovered in the appointment or qualification of a director; in the article the condition is that it is afterwards discovered that there was some defect in the appointment of a director or person acting as a director or that he was disqualified to act as a director. Though the language of the section differs in some respects from that of the article, it does not appear that the difference is material for the purpose of the present case.

The facts relevant to the question now under consideration have already been stated. I will very briefly tabulate them: (1) On February 1, 1940, Cromie and Kanssen were the only directors and the only shareholders holding one share each. (2) On or about that date the fraudulent, assumption of office by Strelitz and a minute concocted to record an appointment which did not take place. (3) On April 9, 1940, an ineffective attempt to expel Kanssen from his office. (4) On April 12, [471] 1940, the ineffective allotment of one share to Strelitz and seven shares to Cromie at a purported meeting of directors. (5) On April 26, 1940, an extraordinary general meeting of the company at which as I have pointed out nothing was effectively done. (6) At the end of 1941 the determination of the term of office of Cromie and Kanssen and of Strelitz, if he was a director, and from that date no directors of the company.

It is in these circumstances that the question arises whether the section or article can be called in aid by Morris in order to validate the transactions of March 30, 1942, namely, the allotment to him of shares or the appointment of him as a director. Do the facts that I have stated establish a defect in the appointment or qualification of Cromie or Strelitz? There is, as it appears to me, a vital distinction between (a) an appointment in which there is a defect or, in other words, a defective appointment, and (b.) no appointment at all. In the first case it is implied that some act is done which purports to be an appointment but is by reason of some defect inadequate for the purpose; in the second case there is not a defect, there is no act at all. The section does not say that the acts of a person acting as director shall be valid notwithstanding that it is afterwards discovered that he was not appointed a director. Even if it did, it might well be contended that at least a purported appointment was postulated. But it does not do so, and it would, I think, be doing violence to plain language to construe the section as covering a case in which there has been no genuine attempt to appoint at all. These observations apply equally where the term of office of a director has expired, but he nevertheless continues to act as a director, and where the office has been from the outset usurped without the colour of authority. Cromie's acts after the end of 1941 were not validated by the section: Strelitz's acts were at no time validated. I have so far dealt with defect in 'appointment' and what I have said in regard to the section covers the article also where the same words are repeated. Some argument was founded by counsel for the appellant upon the words in the section 'or qualification' and in the article 'disqualified'. This argument is not easy to follow. So far as both Cromie and Strelitz were concerned, there was no defect in their qualification after the end of 1941. They were not disqualified. They were, so far as I know, qualified to act, but they had not been appointed. [472] I do not suggest that qualification refers only to the holding of qualification shares. But whatever extended meaning may be given to 'qualification' or 'disqualified' I find it impossible to say that it covers the case of Cromie or of Strelitz. The point may be summed up by saying that the section and the article, being designed as machinery to avoid questions being raised as to the validity of transactions where there has been a slip in the appointment of a director, cannot be utilized for the purpose of ignoring or overriding the substantive provisions relating to such appointment.

Note: In *Re New Cedos Engineering Co. Ltd.* [1994] 1 B.C.L.C. 797 Oliver J. similarly held that the transactions of the purported directors were invalid.

DIRECTORS' APPOINTMENT AND TENURE

See *Company Law*, pp. 109–122.

Companies Act 1990, section 160(2)

Appointment and remuneration of auditors

(2) Where the court is satisfied in any proceedings or as a result of an application under this section that—

(a) a person has been guilty, while a promoter, officer, auditor, receiver, liquidator or examiner of a company, of any fraud in relation to the company, its members or creditors; or

(b) a person has been guilty, while a promoter, officer, auditor, receiver, liquidator or examiner of a company, of any breach of his duty as such promoter, officer, auditor, receiver, liquidator or examiner; or

(c) a declaration has been granted under section 297A of the Principal Act (inserted by section 138 of this Act) in respect of a person; or

(d) the conduct of any person as promoter, officer, auditor, receiver, liquidator or examiner of a company, makes him unfit to be concerned in the management of a company; or

(e) in consequence of a report of inspectors appointed by the court or the minister upon the Companies Acts, the conduct of any person makes him unfit to be concerned in the management of a company; or

(f) a person has been persistently in default in relation to the relevant requirements;

the court, may of its own motion, or as a result of the application, makes a disqualification order against such a person for such period as it sees fit.

Companies Act 1963, section 182(1) and (7)

Removal of directors

182.—(1) A company may by ordinary resolution remove a director before the expiration of his period of office notwithstanding anything in its articles or in any agreement between it and him, so however, that this subsection shall not, in the case of a private company, authorise the removal of a director holding office for life.

(7) Nothing in this section shall be taken as depriving a person removed thereunder of compensation or damages payable to him in respect of the determination of his appointment as director or compensation or damages payable to him in respect of the determinaton of any appointment terminating with that as director or as derogating from any power to remove a director which may exist apart from this section.

Table A articles 77, 91–100 and Part 11 articles 9

77. The shareholding qualification for directors may be fixed by the company in general meeting and unless and until so fixed, no qualification shall be required.

Disqualification of Directors

91. The office of director shall be vacated if the director–

(*a*) ceases to be a director by virtue of section 180 of the Act; or

(*b*) is adjudged bankrupt in the State or in Northern Ireland or Great Britain or makes any arrangement or composition with his creditors generally; or

(*c*) becomes prohibited from being a director by reason of any order made under section 184 of the Act; or

(*d*) becomes of unsound mind; or

(*e*) resigns his office by notice in writing to the company; or

(*f*) is convicted of an indictable offence unless the directors otherwise determine; or

(*g*) is for more than 6 months absent without permission of the directors from meetings of the directors held during that period.

Rotation of Directors

92. At the first annual general meeting of the company all the directors shall retire from office, and at the annual general meeting in every subsequent Year, one-third of the directors for the time being, or, if their number is not three or a multiple of three, then the number nearest one-third shall retire from office.

93. The directors to retire in every year shall be those who have been longest in office since their last election but as between persons who became directors on the same day, those to retire shall (unless they otherwise agree among themselves) be determined by lot.

94. A retiring director shall be eligible for re-election.

95. The company, at the meeting at which a director retires in manner aforesaid, may fill the vacated office by electing a person thereto, and in default the retiring director shall, if offering himself for re-election, be deemed to have been re-elected, unless at such meeting it is expressly resolved not to fill such vacated office, or unless a resolution for the re-election of such director has been put to the meeting and lost.

96. No person other than a director retiring at the meeting shall, unless recommended by the directors, be eligible for election to the office of director at any general meeting unless not less than three nor more than 21 days before the day appointed for the meeting there shall have been left at the office notice in writing signed by a member duly qualified to attend and vote at the meeting for which such notice is given, of his intention to propose such person for election and also notice in writing signed by that person of his willingness to be elected.

97. The company may from time to time by ordinary resolution increase or reduce the number of directors and may also determine in what rotation the increased or reduced number is to go out of office.

98. The directors shall have power at any time and from time to time to appoint any person to be a director, either to fill a casual vacancy or as an addition to the existing directors, but so that the total number of directors shall not at any time exceed the number fixed in accordance with these regulations. Any director so appointed shall hold office only until the next following annual general meeting, and shall then be eligible for re-election but shall not be taken into account in determining the directors who are to retire by rotation at such meeting.

99. The company may, by ordinary resolution, of which extended notice has been given in accordance with section 142 of the Act, remove any director before the expiration of his period of office notwithstanding anything in these regulations or in any agreement between the company and such director. Such removal shall be without prejudice to any claim such director may have for damages for breach of any contract of service between him and the company.

100. The company may, by ordinary resolution, appoint another person in place of a director removed from office under regulation 99 and without prejudice to the powers of the directors under regulation 98 the company in general meeting may appoint any person to be a director either to fill a casual vacancy or as an additional director. A person appointed in place of a director so removed or to fill such a vacancy shall be subject to retirement at the same time as if he had become a director on the day on which the director in whose place he is appointed was last elected a director.

PART II

9. Any director may from time to time appoint any person who is approved by the majority of the directors to be an alternate or substitute director. The appointee, while he holds office as an alternate director, shall be entitled to notice of meetings of the directors and to attend and vote thereat as a director and shall not be entitled to be remunerated otherwise than out of the remuneration of the director appointing him. Any appointment under this regulation shall be effected by notice in writing given by the appointer to the secretary. Any appointment so made may be revoked at any time by the appointer or by a majority of the other directors or by the company in general meeting. Revocation by an appointer shall be effected by notice in writing given by the appointer to the secretary.

Runciman v. Walter Runciman plc
[1992] B.C.L.C. 1084

This case concerns the procedures to be followed when determining the duration of a director's service contract and his remuneration. The plaintiff had been chairman of the company. It had been acquired as a result of a hostile take-over bid and he was dismissed. The company eventually conceded that the dismissal had been unfair but a dispute arose as to the amount of damages awardable. The company contended that a purported extension in 1987 of his contract of service to five years was invalid because (a) the extension had not been authorised by the directors as was required by the company's articles of association, (b) that even if the extension had been properly authorised the contract was voidable because the plaintiff had not made disclosure of his interest in it, or (c) the extension had not been made in the interests of the company. Similar objections were made with respect to ancillary benefits (car, health insurance, telephone facility).

SIMON BROWN J.: [1089] Against that background of evidence let me now turn to deal in greater detail with the legal arguments.

The first two issues, as to whether there ever was any properly authorised agreement to increase the notice term and as to whether the plaintiff was required to declare an interest in this increase, require reference to the company's articles of association. Article 85 (similar to arts. 83–86 of 1963 Act's Table A – see *post*, p. 269) in particular is crucial:

"85(1) A director who is in any way, whether directly or indirectly, interested [1090] in a contract or proposed contract with the Company shall declare the nature of his interest at a meeting of the Directors in accordance with section 199 of the Act (i.e. section 194 of the 1963 Act).

(2) A director shall not vote in respect of any contract or arrangement in which he is interested, and if he shall do so his vote shall not be counted.

(3) A director may hold any other office or place of profit under the company (other than the office of auditor) in conjunction with his office of director for such period and on such terms (as to remuneration and

otherwise) as the directors may determine. No director or intending director shall be disqualified by his office from contracting with the company, either with regard to his tenure of any such other office or place of profit, or as vendor, purchaser or otherwise. No such contract, and no contract or arrangement entered into by or on behalf of the company, in which any director is in any way interested, shall be liable to be avoided, nor shall any director so contracting or being so interested be liable to account to the company for any profit realised by any such contract or arrangement by reason of such director holding that office or of the fiduciary relation thereby established.

(4) A director, notwithstanding his interest, may be counted in the quorum present at any meeting whereat he or any other director is appointed to hold any such office or place of profit under the company or whereat the terms of any such appointment are arranged, and he may vote on any such appointment or arrangement other than his own appointment or the arrangement of the terms thereof."

Several other articles were discussed in course of argument but I have come to conclude that they bear only marginally on the points at issue.

The defendant's first argument focuses essentially upon art 85(3) and in particular its provision that an office held by a director, here the plaintiff's office of executive chairman, is held 'on such terms (as to remuneration and otherwise) as the directors may determine'. 'The directors' are defined by art 2 to be 'the directors for the time being of the company as a body, or a quorum of the directors present at a meeting of the directors'. I should perhaps note in passing art 89(3), a provision complementary to art 85(3), although in the end it adds little to the debate:

"89(3) A managing director or any director holding any such other office or place of profit shall receive such remuneration or emoluments as the directors may determine." (similar to art. 111 in 1963 Act's Table A).

Given that the relevant terms here were never decided at a directors' meeting, the critical question raised is, of course, this: did the directors as a body, i.e. all of them, determine that the plaintiffs notice term should be increased to five years? The plaintiff says Yes, the defendants No.

Let it be said at once that if the answer is indeed No, then the purported agreement is clearly void. Many are the authorities and extensive the academic commentary establishing that. Prominent amongst the cases are *Re Richmond Gate Property. Co. Ltd.* [1965] 1 W.L.R. 335 and *Guinness plc v. Saunders* [1990] 2 A.C. 633 (see *infra*, p. 236).

[1091] Was there then a failure here to determine the variation of the plaintiffs notice period in accordance with article 85(3)? Contending that there was, Mr Charles Falconer QC, counsel for the defendants, submits that it would be wrong to conclude that when the plaintiff finally notified Mr Johnson and Mr McIntyre-Brown of the results of his (and Mr Haley's) consultation with the non-executive directors he was in any sense involving them personally in the decision-making process, wrong even to conclude that they were approving the various increases of pay or notice term. They never participated in the decision: they simply took their own individual benefits from it. The reality, Mr Falconer submits, is to be found in the evidence: As Mr Haley put it, 'Once the non-executives approved them, without more ado the increases would be put into effect'. And as the plaintiff stated in his memorandum of 20 November 1987, after noting the non-executive directors' agreement to the increases: 'I will be writing individual letters confirming these figures.' To similar effect is the plaintiff's letter to Mr Grant dated 21 November 1989: 'I should like to let people know what has been decided early in December and should therefore be grateful if I could have your reaction by the end of this month.' And entirely consistently with all this, submits Mr Falconer, are the minutes of a board meeting of 24 May 1988 with regard to pensions. . . .

[1092] None of this, the argument runs, suggests that Mr Johnson and Mr McIntyre-Brown were themselves party to the determination of their colleagues' salary levels or other terms of contract. (They could not, of course, under the articles, determine their own terms). The reality was rather that the decision was taken before ever these particular directors were notified of it. There was thus no unanimous determination by the board as a whole.

Powerfully although the argument was urged upon me, I have concluded that it fails. And for this reason above all. The articles say nothing as to how or when the directors are to arrive at their determination. In my judgment, therefore, provided only and always that by that time the term relied upon is sought to be enforced all the other directors can be shown to have concurred in the agreement of that term, it can then fairly and properly be said that they have indeed determined it as the article requires.

That directors, provided they act unanimously, can act informally appears clearly established – *Re Bonnelli's Telegraph Co, Collie's claim* (1871) L.R. 11 Eq. 246 and *Charterhouse Investments Trust Ltd. v. Tempest Diesels Ltd.* [1986] B.C.L.C. 1 so decide, the latter on the basis that informal acquiescence by other board members in an otherwise unauthorised agreement by one of their number binds the company. So in my judgment in the present case. And, indeed, I conclude that Mr Johnson's and Mr McIntyre-Brown's involvement went beyond mere informal acquiescence. As the plaintiff told me in evidence, when they were acquainted with the proposals following approval by the non-executive directors they, as directors, had the opportunity to query them. The mere fact that they never apparently did so and that their views were not more explicitly canvassed seems to me nothing to the point: by the time of the implementation of the various salary increases, and more obviously still by the time the plaintiff came to assert his notice term, such terms were indeed 'as determined' by the other board members, and none of them could possibly have been heard to assert the contrary.

Mr Elias, counsel for the plaintiff, put the case here in favour of my finding a binding agreement in a number of different ways. These included the submission that the decision making process regarding a director's term of service can lawfully be delegated (see arts 89(4) and 110) and that the company would be bound if all the directors acquiesced in such an arrangement. Although, having regard to my already stated conclusion, it is unnecessary to deal with these various alternative arguments in any detail, I should nevertheless observe that there seem to me insuperable difficulties in the plaintiff here seeking to rely on general powers of delegation under the articles, *Guinness* is to my mind indistinguishable in this regard. What really serves to distinguish *Guinness* from this case is not the different articles of association in play, not the different kind of remuneration in question, not (on this issue) the absence of knowledge on the part of the other members of the Guinness board, but rather that the decision there was taken by a committee so that the matter was never determined by the board as a whole whereas in the present case I have found that it was.

I pass to the defendants' second argument which centres on art 85(1). Section [1093] 199 of the Act (of 1948) there referred to, has been superseded by section 317 of the Companies Act 1985 (same as section 174 of the 1963 Act) – as recognised in *Guinness*, not for present purposes a significantly different. The argument here is that the plaintiff was required by art 85(1) (same as in 1963 Act's Table A) to declare at a directors' meeting the nature of his interest in the relevant variations to his service agreement, that he failed to do so, and that accordingly the variations relied upon, both as to the period of notice and the fringe benefits (the salary increases, I repeat are not challenged in these proceedings), are voidable at the suit of the company, unenforceable by the plaintiff against it.

Once again there is ample authority for the proposition that non-compliance with a requirement such as that imposed here by art 85(1) leaves the contract voidable at the option of the company: see most notably *Hely-Hutchinson v. Brayhead* [1968] 1 Q.B. 549 and *Guinness*.

But once again there is a dispute here as to whether the article has in fact been breached. And even if it has, submits Mr Elias, there are compelling reasons why the court should not permit the defendants now to avoid the contract.

Four particular questions are raised upon this part of the case. First, as to whether section 317 (and therefore art 85(1)) has any application to service contracts between a company and its own directors. Second, assuming it has, whether it applies to the variation of an existing contract. Third, again assuming it does, whether disclosure was made here by the plaintiff in conformity with the section. Fourth, assuming that the plaintiff was in breach of a duty to disclose, whether it is equitable to permit the defendants now to rescind.

Although these four questions were argued before me at very considerable length, I shall hope to be forgiven for dealing with them relatively shortly. The reason I do so is quite simply this. Whatever may have been the strict legal requirements of the position, on the particular facts of this case I am perfectly satisfied that for the plaintiff to have made a specific declaration of interest before agreement of the variations here in question would have served no conceivable purpose. It would have been mere incantation. Any non-compliance with art 85(1) was accordingly wholly technical. Nothing could be less just than that the new owners of the company after take-over should now benefit from their adventitious discovery of such breach. To allow them to do so would be to sacrifice the plaintiffs legitimate interests on the altar of slavish adherence to ritualistic form.

To revert, however, to the questions. Does section 317 apply to service contracts? (Section 317 I propose to take as read rather than lengthen this judgment by its detailed recitation). The plaintiff argues not, on the footing that self-evidently an executive director is interested in his own service contract so that it could never be necessary for him to declare that interest at a meeting. Mr Elias prays in aid in this regard section 317(3) which permits a director in certain circumstances to give a general notice which is then deemed a sufficient declaration of interest for future purposes. True, Mr Elias accepts, that subsection has no direct application to this case but, the argument runs, it appears at least to suggest that the legislation is concerned with realities rather than form. Compelling although at first blush I confess to have found this argument, I have regretfully come to reject it. Not only is it inconsistent with the plain language of the section, but there is ample authority for the proposition that the mere obviousness of a director's interest in a particular contract is no reason for non-compliance with [1094] the requirements of the section. That, indeed, is implicit in decisions like *Hely-Hutchinson* and *Guinness* each of which concerned contracts directly between a director and his company, contracts respectively of guarantee and for services. True, the contracts there in issue were made without knowledge on the part of some at least of the board's members. But that consideration cannot logically affect the question whether or not a particular type of contract falls within the legislation. And section 317(5), referring as it does to other transactions or arrangements in which a director is interested (such as loans to directors), points to the same conclusion. Furthermore, as Mr Falconer points out, to exclude service contracts from the ambit of section 317 would involve ridiculous and pointless distinctions being drawn, (a) between the employed and the self-employed director; and (h) between benefits given to a director as part of his contract of employment and those given separately. Finally on this point the defendants drew my attention to *Foster v. Foster* [1916] 1 Ch. 532, a decision holding in terms that the statutory predecessor to section 317 applied to service contracts.

Does section 317 apply to variations? The plaintiffs' contention that it does not again on analysis relies heavily on the apparent absurdity of requiring a declaration of interest in regard to such an agreement. Why declare an interest in the variation of a contract which the company already knows is one in which the director is interested? In addition, submits Mr Elias, if section 317 was intended to cover variations it would have said so expressly, in the same way that sub-s (10) of section 318 expressly applies subs. (1) and (5) of that section to a variation of a contract of service as to the contract itself. But those arguments too must in my judgment fail. So far as the analogy with section 318 goes, I accept the defendants' submission that section 318(10) was necessary because section 108(1) and (5) deal specifically with contracts of service and a variation of such a contract, albeit a contract, might well not in itself be regarded as a contract of service. And I accept too the defendants' fundamental argument that a variation of contract is itself a contract and that to construe section 317 otherwise would lead to pointless debate about whether a given agreement constitutes a variation or a fresh contract. Looking moreover to the purpose of the legislation and the mischief against which it is directed, there will certainly be cases where it is as necessary for an interest to be declared in a variation of contract as in the making of the contract in the first place: take *Guinness* and suppose that the consideration for Ward's services had initially and in conformity with the articles been agreed at £5,000 and only later varied to the eventual figure of £5.2m.

Was, then, disclosure made in the present case? Given as already stated that agreements such as those here in question need not themselves be determined at a directors' meeting, there is, submits Mr Elias, implicit disclosure of an executive director's interest in his service contract merely by the fact of his attendance at the first board meeting after his appointment. And, the submission continues, that disclosure is implicitly made afresh at every subsequent meeting which he attends, disclosure which would meet any statutory requirement in regard to later variations. Mr Elias further submits that the plaintiff here made in addition what was akin to express disclosure in that the company's letters to shareholders, advising them to reject respectively the Telfos bid in 1988 and the Avena bid (initially) in 1990, stated in terms that each of the four directors' contracts 'may be terminated by the company giving not less than five years previous notice in writing', a statement expressly agreed (as were the letters as a whole) at board [1095] meetings where the individual directors' interests in their contractual provisions were of course obvious.

Not so, argue the defendants. There was never here anything said or done which even purported to constitute a declaration of interest. To infer such declaration would involve a fiction. Rather, Mr Falconer submits, for there to be compliance with the legislation all contracts or arrangements between a company and one of its directors must at some stage come before the board and a specific declaration of interest then be made in respect of them. That is what section 317 on its proper construction and application requires. Nothing short of it will do. And, counsel argues, there are good policy reasons for this, amongst them these:

(1) That a director with an interest is obliged to acknowledge formally his involvement in a transaction which may be inimicable to the company and its shareholders;

(2) The director's interest will then be considered by the board and other directors will be reminded of their duty to consider the company's interest as distinct from their colleague's;

(3) Declarations of interest and their consideration will be minuted under the provisions of section 382 of the 1985 Act, and a permanent record kept.

Support for such an approach appears to be found in the authorities. Mr Falconer relies on two in particular. First the leading judgment of Fox L.J. in the Court of Appeal in *Guinness* [1988] 2 All E.R. 940 at 944 which includes this passage:

> "It is said, as I understand it, on behalf of Mr Ward, that disclosure to the full board would be an absurdity because the board, or at any rate the executive committee of the board for the purpose of the bid, knew about the payment. Assuming that it were true that all the members of the board knew about the payment, that does not alter the fact that the requirement of the statute that there be a disclosure to "a meeting of the directors of the company" (which is a wholly different thing from knowledge by individuals and involves the opportunity for positive consideration of the matter by the board as a body) was not complied with. I conclude, therefore, that the statute required disclosure to a duly convened meeting of the full board of Guinness."

Albeit the House of Lords held that the Court of Appeal had proceeded on a wrong footing, their decision in particular being inconsistent *with Hely Hutchinson v. Brayhead Ltd*, that passage in Fox L.J.'s judgment was not itself criticised and remains, it is submitted, valid. Second, Mr Falconer invites my attention to *Lee Panavision Ltd. v. Lee Lighting Ltd.* [1991] B.C.L.C. 575 at 584, where Harman J. adopted substantially the same approach.

I readily acknowledge the apparent weight of these arguments. And yet I remain profoundly reluctant to conclude that a director must solemnly declare an interest in his own service agreement, a contract which by its very nature involves his interest, before any variation is made concerning his salary or other terms of employment, Is there really, irrespective of the common-sense of the position, a statutory requirement for such formal declaration? I do not believe that the point is free from doubt. Lord Goff, for instance, spoke in Guinness of the 'very serious difficulties arising on the construction of section 317'. And when *Lee* [1096] *Panavision* got to the Court of Appeal, Dillon L.J. ([1992] B.C.L.C. 22 at 33) similarly recognised the problems in the legislation and, wisely is I believe, declined counsel's urgent invitation to express a view on the construction and a effect of art 85 in the light of section 317 despite blandishments that it was necessary to do so to resolve difficulties for all practitioners. Against that background it would surely be rash indeed for me needlessly to venture a definitive view upon this troublesome issue.

As stated, it is upon the fourth question that I have reached the clearest conclusion. It is at this point that Dillon L.J.'s comments on section 317 becomes most pertinent ([1992] B.C.L.C. 22 at 33):

> ". . . if the judge was entitled to make the findings of non-disclosure and non-declaration of interests that he did, the position is that each of the directors has failed to disclose formally at the board meeting an interest common to all the directors and, ex hypothesi, already known to all the directors. I would hesitate to hold that such apparently technical non-declaration of an interest in breach of section 317 has the inevitable result, as to which the court has no discretion, that the second management agreement is fundamentally flawed and must be set aside if Lee Lighting chooses to ask sufficiently promptly that it be set aside."

As it seems to me, the (assumed) non-declaration of the plaintiffs interest in the variations here in question was as purely technical as it could ever be. Whatever may be the suggested advantages of a strictly formal approach to the section, such as a record of the proceedings and a reduced risk of directors abusing their position, no such advantage would have accrued here. It is certainly not suggested in this case that the plaintiff or his fellow directors in any way abused their position. Rather the basis of Mr Falconer's case for holding the plaintiff unable to enforce his increased notice term is the contention that the strict rule should invariably be applied save only where the right of rescission must in law be regarded as lost – by acquiescence, delay, the impossibility of making restitutio in integrum, or on some other similarly recognised ground. Here it is submitted that no such reason exists. In reality, submits Mr Falconer, there has been no delay and no acquiescence: it was not until after Averia's take-over that the new management and shareholders learned of the circumstances in which the service agreements came to be varied, and in particular of the plaintiff's failure to disclose his interest. In this context he draws my attention to the decision of the House of Lords in *Erlanger v. New Sombrero Phosphate Co.* (1878) 3 App. Cas. 1218 at 1279–1180 and Lord Blackburn's speech where, dealing with the question of laches by a corporation, he said:

> ". . . it should be recollected that shareholders who seek to set aside a contract made by the governing body, have practically first to change that governing body, and must have time to do so."

The force of that observation is plain. But it must be read in the context of this earlier passage in the speech:

". . . I think, from the nature of the enquiry, it must always be a question [1097] more or less, depending upon the degree of diligence which might reasonably be required, and the degree of change which has occurred, whether a the balance of justice or injustice is in favour of granting the remedy or withholding it. The determination of such a question must largely depend upon the turn of mind of those who have to decide, and must therefore be subject to uncertainty; but that, I think, is inherent in the nature of the enquiry."

If then one poses the simple question: what does the balance of justice require in the present case, I am left in no doubt whatever as to the proper answer. The plain fact is that this plaintiff continued, from 1987 to 1990, to serve the company as its chairman understanding that his notice term had been increased to five years; that equally was the understanding of all his fellow directors; and Avena too, at the time of their take-over of the company, clearly understood that to be the position an understanding in their case derived from the company's explicit letter published earlier in opposition to the bid. To hold in these circumstances that what was at most a merely technical breach of a statutory duty of disclosure should render that variation unenforceable would to my mind involve the most patent injustice.

I turn to the defendants' third argument, that the increase in the notice term should be set aside as having been made in breach of the directors' fiduciary duty, i.e. the duty of the plaintiffs fellow directors to exercise their powers bona fide in the interests of the company as a whole and for a proper corporate purpose.

The principles of law here in play are not in doubt. They are stated in *Palmer's Company Law* (25th ed.) para. 8.508 as follows:

"The duty imposed upon directors to act bona fide in the interests of the company is a subjective one. As Lord Greene, MR put it in *Re Smith and Fawcett Ltd.* [1942] Ch. 304 directors must act "bona fide in what they consider – not what a Court may consider – is in the interests of the company." So long as the directors have correctly informed themselves as to how the company is defined in law (for this purpose, present and future shareholders), it is left to the directors in the exercise of their business judgment to decide how the interests of the company may best be promoted. The Courts will interfere only if no reasonable director could possibly have concluded that a particular course of action was in the interests of the company."

In *Howard Smith Ltd. v. Ampol Petroleum Ltd.* [1974] A.C. 811 (see *post*, p. 273) at 835 Lord Wilberforce put it thus:

". . . it is then necessary for the Court, if a particular exercise of [power] is challenged, to examine the substantial purpose for which it was exercised, and to reach a conclusion whether that purpose was proper or not. In doing so it will necessarily give credit to the bona fide opinion of the directors, if such is found to exist, and will respect their judgment as to matters of management; having done this, the ultimate conclusion has to be as to the side of a fairly broad line on which the case falls."

[1098] The defendants here argue that it was quite unnecessary for the plaintiff's and Mr Haley's notice terms to be increased merely because such variation was thought necessary for the other two directors. Mr Falconer points to various other very substantial benefit increases conferred on the plaintiff in the 1987-88 period: an increase in salary from £48,000 to £75,000 with effect from 1 January 1988, an increased share option from 10,000 to 75,000 shares during 1987, and a reduction in the normal retiring age under the company's pension scheme from 65 to 6o at no additional cost to himself. Against that background, it is submitted, it was wrong to improve the plaintiff's notice term merely to achieve symmetry across the board. Mr Falconer does not suggest that the plaintiff's term was increased for any impermissible ulterior purpose; only that symmetry is not in itself a proper or sufficient purpose, rather it needlessly burdens the company with high potential liability, just as has occurred.

This argument too I reject. Given the accepted bona fides of the directors, and given that it is essentially for them and not the court to decide what is in the company's interests, I find it quite impossible to say that this board in 1987 reached a view of the matter which was simply not open to them. Mr Grant told me in terms that he thought it right to make no distinction between the four working directors, that it would have been invidious to have done so. Am I really to say that such a view was plainly wrong? On the contrary, in the context of this small and close knit executive team, the approach taken seems to me eminently understandable. As Mr Elias points out, the position is really not unlike that arising when salary increases are in question: merely because one particular director may have reached an age when his prospects of alternative employment have faded would hardly be a sufficient, let alone a compelling, reason for denying him an increase otherwise required to maintain his appropriate position in the overall salary scale. Yet on Mr Falconer's argument, if there were no risk of his leaving the company, it would be unnecessary and therefore impermissible, in breach of his fellow directors' fiduciary duty, to pay him his increase.

It follows from all this that in my judgment the plaintiff is entitled to rely upon his five-year notice term.

Re Dairy Lee Ltd., Stakelum v. Canning
[1976] I.R. 314

Is a full time executive director a company employee or is he a self-employed office holder? The company was unable to pay its debts and passed a resolution for voluntary winding-up. Its liquidator brought proceedings for a decision as to whether the respondent's claim for accrued holiday remuneration should be treated as a debt ranking in priority under section 285 of the Companies Act, 1963. The respondent, who held 3,000 shares of £1 each in the company which had an issued capital of £6,452, was a director of the company. He worked full time for it and was responsible for the day-to-day running of the business though he was not the managing director. He was paid £225 a month by the company but there are no entries in the minute book to show whether these payments were salary or director's fees. The respondent, who did not have any service agreement with the company, regarded the payments as salary. His employment was terminated by the applicant, and he claimed accrued holiday remuneration.

KENNY J.: . . . [316] A director holds his office under the articles of association of the company and so, as a director, is not an employee or a clerk or servant of the company. Article 85 of the articles in Table 'A', which applies to this company, permits him to hold any other office or place of profit under the company in conjunction with his office of director for such period and on such terms as to remuneration and otherwise as the directors may determine. The result is that a director may be employed by the company not as a director but as a salaried employee.

When a person who is a director claims priority under section 285 of the Act of 1963, the relevant questions are whether he was a director only or a director and a salaried employee. When deciding this, it is relevant to consider whether the moneys received by him were paid as director's fees or as salary. If he was a director and a salaried employee, he is entitled to priority under section 285 for salary and accrued holiday remuneration. When a person who is a director but is not a managing director is working whole-time with the company, the inference that he was a director and a salaried employee seems to me to be justified unless there is evidence that he was a whole-time director only and was paid as such.

It is impossible to reconcile all the decided cases but the view which I have expressed is supported by the modem authorities. Some of the confusion arises from the fact that in the 19th century the concept of an executive or whole-time director (other than a man ageing director) was almost unknown, and the earlier cases were dealing with the question whether a part-time director was a clerk or a servant. In *Hutton v. West Cork Railway Co.* (1883) 23 Ch. D. 654, Bowen L.J. said that a director is not a servant of the company but a person who is doing business for the company but not on ordinary terms. In *Re News-*

paper Proprietary Syndicate Ltd. [1900] 2 Ch. 349, Cozens-Hardy J. held that a managing director was not a clerk or servant of the company although he had entered into an agreement with it by which he was appointed managing director for three years at a salary. The judge said that a managing director is only (*sic*) an ordinary director entrusted with some special powers, and that it was not relevant that he was entitled to remuneration by virtue of a special bargain or that his remuneration was [317] described as salary. This reasoning cannot be reconciled with that in the later, and more authoritative, decision of the Inner House of the Court of Session and the case should now be regarded as having been wrongly decided. In *Normandy v. Ind. Coope and Co. Ltd.* [1908] 1 Ch. 84, Kekewich J. said that a managing or other director is not a person in the employment of the company. In *Re Beeton & Co. Ltd.* [1913] 2 Ch. 279, the articles of association of a company provided that no director should be disqualified by his office from contracting with, or being employed by, the company, and that a director might hold any other office or place of profit under the company in conjunction with his office as director. The minutes of the board of directors showed that one of the directors was to do other work for the company. Mr Justice Neville said that there was a special contract outside the office of director under which the claimant had to perform duties and that, although qua director she had no valid claim to preferential payment, yet in her other capacity as a servant of the company she was entitled to it. This decision seems to me to have been correct and to recognise the difference between moneys due to a person as director and sums due to an employee who is a director. In *Re Lee, Behrens & Co. Ltd.* [1932] 2 Ch. 46, Eve J. said that a director is not a servant of the company, but this decision was subsequently dissented from by Lord Normand.

In *Anderson v. Yames Sutherland (Peterhead) Ltd.* (1941) S.C. 203, the articles of association provided that, whenever any member of the company who was employed by the company in any capacity was dismissed for misconduct, the directors might resolve that such person should cease to be a member of the company and should be deemed to have served the other members with an offer of his shares. The managing director, who held shares in the capital of the company, was removed from his post as managing director and, when the directors 'decided to acquire his shares, he resisted the claim because, he said, he was not employed by the company. The members of the Inner House rejected this argument. The Lord President (Lord Normand) said that while he accepted the view that a director as such is not the servant or employee of the company, he might occupy an employment subordinate to that of director and in that capacity have different functions from a director. He added that a managing director has two functions and two capacities. Qua managing director, he is a party to a contract with the company which is a contract of employment and of service. There is nothing anomalous in this because, as Lord Normand said: 'it is a [318] common place of our law that the same individual may have two or more capacities each including special rights and duties in relation to the same thing or matter or in relation to the same persons.' A striking illustration of this distinction is given by the advice of the Privy Council in *Lee v. Lee Air Farming Ltd.* [1961] A.C. 12 (see *ante*, p. 68). Mr Lee, who was a pilot, was governing director of the company. As governing director he gave an instruction to himself to act as pilot. He was killed while flying and his widow claimed that he was a worker and was employed by the company. The Privy Council held that a person who is a governing director of a company may have a contract of service with it, not as governing director, but as an employee.

In this case the only reasonable inference is that the respondent was a director and a salaried employee, and that the money he received was salary and not director's fees. He was therefore an employee and servant of the company and I will declare that he is entitled to priority under section 285, sub-s. 2(d), of the Companies Act, 1963, in respect of his claim in the winding up for accrued holiday remuneration.

Bushell v. Faith
[1970] A.C. 1099

See *ante*, p. 165.

Carvill v. Irish Industrial Bank Ltd.
[1968] I.R. 325

This and the following two cases. *Glover* and *Schindler*, concern when may a director be lawfully removed from office without being given the due notice under his service agreement? The articles of association of the company provided that it could remove a director before the expiration of his term of office, that the directors of the company could appoint a director to be the managing director for a fixed term or indefinitely, that the provisions of the articles relating to the removal of directors should apply to a managing director 'subject to the provision of any contract between him and the company', and that a managing director would cease to hold that office upon ceasing to hold the office of director. The plaintiff was not appointed to be managing director of the company but he had acted as such and he had been remunerated and treated by the company as its managing director.

While so acting he bought a new carpet for his own house and at the same time he instructed the suppliers to take an old carpet from the house, to alter the old carpet and to re-lay it in the company's premises. The total cost of these transactions was £129 15s, of which £90 15s was apportioned by him as a debt due by the company to the suppliers. The company paid that sum to the suppliers without having been informed of the plaintiff's interest in the matter. Later the company duly resolved that he be removed from the office of director, without being aware of any misconduct by him and without giving him any notice of his removal. He sued claiming damages, amounting to 12 months salary, for wrongful dismissal. At the hearing of the action, he conceded that the defendant company could justify the dismissal by proof of sufficient misconduct by him prior to the dismissal, while the company conceded that (if any notice were required) twelve months notice of dismissal was reasonable, and the company justified the dismissal on the ground of the plaintiffs conduct in the carpet transaction.

Held by Kenny J., in dismissing the plaintiffs claim, that the company had been entitled to terminate the contract of employment as a salaried employee, who was called the managing director, without giving the plaintiff 12 months notice of such termination, which otherwise would have been necessary. The plaintiff appealed.

O'KEEFFE J.: . . . [339] [T]he plaintiff alleged that he was managing director of the company, and this was not denied by the defendants. Mr. Justice Kenny held that the plaintiff was not the managing director of the company, but that he was a director and also a salaried employee of the company. At the trial the defendants had applied for leave to amend their defence by inserting, at the beginning of para. 5 of the defence, the following plea:

> "The defendant admits that the plaintiff was employed as managing director but denies that he was so employed from year to year or for any fixed or definite term and further denies that such employment was at the salary and emoluments mentioned in the statement of claim. The defendant further denies that the plaintiff was employed under any contract, express or implied. If (which is denied) the plaintiff was employed under any contract, it was not an implied term or condition of the said contract or employment that the said employment of the plaintiff should be determinable by the defendant company only by reasonable notice to the plaintiff or that the plaintiff [340] should be entitled to continue in such employment until the expiration of such notice."

Leave to make this amendment was refused, and from this refusal the defendants have appealed in their cross-appeal. It appears to me that this amendment was necessary to enable the real dispute between the parties to be decided, and that it should have been allowed although, for the reasons which I set out hereafter, the amendment may not materially affect the result of the proceedings.

The finding of Mr Justice Kenny, that the plaintiff was not managing director of the company, appears to me to be neither in accord with the pleadings nor in accord with the facts as adduced in evidence. The reasons for this view are as follows.

Article 106 of the articles of association of the company provided that the directors may from time to time appoint one or more of their body to be managing director or managing directors, or to discharge any technical, advisory or other special duties (such persons to be called 'Special Directors'), and either for a fixed term or without any limitation as to the period for which he or they is or are to hold any such office and may from time to time remove or dismiss him or them from office and appoint another or others in his or their place or places. Article 107 provides as follows 'A Special Director shall not, while he continues to hold that office, be subject to retirement by rotation and he shall not be taken into account in determining the rotation by retirement of directors, but he shall (subject to the provisions of any contract between him and the company) be subject to the same provisions as to resignation and removal as the other directors of the company, and if he cease to hold the office of director from any cause he shall *ipso facto*, and immediately, cease to be a Special Director.'

There is no evidence of a formal appointment of the plaintiff as managing director by resolution of the board, but there was evidence that he had acted as such and had described himself and had been described by the defendants as such, and had received remuneration from the defendants appropriate to the position of managing director. The resolutions put in evidence fixing the remuneration of the plaintiff did not in terms describe him as managing director, but a resolution of the board passed on 6th July, 1961, purported to remove him from office as managing director and to appoint a new managing director in his stead. I take the view that, if there is compelling evidence of a consensus of opinion among the directors, a formal resolution need not be proved in order to justify a finding in accordance with that consensus of opinion. In the present case, I consider that it is clearly established by the evidence that the plaintiff was regarded by his co-directors as appointed to the office of managing [341] director, and that he should be held to be validly appointed to that office, even though no formal resolution appointing him appears among the minutes of the meetings of the board of directors. Not only is this in accordance with the facts, but it is, I think, the case which both the plaintiff and the defendants wished to make on their respective pleadings.

The real dispute between the plaintiff and the defendants is not as to whether the plaintiff was a managing director, but as to the terms upon which he held that office. The plaintiff alleges that one of the terms of his appointment as such was that he should not be removed from office save on notice of not less than twelve months duration, while the defendants allege that the plaintiff could be removed from office at any time. Each party in turn relies upon Article 107 of the articles of association. The plaintiff says that the provisions in that Article were expressed to be subject to his contract with the company, and that that contract required notice of not less than twelve months to determine it. The defendants say that there was no contract or, alternatively, that there was no contract which required any notice; and they say that, on his ceasing to be a director, the plaintiff automatically ceased to hold his position as managing director.

Reference was made to a number of authorities. On the one hand reliance was placed on such cases as *Nelson v. James Nelson and Sons Ltd.* [1914] 2 K.B. 770, *Southern Foundries (1926) Ltd. v. Shirlaw* [1940] A.C. 701, and *Shindler v. Northern Raincoat Co. Ltd.* [1960] 1 W.L.R. 1038, (see *post*, p. 226) where it was held that a company which had appointed a managing director for a fixed term could not, without being liable for damages for breach of contract, put an end to his employment as managing director during that term, even by altering its articles of association. On the other hand reference was made to *Read v. Astoria Garage (Streatham) Ltd.* [1952] Ch. 637 in which the plaintiff had been appointed managing director at a salary of £7 per week, which salary was later increased. He continued in office for many years, but finally it was resolved by the directors that his employment be terminated, and he was given a month's notice. His salary was paid for approximately four months. He brought an action for wrongful dismissal on the ground that he had not been given reasonable notice. Article 68 of Table 'A' to the Companies Act, 1929, applied to the company. That Article provided: 'The directors may from time to time appoint one or more of their body to the office of managing director or manager for such term and at such remuneration [342] (whether by way of salary, or commission, or participation in profits, or partly in one way and partly in another) as they may think fit, and a director so appointed shall not, while holding that office, be subject to retirement by rotation, or taken into account in determining the rotation or retirement of directors; but his appointment shall be subject to determination *ipso facto* if he ceases from any cause to be a director, or if the company in general meeting resolve that his tenure of the office of managing director or manager be determined.' Harman J. held that, on an article of association in that form, it was not open to the directors to appoint a managing director on terms which would deprive the company of its power to revoke the appointment *ipso facto* by removing the director from his office. This decision was upheld by the Court of Appeal, which distinguished the *Southern Foundries* case on two grounds, first, that in that case there was a contract of service between the company and the managing director *dehors* the articles of association and, secondly, the contract was sought to be determined by a power which was not present in the articles of association of the company as they stood at the date of the contract, but which had been inserted in the articles by subsequent alteration.

In *Shindler's* Case, Diplock J. (as he then was) regarded himself bound by the decision in the *Southern Foundries* case and considered that Harman J. had arrived at a decision which could not be reconciled with that earlier decision. In the present case it is not necessary to decide whether Diplock J., was correct in this. The articles which was construed in *Read v. Astoria Garage (Streatham) Ltd.* did not contain the important phrase 'subject to the provisions of any contract between him and the company' which appear in Article 107 of the articles of association of the defendant company, and these words make an important difference. Once these words appear, it is open to the directors to enter into a contract with the managing director the effect of which may be to deprive the company in general meeting of the power to remove him from office without being liable to pay damages. The question is whether there is such a contract in the present case.

It appears to me that a person who is a director, and who is appointed by the board of directors to the office of managing director, must be deemed to hold that office under some contract, either express or implied. The contract may be for a fixed term, in which case it cannot properly be terminated before the expiration of that term without a liability [343] to pay damages. It may be for no fixed term and, indeed, may be for so long only as the person holds office as director, in which case, if the person concerned ceases to be a director, his office as managing director also comes to an end. An express contract might well provide that the office could be held without limitation as to term, but with a provision for notice to determine it, and in that case there would be implied a term that, until the proper notice had been given, the person concerned would not be removed from the position of director so as to bring his appointment as managing director to an end.

What were the terms of the plaintiffs contract in the present case? . . . .

[344] I then find a situation in which the plaintiff is appointed managing director and his salary if fixed on a yearly basis and, while the figure is altered by increasing it first to £2,000 and then to £2,000 with a percentage of profits, it remains fixed on a yearly basis. I think that the plaintiff must be regarded as employed under a contract from year to year as managing director, and that it must be implied also that such contract could not be determined without such notice as is appropriate to an engagement of the kind mentioned. The trial judge considered that a year's notice (or salary in lieu of notice) was appropriate, and the defendants have not submitted that such length of notice was excessive, although they have contended that no notice at all was required. In the circumstances I see no reason for disturbing the finding of the trial judge that the appropriate period of notice was a year, although I might not myself have fixed so long a period. I think, however, that the salary payable during the period of notice would be £2,000 p.a., not £2,500 p.a. If the plaintiff is entitled to damages this is the figure which I would award.

The plaintiff was dismissed summarily, and no reason was assigned at the time. The defendants subsequently sought to justify the dismissal on the ground that the plaintiff misconducted himself in his employment before his removal and that he was discharged because of this. Particulars of the misconduct were sought, and they were furnished by letters dated the 28th October, 1963, and the 21st January, 1964. The particulars of misconduct were given as follows: '4. The defendants maintain that the plaintiff's management of the affairs of the Company was incompetent and in particular the following matters appeared to the Board to be extremely unsatisfactory. . . .' There followed particulars of twelve matters which the defendants wished to question. These matters were dealt with at the trial and the trial judge found, in respect of all except one, that they would not justify the plaintiffs summary dismissal. He found against the plaintiff on that one, and because of this he held that the plaintiff was lawfully dismissed summarily, and did not award him any damages for wrongful dismissal.

The plaintiff has appealed against the finding of the trial judge on the last-mentioned item, and the defendants cross-appealed against the findings of the trial judge in relation to the other eleven items. At the hearing of the appeal the defendants confined their submissions to five of the twelve items.

As I have already said, no reason for the plaintiffs summary dismissal was assigned at the time, but the defendants sought to justify the dismissal on the grounds of 'misconduct' and gave particulars of this alleged misconduct, [345] and gave evidence in support of their plea. There was no evidence that at the time of the dismissal any of the matters complained of subsequently were within the knowledge of the defendants, but the defendants relied upon the statement of the law contained in text books to the effect that it is not necessary that a master, dismissing a servant for good cause, should state the ground for such dismissal; and that provided good ground existed in fact, it is immaterial whether or not it was known to the employer at the time of the dismissal. Counsel for the plaintiff submitted that this statement of the law was erroneous, and this point was fully argued by both sides. The plaintiffs counsel submitted that, while a master need not assign any ground for the summary dismissal of a servant, he could not later justify the dismissal on a ground which was not within his knowledge at the time of the dismissal. Support for this view is to be found in the judgment of Parke B. in *Cussons v. Skinner* (11 M. & W. 16 1) at p. 172 of the report where he says: '. . . it would be necessary for the defendants, who justify the discharge, to shew that at the time the discharge took place in January, 1841, they knew at least of this act of misconduct.' Support for the proposition relied upon by the defendants, and stated in the text books, is to be found in a number of cases but particularly in the judgment of Cotton L.J. in *Boston Deep Sea Fishing & Ice Co. v. Ansell* 39 Ch. D. 339. The Court was referred to the statement of the law in *Smith on Master and Servant* and it appears that, in the first and second editions, the author considered that a master could not rely on an act of misconduct to justify a dismissal unless he at least knew of the act at the time of dismissal; but that in the third edition (published in 1870) and in later editions of the work the author considered that a master might rely on an act of misconduct to justify a dismissal even if he did not know of it at the time of the dismissal.

In principle it is difficult to understand how an act can be relied upon to justify a dismissal unless it is known at the time of the dismissal. It must be conceded that there can be some breaches of contract so fundamental as to show that the contract is entirely repudiated by the party committing them, and that such an act might be relied upon in an action for wrongful dismissal, not as justifying the dismissal, but as supporting a plea that the dismissed servant had himself put an end to the contract. Where the act is not of so fundamental a character but would warrant the dismissal of the servant at the option of the employer, it appears to me to be quite illogical to say that an employer may be heard to [346] say that he dismissed his servant on a ground unknown to him at the actual time of dismissal. This is the reasoning of Lord Abinger C.B. in *Cussons v. Skinner* at page 168 of the report where he says: 'This plea alleges disobedience to be the cause of the plaintiffs discharge. What act of disobedience is shewn in this case, excepting the act alleged, which is said to be proved by the plaintiffs own letter? But it is admitted by the counsel on both sides, that the defendants never discovered that act till after they discharged him. How, then, can they urge that that was the cause of his discharge? It is agreed that the plea could only be sustained by evidence that that was the cause of his discharge. If the defendants knew it before, and passed it over, and allowed the plaintiff to remain to the 1st of August, he would still be entitled to all his wages up to that time. If the defendants did not know it, it clearly was not the cause of his discharge.' I should mention that in *Boland v. Dublin Corporation* [1946] I.R. 88, where the question of wrongful dismissal was discussed incidentally in the Supreme Court, the case of *Cussons v. Skinner* appears not to have been mentioned in the course of the argument.

In my opinion, therefore, an employer cannot, as a defence to an action for wrongful dismissal, rely on an act of misconduct on the part of his servant, which was unknown to him at the time of the dismissal, unless the act is of so fundamental a character as to show a repudiation of the contract of employment by the servant. This does not mean that the employer is without rights in respect of the misconduct. He can, in my view, rely on it as a ground for reduction of damages, and in a proper case the result may be to reduce the damages to the point of extinction.

[His Lordship referred to four of the five allegations of misconduct upon which the defendants relied in support of their cross-appeal and, having expressed his agreement with the findings of Kenny J. with regard to those four allegations, continued as follows:]

I now come to the carpet transaction. I have to examine this transaction in some detail, though I need not repeat all the facts. Counsel for the plaintiff have relied strongly on the fact that fraud or dishonesty on the part of the plaintiff was not pleaded and in my opinion this is so, if one is to have regard to the nature of the fraud or dishonesty which the evidence was tendered to establish. When particulars in relation to this matter were furnished they were as follows: 'In April, 1961, a carpet was supplied to the plaintiffs house by Messrs. Strahan & Co. together with an [347] underfelt and an old carpet from the plaintiffs house was fitted in the defendant's premises at a total cost of £129 15s. 0d. Part of this sum (£90) was charged to the defendants. This was done without the knowledge or consent of the board of the defendant company.' The complaint made is apparently that the plaintiff did not disclose his financial interest in the transaction. No complaint is made in the particulars that what the defendants obtained was worth less than the £90 paid for it. The failure to disclose his interest to his co-directors was a rather trivial matter, and would not warrant his dismissal, but at the trial the defendants put forward a case in excess of that covered by the particulars, and alleged in effect that the company had been defrauded by charging it with an amount greatly in excess of the value of the second-hand carpet. I do not think that this should have been permitted. If fraud is to be relied on, it must always be clearly pleaded and clearly established. Here it was not, in my view, pleaded at all. Furthermore, the evidence to establish it was unsatisfactory. The carpet was fitted early in 1961. Mr Gillespie, of Strahan & Co., had looked at it for the purpose of the case sometime between the 28th and the 31 st January, 1964. When he was asked what its highest value was in April, 1961, he said: 'Well, it would be difficult to say in so far as I did not pay particular attention to it then. I would imagine possibly £30 to £35.' This is obviously not the considered opinion of an expert to be relied upon as bringing home to the plaintiff the fraud which the defendants sought to impute to him, but an opinion casually given to a question for which the witness was, apparently quite unprepared. Even if fraud were properly pleaded, I would be reluctant to convict the plaintiff on such evidence. In the result I find myself at variance with the trial judge in respect of this transaction, and I would not regard the defendants as having established in respect of it a ground for dismissing the plaintiff.

It follows that even had all these matters been within the knowledge of the defendants at the time of dismissal, they have failed to make out a sufficient case to warrant the summary dismissal of the plaintiff and accordingly the plaintiff is, in my view, entitled to damages for wrongful dismissal. I have already indicated that the amount should be £2,000 and not £2,500.

Glover v. B.L.N. Ltd.
[1973] I.R. 388

A holding company and its three subsidiaries appointed the plaintiff to be technical director of the four companies for a period of five years at an agreed salary, subject to termination in accordance with clause 12(c) thereof. That clause provided that his appointment might be terminated, without giving rise to compensation, if he should be guilty of any serious misconduct or serious neglect in the performance of his duties which, in the unanimous opinion of the board of directors of the holding company, affected injuriously the business or property of the holding company or of any of the subsidiaries. Having considered several serious complaints made against him, the board of the holding company found unanimously that he had been guilty of serious misconduct and neglect affecting the business of one of the subsidiaries, and terminated his appointment. Each of the subsidiaries terminated appointments too. But he was never given any prior notice of the complaints made against him. He claimed damages from the four companies for wrongful dismissal and breach of contract, it was

Held by Kenny J., in deciding the issue of liability for damages;

1. That the decision of the board of the holding company was amenable to review by the court.

2. That, in making their decision, the board of the holding company could only take into account the matters known on the 5th July, 1966.

3. That the evidence of the matters known to the board of the holding company on that date established that the plaintiff had been guilty of serious misconduct and neglect affecting injuriously the business of one of the subsidiaries.

4. That the plaintiffs position as the holder of an office, as distinct from being only an employee, required the application of the rules of natural justice to the termination of his appointment as technical director.

5. That since, in breach of such rules, the plaintiff had not been given prior notice of the charges made against him, his dismissal was invalid and he was entitled to damages.

The defendants appealed.

WALSH J.: . . . [423] For the purpose of this limited appeal only, it is unnecessary to go into details of the particular complaints. I proceed on the assumption that the learned trial judge's assessment of the facts and his conclusion that the plaintiff was guilty of serious neglect of duty and of serious misconduct were correct, and that the nature of the neglect and misconduct was such that the directors could reasonably have considered them to have injuriously affected the business, property and management of the operating company.

At the time the plaintiff was given his notice of dismissal he knew nothing of these charges because he was not given notice of them nor was he given any opportunity to answer them. In fact, he did not find out what the charges were until April, 1967. On the 27th July, 1966, the plaintiff issued proceedings for damages for wrongful dismissal. His statement of claim was delivered on the 15th December, 1966. The defendants delivered their defence on the 9th March, 1967, and alleged that the plaintiff was guilty of misconduct and neglect and that the defendants acted in lawful exercise of their rights under the agreement. On the 13th March the plaintiffs solicitor asked for particulars of the alleged misconduct and neglect and, in a long and detailed reply of the 12th April from the defendants' solicitors, the plaintiff learned for the first time the charges upon which the defendants sought to justify his dismissal. The plaintiff in his reply, which was delivered on the 24th May, denied that he was guilty of the alleged or any misconduct, or neglect and claimed that the boards were acting in excess of the authority vested in them under the service agreement to dismiss the plaintiff. The reply also claimed that the opinion formed by the board was not a *bona fide* one based upon any fair or proper inquiry or investigation into the circumstances of the case or upon any reasonable or justifiable grounds, and that it was formed without [424] reasonable or probable cause. It also claimed that the several boards of directors, in passing the resolutions, acted contrary to the principles of natural justice.

Mr Justice Kenny held that, as the plaintiff did not get notice of the charges against him and as the directors of the holding company did not give him an opportunity to make his defence, the termination of the plaintiffs contract by the resolution of the 5th July and the letter of the 8th July, 1966, was invalid; the judge held that the plaintiff was entitled to damages against the defendants. Mr. Justice Kenny reviewed the various cases he mentioned in his judgment, in particular the decision of the House of Lords in *Ridge v. Baldwin* [1964] A.C. 40; the speech of Lord Reid in that decision led him to the conclusion that the plaintiffs position should be equated to that of the holder of an office, and not that of an employee only, and that the principles of natural justice applied to a termination under clause 12 (c) of the plaintiffs agreement.

In my opinion, this case hinges entirely upon clause 12 (c) of the service agreement. The defendants have relied upon this particular clause to justify their summary dismissal of the plaintiff. I agree with Mr Justice Kenny when he states that, because of the express provisions of this clause, no implied term is to be read into the contract that the plaintiff might be summarily dismissed for misconduct. On the contrary, the clause expressly provides that the plaintiff could not be validly dismissed for misconduct unless it was serious misconduct and was of a kind which, in the unanimous opinion of the board of directors of the holding company present and voting at the meeting, injuriously affected the reputation, business or property of either that company or of the subsidiary companies. The question of whether or not such a contract could be terminated summarily for breach of fundamental condition on the part of the plaintiff was not raised in this case and was not relied upon by the defendants so I do not feel any need to offer any view upon that point. It appears to me quite clear that the operation of clause 12(c) would necessarily involve (a) the ascertainment of the facts alleged to constitute serious misconduct, (b) the determination [425] that they did in fact constitute serious misconduct, and (c) that the members of the board present and voting should be unanimously of opinion that the serious misconduct injuriously affected the reputation, business or property of the holding company or of the subsidiary companies. The parties by their conduct explicitly set up the machinery for dismissal specified in clause 12(c); that machinery designated the board of directors as the tribunal, and required unanimity of opinion upon the effect of such serious misconduct if it should be proved.

In my view, it was necessarily an implied term of the contract that this inquiry and determination should be fairly conducted. The arguments and submissions in this Court ranged over a very wide field particularly in the field of constitutional justice: see the judgments of this Court in *McDonald v. Bord na gCon* [1965] I.R. 265 and *East Donegal Co-operative v. The Attorney Gen-*

eral [1970] I.R. 317. The Constitution was relied upon; in particular Article 40, section 3, of the Constitution. This Court in *In re Haughey* [1971] I.R. 217 held that that provision of the Constitution was a guarantee of fair procedures. It is not, in my opinion, necessary to discuss the full effect of this Article in the realm of private law or indeed of public law. It is sufficient to say that public policy and the dictates of constitutional justice require that statutes, regulations or agreements setting up machinery for taking decisions which may affect rights or impose liabilities should be construed as providing for fair procedures. It is unnecessary to decide to what extent the contrary can be provided for by agreement between the parties. In the present case the provisions of clause 12(c) do not seek expressly or by implication to exclude the right of any of the parties to a fair procedure.

The plaintiff was neither told of the charges against him nor was he given any opportunity of dealing with them before the board of directors arrived at its decision to dismiss him. In my view this procedure was a breach of the implied term of the contract that the procedure should be fair, as it cannot be disputed, in the light of so much authority on the point, that failure to allow a person to meet the charges against him and to afford him an adequate [426] opportunity of answering them is a violation of an obligation to proceed fairly.

Having regard to the evidence which was given at the trial, one could not say with any degree of certainty that the members of the board of directors would have come to the same conclusion on the facts as Mr Justice Kenny did, or that they would have arrived at a unanimity of opinion on the effects of such misconduct as they might have found proved, particularly when one has regard to the close personal relationships which existed between some members of the board and the plaintiff and their knowledge of his activities in the firm since he joined it. But even if one could say with certainty that, if he had been given a fair hearing, the result would still have been the same, in my view that does not offer any ground for validating retroactively a procedure which was clearly invalid. It is to be noted that the board acted with great haste in dismissing the plaintiff, and on a report which did not contain complaints or allegations of misconduct set out with the particularity with which they were set out subsequently in the reply to the plaintiff's notice for particulars. Furthermore, as was settled by this Court in *Carvill v. Irish Industrial Bank Ltd.* [1968] I.R. 325 (*ante*, p. 213), an employer, in defending an action by an employee for wrongful summary dismissal, cannot rely upon misconduct which was not known by the employer at the time of the dismissal. I would add that the misconduct, if known but not in fact used as a ground for dismissal at the time, cannot be relied upon afterwards in an effort to justify the dismissal.

For the reasons I have already stated, I am of opinion that the plaintiff was wrongfully dismissed in that the dismissal was a violation of the provisions of clause 12(c) of the service agreement because of the failure to inform him of the charges against him and the failure to give him an adequate opportunity of answering them.

I am conscious of the fact that Mr Justice Kenny's conclusion that the defendants had acted in breach of the contract is based on somewhat different grounds and, therefore, I should deal with Mr Justice Kenny's reasons. He places great reliance upon the speech of Lord Reid in *Ridge v. Baldwin* and quoted with apparent approval the [427] passage at p. 65 of the report in which Lord Reid said: 'The law regarding master and servant is not in doubt. There cannot be specific performance of a contract of service, and the master can terminate the contract with his servant at any time and for any reason or for none. But if he does so in a manner not warranted by the contract he must pay damages for breach of contract.' This particular point does not arise for decision in this case but I wish to expressly reserve my opinion on the correctness of this statement if it is intended to convey that a court cannot make a declaration which would have the effect of reinstating a person wrongfully dismissed. I do not think that the decision in *Ridge v. Baldwin* is directly applicable to the present case. In that case the appellant was a Chief Constable and by a statutory provision the watch committee had power to suspend or dismiss him when they thought him negligent in the discharge of his duty or otherwise unfit for the same. The Chief Constable was not the servant of the watch committee, or of any one else, and he was the holder of an office from which he could be only dismissed in accordance with statutory provisions. It was held that the power of dismissal of this officer, contained in the Municipal Corporations Act, 1882, could not have been exercised until the watch committee had informed the officer of the grounds on which they proposed to proceed and had given him a proper opportunity to present his case in defence. It was a prerequisite that the question of neglect of duty should be considered in a judicial spirit and that could not be done without giving the officer in question the opportunity to defend himself against such a charge, and he would therefore have to be told what was alleged neglect of duty. As that had not been done the decision was a nullity.

Unlike the present case, *Ridge v. Baldwin* was not governed by the terms of a contract. In my view, once the matter is governed by the terms of a contract between the parties, it is immaterial whether the employee concerned is deemed to be a servant or an officer in so far as the distinction may be of relevance depending on whether the contract is a contract for services or a contract of service. In the present case it is immaterial whether the [428] plaintiff is an officer or a servant of his employers and, in my view, the case does not fall to be decided upon that distinction but rather upon the actual terms of the contract for the reasons I have already given.

Mr Justice Kenny attached importance to the fact that the plaintiffs position with any of the four companies involved could be terminated by the directors of one of them (namely, the holding company) and that this was a characteristic which equated his position to that of an officer. This particular position was the result of a contract between the parties, including the plaintiff, and clause 12(c) of the service agreement gave the directors of the holding company the final decision in whether or not he should be dismissed. I agree with Mr Justice Kenny in so far as he says that this situation strengthened the plaintiffs position in his claim to have a fair hearing, but it leads me to the conclusion that this right was an implied term of the contract by reason of the particular machinery set up by clause 12(c) and, therefore, it is not necessary to examine what might have been the plaintiffs position if such a machinery had not been provided. The relationship between the plaintiff and the defendants was a contractual one in so far as this particular matter is concerned.

Even if there had not been a pre-existing contractual relationship and the plaintiff had been invited to attend such an inquiry it is probably correct to say, as Harman J. held in *Byrne v. Kinematograph Renters Society* [1958] 1 W.L.R. 762, that a contract between the plaintiff and the defendants that the inquiry would be fairly conducted could be implied. It never appears to have been doubted in cases decided in England that, if the basis of the jurisdiction to conduct such an inquiry was based on statute or on the agreement of the parties, public policy prevents the exclusion of the rules of what in England is called natural justice where they ought to be observed. It is unnecessary in this case to enter into an examination of the other aspects of this problem which have engaged English courts, namely, whether the obligation to observe the rules of natural justice can be relied upon in a case where the relationship [429] between the parties is not founded either on statute or on contract.

Lastly, I come to deal with the defendant's contention that, if a hearing had been given to the plaintiff, there was nothing he could usefully have said and the result would have been the same. I think this proposition only has to be stated to be rejected. The obligation to give a fair hearing to the guilty is just as great as the obligation to give a fair hearing to the innocent. Furthermore, in this case, by reason of the provisions of clause 12(c), it would not be simply a case of established guilt or innocence, because the most important and effective power of the board of the holding company was one which was mainly a discretionary power, namely, to form the opinion or not that the plaintiffs misconduct injured any of the four companies.

For the reasons I have already given, I am of opinion that the defendants' appeal on all the matters set out in para. (1) of the said notice of appeal should be dismissed. This appeal, which took the form of an appeal confined in the first instance to the issues set out in the said paragraph of the notice of appeal, was heard pursuant to the order of this Court of the 13th March, 1970, which gave liberty to the parties to have the appeal on these issues heard in the first instance. Summarised briefly, the issues set out in para. (1) of the notice of appeal were whether the plaintiff was entitled to receive notice of the charges against him and to be given an opportunity to reply to the same, by virtue of clause 12(c) of the service agreement, before he could be dismissed; and whether he was entitled to damages for wrongful dismissal when he did not receive such notice before his dismissal. I am expressing no view on what damages the plaintiff should receive, or on what basis they should be calculated, as that aspect of the appeal has not yet been heard.

Shindler v. Northern Raincoat Co. Ltd.
[1960] 2 All E.R. 239

The plaintiff was appointed managing director of the company for a 10 year period. Following a subsequent take over of the company and disagreements between him and the new controllers, resolutions were passed removing him from his office as a director and terminating his service agreement in so far as that may still be subsisting. The company's articles of association included clauses along the lines of articles 99 and 110 of Table A.

DIPLOCK J.: . . . [240] The argument for the defendant company on this matter derives some support from the cases referred to and from another case, *Nelson v. James Nelson & Sons, Ltd.* [1914] 2 K.B. 770. The argument is put thus – where a company's articles of association include art. 68, the directors have no power to appoint a managing director on terms which purport to exclude the company's right to terminate his appointment ipso facto on either his ceasing to be a director or if the company shall by resolution in general meeting resolve that his tenure of office as managing director be determined. That argument can be put in alternative ways, either that the agreement for a fixed term which does not incorporate the right of the company set out in art. 68 is ultra vires, or else that the agreement for a fixed period of employment must be subject to the implied term that it is determinable in either of the circumstances set out at the end of art. 68.

It seems to me that this point is concluded against the defendant company by the decision of the House of Lords in *Southern Foundries (1926) Ltd. v. Shirlaw* [1940] A.C. 701. That case was somewhat complicated and gave rise to a division of opinion in the House of Lords. Two of their Lordships (Viscount Maugham and Lord Romer) who were most familiar with the Chancery side came to one conclusion and three of their Lordships (Lord Atkin, Lord Wright and Lord Porter) who were perhaps more familiar with the common law side, came to another. There are some references in subsequent cases in the Chancery Division which suggest that it is difficult to ascertain what *Southern Foundries (1926), Ltd. v. Shirlaw* determined. It does, however, seem to me that all five of their Lordships in the Southern Foundries case were agreed on one principle of law which is vital to the defendant company's contention in the present case. That principle of law is that laid down in *Stirling v. Maitland* (5 B. & S. 840), where Cockburn, C.J., said:

"... if a party enters into an arrangement which can only take effect by the continuance of a certain existing state of circumstances, there is an implied engagement on his part that he shall do nothing of his own motion to put an end to that state of circumstances, under which alone the arrangement can be operative."

Applying that respectable principle to the present case, there is an implied engagement on the part of the defendant company that it will do nothing of its own motion to put an end to the state of circumstances which enables the plaintiff to continue as managing director. That is to say, there is an implied undertaking that it will not revoke his appointment as a director, and will not resolve that his tenure of office be determined.

Directors' Remuneration, Expenses and Loans

See *Company Law*, pp. 122-13 6.

Companies Act 1963, section 186

Approval of company necessary for payment by it to director for loss of office

186.—It shall not be lawful for a company to make to any director of the company any payment by way of compensation for loss of office, or as consideration for or in connection with his retirement from office, without particulars relating to the proposed payment (including the amount thereof) being disclosed to the members of the company and the proposal being approved by the Company in general meeting.

Companies Act 1990 Act, sections 31(1) and 36

Prohibition of loans etc. to directors and connected persons

31.—(1) Except as provided by sections 32 to 37, a company shall not –

(*a*) make a loan or a quasi-loan to a director of the company or of its holding company or to a person connected with such a director;

(*b*) enter into a credit transaction as creditor for such a director or a person so connected;

(*c*) enter into a guarantee or provide any security in connection with a loan, quasi-loan or credit transaction made by any other person for such a director or a person so connected.

Directors' expenses

36.—(1) Section 31 shall not prohibit a company from doing anything to provide any of its directors with funds to meet vouched expenditure properly incurred or to be incurred by him for the purposes of the company or the purpose of enabling him properly to perform his duties as an officer of the company or doing anything to enable any of its directors to avoid incurring such expenditure.

(2) Where a company enters into any transaction pursuant to subsection (1), any liability falling on any person arising from any such transaction shall be discharged by him within six months from the date on which it was incurred.

Table A articles 76, 90, 110, 138

76. The remuneration of the directors shall from time to time be determined by the company in general meeting. Such remuneration shall be deemed to accrue from day to day. The directors may also be paid all travelling, hotel and other expenses properly incurred by them in attending and returning from meetings of the directors or any committee of the directors or general meetings of the company or in connection with the business of the company.

90. The directors on behalf of the company may pay a gratuity or pension or allowance on retirement to any director who has held any other salaried office or place of profit with the company or to his widow or dependants, and may make contributions to any fund and pay premiums for the purchase or provision of any such gratuity, pension or allowance.

110. See ante p. 190 (managing director)

138. Every director, managing director, agent, auditor, secretary and other officer for the time being of the company shall be indemnified out of the assets of the company against any liability incurred by him in defending any proceedings, whether civil or criminal, in relation to his acts while acting in such office, in which judgment is given in his favour or in which he is acquitted or in connection with any application under section 391 of the Act in which relief is granted to him by the court.

Re Halt Garage (1964) Ltd.
[1982] 3 All E.R. 1016

This decision contains the most extensive modern analysis of the *ultra vires* principle's application to the question of directors' remuneration. A husband and wife were the company's only directors and shareholders. Early on in the company's existence, both worked in the business and drew directors' remuneration. Then she became ill and ceased working, but she remained a director and continued drawing remuneration. In the following year the company started to incur losses, and three years later it was wound up as insolvent. The liquidator contended that she should not have been remunerated when she was not actively engaged in the business, and that her husband's remuneration was excessive.

OLIVER J.: . . . [1023] [T]he claim originally made under section 332 of the Companies Act 1948 (same as section 297 of the 1963 Act) has not been proceeded with and the present claim is restricted to a claim for misfeasance and breach of trust under section 333 (same as section 298 of the 1963 Act). So it has to be shown that in making these payments the directors were in breach of some fiduciary duty which they owed to their beneficiary, which either was not or could not be sanctioned by that beneficiary. In relation to this claim, although it is alleged that the respondents (and that means, effectively, Mr Charlesworth) knew that the company was making losses and was unable to pay its debts without at least a further injection of funds or a measure of forbearance on the part of its major creditors, there is no allegation of fraud. . . .

The company's articles in the present case incorporate reg 76 of Table A, Part 1 (same in 1963 Act's Table A), which provides that the remuneration of the directors shall from time to time be determined by the company in general meeting and shall be deemed to accrue from day to day. The directors, qua directors, are not, therefore, entitled as of right to any remuneration for their services, and in so far as remuneration has been drawn without the proper authority, they are bound to account to the company for it or to pay damages.

Obviously in the case of a lady who is as ill as Mrs Charlesworth is and whose illness, so far as the evidence goes, appears to have been contributed to by the long hours of work and irregularity of meals which she underwent whilst working up the business, the claim is not a very attractive one, but a liquidator has no discretion about the performance of his duties and if the claim is good in law it must succeed. If charity has, to use the words of Bowen L.J. in *Hutton v. West Cork Rly Co.* (1883) 23 Ch.D. 654 at 673, no business to sit at the board of directors, equally sympathy has no voice at the Bar of the court.

Counsel for the respondents takes his stand on the fact that the company has, by its constitution, an express power to determine and pay directors' remuneration, a power, moreover, which is recognised expressly in the case of every limited company by the Companies Act, 1948 (see, for instance, ss. 189 and 196). While it is true that a director, under an article in this form, has no entitlement to remuneration, nevertheless his agreement with the company when he accepts office is, impliedly, to serve the company as a director and to take the responsibilities which that office entails at whatever remuneration the company in general meeting may choose to vote to him, be it mean or generous, liberal or illiberal. It may vote nothing. But, if it votes him something, he is entitled to have it and it cannot be recovered from him in misfeasance proceedings, even if it is very greatly in excess of any possible value attributable to his services.

In the absence of fraud on the creditors or on minority shareholders, the quantum of such remuneration is a matter for the company. There is no implication or requirement that it must come out of profits only and indeed, any requirement that it must be so restricted would, in many cases, bring business to a halt and prevent a business which had fallen on hard times from being brought round.

There is, counsel for the respondents submits, no principle of law which establishes [1024] that the payment of a scale of remuneration which the court may consider overgenerous, having regard to the services performed by a particular director, is ultra vires the company, either in toto or pro tanto, and indeed it is not for the courts to decide how far remuneration is reasonable, absent some plea that its payment is a fraud on the creditors or on minority shareholders. As long as it is acting within its express powers, a company may be unwise, at least so long as it is honest, and, as I have said, there is now no suggestion of mala fides here. . . . [1029] I cannot help thinking, if I may respectfully say so, that there has been a certain confusion between the requirements for a valid exercise of the fiduciary powers of directors (which have nothing to do with the capacity of the company but everything to do with the propriety of acts done within that capacity), the extent to which powers can be implied or limits be placed, as a matter of construction, on express powers, and the matters which the court will take into consideration at the suit of a minority shareholder in determining the extent to which his interests can be over ridden by a majority vote. These three matters, as it seems to me, raise questions which are logically quite distinct [1030] but which have sometimes been treated as if they demanded a single, universal answer leading to the conclusion that, because a power must not be abused, therefore, beyond the limits of propriety it does not exist.

Nevertheless, it cannot, I think, be doubted that, whether it be logically defensible or not and whether it be labelled an application of the ultra vires doctrine of the protection of minorities, the courts have over the past hundred years evolved a series of principles which have been stated to be of general application to gratuitous dispositions of the property of trading companies. . . .

[1033] It is a commonplace in private family companies, where there are substantial profits available for distribution by way of dividend, for the shareholder directors to distribute those profits by way of directors' remuneration rather than by way of dividend, because the latter course has certain fiscal advantages. But such a distribution may, and frequently does, bear very little relation to the true market value of the services rendered by the directors and if one is to look at it from the point of view of the benefit of the company as a corporate entity, then it is wholly unjustifiable, because it deprives the company of funds which might otherwise be used for expansion or investment or contingency reserves.

Yet unless it is to be said that the *Lee, Behrens & Co.* [1932] 2 Ch. 46 test is to be applied also even to a unanimous exercise of the power of the company in general meeting to distribute profits by way of dividend (which I should hardly have thought was arguable) it is very difficult to see why the payment of directors' remuneration, on whatever scale the company in general meeting chooses, out of funds which could perfectly well be distributed by way of dividend, should be open to attack merely because the shareholders, in their own interests, choose to attach to it the label of directors' remuneration. After all, the close company provisions of the Income Tax Acts are specifically designed to compel distributions and deem them to have taken place if they fall short of the standard required. Is it then to be said that subsequently, perhaps years later, the company, by its liquidator or possibly at the instance of a purchaser of the shares, can come along and demand back profits paid out as remuneration with the active assent and concurrence of all the shareholders at the time because their payment was ultra vires? . . .

[1034] If it is truly beyond a company's capacity to make any gratuitous payment out of its funds that is not, viewed objectively, for the benefit of the company and to promote its business, then such a payment cannot logically be sanctioned or ratified even by all the shareholders acting in unison and it cannot logically matter how the company came by the funds. Company funds are company funds whether they are in the form of cash and representing profits earned by trading or in the form of credit from suppliers of moneys drawn on loan from the company's bankers. They do not belong to the shareholders unless and until they are paid to them by way of a properly declared dividend.

I do not find it altogether easy to reconcile the cases or to extract the principle from them, and it is not in this case of merely academic interest to seek to do so, because the payments under attack here were expressly sanctioned by all the shareholders and the liquidator's claim relates in part to a period when there were divisible profits from which the payments could be made and in part to a period when there were not. . . .

[1036] It does not appear to me that the group of cases culminating in *Parke v. Daily News* [1962] Ch. 927 really has much bearing on a case where what has been done is something expressly authorised by the company's constitution and has been expressly sanctioned by the unanimous vote of all the shareholders in general meeting. Counsel for the liquidator, however, submits that the liquidator is, in effect, in the position of a minority shareholder. Suppose, he suggests, that the directors of a company vote themselves a present and then use their majority votes as shareholders to override a dissentient minority. Suppose that before the minority can act to challenge this the company is wound up. Can it be said, he asks, that the liquidator cannot pursue a claim on their behalf. That may be perfectly right, but it does not seem to me that it really is of any help in the context of a case where there is not and never has been any minority shareholder. . . .

[1037] No doubt the effectiveness even of a resolution in general meeting will depend on its bona fides. Fraud opens all doors and the court will not uphold or permit the fraudulent exercise of a power. *Re George Newman & Go.* [1895] 1 Ch. 674 was a clear case of dishonesty, and it is not surprising to find in the judgment of the court the doubt expressed whether what was done there could have been sanctioned even by all the shareholders, although the point was not actually decided. But there is no suggestion of bad faith in this case and, as is shown by *Re British Seamless Paper Box Co.* (1881) 17 Ch. D. 467, which is referred to in the judgment of Lindley L.J. in the *George Newman* case, the position is quite different where the transaction is honest and is sanctioned by all members of the company at the time . . .

[E]ven given a bona fide unanimous resolution in general meeting, it still must be a resolution to do something which the company can lawfully do. It cannot, for instance, lawfully return money to its shareholders out of capital. . . . In the context of the instant case, however, counsel for the liquidator submits that since (at any rate during most of the material time) there were no profits available in the company for distribution and since directors' emoluments are always gratuities, except where payable under contract, and since the directors were shareholders as well, every payment to them constituted an illegal reduction of capital except to the extent to which it can be justified by the test of benefit to the company. One difficulty about that, even accepting the submission for the moment, is that if 'the benefit of the company' means, as Plowman J. suggested in *Parke v. Daily News*, 'the benefit of the shareholders as a whole', it leads him nowhere.

I accept entirely the submission of counsel for the liquidator that a gratuitous payment out of the company's capital to a member, qua member, is unlawful and cannot stand, even if authorised by all the shareholders. What I find difficulty in accepting is that, assuming a sum to be genuinely paid to a director-shareholder as remuneration under an express power, it becomes an illegal return of capital to him, qua member, if it does not satisfy some further test of being paid for the benefit of the company as a corporate entity. If he genuinely receives the money as a reward for his directorship, the question whether the payment is beneficial to the company or not cannot, as I see it, alter the capacity in which he receives it: see, for instance, *Cyclists' Touring Club v. Hopkinson* [1910] 1 Ch. 179. . . .

[1039] [A]ssuming that the sum is bona fide voted to be paid as remuneration, it seems to me that the amount, whether it be mean or generous, must be a matter of management for the company to determine in accordance with its constitution which expressly authorises payment for directors' services. Shareholders are required to be honest, but as counsel for the respondents suggests, there is no requirement that they must be wise and it is not for the court to manage the company.

Counsel for the liquidator submits, however, that if this is right it leads to the bizarre result that a meeting of stupid or deranged but perfectly honest shareholders can, like Bowen L.J.'s lunatic director, vote to themselves, qua directors, some perfectly outlandish sum by way of remuneration and that in a subsequent winding up the liquidator can do nothing to recover it. It seems to me that the answer to this lies in the objective test which the court necessarily applies. It assumes human beings to be rational and to apply ordinary standards. In the postulated circumstances of a wholly unreasonable payment, that might, no doubt, be prima facie evidence of fraud, but it might also be evidence that what purported to be remuneration was not remuneration at all but a dressed-up gift to a shareholder out of capital, like the 'interest' payment in the *Ridge Securities* case which bore no relation to the principal sums advanced.

This, as it seems to me, is the real question in a case such as the present. I do not think that in circumstances such as those in the instant case the authorities compel the application to the express power of a test of benefit to the company which, certainly construed as Plowman J. held that it should be construed, would be largely meaningless. The real test must, I think, be whether the transaction in question was a genuine exercise of the power. The motive is more important than the label. Those who deal with a limited company do so on the basis that its affairs will be conducted in accordance with its constitution, one of the express incidents of which is that the directors may be paid remuneration. Subject to that, they are entitled to have the capital kept intact. They have to accept the shareholders' assessment of the scale of that remuneration, but they are entitled to assume that, whether liberal or illiberal, what is paid is genuinely remuneration and that the power is not used as a cloak for making payments out of capital to the shareholders as such.

[1040] Turning now to the facts of the instant case, it seems to me that the question which I have to determine is whether, on the evidence before me, I can say that the payments made to Mr Charlesworth and to Mrs Charlesworth were genuinely exercises of the company's power to pay remuneration, and counsel for the liquidator very properly concedes that he is in some difficulties as regards the case of Mr Charlesworth. Despite some rather confusing statements made by Mr Charlesworth to the Official Receiver which indicate the contrary (at any rate as regards part of the relevant time), I am satisfied on the evidence that, except for the period from December 1967 to March 1968 when Mr Gore was in charge and the period from September 1970 to March 1971 when he was away (save for two weeks or so in December), he was working more or less full-time in the business. . . .

[1041] I do not think that, in the absence of evidence that the payments made were patently excessive or unreasonable, the court can or should engage on a minute examination of whether it would have been more appropriate or beneficial to the company to fix the remuneration at £X rather than £Y, so long as it is satisfied that it was indeed drawn as remuneration. That is a matter left by the company's constitution to its members. In my judgment, a general meeting was competent to sanction the payments which he in fact drew and the claim in misfeasance against Mr Charlesworth under this head must fail.

I have felt considerably greater difficulty over the payments to Mrs Charlesworth. . . . It was known from, at the latest, December 1967 onwards, that Mrs Charlesworth could never return to render any services in the actual conduct of the company's business, and she was never thereafter called on, nor was she ever expected, to fulfil any function save that of being a director and carrying out such minimal formal acts as the holding of that office entailed. Mr Charlesworth in his evidence admitted that the company derived no benefit at all from the payments made to her, save such as may be thought to flow from the fact that she held office. She was incurably ill and living at a distance of several hundred miles from the company's place of business. Yet in each of the years 1968-69 and 1969-70 she received a sum of some £1,500 and in the year 1970-71 something over £500. It is true that Mr Charlesworth said in his evidence that it had always been the company's practice to continue the payment of full wages to employees who were off sick, and indeed the company's memorandum of association contains a wide express power in these terms:

> "To pay gratuities or pensions or allowances on retirement to any directors who have held any other salaried office or place of profit with the company or to their widows or dependants and to make contributions to any fund and to pay premiums [1043] for the purchase or provision of any such gratuity, pension or allowance and to promote or assist, financially, whether by way of contributions, donations, the payment of premiums or otherwise, any fund or scheme for the benefit, wholly or in part, of directors, ex-directors, or employees, or ex-employees, of the company, or their dependants or relatives, or for charitable purposes generally."

But it cannot be contended, I think, that Mrs Charlesworth came within that clause. She had never held any office other than that of director and that she retained. Moreover, Mr Charlesworth was not prepared to say that this practice of the company to which he referred had, or was thought to have, any effect on the loyalty of his staff.

The fact is that, however valuable and exacting may have been the services which Mrs Charlesworth had rendered in the past, her continued directorship contributed nothing to the company's future, beyond the fact that she was and remained responsible as a director and was able to make up the necessary quorum for directors' meetings (of which remarkably few took place if the minutes are any accurate guide).

On the other hand, it is said that the Companies Act 1948 imposes on every company incorporated under its provisions an obligation to have a director and it contemplates that those who assume the responsibilities of office, whether they carry them out well or ill, may be paid for that service in such way and in such measure as the company's regulations prescribe or permit. Here the company's constitution conferred on it in express terms a power to award to a director as reward or remuneration for the bare fact of holding office, and that power the company purported to exercise. If it be legitimate for the company to award some remuneration, however nominal, to Mrs Charlesworth for acting as a director and taking on herself, for good or ill, the responsibilities which that office entails, at what point, counsel for the respondents asks, does it become beyond the company's power to do that which its constitution permits it to do and how can the court take on itself the discretion as to quantum which is vested in the shareholders, there being, ex concessis, no mala fides? I have not found the point an easy one, but on the view that I take of the law the argument of counsel for the respondents is very difficult to meet *if* the payments made really were within the express power conferred by the company's constitution.

But of course what the company's articles authorise is the fixing of 'remuneration', which I take to mean a reward for services rendered or to be rendered; and, whatever the terms of the resolutions passed and however described in the accounts of the company's books, the real question seems to me to be whether the payments really were 'directors' remuneration' or whether they were gratuitous distributions to a shareholder out of capital dressed up as remuneration.

I do not think that it can be said that a director of a company cannot be rewarded as such merely because he is not active in the company's business. The mere holding of office involves responsibility even in the absence of any substantial activity, and it is indeed in part to the mere holding of office that Mrs Charlesworth owes her position as a respondent in these proceedings. I can see nothing as a matter of construction of the article to disentitle the company, if the shareholders so resolve, from paying a reward attributable to the mere holding of the office of director, for being, as it were, a name on the notepaper and attending such meetings or signing such documents as are from time to time required. The director assumes the responsibility on the footing that he will receive whatever recompense the company in general meeting may think appropriate. In this case, however, counsel for the liquidator is entitled to submit that the sums paid to Mrs Charlesworth were so out of proportion to any possible value attributable to her holding of office that the court is entitled to treat them as not being genuine payments of remuneration at all but as dressed-up dividends out of capital. . . .

Guinness plc v Saunders
[1990] 2 A.C. 663

The matter in issue here is the procedures to be followed when agreeing directors' remuneration. Both defendants and another director of the plaintiff company, as a committee of the board of directors, agreed to pay the second defendant (Mr. Ward) £5.2m for his services in connection with a take-over bid being made by the plaintiffs. Following the successful completion of the bid, the company paid him the money. It claimed recovery of the money on the ground that he had received the payment in breach of his fiduciary duty as a director, in that he had not disclosed his interest in the agreement to the board of directors, as is required by the equivalent of section 194 of the 1963 Act.

LORD TEMPLEMAN: – [686] Mr. Ward admits receipt of £5.2m from Guinness and pleads an agreement by Guinness that he should he paid this sum for his advice and services in connection with the bid. Mr. Ward admits that payment was not authorised by the board of directors of Guinness.

The articles of association of Guinness provide:

> "Remuneration of directors 90. The board shall fix the annual remuneration of the directors provided that without the consent of the company in general meeting such remuneration (excluding any special remuneration payable under article 91 and article 92) shall not exceed the sum of £100,000 per annum. . . . 91. The board may, in addition to the remuneration authorised in article 90, grant special remuneration to any director who serves on any committee or who devotes special attention to the business of the company or who otherwise performs services which in the opinion of the board are outside the scope of the ordinary duties of a director. Such special remuneration may be made payable to such director in addition to or in substitution for his ordinary remuneration as a director, and may be made payable by a lump sum or by way of salary, or commission or participation in profits, or by any or all of those modes or otherwise as the board may determine."

Articles 90 and 91 of the articles of association of Guinness depart from the Table A articles recommended by statute, which reserve to a company in general meeting the right to determine the remuneration of the directors of the company. But by article 90 the annual remuneration which the directors may award themselves is limited and by article 91 special remuneration for an individual director can only be authorised by the board. A committee, which may consist of only two or, as in the present case, three members, however honest and conscientious, cannot assess impartially the value of its work or the value of the contribution of its individual members. A director may, as a condition of accepting appointment to a committee, or after he has accepted appointment, seek the agreement of the board to authorise payment for special work envisaged or carried out. The shareholders of Guinness run the risk that the board may be too generous to an individual director at the expense of the shareholders but the shareholders have, by article 91 chosen to run this risk and can protect themselves by the number, quality and impartiality of the members of the board who will consider whether an individual director deserves special reward. Under article 91 the shareholders of Guinness do not run the risk that a committee may value its own work and the contribution of its own members. Article 91 authorises the board, and only the board, to grant special remuneration to a director who serves on a committee.

It was submitted that article 2 alters the plain meaning of article 91. In article 2 there are a number of definitions each of which is expressed to apply "if not inconsistent with the subject or context." The expression "the board" is defined as [687]

> "The directors of the company for the time being (or a quorum of such directors assembled at a meeting of directors duly convened) or any committee authorised by the board to act on its behalf."

The result of applying the article 2 definition to article 91, it is said, is that a committee may grant special remuneration to any director who serves on a committee or devotes special attention to the business of the company or who otherwise performs services which in the opinion of the committee are outside the scope of the ordinary duties of a director. In my opinion the subject and context of article 91 are inconsistent with the expression "the board" in article 91 meaning anything except the board. Article 91 draws a contrast between the board and a committee of the board. The board is expressly authorised to grant special remuneration to *any* director who serves on *any* committee. It cannot have been intended that any committee should be able to grant special remuneration to any director, whether a member of the committee or not. The board must compare the work of an individual director with the ordinary duties of a director. The board must decide whether special remuneration shall be paid in addition to or in substitution for the annual remuneration determined by the board under article 90. These decisions could only be made by the board surveying the work and remuneration of each and every director. Article 91 also provides for the board to decide whether special remuneration should take the form of participation in profits; the article could not intend that a committee should be able to determine whether profits should accrue to the shareholders' funds or be paid out to an individual director. The remuneration of directors concerns all the members of the board and all the shareholders of Guinness. Article 2 does not operate to produce a result which is inconsistent with the language, the subject and the context of article 91. Only the board possessed power to award £5.2m. to Mr. Ward.

Reliance was next placed on article 110 which provides:

> "The directors may establish any committees, local boards or agencies for managing any of the affairs of the company, either in the United Kingdom, or elsewhere. and may appoint any persons to be members of such local boards, or as managers or agents, and fix their remuneration, and may delegate to any committee, local board, managers or agent 'any of the powers, authorities and discretions vested in the board. with power to sub-delegate, and may authorise the members of any local board, or any of them to fill any vacancies therein, and to act notwithstanding vacancies, and any such appointment or delegation may be made upon such terms and subject to such conditions as the directors may think fit . . ."

Therefore, it is said, the board may delegate to a committee the power conferred on the board by article 91 to grant special remuneration to a director. But article 110 could not have been intended to allow a local board or agency or manager to fix the remuneration of a director and article 110 expressly provides that remuneration shall be fixed by the board. Article 110 does not enable the board to delegate the power of deciding directors' remuneration which by articles 90 and 91 is vested in the board alone.

[688] Next, reliance was placed on article 100(D) which is in the following terms:

> "Any director may act by himself or his firm in a professional capacity for the company and any company in which the company is interested, and he or his firm shall be entitled to remuneration for professional services as if he were not a director; provided that nothing herein contained shall authorise a director or his firm to act as auditor to the company or any subsidiary."

Article 91 deals with directors' remuneration; article 100(D) deals with directors' charges for professional services. There is a distinction between remuneration and professional charges. Remuneration depends on an assessment of the value of the individual and the perceived quality of his work. Professional charges can be checked by taxation in the case of lawyers and in other instances by professional recommendations and standards of comparison. Mr. Ward nowhere alleges in his pleadings that he provided professional services. Counsel on his behalf stated that Mr. Ward was a member of a New York firm of attorneys. The professional charges of that firm in connection with the bid were paid to the firm pursuant to article 100(D). If Mr. Ward had performed legal professional services separately from the services rendered by his firm, then article 100(D) would apply. The advice and services upon which Mr. Ward relies in these proceedings were not legal professional services. Counsel informed the House that Mr. Ward was one of a number of experts who advise and negotiate, implement or frustrate take-over bids. Counsel did not suggest that these experts are all lawyers or that they constitute a profession or that they possessed the indicia of a profession, namely, an organisation which controls entry and membership, provides educational and training qualifications, insists upon a standard of work and behaviour, imposes disciplinary sanctions for misconduct and, above all, acknowledges and enforces a duty to the public over and above the duty common to all of obeying the law. The services pleaded by Mr. Ward were the services he was bound to carry out and which any member of the board is entitled and bound to carry out as a member of a committee established by the board. Guinness admit for the purposes of this application that Mr. Ward performed services which were of value to Guinness, although if it were necessary to do so Guinness would attempt to prove, and Mr. Ward would deny, that Mr. Ward has exaggerated the value of his services and that some of his activities were improper and caused damage to Guinness. For present purposes it suffices that Mr. Ward seeks remuneration for his services as a member of a committee; he is not seeking remuneration for professional services provided in a professional capacity. Failure to comply with article 91 cannot be disguised as an application of article 100(D).

Mr. Ward also pleads that Mr. Saunders possessed implied actual authority or ostensible authority to agree on behalf of Guinness that Mr. Ward should be paid for his services. This allegation is inconsistent with the express terms of the resolution dated 19 January 1986 whereby the board conferred power in relation to the bid on the committee and not on Mr. Saunders. The board could not confer on the committee the [689] right to agree or to award special remuneration to a director. The board could not confer such a right on Mr. Saunders. The resolution dated 19 January 1986 does not purport to confer on anybody a power which the board could not confer. The articles of Guinness are binding on the board, on the committee, on Mr. Saunders and on Mr. Ward. Mr.Ward was not entitled to assume that Mr. Saunders possessed an authority inconsistent with the articles of Guinness, inconsistent with the appointment of the committee and inconsistent with the terms of the appointment of the committee. If before or at the board meeting on 19 January 1986 the board had been requested to agree to grant special remuneration to Mr. Ward, such a request might well have met with a favourable response. If the bid for Distillers had not led to allegations of misconduct by Guinness it is possible that the payment of £5.2m to Mr. Ward's company, apparently for services rendered by his company, would not have been questioned or, at any event, that Mr. Ward would not have been required to repay that sum. But there never was any contract by Guinness to pay special remuneration to Mr. Ward for services rendered in connection with the bid for Distillers. Since, for the purposes of this application, Guinness concede that Mr. Ward performed valuable services for Guinness in connection with the bid, counsel on behalf of Mr. Ward submits that Mr. Ward, if not entitled to remuneration pursuant to the articles, is, nevertheless, entitled to be awarded by the court a sum by way of quantum meruit or equitable allowance for his services. Counsel submits that the sum awarded by the court might amount to £5.2m or a substantial proportion of that sum; therefore Mr. Ward should be allowed to retain the sum of £5.2m which he has received until, at the trial of the action, the court determines whether he acted with propriety and, if so, how much of the sum of £5.2m he should be permitted to retain; Mr. Ward is anxious for an opportunity to prove at a trial that he acted with propriety throughout the bid. It is common ground that, for the purposes of this appeal, it must be assumed that Mr. Ward and the other members of the committee acted in good faith and that the sum of £5.2m was a proper reward for the services rendered by Mr. Ward to Guinness.

My Lords, the short answer to a quantum meruit claim based on an implied contract by Guinness to pay reasonable remuneration for services rendered is that there can be no contract by Guinness to pay special remuneration for the services of a director unless that contract is entered into by the board pursuant to article 91. The short answer to the claim for an equitable allowance is the equitable principle which forbids a trustee to make a profit out of his trust unless the trust instrument, in this case the articles of association of Guinness, so provides. The law cannot and equity will not amend the articles of Guinness. The court is not entitled to usurp the functions conferred on the board by the articles.

The 28th edition (1982) of *Snell's Principles of Equity*, first published in 1868, contains the distilled wisdom of the author and subsequent editors, including Sir Robert Megarry, on the law applicable to trusts and trustees. It is said, at p. 244, that:

> [690] "With certain exceptions, neither directly nor indirectly may a trustee make a profit from his trust. . . . The rule depends not on fraud or *mala fides*, but on the mere fact of a profit made."

The 24th edition (1987) of *Palmer's Company Law*, first published in 1898, contains the distilled wisdom of the author and subsequent editors concerning the law applicable to companies and directors. It is said, in volume 1, at pp. 943-944, that:

> "Like other fiduciaries directors are required not to put themselves in a position where there is a conflict (actual or potential) between their personal interests and their duties to the company. . . . the position of a director. vis-à-vis the company, is that of an agent who may not himself contract with his principal, and . . . is similar to that of a trustee who, however fair a proposal may be, is not allowed to let the position arise where his interest and that of the trust may conflict. . . he is, like a trustee, disqualified from contracting with the company and for a good reason: the company is entitled to the collective wisdom of its directors, and if any director is interested in a contract, his interest may conflict with his duty, and the law always strives to prevent such a conflict from arising."

The application of these principles to remuneration in the case of a trustee is described by *Snell*, 28th ed., at p. 252:

"As a result of the rule that a trustee cannot make a profit from his trust, trustees and executors are generally entitled to no allowance for their care and trouble. This rule is so strict that even if a trustee or executor has sacrificed much time to carrying on a business as directed by the trust, he will usually be allowed nothing as compensation for his personal trouble or loss of time."

The application of these principles to remuneration in the case of a director is described by *Palmer*, 24th ed., at p. 902:

"Prima facie, directors of a company cannot claim remuneration, but the articles usually provide expressly for payment of it . . . and, where this is the case, the provision operates as an authority to the directors to pay remuneration out of the funds of the company; such remuneration is not restricted to payment out of profits."

The following also appears, at p. 903:

"The articles will also usually authorise the payment by the directors to one of their number of extra remuneration for special services. Where such provision is made, it is a condition precedent to a director's claim for additional remuneration that the board of directors shall determine the method and amount of the extra payment; it is irrelevant that the director has performed substantial extra services and the payment of additional remuneration would be reasonable."

So far as contract is concerned. Lord Cranworth L.C., in *Aberdeen Railway Co. v. Blaikie Bros.* (1854) 1 Macq. H.L. 461, considered, at pp. 471-472:

[691] "the general question, whether a director of a railway company is or is not precluded from dealing on behalf of the company with himself, or with a firm in which he is a partner. The directors are a body to whom is delegated the duty of managing the general affairs of the company. A corporate body can only act by agents, and it is of course the duty of those agents so to act as best to promote the interests of the corporation whose affairs they are conducting. Such agents have duties to discharge of a fiduciary nature towards their principal. And it is a rule of universal application, that no one, having such duties to discharge, shall be allowed to enter into engagements in which he has, or can have, a personal interest conflicting, or which possibly may conflict, with the interests of those whom he is bound to protect. So strictly is this principle adhered

to, that no question is allowed to be raised as to the fairness or unfairness of a contract so entered into. It obviously is, or may be, impossible to demonstrate how far in any particular case the terms of such a contract have been the best for the interest of the cestui que trust, which it was possible to obtain. It may sometimes happen that the terms on which a trustee has dealt or attempted to deal with the estate or interests of those for whom he is a trustee, have been as good as could have been obtained from any other person-they may even at the time have been better. But still so inflexible is the rule that no inquiry on that subject is permitted. . . .

[692] Equity forbids a trustee to make a profit out of his trust. The articles of association of Guinness relax the strict rule of equity to the extent of enabling a director to make a profit provided that the board of directors contracts on behalf of Guinness for the payment of special remuneration or decides to award special remuneration. Mr. Ward did not obtain a contract or a grant from the board of directors. Equity has no power to relax its own strict rule further than and inconsistently with the express relaxation contained in the articles of association. A shareholder is entitled to compliance with the articles. A director accepts office subject to and with the benefit of the provisions of the articles relating to directors. No one is obliged to accept appointment as a director. No director can be obliged to serve on a committee. A director of Guinness who contemplates or accepts service on a committee or has performed outstanding services for the company as a member of a committee may apply to the board of directors for a contract or an award of special remuneration. A director who does not read the articles or a director who misconstrues the articles is nevertheless bound by the articles. Article 91 provides clearly enough for the authority of the board of directors to he obtained for the payment of special remuneration and the submissions made on behalf of Mr. Ward, based on articles 2, 100(D) and 110 are more ingenious than plausible and more legalistic than convincing. At the board meeting held on 19 January 1986, Mr. Ward was present but he did not seek then or thereafter to obtain the necessary authority of the board of directors for payment of special remuneration. In these circumstances there are no grounds for equity to relax its rules further than the articles of association provide. Similarly, the law will not imply a contract between Guinness and Mr. Ward for remuneration on a quantum meruit basis awarded by the court when the articles of association of Guinness stipulate that special remuneration for a director can only be awarded by the board.

It was submitted on behalf of Mr. Ward that Guinness, by the committee consisting of Mr. Saunders, Mr. Ward and Mr. Roux, entered into a voidable contract to pay remuneration to Mr. Ward and that since Mr. Ward performed the services he agreed to perform under this voidable contract there could be no *restitutio integrum* and the contract [693] cannot be avoided. This submission would enable a director to claim and retain remuneration under a contract which a committee purported to conclude with him. notwithstanding that the committee had no power to enter into the contract. The fact is that Guinness never did contract to pay anything to Mr. Ward. The contract on which Mr. Ward relies is not voidable but non-existent. In support of a quantum meruit claim, counsel for Mr. Ward relied on the decision of Buckley J. in *In re Duomatic Ltd.* [1969] 2 Ch. 365. In that case a company sought and failed to recover remuneration received by a director when the shareholders or a voting majority of the shareholders had sanctioned or ratified the payment. In the present case there has been no such sanction or ratification either by the board of directors or by the shareholders. Mr. Ward also relied on the decision in *Craven-Ellis v. Canons Ltd.* [1936] 2 K.B. 403. In that case the plaintiff was appointed managing director of a company by an agreement under the company's seal which also provided for his remuneration. By the articles of association each director was required to obtain qualification shares within two months of his appointment. Neither the plaintiff nor the other directors obtained their qualification shares within two months or at all and the agreement with the managing director was entered into after they had ceased to be directors. The plaintiff having done work for the company pursuant to the terms of the agreement was held to be entitled to the remuneration provided for in the agreement on the basis of a quantum meruit. In *Craven-Ellis* the plaintiff was not a director, there was no conflict between his claim to remuneration and the equitable doctrine which debars a director from profiting from his fiduciary duty, and there was no obstacle to the implication of a contract between the company and the plaintiff entitling the plaintiff to claim reasonable remuneration as of right by an action in law. Moreover, as in *In re Duomatic Ltd.*, the agreement was sanctioned by all the directors, two of whom were beneficially entitled to the share capital of the company. In the present case Mr. Ward was a director, there was a conflict between his interest and his duties, there could be no contract by Guinness for the payment of remuneration pursuant to article 91 unless the board made the contract on behalf of Guinness and there was no question of approval by directors or shareholders.

In support of a claim for an equitable allowance, reference was made to the decision of Wilberforce J. in *Phipps v. Boardman* [1964] 1 W.L.R. 993. His decision was upheld by the Court of Appeal [1965] Ch. 992 and ultimately by this House under the name of *Boardman v. Phipps* [1967] 2 A.C. 46. In that case a trust estate included a minority holding in a private company which fell on lean times. The trustees declined to attempt to acquire a controlling interest in the company in order to improve its performance. The solicitor to the trust and one of the beneficiaries, with the knowledge and approval of the trustees, purchased the controlling interest from outside shareholders for themselves with the help of information about the shareholders acquired by the solicitor in the course of acting for the trust. The company's position was improved and the shares bought by the solicitor and the purchasing beneficiary were ultimately sold at a profit. A complaining [694] beneficiary was held to be entitled to a share of the profits on the resale on the grounds that the solicitor and the purchasing beneficiary were assisted in the original purchase by the information derived from the trust. The purchase of a controlling interest might have turned out badly and in that case the solicitor and the purchasing beneficiary would have made irrecoverable personal losses. In these circumstances it is not surprising that Wilberforce J. decided that in calculating the undeserved profit which accrued to the trust estate there should be deducted a generous allowance for the work and trouble of the solicitor and purchasing beneficiary in acquiring the controlling shares and restoring the company to prosperity. *Phipps v. Boardman* decides that in exceptional circumstances a court of equity may award remuneration to the trustee. Therefore, it is argued, a court of equity may award remuneration to a director. As at present advised, I am unable to envisage circumstances in which a court of equity would exercise a power to award remuneration to a director when the relevant articles of association confided that power to the board of directors. Certainly, the circumstances do not exist in the present case. It is in this respect that section 317 of the Companies Act 1985 (same as section 194 of the 1963 Act) is relevant. By that section:

> "(1) It is the duty of a director of a company who is in any way, whether directly or indirectly. interested in a contract or proposed contract with the company to declare the nature of his interest at a meeting of the directors of the company . . . . (7) A director who fails to comply with this section is liable to a fine . . ."

In *Hely-Hutchinson v. Brayhead Ltd.* [1968] 1 Q.B. 549, the Court of Appeal held that section 317 renders a contract voidable by a company if the director does not declare his interest. Section 317 does not apply directly to the present case because there was no contract between Guinness and Mr. Ward, But section 317 shows the importance which the legislature attaches to the principle that a company should be protected against a director who has a conflict of interest and duty. There is a fundamental objection to the admission of any claim by Mr. Ward whether that claim he based on article 100(D), a quantum meruit, section 727 of the Act of 1985 or the powers of a court of equity. The objection is that by the agreement with the committee, which is the foundation of Mr. Ward's claim to any relief, he voluntarily involved himself in an irreconcilable conflict between his duty as a director and his personal interests. Both before and after 19 January 1986, Mr. Ward owed a duty to tender to Guinness impartial and independent advice untainted by any possibility of personal gain. Yet by the agreement, which Mr. Ward claims to have concluded with the committee and which may have been in contemplation by Mr. Ward even before 19 January 1986, Mr. Ward became entitled to a negotiating fee payable by Guinness if, and only if, Guinness acquired Distillers and, by the agreement, the amount of the negotiating fee depended on the price which

Guinness ultimately offered to the shareholders of Distillers. If such an agreement had been concluded by the board of directors, it would have been binding on Guinness under article 91 but foolish in that the agreement perforce made Mr. Ward's advice to Guinness [695] suspect and biased. But at least the conflict would have been revealed to the board. As it was, the agreement was not made by the board and was not binding on Guinness. The agreement was made by the committee and ought not to have been made at all. By the agreement Mr. Ward debarred himself from giving impartial and independent advice to Guinness. Mr. Ward was a director of Guinness and in that capacity was able to negotiate his own agreement with the committee of which he was a member, and was able to discuss the bid by Guinness for Distillers with the other directors, to advise and participate in decisions on behalf of Guinness relevant to the bid (including a decision to increase the amount of the offer) and to procure the acquisition by Guinness of Distillers and thus to claim £5.2m. from Guinness. I agree with my noble and learned friend Lord Goff of Chieveley that for the purposes of this appeal it must be assumed that Mr. Ward acted in good faith, believing that his services were rendered under contract binding on the company, and that in that mistaken belief Mr. Ward may have rendered services to Guinness of great value and contributed substantially to the enrichment of the shareholders of Guinness. Nevertheless, the failure of Mr. Ward to realise that he could not properly use his position as director of Guinness to obtain a contingent negotiating fee of £5.2m from Guinness does not excuse him or enable him to defeat the rules of equity which prohibit a trustee from putting himself in a position in which his interests and duty conflict and which insist that a trustee or any other fiduciary shall not make a profit out of his trust.

Finally, judgment against Mr.Ward on this application was resisted in reliance on section 727 of the Act of 1985 (same as section 391 of the 1963 Act). That section provides:

> "(1) If in any proceedings for negligence, default, breach of duty or breach of trust against an officer of a company or a person employed by a company as auditor . . . it appears to the court hearing the case that that officer or person is or may be liable in respect of the negligence, default, breach of duty or breach of trust, but that he has acted honestly and reasonably, and that having regard to all the circumstances of the case (including those connected with his appointment) he ought fairly to be excused for the negligence, default, breach of duty or breach of trust, that court may relieve him, either wholly or partly, from his liability on such terms as it thinks fit."

Mr. Ward requested the committee to pay him and received from the committee out of moneys belonging to Guinness the sum of £5.2m as a reward for his advice and services as a director. Mr. Ward had no right to remuneration without the authority of the board. Thus the claim by Guinness for repayment is unanswerable. If Mr. Ward acted honestly and reasonably and ought fairly to be excused for receiving £5.2m without the authority of the board, he cannot be excused from paying it back. By invoking section 727 as a defence to the claim by Guinness for repayment, Mr. Ward seeks an order of the court which would entitle him to remuneration without the authority of the board. The order would be a breach of the articles which protect shareholders. . . .

Runciman v. Walter Runciman p.l.c.
[1992] B.C.L.C. 1984

See *ante*, p. 201.

Taupo Totara Timber Co. Ltd. v. Rowe
[1978] A.C. 537

As well as the equitable principles explained in the *Guinness* case (*supra*), the payment of what are colloquially described as 'golden handshakes' are also regulated by provisions in the Companies Acts. The plaintiff was hired as the defendant company's managing director for a five year period. It was provided in the service contract that, in the event of the company ever being taken over during the contract period, the plaintiff could resign, and would thereupon become entitled to a sum equivalent to five times his annual salary. The company was taken over, whereupon he resigned and claimed that sum.

LORD WILBERFORCE: . . . [545] [T]he company's contention [is] that payment of the sum claimed by the respondent would be unlawful by virtue of section 191 of the Companies Act 1955 (cf. section 186 of the 1963 Act). This is as follows:

> "*Approval of the company requisite for payment by it to director for loss of office, etc.* – It shall not be lawful for a company to make to any director of the company any payment by way of compensation for loss of office, or as consideration for or in connection with his retirement from office, without particulars with respect to the proposed payment (including the amount thereof being disclosed to members of the company and the proposal being approved by the company in general meeting."

This section is identical with section 191 of the Companies Act 1948 (U.K.) and, with one qualification, with section 129 of the Companies Act 1961 (Victoria). That qualification is that the Victorian section adds, after 'compensation for loss of office,' the words 'as director', and refers to 'retirement from such office'. These changes may be either clarificatory or restrictive. Since there is no obvious reason why Australian legislatures should wish to narrow the scope of the section, the former alternative seems more likely. The belief of the draftsman as to what the section was intended to mean is of course not decisive.

The New Zealand section raises two questions. First, whether it extends to payments made to persons who are directors in connection, not simply with the office of director, but also with some employment held by the director. Secondly, whether it applies to payments which the company is obliged, under contract, to make, or is limited to payment which the company, not being obliged to make, proposes to make. Although the section deals first with 'compensation for loss of office,' which is a well enough known type of transaction popularly described as a golden handshake, it is said that in continuing with a reference to payments as consideration for, or in connection with, retirement from office, the section is casting a wider net, capable of including contractual payments.

There is only one reported case, to their Lordships' knowledge, in which these points have been considered: the Victorian case of *Lincoln Mills (Aust.) Ltd. v. Gough* [1964] V.R. 193, a case like the present concerned with a managing director. Hudson J. gave a careful judgment, the relevant part (at p. 199) of which was fully quoted by Richmond P., in which he decided, on both the points above mentioned, that the payment was not illegal.

Their Lordships agree with the judgment of Hudson J., and, although [546] unassisted by the additional words appearing in the Victorian statute, would apply it to the present case. The respondent, as well as being a director, was an employee, and, as other employees with this company, had the benefit of a service agreement; he was described as 'employee' in it. In certain events, which might not happen, he could become contractually entitled to a sum of money, on resignation or dismissal, the amount of which was not fixed by the agreement and could only be ascertained if and when the event happened. The directors had full power under article 116 to appoint him as managing director on such terms as they thought fit. There was no obligation on them to seek approval of this agreement by the company in general meeting; to do so indeed would be both unusual and possibly undesirable. Then, if the agreement was, as (subject to any point as to vires; see below) it undoubtedly was, valid in itself, does section 191 require the directors to seek approval of a general meeting for carrying it out? Presumably this approval would be sought at a time when the obligation to make the payment had arisen and when its amount was known, but meanwhile the position of the employee would be uncertain and difficult. In their Lordships' view the section imposes no such requirement. The section as a whole read with sections 192 and 193 which are in similar form and the words 'proposed payment' and 'proposal' point to a prohibition of uncovenanted payments as contrasted with payments which the company is legally obliged to make. Their Lordships note that this contrast is drawn by the authoritative Report of the Jenkins Committee (1962) (Cmnd. 1749), para. 93; there is also textbook support for it. Their Lordships on this point also agree with the Court of Appeal.

There remains an argument based upon vires. It was suggested that the agreement was ultra vires the company or ultra vires the directors of the company. Their Lordships cannot accept either of these contentions. There can be no doubt as to the general power of the company to engage servants and to enter into service agreements with them. There is no question as to the bona fides of the directors in entering into this particular agreement. It was shown that similar agreements had been entered into with other employees and that to do so had been the company's policy for several years. The view that inclusion of a provision giving protection in the event of a take-over was in the interests of the company, was clearly one that reasonable and honest directors might take. In its absence, the staff might be likely to go elsewhere. In the case of the respondent, as had been noted, an agreement in substantially similar form had been entered into in 1969 and there could be nothing suspicious, or open to criticism, in replacing that agreement in 1972 when he became managing director. As has been pointed out, there is explicit power in the articles to appoint a managing director on such terms as the directors – acting of course bona fide – think fit.

DIRECTORS' POWERS AND RIGHTS

See *Company Law*, pp. 136–139.

Table A articles 79–82, 115

79. The directors may exercise all the powers of the company to borrow money, and to mortgage or charge its undertaking, property and uncalled capital, or any part thereof, and to issue debentures, debenture stock and other securities, whether outright or as security for any debt, liability or obligation of the company or of any third party, so, however, that the amount for the time being remaining undischarged of moneys borrowed or secured by the director as aforesaid (apart from temporary loans obtained from the company's bankers in the ordinary course of business) shall not at any time, without the previous sanction of the company in general meeting, exceed the nominal amount of the share capital of the company for the time being issued, but nevertheless no lender or other person dealing with the company shall be concerned to see or inquire whether this limit is observed. No debt incurred or security given in excess of such limit shall be invalid or ineffectual except in the case of express notice to the lender or the recipient of the security at the time when the debt was incurred or security given that the limit hereby imposed had been or was thereby exceeded.

80. Printed *ante*, p. 178 (general power to manage the business).

81. (A power to appoint attorneys).

82. The company may exercise the powers conferred by section 41 of the Act with regard to having an official seal for use abroad, and such powers shall be vested in the directors.

115. The seal shall be used only by the authority of the directors or of a committee of directors authorised by the directors in that behalf, and every instrument to which the seal shall be affixed shall be signed by a director and shall be countersigned by the secretary or by a second director or by some other person appointed by the directors for the purpose.

Coubrough v. James Panton & Co. Ltd.
[1965] I.R. 272

At times disputes arise among directors and some of them seek to exclude others from board meetings on the grounds that those were never properly appointed as, or have ceased to be, directors. The plaintiff was a director of and a large shareholder in the company. An extraordinary resolution was required by the Articles of Association for the removal of him from office before the expiration of his period of office, but such resolution could not be carried without his concurrence. Despite his objection, an ordinary resolution that the existing directors should retire and offer themselves for re-election was proposed and passed. Thereafter the four individual defendants were elected as directors and the plaintiff was excluded from meetings of the board. He sought a declaration that the resolution purporting to remove the directors from office was invalid; a declaration that he was still a director and an order restraining the defendants from excluding him from meetings of the board. At the trial the defendants conceded that the plaintiff was still a director of the company but, nevertheless, they contended that, in view of the opposition to him acting as director, the Court should not restrain them by injunction from excluding him from meetings of the board.

BUDD J.: . . . [274] The plaintiff and the individual defendants own between them all the shares in the defendant company. It is convenient here to refer to Article 104 of the company's Articles as it is important in relation to what follows. The relevant part reads: '104. The company may by extraordinary resolution remove any director before the expiration of his period of office, and appoint another qualified person in his stead.' The position is that the company could not carry such a resolution against the plaintiff as the remaining shareholders had not a sufficient holding of votes to achieve the required majority. So the resolution of the 9th June, 1961, in so far as it purported to remove the plaintiff was invalid. Now the contention of the defendants is that, notwithstanding that the resolution may be invalid, if all the shareholders other than the plaintiff approve the resolution which plainly shows that they do not wish him to take part in the affairs of the company as a director, then I should not grant him an injunction restraining them from excluding him from their meetings. They make the further point that, notwithstanding that the resolution may be invalid, yet if in reality and *de facto* they have expressed a wish to exclude him, then that is sufficient to exclude him under the Articles for the reason that he is a trustee of the shareholders and owes a duty to them and he should not act contrary to their wishes by participating in the Company's affairs.

The position therefore is that the plaintiff is now accepted as a director. That being so, may the other directors exclude him from meetings? . . . .

On the question as to whether directors of a company may exclude one of their fellow directors several cases were cited and a question of some difficulty arises. The first case cited was *Pulbrook v. Richmond Consolidated Mining Company* (1878) 9 Ch.D. 610. The relevant portion of the head-note reads: 'A director of a company can, if qualifies sustain an action in his own name against the other directors, on the ground of an individual injury to himself, for an injunction to restrain them from wrongfully excluding him from acting as a director.' The matter came before Jessel M.R. who at the beginning of his judgment stated the issue in the following words: 'The first question is, whether a director who is improperly and without cause excluded by his brother directors from the board from which they claim the right to exclude him, is entitled to an order restraining his brother directors from so excluding him.' He then continued: 'In this case a man is necessarily a shareholder in order to be [276] a director, and as a director he is entitled to fees and remuneration for his services, and it might be a question whether he would be entitled to the fees if he did not attend meetings of the board. He has been excluded. Now, it appears to me that this is an individual wrong, a wrong that has been done to an individual. It is a deprivation of his legal rights for which the directors are personally and individually liable. He has a right by the constitution of the company to take a part in its management, to be present, and to vote at the meetings of the board of directors. He has a perfect right to know what is going on at these meetings. It may affect his individual interest as a shareholder as well as his liability as a director, because it has been sometimes held that even a director who does not attend board meetings is bound to know what is done in his absence. Besides that, he is in the position of a shareholder, of a managing partner in the affairs of the company, and he has a right to remain managing partner, and to receive remuneration for his services. It appears to me that for the injury or wrong done to him by preventing him from attending board meetings by force, he has a right to sue. He has what is commonly called a right of action. . .'. And finally at page 616 he said: 'It appears to me that Mr Pulbrook is a director, lawfully elected, and that he has not vacated his office. Therefore I think he is entitled to an injunction to restrain the directors as asked.' The facts in that case are similar to the present in as much as the plaintiff was a shareholder and entitled to remuneration and by the action of the other directors was excluded from meetings which he had a right to attend under the constitution of the Company.

The second report that I wish to refer to is *Hayes v. Bristol Plant Hire Ltd.* [1957] 1 All E.R. 685. The head-note sets out the facts. By resolution of the board of the defendant company, passed by certain defendant directors in the absence of the plaintiff, who was also a director, the exclusion of the plaintiff from the board for his absence from board meetings, was confirmed. The consequences of the resolution, if it were valid, was that the plaintiffs office as a director of the company would be vacated. The articles of association did not require a director to hold a share qualification and did not confer on directors the right to any specified remuneration, but provided that, subject to the terms of any agreement between a director and the company, the directors should be paid, by way of remuneration for their services, such sums as the company in general meeting might prescribe. The plaintiff had no service agreement with the company. He was a shareholder in the [277] company. In an action for a declaration, among other declarations, that the resolution confirming the exclusion of the plaintiff was invalid, and for consequential relief by injunction, the defendants objected, as a preliminary point, that the plaintiff had no such proprietary interest as entitled him to equitable relief by declaration and injunction. It was held that the action would not be stopped on the preliminary objection because, although the articles of association of the company did not require a director to hold a share qualification and although they did not confer on directors a right to specified remuneration, yet the plaintiff had a sufficient proprietary interest to enable him to pursue an action for relief by way of declaration and injunction against his exclusion from the board.

That decision follows *Pulbrook's* case and it was decided as recently as 1957. It will be helpful to read a few of the observations of Wynn-Parry J. which are relevant to the facts of this case. He first deals with the facts stating that it was the fact that the articles of association did not require a director to be a shareholder, nor did they provide any direct right to a stipulated amount for remuneration, they merely provided for the payment of such amount as the company in general meeting might prescribe. I digress for a moment to say that under the articles of the defendant company a director is entitled to such sum as the company in general meeting shall from time to time prescribe. Then (at the bottom of page 686) he says: 'On those facts counsel for the defendants contends that there is no, or no sufficient, proprietary interest vested in the plaintiff as director. He cited to me a number of cases the principles underlying which I wholly accept. It is perfectly clear that in the case of any relationship which involves a personal relationship this court will not intervene by way of injunction to enforce on a person or on a limited company in the position of an employer a person whom the employer or the company, expressing its view through the shareholders, does not want; and it is perfectly true also to say that the cases establish that the basis of the court's interference is the existence of some right of property in the person seeking relief ' Then he goes on to deal with *Pulbrook's* case and points out that the Master of the Rolls did not base his decision on the fact that in that case a director was necessarily a shareholder, but that his reasoning applied equally where the articles did not require a director to be a shareholder. He also took the view that the reasoning of the Masters of the Rolls in *Pulbrook's* case applied equally well to cases where the [278] articles of association of a company did not give an express right to specified remuneration but merely provides for a director being paid such remuneration as the company may prescribe. He therefore held the plaintiff entitled to proceed. It is right to add that the learned judge made it clear that he was not dealing with the case on the basis that the majority of the company did not wish the plaintiff to continue as a director. The case was really decided on the basis of a sufficient proprietary interest to maintain an action. Reading the two cases together they go this far in my view – that the plaintiff in the present proceedings has a sufficient proprietary right to maintain this action. However, the question still remains whether the Court should grant the relief claimed in the circumstances existing.

The next case I wish to refer to is *Bainbridge v. Smith* 41 Ch. D. 462. I do not intend to brush it lightly aside, but it does not in my view deal with the same facts as are in issue here. The ratio decidendi is to be found on, page 474, where Cotton L.J. says: 'But I think it right to say that in my opinion, and I believe that my learned Brother agrees with me, if the company says that even if the plaintiff has the qualification they do not desire him to act as one of their managing directors, we should not grant an injunction, because it would be contrary to the principles on which this Court acts to grant specific performance of this contract by compelling this company to take this gentleman as managing director, although he was qualified so to act, when they do not desire him to act as such.' It is clear that the plaintiffs rights in that case were rights under a contract and not rights arising out of the articles of association, or rights of directors or shareholders inter se. That case does not therefore advance matters very much.

But the next case, *Harben v. Phillips* (1883) 23 Ch. D. 14, does require careful consideration. The facts are complicated but may be stated briefly as follows: at the annual general meeting of the company concerned, two opposing groups arose relating to the number of directors, the persons to be elected as directors, the amount of dividend to be declared and the port of operation of the company's ships. Votes were taken and polls were demanded on them. The chairman ruled proxies valid which did not comply with the Articles. Had the proxies not been admitted, the plaintiffs' opponents would have been defeated and the five plaintiffs would have been elected to the board. The plaintiffs brought proceedings seeking declarations that their motions had been carried, that they had been elected directors and claiming *inter alia* an injunction to restrain the [279] other directors from excluding them from board meetings. On the hearing of an interlocutory motion before Chitty J. and the Court of Appeal it was held that the proxies ruled valid by the chairman were invalid. Chitty J. granted the injunction above-mentioned and other relief. His order was discharged by the Court of Appeal and a series of orders made and undertakings exacted designed to preserve the *status quo* until a meeting of the shareholders, convened with the concurrence of all parties, had been held to deal with the matters in dispute. The extraordinary general meeting was held and a motion carried rescinding the appointment of the plaintiffs as directors. On the matter coming on again before the Court of Appeal, it was agreed that the shareholders' resolution was ineffectual for removing the plaintiffs from office, and the plaintiffs renewed their claim for an injunction to restrain the other directors from excluding them. It was held that the injunction should not be granted, for reasons which will later appear.

The facts therefore are somewhat similar to those of the present case, particularly in that there was an ineffective resolution of the shareholders to remove a director. Mr McWilliam relies on part of the judgment of Cotton L.J. as showing that he is entitled to succeed and that I should not in any event grant an injunction. The relevant portion of the judgment of Cotton L.J. is at page 39 of the report, where he says:

"If there is no power given by the articles of association to remove a director, all the shareholders cannot say effectually that he is to be removed, for it has been decided that there is no power to remove a director unless it is given by the articles of association; but no one can doubt that the wish of a corporation that certain persons should not be directors may effectually be expressed by any meeting of the shareholders duly called for such purpose, although such wish may not be effectual to remove the persons appointed to the office of directors. Then it comes to this, that we have in the resolution of the meeting an expression by the majority of the shareholders of the company of a desire that the plaintiffs should not be directors, and that the policy advocated by the plaintiffs should not be that which should be adopted by the company, and what this Court is asked to do is, as against the wish to the majority of the shareholders, to interfere by injunction to compel in fact the company and the other members of the board to allow the plaintiffs to act as directors."

Mr McWilliam asks me to interpret that passage as a statement of the law that the Court should not force a director on the board of a company where the

shareholders have made it [280] clear that they do not want him. Mr Parke's
answer to that is this: Cotton, L.J. was not in fact laying down the law as Mr
McWilliam claims; the Lord justice was posing the problem which had arisen
on an interlocutory application and there is no way of knowing what action
the Court might have taken on a full trial of the action. The only clear view of
what might have been done appears in the judgment of Bowen L.J., at page
42, where he says: 'I am not satisfied if it had now to be decided, that, assuming the plaintiffs to make out their case in other respects, this is a matter in
which perpetual injunction is the relief to which they are entitled, but I wish to
leave that entirely open, and to decide this case on the grounds simply that
although there is a great inconvenience whichever way we decide, I am by no
means satisfied that the balance of convenience is in favour of granting an
injunction. One cannot help seeing that this company has got into a very unfortunate position for the transaction of even its most ordinary business, and it
is difficult to say what can be done to relieve it so long as both parties insist on
prosecuting their own views of their legal rights, but on the whole the best
thing to do is, I think, to leave the matter to stand as it is and refuse the application of the plaintiffs, Mr Macnaghten giving the undertaking that the two
directors whom he represents, and whose election is open to doubt, should not
act until the hearing.' In short, the matter was left open.

Now in support of the view that Cotton L.J. was merely posing a question
as to what might happen if shareholders did express a wish, Mr Parke points
out that the Lord justice proceeded as follows, at page 40 of the report: 'Now,
in determining whether the Court should so interfere, we must not only consider the expression of the wish of the majority of the shareholders as shewn at
that last meeting, but in my opinion we must also consider how it was that the
plaintiffs came to be appointed to be directors.' So Cotton L.J. in Mr Parke's
submission, did not decide as a matter of law that the shareholders' wish ends
the matter, for that would have been the end of the case. It was only one matter
to be considered.

And the Lord Justice went on to say:

> "I assume that they were effectually appointed directors of this com-
> pany, although of course at the hearing we can listen to any argument
> which the defendants may think fit to advance to shew that they were not
> properly elected. But then assuming they were rightly elected, the elec-
> tion was only an accident arising from many of the shareholders who
> desired that some one else should be appointed, sending their proxies in
> such a way that the votes expressed by them could not be legally [281]
> used. Taking that, as I do, into consideration, this Court ought not, in my
> opinion, to interfere on this motion by compelling the company to put
> the management of its affairs into the hands of the plaintiffs, or by re-
> quiring the other directors to receive the plaintiffs as co-directors. Cases
> were referred to, to shew there was authority for the Court to so inter-

fere; but there was no case which touched the point on which I decide this."

Now I think it is clear from that passage that Mr McWilliam is not correct in suggesting that Cotton L.J. had decided as a matter of law that if the shareholders are opposed to a director the Court will not assist him to enforce his rights. It was a matter concerning the control of the company and he pointed out that the plaintiffs were directors only by the accident of the invalid proxies. That does not apply in this case. And in this case a director can only he removed by a three-fourths majority of the Company on an extraordinary resolution. I am then of opinion that *Harben v. Phillips* is not an authority for the proposition that if the shareholders are opposed to a director the Court will not act to aid that director. To take an extreme illustration, suppose a company had five directors and as a result of prolonged differences of opinion a resolution was passed by the shareholders in general meeting that they did not want any of the directors to act. Then there would be nobody to carry on the affairs of the company. But directors have a duty to conduct their company's affairs. And further, if Mr McWilliam were right, it would make nonsense of Article 194 which provides that directors can only be removed by extraordinary resolutions. It would mean that while a director could not be legally removed, nevertheless the same result could be achieved by barring him from attending meetings by a bare majority. Articles 114 and 115 provide that the management and control of the company shall be vested in the directors. So that to accede to Mr McWilliam's argument and not grant the relief claimed would be to exclude the plaintiff from his right to act as a director; and one must remember that he would, as a director, be responsible for decisions of the board at a time when he was not allowed to attend and to give his advice and vote.

In my view, being a large shareholder and a director, the plaintiff is in fairness entitled to know what is happening and to vote at meetings. There is the further consideration that resolutions of the board may possibly be ineffectual and invalid if a person entitled to be present is excluded from meetings at which the resolutions are passed. So I have come [282] to the conclusion, on the basis of the cases of *Pulbrook v. Richmond Consolidate Mining Company* and *Hayes v. Bristol Plant Hire Ltd.* that in proper circumstances a director has a right to attend board meetings which may be enforced against the other directors. What was said in *Harben v. Phillips*, an interlocutory application, is not sufficient to prevent me granting relief. I think it is clearly distinguishable on the facts from the present case.

So the plaintiff is in the position of being a director, not validly excluded from meetings. And he is also a large shareholder. He is in consequence deprived of information on the affairs of the company, and important decisions are made in his absence. In all the circumstances I feel I should exercise my discretion in favour of the plaintiff and grant him the relief claimed relevant to that part of the action that I am dealing with.

Healy v. Healy Homes Ltd.
[1973] I.R. 309

The plaintiff, who was a director of the defendant company, claimed an injunction to restrain the defendants from preventing him and his accountant from examining and inspecting the statutory books and accounts of the company and its share register, register of members and minute books.

KENNY J.: [310] The plaintiff and the second defendant are directors of the defendant company. The plaintiff, who complains that he has been excluded from the management of the company, sought an inspection of the register of members, the minute book and the books of account of the company, and wished to have an accountant with him when he was doing this. The defendants refused to allow anyone except the plaintiff to see the books of account. The right of the plaintiff and his accountant to inspect the register of members and the minute book of general meetings was not disputed, and the debate was limited to the question whether the right of inspection of the books of account is personal to a director or whether he may be accompanied by an accountant when exercising it. The parties have wisely agreed that this point should be decided under Order 25 of the Rules of the Superior Courts. . . .

[311] The purpose of the section [s. 147 of the Companies Act, 1963] is to compel companies to keep proper books of account: one of the ways in which this important object is achieved is by imposing an obligation on each director to make sure that this is being done. But a director who has not had a training in accountancy cannot decide whether proper books of account are being kept unless an accountant is allowed to inspect them; the phrase 'proper books of account' means books which give a true and fair view of the state of the company's affairs and which explain its transactions. It follows that a director's right to inspect the books of account necessarily involves that an accountant nominated by him may do this. The accountant may do this when he is accompanied by the director or when the accountant has been given a written authority to do so, and he may be required to give a written undertaking that the knowledge which he gets will not be used for any purpose except that of giving confidential advice to his employer in relation to the matter in connection with which he has been retained.

The purpose of the section shows that this is the correct interpretation of it. This view gets support from the judgment of Collins L.J. in the Court of Appeal in England in *Bevan v. Webb* [1901] 2 Ch. 59, where, at p. 68 of the report, he said that a permission to a man to do something which he cannot do effectually without an agent to help him carries with it the right to employ an agent. The right of a director to inspect the books of a company, when he has an obligation imposed on him the breach of which may involve him in criminal liability, necessarily implies that he has the right to employ a qualified agent to advise him. The question whether proper books are being kept is one on which an accountant is the only person qualified to advise as most directors would not be able to form a correct judgment on [312] the matter. The director and his accountant are also entitled to make copies of the books of account or any part of them. *Bevan v. Webb* was a decision that the right of a partner to inspect the books of account of the partnership may be exercised by his agent also. It was decided on section 24, sub-s. 9, of the Partnership Act, 1890, which provided that the partnership books were to be kept at the place of business of the partnership and that every partner might, when he thought fit, have access to and inspect and copy any of them. The court held that the right to inspect was not confined to the partners personally but that any of them could appoint an agent who was entitled to make the inspection if he was prepared to give the undertaking which I have already mentioned.

In this case the plaintiff is prepared to have his accountant with him when he is making the inspection. *Bevan v. Webb* decided that the accountant is entitled to make the inspection though he is not accompanied by his employer if he has the necessary authority from him.

Battle v. Irish Art Promotion Centre Ltd.
[1968] I.R. 242

In the course of proceedings being brought against the defendant company, its managing director, who was also its principal shareholder, applied for liberty to conduct the company's defence at the hearing.

Ó DÁLAIGH C.J.: [243] The appellant says the company has not now sufficient assets to permit of solicitor and counsel being engaged to present the company's defence; he also says that the company has a good defence to the action and that if, in the absence of solicitor and counsel to conduct the defence, the company were to be decreed, it would be a reflection on the appellant's reputation and standing as a business man. It would appear that the appellant is now managing director of another company of which he is also the major shareholder. The appellant was unable to refer the Court to any authorities touching on his application; and in these circumstances the Court allowed the application to stand over in order that it might have an opportunity of examining the law.

I have not found any reported Irish case which bears on the Court's problem; but there are at least three English decisions. The first, *Scriven v. Jescott Leeds Ltd.* (53 Sol. Jo. 101) is reported as a note. The managing director sought a right of audience to represent the company. Bray J. is reported as having held that a company can only be represented by attorney and that it is not in the same position as a litigant in person. In *London County Council and London Tramways Company* (13 T.L.R. 254) the objection was taken but not ruled.

The point arose again in *Frinton and Walton U.D.C. v. Walton and District Sand and Mineral Co. Ltd.* [1938] 1 All E.R. 649 and it was again ruled in the same sense by Morton J. who said: 'the points to which my attention has been drawn are sufficient to satisfy me that a company cannot appear in person.' Lastly, the matter was the subject of a ruling in *Tritonia Ltd. v. Equity and Law Life Assurance Society* [1943] A.C. 584. Viscount Simon L.C. in his speech (with which all his brethren concurred) said at p. 586 of the report: 'In the case of a corporation, inasmuch as the artificial entity cannot attend and argue personally the right of audience is necessarily limited to counsel instructed on the corporation's behalf.' Having referred to an apparent exception in the case of the Appeal Committee (whose practice it was to hear agents in incidental petitions and other matters dealt with by the committee, but not in argument on the substantial appeal), he said that this 'cannot be held to constitute a real exception to the long established rule that an appeal cannot be argued on behalf of a party by any one except the party himself (if not a corporation) or by counsel.'

[2440] I should also avert the case of *Charles P. Kinnell & Co. v. Harding, Wace & Co.* [1918] 1 K.B. 405, where it was held that in the English County Court a limited company may lawfully employ an agent who is not a solicitor to institute proceedings and file the necessary *praecipe* on its behalf and, with the leave of the judge, represent it in Court. The proceedings were to set aside a judgment which had been entered on default of appearance at the hearing by the defendant. The plaintiff company had, for the purpose of filing the necessary *praecipe* and affidavit, employed one of their own clerks instead of a solicitor. This was relied upon by the defendants as an irregularity such as to entitle them to have the judgment set aside. The Court of Appeal, hearing an appeal from a divisional court which refused the motion, examined the wider question on the right of a limited company to appear in the county court by its officer or agent, and the judges found warrant for their view that it could in the express provision of section 72 of the County Courts Act, 1888.

This survey of the cases indicates clearly that the law is, as we apprehended it to be when this application was first made to us, *viz.* that, in the Absence of statutory exception, a limited company cannot be represented in court proceedings by its managing director or other officer or servant. This is an infirmity of the company which derives from its own very nature. The creation of the company is the act of its subscribers; the subscribers, in discarding their own *personae* for the *persona* of the company, doubtless did so for the advantages which incorporation offers to traders. In seeking incorporation they thereby lose the right of audience which they would have as individuals; but the choice has been their own. One sympathises with the purpose which the appellant has in mind, to wit, to safeguard his business reputation; but, as the law stands, he cannot as major shareholder and managing director now substitute his *persona* for that of the company. The only practical course open to him would, it appears, be for him personally to put the company in funds for the purpose of presenting its defence. The Court in my judgment should refuse this application.

Note: Variations on this theme include *Arbuthnot Leasing Int'l Ltd. v. Havelet Leasing Ltd.* [1992] 1 W.L.R. 455 and *Jonathan Alexander Ltd. v. Proctor* [1996] 2 B.C.L.C. 91.

DIRECTORS' DUTIES AND LIABILITIES

See *Company Law*, pp. 139–174.

Negligence

Re City Equitable Insurance Co. Ltd.
[1925] 1 Ch. 407

This case concerns a notorious financial scandal of the 1920s when, in consequence of management fraud, a large insurance company collapsed and was heavily insolvent. Many of its directors and also its auditors were sued for negligence and breach of duty. In the winding up by the Court of the company, an investigation of its affairs disclosed a shortage in the funds, of which the company should have been possessed, of over £1,200,000, due in part to depreciation of investments, but mainly to the instrumentality of the managing director and largely to his deliberate fraud, for which he had been convicted and sentenced.

Article 150 of the company's articles of association provided (*inter alia*) that none of the directors, auditors, secretary or other officers for the time being of the company should be answerable for the acts, receipts, neglects or defaults of the others or other of them, or for any bankers or other persons with whom any moneys or effects belonging to the company should or might be lodged or deposited for safe custody, or for insufficiency or deficiency of any security upon which any moneys of or belonging to the company should be placed out or invested, or for any other loss, misfortune, or damage which might happen in the execution of their respective offices or trusts, or in relation thereto, unless the same should happen by or through their own wilful neglect or default respectively.

On a misfeasance summons under section 215 of the Companies (Consolidation) Act 1908 (same as section 298 of the 1963 Act) the Official Receiver as liquidator sought to make the respondent directors, all of whom (except the managing director) had admittedly acted throughout, liable for negligence in respect of losses occasioned by investments and loans, and of payment of dividends out of capital.

In determining the questions of the liability of the respondent directors raised by the summons, Romer J. enunciated and adopted the following principles relative to the duties of directors and to the meaning to be attached to the words 'wilful neglect or default' in art. 150. (The extract below is from the headnote in the law report).

Duties of Directors

The manner in which the work of a company is to be distributed between the board of directors and the staff is a business matter to be decided on business lines. The larger the business carried on by the company the more numerous and the more important the matters that must of necessity be left to the managers, the accountants, and the rest of the staff.

In ascertaining the duties of a company director, it is necessary to consider the nature of the company's business and the manner in which the work of the company is, reasonably in the circumstances and consistently with the articles of association, distributed between the directors and the other officials of the company.

In discharging those duties, a director (a) must act honestly, and (b) must exercise such degree of skill and diligence as would amount to the reasonable care which an ordinary man might be expected to take, in the circumstances, on his own behalf. But, (c) he need not exhibit in the performance of his duties a greater degree of skill than may reasonably be expected from a person of his knowledge and experience; in other words, he is not liable for mere errors of judgment; (d) he is not bound to give continuous attention to the affairs of his company; his duties are of an intermittent nature to be performed at periodical board meetings, and at meetings of any committee to which he is appointed, and though not bound to attend all such meetings he ought to attend them when reasonably able to do so; and (e) in respect of all duties which, having regard to the exigencies of business and the articles of association, may properly be left to some other official, he is, in the absence of grounds for suspicion, justified in trusting that official to perform such duties honestly.

A director who signs a cheque that appears to be drawn for a legitimate purpose is not responsible for seeing that the money is in fact required for that purpose, or that it is subsequently applied for that purpose, assuming, of course, that the cheque comes before him for signature in the regular way, having regard to the usual practice of the company. A director must of necessity trust to the officials of the company to perform properly and honestly the duties allocated to them.

Before any director signs a cheque, or parts with a cheque signed by him, he should satisfy himself that a resolution has been passed by the board, or committee of the board (as the case may be), authorizing the signature of the cheque; and where a cheque has to be signed between meetings, he should obtain the confirmation of the board subsequently to his signature.

The authority given by the board or committee should not be for the signing of numerous cheques to an aggregate amount, but a proper list of the individual cheques, mentioning the payee and the amount of each, should be read out at the board or committee meeting and subsequently transcribed into the minutes of the meeting.

It is the duty of each director to see that the company's moneys are from time to time in a proper state of investment, except so far as the articles of association may justify him in delegating that duty to others.

Before presenting their annual report and balance sheet to their shareholders, and before recommending a dividend, directors should have a complete and detailed list of the company's assets and investments prepared for their own use and information, and ought not to be satisfied as to the value of their company's assets merely by the assurance of their chairman, however apparently distinguished and honourable, nor with the expression of the belief of their auditors, however competent and trustworthy.

It is not the duty of a director of a big insurance company to supervise personally the safe custody of the securities of the company. It would be impracticable, on every purchase of securities, for actual delivery thereof to be made to the directors, or, on every sale, for the delivery to the brokers of the securities sold to await a meeting of the board or of a committee of directors. The duty of seeing that the securities are in safe custody must of necessity be left to some official of the company in daily attendance at the office of the company, such as the manager, accountant, or secretary.

A director is not responsible for declaring a dividend unwisely. He is liable if he pays it out of capital, but the onus of proving that he has done so lies upon the liquidator who alleges it.

Wilful Neglect or Default
An act, or an omission to do an act, is wilful where the person who acts, or omits to act, knows what he is doing and intends to do what he is doing, but if that act or omission amounts to a breach of that person's duty, and therefore to negligence, he is not guilty of wilful neglect or default unless he knows that he is committing, and intends to commit, a breach of his duty, or is recklessly careless in the sense of not caring whether his act or omission is or is not a breach of his duty.

That the immunity afforded by art. 150 was one of the terms upon which the directors held office in the company, and availed them as much on a misfeasance summons by the Official Receiver under section 215, as it would have done in an action by the company against them for negligence; and

Upon the evidence and in accordance with the principles enunciated above, that none of the respondent directors (other than the managing director) was liable for the losses covered by the points of claim, and that in those instances in which all or some of the directors had been guilty of negligence, such negligence was not wilful and art. 150 applied to exonerate them from liability.

Land Credit Co. of Ireland v. Lord Fermoy
(1870) L.R. 5 Ch. App. 763

The company's directors set up an executive sub-committee of the board. That committee, with the intention of raising the price of its shares in the market and keeping up fictitious appearance of credit, determined to use company money in the purchase its own shares, and brokers were directed to purchase shares in the company at a premium. In order to conceal the irregularity, the committee determined to use other persons' names and untruly to represent those payments in the company's books as loans. The shares were paid for with cheques drawn on the company's bank account. At a board meeting, the secretary reported to the directors that various cheques had been paid, including the above-mentioned cheques.

LORD HATHERLEY L.C.: [770] I am exceedingly reluctant in any way to exonerate directors from performing their duty, and I quite agree that it is their duty to be awake, and that their being asleep would not exempt [771] them from the consequences of not attending to the business of the company. But we must look at the nature of the business of this company.

It appears that under the trust-deed they had the power of making loans, and the power of appointing a committee, to whom they might delegate all the powers they thought proper; and that, in fact, a committee was appointed, called the executive committee, and that the functions of the directors were transferred to this committee, so far as regarded proposals for business, and for loans and other matters. The committee from time to time reported to the directors, and the directors had a right to ask proper questions, and to decide thereon according to their discretion; and the directors must be tried as any other trustees accused of neglecting their duty. Now, setting aside all that was concealed by the executive committee, there was laid before the board a statement that the cheques for £2000 and £1733 11s 3d had been signed by the executive committee, and then, before the chairman, a paper, on which was written, amongst the agenda for the day, 'Loans to Mr. *Costelloe* and Mr *Oliphant.* 'This we must take to have been read out, and it must have been stated that these loans had received the sanction of the executive committee, and that the sanction of the directors was sought. Now, suppose that Mr *Munster* is bound by everything which appears upon the books to have been discussed by the directors? He must be taken to have known of these loans; and the question is, how far he ought to have pursued his investigation? If there had been anything unreasonable or extravagant in the matter, or the loans had been of an unusual amount, one would expect further questions to be asked, but the loans amounted to £3,733 only, and it would have been useless to ask the executive committee, who had already recommended the loans, whether the security was good. But the charge is, that the directors did not see to the application of these loans. The money was actually placed to the credit of these persons, and, in form, all was done that was recommended by the executive committee. The real transaction was, that the executive committee had adopted the very improper course of purchasing shares in their own company, and now wanted to pay for them by means of these apparent loans to *Oliphant* and *Costelloe*.

[772] But it would be carrying the doctrine of liability too far to say that the directors are liable for negligence, not because they did not ask whether *Costelloe* and *Oliphant* were solvent and respectable, but because they did not inquire what they were going to do with the money. To do this would be carrying the doctrine of the responsibility of directors far beyond anything laid down in this Court. Whatever may be the case with a trustee, a director cannot be held liable for being defrauded; to do so would make his position intolerable.

The question, then, is, whether this was concealed. *Oliphant* says it was not; but this is denied by the evidence of others, and I think that it was in fact concealed: it was very unlikely that the executive committee would disclose their scheme to the other directors. Mr *Munster* has denied that the matter was ever brought before him, or that he had any knowledge of the transactions; and I give full belief to his denial.

The Plaintiffs have failed to establish against Mr *Munster* the thing which it was essential for them to establish; and the bill, as against him, must be dismissed with costs.

Jackson v. Munster Bank Ltd.
(1885) 15 L.R.Ir. 356

This action was brought by certain shareholders of the bank for a declaration that the making of advances out of the funds of the company to the directors, or to past directors while holding office, or to firms of which, while holding office, they were partners, constituted a breach of trust on the part of the board of directors, and that the defendants, other than the company, or such of them as might appear to the Court to be liable thereto, should be ordered to repay and make good to the company the amount of such advances not adequately secured. No advances had been made by the bank to Mr Dease or to any firm of which he was a partner; but very substantial advances had been made to all the other directors, with the exception of one. Some of these advances were made on dates after Mr Dease was appointed a director but such advances were not made by his direct permission or authority. The question whether, he being a director, such advances were made by his permission or authority was at the desire of the plaintiffs, and the defendant Mr Dease reserved for the consideration of the Court on the further consideration of the action.

CHATTERTON V.C.: [360] The only question I have now to decide is whether the defendant Edmund G. Dease is liable for the advance made, without security, to the directors of the Munster Bank at any time since he was appointed director. It appears that Mr Dease was nominated to be a director of the bank in the month of February, 1881, and that his appointment was confirmed at the half-yearly meeting held in Cork in the subsequent July. There can be no doubt that it was intended at the time that his services were to be made use of principally, at any rate, in Dublin, and I have now to decide how far he is responsible for the very great misfeasance and breaches of trust which were committed by his co-directors in Cork since the date of his appointment. . . .

It is not a universal rule that a trustee is bound to make himself acquainted with all the circumstances relating to the trust fund, and the authorities cited [361] by Mr Robertson undoubtedly show that the directors of companies are not, in all respects, under the same liabilities as other trustees. In this case, however, the only doubt present to my mind is where the point of liability commences. There is much to be said in excuse for Mr Dease's inaction with reference to the transactions that occurred previously to the 11th January, 1883. It was expected of him that he would remain in Dublin, and there certainly was plenty of business to occupy him there. That enables a reasonable excuse to be urged for his not having taken a more active part in the business at Cork. I agree with the contention of the plaintiffs that he was bound to perform the duties of his post, no matter how arduous; but the fact of his having been actively engaged in the business of the company in Dublin may be an excuse for his non-intervention in the business at Cork, where no other would avail him. There can, however, be no reason for exempting him from liability from an early period in the year 1883.

On the 11th January, 1883, the following letter was written by Mr Thomas Fitzgerald, one of the Plaintiffs, to Mr La Touche, and this letter was shown to Mr Dease. [His Lordship here read the letter.] Here was a statement which, if Mr Dease had been hitherto ignorant of the affairs of the company, should have startled him very much. It is strange that he should have been ignorant of them before; but, at any rate, after the receipt of that letter, he was bound at once to set about investigating all this misfeasance. If he had then gone down to Cork and done his duty and examined the accounts, he would have found that there had been a systematic fraudulent misappropriation of the property of the bank, and the money of the customers of the bank, extending over a period of years, conducted principally by the chairman of the bank, with the assistance of one who had been a manager, and was afterwards appointed a director of it, and with the concurrence of several other directors who formed the local board in Cork. A firm man going down in the exercise of his duty, mastering the facts, and remonstrating with his brother directors, could have put a stop to this nefarious system, and the bank would, from that time out, have been protected against the fraudulent misconduct of its directors. Mr Dease did not do so. He [362] attended at the general meeting, and was silent. He sat by and heard as false a statement as ever was made by a person in the same situation which he knew to be false, and for his own benefit put forward. That was the statement made by the chairman of the company to the meeting, that all these statements about overdrafts to the directors were utterly without foundation, the account of that gentleman being actually overdrawn nearly £100,000 at the time the statement was made. Subsequently to this meeting Mr Dease was appointed to make an examination of the accounts of the directors with the company, but he did not go down to Cork for this purpose for some months afterwards. It was his bounden duty to have gone at once into an investigation of these transactions, and to have put a stop to them, and I can listen to no excuse for his not having done so. If no better course was open to him, he was, in my opinion, bound to institute a suit in Chancery to put a stop to these proceedings. He did nothing of the kind. Mr Dease is liable from February, 1883.

Dorchester Finance Co. Ltd v. Stebbing
[1989] B.C.L.C. 498

S, P and H were directors of the first plaintiff, which was a subsidiary of the second plaintiff. S and P were chartered accountants and H had considerable accounting experience. P and H were non-executive directors and left the management of its affairs to S. Because P and H infrequently visited the company's head office, they often signed cheques in blank to be signed by S at some later date. The company brought an action against S, P and H alleging that they had been negligent in the management of the company's affairs and seeking damages.

FOSTER J.: [501] I am therefore left with the question: 'Were the first three defendants negligent in their duties as directors of Dorchester?' The plaintiffs originally sought, in addition to the negligence claim, to accuse the defendants of breaches of section 54 of the Companies Act 1948 by Dorchester lending moneys to persons to purchase shares in Talbex and of breaches of other statutory requirements, but it may be that these allegations if proved do not lead to damages for negligence and they were not pressed by the plaintiffs. On the other hand, all three defendants sought to be excused if they were negligent under section 448 of the Companies Act 1948 (same as section 391 of the 1963 Act), a plea which I will deal with later.

The law

For the plaintiffs three main submissions were made in regard to the duties of the directors. (a) A director is required to exhibit in performance of his duties such a degree of skill as may reasonably be expected from a person with his knowledge and experience. (b) A director is required to take in the performance of his duties such care as an ordinary man might be expected to take on his own behalf. (c) A director must exercise any power vested in him as such honesty, in good faith and in the interests of the company and reliance was placed on *Re City Equitable Fire Insurance Co Ltd.* [1925] Ch. 407, *Re Sharpe* [1892] 1 Ch. 154, and *Re Smith & Fawcett Ltd.* [1942] Ch. 304.

For the first defendant it was submitted that mere negligence was insufficient and the court had to be satisfied that there had been crassa neglentia or gross negligence and reliance for this submission was placed on *Turquand v. Marshall* (1869) LR 4 Ch. App. 376, *Overend & Gurney Co v. Gibb* (1872) LR 5 HL 480, *Sheffield and South Yorkshire Permanent Building Society v. Aizlewood* (1889) 44 Ch. D. 41, *Re New Mashonaland Exploration Co* [1892] 3 Ch. 577 and *Lagunas Nitrate Co v. Lagunas Syndicate* [1899] 1 Ch. 391. In none of those cases was there a suggestion of dishonesty or recklessness on the part of the directors. In those cases the directors were charged with what might be called errors of judgment. In the *New Mashonaland* case [1892] 3 Ch. 577 at 586 Vaughan Williams J. says:

> "If I had arrived at the conclusion that that was done, I should have said that the director who advanced motley on a security, without waiting for the security, could not have used any discretion or judgment at all. For to advance money on security without waiting for the security is so unbusinesslike an act that it cannot be called a mere error of judgment or all imprudent act."

I find myself in agreement with Romer J. in the *City Equitable* case [1925] Ch. 407 at 427-428 where he says:

> "For myself, I confess to feeling some difficulty in understanding the difference between negligence and gross negligence, except in so far [502] as the expressions are used for the purpose of drawing a distinction between the duty that is owed in one case and the duty that is owed in another."

I accept the plaintiffs' three submissions as accurately stating the law applicable, and counsel for the first defendant conceded that I could take into account the fact that of the three directors two are chartered accountants and the third has considerable experience of accountancy.

Note: A completely distinct issue is the circumstances in which directors owe a duty of care to persons other than the company itself, i.e. where directors are dealing with others in relation to company business, when have those others a right of action against the directors themselves and not just against the company? Instances where directors have been held liable in negligence to others include *New Zealand Guardian Trust Co. Ltd. v. Brooks* [1995] 2 B.C.L.C. 242; contrast *Williams v. Natural Life Health Foods Ltd.* [1998] 1 W.L.R. It was held by the Court of Appeal in *C. Evans & Sons Ltd. v. Spritebrand Ltd.* [1985] B.C.L.C. 105 that where a director authorised, directed and procured a breach of copyright by a company, there could be circumstances where he would be personally liable to the copyright-owner. In *Circuit Systems Ltd. v. Zuken-Redok (U.K.) Ltd.* [1996] 2 B.C.L.C. 349, the Court of Appeal struck out a claim by the substantial majority shareholder in a company that its directors owned a, duty of care to him as well as to the company.

Fiduciary Duties

Companies Act 1963, section 194(1)

Duty of director to disclose his interest in contracts made by the company

194.—(1) It shall be the duty of a director of a company who is in any way, whether directly or indirectly, interested in a contract or proposed contract declare to the nature of his interest at a meeting of the directors of the company.

Companies Act 1990, sections 29(1), 52 and 108(1)–(5)

Substantial property transactions involving directors

29.—(1) Subject to subsections (6), (7) and (8), a company shall not enter into an arrangement–

(*a*) whereby a director of the company or its holding company or a person connected with such a director acquires or is to acquire one or more non-cash assets of the requisite value from the company; or

(*b*) whereby the company acquires or is to acquire one or more non-cash assets of the requisite value from such a director or a person so connected;

unless the arrangement is first approved by a resolution of the company in general meeting and, if the director or connected person is a director of its holding company or a person connected with such a director, by a resolution in general meeting of the holding company.

Directors to have regard to interests of employees

52. (1) The matters to which the directors of a company are to have regard in the performance of their functions shall include the interests of the company's employees in general, as well as the interests of its members.

(2) Accordingly, the duty imposed by this section on the directors shall be owed by them to the company (and the company alone) and shall be enforceable in the same way as any other fiduciary duty owed to a company by its directors.

Unlawful dealings in securities by insiders

108.—(1) It shall not be lawful for a person who is, or at any time in the preceding six months has been, connected with a company to deal in any securities of that company if by reason of his so being, or having been, connected with that company he is in possession of information that is not generally available, but, if it were, would be likely materially to affect the price of those securities.

(2) It shall not be lawful for a person who is, or at any time in the preceding 6 months has been, connected with a company to deal in any securities of any other company if by reason of his so being, or having been, connected with the first-mentioned company he is in possession of information that-

(*a*) is not generally available but, if it were, would be likely materially to affect the price of those securities, and

(*b*) relates to any transaction (actual or contemplated) involving both those companies or involving one of them and securities of the other, or to the fact that any such transaction is no longer contemplated.

(3) Where a person is in possession of any such information as is mentioned in subsection (1) or (2) that if generally available would be likely materially to affect the price of securities but is not precluded by either of those subsections from dealing in those securities, it shall not be lawful for him to deal in those securities if he has received the information, directly or indirectly, from another person and is aware, or ought reasonably to be aware, of facts or circumstances by virtue of which that other person is then himself precluded by subsection (1) or (2) from dealing in those securities.

(4) It shall not be lawful for a person at any time when he is precluded by subsection (1), (2) or (3) from dealing in any securities, to cause or procure any other person to deal in those securities.

(5) It shall not be lawful for a person, at any time when he is precluded by subsection (1), (2) or (3) from dealing in any securities by reason of his being in possession of any information, to communicate that information to any other person if he knows, or ought reasonably to know, that the other person will make use of the information for the purpose of dealing, or causing or procuring another person to deal, in those securities.

Table A articles 78 and 83–87, and Part II articles 7 and 8

78. A director of the company may become other officer of or otherwise interested in, any company promoted by the company or in which the company may be interested as shareholder or otherwise, and no such director shall be accountable to the company for any remuneration or other benefits received by him as a director or officer of, or from his interest in, such other company unless the company otherwise directs.

83. A director who is in any way, whether directly or indirectly, interested in a contract or proposed contract with the company shall declare the nature of his interest at a meeting of the directors in accordance with section 194 of the Act.

84. A director shall not vote in respect of any contract or arrangement in which he is so interested, and if he shall so vote, his vote shall not be counted, nor shall he be counted in the quorum present at the meeting but neither of these prohibitions shall apply to–

    (*a*) any arrangement for giving any director any security or indemnity in respect of money lent by him to or obligations undertaken by him for the benefit of the company; or

    (*b*) any arrangement for the giving by the company of any security to a third party in respect of a debt or obligation of the company for which the director himself has assumed responsibility in whole or in part under a guarantee or indemnity or by the deposit of a security; or

    (*c*) any contract by a director to subscribe for or underwrite shares or debentures of the company; or

    (*d*) any contract or arrangement with any other company in which he is interested only as an officer of such other company or as a holder of shares or other securities in such other company;

and these prohibitions may at any time be suspended or relaxed to any extent and either generally or in respect of any particular contract, arrangement or transaction by the company in general meeting.

85. A director may hold any other office or place of profit under the company (other than the office of auditor) in conjunction with his office of director for such period and on such terms as to remuneration and otherwise as the directors may determine, and no director or intending director shall be disqualified by his office from contracting with the company either with regard to his tenure of any such other office or place of profit or as vendor, purchaser or nor shall any such contract or any contract or arrangement entered into by or on behalf of the company in which any director is in any way interested, be liable to be avoided, nor shall any director so contracting or being so interested be liable to account to the company for any profit realised by any such contract or arrangement by reason of such director holding that office or of the fiduciary relation thereby established.

86. A director, notwithstanding his interest, may be counted in the quorum present at any meeting whereat he or any other director is appointed to hold any such office or place of profit under the company or whereat the terms of any such appointment are arranged, and he may vote on any such appointment or arrangement other than his own appointment or the arrangement Of the terms thereof.

87. Any director may act by himself or his firm in a professional capacity for the company, and he or his firm shall be entitled to remuneration for professional services as if he were not a director; but nothing herein contained shall authorise a director or his firm to act as auditor to the company.

PART II

7. A director may vote in respect of any contract, appointment or arrangement in which he is interested, and he shall be counted in the quorum present at the meeting.

8. The directors may exercise the voting powers conferred by the shares of any other company held or owned by the company in such manner in all respects as they think fit and in particular they may exercise the voting powers in favour of any resolution appointing the directors or any of them as directors or officers of such other company or providing for the payment of remuneration or pensions to the directors or officers of such other company. Any director of the company may vote in favour of the exercise of such voting rights, notwithstanding that he may be or may be about to become a director or officer of such other company and as such or in any other manner is or may be interested in the exercise of such voting rights in manner aforesaid.

Fulham Football Club Ltd v. Cabra Estates plc
[1994] 1 B.C.L.C. 363

This case concerns the principle that prevents directors from unduly fettering their discretion with regard to managing their company's affairs. Here the company, which owned a valuable site, and its directors agreed with a property developer to support the developer's plans in relation to that site. *Inter alia*, the directors undertook to use their powers and rights as directors and members to provide that support in a particular manner. In the event, they did not give that support and the company was sued by the developers for breach of contract.

NEILL L.J.: [392] It is trite law that directors are under a duty to act bona fide in the interests of their company. However, it does not follow from that proposition that directors can never make a contract by which they bind themselves to the future exercise of their powers in a particular manner, even though the contract taken as a whole is manifestly for the benefit of the company. Such a rule could well prevent companies from entering into contracts which were commercially beneficial to them.

The true rule was stated by the High Court of Australia in *Thorby v. Goldberg* (1964) 112 CLR 597. The relevant part of the headnote reads:

"If, when a contract is negotiated on behalf of a company, the directors bona fide think it in the interests of the company as a whole that the transaction should be entered into and carried into effect they may bind themselves by the contract to do whatever is necessary to effectuate it."

Kitto J. stated the argument in that case in the following passage from his judgment (112 CLR 597 at 601):

"They [the appellant defendants] say . . . that because it [the alleged contract] purports to bind the directors of a company as to the manner in which they shall exercise a discretion of a fiduciary nature it is void for illegality."

He dealt with that argument (112 CLR 597 at 605-606):

"The argument for illegality postulates that since the discretionary powers of directors are fiduciary, in the sense that every exercise of them is required to be in good faith for the benefit of the company as a whole, an agreement is contrary to the policy of the law and void if thereby the directors of a company purport to fetter their discretion in advance . . . There may be more answers than one to the argument, but I content myself with one. There are many kinds of transactions in which the proper

time for the exercise of the directors' discretion is the time of the negotiation of a contract, and not the time at which the contract is to be performed. A sale of land is a familiar example. Where all the members of
a company desire to enter as a group into a transaction such as that in the
present case, the transaction being one which requires action by the board
of directors for its effectuation, it seems to me that the proper time for
the directors to decide whether their proposed action will be in the interests of the company as a whole is the time when the transaction is being
entered into, and not the time when their action under it is required. If at
the former time they are bona fide of opinion that it is in the interests of
the company that the transaction should be entered into and carried into
effect, I see no reason in law why they should not bind themselves to do
whatever under the transaction is to [393] be done by the board. in my
opinion the defendants' contention that the agreement is void for illegality should be rejected."

McTiernan and Windeyer JJ. agreed with Kitto) and Owen J. supported this
particular point of the judgment of Kitto) in the following passage (112 CLR
597 at 617-618):

"For all that appears from the plea, the directors of the Company may,
before the execution of the agreement, have given proper consideration
to the desirability of entering into it and decided that it was in the best
interests of the Company that it should be made. If so, it would be impossible to argue that they had, by executing the document, improperly
fettered the future exercise of their discretion. In fact they would already
have exercised it and, in the absence of ail allegation that they had done
so improperly, the suggested defence could not be sustained."

For a general discussion of this question see *Finn on Fiduciary Obligations*
(1977) pp. 25-30.

In the present case the undertakings given by the directors were part of the
contractual arrangements made on 29 January 1990 which conferred substantial benefits on the company. In those circumstances it cannot be said that the
directors improperly fettered the future exercise of their discretion, nor is there
any scope for the implication of any such term as is suggested by the plaintiffs.

The judge rejected the plaintiffs' arguments under these heads on the somewhat different ground that the undertaking in the present case was to use powers as members as well as directors, and that all the members of the company
were parties to the undertaking. He referred to a passage from the judgment of
Menzies J. in *Thorby v. Goldberg* (1964) 112 C.L.R. 597 at 616 which relied
on the fact that in that case all the shareholders were party to the agreement,
and what the directors undertook to do was what all the shareholders commit-

ted themselves to ensure that they did.

We find some difficulty in supporting this reasoning. The duties owed by the directors are to the company and the company is more than just the sum total of its members. Creditors, both present and potential, are interested, while section 309 of the Companies Act 1985 (same as section 52 of the 1990 Act) imposes a specific duty on directors to have regard to the interests of the company's employees in general. Accordingly we prefer to reject the plaintiffs' arguments on the more general grounds set out above.

We were referred to two English cases at first instance where in each the court held that an undertaking by directors to use their best endeavours to ensure that their shareholders should approve a particular deal by the company (in one case a purchase, in the other a sale) was unenforceable. The cases are *Rackham v. Peek Foods Ltd. (1977)* [1990] B.C.L.C. 895 and *John Crowther Group plc v. Carpets International plc* [1990] B.C.L.C. 460. In neither case was *Thorby v. Goldberg* cited. It may be that these decisions can be justified on their particular facts, but they should not be read as laying down a general proposition that directors can never bind themselves as to the future exercise of their fiduciary powers. If they could be so read then they would be wrong.

Howard Smith Ltd. v. Ampol Ltd
[1974] A.C. 821

Prior to the enactment of sections 20 and 23 of the 1983 Act (see *post*, p. 273), the discretion that directors had regarding the issue and allotment of shares in their companies engendered considerable litigation, of which this case is the leading authority on the point. A company ('Millers Ltd.') that was somewhat short of funds was the subject of a take-over bid from an associate of its principal shareholder (Ampol Ltd.), which controlled 55 per cent of its shares. Another company (Howard Smith Ltd.) then made a take-over bid for Millers Ltd. In order to block the Ampol Ltd. bid, and to raise funds for the company, Millers Ltd.'s directors decided to make a substantial allotment of shares in the company to Howard Smith Ltd., and the effect of the allotment was to convert Ampol Ltd. and its associates into minority shareholders. Proceedings were brought to set aside the allotment.

LORD WILBERFORCE: . . . [831] The central findings of the judge, directed as they are to a determination of the purpose of the Millers' board of directors in making the disputed issue, and based as they are upon his estimate of the individual directors as seen in the witness box, are such as an appellate tribunal would necessarily respect. Their Lordships in fact are of opinion that upon the evidence given at the trial these findings are not only supportable, but inevitable. They will first endeavour to summarise them and will then consider to what conclusion they should lead in law.

Findings of fact

1. The judge found, as their Lordships think it right to make clear at once, that the Millers' directors were not motivated by any purpose of personal gain or advantage, or by any desire to retain their position on the board. The judge said:

> "I discard the suggestion that the directors of Millers allotted these shares to Howard Smith in order to gain some private advantage for themselves by way of retention of their seats on the board or by obtaining a higher price for their personal shareholding. Personal considerations of this nature were not to the forefront so far as any of these directors was concerned, and in this respect their integrity emerges unscathed from this contest."

2. He then proceeded to consider the main issue which he formulated in accordance with the principle stated in the High Court of Australia by Dixon J. in *Mills v. Mills* (1938) 60 C.L.R. 150, 185-186. This was to ascertain the substantial object the accomplishment of which formed the real ground of the board's action. The issue before him he considered to be whether the primary purpose of the majority of directors was to satisfy Millers' need for capital or whether their primary purpose was to destroy the majority holding of Ampol and [its associate].

[832] In order to assist him in deciding upon the alternative motivations contended for, the judge considered first, at some length, the objective question whether Millers was in fact in need of capital. This approach was criticised before their Lordships: it was argued that what mattered was not the actual financial condition of Millers, but what the majority directors bona fide considered that condition to be. Their Lordships accept that such a matter as the raising of finance is one of management, within the responsibility of the directors: they accept that it would be wrong for the court to substitute its opinion for that of the management, or indeed to question the correctness of the management's decision, on such a question, if bona fide arrived at. There is no appeal on merits from management decisions to courts of law: nor will courts of law assume to act as a kind of supervisory board over decisions within the powers of management honestly arrived at.

But accepting all of this, when a dispute arises whether directors of a company made a particular decision for one purpose or for another, or whether, there being more than one purpose, one or another purpose was the substantial or primary purpose, the court, in the Lordships' opinion, is entitled to look at the situation objectively in order to estimate how critical or pressing, or substantial, or, per contra, insubstantial an alleged requirement may have been. If it finds that a particular requirement, though real, was not urgent, or critical, at the relevant time, it may have reason to doubt, or discount, the assertions of individuals that they acted solely in order to deal with it, particularly when the action they took was unusual or even extreme. . . .

[833] [The judge] found that the primary purpose so far as the management team was concerned (this is not the directors . . .) was to issue shares to Howard Smith so as to enable the Howard Smith takeover to proceed. As to the Millers' majority directors he said:

> "They had found themselves enmeshed in a takeover struggle. The greater part, if not the whole, of their thinking in the critical days up to and including July 6 was directed to this takeover situation. It is unreal and unconvincing to hear them assert in the witness box that their dominant purpose was to obtain capital rather than to promote the Howard Smith's takeover offer, and I do not believe these assertions."

The conclusion that I have reached is that the primary purpose of the four directors in voting in favour of this allotment was to reduce the proportionate combined shareholding of Ampol and [its associates] in order to induce Howard Smiths to proceed with its takeover offer. There was a majority bloc in the share register. Their intention was to destroy its character as a majority. The directors were, and had for some weeks been, concerned at the position of strength occupied by Ampol and Bulkships together. They were aware that in the light of the attitude of these two shareholders Howard Smiths could not be expected to proceed with its takeover offer that these directors regarded as attractive. They issued the shares so as to reduce the interest of these two shareholders to something significantly less than that of a majority. This was the immediate purpose. The ultimate purpose was to procure the continuation by Howard Smith's of the takeover offer made by that company.

Their Lordships accept these findings.

[834] *The law*
The directors, in deciding to issue shares, forming part of Millers' unissued capital, to Howard Smith, acted under clause 8 of the company's articles of association. This provides, subject to certain qualifications which have not been invoked, that the shares shall be under the control of the directors, who may allot or otherwise dispose of the same to such persons on such terms as the directors think fit. Thus, and this is not disputed, the issue was clearly intra vires the directors. But, intra vires though the issue may have been, the directors' power under this article is a fiduciary power: and it remains the case that an exercise of such a power though formally valid, may be attacked on the ground that it was not exercised for the purpose for which it was granted. It is at this point that the contentions of the parties diverge. The extreme argument on one side is that, for validity, what is required is bona fide exercise of the power in the interests of the company: that once it is found that the directors were not motivated by self-interest – *i.e.* by a desire to retain their control of the company or their positions on the board – the matter is concluded in their

favour and that the court will not inquire into the validity of their reasons for making the issue. All decided cases, it was submitted, where an exercise of such a power as this has been found invalid, are cases where directors are found to have acted through self-interest of this kind.

On the other side, the main argument is that the purpose for which the power is conferred is to enable capital to be raised for the company, and that once it is found that the issue was not made for that purpose, invalidity follows.

It is fair to say that under the pressure of argument intermediate positions were taken by both sides, but in the main the arguments followed the polarisation which has been stated.

In their Lordships' opinion neither of the extreme positions can be maintained. It can be accepted, as one would only expect, that the majority of cases in which issues of shares are challenged in the courts are cases in which the vitiating element is the self-interest of the directors, or at least the purpose of the directors to preserve their own control of the management; see *Fraser v. Whalley* (1864) 2 Hem. & M. 10; *Punt v. Symons & Co. Ltd.* [1903] 2 Ch. 506; *Piercy v. S. Mills & Co. Ltd.* [1920] 1 Ch. 77; *Ngurli Ltd. v. McCann* (1953) 90 C.L.R. 425 and *Hogg v. Cramphorn Ltd.* [1967] Ch. 254, 267.

Further it is correct to say that where the self-interest of the directors is involved, they will not be permitted to assert that their action was bona fide thought to be, or was, in the interest of the company; pleas to this effect have invariably been rejected (*e.g. Fraser v. Whalley*, 2 Hem. & M. 10 and *Hogg v. Cramphorn Ltd.* [1967] Ch. 254) – just as trustees who buy trust property are not permitted to assert that they paid a good price.

But it does not follow from this, as the appellants assert, that the absence of any element of self-interest is enough to make an issue valid. Self-interest is only one, though no doubt the commonest, instance of improper motive: and, before one can say that a fiduciary power has been exercised for the purpose for which it was conferred, a wider investigation may have to be made. This is recognised in several well-known statements [835] of the law. Their Lordships quote the clearest which has so often been cited:

Where the question is one of abuse of powers, the state of mind of those who acted, and the motive on which they acted, are all important, and you may go into the question of what their intention was, collecting from the surrounding circumstances all the materials which genuinely throw light upon that question of the state of mind of the directors so as to show whether they were honestly acting in discharge of their powers in the interests of the company or were acting from some bye-motive, possibly of personal advantage, or for any other reason. (*Hindle v. John Cotton Ltd.* (1919) 56 Sc.L.R. 625, 630-63 1, *per* Viscount Finlay).

On the other hand, taking the respondents' contention, it is, in their Lordships' opinion, too narrow an approach to say that the only valid purpose for which shares may be issued is to raise capital for the company. The discretion is not in terms limited in this way: the law should not impose such a limitation on directors' powers. To define in advance exact limits beyond which directors must not pass is, in their Lordships' view, impossible. This clearly cannot be done by enumeration, since the variety of situations facing directors of different types of company in different situations cannot be anticipated. No more, in their Lordships' view, can this be done by the use of a phrase – such as 'bona fide in the interest of the company as a whole,' or 'for some corporate purpose.' Such phrases, if they do anything more than restate the general principle applicable to fiduciary powers, at best serve, negatively, to exclude from the area of validity cases where the directors are acting sectionally, or partially: *i.e.* improperly favouring one section of the shareholders against another. Of such cases it has been said:

The question which arises is sometimes not a question of the interest of the company at all, but a question of what is fair as between different classes of shareholders. Where such a case arises some other test than that of the 'interests of the company' must be applied . . . (*Mills v. Mills*, 164, *per* Latham C.J.).

In their Lordships' opinion it is necessary to start with a consideration of the power whose exercise is in question, in this case a power to issue shares. Having ascertained, on a fair view, the nature of this power, and having defined as can best be done in the light of modern conditions the, or some, limits within which it may be exercised, it is then necessary for the court, if a particular exercise of it is challenged, to examine the substantial purpose for which it was exercised, and to reach a conclusion whether that purpose was proper or not. In doing so it will necessarily give credit to the bona fide opinion of the directors, if such is found to exist, and will respect their judgment as to matters of management; having done this, the ultimate conclusion has to be as to the side of a fairly broad line on which the case falls.

The application of the general equitable principle to the acts of directors managing the affairs of a company cannot be as nice as it is [836] in the case of a trustee exercising a special power of appointment. (*Mills v. Mills*, 185-186, *per* Dixon J.).

The main stream of authority, in their Lordships' opinion, supports this approach. In *Punt v. Symons & Go. Ltd.* Byrne J. expressly accepts that there may be reasons other than to raise capital for which shares may be issued. In the High Court case of *Harlowe's Nominees Pty. Ltd. v. Woodside (Lakes Entrance) Oil Co. N.L.* (1968) 121 C.L.R. 483, an issue of shares was made to a large oil company in order, as was found, to secure the financial stability of the company. This was upheld as being within the power although it had the effect of defeating the attempt of the plaintiff to secure control by buying up the company's shares. The joint judgment of Barwick C.J., McTiernan J. and Kitto J. contains this passage, at p. 493:

"The principle is that although primarily the power is given to enable capital to be raised when required for the purposes of the company, there may be occasions when the directors may fairly and properly issue shares for other reasons, so long as those reasons relate to a purpose of benefiting the company as a whole, as distinguished from a purpose, for example, of maintaining control of the company in the hands of the directors themselves or their friends. An inquiry as to whether additional capital was presently required is often most relevant to the ultimate question upon which the validity or invalidity of the issue depends; but that ultimate question must always be whether in truth the issue was made honestly in the interests of the company. Directors in whom are vested the right and the duty of deciding where the company's interests lie and how they are to be served may be concerned with a wide range of practical considerations, and their judgment, if exercised in good faith and not for irrelevant purposes, is not open to review in the courts. Thus in the present case it is not a matter for judicial concern, if it be the fact, that the allotment to Burmah would frustrate the ambitions of someone who was buying up shares as opportunity offered with a view to obtaining increased influence on the control of the company, or even that the directors realised that the allotment would have that result and found it agreeable to the personal wishes. . . ."

Their Lordships were referred to the recent judgment of Berger J. in the Supreme Court of British Columbia, in *Teck Corporation Ltd. v. Millar* (1972) 33 D.L.R. (3d) 288. This was concerned with the affairs of Afton Mines Ltd. in which Teck Corporation Ltd., a resource conglomerate, had acquired a majority shareholding. Teck was indicating an intention to replace the board of directors of Afton with its own nominees with a view to causing Afton to enter into an agreement (called an 'ultimate deal') with itself for the exploitation by Teck of valuable mineral rights owned by Afton. Before this could be done, and in order to prevent it, the directors of Afton concluded an exploitation agreement with another company 'Canex'. One of its provisions, as is apparently common in this type of agreement in Canada, provided for the issue to Canex of a large number of shares in Afton, thus displacing Teck's majority. Berger J. found, at p. 328:

> [837] "their [*sc.* the directors'] purpose was to obtain the best agreement they could while . . . still in control. Their purpose was in that sense to defeat Teck. But, not to defeat Teck's attempt to obtain control, rather it was to foreclose Teck's opportunity of obtaining for itself the ultimate deal. That was . . . no improper purpose."

His decision upholding the agreement with Canex on this basis appears to be in line with the English and Australian authorities to which reference has been made.

In relation to a different but analogous power, to refuse registration of a transfer, the wide range of considerations open to directors, and to the court upon challenge to an exercise of the power, is set out in the judgment of the High Court of Australia in *Australian Metropolitan Life Assurance Co. Ltd. v. Ure* (1923) 33 C.L.R. 199. By contrast to the cases of *Harlowe* and *Teck*, the present case, on the evidence does not, on the findings of the trial judge, involve any considerations of management, within the proper sphere of the directors. The purpose found by the judge is simply and solely to dilute the majority voting power held by Ampol and Bulkships so as to enable a then minority of shareholders to sell their shares more advantageously. So far as authority goes, an issue of shares purely for the purpose of creating voting power has repeatedly been condemned: *Fraser v. Whalley; Punt v. Symons & Co. Ltd.; Piercy v. S. Mills & Co. Ltd.* ('merely for the purpose of defeating the wishes of the existing majority of shareholders') and *Hogg v. Cramphorn Ltd.* In the leading Australian case of *Mills v. Mills*, it was accepted in the High Court that if the purpose of issuing shares was solely to alter the voting power the issue would be invalid. And, though the reported decisions, naturally enough, are expressed in terms of their own facts, there are clear considerations of principle which support the trend they establish. The constitution of a limited company normally provides for directors, with powers of management, and shareholders with defined voting powers having power to appoint the directors, and to take, in general meeting, by majority vote, decisions on matters not reserved for management. just as it is established that directors, within their management powers, may take decisions against the wishes of the majority of shareholders, and indeed that the majority of shareholders cannot control them in the exercise of these powers while they remain in office *Automatic Self-Cleansing Filter Syndicate Co. Ltd. v. Cuninghame* [1906] 2 Ch. 34), so it must be unconstitutional for directors to use their fiduciary powers over the shares in the company purely for the purpose of destroying an existing majority, or creating a new majority which did not previously exist. To do so is to interfere with that element of the company's constitution which is separate from and set against their powers. If there is added, moreover, to this immediate purpose, an ulterior purpose to enable an offer for shares to proceed which the existing majority was in a position to block, the departure from the legitimate use of the fiduciary power becomes not less, but all the greater. The right to dispose of shares at a given price is essentially an individual right to be exercised on individual decision and on which a majority, in the absence [838] of oppression or similar impropriety, is entitled to prevail. Directors are of course entitled to offer advice, and bound to supply information, relevant to the making of such a decision, but to use their fiduciary power solely for the purpose of shifting the power to decide to whom and at what price shares are to be sold cannot be related to any purpose for which the power over the share capital was conferred upon them. That this is the position in law was in effect recognised by the majority directors themselves when they attempted to justify the issue as made primarily in order to obtain much needed capital for the company. And once this primary purpose was rejected, as it was by Street J., there is nothing legitimate left as a basis for their action, except honest behaviour. That is not, in itself, enough.

Their Lordships therefore agree entirely with the conclusion of Street J. that the power to issue and allot shares was improperly exercised by the issue of shares to Howard Smith. It was not disputed that an action to set aside the allotment and for rectification of the register was properly brought by Ampol as plaintiff.

Cook v. Deeks
[1916] A.C. 554

The question of directors by-passing their company and taking for themselves what are often referred to as 'corporate opportunities' is a perennial bone of contention, as is illustrated by this and the next two cases, *Regal (Hastings) Ltd v. Gulliver* and *I.DC. v. Cooley*. A construction company had prospered from contracts it had executed for the Canadian Pacific Railway Co. and its related enterprises. When a major new contract was being negotiated with the C.P.R. Co., three of the company's directors (who between them had a majority of the company's shares) succeeded in having the contract eventually being awarded to themselves rather than to their company. They never gave the company even an opportunity of having the contract for itself and they concealed from the plaintiff (the remaining director and shareholder) all circumstances regarding the negotiations.

LORD BUCKMASTER L.C.: . . . [560] The negotiations for this contract were opened by a telephone message sent through to Mr Hinds at the Toronto Construction Company's office. Upon receipt of that message certain units of price were prepared in the company's office, and, the prices being ultimately fixed, the defendant Hinds was informed by Mr Leonard that, although the prices had been agreed to, the contract would not be then immediately let, as it was necessary that there should be an appropriation of the necessary cash made to authorize the contract by the Canadian Pacific Railway Company.

During the whole of this discussion, up till the time when these prices were fixed, it does not appear that at any moment the representatives of the Canadian Pacific Railway Company were told that this contract was in any way different from the others that had been negotiated in the same manner on behalf of the Toronto Construction Company, although it was plain that Mr Leonard had been told by Mr Deeks, when he was engaged on the Georgian Bay and Seaboard line, that when it was finished Messrs. Deeks and Hinds intended to go on their own account and leave Mr Cook. But after all the necessary preliminaries of the contract had been concluded Mr Hinds made to

Mr Leonard this statement: 'Remember, if we get this contract it is to be Deeks and I, and not the Toronto Construction Company.'

On March 12, 1912, the Canadian Pacific Railway Company made the necessary appropriation for the contract, and this was communicated to Mr Deeks by Mr Ramsay, that company's engineer of construction, who said that they might proceed with the contract at once. As from this moment, although the formal contract was not signed until April 1, 1912, the defendants became certain of their position, and knew that they had obtained the contract for themselves. They then for the first time informed the plaintiff of what had happened. He protested without result, and the defendant the Dominion Construction Company was formed by the three defendants G.S. Deeks, G. M. Deeks, and T. R. Hinds, to carry out the work. The contract was accordingly taken over by this company, by whom the work was carried out and the profits made. . . .

[562] In other words, they intentionally concealed all circumstances relating to their negotiations until a point had been reached when the whole arrangement had been concluded in their own favour and there was no longer any real chance that there could be any interference with their plans. This means that while entrusted with the conduct of the affairs of the company they deliberately designed to exclude, and used their influence and position to exclude, the company whose interest it was their first duty to protect. . . .

[563] It is quite right to point out the importance of avoiding the establishment of rules as to directors' duties which would impose upon them burdens so heavy and responsibilities so great that men of good position would hesitate to accept the office. But, on the other hand, men who assume the complete control of a company's business must remember that they are not at liberty to sacrifice the interests which they are bound to protect, and, while ostensibly acting for the company, divert in their own favour business which should properly belong to the company they represent.

Their Lordships think that, in the circumstances, the defendants T.R. Hinds and G.S. and G.M. Deeks were guilty of a distinct breach of duty in the course they took to secure the contract, and that they cannot retain the benefit of such contract for themselves, but must be regarded as holding it on behalf of the company.

Regal (Hastings) Ltd v. Gulliver
[1967] 2 A.C. 134n

In order to enhance the plaintiff company's asset value (its business being running cinemas) with a view to selling the entire enterprise, the directors decided to take a lease on other cinemas. Because the company did not have sufficient funds to provide the lessor with security, its then directors and solicitor came to its assistance by putting some of their own money into the company's subsidiary, which then acquired the lease. Subsequently, the company and the subsidiary were taken over, and the directors and solicitor made substantial profits on their brief investment. The company then sued them to recover those profits.

VISCOUNT SANKEY: . . . [137] The appellants say they are entitled to succeed: (i) because the respondents secured for themselves the profits upon the acquisition and sale of the shares in Amalgamated by using the knowledge acquired as directors and solicitors respectively of Regal and by using their said respective positions and without the knowledge or consent of Regal; (ii) because the doctrine laid down with regard to trustees is equally applicable to directors and solicitors. Although both in the court of first instance and the Court of Appeal the question of fraud was the prominent feature, the appellants' counsel in this House at once stated that it was no part of his case and quite irrelevant to his arguments. His contention was that the respondents were in a fiduciary capacity in relation to the appellants and, as such, accountable in the circumstances for the profit which they made on the sale of the shares.

As to the duties and liabilities of those occupying such a fiduciary position, a number of cases were cited to us which were not brought to the attention of the trial judge. In my view, the respondents were in a fiduciary position and their liability to account does not depend upon proof of mala fides. The general rule of equity is that no one who has duties of a fiduciary nature to perform is allowed to enter into engagements in which he has or can have a personal interest conflicting with the interests of those whom he is bound to protect. If he holds any property so acquired as trustee, he is bound to account for it to his cestui que trust. The earlier cases are concerned with [138] trusts of specific property: *Keech v. Sandford* (1726) Sel. Cas. Ch. 261 per Lord King L.C. The rule, however, applies to agents, as, for example, solicitors and directors, when acting in a fiduciary capacity. . . .

[139] It is not, however, necessary to discuss all the cases cited, because the respondents admitted the generality of the rule as contended for by the appellants, but were concerned rather to confess and avoid it. Their contention was that, in this case, upon a true perspective of the facts, they were under no equity to account for the profits which they made. I will deal first with the respondents, other than Gulliver and Garton. We were referred to *Imperial Hydropathic Hotel Co., Blackpool v. Hampson* (1882) 23 Ch.D. 1 where Bowen L.J., drew attention to the difference between directors and trustees, but the case is not an authority for contending that a director cannot come within the general rule. No doubt there may be exceptions to the general rule as for example, where a purchase is entered into after the trustee had divested himself of his trust sufficiently long before the purchase to avoid the possibility of his making use of special information acquired by him as trustee (see the remarks of Lord Eldon in *Ex parte James* (1803) 8 Ves.337) or where he purchases with full knowledge and consent of his cestui que trust. *Imperial Hydropathic*

Hotel Co., Blackpool v. Hampson makes no exception to the general rule that a solicitor or director, if acting in a fiduciary capacity, is liable to account for the profits made by him from knowledge acquired when so acting.

It was then argued that it would have been a breach of trust for the respondents, as directors of Regal, to have invested more than £2,000 of Regal's money in Amalgamated, and that the transaction would never have been carried through if they had not themselves put up the other £3,000. Be it so, but it is impossible to maintain that, because it would have been a breach of trust to advance more than £2,000 from Regal and that the only way to finance the matter was for the directors to advance the balance themselves, a situation arose which brought the respondents outside the general rule and permitted them to retain the profits which accrued to them from the action they took. At all material times they were directors and in a fiduciary position, and they used and acted upon their exclusive knowledge acquired as such directors. They framed resolutions by which they made a profit for themselves. They sought no authority from the company to do so, and, by reason of their position and actions, they made large profits for which, in my view, they are liable to account to the company.

LORD RUSSELL OF KILLOWEN: . . . [144] The rule of equity which insists on those, who by use of a fiduciary position make a profit, being liable to account for that profit, in no way depends on fraud, or absence of bona fides; or upon such questions or considerations as whether the profit would or should otherwise have gone to the plaintiff, or whether the profiteer was under a duty to obtain the source of the profit for the plaintiff, or whether he took a risk or acted as he did for the benefit of the plaintiff, or whether the plaintiff has in fact been damaged or benefited by his action. [145] The liability arises from the mere fact of a profit having, in the stated circumstances, been made. The profiteer, however honest and well-intentioned, cannot escape the risk of being called upon to account.

The leading case of *Keech v. Sandford* is an illustration of the strictness of this rule of equity in this regard, and of how far the rule is independent of these outside considerations. A lease of the profits of a market had been devised to a trustee for the benefit of an infant. A renewal on behalf of the infant was refused. It was absolutely unobtainable. The trustee, finding that it was impossible to get a renewal for the benefit of the infant, took a lease for his own benefit. Though his duty to obtain it for the infant was incapable of performance, nevertheless he was ordered to assign the lease to the infant, upon the bare ground that, if a trustee on the refusal to renew might have a lease for himself, few renewals would be made for the benefit of cestuis que trust. Lord King L.C. said:

"This may seem hard, that the trustee is the only person of all mankind who might not have the lease: but it is very proper that the rule should be strictly pursued, and not in the least relaxed. . . ." [147]

My Lords, I have no hesitation in coming to the conclusion, upon the facts of this case, that these shares, when acquired by the directors, were acquired by reason, and only by reason of the fact that they were directors of Regal, and in the course of their execution of that office.

It now remains to consider whether in acting as directors of Regal they stood in a fiduciary relationship to that company. Directors of a limited company are the creatures of statute and occupy a position peculiar to themselves. In some respects they resemble trustees, in others they do not, In some respects they resemble agents, in others they do not. In some respects they resemble managing partners, in others they do not. In *In re Forest of Dean Coal Mining Co.* (1878) 10 Ch. D. 450 a director was held not liable for omitting to recover promotion money which had been improperly paid on the formation of the company. He knew of the improper payment, but he was not appointed a director until a later date. It was held that, although a trustee of settled property which included a debt would be liable for neglecting to sue for it, a director of a company was not a trustee of debts due to the company and was not liable. I cite two passages from the judgment of Sir George Jessel M.R.

Directors have sometimes been called trustees, or commercial trustees, and sometimes they have been called managing partners, it does not matter what you call them so long as you understand what their true position is, which is that they are really commercial men managing a trading concern for the benefit of themselves and all other shareholders in it.

Later, after pointing out that traders have a discretion whether they shall sue for a debt, which discretion is not vested in trustees of a debt under a settlement, he said:

> "Again directors are called trustees. They are no doubt trustees of assets which have come to their hands, or which are under their control, but they are not trustees of a debt due to the company. . . . A director is the managing partner of the concern, and although a debt is due to the concern I do not think it right to call him a trustee of that debt which remains unpaid, though his liability in respect of it may in certain cases and in some respects be analogous to the liability of a trustee. . . ." [149]

In the result, I am of opinion that the directors standing in a fiduciary relationship to Regal in regard to the exercise of their powers as directors, and having obtained these shares by reason and only by reason of the fact that they were directors of Regal and in the course of the execution of that office, are accountable for the profits which they have made out of them. The equitable rule laid down in *Keech v. Sandford* and *Ex parte James* and similar authorities applies to them in full force. It was contended that these cases were distinguishable by reason of the fact that it was impossible for Regal to get the shares owing to lack of funds, and that the directors in taking the shares were really acting as members of the public. I cannot accept this argument. It was impossible for the cestui que trust in *Keech v. Sandford* to obtain the lease, nevertheless the trustee was [150] accountable. The suggestion that the directors were applying simply as members of the public is a travesty of the facts. They could, had they wished, have protected themselves by a resolution (either antecedent or subsequent) of the Regal shareholders in general meeting. In default of such approval, the liability to account must remain. . . . [152]

There remains to consider the case of *Garton*. He stands on a different footing from the other respondents, but, in my opinion, he has a short but effective answer to the plaintiffs' claim. He was requested by the Regal directors to apply for 500 shares. They arranged that they themselves should each be responsible for £500 of the Amalgamated capital, and they appealed, by their chairman, to Garton to subscribe the balance of £500 which was required to make up the £3,000. In law his action, which has resulted in a profit, was taken at the request of Regal, and I know of no principle or authority which would justify a decision that a solicitor must account for profit resulting from a transaction which he has entered into on his own behalf, not merely with the consent, but at the request of his client.

Industrial Development Consultants Ltd v. Cooley
[1972] 2 All E.R. 162

The defendant, who was a managing director of an engineering company, was approached privately and offered a lucrative engineering contract for himself. He was told that in no circumstances would that contract ever be offered to his company. On the pretext of being ill, he resigned from the company, and he took up the contract himself.

ROSKILL C.J.: . . . [166] There can be no doubt that the defendant got this Eastern Gas Board contract for himself and got it as a result of work which he did whilst still the plaintiffs' managing director. It is, of course, right to say that the contract for that work was not concluded until after he had left the plaintiffs. That work, as I have already said, was work which the plaintiffs would very much have liked to have had and, indeed, was in substance the same work as they had unsuccessfully tried to get in 1968. . . .

[167] At that time the defendant was still their managing director. He was still their managing director not only at the time when he met Mr Smettom on 13th June but when he prepared the documents over the ensuing. weekend, sending them off on 17th June so as to get this work for himself. There was a point to make that on 13th June he went down to Watford in the plaintiffs' time and in the plaintiffs' car. That is, if I may use the phrase, and without wishing to condone such conduct, fiddling. It would be wrong to hold that sort

of thing against the defendant, although perhaps it is not in accord with the strictest ethics, and I do not do so. However, at the meeting of 13th June Mr Smettom had made it absolutely plain to the defendant that no commitment was being made with the project, the time-table was likely to be urgent, it was necessary before there was any possibility of commitment being made, for the defendant to satisy Mr Smettom that he (the defendant) was free of all obligations to the plaintiffs and it was up to the defendant to do whatever was necessary to obtain that freedom.

It is plain that at the meeting of 13th June the defendant became possessed of knowledge and information which was not possessed by his employers, the plaintiffs, knowledge which the plaintiffs would have wished to possess. . . .

Counsel for the defendant has forcefully described the cause of action for an account which is relied on in this case as misconceived. His admirable argument ran thus. True some directors are in a fiduciary relationship with their companies but when the defendant saw Mr Smettom on 13th June Mr Smettom made it plain that he was consulting the defendant not as managing director of the plaintiffs, but in a private capacity. Therefore, what the defendant did on 13th June and thereafter was not done qua managing director of the plaintiffs. The information he received was not received qua managing director of the plaintiffs. On the contrary the information was given and received in a purely private capacity. There was thus no breach of any duty, even the barest contractual duty, in failing to pass that information on to the plaintiffs. Still less was there any breach of any fiduciary duty because, [168] having regard to the fact this information was received by the defendant in his private capacity, there could be no fiduciary obligation to pass on this information to Mr Hicks or to his employers generally. The argument continued that, that being the position, the defendant did not and could not have got this valuable Eastern Gas Board work by virtue of his position as managing director of the plaintiffs. Indeed, the converse of that was true because the defendant could never have got that work so long as he was their managing director. . . .

Counsel for the defendant summarised his argument in this way. Any duty which might otherwise have been owed to the plaintiffs by the defendant was eliminated by the nature of Mr Smettom's approach which was from the outset a private approach. He pointed out that the contracts in this connection fell into two different classes, first, contracts with a company in which the director is interested – in relation to those counsel for the defendant said there was what he described as an inherent and inevitable conflict of interest and, therefore, there was a duty to disclose and a consequential liability in the event of a failure to disclose – and, secondly, contracts with a third party with which alone he submitted the court was concerned in this case. The relevant contract was not, as he put it, a contract with the plaintiffs at all. It was a contract with a third party and being a third party there was no inherent conflict between interest and duty unless it could be said that this contract was equally available to the plaintiffs as his employers. As it was a contract which was not available to the plaintiffs and with a third party there could be no duty to account. . . .

The first matter that has to be considered is whether or not the defendant was in a fiduciary relationship with his principals, the plaintiffs. Counsel for the defendant argued that he was not because he received this information which was communicated to him privately. With respect, I think that argument is wrong. The defendant had one capacity and one capacity only in which he was carrying on business at that time. That capacity was as managing director of the plaintiffs. Information which came to him while he was managing director and which was of concern to the plaintiffs and was relative for the plaintiffs to know, was information which it was his duty to pass on to the plaintiffs because between himself and the plaintiffs a [174] fiduciary relationship existed. . . .

It seems to me plain that throughout the whole of May, June and July 1969 the defendant was in a fiduciary relationship with the plaintiffs. From the time he embarked on his course of dealing with the Eastern Gas Board, irrespective of anything which he did or he said to Mr Hicks, he embarked on a deliberate policy and course of conduct which put his personal interest as a potential contracting party with the Eastern Gas Board in direct conflict with his pre-existing and continuing duty as managing director of the plaintiffs. That is something which for over 200 years the courts have forbidden. The principle goes back far beyond the cases cited to me from the last century. The well-known case of *Keech v. Sandford* is perhaps one of the most striking illustrations of this rule. . . .

[175] Therefore, I feel impelled to the conclusion that when the defendant embarked on this course of conduct of getting information on 13th June, using that information and preparing those documents over the weekend of 14th/15th June and sending them off on 17th June, he was guilty of putting himself into the position in which his duty to his employers, the plaintiffs, and his own private interests conflicted and conflicted grievously. There being the fiduciary relationship I have described it seems to me plain that it was his duty once he got this information to pass it to his employers and not to guard it for his own personal purposes and profit. He put himself into the position when his duty and his interests conflicted. As Lord Upjohn himself put it: 'It is only at this stage that any question of accountability arises.'

Does accountability arise? It is said: 'Well, even if there were that conflict of duty and interest, nonetheless, this was a contract with a third party in which the plaintiffs never could have had any interest because they would have never got it.' That argument has been forcefully put before me by counsel for the defendant.

The remarkable position then arises that if one applies the equitable doctrine on which the plaintiffs rely to oblige the defendant to account, they will receive a benefit which on Mr Smettom's evidence at least it is unlikely they would have got for themselves had the defendant complied with his duty to them. On the other hand, if the defendant is not required to account he will have made a large profit as a result of having deliberately put himself into a position on which his duty to the plaintiffs who were employing him and his personal interests conflicted. I leave out of account the fact that he dishonestly tricked Mr Hicks into releasing him on 16th June although counsel for the plaintiffs urged that that was another reason why equity must compel him to disgorge his profit. It is said that the plaintiffs' only remedy is to sue for damages either for breach of contract or maybe for fraudulent misrepresentation. Counsel for the plaintiffs has been at pains to disclaim any intention to claim damages for breach of contract save on one basis only and he has disclaimed specifically any claim for damages for fraudulent misrepresentation. Therefore, if the plaintiffs succeed they will get a profit which they probably would not have got for themselves had the defendent fulfilled his duty. If the defendant is allowed to keep that profit he will have got something which he was able to get solely by reason of his breach of fiduciary duty to the plaintiffs.

When one looks at the way the cases have gone over the centuries it is plain that the question whether or not the benefit would have been obtained but for the breach of trust has always been treated as irrelevant. I mentioned *Keech v. Sandford* a few moments ago and this fact will also be found emphasised if one looks at some of the speeches in *Regal (Hastings) Ltd. v. Gulliver* [1967] A.C. 134, (*ante*, p. 281) although it is true, as was pointed out to [176] me, that if one looks at some of the language used in the speeches in *Regal* such phrases as 'he must account for any benefit which he obtains in the course of and owing to his directorship' will be found. In one sense the benefit in this case did not arise because of the defendant's directorship; indeed, the defendant would not have got this work had he remained a director. However, one must, as Lord Upjohn pointed out, look at the passages in the speeches in *Regal* having regard to the facts of that case to which those passages and those statements were directed. I think counsel for the plaintiffs was right when he said that it is the basic principle which matters. It is an overriding principle of equity that a man must not be allowed to put himself in a position in which his fiduciary duty and his interests conflict. The variety of cases where that can happen is infinite. The fact there has not previously been a case precisely of this nature with precisely similar facts before the courts is of no import. The facts of this case are, I think, exceptional and I hope unusual. They seem to me plainly to come within this principle.

I think, although perhaps the expression is not entirely precise, counsel for the plaintiffs put the point well when he said that what the defendant did in May, June and July was to substitute himself as an individual for the company of which he was managing director and to which he owed a fiduciary duty. It is on the ground which I have stated that I rest my conclusion in this case. Perhaps it is permissible to say that I have less reluctance in reaching that conclusion on the application of this basic principle of equity since I know that what happened was enabled to happen because a release was obtained by the defendant from a binding contractual obligation by the dishonest and untrue misrepresentations which were made to Mr Hicks on 16th June. In my judgment, therefore, an order for an account will be issued because the defendant made and will make his profit as a result of having allowed his interests and his duty to conflict.

Re Dominion International Group
[1996] 1 B.C.L.C. 572

Where a company is about to become party to a contract, in which one or more of its directors have some private interest of their own, they are required to duly declare that interest to the board and the making of that declaration must be recorded. One of the issues that arose in proceedings to have directors disqualified was whether payments made by the company to one charity, which in turn were paid on to another charity, should have been the subject of a declaration of interest because the latter charity awarded scholarships to the directors' children.

KNOX J.: [597] The next allegation was that Mr Lewinsohn was guilty of a breach of section 317(1) (same as section 194 of the 1963 Act – see *ante*, p. 267). The duty of a director is to disclose the nature of his interest when he is in any way directly or indirectly interested in a contract or proposed contract with the company and for this purpose the expression 'contract' is enlarged to include any arrangement whether or not constituting a contract. Miss Gloster correctly identified the question on this issue as being whether Mr Lewinsohn was directly interested in the arrangement between DIG and Cygnus whereby DIG or its subsidiary DSL made payments to Cygnus. She submitted he was not because section 317 being penal should be construed strictly and that Mr Lewinsohn's interest was too uncertain, remote and contingent to constitute an interest for the purposes of section 317. In that context she referred to the Queensland authority *Baker v. Palm Bay Island Resort Pty Ltd. (No 2)* [1970] Qd R 210 where it was held that an agreement between a director of a company selling property and the purchaser of the property that if the sale went through the director would be given an opportunity to subscribe for shares in the acquiring company and be employed by it was too uncertain, remote and contingent an interest to constitute such a breach of duty on his part as to entitle the vendor company to resist a decree of specific performance. Miss Gloster relied upon the fact that all that Mr Lewinsohn had as a matter of law was a hope that scholarship payments would be made in his children's favour. I do not consider that *Baker's* case is authority for the proposition that an expectation however strong can never constitute an interest for the purposes of section 317 and if it is I should decline to follow it. It does not seem to me that this is an appropriate field in which to draw technical distinctions between vested and contingent interests and mere hopes or expectations. What is needed is a realistic appraisal of the nature of the interest and to see whether it is real and substantial or merely theoretical and insubstantial. Thus the expectation of Mr Lewinsohn seems to me comparable to that of a healthy young person entitled as the sole next of kin on the prospective intestacy of an incurable lunatic in the last stages of a fatal disease. Technically in each case there is a mere expectancy. In practice there was what I might perhaps describe as a racing certainty.

Support for such a practical approach is in my view to be found in the judgment of Upjohn LJ in *Boulting v. Association of Cinematograph, Television and Allied Technicians* [1963] 2 QB 606 where in describing the rule of equity that a person in a fiduciary capacity may not place himself in a position where his interests may conflict with the interests of the person to whom the fiduciary duty is owed he said ([1963] 2 QB 606 at 637-638):

> "However, a broad rule like this must be applied with common sense and with an appreciation of the sort of circumstances in which, over the last two hundred years and more it has been applied and thrived. It must be applied realistically to a state of affairs which discloses a real conflict of duty and interest, and not to some theoretical or rhetorical conflict."

Another point taken by Miss Gloster on section 317 was that subs. (6), which provides that a transaction or arrangement of a kind described in section 330 [598] (prohibitions of loans, quasi-loans etc to directors) made by a company for a director of the company or a person connected with such a director is treated as a transaction or arrangement in which that director is interested, shows a that a director does not automatically have an interest in a transaction or arrangement for the benefit of his children. I accept the submission but it does not meet the point that the discharge of a liability to pay fees is a benefit.

I therefore conclude that there was a duty to disclose the nature of Mr Lewinsohn's interest. I have found that there was no such formal disclosure to the directors of the board as the 1985 Act in terms required. On the other hand it has been held that where the directors are all in fact sufficiently aware of the matter that should be formally disclosed, the absence of format disclosure may not amount to more than a technical non-declaration of an interest. This was the expression used by Dillon L.J. in *Lee Panavision Ltd. v. Lee Lighting Ltd.* [1992] B.C.L.C. 22 at 33 when he said:

> "Apart from that, however, if the judge was entitled to make the findings of non-disclosure and non-declaration of interests that he did, the position is that each of the directors has failed to disclose formally at the board meeting an interest common to all the directors, and *ex hypothesi*, already known to all the directors. I would hesitate to hold that such apparently technical non-declaration of an interest in breach of section

317 has the inevitable result, as to which the court has no discretion, that the second management agreement is fundamentally flawed and must be set aside if [the plaintiff] chooses to ask sufficiently promptly that it be set aside."

That passage is clearly obiter.

In *Neptune (Vehicle Washing Equipment) Ltd. v. Fitzgerald* [1995] 3 W.L.R. 108 a problem arose regarding declarations of interest under section 317 of the 1985 Act, or its predecessor section 199 of the Companies Act 1948, where there was only one director. Lightman J., as well as holding that the obligation to make disclosure at a meeting applied where a sole director was the only person present at the meeting, which is not relevant to these proceedings, emphasised the importance of compliance with the formal requirements of section 317 of the 1985 Act. He said [1995] 3 W.L.R. 108 at 114-115):

"The object of section 317 is to ensure that the interest of any director and of any shadow director in any actual or proposed contract shall (unless the procedure has been adopted of giving a general declaration under subs. (3)) be an item of business at a meeting of the directors. Where a director is interested in a contract, the section secures that three things happen at a directors meeting. First, all the directors should know or be reminded of the interest; second, the making of the declaration should be the occasion for a statutory pause for thought about the existence of the conflict of interest and of the duty to prefer the interests of the company to their own; third, the disclosure or reminder must be a distinct happening at the meeting which therefore must be recorded in the minutes of the meeting under section 382 and cl 86 of Table A (consider in particular section 382(3)). Failure to record the declaration (if made) exposes [599] the company and every officer in default to a fine (see section 382(5) (see section 194(5) of the 1963 Act)) but does not preclude proof that the declaration was made and that section 317 was complied with. The existence of this record operates as a necessary caution to directors and shadow directors who might otherwise think that their interest might pass unnoticed if the contract falls to be scrutinised at some later date; and it affords valuable information as to the existence of any interest and its disclosure and thereby protection for shareholders and creditors alike in case they later wish to investigate a contract."

He also observed, in connection with a meeting of one director, but the statement is of general application [1995] 3 W.L.R. 108 at 116):

"The court may well find it difficult to accept that the declaration has been made if it is not so recorded, that is to say in the minutes."

Similarly Simon Brown J. in *Runciman v. Walter Runciman plc* [1992] B.C.L.C. 1084 (see *supra*, p. 201) recognised and applied the rule that directors, provided they act unanimously, can act informally in holding that an extension of a director's employment contract was validly effected because on the facts all the directors agreed to it. He went on to consider a defence under an article to the same effect as section 317 of the 1985 Act, based on the failure to make formal disclosure of what he had already held had been agreed to by all the directors. In relation to this he said (at 1093):

> "Whatever may have been the strict legal requirements of the position, on the particular facts of this case I am perfectly satisfied that for the plaintiff to have made a specific declaration of interest before agreement of the variations here in question would have served no conceivable purpose. It would have been mere incantation. Any non-compliance with art 85(1) was accordingly wholly technical. Nothing could be less just than that the new owners of the company after take-over should now benefit from their adventitious discovery of such breach. To allow them to do so would be to sacrifice the plaintiff's legitimate interests on the altar of slavish adherence to ritualistic form."

He went on to reject the arguments that the article based on section 317 did not apply but held that what was at most a merely technical breach did not render the agreed variation unenforceable.

I observe in passing that Miss Gloster relied upon art 94 of DIG's articles which is in common form taken from art 84(3) in Table A to the Companies Act 1948, and relieves directors (inter alia) from having to account for profits from dealing with the company. Put shortly, it relieves directors against the consequences of the self dealing rule. But it has no relevance to the duty to disclose interests, which is in fact expressly preserved by art 96 of DIG's articles. No one suggests that it would not have been possible if proper disclosure was made and if the other directors considered it in the interests of DIG for scholarship payments to be obtained for the chairman's children through payments to Cygnus. There is nothing illegal about such provision by direct means, and if it can be done directly it must be possible for it to be [600] done indirectly. But all that is subject to disclosure requirements and it is with them that this issue is concerned.

The authorities cited above do establish that where there is genuine informed consent by all directors, a failure to make the declaration required by section 317 will be a technical rather than a substantive default and I am satisfied that, whatever the consequences in law of such technical defaults upon the enforceability of contracts with the company, such a purely technical default would not in general constitute grounds for finding a director unfit under the Disqualification Act. In effect, therefore, the issue comes back to the extent to which all the directors did indeed give their informed consent. As to that, in the light of the factual findings which I have made earlier, I find that Mr Neville and Mr Palmer did give a sufficiently informed consent but that the other directors' consent was not sufficiently informed to make the failure to disclose Mr Lewinsohn's interest in the arrangement between DIG and Cygnus a purely technical default. There is no illegality or impropriety involved in taking advice upon and arranging the relations between a company and its directors with a view to minimising the liability to tax of either or both of them, but where schemes are evolved for achieving those ends it is critically important that matters should he entirely above board both in the sense of not involving any dishonesty and in the sense of being conducted with all relevant informed consents.

Guinness p.l.c. v. Saunders
[1990] 2 A.C.683; [1901] B.C.L.C.

See *ante*, p. 236.

Percival v. Wright
[1902] 1 Ch. 421

This is one of the few reported cases on what is often described as 'Insider dealing', before the law was radically tightened up by Part V of the 1990 Act (see section 108, *ante*, p. 268). The company was a private company and shares in it could not be transferred without the board's consent. Some shareholders offered to sell their shares to the directors at a stipulated price. The directors agreed to buy those shares, but at the time the directors were engaged in negotiations to have the company taken over at a much higher price per share. On discovering this, the plaintiffs sought to have the agreements to sell their shares set aside.

SWIFTEN EADY J.: [425] The position of directors of a company has often been considered and explained by many eminent equity judges. In *Great Eastern Ry. Co. v. Turner* (1872) L.R. 8 Ch. 149, 152, Lord Selborne L.C. points out the twofold position which directors fill. He says: 'The directors are the mere trustees or agents of the company – trustees of the company's money and property – agents in the transactions which they enter into on behalf of the company.' In *In re Forest of Dean Coal Mining Co.* (1878) 10 Ch.D. 450, 453, Jessel M.R. says: 'Again, directors are called trustees. They are no doubt trustees of assets which have come into their hands, or which are under their control, but they are not trustees of a debt due to the company. The company is the creditor, and, as I said before, they are only the managing partners.' Again, in *In re Lands Allotment Co.* [1894] 1 Ch. 616, 631, Lindley L.J. says:

> "Although directors are not properly speaking trustees, yet they have always been considered and treated as trustees of money which comes to their hands or which is actually under their control; and ever since joint stock companies were invented directors had been held liable to make good moneys which they have misapplied upon the same footing as if they were trustees, and it has always been held that they are not entitled to the benefit of the old Statute of Limitations because they have committed breaches of trust, and are in respect of such moneys to be treated as trustees."

It was from this point of view that *York and North Midland Ry. Co, v. Hudson* 16 Beav. 485, 491, 496, and *Parker v. McKenna* (1874) L.R. 10 Ch. 96, were decided. Directors must dispose of their company's shares on the best terms obtainable, and must not allot them to themselves or their friends at a lower price in order to obtain a personal benefit. They must act bona fide for the interests of the company.

The plaintiffs' contention in the present case goes far beyond this. It is urged that the directors hold a fiduciary position as trustees for the individual shareholders, and that, where negotiations for sale of the undertaking are on foot, they are [426] in the position of trustees for sale. The plaintiffs admitted that this fiduciary position did not stand in the way of any dealing between a director and a shareholder before the question of sale of the undertaking had arisen, but contended that as soon as that question arose the position was altered. No authority was cited for that proposition, and I am unable to adopt the view that any line should be drawn at that point. It is contended that a shareholder knows that the directors are managing the business of the company in the ordinary course of management, and impliedly releases them from any obligation to disclose any information so acquired. That is to say, a director purchasing shares need not disclose a large casual profit, the discovery of a new vein, or the prospect of a good dividend in the immediate future, and similarly a director selling shares need not disclose losses, these being merely incidents in the ordinary course of management. But it is urged that, as soon as negotiations for the sale of the undertaking are on foot, the position is altered. Why? The true rule is that a shareholder is fixed with knowledge of all the directors' powers, and has no more reason to assume that they are not negotiating a sale of the undertaking than to assume that they are not exercising any other power. It was strenuously urged that, though incorporation affected the relations of the shareholders to the external world, the company thereby becoming a distinct entity, the position of the shareholders inter se was not affected, and was the same as that of partners or shareholders in an unincorporated company. I am unable to adopt that view. I am therefore of opinion that the purchasing directors were under no obligation to disclose to their vendor share-holders the negotiations, which ultimately proved abortive. The contrary view would place directors in a most invidious position, as they could not buy or sell shares without disclosing negotiations, a premature disclosure of which might well be against the best interests of the company. I am of opinion that directors are not in that position.

There is no question of unfair dealing in this case. The directors did not approach the shareholders with the view of obtaining their shares. The share-holders approached the directors, and named the price at which they were desirous of selling. The plaintiffs' case wholly fails, and must be dismissed with costs.

CHAPTER 6

Finance and Raising Capital

There are various ways in which companies finance their operations, such as through shareholders' funds, money borrowed either from shareholders or from outside lenders, retained earnings ploughed back into the business, and different kinds of state grants and aids. The Companies Acts contain elaborate provisions about companies issuing their shares and debentures, especially where securities are offered to the general investing public. Among the principal concerns of these rules is to ensure that existing shareholders control allotments of unissued shares being made by the directors, and to insure that investors are not deceived or misled into acquiring shares.

SOURCES OF FINANCE

See *Company Law*, pp. 176–182.

ISSUING SECURITIES

See *Company Law*, pp. 182–192.

Table A articles 2 and 5

2. Without prejudice to any special rights previously conferred on the holders of any existing shares or class of shares, any share in the company may be issued with such preferred, deferred or other special rights or such restrictions, whether in regard to dividend, voting, return of capital or otherwise, as the company may from time to time by ordinary resolution determine.

5. Subject to the provisions of these regulations relating to new shares, the shares shall be at the disposal of the directors, and they may (subject to the provisions of the Companies Acts, 1963 to 1983) allot, grant options over or otherwise dispose of them to such persons, on such terms and conditions and at such times as they may consider to be in the best interests of the company and its shareholders, but so that no share shall be issued at a discount and so that, in the case of shares offered to the public for subscription by a public limited company, the amount payable on application on each share shall not be less than one-quarter of the nominal amount of the share and the whole of any premium thereon.

Note: There are several leading cases on the controversial question of whether, in the circumstances, issuing additional shares in the company to either particular members or to an outsider constitutes, a breach of directors' duties, *e.g. Howard Smith Ltd. v. Ampol Petroleum Ltd.* [1974] A.C. 821 (*ante*, p. 273), *Nash v. Lancegaye Safety Glass (Ireland) Ltd.*, 92 I.L.T.R. 11 (1958) and *Clemens v. Clemens Bros. Ltd.* [1976] 2 All E.R. 268.

Companies Act 1983, section 20(1)-(3) and (10)

Authority of company required for allotment of certain securities by directors

20.—(1) The directors of a company shall not exercise any power of the company to allot relevant securities, unless the directors are, in accordance with this section, authorised to do so by-

(a) the company in general meeting; or

(b) the articles of the company.

(2) Authority for the purposes of this section may be given for a particular exercise of that power or for the exercise of that power generally, and may be unconditional or subject to conditions.

(3) Any such authority shall state the maximum amount of relevant securities that may be allotted thereunder and the date on which the authority will expire, which shall be not more than five years from whichever is relevant of the following dates–

(a) in the case of an authority contained at the time of the original incorporation of the company in the articles of the company, the date of that incorporation; and

(b) in any other case, the date on which the resolution is passed by virtue of which that authority is given;

but any such authority (including an authority contained in the articles of the company) may be previously revoked or varied by the company in general meeting.

(10) In this section "relevant securities" means in relation to a company,–

(a) shares in the company other than shares shown in the memorandum to have been taken by the subscribers thereto or shares allotted in pursuance of an employees' share scheme, and

(b) any right to subscribe for, or to convert any security into, shares in the company other than shares so allotted;

and any reference to the allotment of relevant securities shall include a reference to the grant of such a right but shall not include any reference to the allotment of shares pursuant to such a right.

Note: It was held by the European Court of Justice in *Karella v. Minister of Industry* [1994] 1 B.C.L.C. 774 that article 25 of the E.C. Second Directive, which requires that increases in a company's capital obtain the approval of the shareholders, was sufficiently precise to have 'direct effect' against any public authority.

Hilder v. Dexter
[1902] A.C. 474

Immediately after its incorporation, the company issued £1 shares to raise working capital. Under the terms of issue, the shares were allotted at par and the allottees would have the option at some later stage to subscribe for additional shares at par. Some time later when the shares were worth over £2, the defendant sought to exercise his option.

LORD DAVEY: . . . [478] [T]here is nothing whatever in the case to throw doubt upon the good faith of the directors in selecting this mode of issuing the shares of the company, in preference to offering them for public subscription in the ordinary way, or to impeach their exercise of the discretion vested in them by the articles. It appears from the affidavits that the scheme was to raise the necessary working capital by the issue of one-half of the share capital for cash, the other half being used for the purpose of payment in shares credited as fully paid up for the concessions to be purchased by the company. But it was said that this mode of raising the sum required for working capital is prohibited by section 8(2) of the recent Act of 1900, and is therefore beyond the power of the company. This is the only question which has been argued at the bar.

Now, before construing the words of the section which is relied on, your Lordships are entitled to consider the state of the law before the section was passed, with a view to ascertaining the mischief to which the enactment is directed. It was decided by this House in *Ooregum v. Roper* [1892] A.C.125 that a stipulation or agreement that a less cash sum than the nominal amount of the share shall be accepted as payment for the share is repugnant and void. On the other hand, there was authority for saying that the payment of a commission to brokers or others who undertook to procure subscriptions, or in default to subscribe for a certain number of shares, was legitimate. . . .

[480] The argument seems to be that the company, by engaging to allot shares at par to the shareholder at a future date, is applying or using its shares in such a manner as to give him a possible benefit at the expense of the company in this sense, that it foregoes the chance of issuing them at a premium. With regard to the latter point, it may or may not be at the expense of the company. I am not aware of any law which obliges a company to issue its shares above par because they are saleable at a premium in the market. It depends on the circumstances of each case whether it will be prudent or even possible to do so, and it is a question for the directors to decide. But the point which, in my opinion, is alone material for the present purpose is that the benefit to the shareholder from being able to sell his shares at a premium is not obtained by him at the expense of the company's capital. The prohibited application of the shares may be direct by allotting them as fully or partly paid up to the person underwriting the shares, or by allotting them in some other way with the intention that they shall ultimately find their way to such person or be applied in payment of his commission.

[481] My Lords, it may be that in some particular case a contract such as that which your Lordships have before you would be open to impeachment as improvident, or an abuse, or in excess of the powers of management committed to the directors. In this case the question is as to the powers of the company itself, and not as to the the the due exercise of the directors' powers. I have come to the conclusion from a consideration of the language of s.8, sub-s.2, that the prohibition therein contained extends only to the application, direct or indirect, of the company's capital in payment of a commission by the company, and the transaction impeached in this case is not within it.

Mutual Life Insurance Co. of New York v. Rank Organisation Ltd.
[1985] B.C.L.C. 11

The defendant company proposed to issue additional shares but without giving all of its shareholders a first option on them. Principally in order not to be obliged to comply with U.S. securities regulations, it proposed to offer the new shares *pro rata* to all its members except for the U.S.-based shareholders. A New York based shareholder challenged the proposal.

GOULDING J.: . . . [18] The main support of counsel for the plaintiffs argument was an anthology of judicial pronouncements regarding the equality of a company's individual shareholders in point of rights save as otherwise clearly provided by its constitution. On the basis of such authority, he submitted that shareholders of one and the same class are to be given equal treatment, having in that respect an individual right which any shareholder can enforce against the company, a right, moreover, that is broken if the company by its directors or even by resolution of a general meeting, gives some shareholders an advantage not given to others of the same class, whether or not those others suffer any disadvantage beyond such mere denial of the advantage. So, counsel for the plaintiffs contends, shareholders not connected with North America received here in their capacity as shareholders an advantage not allowed to Guaranty, and Guaranty has a right of action against Rank accordingly. . . .

[21] I do not, of course, disagree with any of the judicial statements that I have recited. I think they were all clearly right in the respective contexts in which they were uttered, but they and other authorities that have been used in argument do not in my opinion justify the inference of an overriding term in the membership contract of the sort which the plaintiffs assert. To my mind the wide powers and provisions contained in art. 7, being themselves an express term of the membership contract which the members have accepted, ought not to be whittled down by any implication beyond what is required in the circumstances of the membership contract by the ordinary principles of the law of contract. That law in such circumstances, and so far as relevant to this action, requires in my judgment but two implied terms. First, the time honoured rule that the directors' powers are to be exercised in good faith in the interests of the company, and secondly that they must be exercised fairly as between different shareholders. I doubt whether it is possible to formulate either of the stipulations more precisely because of the infinity of circumstances in which they may fall to be applied. . . .

[23] The making of the offer was clearly actuated by a genuine belief that Rank needed more equity capital and less indebtedness to banks.

Then as to its terms, did the directors exercise their discretionary power under art. 7 in good faith in the interests of the company? In my opinion it is abundantly clear that they did so. The motive for refusing applications from North American members of the public appears in great detail from the documentary evidence, and it is in my judgment perfectly plain that they were excluded only to avoid legal requirements that the directors reasonably considered it would be disadvantageous for Rank to comply with. . . .

[24] I turn to the remaining test which I have proposed, namely, that of fairness between different shareholders. It must be borne in mind that in my view the equality of individual shareholders in point of right, does not always require an identity of treatment. Compare the first of the passages that I cited from Lord Macnaghten's speech in the *British and American Trustee case* [1894] A.C. 399. After reflection on all that counsel for the plaintiffs said in argument I remain of opinion that the North American shareholders were fairly treated on the occasion of the offer for sale, notwithstanding their exclusion

from participation along with their compatriots who were not already share-holders. Such exclusion did not in any way affect the existence of a sharehold-er's shares nor the rights attached to them. I do not know whether the transaction had any effect upon their market price. None has been alleged by the plain-tiffs, and counsel for the plaintiffs disclaimed any suggestion that the terms of the offer for sale were improvident, heavily oversubscribed though it was. In any case, no shareholder in Rank, while its articles of association retain their present form, has any right to expect that his fractional interest in the company will remain forever constant. Moreover, the reason why North American share-holders were excluded was because of a difficulty resulting only from their own personal situation. It was not the fault of Rank that they were nationals or residents of countries whose laws impose onerous obligations.

Finally, it is not in my judgment unfair to the North American shareholders that Rank should raise capital in the way which it was advised, and its direc-tors believed, was most advantageous for the purposes of maintaining its in-vestment programme, since the successful fulfilment of the programme would give a prospect of continuing benefit to all members whatever their personal situation.

Companies Act 1983, section 23(1)

Pre-emption rights

23.—(1) Subject to the following provisions of this section and sections 24 and 25, a company proposing to allot any equity securities-

(*a*) shall not allot any of those securities on any terms to any person unless it has made an offer to each person who holds relevant shares or relevant employee shares to allot to him on the same or more favourable terms a proportion of those securities which is as nearly as practicable equal to the proportion in nominal value held by him of the aggregate of relevant shares and relevant employee shares; and

(*b*) shall not allot any of those securities to any person unless the period during which any such offer may be accepted has expired or the company has received notice of the acceptance or refusal of every offer so made

Table A article 130A

130A. The company in general meeting may on the recommendation of the directors resolve that it is desirable to capitalise any part of the amount for the time being standing to the credit of any of the company's reserve accounts or to the credit of the profit and loss account which is not available for distribution by applying such sum in paying up in full unissued shares to be allotted as fully paid bonus shares to those members of the company who would have been entitled to that sum if it were distributed by way of dividend (and in the same proportions, and the directors shall give effect to such resolution.

Table A, articles 15–21

Calls of shares

15. The directors may from time to time make calls upon the members in respect of any moneys unpaid on their shares (whether on account of the nominal value of the shares or by way of premium) and not by the conditions of allotment thereof made payable at fixed times, provided that no call shall exceed one-fourth of the nominal value of the share or be payable at less than month from the date fixed for the payment of the last proceeding call, and each member shall (subject to receiving at least 14 days' notice specifying the time or times and place of payment) pay to the company at the time or times and place so specified the amount called on his shares. A call may be revoked or postponed as the directors may determine.

16. A call shall be deemed to have been made at the time when the resolution of the directors authorising the call was passed and may be required to be paid by instalments.

17. The joint holders of a share shall be jointly and severally liable to pay all calls in respect thereof.

18. If a sum called in respect of a share is not paid before or on the day appointed for payment thereof, the person from whom the sum is due shall pay interest on the sum from the day appointed for payment thereof to the time of actual payment at such rate, not exceeding 5 per cent per annum, as the directors may determine, but the directors shall be at liberty to waive payment of such interest wholly or in part.

19. Any sum which by the terms of issue of a share becomes payable on allotment or at any fixed date, whether on account of the nominal value of the share or by way of premium, shall, for the purposes of these regulations, be deemed to be a call duly made and payable on the date on which, by the terms of issue, the same becomes payable, and in case of non-payment all the relevant provisions of these regulations as to payment of interest and expenses, forfeiture or otherwise, shall apply as if such sum had become payable by virtue of a call duly made and notified.

20. The directors may, on the issue of shares, differentiate between the holders as to the amount of calls to be paid and the times of payment.

21. The directors may, if they think fit, receive from any member willing to advance the same, all or any part of the moneys uncalled and unpaid upon any shares held by him, and upon all or any of the moneys so advanced may (until the same would, but for such advance, become payable) pay interest at such rate not exceeding (unless the company in general meeting otherwise directs) 5 per cent. per annum, as may be agreed upon between the directors and the member paying such sum in advance.

INVESTOR PROTECTION

Gluckstein v. Barnes
[1900] A.C. 240

This is one of the several leading cases decided around the turn of the century concerning defrauding investors by issuing them shares which were worth far less than they we represented to be, or where, as here, the promoters made substantial secret profits for themselves from their dealings with investors. The defendant was a member of a syndicate that bought the Olympia exhibition hall for £140,000, then formed a company and sold it the hall for £180,000, disclosing a profit of £40,000. But no disclosure was made of a profit of £20,000 he made by previously having bought up various charges on the property.

LORD MACNAGHTEN: . . . [248] These gentlemen set about forming a company to pay them a handsome sum for taking off their hands a property which they had contracted to buy with that end in view. They bring the company into existence by means of the usual machinery. They appoint themselves sole guardians and protectors of this creature of theirs, half-fledged and just struggling into life, bound hand and foot while yet unborn by contracts tending to their private advantage, and so fashioned by its makers that it could only act by their hands and only see through their eyes. They issue a prospectus representing that they had agreed to purchase the property for a sum largely in excess of the amount which they had, in fact, to pay. On the faith of this prospectus they collect subscriptions from a confiding and credulous public. And then comes the last act. Secretly, and therefore dishonestly, they put into their own pockets the difference between the real and the pretended price. After a brief career the company is ordered to be wound up. In the course of the liquidation the trick is discovered. Mr Gluckstein is called upon to make good a portion of the sum which he and his associates had misappropriated. Why Mr Gluckstein alone was selected for attack I do not know any more than I know why he was only asked to pay back a fraction of the money improperly withdrawn from the coffers of the company.

However that may be, Mr Gluckstein defends his conduct, or, rather I should say, resists the demand, on four grounds, [249] which have been gravely argued at the bar. In the first place, he says that he was not in a fiduciary position towards Olympia Limited, before the company was formed. Well, for some purposes he was not. For others he was. A good deal might be said on the point. But to my mind the point is immaterial, for it is not necessary to go back beyond the formation of the company.

In the second place, he says, that if he was in a fiduciary position he did in fact make a proper disclosure. With all deference to the learned counsel for the appellant, that seems to me to be absurd. 'Disclosure' is not the most appropriate word to use when a person who plays many parts announces to himself in one character what he has done and is doing in another. To talk of disclosure to the thing called the company, when as yet there were no shareholders, is a mere farce. To the intended shareholders there was no disclosure at all. On them was practised an elaborate system of deception.

The third ground of defence was that the only remedy was rescission. That defence, in the circumstances of the present case, seems to me to be as contrary to common sense as it is to authority. . . .

The last defence of all was that, however much the shareholders may have been wronged, they have bound themselves by a special bargain, sacred under the provisions of the Companies Act, 1862, to bear their wrongs in silence. In other words, Mr Gluckstein boldly asserts that he is entitled to use the provisions of an Act, of Parliament, which are directed to a very different purpose, as a shield and shelter against the just consequences of his fraud.

LORD ROBERTSON: . . . [256] To my thinking, the central fact in the history is, that while the object of the syndicate was to make profit out of the resale of Olympia, it was an essential part of the enterprise, as originally designed and as actually carried out, that the same individuals who sold as syndicate should buy as directors.

[W]here speculators have formed, exclusively of themselves, the directorate of a company, to be immediately floated for the purpose of buying the property which those same individuals are associated to acquire and resell, they have brought themselves directly within Lord Cairns's statement of the law in *Erlanger's* case (1878) 2 App. Cas. 1218. They have taken a decisive step in shaping and limiting the company. It may well be asked, if this be not an act of promotion what is? The hypothesis of all the law which we are considering is that the company is not yet formed; and unless these gentlemen had registered the company (and thus passed out of this stage altogether) it is difficult to see what more overt acts of promoting and forming the company they could have done.

[257] And now I pass to the next stage of the case. Assuming the members of the syndicate to have been promotors at the date of the purchase of the

mortgages, did they properly disclose it? In the skilful argument for the appellant the duty of disclosure on this hypothesis was conceded. But his concession must not disarm the criticism which, in considering the adequacy of the disclosure, first ascertains the relevancy of the transaction to the question what sum ought to be paid by the directors for the mortgaged property.

The theory of the appellant is that the purchase of the mortgages was a collateral and independent transaction. It seems to me, on the contrary, to be an essential and inseparable part of one and the same transaction, and for this plain reason that the syndicate's gain on the mortgages had to be paid by the company. The relevancy of the mortgage transaction to the [258] question solved by the syndicate sitting as directors is this – a company, or any one else, considering what price shall be paid draws inferences as to the true value from the price paid by the seller and the proposed advance on that price. In short, what the possible buyer wants to know is the profit to be made by his seller. . . . I consider that the transaction in mortgages was so relevant to the question what price should the company pay for the property that it was necessary that it should be disclosed to the company completely and in detail, and the question is whether this was done. There are several overwhelming reasons for a negative answer.

In the normal case, where the directors are truly and not merely in name the executive of the company, it may be assumed that they will be vigilant and critical of the particulars of a bargain of such paramount importance as the purchase of the property to be traded with, and that, dealing at arm's length, they will examine into anything bearing on that matter that does not tell its own story in its face. But, in the present case, the company was paralyzed so far as vigilance and criticism were concerned; for the board-room was occupied by the enemy. [259] Now, the question whether adequate disclosure had been made to a company by a vendor bound to do so must necessarily depend upon the intelligence brought to bear on the information. And if, by his own act, the promoter has weakened, or, as here, has annulled the directorate, his case on disclosure becomes extremely arduous – for he has to make out such disclosure to shareholders as makes directors unnecessary. How this could be done we have no occasion to consider, for the appellant is not within sight of doing it. Indeed, the case is so clear that I do not think it is a case of inadequate disclosure, but of direct misrepresentation.

Prospectus of the Components Tube Co. Ltd.

which was considered in *Components Tube Co. Ltd. v. Naylor* [1900] 2 I.R. 1 (*infra*, p. 315).

The List of Applications will OPEN on MONDAY, the 1st FEBRUARY, and CLOSE on or before WEDNESDAY the 3rd of FEBRUARY 1897, for London, and on or before the following day for Country.

THE COMPONENTS TUBE COMPANY, LIMITED
INCORPORATED UNDER THE COMPANIES ACTS, 1862 to 1893.

CAPITAL: £150,000, in Ordinary Shares of £1 each, payable: 2s.6d. on Application; 7s.6d. on Allotment; Balance, 10s., on 1st March.

Directors: *Harvey Du Cros, Junr., Metchley House, Edgbaston, Birmingham, (Managing Director, Cycle Components Manufacturing Company, Limited). *Frederick Faber MacCabe, M.B., Belleville, Donnybrook, Dublin (Director, Singer Cycle Company, Limited). Richard James Mecredy, Gortmore, Dundrum, Co. Dublin (ex-Director, Pneumatic Tyre Company, Limited), Charles Sangster, Bristol Road, Edgbaston, Birmingham (Director, Cycle Components Manufacturing Company, Limited). Alexis M. DeBeck, St. joseph's, Edgbaston, Birmingham (Managing Director, Singer Cycle Company (Russia), Limited). Benjamin B. Tuke, Coventry (Director Austral Cycle Agency, Limited).

Bankers: Lloyds Bank, Limited, 222 Strand, London; and all other Branches. National Bank, Limited, College Green, Dublin, and all Country Branches.

Solicitor: John B. Purchase, 11 Queen Victoria-street, London, E.C.

Brokers: *London* – Basil Montgomery & Co., 19, Throgmorton Avenue, E.C., and Stock Exchange. *Birmingham* – W. & F. Cuthbert, 103, Colmorerow, and Stock Exchange. *Dublin* – Daniel D. Bulger, 16 College Green, and Stock Exchange. *Limerick* – Thomas McSwiney, George's-street, Limerick.

Auditors: Felton & Walker, Chartered Accountants, 5, Waterloo-street, Birmingham.

Secretary (pro. tem): Charles Freake.

Offices (pro tem): 5, Waterloo-street, Birmingham.

Registered Offices: The Works, Bournbrook, Birmingham.

PROSPECTUS

This Company has been formed to acquire, carry on, and develop the well known profitable and extending Tube manufacturing business carried on by The Cycle Components Manufacturing Company, Limited, at Bournbrook, Birmingham. This business was established by Mr James Hudson in 1882, and carried on by him till 1892, when it was converted into a Company under the title of Hudson & Company, Limited, and successfully carried on by that Company till taken over by The Cycle Components Manufacturing Company, Limited in 1894.

In dealing with the acquisition of Hudson & Co., Limited, the Prospectus of The Cycle Components Manufacturing Company, Limited, said: 'It would be difficult to exaggerate the importance of this purchase in view of the improvements contemplated and the exceptional facilities of which the amalgamation has obtained control. This Company has hitherto depended almost exclusively upon the demands of the cycle trade for tubing; but it is now intended to develop other branches of the tube trade, such as boiler tubes, tubes for gas conveyance, tubular shafting and a multitude of other articles which are made from weldless steel tube.'

The manufacture of weldless tubing has become such an important feature of businesses, other than the cycle industry, that it is desirable that a separate Company should be formed to work and extend this important and long established business, which, under the style of Hudson & Co., Limited, and later as a branch of The Cycle Components Manufacturing Co., Limited, has maintained a great reputation for tubing of the highest grade.

Since the date of sale of this branch of the business by The Cycle Components Manufacturing Company, Limited, contracts for the alteration and extension of the machinery and plant are being entered into at a cost of £20,000, which when complete will be capable of increasing the output from the present figure £35,000 to about 100,000 feet per week.

This sum has been guaranteed by the Vendor out of the purchase moneys.

An additional £20,000 will be reserved for working capital, and will be provided out of the first subscriptions to the capital of the Company.

The Company will thus be strengthened by the addition of £40,000 of fresh capital, and the Directors claim that this sum will place the Company in the forefront of the tube trade and enable it to compete most successfully with any other concern.

Orders for tubing at remunerative prices have been received from the following Companies:

Singer Cycle Co. Ltd.	Riley Cycle Co. Ltd.
Swift Cycle Co. Ltd.	Allday & Onions Engineering Co. Ltd.
Birmingham Small Arms, Ltd.	Raglan Cycle and Anti-Friction Ball
Triumph Cycle Co. Ltd.	Co. Ltd.
Bayliss Thomas Ltd.	Fulwell Cycle Co. Ltd.
Thomas Smyth & Sons Ltd.	Tyne Cycle Mfg. Syndicate Ltd.
New Buckingham & Adams	B.F. Williams, Wolverhampton.
Cycle Co.	

In addition to these Orders the Cycle Components Manufacturing Company, Limited, has undertaken to take the whole of the balance of the output for the current season, after all orders received by the Company have been satisfied.

The Cycle Components Manufacturing Company, Limited, one of the largest consumers of Weldless Steel Tube, has also undertaken to purchase, at remunerative prices to this Company, its full requirements for the subsequent two years.

It will thus be seen that the Company starts under most favourable and exceptional circumstances. In addition to its already large clientele, new and important markets are being exploited.

It is also contemplated to lay down plant for the drawing of aluminium tubes, for which there is an increasing demand. The Directors anticipate that the next development in cycle and other light vehicle construction will be in this direction.

The works are situated alongside the works of the Cycle Components Manufacturing Company, Limited, at Boumbrook, within easy reach of the centre of the city of Birmingham. Important railway and canal communication adjoins the premises. The property comprises an area of about 9040 square yards, and is held under lease for 21 years from the Cycle Components Manufacturing Company, Limited, at an annual rental of £400, with the option of renewal or purchase on very favourable terms.

The business will be taken over as a going concern as from the 1st September, 1896, and all profits accruing from that date will belong to the Company.

The purchase price has been fixed by the Vendor at £130,000, out of which he provides the £20,000 above-mentioned for alteration and extension of the plant and machinery. The Vendor undertakes to accept payment of the purchase-money in cash or shares at the option of the Directors, but he stipulates that he may subscribe for and require the Directors to allot to him at least a third of the capital.

The Company has been fortunate in securing the valuable services of Mr Harvey Du Cros, junior, who has undertaken to give every assistance in his power, and to at all times place the benefit of his experience at the disposal of the Directorate. The Vendor fully recognising the great importance of Mr Du Cros' experience, has, at his own expense, entered into a contract with Mr Du Cros, securing his services, as above, to the Company.

Mr Charles Sangster, who has been so prominently connected with the economic and energetic management of the Cycle Components Manufacturing Company as Works Manager, is taking a seat on the Board. This ensures a continuance of the same energetic supervision.

Mr Harvey Du Cros, junior, having made an agreement with the Vendor, will receive no payment beyond the ordinary fees to each Director. Mr Chas. Sangster, whose services might easily be valued at a higher figure, is also content to take only the ordinary Director's fees. The Company is therefore saved very heavy salaries which would otherwise have been incurred.

The following contracts have been entered into, viz.:

(1) Dated the 1st day of October, 1896, between the Cycle Components Manufacturing Company, Limited, of the one part, and Ernest Terah Hooley, of the other part.

(2) Dated the 27th day of January, 1897, between Ernest Terah Hooley, of the one part and William Henry Weekes of the other part.

(3) Dated the 28th day of January, 1897, between William Henry Weekes, of the one part, and Ernest Piercy, as Trustee for and on behalf of the Company, of the other part.

(4) Dated the 27th day of January, 1897, between William Henry Weekes, of the one part, and Harvey Du Cros, junior, of the other part.

(5) Dated the 27th day of January, 1897, between the Cycle Components Manufacturing Company, Limited, of the one part, and the said Ernest Pierey, of the other part.

The Vendor will pay all expenses up to and including the final allotment of shares.

There may be also other contracts, including certain trade contracts, particulars of which, for obvious reasons, the Directors deem it inadvisable to specify, relating to the formation of the Company, and subscriptions to the capital and otherwise, which may technically fall within Section 38 of the Companies Acts, 1867. Subscribers will be held to have had notice of all these contracts, and to have waived all right to be supplied with particulars of such contracts, and to have agreed with the Company as Trustee for the Directors and other persons liable not to make any claim whatsoever, or to take any proceedings under the said section in respect of any non-compliance therewith.

Application for a special settlement and quotation will be made in due course.

Applications for shares should be made on the forms enclosed, and forwarded to the bankers of the Company, with the amount of the deposit.

If no allotment is made the deposit will be returned in full, and where the number of shares allotted is less than the number applied for, the balance will be applied towards payment due on allotment, and any excess will be returned to the applicant.

Copies of the Prospectus, with Forms of Application for Shares, can be obtained at the offices of the Company, or from their bankers, brokers, or solicitors.

The Memorandum and Articles of Association, and contracts specified above, can be seen at the offices of the solicitor to the Company.

30th January, 1897.

Note: Prospectuses being issued today must contain far more information than that contained in the one reproduced *supra*. If the shares are to be traded on the Stock Exchange, the listing particulars must inter alia comply with Chapter 5 of the *Yellow Book*.

Jury v. Stoker
(1882) 9 L.R. Ir. 385

When the Cork Milling Co. Ltd.'s shares were offered for sale to the public, a prominent member of the company's board had become a director in consequence of an agreement that he would get 150 shares in the company for joining its board. This fact was not disclosed either in the prospectus or to the registrar of companies

SIR EDWARD SULLIVAN M.R.: . . . [400] A serious question is raised whether this prospectus is not expressly fraudulent within the thirty-eighth section of the Companies Act, 1867. It is a question of very great importance as between those who launch Companies before the public and those who take shares in them. The section was passed for the protection of honest shareholders. All the judges agree with that view. of it. The section is a very short one, and it is a curious illustration of the difficulty there is in framing a set of words on which there could be no difference of opinion. Here are the words of the section: 'Every prospectus of a Company, and every notice inviting persons to subscribe for shares in any joint Stock Company shall specify the dates and the names of the parties to any contract entered into by the Company, or the promoters, directors, or trustees thereof, before the issue of such prospectus or notice, whether subject to adoption by the directors of the Company, or otherwise; and any prospectus or notice not specifying the same shall be deemed fraudulent on the part of the promoters, directors, and officers of the Company knowingly issuing the same, as regards any person taking shares in the Company on the faith of such prospectus, unless he shall have notice of such contract.' The object of that section was to compel promotors, directors, or trustees, of a Company to tell the public what their contracts were when they issued the prospectus. It is a most important provision. When a man sees in a prospectus the names of men like Stoker and Sikes, men of credit and position in the city of Cork, he would naturally say, 'this is a perfectly safe concern; can I imagine that this is not a good concern when I see the names of two such men in it?' Apart from the statute, the contracts with Stoker and Sikes would be most vital and most material for any person thinking of taking shares in this Company to know. It was material to know that Stoker's and Sikes' names were bought by Jackson; that Jackson, who was the getter up of the Company, made Stoker trustee for the Company for the purpose of making a contract with himself – Jackson being the whole Company, with Stoker's name as director in his pocket, and Stoker being the only person on the other side of the business acting for the intended Company. Such a state of facts never arose before: Jackson was about to start a Company, he was about to sell the mills to the Company, but before the sale he makes sure of Stoker [401] as a director; he makes an arrangement to give him one hundred and fifty fully paid-up shares in hand for allowing his name to be used as director, and then Jackson agrees with Stoker as trustee for the Company to sell his interest in the mills for two thousand five hundred shares. Was it not material for a man before he became a shareholder to know all this? I would say nothing could be more material for the public to know; and my impression is that, if any man in Cork had an idea of taking shares in the Company, the moment he heard that Stoker's name had been bought by Jackson he would not have taken shares, or have had anything to do with a Company based on a contract between men so circumstanced.

However, the material question is, is this contract within the section? What is the nature of a contract which brings it within the 38th section? On that question the judges in England have differed. Some of them held that it must be a contract affecting the Company or its assets or property. Others put a wider interpretation on the words of the section, and held that a contract affecting the position of the promoters, directors, or trustees of the property, which it is material for intended shareholders and the public to know, are within the mischief and express provisions of the section. I am of opinion that the strong weight of authority is in favour of the extended construction. There is high authority on both sides, but my opinion is strongly with the judges who put the extended construction on the statute. As to contracts with the Company, the question is closed by authority. The case which, in my opinion, rules the present is *Sullivan v. Metcalfe*, decided by the Court of Appeal in England, and reported 5 C.P.Div. 455. In that case there was, no doubt, a difference of opinion. The case was this, as it appears by the headnote. B and C, being possessed of a patent, agreed to sell it to the Company for £56,000, but by a series of contracts it was arranged that only £2,000 out of that sum should be retained by them for their own use, and that £54,000 should be divided between the promotors of the Company. The prospectus issued on behalf of the Company did not mention the contracts relating to the disposal of the purchase-money of the patent. The defendants were promoters and directors of the Company. The plaintiff [402] subcribed for shares, but he afterwards sued the defendants to recover the price of the shares subscribed for by him. It was held, upon demurrer, by Baggallay and Thesiger, L.JJ. (Bramwell, L.J., dissenting), that the contracts as to the disposal of the purchase-money of the patent ought to have been specified in the prospectus, pursuant to the Companies Act, 1867, s.38, and that the defendants were liable to the plaintiff for the price of his shares. The judgments of the majority of the Court of Appeal are given at length in the report, as well as the judgment of the dissentient Lord justice, which is of less moment, for – as in the House of Lords, where there is a division of opinion – it is the opinion of the majority we must look to as the decision in the case; and, although the judgment of Lord Justice Bramwell in the case contains most elaborate and able arguments, I am bound to say that the construction of the section adopted by Thesiger and Baggallay, L.JJ., appears to me the right one; and if I was free myself to lay down what contracts are within the 38th section, I would adopt the language of Lord Justice Baggallay, at p.465 of the report: 'Upon the construction, then, of the language of the section, I am prepared to hold that every contract which, upon a reasonable construction of its purport and effect, would assist a person in determining whether he would become a shareholder in the Company is a contract within the meaning of the 38th section of the Act of 1867; and having arrived at this conclusion from the considerations which I have mentioned, I abstain from saying more in support of it, as it is in accordance with the conclusions which have been arrived at by other judges, whose opinions on the subject are to be found in the published reports.'

Lord Justice Thesiger, after reviewing the opinions of the judges in *Twycross v. Grant* (1877) 2 C.P.D. 469 lays down a rule for himself thus (pp. 460, 46 1): ' I am therefore content to put the condition, which would otherwise attach only to the remedy for non-disclosure of a contract as a further limitation or restriction upon the generality of the description of the contract itself, and to adopt the view that every contract relating to the formation of a Company, or its promoters or vendors, of the directors, or other (403) officers of the Company, and which is material to be made known to persons invited to take shares, in order to enable them to form a judgment as to the policy of so doing, is a contract within the meaning of section 38 of the Companies Act, 1867, and as such must be disclosed under the circumstances and to the extent which the section points out; provided that one of the parties to it is, at its date, or subsequently becomes, a promoter, director, or trustee of the Company.' The contract here was made between Stoker, who assumed the character of a trustee for the Company, and Jackson, who was the real promoter of the Company. I entertain no doubt that, if he had known that Stoker had got £750 for allowing himself to be named as a director of the Company, he would have hesitated before he advanced his money in a concern which could bring nothing but danger and loss to him. But that is not the point. The question is, was this contract a thing which a man who was about to subscribe his money to the concern ought to have known? I am clearly of opinion that it was, and that this was a contract within the 38th section of the Companies Act, 1867.

Aaron's Reefs Ltd. v. Twiss
[1896] A.C. 273

A prospectus was issued by a company in Februay 1890 offering 200,000 £1 shares for sale. The company had acquired a gold mine of doubtful value in Venezuela. The prospectus promised in so many words that handsome dividends would be paid, once the mine got under way, and the defendant subscribed for one hundred shares. When a year later a call of four shillings per share was made, he refused to pay it; when the company then sued him in respect of the unpaid calls, his defence was that the prospectus was untrue in material respects and he claimed rescission.

LORD HALSBURY L.C.: . . . [280] Was there evidence for the jury that this contract was obtained by fraud of the plaintiff company? And was there evidence for the jury of the falsehood of the statements which are contained in the prospectus? My Lords, I cannot entertain the smallest doubt upon either of those questions. With reference to the first, whether the contract was obtained by fraud of the company, assuming there to be a fraud (a matter with which I will deal in a moment) I cannot entertain the least doubt that this was a very fascinating prospectus: there were statements in it which I will deal with more particularly hereafter, but they were statements calculated to shew that it was a very good thing – that it was a commercial adventure which was likely to produce very large profits, perhaps not 100 per cent., but at all events large profits. But I must protest against it being supposed that in order to prove a case of this character of fraud, and that a certain course of conduct was induced by it, a person is bound to be able to explain with exact precision what was the mental process by which he was induced to act. It is a question for the jury. If a man said he was induced by such and such an inducement held out in the prospectus, I should not think that conclusive. It must be for the jury to say what they believed upon the evidence. Looking at the evidence in this case, I should say if I were a juryman that this was a very fascinating prospectus, and was [281] calculated to induce any one who believed the statements in it to invest his money in the concern.

Then, inasmuch as the jury have found that, I think, upon very good evidence in the prospectus itself, it remains only to consider the final question, namely, whether or not there was evidence for the jury which would justify them in finding that this was a fraudulent prospectus – that these statements were fraudulent and false. Now, in dealing with that question, again I say I protest against being called on only to look at some specific allegation in it; I think one is entitled to look at the whole document and see what it means taken together. Now, if you look at the whole document taken together, knowing what we now know and what the jury had before them, I suppose nobody can doubt that this was a fraudulent conspiracy. I observe that one or two of the learned judges below used very plain language upon it, and remarked upon the fact that Mr Gilbert, who seems to have been the head and front of it, was not subjected to an inquiry in a criminal court. But, be that as it may, the question before your Lordships now is whether the jury were justified in finding with these facts before them what they did find.

It is said there is no specific allegation of fact which is proved to be false. Again I protest, as I have said, against that being the true test. I should say, taking the whole thing together, was there false representation? I do not care by what means it is conveyed – by what trick or device or ambiguous language: all those are expedients by which fraudulent people seem to think they can escape from the real substance of the transaction. If by a number of statements you intentionally give a false impression and induce a person to act upon it, it is not the less false although if one takes each statement by itself there may be a difficulty in shewing that any specific statement is untrue.

But I do not shrink from the question whether any of these statements are untrue. I think some of them are absolutely untrue. I will take one or two for example, although I think that the whole thing exhibits falsehood. I observed in the prospectus there is a statement to the effect that reports of the [282] most favourable character had been made upon this mine. That is not true. I only mention it in passing – I do not propose to rely upon it. The reports were made in respect of another company, and made some of them eight or nine years before. That is untrue, and, of course, even assuming what I shall deal with in a moment and what the words 'proved to be rich' may imply – assuming that there had been an inquiry into the state of the mine, a prospecting, as it is called, eight or nine years before – to treat that as something which had happened at the formation of this company is of itself a gross misrepresentation. Much may have happened in the eight or nine years intervening; and we now know as a fact that much did happen in those eight or nine years, shewing that, whatever opinion might reasonably have been entertained eight or nine years before, there was no ground for thinking that such a belief would have been entertained by skilled persons if they had just been inquiring into the state of this concession at the time when the company was formed. . . .

[283] But further than that, I wish to say for myself I do not think any particular form of words is necessary to convey a false impression. Supposing a person goes to a bank where the people are foolish enough to believe his words, and says, 'I want a mortgage upon my house, and my house is not completed, but in the course of next week I expect to have it fully completed.' Suppose there was not a house upon his land at all, and no possibility, therefore, that it could be fully completed next week, can anybody say that that was not an affirmative representation that there was a house which was so near to completion that it only required another week's work upon it to complete it? Could anybody defend himself if he was charged upon an indictment for obtaining money under false pretences, the allegation in the indictment being that he pretended that there was a house so near completion that it only required a week's work upon it, by saying that he never represented that there was a house there at all? So here, when I look at the language in which this prospectus is couched, and see that it speaks of a property which requires only the erection of machinery to be either at once or shortly in a condition to do work so as to obtain all this valuable metal from the mine, it seems to me that, although it is put in ambidextrous language, it means as plainly as can be that this [284] is now the condition of the mine, that such and such additions to it will enable it shortly to produce all those great results, and that that is a representation of an actually existing fact. I should quite agree with the proposition that the Lord Chancellor of Ireland and the Master of the Rolls put forward – if you are looking to the language as only the language of hope, expectation, and confident belief, that is one thing; but it does not seem to have been in the minds of the learned judges that you may use language in such away as, although in the form of hope and expectation, it may become a representation as to existing facts; and if so, and if it is brought to your knowledge that these facts are false, it is a fraud.

My Lords, as to the rest of the case, if there was evidence for the jury no one can doubt that the jury were right in coming to the conclusion to which they came. The whole of this transaction seems to me to have been fraudulent to the last degree, and I entirely concur with those learned judges who, in very plain language, said that the persons engaged in this transaction were guilty of a fraudulent conspiracy, and might have been indicted for it.

Components Tube Co. Ltd. v. Naylor
[1900] 2 I.R. 1

The company issued a prospectus (see *supra*, p. 305) on foot of which the defendant subscribed for and was allotted shares in the company. But the defendant refused to pay calls made in respect of those shares, claiming that the prospectus had been so misleading as to entitle him to rescission.

PALLES C.B.: . . . [37] After the incorporation of the company, the directors adopted the prospectus which had been previously prepared, issued it to the public, and upon the faith of it obtained a subscription from the defendant. Those directors were the agents of the company, and, in issuing the prospectus, they acted within the scope of their authority as such.

The defendant alleges: first, that the prospectus contains representations of fact which were untrue to the knowledge of the directors, or some of them, that is, fraudulent misrepresentations; secondly, that the directors concealed from, and omitted to state in the prospectus material facts which were within their knowledge, and which it is reasonable to hold would, if stated, have so operated upon the minds of those to whom the prospectus was addressed as to prevent them from applying for shares.

From the scope of the argument before us, I am driven to refer to principles absolutely elementary. What is the principle upon which a contract such as this, made by a company, is voidable, if induced by the fraud of its directors? It is not that the fraud of the directors is imputed to the company, but it is that even an innocent person is not permitted to retain a benefit obtained through the fraud of an agent, if the contract be repudiated within a reasonable time. Such a principal is not liable in an action for damages for the fraud of his agent, but, in relation to retaining a benefit obtained through the fraud, he cannot be in a better position than the fraudulent agent himself. The law is luminously stated by Lord Selborne in *Houldsworth v. City of Glasgow Bank* (1880) 5 App. Cas. 317. (*post*, p. 332).

In equity, one of the main heads of which has always been the redress of fraud, the constructive imputation of fraud to persons not really guilty of it has never been treated as a ground of relief, though the law of agency was administered according to the same rules in equity as at common law, and though in equity, as well as at law, an innocent principal might suffer for the [38] fraud of an agent . . . Vice-Chancellors Knight Bruce and Parker, and Lord Chancellor Campbell (all very eminent judges), said (as Lord Cranworth and Lord Chelmsford also said in this House), that the law does not impute the fraud of Directors to a company; and the same proposition would, I apprehend, be equally true, in the sense in which they intended it, if the principal whose agent was guilty of fraud were not a corporation, but an individual. The real doctrine which Lord Cranworth, in *Addie's* case, meant (as I understand him) to affirm, was one of substance and not of form: 'An attentive consideration' (he said) 'of the cases has convinced me that the true principle is that these corporate bodies, through whose agents so large a portion of the business of the country is now carried on, may be made responsible for the frauds of those agents, to the extent to which the companies have profited by those frauds, but that they cannot be sued as wrongdoers, by imputing to them the misconduct of those whom they have employed.' . . . The words in this passage, 'to the extent to which the companies have profited by those frauds', may perhaps require some enlargement or explanation; but, subject to that qualification, I am of opinion that this doctrine is in principle right.

The same principle is thus stated by Lord Hatherley in the same case:

> "I think that the following points may be considered as concluded by authority; at all events, I shall assume them so to be for the purposes of the case before the House. First, that an agent, acting within the scope of his authority, and making any representation whereby the person with whom he deals on behalf of his principal is induced to enter into a contract, binds his principal by such representation *to the extent of rendering the contract voidable*, if the representation be false, and the contracting party take proper steps for avoiding it whilst a *restitutio in integrum* is possible. Secondly, that a corporation is bound by the wrongful act of its agent, no less than an individual, and that, such misrepresentation by the agent being a wrongful act, the result of such misrepresentation must take effect in the same manner against the corporation as it would against an individual."

The company being thus, *quoad* the rescission of the contract, responsible for the frauds of its directors, the next question is, Was there evidence that the directors were guilty of fraud? To determine this question, it is essential to consider what is the exact obligation of the company to those whom it invited to apply for its shares? . . . [39]

In giving judgment in *The Central Railway Co. of Venezuela v. Kisch* (L.R. 2 H.C. 99) Lord Chelmsford C., said:

> "But although, in its introduction to the public, some high colouring, and even exaggeration, in the description of the advantages which are likely to be enjoyed by the subscribers to an undertaking, may be expected, yet no mis-statement or *concealment* of any material facts or circumstances ought to be permitted. In my opinion, the public, who are invited by a prospectus to join in any new adventure, *ought to have the same opportunity of judging* of everything which has a material bearing on its true character *as the promoters themselves possess*. It cannot be too frequently or too strongly impressed upon those who, having projected any undertaking, are desirous of obtaining the co-operation of persons who have no other information on the subject than that which

they choose to convey, that the utmost candour and honesty ought to
characterize their published statements. As was said by Vice-Chancellor
Kindersley, in the case of *The New Brunswick and Canada Railway Co.
v. Muggeridge*, 'Those who issue a prospectus holding out to the public
the great advantages which will accrue to persons who will take shares
in a proposed undertaking, and inviting them to take shares on the faith
of the representations therein contained, are bound to state everything
with strict and scrupulous accuracy, and not only to abstain from stating
as fact that which is not so, but to omit no one fact within their knowledge, the existence of which might in any degree affect the nature, or
extent, or quality of the privileges and advantages which the prospectus
holds out as inducements to take shares." . . .

[56] The *New Sombrero Phosphate Company v. Erlanger* (5 Ch. D. 73) was a
decision of Sir George Jessel, Lord Justice James, and Lord Justice Baggallay,
which was affirmed in the House of Lords by Lord Cairns, C., Lord Penzance,
Lord Hatherley, Lord O'Hagan, and Lord Blackburn; and in its circumstances
has a strong similarity to the present. The question there was in reference to
the purchase of an island in the West Indies, which on the 30th August, 1871,
the liquidator of the company, then in the course of being wound up, contracted to sell for £60,000, subject to the sanction of the court of Chancery, to
one Evans, who was the agent of Baron Erlanger, and who purchased for a
syndicate of speculators. This contract was confirmed by the judge in cham-
bers on the 15th September following; and upon the 20th of the same month
Evans agreed to sell the same property for £110,000 to one Francis Pavy, who
purchased as a trustee for a then intended company. There were five directors
named in the articles of association. Two were away from England when the
company was formed, and took no part in the management till after the purchase was completed. Another [57] was Evans, the trustee who purchased on
behalf of the syndicate. A fourth, by arrangement made before the registration
of the company, obtained his share qualification by gift or loan from Baron
Erlanger, the principal member of the syndicate, who in fact, directly or indirectly, selected all the directors. The fifth was independent of the syndicate.
The three directors who were in England, at a Board meeting of the 29th September, adopted the contract for purchase. The bill was by the company, against
the syndicate and directors, to set aside the purchase. Of course *Gover's* case
(1 Ch.D. 182) was cited. It was argued for the plaintiffs that the fact showed
conclusively that Erlanger was the promoter of the company.

It will, perhaps, be suggested (said the plaintiffs counsel) that the law has
been changed by *Gover's* case and that it is necessary to show that when the
first contract was entered into the company was actually in course of formation. But *Gover's* case only decided that an application by contributories to be
relieved from liability on shares could not be granted on the ground that the
contract was made with a person who afterwards became a promoter of the

company, though some of the dicta may lend colour to the argument sought to be founded on that case. Here the company was entirely the creation of Erlanger, and the inception of it must be carried back to the time of the purchase by the syndicate.

Lord Justice James says:

> "In this case the Vice-Chancellor appears to have proceeded, to a great extent, upon what was supposed to have been said in *Gover's* case. Now, I adhere entirely to what I have said in *Gover's* case, that is to say, it is quite open to a man to buy any property, at any price he likes, with a view or in the hope of selling that property to any company that he can get to buy it . . . but that has nothing whatever, as it appears to me, to do with the question in this case, which is, whether a man who has bought at a low price has obtained a higher price fairly and properly in accordance with the view which the Court of Equity takes of such transactions . . . A promoter is, according to my view of the case, in a fiduciary relation to the company which he promotes or causes to come into existence. If that promoter has a property which he desires to sell to the company, it is quite open for him to do so; but upon him, as upon any other person in a fiduciary position, it is incumbent to make full and fair disclosure of his interest and position with respect to the property. I can see no difference in this respect [58] between a promoter and a trustee, steward or agent. Such full and fair disclosure was not made in this case by the syndicate, which syndicate, it is admitted, were the promoters."

Later on he says:

> "Therefore it is not a technical rule at all which requires that a vendor who in any respect is in a fiduciary position should tell the exact truth, should say he is the vendor, or state the interest that he has."

The case was then brought to the House of Lords, where the judgment was affirmed . . . [59]

[N]one of the cases, either those mentioned by our own Master of the Rolls in *Aaron's Reefs v. Twiss* or those referred to in Lord Justice Lindley's book on Company Law, or *Gover's* Case as explained in *The New Sombrero Phosphate Co. v. Erlanger*, establish the proposition for which they are cited.

In my opinion, the result of all these cases is:

1. That where the circumstances are such that there can be rescission, and *restitutio in integrum*, the rule as to disclosure is that laid down in *The New Brunswick and Canada Railway Co. v. Muggeridge*, and *The Central Railway Co. of Venezuela v. Kisch*;

2. That, where the question is not the right of rescission, but is the right to damages for deceit, evidence must be given of active fraudulent misrepresen-

tation, and that mere concealment, although fraudulent, is not sufficient; but -

3. That this second rule, as applicable to an action for deceit, is subject to this explanation, that omissions may, upon the construction of the entire document, render false a statement which would have been true had the omitted statement been contained in the document; and that, where the omission is of this character, the deceived party has a right not only to rescind the contract [60] which he would have been entitled to do even had the representation not been of this character, but in addition he can treat it as active misrepresentation, as distinguished from mere concealment, and therefore make it the ground of an action for damages for deceit – an action which mere concealment would not be sufficient to maintain. My object in thus travelling through this long line of cases is not to establish a mere abstract proposition of law, but because the true principle, when once ascertained, is conclusive upon the case before us, and renders it unnecessary for us to critically examine small matters which are found upon the fringe of the gigantic fraud perpetrated here. It goes to the root of that which every commercial man, reading the prospectus, must know and recognise as the real fraud. It is not that a syndicate of promoters, having it in their power to acquire an undertaking for £50,000, by themselves and their creatures invite the public to become shareholders in a company formed by them to purchase the undertaking, at a profit to the promoters of £60,000. That might have been done, possibly, in such a way as to be consistent with honesty, morality, and law. But the real fraud is that their invitation to the public suppresses the two material facts: 1, that the real vendors are the promoters themselves; and 2, that their sale to the company is part of one entire transaction, by the other part of which they acquire the undertaking at £60,000 less than the price at which they offer it to the public. A contract obtained by such suppression we cannot uphold without violating the most elementary principles of common law and of justice. . . . [61]

Courts of Equity have always applied the rule of caveat emptor, in relation to the only subject-matters to which they held it applicable, viz. sales between parties who stood at arm's length from one another. In *Walters v. Morgan* (3 De G.F. & J. 718), Lord Campbell lays down:

> "There being no fiduciary relation between vendor and purchaser in the negotiation, the purchaser is not bound to disclose any fact exclusively within his knowledge which might reasonably be expected to influence the price of the subject to be sold. Simple reticence does not amount to legal fraud, however it may be viewed by moralists. But a single word, or (I may add) a nod or a wink, or a shake of the head, or a smile from the purchaser intended to induce the vendor to believe the existence of a non-existing fact, which might influence the price of the subject to be sold, would be sufficient ground for a Court of Equity to refuse a decree for a specific performance of the agreement . . .

The fifth question left to the jury was: 'Was the prospectus as a whole substantially misleading and calculated to deceive?' It is found in the affirmative. . . . [68] There is no evidence of the fixing of terms, or of any agreement whatsoever. The terms in the prospectus were those of the promoters only. Upon the evidence, the other directors did little more than consent to become such, and agree to the prospectus; but these matters, taken together, will not amount to such a contract as a court of equity will hold to be binding upon a subsequently formed company. . . ." [69]

Having now gone back behind these writings, and having ascertained the truth of the transaction, it is right to recall to mind the views which, before the judicature Act, a Court of Equity, and since that Act, any Division of the High Court, would be bound to take of such a matter, if, under the circumstances, the transaction really amounted to a contract.

The following are the words of Lord Cairns. L.C., in the case already referred to – *Erlanger v. New Sombrero Phosphate Co.*:

"They (*i.e.* the promoters of a company) stand, in my opinion, undoubtedly in a fiduciary position. They have in their hands the creation and moulding of the company; they have the power of defining how and when, and in what shape, and under what supervision, it shall start into existence, and begin to act as a trading corporation. If they are doing all this in order that the company may, as soon as it starts into life, become, through its managing directors, the purchasers of the property themselves, it is, in my opinion, incumbent upon the promoters to take care that in forming the company they provide it with an executive, that is to say, with a board of directors, who shall both be aware that the property which they are asked to buy is the property of the promoters, and who shall be competent and impartial judges as to whether the purchase ought or ought not to be made. I do not say that the owner of property may not promote and form a joint stock company, and then sell his property to it, but I do say that if he does he is [70] bound to take care that he sells it to the company through the medium of a board of directors who can and do exercise an independent and intelligent judgment on the transaction.

Unquestionably, the proof of the affirmative of these propositions lies upon him who attempts to support the transaction; and so far from there being evidence that the directors here were 'competent and impartial judges as to whether the purchase ought or ought not to be made,' or that they 'could or did exercise an independent and intelligent judgment on the transaction,' the inferences to be drawn from the facts proved are entirely the other way. . . ."

It may be said that the present case is distinguishable from *Erlanger v. New Sombrero Phosphate Co.*, because the present case is not one between the promoters and the company. No doubt this distinction exists, but in my opinion it is not material; and I arrive at that conclusion for the following reasons. By accepting the allotment of shares, the defendant here agreed that £130,000, upwards of four-fifths of the capital, should be applied in a payment under an alleged contract, which is called a purchase, but which in fact was an unreality and a fraud, which was not binding upon the company. When the case I have referred to was before the Court of Appeal both Sir George Jessel, M.R., and James, L.J., considered it as well in reference to the rights of individual shareholders, as of the company in its corporate capacity. It was necessary to do so, because it was urged in the argument that as there may have been many shareholders of the company who were parties to the fraud, the company itself was not the proper plaintiff, and that it was impossible to do equity between the defendants and the different shareholders, unless every shareholder filed his own bill or brought [71] his own action against the parties who misled him. Sir George Jessel shows how the representation to the shareholders could be relied upon there, although the action was one by the company. He says:

> "How does the representation made by the prospectus to the shareholders become material? It is a question of substance. These gentlemen who were nominated as directors had a duty to perform, not to the then nominal shareholders, who are nobodies – there were really none, although there were persons who had agreed to take shares – but the future shareholders, who were to form the real company."

James, L.J. says:

> "The ordinary remedy of a shareholder, in a case of this kind would be to say: 'You, the company, through and by your directors, led us into the thing, – we want to rescind the contract by which we became shareholders.' The remedy of the shareholder is to be relieved of his character of shareholder, and the company alone has the right to deal with the contract to which the company as a company is a party."

These passages seem to be express authorities that such a misrepresentation as that the alleged contract of purchase here was a bona fide contract is a sufficient ground for rescission.

I am of the opinion that it was competent to the jury, upon the evidence, to find that there was a misrepresentation as to the motive for floating the company; and that, in relation to the contract to purchase, there were at least four distinct misrepresentations.

They might have held –

1. That there was a misrepresentation, because, in truth and fact, there was no contract at all.

2. Because, if there were the *factum* of a contract, it was not an honest or

binding one, or one which the directors, acting for the company, could honestly adopt.

3. Because, even if honest and binding, it was a contract not with Weekes, but the promoters.

4. Because it was not a contract for purchase at £130,000, but a contract in which the real purchase-money was fraudulently swollen, by an addition to it of £60,000, either as plunder or as commission. . . . [74]

Admitting, as I have in the commencement of my judgment, that the frauds of the promoters and directors cannot be imputed to the company, the company cannot retain benefits which were procured through the fraud of its authorised agents. Secondly, even assuming that, as MacCabe and Du Cros were not directors until after the allotment, they were not authorised agents of the company at the time of the issue of the prospectus and the payment by the defendant of his deposit, I hold that the company cannot retain benefits which have been obtained by the misrepresentation of persons purporting, although without authority, to act their part; and further that, as the directors, and MacCabe and Du Cros were acting together for a common purpose, the floating of the company, their acts are admissible to show the object and intention of the directors who were acting with them towards the common purpose.

Houldsworth v. City of Glasgow Bank
(1880) 5 App. Cas. 317

The plaintiff bought shares in the defendant bank from the bank itself, which was an unlimited company. In the following year the bank failed and was put into liquidation with an enormous deficiency. The plaintiff, who was liable to the company for calls on his shares, sued it for damages in fraud; he alleged that he had been induced by the bank's own fraud to buy its shares.

EARL CAIRNS L.C.: . . . [324] A man buys from a banking company shares or stock of such an amount as that he becomes, we will say, the proprietor of one hundredth part of the capital of the company. A representation is made to him on behalf of the company that the liabilities of the company are £100,000, and no more. His contract, as between himself and those with whom he becomes a partner, is that he will be entitled to one hundredth part of all the property of the company, and that the assets of the company shall be applied in meeting the liabilities of the company contracted up to the time of his joining them, whatever their amount may be, and those to be contracted afterwards, and that if those assets are deficient the deficiency shall be made good by the shareholders rateably in proportion to their shares in the capital of the company. This is [325] the contract, and the only contract, made between him and his partners, and it is only through this contract, and through the correlative contract of his partners with him, that any liability of him or them can be enforced. . . .

[But H]e finds out, however, after he joins the company, that the liabilities were not £100,000 but £500,000. He is entitled thereupon, as I will assume, to rescind his contract, to leave the company, and to recover any money he has paid or any damages he has sustained; but he prefers to remain in the company and to affirm his contract, that is to say, the contract by which he agreed that the assets of the company should be applied in paying its antecedent debts and liabilities. He then brings an action against the company to recover out of its assets the sum, say £4,000, which will fall upon his share to provide for the liabilities, over and above what his share would have had to provide had the liabilities been as they were represented to him. If he succeeds in that action, this £4,000 will be paid out of the assets and contributions of the company. But he has contracted, and his contract remains, that these assets and contributions shall be applied in payment of the debts and liabilities of the company, among which, as I have said, this £4,000 could not be reckoned. The result is, he is making a claim which is inconsistent with the contract into which he has entered, and by which he wishes to abide; in other words, he is in substance, if not in form, taking the course which is described as approbating and reprobating, a course which is not allowed either in Scotch or English law.

LORD SELBOURNE: . . . [329] This is not a case of parties at arm's length with each other, one of whom has suffered a wrong of which damages are the simple and proper measure, and which may be redressed by damages without any unjust or inconsistent consequences. For many purposes a corporator with whom his own corporation has dealings, or on whom it may by its agents inflict some wrong, is in the same position towards it as a stranger; except that he may have to contribute, rateably with others, towards the payment of his own claim. But here it is impossible to separate the matter of the Pursuer's claim from his status as a corporator, unless that status can be put an end to by rescinding the contract which brought him into it. His complaint is, that by means of the fraud alleged he was induced to take upon himself the liabilities of a shareholder. The loss from which he seeks to be indemnified by damages is really neither more nor less than the whole aliquot share due from him in contribution of the whole debts and liabilities of the company; and if his claim is right in principle I fail to see how the remedy founded on the principle can stop short of going to this length. But it is of the essence of the contract between the shareholders (as long as it remains unrescinded) that they should all contribute equally to the payment of all the company's debts and liabilities.

Such an action of damages as the present is really not against the corporation as an aggregate body, but is against all the members of it except one, viz., the Pursuer; it is to throw upon them the Pursuer's share of the corporate debts and liabilities. Many of those shareholders (as was observed by Lord Cranworth in *Addie's* Case (L.R. 1 H.L. Sc. 145), may have come and probably did come into the company after the Pursuer had acquired his shares. They are all as innocent of the fraud as the Pursuer himself; if it were imputable to them it must, on the same principle, be imputable to [330] Pursuer himself as long as he remains a shareholder; and they are no more liable for any consequences of fraudulent or other wrongful acts of the company's agent than he is. Rescission of the contract in such a case is the only remedy for which there is any precedent, and it is in my opinion the only way in which the company could justly be made answerable for a fraud of this kind. But for rescission the Appellant is confessedly too late.

Note: The Bank's articles of association gave it the 'quasi-partnership power' of dealing in its own shares. It does not appear that the plaintiff had responded to a prospectus that the Bank had issued. *Houldsworth* was distinguished in *Soden v. British and Commonwealth Holdings p.l.c.* [1998] A.C. 298, where the plaintiff had purchased the entire share capital in the company in question from a third party; he sought damages not alone from the vendor but also from the company, which had gone into liquidation. It was held that *Houldsworth* was not a bar to him proving in the liquidation for the damages due to him.

Jury v. Stoker
(1882) 9 L.R. Ir. 385

The plaintiff subscribed for shares in the newly formed company on foot of a prospectus which contained the following:

CORK MILLING COMPANY, LIMITED

> The above Company have acquired the very valuable concern described below, with the vendor's trade business and good-will, on exceptionally favourable terms, *viz.*:
> For the small sum of £8000, payable by the debentures of the Company, at 6 per cent. per annum, redeemable in three years, and one thousand fully paid-up shares; in addition to which the vendor will purchase fifteen hundred shares fully paid up, thus putting a cash capital of £7500 into the concern.
> No promotion money has or will be paid.

Contrary to what was stated there, the vendor never did agree to invest in the company. The company eventually went into liquidation and the plaintiff lost his entire investment. He sued the defendant, who was responsible for issuing the prospectus, claiming damages for deceit.

SIR EDWARD SULLIVAN M.R.: . . . [396] [Then one reads the prospectus, it represents that the cash capital of £7500 was not arising out of a sale by him, but to arise by a future transaction, whereby he was not to put in, but to purchase, one thousand five hundred shares. That is Jackson, after the Company was formed, was to apply for one thousand five hundred shares, and was at once, without call or instalment, to place on its table £7500 in cash. Now, Stoker's counsel of course have done all they could to gloss that passage in the prospectus, and to make it in conformity with the facts of the case; but they have failed to do so. It is manifest beyond a doubt that it was a deliberate misrepresentation, and entirely false; and I have as little doubt that it was deliberately [397] done with a view to make the company attractive in the eyes of the public, putting on the face of the prospectus an untrue allegation that the company was to start with £7500 down, which was to be paid by one person. That prospectus was for several weeks in preparation, and was the subject of deliberation, and it is essential to the Defendant's case to make it consistent with the original agreement of the 10th of July, 1877; but it is impossible to do so. It is impossible, in any view, to justify the insertion, in the passage of the prospectus which I have read, of the word 'cash' before 'capital'. In my opinion, it was a false representation. In my opinion, it was a fraudulent misrepresentation, and Jackson and Stoker are responsible for it. The Plaintiff jury acted on that statement, and on the authorities I hold the Defendants answerable for the false representation.

My view of the law is that contained in the three propositions laid down in *Barry v. Croskey* (2 John & Hem. 1). Lord Hatherley says: First. Every man must be held responsible for the consequences of a false representation made by him to another, upon which the other acts, and, so acting, is injured or damnified. Secondly. Every man must be held responsible for the consequences of a false representation made by him to another, upon which a third person acts, and, so acting, is injured or damnified; provided it appear that such false representation was made with intent that it should be acted upon by such a third person in the manner that occasions the injury or loss. In *Langridge v. Levy* (2 M. & W. 519) the false representation was made to the father; the party who sustained the injury was the son; but the son brought the action, and recovered damages. The Court treated the representation as made by the defendant with the intent that it should be acted upon by the son in the manner that occasioned the injury. In warranting the gun 'to have been made by Nock, and to be a good, safe, and secure gun,' the defendant must have contemplated, as a natural consequence, that the father, confiding in that warranty, might place the gun in the hands of his son, or of any other third person; and, such third person using the gun, and sustaining injury by using it, the [398] defendant was liable for that injury as a consequence of his false warranty. Thirdly. But, to bring it within the principle, the injury, I apprehend, must be the immediate, and not the remote, consequence of the representation thus made. To render a man responsible for the consequences of a false representation made by him to another, upon which a third person acts, and, so acting, is injured or damnified, it must appear that such false representation was made with the direct intent, that it should be acted upon by such third person in the manner that occasions the injury or loss. In my opinion, the shareholders of this Company were entitled to have all the circumstances bearing on the affairs and formation of the company in the prospectus. There is no document in which it is of more consequence to state fully and fairly the real facts than the prospectus of a projected Company. Some men will speculate by taking shares in a Company, no mater how ridiculous it may be. But the law was not made for such persons. Thousands of persons of small property are striving to increase their income by investment in the shares of a Company, and in nine cases out of ten, persons who are not lawyers act on the prospectus, which ought to be a fair resumé of the affairs of the Company.

The law, as stated by Lord Hatherley, in *Barry v. Croskey* is not new law. That case was decided in 1861. In *Scott v. Dixon*, which was decided in 1855, and which is reported in a note to *Bedford v. Bagshaw* (29 L.J. (N.S.) Exch. 62), Lord Campbell and the other judges of the Court of Queen's Bench in England held that, if there be a false and untrue representation in the report of the directors of a banking company, the persons issuing the report must answer for it. And in *Bedford v. Bagshaw* (4 H. & N. 538), decided in 1859, will be found the judgments of Chief Baron Pollock and Baron Bramwell to the same effect. Chief Baron Pollock says, p. 548, 'The defendant acted fraudulently, and made representations to the committee of the Stock Exchange with a view to induce persons to believe the existence of a particular state of things as to these shares. All persons buying [399] shares on the Stock Exchange must be considered as persons to whom it was contemplated that the representation would be made. I am not prepared to lay down as a general rule, that if a person makes a false representation, every one to whom it is repeated, and who acts upon it may sue him. But it is a different thing where a director of a Company procures an artifical and false value to be given to the shares in the Company which he professes to offer to the public. Generally, if a false and fraudulent statement is made with a view to deceive the party who is injured by it, that affords a ground of action. But I think that there must always be this evidence against the person to be charged, viz. that the plaintiff was one of the persons to whom he contemplated that the representation should be made, or a person whom the defendant ought to have been aware he was injuring or might injure. If a director of a Company, one of the persons who puts the shares forth into the world, deliberately adopts a scheme of falsehood and fraud, the effect of which is that parties buy the shares in consequence of the falsehood, I should feel no difficulty in saying that in such a case an action is maintainable.'

The law was laid down in the same manner in a series of subsequent cases; but so far back as 1855 the law on the subject was settled. In my opinion the prospectus was deliberately and fraudulently adopted to make the concern attractive. The Plaintiff Jury acted on the prospectus and took the shares. I have a very strong opinion that the representation was false and fraudulent, to induce men to take shares in this Company, and if loss has resulted from it, the person who made the false representation should be made to answer for the loss, even if the matter rested at common law, and outside any statute. The representation was false, fraudulent, and material, made to induce a man to take the shares, and loss has resulted to the Plaintiff. The Defendant who makes such a representation cannot be heard to say, 'Oh you might have found out that it was wrong if you had gone to the office and seen the instrument itself.' I am, therefore, clearly of the opinion, on the first part of the case, that Mr Stoker is answerable to the Plaintiff for the loss which he has sustained by the false statement in the prospectus as to the cash capital of £7500.

Seddon v. North Eastern Salt Co. Ltd.
[1905] 1 Ch. 326

Unlike in the previous five cases, where the plaintiffs had acquired their shares directly from the companies in question, the plaintiffs here bought the shares from a third party. The net issue was whether vendors of shares are subject to a similar quasi-fiduciary duty of full disclosure as applies to companies and their agents when seeking to induce investors to subscribe for shares. Contending that there had been a misrepresentation, the plaintiffs claimed rescission of the contract and recovery of the purchase price.

JOYCE J.: . . . [332] [I]t appears to me, as it has done all through, that the plaintiffs way to succeeding in his claim is beset with difficulties. Now, in the first place, there is no allegation of fraud, and, in point of fact, the imputation of fraud upon the defendants has been expressly disclaimed, and properly so. Well, then, it is a claim to rescind or set aside for an innocent misrepresentation a contract for the sale of property, not executory, but executed, and under which nothing whatever still remains to be done. Lord Campbell states the rule on the question. In *Wilde v. Gibson* (1 H.L.C. 632), he says: 'My Lords, after the very attentive and anxious consideration which this case has received, I have come to the clear conclusion that the decree appealed against ought to be reversed; and I must say that in the Court below the distinction between a bill for carrying into execution an executory contract, and a bill to set aside a conveyance that has been executed, has not been very distinctly borne in mind.

With regard to the first: If there be, in any way whatever, misrepresentation or concealment, which is material to the purchaser, a Court of Equity will not compel him to complete the purchase; but where the conveyance has been executed, I apprehend, my Lords, that a Court of Equity will set aside the conveyance only on the ground of actual fraud.' Lord Selborne in *Brownlie v. Campbell* (5 App. Cas. 936), to which I have been referred, says, after explaining the circumstances of that particular case: 'The contract is ultimately entered into upon those terms. Passing from the stage of correspondence and negotiation to the stage of written agreement, the purchaser takes upon himself the risk of errors. I assumed them to be errors unconnected with fraud in the particulars, and when the [333] conveyance takes place it is not, as far as I know, in either country' – that means in Scotland or England – 'the principle of equity that relief should afterwards be given against that conveyance, unless there be a case of fraud.' Now I do not entertain the slightest doubt about that being a correct statement of the law. It has been acted upon by Cotton L.J. in *Soper v. Arnold* (37 Ch. D. 96). But the rule is not only a rule of equity, it is also a rule of law. In *Kennedy v. Panama, New Zealand and Australian Royal Mail Co.* (L.R. 2 QB. 580) Blackburn J. delivers die judgment of the court. He says: 'There is, however, a very important difference between cases where a contract may be rescinded on account of fraud, and those in which it may be rescinded on the ground that there is a difference in substance between the thing bargained for and that obtained. It is enough to shew that there was a fraudulent representation as to *any part* of that which induced the party to enter into the contract which he seeks to rescind; but where there has been an innocent misrepresentation or misapprehension, it does not authorise a rescission unless it is such as to shew that there is a complete difference in substance between what was supposed to be and what was taken, so as to constitute a failure of consideration. For example, where a horse is bought under a belief that it is sound, if the purchaser was induced to buy by a fraudulent representation as to the horse's soundness, the contract may be rescinded. If it was induced by an honest misrepresentation as to its soundness, though it may be clear that both vendor and purchaser thought that they were dealing about a sound horse and were in error, yet the purchaser must pay the whole price, unless there was a warranty; and even if there was a warranty, he cannot retain the horse and claim back the whole price, unless there was a condition to that effect in the contract.' And of course there can be no successful claim, after completion, for damages for misrepresentation unless that misrepresentation was fraudulent.

It appeared to me from the first, upon this case, that this fact – the absence of fraud and the absence of any allegation of fraud – was a fatal objection to the action, and I should be [334] perfectly justified in disposing of it on those grounds alone, and saying no more about the facts of the case. But I will add just a few words about the facts as they have been gone into so fully. If the plaintiff be right, the contract in question, of course, is not void but voidable only, and it was the duty of the plaintiff, bearing in mind the peculiar nature of the property, to repudiate the contract at the very earliest possible moment when he found out that any misrepresentation had been made, if, in fact, any was made. In my opinion the plaintiff did not do this, but, taking possession, he went on treating the property as his own in many ways for many months, and continued to do so long after the time when he had the information which would lead him, and ought to have led him, at once to the conclusion that he had been misinformed, if, in fact, he had been misinformed. It is quite plain to my mind that the correspondence between the plaintiff and Mr Storr does not amount to an arrangement that the plaintiff is to be entitled to go on dealing with the property as his own without prejudice to the question of whether he is to be entitled to rescind the contract and repudiate the property or not. Really, as far as I understand it, there never was a suggestion about repudiating the property and rescinding the contract until the commencement of the action. In the solicitor's letter which precedes the commencement of the action there is not even a suggestion of repudiating the property and rescinding; but all that he says is, 'I am going to commence an action and claim against you compensation in damages.'

I think I ought to add also that upon the whole evidence I am not satisfied that there was any misrepresentation that induced the plaintiff to enter into the contract. I very much doubt whether there was any misrepresentation at all.

Securities Trust Ltd. v. Hugh Moore & Alexander Ltd
[1964] I.R. 417

As in the *Seddon* case, *supra*, the plaintiffs here bought the company's shares not from the company itself but a third party. However, instead of (as in *Seddon*) suing the vendor, he sued the company. K.A.who was a registered shareholder of the company, applied for and obtained from it a copy of its memorandum and articles of association. He held his shares in the company as trustee for the plaintiff. His application for the memorandum and articles was in his own name and the defendant was unaware that he held his shares in trust. The copy articles supplied to him contained an error which suggested that, on a winding up of the defendant, both ordinary and preference shareholders would participate in a distribution of surplus assets. On the faith of this copy of the articles, the plaintiff made several purchases of preference shares in the defendant at prices in excess of their true value. Subsequent to these purchases, that error was discovered by the defendant and it notified K.A. that the error existed in the copy articles supplied to him. On the winding up of the defendant, the plaintiff claimed to be entitled to participate in the distribution of surplus assets in respect of their holding of preference shares but the liquidator refused to allow their claim. The plaintiff commenced proceedings for damages for negligent misrepresentation.

DAVITT P.: ... [421]The law to be applied in this case is not in controversy. It would appear that the proposition that innocent (*i.e.* non-fraudulent) misrepresentation cannot give rise to an action for damages is somewhat too broadly stated, and is based upon a misconception of what was decided by the House of Lords, in *Derry v. Peek* (14 App. Cas. 337). Such action may be based on negligent misrepresentation which is not fraudulent. This was pointed out in *Nocton v. Lord Ashburton* [1914] A.C. 932, particularly in the speech of Haldane L C At page 948 he says:

"Although liability for negligence in word has in material respects been developed in our law differently from liability for negligence in act, it is none the less true that a man may come under a special duty to exercise care in giving information or advice. I should accordingly be sorry to be thought to lend countenance to the idea that recent decisions have been intended to stereotype the cases in which people can be held to have assumed such a special duty. Whether such a duty has been assumed must depend on the relationship of the parties, and it is at least certain that there are a good many cases in which that relationship may be properly treated as giving rise to a special duty of care in statement."

It was apparently considered in some quarters that such a special duty could arise only from a contractual or fiduciary relationship. In *Robinson v. National Bank of Ireland* (1916) S.C. (H.L.) 150, Haldane L.C. was at pains to dispel this idea. At page 157 he said:

"The whole of the doctrine as to fiduciary relationships, as to the duty of care arising from implied as well as express contracts, as to the duty of care arising from other special relationships which the Courts may find to exist in particular cases, still remains, and I should be very sorry if any word fell from me which would suggest that the Courts are in any way hampered in recognising that the duty of care may be established when such cases really occur."

The proposition that circumstances may create a relationship between two parties in which, if one seeks information from the other and is given it, that other is under a duty to take reasonable care to ensure that the information given is correct, has been accepted and applied in the case of *Hedley Byrne & Co. Ltd. v. Heller and Partners Ltd.* [1964] A.C. 465. Counsel for the defendant [422] Company did not seek to dispute the proposition. He submitted, however, that the circumstances of this case created no such special relationship.

Sect. 18, sub-s. 1, of the Companies (Consolidation) Act, 1908, provides:

"Every company shall send to every member, at his request, and on payment of one shilling or such less sum as the company may prescribe, a copy of the memorandum and of the articles (if any)."

At the time that Mr Anderson made his request to the secretary of the defendant Company for a copy of their Memorandum and Articles of Association he was a shareholder. The plaintiff company had not then been registered as owner of any shares. He was a member of the defendant Company; his company was not. The position was that he was entitled to receive a copy of the Memorandum and Articles; his company was not. He was entitled to receive it personally *qua* member; he was not entitled to receive it qua agent of the plaintiff company. In these circumstances I must, I think, conclude that the copy was requested and supplied, in accordance with the provisions of section 18, subs. 1 of the Act, by the defendant company to Mr Anderson personally and not as agent for the plaintiff company. It seems to me that there was no relationship between the parties in this case other than such as would exist between the defendant company and any person (other than Mr Anderson) who might chance to read the copy supplied to him; or, indeed, between that company and any member of the community at large, individual or corporate, who chanced to become aware of the last sentence in Article 155 of the defective reprint of the Memorandum and Articles. It can hardly be seriously contended that the defendant company owed a duty to the world at large to take care to avoid mistakes and printer's errors in the reprint of their Articles. In my opinion, counsel is correct in his submission that in this case the defendant company owed no duty to the plaintiff company to take care to ensure that the copy of the Articles supplied to Mr Anderson was a correct copy. For these reasons there must, in my opinion, be judgment for the defendant company.

Possfund Custodian Trustee v. Diamond
[1996] 2 B.C.L.C. 665

As in *Seddon* (*supra*) and in *Securities Trust* (*supra*), the shares in question were not acquired directly from the company but were purchased from a third party. But instead of suing the vendor (as in *Seddon*), the purchaser sued officers and agents of the company in question, contending that there had been reliance on a prospectus published earlier on behalf of the company. In 1989 a prospectus was published when the company floated its shares on the unlisted securities market. The plaintiff subscribed for and was allotted shares at that time and, in 1992, bought further shares in the market. The shares turned out to be worthless and the plaintiff sought damages against the company's directors, auditors and financial advisers on the grounds that there had been misrepresentations in the prospectus.

LIGHTMAN J.: [1358] It is common ground for the purposes of these applications that the plaintiffs' pleadings disclose a cause of action in respect of the placing. The issue is whether such a cause of action is disclosed in respect of the after market purchases.

I propose to approach this question in three stages. First, I shall consider in outline the common law and statutory schemes providing protection to investors in respect of prospectuses. Second, I shall examine the pleadings. Third, I shall look in more detail at the authorities so far as they provide guidance on the scope of the common law duty of care owed to investors and in particular whether it is arguable that the tort of negligence provides the protection pleaded by the plaintiffs.

(A) The common law and statutory scheme
In the nineteenth century when the issue of prospectuses first became a common feature of commercial life, the common law allowed a claim in damages to the investor who incurred a loss after investing in reliance on the contents of a false or misleading prospectus (in the absence of a breach of a fiduciary or contractual duty owed to the investor) only if he [1359] could establish the tort of deceit; see *Derry v. Peek* (1889) 14 App Cas 337. . . . The prospectus was an invitation issued to the public to subscribe for shares, and not to purchase shares in the market, and without more the prospectus could only found liability if relied on for the purpose for which it was issued, namely making the decision whether to subscribe, and not if relied on for the purpose of deciding whether or not to make purchases in the market; see *Peek v. Gurney* (1873) LR 6 HL 377. . . . The principle was graphically expressed in the expression that the representations contained within the prospectus were exhausted upon the allotment being completed.

The legislature evidently considered that the common law provided inadequate protection to placees, and the Directors Liability Act 1890 provided that: (1) directors, promoters and persons authorising the issue of a prospectus should be liable to pay compensation to all persons who should subscribe for shares on the faith of a prospectus for the loss or damage they sustained by reason of any untrue statement in the prospectus; and (2) they should have a statutory defence (in respect of which the onus should be upon them) that they had reasonable grounds to believe and did believe that the statement was true or the fair representation of the views of an expert. No statutory protection was afforded to after-market purchasers.

The provisions of the 1890 Act were brought into the mainstream of companies legislation in 1908 in the form of section 84 of the Companies (Consolidation) Act 1908 and re-enacted by section 37 of the Companies Act 1929, in each case without any material change.

The Companies Act 1948 supplemented the previous statutory provisions in three relevant respects. First, it provided that it should be unlawful to make an invitation to the public to subscribe for shares without issuing a prospectus containing certain specified information. Secondly, it added experts who consented to the use of their reports in the prospectus to the class of those liable to persons subscribing on the faith of a prospectus, and such experts were likewise afforded a statutory defence if they could prove the existence of reasonable grounds for believing their statements to be true. Thirdly, section 45(1) introduced the provision (now in section 58 of the Companies Act 1985 – same as section 51 of the 1963 Act) whereby the protection previously afforded to subscribers was extended to cover the loophole that might otherwise exist where shares were first allotted to an issuing house for sale to the public.

This was done by deeming the offer for sale to the public to be an offer for subscription and the purchasers to be subscribers.

In 1963 the House of Lords in *Hedley Byrne & Go Ltd v. Heller & Partners Ltd* [1964] A.C. 465 established that at common law a cause of action exists enabling the recovery of damages in respect of a negligent misrepresentation occasioning damage and loss where the necessary proximity exists between the representor and representee. It is clearly established (and indeed common ground on these applications) [674] that in a case such as the present, where the defendants have put a document into more or less general circulation and there is no special relationship alleged between the plaintiffs and the defendants, foreseeability by the defendants that the plaintiffs would rely on the prospectus for the purpose of deciding whether to make after-market purchases is not sufficient to impose upon the defendants a duty of care to the plaintiffs in respect of such purchases (see *Caparo Industries plc v. Dickman* [1990] 2 A.C. 605 – see *post*, p. 369). The imposition of a duty of care in such a situation requires a closer relationship between representor and representee, and its imposition must be fair, just and [1360] reasonable. I shall come back to consider whether in this context the existence of an intention on the part of the defendants that investors should rely on the prospectus for this purpose is sufficient to establish the necessary proximity, for that is the crux of the present applications.

The Companies Act 1985 (in force at the time of the prospectus) in section 56 to 71 re-enacted the provisions of the 1948 Act (for present purposes) without any material change. Section 67 contains the provisions for payment of compensation to placees.

Following Professor Gower's review, there was enacted the Financial Services Act 1986. This Act drew a sharp distinction between listing particulars (which effectively replace prospectuses) in respect of shares to be admitted to the official list of The Stock Exchange (listed securities) and prospectuses in respect of unlisted securities, which include shares to be listed on the USM. Part IV of the Act related to listed and Pt V to unlisted. Part IV was brought into force, but Pt V never was. In the case of listed securities, the Act and the listing rules (which the Act required to be complied with) required listing particulars to be constantly updated in respect of any information affecting, inter alia, the value of the listed securities. Section 150 gave a remedy against the 'persons responsible' for listing particulars-

> "to any person who has acquired any of the securities in question [i.e. the listed securities] and suffered loss in respect of them as a result of any untrue or misleading statement in [the listing particulars] or the omission from them of any matter required to be included . . ."

In short, protection was afforded to all purchasers of listed securities (whether placees or after market purchasers) relying on the continuing and updated representations in the listing particulars and the updates.

In the case of unlisted securities, there is no equivalent statutory provision for updating the prospectus, but the USM does in fact require an undertaking to like effect from a company admitted to the USM. Section 166 provides that persons responsible for a prospectus:

> "shall be liable to pay compensation to any person who has acquired the securities to which the prospectus relates and suffered loss in respect of them as a result of any untrue or misleading statement in the prospectus . . ."

Note: In section 49(1) of the 1963 Act, liability is only in favour of those who subscribe for the shares).

For the purpose of determining the ambit of the duty of care under the tort of negligence, I have been invited to consider whether section 166 (albeit not brought into force, but later repealed and re-enacted in 1995) gave a [675] statutory cause of action to after-market purchasers. All I shall say is that as present advised, I do not think that it does. The reference to the 'person who a has acquired the securities to which the prospectus relates', as it seems to me, naturally refers to the placee in respect of the shares originally allotted to him.

To complete the legislative history, the Public Offers of Securities Regulations 1995, SI 1995/1537 (similar to S.I. No. 202 of 1992), made pursuant to Council Directive (EEC) 89/298 (in force on 19 June 1995) on co-ordinating the requirements for the drawing up, scrutiny and distribution of the prospectus to be published when transferable securities are to be offered to the public, laid down a detailed regime in respect of public offers of securities. Any public offer must be accompanied by a prospectus to be made available to the public during the period of the offer, a supplementary prospectus must be published in the event of any significant change or matter arising during the period of the offer, and a remedy in respect of misleading statements in prospectuses for unlisted securities is provided 'to any [1361] person who has acquired the securities to which the prospectus relates'. This provision for compensation is to like effect to that contained in section 166 and is, I think, likewise limited in operation and scope.

(B) Pleadings
Since these applications turn on the sufficiency of the pleadings, I think it right to set out the relevant passages in the pleadings in the two actions. . . .

[1363] Mr Falconer after an adjournment provided both the particulars and the affidavit. Put very shortly, his case thus revealed is that, whatever the situation at the time of the decision in *Peek v. Gurney* (1873) LR 6 HL 377, by 1989 company and commercial practice in respect of prospectuses and market conditions and perceptions had changed and with them the purpose of a prospectus: the established purpose of a prospectus and its contents were no longer confined to inducing investors to become placees, but extended to inducing the public to make after-market purchases. A significant factor in this context was the requirement of The Stock Exchange for the entire prospectus to be printed on Extel cards for Extel Statistical Services Ltd for the purposes of that company making them available to all subscribers and investors who want to look at them. Read in this light and against this background, the intention of the defendants reasonably to be inferred and as reasonably understood by the plaintiffs was to induce the plaintiffs, as well as to accept shares on the allotment, to make [678] after-market purchases. The affidavit in support is from Mr John Herring, a director of Kleinwort Benson Securities Ltd. His affidavit verifies the particulars and is to the effect that in the market today a prospectus is perceived as intended to be acted upon for the purposes of after-market purchases and that indeed is the intention of those who prepare and are responsible for them.

Mr Barnes for AA accepted that the particulars did now furnish a sufficiently pleaded case that the purpose of the prospectus and the intention of the defendants was to induce such purchases. Mr Gillyon for APCS objected to the pleadings as still insufficiently particularising the facts relied on in support of the contention. I think that the pleading is sufficient.

The plaintiffs case, as Mr Falconer made clear and as is now apparent from the pleadings, is one applicable to any ordinary prospectus today and turns exclusively on expert evidence as to the perception in current practice of the purpose of a prospectus. The defendants know sufficiently the case they have to meet from the particulars, supplemented by the affidavit of Mr Herring.

The issue before me is accordingly whether it is arguable that persons responsible for a prospectus owe a duty of care to (and may be liable in [1364] damages at the instance of) an after-market purchaser if it is established that such purchaser was intended to rely on the prospectus for this purpose, and in particular whether the necessary proximity exists in such a situation between those responsible for the prospectus and the purchaser.

(1) Intention

For the purpose of the torts of deceit and negligent misrepresentation, it is necessary to establish a material misrepresentation intended to influence, and which did in fact influence the mind of the representee and on which the representee reasonably relied.

There has been much argument before me whether the required intention of the representor should be objectively ascertained, as the intention reasonably to be inferred from his words or action (or inaction), or whether the subjective intention of the representor to induce is sufficient. The authorities and textbooks do not provide any clear guidance. For example, in 31 *Halsbury's Laws* (4th ed.) para 1042 it is stated that the intention may be actual or presumptive. Whilst in *Clerk and Lindsell on Torts* (17th ed., 1995) para 7.65 it is categorically stated: 'The defendant's intention must be assessed objectively.'

A footnote makes reference to a dictum of Lord Goff in *Henderson v. Merrett Syndicates Ltd.* . . . [1995] 2 A.C. 145 at 181 to the effect that in determining whether a party has 'assumed responsibility' an objective test of intention must be applied.

Whether or not theoretically a subjective intention is sufficient, for all practical purposes, as it seems to me, the intention must in all cases be objectively established. Such intent is objectively established if the representor expressly communicates intent to the representee. On the other hand, where it is not expressly communicated, the representee must establish that he reasonably relied on the representation and that he reasonably believed that the representor intended him to act upon it. Accordingly, if the subjective intention of the representor is not expressly communicated to him, the existence of a subjective intention alone is insufficient to found an action [679] unless the existence of such an intention on the part of the representor was reasonably to be inferred by the representee: i.e. the objective test must be a satisfied. If in all cases the objective test must be satisfied, the subjective (uncommunicated) intention of the representor adds nothing as a matter of law. As a matter of fact, if established it may perhaps assist in establishing what reasonable inference should be drawn from his conduct; and of course it is relevant if the actual state of mind of the representor is in issue (*e.g.* a fraudulent intent).

(2) Proximity
The law has drawn a distinction between representations made to specific persons for specific purposes and representations to the public (or sections of the public *e.g.* investors). In the case of the former, in general it is sufficient to establish a duty on the part of the representor that he should reasonably have foreseen that the persons concerned would rely on his representation for the purposes in question. But in the latter, generally it is necessary to establish a proximity between the representor and representee beyond the mere foreseeability of reliance by the representee [1365] to render it fair, just and reasonable that such a duty be imposed in respect of the representation. As it seems to me, it is at least well arguable that the necessary proximity in such a case is established if the reliance by the members of public for the purpose in question is intended by the representor. Intention, if not sufficient to establish the necessary proximity, is at the least a very important factor (see *Morgan Crucible Co plc v. Hill Samuel Bank Ltd.* . . . [1991] Ch. 295 at 320 per Slade L.J.). The requirements for imposition of a duty of care of fairness, justice and reasonableness are to a large degree directed to protecting against potential far reaching foreseen, but unintended, consequences: where the consequences are intended, rarely can the representor on these grounds object to his being held responsible for the deliberate consequences of his words. Some support for this view may be found in passages in the judgments of the Court of Appeal in *Morgan Crucible v. Hill Samuel* and *Galoo Ltd (in liq) v. Bright Grahame Murray (a firm).* . . . [1994] 1 W.L.R. 1360 at 1382-1383.

(3) Negligence and prospectus

In *Peek v. Gurney* the House of Lords held that (at common law) the object of a prospectus was to provide the necessary information to enable an investor to make an informed decision whether to accept the offer thereby made to take up shares on the proposed allotment, but not a decision whether to make after-market purchases. The later legislation (including the 1948 and 1965 Acts which required and regulated the contents of prospectuses) had the same objective. The 1986 Act recognises a wider object in the case of listing particulars in respect of listed securities: the object includes properly informing after-market purchasers and creates a corresponding duty of care. Parliament refrained from so widening the object of a prospectus in unlisted securities. The question before me is whether it is properly arguable that the common law can in changed market conditions recognise a duty of care in case of prospectuses for unlisted securities which is substantially equivalent to the duty of care statutorily created in respect of listed securities, but statutorily withheld from unlisted.

[680] The starting point in determining the ambit of the duty of care in respect of a prospectus is the statutory purpose of the prospectus. In the same way the starting point in determining the ambit of the duty of auditors in respect a of their audit and audit report is the limited statutory purpose of that statutory requirement, namely to enable shareholders to exercise their class rights in general meeting in an informed manner (see *Caparo Industries plc v. Dickman* [1990] 2 A.C. 605 at 629-630 (post, p. 369)). But that is only the beginning: it is not necessarily also the end. It does not necessarily preclude a super-added purpose if a super-added purpose can positively be shown to exist. The burden of establishing such a super-added purpose may be heavy or indeed overwhelming, but whether the burden can or cannot be discharged is a matter for the trial.

The plaintiffs say the prospectus must be examined in the light of changed market practice and philosophy current at its date of preparation and circulation. The plaintiffs claim that there has developed and been generally recognised an additional purpose, an additional perceived intention on the part of the issuer and other parties to a prospectus, namely to inform and encourage after-market purchasers, and that this is the basis for the pleaded purpose attributed by the plaintiffs to the [1366] prospectus. If this is established, then it does seem to me to be at least arguable that a duty of care is assumed and owed to those investors who (as intended) rely on the contents of the prospectus in making such purchases. No doubt the court should think carefully before recognising a duty in case of unlisted securities which has been withheld by the legislature. Though the plaintiffs may find some support in the recurring provision in the legislation that it should not affect any liability which a party may incur apart from the legislation (see *e.g.* section 160 of the 1986 Act), I do not think that it provides the complete answer. What is significant is that the courts have since 1873 (before any legislation) recognised a duty of care in case of prospectuses when there is a sufficient direct connection between those responsible for the prospectuses and the party acting in reliance (see *Peek v. Gurney*), and the plaintiffs' claim may be recognised as merely an application of this established principle in a new fact situation. It is highly questionable whether (as contended for by the defendants) recognition of such a duty involves recognition of a novel category of negligence or a massive extension of a duty of care.

I can find nothing in the authorities or textbooks which precludes the finding of such a duty and at least some potential support in them.

(a) As regards the authorities, in the decisions limiting the duty of care to placees, the only pleaded allegation of the purpose of the issue of the prospectus was the inducement to take up the allotted shares (see *e.g. Peek v. Gurney* (1873) LR 6 HL 377 at 395-396 . . . and *Al-Nakib Investments (Jersey) Ltd v. Longcroft* [1990] 1 W.L.R. 1390). In *Peek v. Gurney* itself, support may be found in the speech of Lord Chelmsford for the proposition that the necessary direct connection between issuers and after-market purchasers may be found where the intention is established that after-market purchasers rely on the prospectus (see (1873) LR 6 HL 377 at 398-400). Support for the proposition is also found in the speech of Lord Cairns (see LR 6 HL 377 at 412-413). How the intention is manifested, whether by sale of the prospectus to prospective after-market purchasers (as in *Scott v. Dixon* (1859) 29 LJ Ex. 62n), or by other means (as in *Andrews v. Mockford* [1896] 1 Q.B. 372), surely cannot be crucial. Both these last two cases cited are cases of fraudulent misrepresentation, but it is not self-evident to me that, if the issuers of a prospectus intend investors to rely on it, the issue of proximity should depend on whether the representation was fraudulent or negligent. In case of fraudulent representations, the authorities cited above do support the proposition that intended reliance is sufficient (see also *Clerk and Lindsell*, para. 14.02).

(b) In *Gower on Company Law* (5th edn., 1992) p 498 the view is expressed that, once prospectuses specifically stated that one of their purposes was to lead to an admission to listing on The Exchange, the decision limiting the scope of the duty of care adopted in *Peek v. Gurney* seems outmoded and the decision in *AL-Nakib* should be reviewed by a higher court. This passage in this authoritative work supports the view that the plaintiffs' claim as to the purpose of the prospectus and the duty of care owed today in respect of the prospectus-a prospectus which specifically states that, as part of the same exercise as allotment, the facility will be available for shares in Diamond to be dealt with on the USM-sufficiently merits full consideration at trial.

CHAPTER 7

Capital Integrity

One of the fundamental doctrines of company law is that of capital integrity, which has spawned a number of sub-principles and sub-rules. Many of these were discovered by judges between 1880 and 1900, the evidence for their existence being the underlying scheme of the Companies Acts. Their principal objective is to provide company creditors with a degree of security. As Jessel M.R. explained,

> "[t]he creditor has no debtor but that impalpable thing the corporation, which has no property except the assets of the business. The creditor, therefore . . . gives credit to that capital, gives credit to the company on the faith of the representation that the capital shall be applied only for the purposes of the business. . . ."

That is to say, the law enables persons to do business under the aegis of registered companies which are legally segregated from their owners and almost invariably have limited liability. Accordingly, all that persons dealing with such companies can look to for satisfaction of obligations owing to them is the company's own assets. However, there is always a danger of the shareholders withdrawing funds from the company in the shape of dividends or otherwise, with resultant diminution of the amount creditors can claim against. It, therefore, is necessary to provide that the subscribed capital be protected against the depredations of shareholders and to the detriment of creditors, and indeed of the minority shareholders as well.

We have already come across one distinctive manifestation of the capital integrity principle in *Houldsworth v. City of Glasgow Bank* (*ante*, p. 322) which was decided before most of the leading cases in this field. It was held there that persons who were wrongfully induced by a company to subscribe for shares in it have no remedy in damages against the company once those shares have been allotted to them. The reasons given by the Law Lords are somewhat obscure but one justification for the rule, which flies in the face of the principle of separate legal personality (and *Houldsworth* was decided long before the *Salomon & Co.* case (*ante*, p. 60)) is that awarding damages against the company depletes the fund to which outsiders can look for satisfaction of the company's obligations to them.

The rules regarding capital integrity have been extended significantly by the 1983 Act, which was adopted in response to the E.C. Second Directive, it being based on some major features of French and German law. That Directive's central objective is summed up in its preamble:

> "Whereas Community provisions should be adopted for maintaining the capital, which constitutes the creditors' security, in particular by prohibiting any reduction thereof by distribution to shareholders where the latter are not entitled to it and by imposing limits on the company's rights to acquire its own shares."

Some of this Directive's requirements were already incorporated in the 1963 Act, such as those regarding companies buying and financing the purchase of their own shares. But other parts of that Act had to be drastically amended, notably in respect of paying dividends from capital, requiring that P.L.C.s have a minimum capital and that consideration paid for shares in P.L.C.s must be shown to be adequate.

MINIMUM AMOUNTS

See *Company Law*, pp.223–224.

Companies Act 1983, sections 28(1) and 40(1)

Payment for allotted shares

28.—(1) Subject to subsection (4), a public limited company shall not allot a share except as paid up at least as to one-quarter of the nominal value of the share and the whole of any premiurn on it.

Obligation to convene extraordinary general meeting in event of serious loss of capital

40.—(1) Subject to subsection (4), where the net assets of a company are half or less of the amount of the company's called-up share capital, the directors of the company shall, not later than 28 days from general meeting in the earliest day on which that fact is known to a director of the company, duly convene an extraordinary general meeting of the company for a date not later than 56 days from that day for the purpose of considering whether, any and if so what, measures should be taken to deal with the situation.

ISSUING SHARES AT A DISCOUNT

See *Company Law*, pp.225–230.

Ooregum Gold Mining Co. of India Ltd. v. Roper
[1892] A.C. 125

The memorandum of association of a company registered under the Act of 1862 stated that the capital of the company was £125,000 divided into 125,000 shares of £1 each, and that the shares of which the original or increased capital might consist might be divided into different classes and issued with such preference, privilege or guarantee as the company might direct. The company being in want of money and the original shares being at a great discount, the directors in accordance with resolutions duly passed issued preference shares of £1 each with 15s. credited as paid, leaving a liability of only 5s. per share. A contract to this effect was registered under the Companies Act 1867 section 25. The transaction was bona fide and for the benefit of the company. In an action by an ordinary shareholder to test the validity of the issue:

Held, affirming the decision of the Court of Appeal, that reading the Companies Acts of 1862 and 1867 together, the issue was beyond the powers of the company, and that the preference shares so far as the same were held by original allottees were held subject to the liability of the holder to pay to the company in cash the full amount unpaid on the shares. A company limited by shares, formed and registered under the Companies Act has no power to issue shares as fully paid up, for a money consideration less than their nominal value.

Note: This principle is now stated in section 27 of the 1983 Act (see *infra*, p. 343).

Re Wragg Ltd.
[1897] 1 Ch. 796

The term 'watering shares' signifies a company issuing shares in exchange for some asset but the real value of that asset is far less than those shares' face value. Wragg and another formed a company, and they sold it their livery-stable business, which the company paid for partly by allotting them its entire capital of 20,000 fully paid £1 shares. When the company failed, the liquidator sought to show that the real value of the business acquired was £18,000 less than what was paid for it and that, accordingly, the issued shares must be treated as only partly paid.

LINDLEY L.J.: . . . [826] It has never been doubted, so far as I know, that the obligation of every shareholder in a limited company to pay to the company the nominal amount of his shares could be satisfied by a transaction which amounted to accord and satisfaction or set-off as distinguished from payment in cash. In 1867 the Legislature rendered all such transactions invalid unless they were made pursuant to a duly registered contract; but if there is such a contract the law is now what it always was.

As regards the value of the property which a company can take from a shareholder in satisfaction of his liability to pay the [827] amount of his shares, there has been some difference of opinion. But it was ultimately decided by the Court of Appeal that, unless the agreement pursuant to which shares were to be paid for in property or services could be impeached for fraud, the value of the property or services could not be inquired into. In other words, the value at which the company is content to accept the property must be treated as its value as between itself and the shareholders whose liability is discharged by its means. . . .

[829] I understand the law to be as follows. The liability of a shareholder to pay the company the amount of his shares is a statutory liability, and is declared to be a specialty debt (Companies Act, 1862, section 16), and a short form of action is given for its recovery (s. 70). But specialty debts, like other debts, can be discharged in more ways than one – *e.g.*, by payment, set-off, accord and satisfaction, and release – and, subject to the qualifications introduced by the doctrine of ultra vires, or, in other words, the limited capacity of statutory corporations, any mode of discharging a specialty debt is as available to a shareholder as to any other specialty debtor. It is, however, obviously beyond the power of a limited company to release a shareholder from his obligation without payment in money or money's worth. It cannot give fully paid-up shares for nothing and preclude itself from requiring payment of them in money or money's worth: *In re Eddystone Marine Insurance Co.* [1893] 3 Ch. 9; nor can a company deprive itself of its right to future payment in cash by agreeing to accept future payments in some other way. It cannot substitute an action for the breach of a special agreement for a statutory action for non-payment of calls.

[830] From this it follows that shares in limited companies cannot be issued at a discount. By our law the payment by a debtor to his creditor of a less sum than is due does not discharge the debt; and this technical doctrine has also been invoked in aid of the law which prevents the shares of a limited company from being issued at a discount. But this technical doctrine, though often sufficient to decide a particular case, will not suffice as a basis for the wider rule or principle that a company cannot effectually release a shareholder from his statutory obligation to pay in money or money's worth the amount of his shares. That shares cannot be issued at a discount was finally settled in the case of the *Ooregum Gold Mining Co. of India v. Roper* [1892] A.C. 125, the judgments in which are strongly relied upon by the appellant in this case. It has, however, never yet been decided that a limited company cannot buy property or pay for services at any price it thinks proper, and pay for them in fully paid-up shares. Provided a limited company does so honestly and not colourably, and provided that it has not been so imposed upon as to be entitled to be

relieved from its bargain, it appears to be settled by *Pell's* case and the others to which I have referred, of which *Anderson's* case is the most striking, that agreements by limited companies to pay for property or services in paid-up shares are valid and binding on the companies and their creditors. The Legislature in 1867 appears to me to have distinctly recognised such to be the law, but to have required in order to make such agreements binding that they shall be registered before the shares are issued.

Note: In *Park Business Interiors Ltd. v. Park* [1992] B.C.L.C. 1035 the principles laid down in *Re Wragg* (*supra*) were applied, where shares were allotted to a company's promoters to reimburse them for expenses they had incurred in preparations for the company's business.

Companies Act 1983, sections 26(1) and (2), 27(1), 29(1), 30(1), 32(1), 34(1)

Description of share capital

26.—(1) Subject to the following provisions of this Part, shares allotted by a company and any premium payable on them may be paid up in money or money's worth (including goodwill and expertise).

(2) A public limited company shall not accept at any time in payment up of its shares or any premium on them, an undertaking given by any person that he or another should do work or perform services for the company or any other person.

Prohibition of allotment of shares at a discount

27.—(1) Subject to *subsection (4)* the shares of a company shall not be allotted at a discount.

Payment of non-cash consideration

29.—(1) A public limited company shall not allot shares as fully or partly paid (as to their nominal value or any premium payable on them) otherwise than in cash if the consideration for the allotment is or includes an undertaking which is to or he performed more than five years after the date of the allotment.

Experts' reports on non-cash consideration before allotment of shares

30.—(1) Subject to *subsection (2)*, a public limited company shall not allot shares as fully or partly paid up (as to their nominal value or any premium payable on them) otherwise than in cash unless–

(*a*) the consideration for the allotment has been valued in accordance with the following provisions of this section;

(*b*) a report with respect to its value has been made to the company by a person appointed by the company in accordance with those provisions during the six months immediately preceding the allotment of the shares; and

(*c*) a copy of the report has been sent to the proposed allottee of the shares.

Expert's report on non-cash assets acquired

32.—(1) A public limited company, other than a company registered under section 12 shall not, unless the conditions mention in subsection (3) have been complied with, enter into a agreement with a relevant person for the transfer by him during the initial period of one or more cash assets to the company or another to be given by the company equal in value at the time of the agreement to at least one-tenth of the nominal value of the company's share capital issued at the time.

Relief

34.—(1) Where any person is liable to a company under section 26, 29, 30 or 32 in relation to payment in respect of any shares in the company or is liable by virtue of any undertaking given to the company in, or in connection with, payment for any such shares, the person so liable may make an application to the court under this subsection to be exempted in whole or in part from that liability.

Note: Applications for relief under the equivalent of section 34 of the 1983 Act were made in *Re Ossory Estates plc* [1988] B.C.L.C. 213 and in *Re Bradford Investments plc (No. 2)* [1991] B.C.L.C. 688.

DIVIDENDS FROM CAPITAL

See *Company Law*, pp.230–23.

Re Exchange Banking Co., Flitcroft's Case
(1882) 21 Ch.D. 519

The directors of a limited company for several years presented to the general meetings of shareholders reports and balance-sheets in which various debts known by the directors to be bad were entered as assets, so that an apparent profit was shewn though in fact there was none. The shareholders, relying on these documents, passed resolutions declaring dividends, which the directors accordingly paid. An order having been made to wind up the company the liquidator applied, under Sect. 165 of the Companies Act 1862, for an order on the directors to replace the amount of dividends thus paid out of capital:

Held, by Bacon V.C., and by the Court of Appeal, that as regards each half-yearly dividend the persons who were directors when it was paid were liable for the whole amount paid for the dividends of that half-year.

The order of Bacon V.C., declared them to be jointly liable, but this was varied on appeal by declaring them jointly and severally liable:

Even if the shareholders had known the true facts, so that their ratification of the payment of dividends would have bound themselves individually, they could not bind the company, for that the payment of dividends out of *corpus* was *ultra vires* the company, and incapable of ratification by the shareholders:

The fact that the capital thus improperly applied was distributed *pro rata* among the whole body of shareholders did not protect the directors, for that the shareholders were not the corporation, and that payment to them would not prevent the corporation before winding-up, or the liquidator after winding-up, from compelling the directors to replace the money that it might be applied to proper purposes.

Re Halt Garage (1964) Ltd.
[1982] 3 All E.R. 1016

See *ante*, p. 228.

Companies Act 1983, sections 45(1)–(3), 46(1), 49(1) and 51 (2)

Profits available for distribution

45.—(1) A company shall not make a distribution (as defined by section 51) except out of profits available for the purpose.

(2) For the purposes of this Part, but subject to section 47(1), a company's profits available for distribution are its accumulated, realised profits, so far as not previously utilised by distribution or capitalisation, less its accumulated,

realised losses, so far as not previously written off in a reduction or reorganisation of capital duly made.

(3) A company shall not apply an unrealised profit in paying up debentures or any amounts unpaid on any of its issued shares.

Restriction on distribution of assets

46.—(1) Subject to section 47, a public limited company may only make a distribution at any time–

(a) if at that time the amount of its net assets is not less than the aggregate of the company's called-up share capital and its undistributable reserves; and

(b) if, and to the extent that, the distribution does not reduce the amount of those assets to less than that aggregate.

Relevant accounts

49.—(1) Subject to the following provisions of this section, the question whether a distribution may be made by a company without contravening section 45, 46 or 47 (the relevant section) and the amount of any distribution which may be so made shall be determined by reference to the relevant items as stated in the relevant accounts and the relevant section shall be treated as contravened in the case of a distribution unless the requirements of this section about those accounts are complied with in the case of that distribution.

Consequences of making unlawful distribution

50.—(1) Where a distribution, or part of one, made by a company to one of its members is made in contravention of the provisions of this Part and, at the time of the distribution, he knows or has reasonable grounds for believing that it is so made, he shall be liable to repay it or that part as the case may be to the company or (in the case of a distribution made otherwise than in cash) to pay the company a sum equal to the value of the distribution or part at that time.

(2) The provisions of this section are without prejudice to any obligation imposed apart from this section on a member of a company to repay a distribution unlawfully made to him.

Ancillary provisions

51.—(2) In this Part "distribution" means every description of distribution of a company's assets to members of the company, whether in cash or otherwise, except distributions made by way of–

(a) an issue of shares as fully or partly paid bonus shares;

(b) the redemption of preference shares out of the proceeds of a fresh issue of shares made for the purposes of the redemption and the payment of any premium on their redemption out of the company's share premium account;

(c) the reduction of share capital by extinguishing or reducing the liability of any of the members on any of its shares in respect of share capital not paid up or by paying off paid up share capital; and

(d) a distribution of assets to members of the company on its winding up.

(5)The provisions of this part are without prejudice to any enactment or rule of law or any provision of a company's memorandum or articles restricting the sums out of which, or the cases in which, a distribution may be made.

Table A article 118

118. No dividend or interim dividend shall be paid otherwise than in accordance with the provisions of Part IV of the Companies (Amendment) Act, 1983 which apply to the company.

Note: In *Precision Dippings Ltd. v. Precision Dippings Marketing Ltd.* [1985] B.C.L.C. 385 the company paid a £60,000 dividend to the defendant, which owned virtually all its issued share capital, at a time when its last audited accounts did not fully comply with the equivalent of s.49 of the 1983 Act; a qualification in the auditors' report had not been partly lifted as envisaged by s.49(3)(c). Two years later the company became insolvent and was put into liquidation. It was held that the company was entitled to recover the £60,000.

In *Re Cleveland Trust Ltd.* [1991] B.C.L.C. 424, a wholly owned subsidiary paid a dividend from a proceeds of a capital profit it made on realisation of assets, although its memorandum of association prohibited paying dividends from such profits; that dividend was held to be *ultra vires*. Further, because the parent company's directors ought to have known that this dividend was *ultra vires*, that sum should not have been included as a profit in its annual accounts, which therefore did not give a 'true and fair view' of the position. Accordingly, when that parent passed on the dividend to its own parent company, its accounts did not fully comply with the equivalent of s 49 of the 1983 Act and, as a result, that dividend that too was *ultra vires* and, in consequence, bonus shares purportedly allotted on foot of those dividends were never properly allotted.

ACQUIRING OWN SHARES

See *Company Law*, pp. 237-243.

Trevor v. Whitworth
(1887) 12 App. Cas. 409

A limited company was incorporated under the Joint Stock Companies Acts with the objects (as stated in its memorandum) of acquiring and carrying on a manufacturing business, and any other businesses and transactions which the company might consider to be in any way conducive or auxiliary thereto or in any way connected therewith. The articles authorised the company to purchase its own shares. The company having gone into liquidation, a former shareholder made a claim against the company for the balance of the price of his shares sold by him to the company before the liquidation and not wholly paid for:

Held, reversing the decision of the Court of Appeal, that such a company has no power under the Companies Acts to purchase its own shares, that the purchase was therefore *ultra vires* and that the claim must fail.

Companies Act 1983, sections 41(1), (2), 42(1) and 43(1), (2)

Restriction on company acquiring its own shares

41.—(1) Subject to the following provisions of this section. no company limited by shares or limited by guarantee and having a share capital shall acquire its own shares (whether by purchase. subscription or otherwise).

(2) A company limited by shares may acquire any of its own fully paid shares otherwise than for valuable consideration.

Acquisition of shares in a company by company's nominee

42.—(1) Subject to subsections (5) and (6), where shares are issued to a nominee of a company referred to in section 41 (1) or are acquired by a nominee of such a company from a third party as partly paid up, then, for all purposes the shares shall be treated as held by the nominee on his own account and the company shall be regarded as having no beneficial interest in them.

Treatment of shares held by or on behalf of a public limited company

43.—(1) Subject to subsections (12) and (15), this section applies to a public limited company-

    (a) where shares in the company are forfeited or are surrendered to the company in lieu, in pursuance of the articles for failure to pay any sum payable in respect of those shares;

    (b) where shares in the company are acquired by the company otherwise than by any of the methods mentioned in *section 41(4)* and the company has a beneficial interest in those shares:

    (c) where the nominee of the company acquires shares in the company from a third person without financial assistance being given directly or indirectly by the company and the company has a beneficial interest in those shares; or

    (d) where any person acquires shares in the company with financial assistance given to him directly or indirectly, by the company for the purpose of or in connection with the acquisition and the company has a beneficial interest in those shares.

(2) In determining for the purposes of subsection (1) (b) and (c) whether a company has a beneficial interest in any shares, there shall be disregarded, in any case where the company is a trustee (whether a personal representative or otherwise), any right of the company (as trustee) to recover its expenses or be renumerated out of the trust property.

Companies Act 1990, section 211

Power of company to purchase own shares

211.—(1) Subject to the following provisions of this Part, a company may, if so authorised by its articles, purchase its own shares shares (including any redeemable shares).

(2) Sections 207 (2), 208 and 209 shall apply in relation to the purchase by a company under this section of any of its own shares as those sections apply in relation to the redemption of shares by a company under section 207.

(3) A company shall not purchase any of its shares under this section if as a result of such purchase the nominal value of the issued share capital which is not redeemable would be less than one tenth of the nominal value of the total issued share capital of the company.

Note: In *Akatos & Hutcheson plc v. Watson* [1995] 1 B.C.L.C. 218 it was held that the equivalent of section 41 of the 1987 Act did not prevent a company from acquiring shares in another company (the acquired company) in circumstances where the sole asset of the latter was shares in the acquiring company. Lightman J. rejected the submission that, to prevent section 41 being circumvented and to ensure that the spirit of capital maintenance is not infringed, the court should lift the corporate veil and treat the company as acquiring its own shares.

In *Vision Express (UK) Ltd. v. Wilson* [1995] 2 B.C.L.C. 419, as part of a settlement of proceedings a company took against a former employee for fraud, the company was to purchase all such rights as he then had in that company's shares, including any options, for £25,000. When the company applied to court for an order that those shares be transferred to it, as agreed, it was held that the transaction contravened the equivalent of section 41 of the 1983 Act.

FINANCING THE PURCHASE OF OWN SHARES

See *Company Law*, pp.243-249 and 252-25 5.

Re M.J. Cummins Ltd.
[1937] I.R. 60

The company ran a very successful business, due largely to the abilities of Mr. C. who was its general manager and secretary. On the death of the company's founder, its shareholders resolved to sell the business to Mr. C. for £3,000. But he had only £200 in cash and ordinarily would not have been able to raise the necessary funds to buy those shares. Accordingly, a 'very ingenious scheme was devised' by which the bank was to advance £2,750 for this purpose; that money was lent to the company, which in turn lent it to W C. and he used it to buy his shares.

JOHNSON L: held that the bank's loan to the company was 'incurred for a purpose which was not one of the objects of the company, and which was clearly *ultra vires*.' Further, 'not only had the bank the fullest knowledge of that purpose, but the local agent of the bank was the person who arranged the ingenious plan by which the loan was carried through; so that so far as bank's participation in the affair is concerned, the case goes far beyond question of mere knowledge.' The judge then went on to consider whether notwithstanding, the bank were entitled to recover all or any of the money so lent. See post p. 574.

Companies Act 1963, section 60(1), (12)–(14)

Giving of financial assistance by a company for the purchase of its shares

60.—(1) Subject to subsections (2), (12) and (13), it shall not be lawful for a company to give, whether directly or indirectly, and whether by means of a loan, guarantee, the provision of security or otherwise, any financial assistance for the purpose of or in connection with a purchase or subscription made or to be made by person of or for any shares in the company, or, where the company is a subsidiary company, in its holding company.

(12) Nothing in this section shall be taken to prohibit the payment of a dividend properly declared by a company or the discharge of a liability lawfully incurred by it.

(13) Nothing in this section shall be taken to prohibit

(a) where the lending of money is part of the ordinary business of the company, the lending of money by the company in the ordinary course of its-business;

(b) the provision by a company, in accordance with any scheme for the time being in force, of money for the purchase of, or subscription for, fully paid shares in the company or its holding company, being a purchase or subscription of or for shares to be held by or for the benefit of employees or former employees of the company or of any subsidiary of the company including any person who is or was a director holding a salaried employment or office in the company or any subsidiary of the company;

(c) the making by a company of loans to persons, other than directors, bona fide in the employment of the company or any subsidiary of the company, with a view to enabling those persons to purchase or subscribe for fully paid shares in the company or its holding company to be held by themselves as beneficial owners thereof.

(14) Any transaction in breach of this section shall be voidable at the instance of the company against any person (whether a party to the transaction or not) who had notice of the facts which constitute such breach.

Table A article 10

10. The company shall not give, whether directly or indirectly, and whether by means of a loan, guarantee, the provision of security or otherwise, any financial assistance for the purpose of or in connection with a purchase or subscription made or to be made by any person of or for any shares in the company or in its holding company, but this regulation shall not prohibit any transaction permitted by section 60 of the Act.

Belmont Finance Corp. v. Williams Furniture Ltd. (No. 2)
[1980] 1 All E.R. 393

One J. owned a group of companies, being 'Belmont', 'Williams' and 'City'. One G. owned another company, 'Maximum'. G. wished to buy Belmont, in order to use its money to finance property development projects. At the same time, J. was anxious to acquire G's expertise and flair in property development for L's companies. Accordingly, it was agreed that Belmont would buy Maximum for £500,000, that G. would buy the share capital in Belmont from City for £489,000, then Williams and City would lend Belmont £200,000 to be secured on Maximum's capital and that City would subscribe for 230,000 £1 preference shares in Belmont out of the £489,000 it was to receive from G. Additionally, G. guaranteed to Belmont that Maximum's aggregate net profits for the next six years would exceed £500,000. F. and J. dealt at arms length but no independent valuations for Maximum were obtained. G.'s solicitors had counsel's opinion that these steps were not unlawful.

BUCKLEY L.J.: [400] The first question for consideration is whether the agreement did contravene section 54 of the 1948 Act (similar to section 60 of the 1963 Act). Only if the answer to that question is affirmative does the question whether the defendants or any of them are guilty of conspiracy arise, for it is the illegality of the agreement, if it be illegal, which constitutes the common intention of the parties to enter into the agreement a conspiracy at law.

There is little judicial authority on the section. In *Re VGM Holdings* [1942] Ch. 235 this Court had to consider whether under the section in the form in which it stood in the Companies Act 1929, which did not contain the word 'subscription', the section covered a case where money which a company had provided had been used to assist a subscription for the company's own shares. Lord Greene MR said [at p. 240]:

> "There could, I think, be no doubt that, if that question were answered in favour of the liquidator, the £15,980 was provided by the company by way of financial assistance, because whether a company provides the money by way of gift or by way of loan or by buying assets from the person who is purchasing the shares at a fraudulent overvalue, all those transactions, it seems to me, would fall within the phrase "financial assistance."

The transaction there in question was a fraudulent one. V G M Holdings Ltd bought all the share capital of Century, which was worthless, from Vanbergen for £8,301 and Vanbergen used the money to pay a call on shares which he held in VGM. The court, [401] however, held that the transaction did not involve a purchase of V C M shares and so was not within the section. In reliance on the reference by Lord Greene MR to a purchase at its a fraudulent overvalue, it was suggested to us that the section does not apply to any case in which the company which is alleged to have given financial assistance got fair value for its money. I think that Lord Greene MR must be understood to have been speaking in the context of the facts of the case before him and not to have intended to attempt to put any limit on the scope of the section.

Our attention was also drawn to a South African case of *Gradwell (Pty) Ltd v. Rostra Printers Ltd* (1959) 5 S.A. 419. The contract in that case was a little complicated, but the facts can be summarised as follows. Company A sold to company B all the shares in company C and a debt of £40,258 due from company C to company A. The price was £32,245. The contract was conditional on company B being able to borrow £30,000 on the security of company C's assets. That sum was to be applied in discharging an existing mortgage of company C's assets and in reducing company C's debt to company A. To the extent that the debt to company A was reduced, the cash so received by company A was to be treated as paid on account of the purchase price, that is to say, the price payable by company B was to be reduced by the amount that the debt to company A, which formed part of the subject-matter of the sale, was reduced. The statutory provision thereunder consideration was for present purposes identical with section 54(1) of the 1948 Act (and section 60 of the 1963 Act).

The case eventually came before the Appellate Division of the Supreme Court of South Africa. in the following passage Rostra is company A, Crowden is company B and 'the company' is company C. Schreiner JA, who delivered what was effectively the judgment of the court, said [at pp. 425-426]:

"We were pressed by counsel for Crowden with the importance of the purpose of the whole transaction. The purpose of Crowden and Rostra was inevitably that of the company, the actions of which were entirely controllable by Rostra. The purpose must be taken to have been to help Crowden to buy and Rostra to sell the company's shares. But this does not carry Crowden to success. Unless what was to be done would amount to giving of financial assistance within the meaning of the sub-section the purpose and the connection would not be important. Having money available the company could part with it in various ways that would enable the recipient to purchase the company's shares with the money. iIt could for instance buy an asset, not required for the purposes of its business, in order to provide the seller of the asset with money with which to buy the shares. It was contended on behalf of Crowden that this would be giving financial assistance. If the purchase of the asset were effected at a price known to be inflated, this would no doubt be the giving of financial assistance. It would indeed be equivalent to a gift and would clearly involve a reduction of the company's capital. It was one of the illustrations given by Lord Greene in *In re V.G.M. Holdings Ltd*. It is, I think, significant that the Master of the Rolls did not mention the case of the purchase of an asset at a fair price with the object of enabling the seller of the asset to buy the shares. But whatever may be the position in such a case the paying off of an existing debt seems to be decidedly more difficult to bring within the notion of giving financial assistance. The payer's assets and liabilities are put into a different form but the balance is unchanged. And the same applies to the financial position of the payee. Here the company would have no more and no less after the completion of the transaction than before. And the same would apply to Rostra. The company would owe more to its mortgagee and correspondingly less to Rostra. The price to be paid by Crowden would be less by the difference in the value of the assets to be acquired. Its financial position would be unchanged-only its investment would be smaller. [402] Where there is an anticipation of the date when a debt becomes due and payable the position may possibly be different, but where the debt is presently due and payable and the debtor can have no answer to the creditor's demand for payment, it would be straining the language to hold that by paying his debt the debtor gives the creditor financial assistance."

In that passage the learned judge reserves the question of what the effect would be if company B were to purchase from company A an asset nor required for the purposes of its business but at a fair price.

Foster J. treated as a proposition of law, accepted by counsel for Belmont, that a company does not give financial assistance in connection with a purchase of its own shares within the meaning of section 54 by reason only of its simultaneous entry into a bona fide commercial transaction as a result of which it parts with money or money's worth, which in turn is used to finance the purchase of its own shares. He went on to find that the negotiations in the present case were at arm's length and that on the one side Mr James genuinely believed that to buy the capital of Maximum for £500,000 was a good commercial proposition for Belmont and on the other side Mr Copeland honestly believed that in October 1963 the value of the capital of Maximum with Mr Grosscurth's guarantee of Maximum's profits under cl 13(h) of the agreement secured on Rentabome's share capital was not less than £500,000. On these findings he reached the conclusion that the agreement was a bona fide commercial transaction, on which ground he dismissed the action.

This reasoning. assumes, as I understand it, that if the transaction under consideration is genuinely regarded by the parties as a sound commercial transaction negotiated at arm's length and capable of justification on purely commercial grounds, it cannot offend against section 54. This is, I think, a broader proposition than the proposition which the judge treated as having been accepted by counsel for Belmont. If A Ltd buys from B a chattel or a commodity, like a ship or merchandise, which A Ltd genuinely wants to acquire for its own purposes, and does so having no other purpose in view, the fact that B thereafter employs the proceeds of the sale in buying shares in A Ltd should not, I would suppose, be held to offend against the section; but the position may be different if A Ltd makes the purchase in order to put B in funds to buy shares in A Ltd. If A Ltd buys something from B without regard to its own commercial interests, the sole purpose of the transaction being to put B in funds to acquire shares in A Ltd, this would, in my opinion, clearly contravene the section, even if the price paid was a fair price for what is bought, and a fortiori that would be so if the sale to A Ltd was at an inflated price. The sole purpose would be to enable (*i.e.* to assist) B to pay for the shares. If A Ltd buys something from B at a fair price, which A Ltd could readily realise on a resale if it wished to do so, but the purpose, or one of the purposes, of the transaction is to put B in funds to acquire shares of A Ltd, the fact that the price was fair might not, I think, prevent the transaction from contravening the section, if it would otherwise do so, though A Ltd could very probably recover no damages in civil proceedings, for it would have suffered no damage. If the transaction is of a kind which A Ltd could in its own commercial interests legitimately enter into, and the transaction is genuinely entered into by A Ltd in its own commercial interests and not merely as a means of assisting B financially to buy shares of A Ltd, the circumstance that A Ltd enters into the transaction with B, partly with the object of putting B in funds to acquire its own shares or with the knowledge of B's intended use of the proceeds of sale, might, I think, involve no contravention of the section, but I do not wish to express a concluded opinion on that point.

The reasoning of the judge's judgment appears to me, with deference to him, to overlook the word 'only' in the suggested proposition of law.

[His Lordship then considered the judge's favourable assessment of Mr James as a witness and the failure of Mr James or any of his associates to obtain a valuation of Maximum and went on to consider an independent valuation made in July 1974 by Mr Howard Williams, a partner in Messrs Mann Judd & Co, a London firm of chartered [403] accountants, who were instructed by Belmont's receiver as if to advise Belmont of a fair price to pay for the share capital of Maximum as at 3rd October 1963. The valuation report of Messrs Mann Judd & Co valued the total issued share capital of Maximum as at 3rd October 1963 at not more than the 'value of the underlying consolidated "tangible" assets of the company, that is, £60,069'. [His Lordship then pointed out that Mr Hames had genuinely believed that the transaction was a good commercial proposition for Belmont without having any good grounds for that belief, and then continued:] After careful consideration I do not feel that we should be justified in disturbing the judge's finding that Mr James genuinely believed that the agreement was a good commercial proposition for Belmont. it was a belief which, on his view of the commercial aspects of the case, Mr James could have sincerely held.

In truth the purchase of the share capital of Maximum was not a commercial transaction in its own right so far as Mr James and his group of companies were concerned: it was part of the machinery by which City obtained £489,000 for the share capital of Belmont, £259,000 in cash and £230,000 by redemption of the redeemable preference shares subscribed in Belmont. It was not a transaction whereby Belmont acquired anything which Belmont genuinely needed or wanted for its own purposes: it was one which facilitated Mr Grosscurth's acquiring Belmont for his own purposes without effectively parting with Maximum. That the purpose of the sale of Maximum to Belmont was to enable Mr Grosscurth to pay £489,000 for Belmont was at all relevant times known to and recognised by Mr James and the members of his team as well as by Mr Copeland. There is no good reason disclosed by the evidence to suppose either that Mr Grosscurth and his associates could have sold Maximum to anyone else for £500,000 or that Belmont could have disposed of Maximum for £500,000 to anyone else at any time. The purchase of the share capital of Maximum may have been intra vires of Belmont (a matter which we have not been invited to consider), but it was certainly not a transaction in the ordinary course of Belmont's business or for the purposes of that business as it subsisted at the date of the agreement. It was an exceptional and artificial transaction and not in any sense an ordinary commercial transaction entered into for its own sake in the commercial interests of Belmont. It was part of a comparatively complex scheme for enabling Mr Grosscurth and his associates to acquire Belmont at no cash cost to themselves, the purchase price being found not from their own funds or by the realisation of any asset of theirs (for Maximum continued to be part of their group of companies) but out of Belmont's own resources. In these circumstances, in my judgment the agreement would have contravened section 54 of the 1948 Act even if £500,000 was a fair price for Maximum. I think, however, that Mr Howard Williams's report and evidence clearly establish that £500,000 was in truth an inflated price. . .

It follows that in my judgment the agreement was unlawful, for it was a contract by Belmont to do an unlawful act, viz to provide financial assistance to Mr Grosscurth and his associates for the purpose of, or in connection with, the purchase of Belmont's own share capital.

Note: In most of the recent U.K. cases on the equivalent prohibition, the severity of which was relaxed when amended in 1981, the transactions were held not to fall foul of section 151 of the Companies Act, 1980, *e.g. Brady v. Brady* [1989] A.C. 755, which concerned the splitting of a group of companies between two brothers by means of a complex reorganisation; *Partlett v.*

Goppys (Bridport) Ltd. [1996] 2 B.C.L.C. 34, where the managing director of a group of companies agreed to transfer his shares in one of those companies to his sons in return for the companies paying him a salary and bonus, and a pension on retirement; *British Commonwealth Holdings plc v. Barclays Bank plc* [1996] 1 W.L.R. 1, which concerned a compromise of substantial debts between the company and banks, involving an option agreement under which the company was to issue redeemable preference shares in substitution for ordinary stock units; *Arab Bank plc v. Merchantile Holdings Ltd.* [1994] Ch. 71, where it was held that the reference to any of its subsidiaries in the equivalent of section 60(1) applied only to subsidiaries that were registered in Britain and not to foreign subsidiaries.

The proper form of the statutory declaration under section 60(2)-(5) was considered in *Re S.H. & Co. (Realisations) 1990 Ltd* [1993] B.C.L.C. 1309 and in *Re N.L. Electrical Ltd.* [1994] 1 B.C.L.C. 23.

SANCTIONS AND REMEDIES

Belmont Finance Corp. v. Williams Furniture Ltd. (No. 2)
[1980] 1 All E.R. 393

For background, see *supra*, p. 352.

BUCKLEY L.J.: . . . [404] The next question is whether in these circumstances the alleged conspiracy is established in respect of those defendants against whom the action is still on foot, i.e. the first three defendants. To obtain in civil proceedings a remedy for conspiracy, the plaintiff must establish (a) a combination of the defendants, (b) to effect an unlawful purpose, (c) resulting in damage to the plaintiff . . .

The unlawful purpose in this case was the provision of financial assistance in contravention of section 54 of the 1948 Act (s. 60 of the 1963 Act). That the purpose of the sale of Maximum to Belmont was to enable Mr Grosscurth to pay £489,000 to City for the share capital of Belmont was known to all concerned. For reasons which I gave in my judgment on the earlier appeal in this action, the alleged conspiracy sued on must, in my view, have preceded the signing of the agreement, but its object is made clear by the agreement, namely that Belmont should give the financial assistance to Mr Grosscurth which the carrying out of the agreement would afford him. Williams and City were parties to the agreement and so, in my opinion, are fixed with the character of parties to the conspiracy. Moreover, Mr James knew perfectly well what the objects of the agreement were. He was director of both Williams and City. Mr Harries and Mr Foley, who also knew the objects of the agreement, were a director and the secretary respectively of City. Mr Foley was also the secretary of Williams. Their knowledge must, in my opinion, be imputed to the companies of which they were directors and secretary, for an officer of a company must surely be under a duty, if he is aware that a transaction into which his company or a wholly-owned subsidiary is about to enter is illegal or tainted with illegality, to inform the board of that company of the fact. Where an officer is under a duty to make such a disclosure to his company, his knowledge is imputed to the company (*Re David Payne & Co Ltd* [1904] 2 Ch. 608, *Re Fenwick, Stobart & Co Ltd* [1902] 1 Ch. 507). In these circumstances, in my opinion, Williams and City must be regarded as having participated with Mr Grosscurth in a common intention to enter into the agreement and to procure that Belmont should enter into the agreement and that the agreement should be implemented. That Mr Grosscurth was a party to that common intention is, in my opinion, indisputable.

In my judgment, the alleged conspiracy is established in respect of these three defendants, and they are not exempt from liability on account of counsel's opinion or because they may have believed in good faith that the transaction did not transgress section 54. If all the facts which make the transaction unlawful were known to the parties, as I think they were, ignorance of the law will not excuse them: see *Churchill v. Walton* [1967] 2 A.C. 224. That case was one of criminal conspiracy, but it seems to me that precisely similar principles must apply to a conspiracy for which a civil remedy is sought. Nor, in my opinion, can the fact that their ignorance of, or failure to appreciate, the unlawful nature of the transaction was due to the unfortunate fact that they were, as I think, erroneously advised excuse them (*Cooper v. Simmons* (1862) 7 H. & N. 707, and see *Shaw v. Director of Public Prosecutions* [1962] A.C. 220, where the appellant had taken professional legal advice).

If they had sincerely believed in a factual state of affairs which, if true, would have made their actions legal, this would have afforded a defence (*Kamara v. Director of Public Prosecutions* [1974] A.C. 104); but in my view of the effect of section 54 in the present case, even if £500,000 had been a fair price for the share capital of Maximum and all other benefits under the agreement, this would not have made the agreement legal. So a belief in the fairness of the price could not excuse them.

I now come to the constructive trust point. If a stranger to a trust (a) receives and becomes chargeable with some part of the trust fund or (b) assists the trustees of a trust with knowledge of the facts in a dishonest design on the part of the trustees to misapply some part of a trust fund, he is liable as a constructive trustee (*Barnes v. Addy* (1874) 9 Ch. App. 1035 per Lord Selborne LC).

A limited company is of course not a trustee of its own funds: it is their beneficial owner; but in consequence of the fiduciary character of their duties the directors of a limited company are treated as if they were trustees of those funds of the company which are in their hands or under their control, and if they misapply them they commit a breach of trust (*Re Lands Allotment Co.* [1894] 1 Ch. 616, per Lindley and Kay LJ.J.), So, if the directors of a company in breach of their fiduciary duties misapply the funds of their company so that they come into the hands of some stranger to the trust who receives them with knowledge (actual or constructive) of the breach, he cannot conscientiously retain those funds against the company unless he has some better equity. He becomes a constructive trustee for the company of the misapplied funds. This is stated very clearly by Jessel MR in *Russell v. Wakefield Waterworks Co*, where he said:

> "In this Court the money of the company is a trust fund, because it is applicable only to the special purposes of the company in the hands of the agents of the company, and it is in that sense a trust fund applicable by them to those special purposes; and a person taking it from them with notice that it is being applied to other purposes cannot in this Court say that he is not a constructive trustee."

In the present case, the payment of the £500,000 by Belmont to Mr Grosscurth, being an unlawful contravention of section 54, was a misapplication of Belmont's money and was in breach of the duties of the directors of Belmont. £489,000 of the £500,000 so misapplied found their way into the hands of City with City's knowledge of the whole circumstances of the transaction. It must follow, in my opinion, that City is accountable to Belmont as a constructive trustee of the £489,000 under the first of Lord Selborne LC's two heads.

Bank of Ireland v. Rockfield Ltd.
[1979] I.R. 21

The bank had agreed to advance money to two individuals to enable them to buy a certain piece of land, and it was intended that the security would be an equitable mortgage of the certificate of tide to the land. In the event, the money was advanced to the order of the defendant company; and since the land was in its name, it deposited the certificate of tide with the bank. The individuals then used the money that was advanced to acquire control of the company. When the bank sought to enforce the equitable charge, the company claimed that the charge was ineffective because it was used to assist financing the purchase of the company's shares.

KENNY J.: . . . [34] McWilliam J . . . held that the agreement of the 30th July, 1973, had been ratified by the defendants, that the plaintiffs had not actual notice that the £150,000 was to be applied in purchasing the shares in the defendant company, that the doctrine of constructive notice did not apply, and that 'notice' in section 60, sub-s. 14, of the [35] Act of 1963 means actual notice; he then went on to say: 'I fully accept the view expressed by Lindley L.J. but it seems to me that there must be some limit to the extent to which a person may fad to accept information available to him or fail to make the inquiries normal in his line of business so as to leave himself in the position that he has no notice of something anyone else in the same line of business would have appreciated.' Counsel for the plaintiffs has complained that this blurs the distinction between actual notice and constructive notice, and I confess that I find considerable difficulty in understanding what the judge meant by this passage. He went on to say that the limit he had mentioned was reached in this case 'and I hold that the plaintiff should have had notice of the purpose for which the money was being applied, namely, the purchase of the defendant's own shares.' This meant that the judge was applying the doctrine of constructive notice to section 60, sub-s. 14, of the Act of 1963.

It was agreed by counsel that the appeal was confined to the questions of ratification and section 60, sub-s. 14, of the Act of 1963.

The principles governing ratification by a principal of an act by an agent when the agent had no authority to act for the principal have been stated by Wright J. at p. 75 of the report of *Firth v. Staines* [1897] 2 Q.B. 70, in a passage which has been cited with approval in many subsequent cases: the passage reads:

> "I think the case must be decided upon the ordinary principles of the doctrine of ratification. To constitute a valid ratification three conditions must be satisfied: first, the agent whose act is sought to be ratified must have purported to act for the principal; secondly, at the time the act was done the agent must have had a competent principal; and, thirdly, at the time of the ratification the principal must be legally capable of doing the act himself."

At the meeting with the plaintiffs on the 5th September, 1973, Mr Costello and Mr Blakemore signed a promissory note which bore on its face over their signatures the words 'for and on behalf of Rockfield Limited'. They were not directors or members of the defendant company at the time when they signed this note but they had agreed to buy all the shares in that company. Mr Blakemore said that he knew that he was going to be a director of that company in a short time. I have no doubt whatever that Mr Blakemore and Mr Costello purported to act for the principal, the defendant company. The first condition in the passage from the judgment of Wright J. is satisfied.

[36] It was strenuously argued by counsel for the defendants that the transaction could not be ratified because it was illegal. The transaction was the borrowing of money; it was not the borrowing of money for the purchase of the shares in the defendant company, and indeed, only part of the money was applied for that purpose. The defendants had power to borrow money and so the agents had a competent principal that was legally capable of doing the act itself. The defendants' argument on this branch of the case confuses two things – the borrowing of the money and the borrowing of the money for the purpose

of buying the shares in the defendant company. The defendants also ratified the transaction by accepting the two cheques of £15,300 and £5,100 which were part of the agreed total advance. The amounts of the loan represented by these two cheques were subsequently repaid and this is also an act of ratification – as was the authorised deposit of the land certificate in May, 1974. I fully agree with the trial judge's finding that Mr Costello and Mr Blakemore did not enter into the transaction on the 5th September, 1973, on behalf of the defendant company; they could not have done so because they had not been authorised but I have no doubt whatever that the judge's finding that the act of agreeing to borrow the money was subsequently validly ratified by the defendants.

I come now to deal with the much more difficult question which arises under the provisions of section 60 of the Act of 1963. In 1963 this section was new to our company law; it was enacted to prevent a limited company from purchasing its own shares or giving assistance to anyone who wanted to buy shares in it. When a company buys its own shares, it is reducing its share capital without the sanction of the court and so damnifying the position of its creditors. The introduction of the section had been recommended in the report of the Company Law Reform Committee.

[The judge referred to the provisions of subss. 1 and 14 of section 60 of the Act of 1963 and continued] Sub-sections 2, 12 and 13 of section 60 have no relevance to this case and, although sub-s. 1 of section 60 appears in the (British) Companies Act, 1948, nothing corresponding to sub-s. 14 appears in that Act. This is the first case, as far as I know, in which the meaning of sub-s. 14 of section 60 has been considered by any court in this country. The onus of proving that the money was advanced for the purchase of shares in the defendant company lies on the person who alleges this. The plaintiffs do not have to prove that they had no notice of facts which constituted a breach of section 60. What has to be established is that the plaintiffs had notice when lending the money that it was to be used for the purchase of shares in the defendant company. The fact [37] which constituted such breach in this case was the application of £150,000 to the purchase of the shares in the defendant company. As the purchase followed the loan, the defendants must establish that the plaintiffs knew at the time when they made the loan that it was to be applied for this purpose. If they got notice of this subsequently, that is irrelevant.

The notice referred to in sub-s. 14 of section 60 is actual notice and not constructive notice. As there has been considerable confusion as to the meaning of the terms 'actual notice' and 'imputed notice' and 'constructive notice' – a confusion which has been pointed out by many judges and text-book writers – I wish to say that I use the term 'actual notice' as meaning in this case that the plaintiff bank, or any of its officials, had been informed, either verbally or in writing, that part of the advance was to be applied in the purchase of shares in the defendant company, or that they knew facts from which they *must* have inferred that part of the advance was to be applied for this purpose. This difficult branch of the law is well summarised at p. 50 of the 27th edition of *Snell's Principles of Equity* (of which the editors were The Hon. Sir Robert Megarry, now the Vice-Chancellor, and Professor Baker) where it is stated:

> "From this it is clear that a purchaser is affected by notice of an equity in three cases:
>
> (1) Actual notice: where the equity is within his own knowledge;
> (2) Constructive notice: where the equity would have come to his own knowledge if proper inquiries had been made; and
> (3) Imputed notice: where his agent as such in the course of the transaction has actual or constructive notice of the equity."

See also section 3 of the Conveyancing Act, 1882. I include in 'actual notice' cases where the agent gets actual notice of the equity.

There is strong authority that the doctrine of constructive notice is not to be extended to commercial transactions. In *Manchester Trust v. Furness* [1895] 2 Q.B. 539, Lindley J., a great authority upon company law, said at p. 545 of the report:

> ". . . as regards the extension of the equitable doctrines of constructive notice to commercial transactions, the Courts have always set their faces resolutely against it. The equitable doctrines of constructive notice are common enough in dealing with land and estates, with which the Court is familiar; but there have been repeated protests against the introduction into commercial transactions of anything like an extension of those doctrines, and the protest is founded on perfect good sense. In dealing with estates in [38] land tide is everything, and it can be leisurely investigated; in commercial transactions possession is everything, and there is no time to investigate tide; and if we were to extend the doctrine of constructive notice to commercial transactions we should be doing infinite mischief and paralyzing the trade of the country."

That passage was approved by Lopes and Rigby J.J. It was cited with approval by Scrutton L.J. in the Court of Appeal in *Greer v. Downs Supply Co.* [1927] 2 Q.B. 28.

Section 60 of the Act of 1963 deals with financial assistance, not with mortgages. The word 'mortgage' does not appear in the section and subs. 14 applies to all commercial transactions. The fact that there was a mortgage involved in this transaction does not mean that the sub-section is to be read in one sense for financial assistance without security and in another sense when a mortgage is involved. That would be a ludicrous interpretation. Therefore 'notice of the facts which constitute such breach' means 'actual notice' in the sense in which I have defined those words.

In the puzzling passage in the trial judge's judgment, he refers to a person failing to accept information available to him or failing to make the inquiries normal in his line of business; but these are the criteria of constructive notice. What he seems to be saying is that constructive notice becomes actual notice at some undefined point. This is incorrect; it is blurring the distinction between actual notice and constructive notice. There is nothing in this case which indicates that the plaintiffs or any of their officials knew that any part of the advance was to be applied to the purchase of shares in the defendant company, and what they did know does not lead to a conclusion that they must have inferred that the money was to be applied for the purchase of shares in the defendant company.

The matters which were relied on as fixing the plaintiffs with constructive notice were, first, the failure to inspect or get a copy of the folio; secondly, the estimate of stamp duty in the estimate of the cost of the transaction which was submitted to them early on in the discussions; thirdly, the fact that planning permission was granted to the defendants in 1972 when application was made for it by them; and, fourthly counsel's opinion which is headed 'Rockfield Limited with Wicklow County Council.' The opinion is dated the 18th January, 1973. I think the failure to get a copy of or to inspect the folio would be held to be constructive notice for this was a matter that the plaintiffs ought to have investigated and, if the doctrine of constructive notice applied, that failure would certainly have fixed them with that type of notice; but, as it [39] is an omission to do something which they ought to have done, it is not actual notice. I confess that I find it incomprehensible why the plaintiffs did not ask for a copy of the folio, but then lawyers tend to think that everyone will take the same precautions as they do. I think that the plaintiffs ought to have inquired as to the estimate of stamp duty but, again, the fact that the stamp duty estimate was 1% of the purchase price was not notice that the money was to be applied for the purchase of the shares in the defendant company; it indicated that the purchase of another company was contemplated but not necessarily the defendant company. Knowledge that the defendants applied in 1973 for planning permission and that it was granted to them by Wicklow County Council was not either actual or constructive notice for, as I have already pointed out, until the 30th July, 1974, when this Court decided otherwise it was generally assumed in the legal, architectural and engineering professions that anybody could apply for planning permission without having any interest in the land. This transaction took place long before that date.

It follows that the plaintiffs are entitled to succeed in this action. Although they had constructive notice that the defendant company was the owner of the land, the plaintiffs had not actual notice and that is the knowledge which is referred to in section 60, subs. 14, of the Act of 1963.

CHAPTER 8

Accounts and Audit

ACCOUNTS

See *Company Law*, pp.257–259.

Companies Act 1990, section 202(1)-(4)

Keeping of books of account

202.—(1) Every company shall cause to be kept proper books of account, whether in the form of documents or otherwise, that–

(*a*) correctly record and explain the transactions of the company,

(*b*) will at any time enable the financial position of the company to be determined with reasonable accuracy,

(*c*) will enable the directors to ensure that any balance sheet, profit and loss account or income and expenditure account of the company complies with the requirements of the Companies Acts, and

(*d*) will enable the accounts of the company to be readily and properly audited.

(2) The books of account of a company shall be kept on a continuous and consistent basis, that is to say, the entries therein shall be made in a timely manner and be consistent from one year to the next.

(3) Without prejudice to the generality of subsections (1) and (2), books of account kept pursuant to those subsections shall contain-

(*a*) entries from day to day of all sums of money received and expended by the company and the matters in respect of which the receipt and expenditure takes place,

(*b*) a record of the assets and liabilities of the company,

(*c*) if the company's business involves dealing in goods–
   (i) a record of all goods purchased, and of all goods sold (except those sold for cash by way of ordinary retail trade), showing the goods and the sellers and buyers in sufficient detail to enable the goods and the sellers and buyers to be identified and a record

of all the invoices relating to such purchases and sales,

(ii) statements of stock held by the company at the end of each financial year and all records of stocktakings from which any such statement of stock has been, or is to be, prepared, and

(d) if the company's business involves the provision of services, a record of the services provided and of all the invoices relating thereto.

(4) For the purposes of subsections (1), (2) and (3), proper books of account shall be deemed to be kept if they comply with those subsections and give a true and fair view of the state of affairs of the company and explain its transactions.

Table A articles 125–129

125.—The directors shall cause proper books of account to be kept relating to–

(a) all sums of money received and expended by the company and the matters in respect of which the receipt and expenditure takes place; and

(b) all sales and purchases of goods by the company; and

(c) the assets and liabilities of the company.

Proper books shall not be deemed to be kept if there are not kept such books of account as are necessary to give a true and fair view of the state of the company's affairs and to explain its transactions.

126.—The books of account shall be kept at the office or, subject to section 147 of the Act, at such other place as the directors think fit, and shall at all reasonable times be open to the inspection of the directors.

127.—The directors shall from time to time determine whether and to what extent and at what times and places and under what conditions or regulations the accounts and books of the company or any of them shall be open to the inspection of members, not being directors, and no member (not being a director) shall have any right of inspecting any account or book or document of the company except as conferred by statute or authorised by the directors or by the company in general meeting.

128.—The directors shall from time to time, in accordance with sections 148, 150, 157 and 158 of the Act cause to be prepared and to be laid before the annual general meeting of the company such profit and loss accounts, balance sheets, group accounts and reports as are required by those sections to be prepared and laid before the annual general meeting of the company.

129.—A copy of every balance sheet (including every document required by law to be annexed thereto) which is to be laid before the annual general meeting of the company together with a copy of the directors' report and auditors' report shall, not less than 21 days before the date of the annual general meeting be sent to every person entitled under the provisions of the Act to receive them.

Note: In *Mehigan v. Duignan* [1997] 1 I.L.R.M. 171 Shanley J. applied section 204 of the 1990 Act, rendering directors of an insolvent company liable for its debts because no proper books and accounts were kept in accordance with section 202 (supra).

AUDIT AND THE AUDITORS

See *Company Law*, pp.259–269.

Companies Act 1990, section 187(1) and (2)

Qualification for appointment as auditor

187.—(1) Subject to section 190, a person shall not be qualified for appointment either as auditor of a company or as a public auditor auditor unless—

(*a*) (i) he is a member of a body of accountants for the time being recognised by the Minister for the purposes of this section and holds a valid practising certificate from such a body, or

(ii) he holds an accountancy qualification that is, in the opinion of the Minister, of a standard which is not less than that required for such membership as aforesaid and which would entitle him to be granted a practising certificate by that body if he were a member of it, and is for the time being authorised by the Minister to be so appointed, or

(iii) he was, on the 31st day of December, 1990, a member of a body of accountants for the time being recognised under section 162 (1) (a) of the Principal Act (provided he holds a valid practising certificate – S.I. No. 259 of 1992), or

(iv) he was authorised by the Minister before the 3rd of February, 1983, and is for the time being authorised by the Minister to be so appointed, or

    (v) he is a person to whom section 188 applies, or

    (vi) he is a person to whom section 189 applies, and is for the time being authorised by the Minister to be so appointed, and

  (b) the particulars required by sections 199 and 200 in respect of such a person have been forwarded to the registrar of companies.

(2) None of the following persons shall be qualified for appointment as auditor of a company–

  (*a*) an officer or servant of the company,

  (*b*) a person who has been an officer or servant of the company within a period in respect of which accounts would fall to be audited by him if he were appointed auditor of the company,

  (*c*) a parent, spouse, brother, sister or child of an officer of the company,

  (*d*) a person who is a partner of or in the employment of an officer of the company,.

  (*e*) a person who is disqualified under this subsection for appointment as auditor of any other body corporate that is a subsidiary or holding company of the company or a subsidiary of the company's holding company, or would be so disqualified if the body corporate were a company,

  (*f*) a person who is disqualified under subsection (3) for appointment as a public auditor of a society that is a subsidiary or holding company of the company or a subsidiary of the company's holding company,

  (*g*) a body corporate.

Table A article 132

132.—Auditors shall be appointed and their duties regulated in accordance with sections 160 to 163 of the Act.

Note: In *Mutual Reinsurance Co. Ltd. v. Peat Marwick Mitchell & Co.* [1997] 1 B.C.L.C. it was held that auditors are officers of a company when appointed under provisions similar to section 160 of the 1963 Act. But they are not officers when not so appointed and are merely retained to carry out an audit function.

Re City Equitable Fire Insurance Co.
[1925] Ch. 407

This case ensued from a notorious financial scandal in the 1920's, in consequence of management fraud, when a major insurance company collapsed and was heavily insolvent. Proceedings for negligence and breach of duty were brought against the directors (see *ante*, p. 259) and its auditors, on a misfeasance summons. In determining the question of liability of the respondent auditors raised by the summons, Romer J. applied the principles enunciated by Lindley L.J. in *In re London and General Bank (No. 2)* [1895] 2 Ch. 673 and also the following further principles relative to the duties of auditors. An auditor is not ever justified in omitting to make personal inspection of securities that are in the custody of a person or company with whom it is not proper that they should be left, whenever such personal inspection is practicable.

A company's stockbrokers, however respectable and responsible they may be, are not proper persons to have the custody of its securities except on such occasions when, for short periods, securities must of necessity be left with them; but immediately such necessity ceases the securities should be lodged in the company's strongroom or with its bank, or placed in other proper and usual safe keeping.

Whenever an auditor discovers that securities of the company are not in proper custody, it is his duty to require that the matter be put right at once, or, if his requirement is not complied with, to report the fact to the shareholders, and this whether he can or cannot make a personal inspection:

Held, (1.) That section 215 was a procedure section only and created no new or additional liability.

(2.) That the measure of the auditor's responsibility depends upon the terms of his engagement. There may be a special contract defining the duties and liabilities of the auditors. If there is, then that contract governs the question. The articles will, however, be looked at if there is no special agreement, because the auditors will presumably have taken their duties upon the terms (among others) set out in the articles. That is not to say that auditors can set aside a statutory obligation. No agreement or article of association can remove an imperative or statutory duty.

(3.) Sect. 113 does not lay down a rigid code. The duty imposed on the auditors by it is not absolute, but depends upon the information given and explanations furnished to them, so that there is abundant scope for discretion. Art. 150 is not in conflict with the section. The onus lies upon the auditors, who would not be excused for total omission to comply with any of the requirements of the section, or for any consequences of deliberate or reckless indifferent failure to ask for information on matters which call for further explanation.

(4.) Auditors should not be content with a certificate that securities are in the possession of a particular company, firm, or person unless the company, etc., is trustworthy, or, as it is sometimes put, respectable, and further is one that in the ordinary course of business keeps securities for its customers. In all these cases the auditor must use his judgment.

Caparo Industries plc v. Dickman
[1996] 2 A.C. 605

This is a leading case on the vexed question of to whom do auditors owe a duty of care in negligence. The plaintiffs, a public limited company, which had accomplished the take-over of F. plc, sued its directors alleging fraudulent misrepresentation and against its auditors claiming that they were negligent in carrying out the audit and making their report, which they were required to do within the terms of the Companies Act. In the statement of claim the plaintiffs alleged that they had begun purchasing shares in F. Plc. a few days before the annual accounts had been published to shareholders, that in reliance on those accounts they made further purchases of shares so as to take over the company, and that the auditors (owed both shareholders and potential investors a duty of care in respect of the certification of the accounts and should have known that as F. Plc.'s profits were not as high as projected and its share price had fallen significantly, that it was susceptible to a take-over bid and that reliance on the accuracy of the accounts would be placed by any potential bidder such as the plaintiffs.

LORD BRIDGE OF HARWICH: [616] In determining the existence and scope of the duty of care which one person may owe to another in the infinitely varied circumstances of human relationships there has for long been a tension between two different approaches. Traditionally the law finds the existence of the duty in different specific situations each exhibiting its own particular characteristics. In this way the law has identified a wide variety of duty situations, all failing within the ambit of the tort of negligence, but sufficiently distinct to require separate definition of the essential ingredients by which the existence of the duty is to be recognised. . . .

[But there has been] introduc[ed] the more modern approach of seeking a single general principle which may be applied in all circumstances to determine the existence of a duty of care. . . .

   [617] The most comprehensive attempt to articulate a single general principle is reached in the well known passage from the speech of Lord Wilberforce in *Anns v. Merton London Borough Council* [1978] A.C. 728. . . .

   But since the *Anns* case a series of decisions of the Privy Council and of your Lordships' House, notably in judgments and speeches delivered by Lord Keith of Kinkel, have emphasised the inability of any single general principle to provide a practical test which can be applied to every situation to determine whether a duty of care is owed and, if so, what is its scope: see *Governors of Peabody Donation Fund v. Sir Lindsay Parkinson & Co. Ltd.* [1985] A.C. 210, 239F-241C; *Yuen Kun Yeu v. Attorney General of Hong Kong* [1988] A.C. 175, 190E-194; *Rowling v. Takaro Properties Ltd.* [1988] A.C. 473, 501D-G; *Hill v. Chief Constable of West Yorkshire* [1989] A.C. 53, 60B-D. What emerges is that, in addition to the foreseeability of damage, necessary ingredients in any situation giving rise to a duty of care are that there [618] should exist between the party owing the duty and the party to whom it is owed a relationship characterised by the law as one of "proximity" or "neighbourhood" and that the situation should be one in which the court considers it fair, just and reasonable that the law should impose a duty of a given scope upon the one party for the benefit of the other. But it is implicit in the passages referred to that the concepts of proximity and fairness embodied in these additional ingredients are not susceptible of any such precise definition as would be necessary to give them utility as practical tests, but amount in effect to little more than convenient labels to attach to the features of different specific situations which, on a detailed examination of all the circumstances, the law recognises pragmatically as giving rise to a duty of care of a given scope. Whilst recognising, of course, the importance of the underlying general principles common to the whole field of negligence, I think the law has now moved in the direction of attaching greater significance to the more traditional categorisation of distinct and recognisable situations as guides to the existence. the scope and the limits of the varied duties of care which the law imposes. . . .

One of the most important distinctions always to be observed lies in the law's essentially different approach to the different kinds of damage which one party may have suffered in consequence of the acts or omissions of another. It is one thing to owe a duty of care to avoid causing injury to the person or property of others. It is quite another to avoid causing others to suffer purely economic loss. . . .

The proposition derives from *Cattle v. Stockton Waterworks Co.* (1875) L.R. 10 QB. 453. It has recently been reaffirmed in *Candlewood Navigation Corporation Ltd. v. Mitsui O.S.K. Lines Ltd.* [1986] A.C. 1 and *Leigh & Sillavan Ltd. v. Aliakmon Shipping Co. Ltd.* [1986] A.C. 785. In the former case Lord Fraser of Tullybelton, delivering the judgment of the Privy Council, said. at p. 25:

> "Their Lordships consider that some limit or control mechanism has to be imposed upon the liability of a wrongdoer towards those [619] who have suffered economic damage in consequence of his negligence. The need for such a limit has been repeatedly asserted in the cases, from *Cattle's* case, L.R. 10 QB. 453, to *Caltex [Oil (Australia) Pty. Ltd. v. Dredge "Willemstad"* (1976)], 136 C.L.R. 529, and their Lordships are not aware that a view to the contrary has ever been judicially expressed."

The damage which may be caused by the negligently spoken or written word will normally be confined to economic loss sustained by those who rely on the accuracy of the information or advice they receive as a basis for action. The question what, if any, duty is owed by the maker of a statement to exercise due care to ensure its accuracy arises typically In relation to statements made by a person in the exercise of his calling or profession. In advising the client who employs him the professional man owes a duty to exercise that standard of skill and care appropriate to his professional status and will he liable both in contract and in tort for all losses which his client may suffer by reason of any breach of that duty. But the possibility of any duty of care being owed to third parties with whom the professional man was in no contractual relationship was for long denied because of the wrong turning taken by the law in *Le Lievre v. Gould* [1893] 1 Q.B. 491 in overruling *Cann v. Willson* (1888) 39 Ch.D. 39. In *Candler v. Crane, Christmas & Co.* [1951] 2 K.B. 164, Denning L.J. in his dissenting judgment, made a valiant attempt to correct the error. But it was not until the decision of this House in *Hedley Byrne & Co. Ltd. v. Heller & Partners Ltd.* [1964] A.C. 465 that the law was once more set upon the right path.

Consistently with the traditional approach it is to these authorities and to subsequent decisions directly relevant to this relatively narrow corner of the field that we should look to determine the essential characteristics of a situation giving rise, independently of any contractual or fiduciary relationship, to a duty of care owed by one party to another to ensure that the accuracy of any statement which the one party makes and on which the other party may foreseeably rely to his economic detriment. . . .

In *Candler v. Crane, Christmas & Co. Ltd.* [1951] 2 K.B. 164 the plaintiff invested money in a limited company in reliance on accounts of the company prepared by the company's accountants at the request [620] of the managing director, which were shown to the plaintiff and discussed with him by the accountants in the knowledge that he was interested as a potential investor in the company. The accounts were inaccurate and misleading and the plaintiff, having invested in the company in reliance upon them, lost his money. Denning L.J., in his dissenting judgment, held the plaintiff entitled to recover damages for the accountants' negligence.

In *Hedley Byrne & Co. Ltd. v. Heller & Partners Ltd.* [1964] A.C. 465 bankers were asked about the financial stability of a customer of the bank. They gave a favourable reference, albeit with a disclaimer of responsibility. The circumstances of the inquiry made it clear to the bankers that the party on whose behalf the inquiry was made wanted to know if they could safely extend credit to the bank's customer in a substantial sum. Acting on the reference given, the plaintiffs extended credit to the bank's customer who in due course defaulted. Although the House held that the bankers were protected by the disclaimer of responsibility, the case provided the opportunity to review the law, which led to the reinstatement of *Cann v. Willson*, the overruling of the majority decision in the *Candler* case and the approbation of the dissenting judgment of Denning L.J. in that case.

The most recent decision of the House, which is very much in point, is that of the two appeals heard together of *Smith v. Eric S. Bush* and *Harris v. Wyre Forest District Council* [1990] 1 A.C. 831. The plaintiffs in both cases were house purchasers who purchased in reliance on valuations of the properties made by surveyors acting for and on the instructions of the mortgagees proposing to advance money to the plaintiffs to enable them to effect their purchases. In both cases the surveyors' fees were paid by the plaintiffs and in both cases it turned out that the inspections and valuations had been negligently carried out and that the property was seriously defective so that the plaintiffs suffered financial loss. . . . The House held that in both cases the surveyor making the inspection and valuation owed a duty of care to the plaintiff house purchaser and that the contractual clauses purporting to exclude liability were struck down by section 2(2) and section 11(3) of the Unfair Contract Terms Act 1977.

The salient feature of all these cases is that the defendant giving advice or information was fully aware of the nature of the transaction which the plaintiff had in contemplation, knew that the advice or information would be communicated to him directly or indirectly and [621] knew that it was very likely that the plaintiff would rely on that advice or information in deciding whether or not to engage in the transaction in contemplation. In these circumstances the defendant could clearly be expected, subject always to the effect of any disclaimer of responsibility, specifically to anticipate that the plaintiff would rely on the advice or information given by the defendant for the very purpose for which he did in the event rely on it. So also the plaintiff, subject again to the effect of any disclaimer, would in that situation reasonably suppose that he was entitled to rely on the advice or information communicated to him for the very purpose for which he required it. The situation is entirely different where a statement is put into more or less general circulation and may foreseeably be relied on by strangers to the maker of the statement for any one of a variety of different purposes which the maker of the statement has no specific reason to anticipate. To hold the maker of the statement to be under a duty of care in respect of the accuracy of the statement to all and sundry for any purpose for which they may choose to rely on it is not only to subject him, in the classic words of Cardozo C.J. to "liability in an indeterminate amount for an indeterminate time to an indeterminate class:" see *Ultramares Corporation v. Touche* (1931) 174 N.E. 441 at 444; it is also to confer on the world at large a quite unwarranted entitlement to appropriate for their own purposes the benefit of the expert knowledge or professional expertise attributed to the maker of the statement. Hence, looking only at the circumstances of these decided cases where a duty of care in respect of negligent statements has been held to exist, I should expect to find that the 'limit or control mechanism . . . imposed upon the liability of a wrongdoer towards those who have suffered economic damage in consequence of his negligence' rested in the necessity to prove, in this category of the tort of negligence, as an essential ingredient of the 'proximity' between the plaintiff and the defendant, that the defendant knew that his statement would be communicated to the plaintiff, either as an individual or as a member of an identifiable class, specifically in connection with a particular transaction or transactions of a particular kind (*e.g.* in a prospectus inviting investment) and that the plaintiff would be very likely to rely on it for the purpose of deciding whether or not to enter upon that transaction or upon a transaction of that kind. . . .

[623] Some of the speeches in the *Hedley Byrne* case derive a duty of care in relation to negligent statements from a voluntary assumption of responsibility on the part of the maker of the statements. In his speech in *Smith v. Eric S. Bush* [1990] 1 A.C. 831, 862, Lord Griffiths emphatically rejected the view that this was the true ground of liability and concluded that:

> "The phrase 'assumption of responsibility' can only have any real meaning if it is understood as referring to the circumstances in which the law will deem the maker of the statement to have assumed responsibility to the person who acts upon the advice."

I do not think that in the context of the present appeal anything turns upon the difference between these two approaches.

These considerations amply justify the conclusion that auditors of a public company's accounts owe no duty of care to members of the public at large who rely upon the accounts in deciding to buy shares in the company. If a duty of care were owed so widely. it is difficult to see any reason why it should not equally extend to all who rely on the accounts in relation to other dealings with a company as lenders or merchants extending credit to the company. A claim that such a duty was owed by auditors to a bank lending to a company was emphatically and convincingly rejected by Millett J. in *Al Saudi Banque v. Clarke Pixley* [1990] Ch. 313. The only support for an unlimited duty of care owed by auditors for the accuracy of their accounts to all who may foreseeably rely upon them is to be found in some jurisdictions in the United States of America where there are striking differences in the law in different states. In this jurisdiction I have no doubt that the creation of such an unlimited duty would be a legislative step which it would be for Parliament, not the courts, to take.

The main submissions for Caparo are that the necessary nexus of proximity between it and the appellants giving rise to a duty of care stems (1) from the pleaded circumstances indicating the vulnerability of Fidelity to a take-over bid and from the consequent probability that another company, such as Caparo, would rely on the audited accounts in deciding to launch a take-over bid, or (2) from the circumstance that Caparo was already a shareholder in Fidelity when it decided to launch its take-over bid in reliance on the accounts.

In relation to the first of these two submissions, Caparo applied. in the course of the hearing, for leave to amend paragraph 16(2) of the statement of claim by adding the words "or alternatively that it was highly probable that such persons would rely on the accounts for that purpose." . . .

[625] The only other English authority to which I need refer in this context in *JEB Fasteners Ltd. v. Marks, Bloom & Co.* [1981] 3 All E.R. 289, a decision at first instance of Woolf J. This was another case where the plaintiffs, who had made a successful take-over bid for a company in reliance on audited accounts which had been negligently prepared, sued the accountants for damages. Woolf J. held that the auditors owed the plaintiffs a duty of care in the preparation of the accounts. He relied on both the *Anns* case [1978] A.C. 728 and *Scott Group Ltd. v. McFarlane* [1978] 1 N.Z.L.R. 553, in reaching the conclusion that the duty could be derived from foreseeability alone. For the reasons already indicated, I do not agree with this. It may well be, however, that the particular facts in the JEB case were sufficient to establish a basis on which the necessary ingredient of proximity to found a duty of care could be derived from the actual knowledge on the part of the auditors of the specific purpose for which the plaintiffs intended to use the accounts. The position of auditors in relation to the shareholders of a public limited liability company arising from the relevant provisions of the Companies Act, 1985 is accurately summarised in the judgment of Bingham L.J. in the Court of Appeal [1989] Q.B. 653, 680-681:

> "The members, or shareholders, of the company are its owners. But they are too numerous. and in most cases too unskilled, to undertake the day to day management of that which they own. So responsibility for day to day management of the company is delegated to directors. The shareholders, despite their overall powers of control, are in most companies for most of the time investors and little more. But it would of course be unsatisfactory and open to abuse if the shareholders received no report on the financial stewardship of their investment save from those to whom the stewardship had been entrusted. So provision is made for the company in general meeting to appoint an auditor (section 384 of the Companies Act 1985), whose duty is to investigate and form an opinion on the adequacy of the company's accounting records and returns and the correspondence between the company's accounting records and returns and its accounts: section 237. The auditor has then to report to the company's members (among other things) whether in his opinion the company's accounts give a true and fair view of the company's financial position: section 236. In carrying out his investigation and in forming his opinion the auditor necessarily works very closely with the directors and officers of the company. He receives his remuneration from the company. He naturally, and rightly, regards the company as his client. But he is employed by the company to exercise his professional skill and judgment

for the purpose of giving the shareholders an independent report on the reliability of the company's accounts and thus on their investment. 'No doubt he is acting antagonistically to the directors [626] in the sense that he is appointed by the shareholders to be a check upon them:' *In re Kingston Cotton Mill Co.* [1896] 1 Ch. 6, 11, per Vaughan Williams J. The auditor's report must be read before the company in general meeting and must be open to inspection by any member of the company: section 241. It is attached to and forms part of the company's accounts: sections 238(3) and 239. A copy of the company's accounts, including the auditor's report, must be sent to every member: section 240. Any member of the company, even if not entitled to have a copy of the accounts sent to him, is entitled to be furnished with a copy of the company's last accounts on demand and without charge: section 246."

No doubt these provisions establish a relationship between the auditors and the shareholders of a company on which the shareholder is entitled to rely for the protection of his interest. But the crucial question concerns the extent of the shareholder's interest which the auditor has a duty to protect. The shareholders of a company have a collective interest in the company's proper management and in so far as a negligent failure of the auditor to report accurately on the state of the company's finances deprives the shareholders of the opportunity to exercise their powers in general meeting to call the directors to book and to ensure that errors in management are corrected, the shareholders ought to be entitled to a remedy. But in practice no problem arises in this regard since the interest of the shareholders in the proper management of the company's affairs is indistinguishable from the interest of the company itself and any loss suffered by the shareholders, *e.g.* by the negligent failure of the auditor to discover and expose a misappropriation of funds by a director of the company, will be recouped by a claim against the auditors in the name of the' company, not by individual shareholders.

I find it difficult to visualise a situation arising in the real world in which the individual shareholder could claim to have sustained a loss in respect of his existing shareholding referable to the negligence of the auditor which could riot he recouped by the company. But on this part of the case your Lordships were much pressed with the argument that such a loss might occur by a negligent undervaluation of the company's assets in the auditor's report relied on by the individual shareholder in deciding to sell his shares at an undervalue. The argument then runs thus. The shareholder, qua shareholder, is entitled to rely on the auditor's report as the basis of his investment decision to sell his existing shareholding. If he sells at an undervalue he is entitled to recover the loss from the auditor. There can be no distinction in law between the shareholder's investment decision to sell the shares he has or to buy additional shares. It follows, therefore, that the scope of the duty of care owed to him by the auditor extends to cover any loss sustained consequent on the purchase of additional shares in reliance on the auditor's negligent report.

I believe this argument to be fallacious. Assuming without deciding that a claim by a shareholder to recover a loss suffered by selling his shares at an undervalue attributable to an undervaluation of the [627] company's assets in the auditor's report could be sustained at all, it would not be by reason of any reliance by the shareholder on the auditor's report in deciding to sell; the loss would he referable to the depreciatory effect of the report on the market value of the shares before ever the decision of the shareholder to sell was taken. A claim to recoup a loss alleged to flow from the purchase of overvalued shares, on the other hand, can only be sustained on the basis of the purchaser's reliance on the report. The specious equation of "investment decisions" to sell or to buy as giving rise to parallel claims thus appears to me to be untenable. Moreover, the loss in the case of the sale would be of a loss of part of the value of the shareholder's existing holding, which, assuming a duty of care owed to individual shareholders, it might sensibly lie within the scope of the auditor's duty to protect. A loss, on the other hand, resulting from the purchase of additional shares would result from a wholly independent transaction having no connection with the existing shareholding.

I believe it is this last distinction which is of critical importance and which demonstrates the unsoundness of the conclusion reached by the majority of the Court of Appeal. It is never sufficient to ask simply whether A owes B a duty of care. It is always necessary to determine the scope of the duty by reference to the kind of damage from which A must take care to save B harmless. "The question is always whether the defendant was under a duty to avoid or prevent that damage, but the actual nature of the damage suffered is relevant to the existence and extent of any duty to avoid or prevent it:" see *Sutherland Shire Council v. Heyman*, 60 A.L.R. 1, 48, *per* Brennan J. Assuming for the purpose of the argument that the relationship between the auditor of a company and individual shareholders is of sufficient proximity to give rise to a duty of care, I do not understand how the scope of that duty can possibly extend beyond the protection of any individual shareholder from losses in the value of the shares which he holds. As a purchaser of additional shares in reliance on the auditor's report, he stands in no different position from any other investing member of the public to whom the auditor owes no duty.

Note: The liability of auditors in negligence remains a vexed question. Recent reported instances include:

James McNaughton Paper Group Ltd. v. Hicks Anderson & Co. [1991] 2 Q.B. 213, concerned 'final drafts' of accounts of a company prepared while negotiations were taking place for its take-over and a statement made by its auditors that it was about 'breaking even'. Following the take-over, several errors were found in the accounts. The buyers sued the auditors for negligence. The Court of Appeal held that in the circumstances there was not sufficient proximity to give rise to a duty of care and also the loss suffered by the plaintiffs was not reasonably foreseeable.

Morgan Crucible Co. plc v. Hill Samuel & Co. Ltd [1991] Ch. 295, also concerned a take-over, where the successful bidder subsequently sued the company's auditors, alleging that they were negligent. On the admitted facts here, during the course of the bid the company issued a profits forecast, which was supported by a letter from the auditors stating that the forecast had been properly compiled in accordance with stated accounting policies. The Court of Appeal held, distinguishing *Caparo* (supra), that the auditors owed a duty of care; that:

> 'If during the course of a contested take-over bid the directors and financial advisers of the target company made express representations after an identified bidder had emerged, intending that the bidder would rely on those representations, they owed the bidder a duty of care not to be negligent in making representations which might mislead him.'

Berg Sons & Co. Ltd v. Mervyn Hampton Adams [1993] B.C.L.C. 1045, concerned the unqualified audit report on an company that about eight months later was wound up with a deficit of about £15.5m. Both the company and one of its principal creditors, a bank, sued the auditors, claiming negligence.

Hobhouse J.. held that,

(1) in the circumstances the accounts should have been qualified for uncertainty;

(2) the company was entitled to only nominal damages because it had not relied on or been misled by the unqualified certificate;

(3) there was no duty of care in tort owed to the bank.

Galoo Ltd. v. Bright Grahame Murray [1994] 1 W.L.R 1360, concerned a company, that purchased 51% of a company and later 44.3% of another company, and also made loans of over £30m. to it and its wholly owned subsidiary. Some years later these were wound up as insolvent. They and the purchaser/lender sued the auditors, claiming negligence in including in the figures for stocks approximately £15.3 for fictitious stock. It was held by the Court of Appeal that:

(1) the two companies' claims should be struck out because, if there were negligence, it did not cause them any loss;

(2) in the circumstances, there could be a duty of care in respect of the first acquisition of shares but the claim in respect of the second acquisition was struck out because negligence was not properly pleaded;

(3) the claim in respect of the loan was also dismissed on pleading grounds.

Anthony v. Wright [1995] 1 B.C.L.C. 236, concerned a firm of insurance brokers with which investors placed money, which was held in trust for them. The company was wound up with a deficiency of £4.5m. The investors, who had not relied on the audits, sued the auditors, claiming negligence in not detecting defalcations by directors of the company. Their claim was struck out by Lightman J.; the fact that their money was held in trust by the company did not have the effect of creating a special relationship between them and the auditors giving rise to a duty of care being owed to them.

Barings plc v. Coopers & Lybrand [1997] 1 B.C.L.C. 427 concerning the collapse of the Barings group, following the losses inflicted, by futures trading, on its Singapore indirect subsidiary due to the defalcations of a bank official employed there. The preliminary question was whether the auditors of the subsidiary's accounts owed a duty of care not alone to it but also to the parent company. The Court of Appeal answered in the affirmative, rejecting the contention that any damages that resulted from the alleged negligence were due only to the subsidiary which actually suffered the loss and not by the parent company, which was only a shareholder.

CHAPTER 9

Shareholder Status and Rights

The Companies Acts contain elaborate provisions concerning what may be called the personal property aspect of company law, *viz.* questions of title to shares, their transfer and transmission. Shareholders generally owe their companies one principal obligation, which is to pay up any unpaid amount on their shares when called upon to do so. Subject to the company in question's own regulations, shareholders generally are entitled to transfer their shares, to vote in general meetings, to a dividend whenever one is declared, and where possible when the company is wound up to a return of their capital and a share in any surplus remaining. Companies with preference shares usually have special rules on these matters.

NATURE OF SHARES

See *Company Law*, pp. 283–285.

Companies Act 1963, section 79

Nature of shares

79.—The shares or other interest of any member in a company shall be personal estate, transferable in manner provided by the articles of the company, and shall, not be of the nature of real estate.

INCIDENTS OF MEMBERSHIP

See *Company Law*, pp. 287–300.

Voting

Table A articles 63–74
(votes of members)
see *ante*, p. 143.

Bushell v. Faith
[1970] A.C. 1099
See ante p. 165.

In *Re Bradford Investments Ltd* [1991] B.C.L.C. 224, one of the issues was whether, in the circumstances, the ordinary shareholders were entitled to vote where the articles of association deprived them of votes whenever any calls or other sums payable in respect of their shares had not been fully paid.

In *Standard Chartered Bank v. Walker* [1992] B.C.L.C. 603, Vinelott J. held that in very extreme circumstances a court would enjoin a shareholder from voting his shares in such manner as he chooses. The company there was in acute financial difficulties and, if a proposed restructuring was not approved by its members, the company would collapse. Compare *Re Swindon Town Football Club Ltd* [1990] B.C.L.C. 467, where Harman J. declined to enjoin directors from voting their shares in their own interests.

Dividends

Table A articles 116–124 and 130–131

Dividends and Reserve

116. The company in general meeting may declare dividends, but no dividend shall exceed the amount recommended by the directors.

117. The directors may from time to time pay to the members such interim dividends as appear to the directors to be justified by the profits of the company.

118. No dividend or interim dividend shall be paid otherwise than in accordance with the provisions of Part IV of the Companies (Amendment) Act 1983, which apply to the company.

119. The directors may, before recommending any dividend, set aside out of the profits of the company such sums as they think proper as a reserve or reserves which shall, at the discretion of the directors, be applicable for any purpose to which the profits of the company may be properly applied, and pending such application may, at the like discretion, either be employed in the business of the company or be invested in such investments as the directors may lawfully determine. The directors may also, without placing the same to reserve, carry forward any profits which they may think it prudent not to divide.

120. Subject to the rights of persons, if any, entitled to shares with special rights as to dividend, all dividends shall be declared and paid according to the amounts paid or credited as paid on the shares in respect whereof the dividend is paid, but no amount paid or credited as paid on a share in advance of calls shall be treated for the purposes of this regulation as paid on the share. All dividends shall be apportioned and paid proportionately to the amounts paid or credited as paid on the shares during any portion or portions of the period in respect of which the dividend is paid; but if any share is issued on terms providing that it shall rank for dividend as from a particular date, such share shall rank for dividend accordingly.

121. The directors may deduct from any dividend payable to any member all sums of money (if any) immediately payable by him to the company on account of calls or otherwise in relation to the shares of the company.

122. Any general meeting declaring a dividend or bonus may direct payment of such dividend or bonus wholly or partly by the distribution of specific assets and in particular of paid up shares, debentures or debenture stock of any other company or in one or more of such ways, and the directors shall give effect to such resolution, and where any difficulty arises in regard to such distribution, the directors may settle the same as they think expedient, and in particular may issue fractional certificates and fix the value for distribution of such specific assets or any part thereof and may determine that cash payments shall be made to any members upon the footing of the value so fixed, in order to adjust the rights of all the parties, and may vest any such specific assets in trustees as may seem expedient to the directors.

123. Any dividend, interest or other moneys payable in cash in respect of any shares may be paid by cheque or warrant sent through the post directed to the registered address of the holder, or, where there are joint holders, to the registered address of that one of the joint holders who is first named on the register or to such person and to such address as the holder or joint holders may in writing direct. Every such cheque or warrant shall be made payable to the order of the person to whom it is sent. Any one of two or more joint holders may give effectual receipts for any dividends, bonuses or other money; payable in respect of the shares held by them as joint holders.

124. No dividend shall bear interest against the company.

Capitalisation of Profits

130. The company in general meeting may upon the recommendation of the directors resolve that any sum for the time being standing to the credit of any of the company's reserves (including any capital redemption reserve fund or share premium account) or to the credit of profit and loss account be capitalised and applied on behalf of the members who would have been entitled to receive the same if the same had been distributed by way of dividend and in the same proportions either in or towards paying up amounts for the time being unpaid on any shares held by them respectively or in paying up in full unissued shares or debentures of the company of a nominal amount equal to the sum capitalised (such shares or debentures to be allotted and distributed credited as fully paid up to and amongst such holders in the proportions aforesaid) or partly in one way and partly in another, so however, that the only purpose for which sums standing to the credit of the capital redemption reserve fund or the share premium account be applied shall be those permitted by sections 62 and 64 of the Act.

130A. The company in general meeting may on the recommendation of the directors resolve that it is desirable to capitalise any part of the amount for the time being standing to the credit of any of the company's reserve accounts or to the credit of the profit and loss account which is not available for distribution by applying such sum in paying up in full unissued shares to be allotted as fully paid bonus shares to those members of the company who would have been entitled to that sum if it were distributed by way of dividend (and in the same proportions), and the directors shall give effect to such resolution.

131. Whenever a resolution is passed in pursuance of regulation 130 or 130a, the directors shall make all appropriations an applications of the undivided profits resolved to be capitalised thereby and all allotments and issues of fully paid shares or debentures, if any, and generally shall do all acts and things required to give effect thereto with full power to the directors to make such provision as they shall think fit for the case of shares or debentures becoming distributable in fractions (and, in particular, without prejudice to the generality of the foregoing, to sell the shares or debentures represented by such fractions and distribute the net proceeds of such sale amongst the members otherwise entitled to such fractions in due proportions) and also to authorise any person to enter on behalf of all the members concerned into an agreement with the company providing for the allotment to them respectively credited as fully paid up of any further shares or debentures to which they may become entitled on such capitalisation or, as the case may require, for the payment up by the application thereto of their respective proportions of the profits resolved to be capitalised of the amounts remaining unpaid on their existing shares and any agreement made under such authority shall be effective and binding on all such members.

Transfer of Shares

Re Discoverers Finance Corp. Ltd., Lindlar's Case
[1910] 1 Ch. 312

Fearing that the company was in difficulties and that he might be obliged to pay further calls on his shares, which were not fully paid up, the owner of 2,000 shares of £1 par sold them for £5 in all to a journeyman tanner. The consideration was never paid, nor even sought. If that agreement was effective to transfer title in the shares to the journeyman, the defendant would escape liability for calls made in respect of those shares.

BUCKLEY L.J.: . . . [316] The decisions upon the branch of the law with which we are here concerned are numerous. Care is necessary to avoid the danger which exists of allowing the attention to be distracted from the principles which underlie all those decisions, and to be drawn into an examination of the minute differences of fact and inferences of fact upon which judges have in different cases acted in forming their conclusions as to the facts to which they are about to apply those principles.

We propose first to state the principles as we understand them. By section 22 of the Companies Act, 1862, which is reproduced as section 22 of the Companies (Consolidation) Act, 1908 (same as section 79 of the 1963 Act), it is provided that the shares in a company under these Acts shall be capable of being transferred in manner provided by the regulations of the company. The regulations of the company may impose fetters upon the right of transfer. In the absence of restrictions in the articles the shareholder has by virtue of the statute the right to transfer his shares without the consent of anybody to any transferee, even though he be a man of straw, provided it is a bona fide transaction in the sense that it is an out and out disposal of the property without retaining any interest in the shares – that the transferor bona fide divests himself of all benefit . . . . [317] It was the policy of these Acts to give a free right of disposition, leaving it to the regulations of the company to impose such restrictions upon its exercise as might be desired. In the absence of restrictions it is competent to a transferor, notwithstanding that the company is in extremis, to compel registration of a transfer to a transferee notwithstanding that the latter is a person not competent to meet the unpaid liability upon the shares. Even if the transfer be executed for the express purpose of relieving the transferor from liability, the directors cannot upon that ground refuse to register it unless there is in the articles some provision so enabling them.

The cases which are generally regarded as the leading cases upon this branch of the law are cases decided before 1862. [Many of those] were cases in which the right to transfer rested not upon the statutory provision which has been mentioned, but upon such rights as arose upon the delivery of an instrument by whose delivery the shares were taken to pass. In the subsequent cases since

1862 (and they have been numerous) we do not remember that reference was made to the difference which arises by reason of the fact that the right to transfer is in cases under the Companies Acts a statutory right. It is a difference which in our judgment gives the transferor a greater right if that be necessary than existed in such a company as was the subject of the [Pre-1862] decision[s].

In that which follows the authorities are divided into three classes. . . .

[318] The first is the case where the articles contain no clause allowing the directors to reject a transferee. In such case the law is that a shareholder may up to the last moment before liquidation, and for the express purpose of escaping liability, transfer his partly-paid shares to a transferee, even though the latter be a pauper, and may compel the directors to register that transfer made avowedly for the purpose of avoiding liability, provided his transfer be an out and out transfer reserving to himself no beneficial right to the shares, direct or indirect. Whether the transfer is of that character is a question of fact. . . . [320] [Any] liability of the transferor in every case arises not from the fact that he has paid or become liable to pay something to the transferee, but upon the fact that he has reserved to himself a benefit in respect of the shares. If that be found not to be the case, then the transfer to a man of straw is effectual to protect the transferor.

The investigation whether the transfer is or is not an out and out transfer, is, of course, an investigation of the true relations subsisting between the transferor and the transferee. But if this inquiry is answered by finding that the transfer is out and out, there is in the absence of an approval clause in the articles, and in the absence of facts which bring the case within the third class presently mentioned, an end of the matter so far as any rights of the liquidator are concerned. Suppose the out and out transfer was procured by misrepresentation practised by the transferor towards the transferee. This will give the latter rights against the former, but with these the liquidator is not concerned. He has no right arising from this cause of action, assuming it to exist as between the other [321] parties. If the transferee initiates against the transferor successful proceedings, the liquidator no doubt can and ought to give his sanction under section 131 of the Act of 1862, or section 205 of the Act of 1908, if the result will be that he will obtain as contributory a solvent transferor in place of an insolvent transferee. But in such case the result is attained not by virtue of any right subsisting in the liquidator, but by the liquidator consenting to the successful assertion of a right subsisting in some one else. . . .

The second class of case is where the articles do contain a clause empowering the directors to reject a transferee whom they do not approve. In these cases the principle is that the transferor cannot escape liability if he has actively by falsehood or passively by concealment, induced the directors to pass and register a transfer (even though it be an out and out transfer) which, if he had not so deceived or concealed, they would have refused to register. Here again the question is one of fact. It is not sufficient to shew that the transferee's address was incorrect or that the description of his occupation was not accurate, or the like. The Court must arrive at the conclusion that therefrom resulted such a state of things as that if the directors had known the truth they would not have registered the transfer.

The third class of case is one which may arise in either one of the two classes of case above mentioned. It is the case in which the transferor has obtained the advantage of executing and registering his transfer to a man of straw upon an opportunity obtained by him fraudulently or in breach of some duty which he owed the corporation. As, for instance, if he (being in a position so to do) has procured the postponement of the commencement of the winding-up in order to get time to execute and tender such a transfer for registration, or if by collusion with the directors he has procured them in breach of their duty to pass a transfer which they ought not to have passed. The last is a ground which might have been material in the present case if it had been proved, which it has not.

Part II of Table A article 3

The directors may in their absolute discretion, and without assigning any reason therefor, decline to register any transfer of any share, whether or not it is a fully paid share.

Tangney v. Clarence Hotels Ltd
[1933] I.R. 51

The company's articles of association empowered the directors to refuse to register any transfer of shares to someone who in their opinion 'is not a desirable person to admit to membership'. The plaintiff, who held some shares in the company bought more shares; but the directors refused to register those shares in his name.

JOHNSTON J.: . . . [59] The first matter that was discussed by counsel for the Company, namely, the point that the plaintiff, being merely the transferee of the shares, has no *locus standi* as such and no right to take proceedings against the Company to compel the Company to register him as the owner of the shares, is wholly unsustainable. The transferee of shares is the proper person to take such a step, and were it not that the transferor has been given a statutory right, notwithstanding the fact that by the transfer the shares have passed from him outright, to apply to the Company to enter the transferee's name on the register, he would have no power whatsoever to do so. A transferee's right and privileges in regard to this matter are perfectly plain when the nature of a public company registered under the Companies Acts is considered and when the provisions of those Acts as to shares, stock and the proprietary interest that a 'member' of the company is entitled to, and the rights of transfer, and the method by which that proprietary interest may be transferred, are taken into account; and I would be prepared to hold, even without the assistance of sects. 28 and 32 of the Companies (Consolidation) Act, 1908, that a transferee's right was as I have stated it.

It is quite idle for this Company and the Directors to contend, as they both have done, that a person to whom a member of a company has transferred his stock or his share has no such privity with the company as would entitle him to go to the company with his deed of transfer and insist upon his being registered as the owner of the shares. Even were sects. 28 and 32 less clear than they are, the whole course of the existing statutory law would point to that conclusion. As a matter of fact, however, the matter has been set at rest by *Skinner's* case (14 Q.B.D. 882) – a case to which I was not referred during the course of the argument. In that case a claim had been brought against [60] a company by a transferor of shares for damages for delay on the part of the company in registering the transfer. It was held by the Court of Appeal (Brett M.R. and Baggalley and Brown L.JJ.) that it was primarily the duty of the transferee to have procured the registration; and, as the consideration appearing on the face of the deed was merely a nominal sum, the plaintiff could, under the particular circumstances, recover only nominal damages from the company. Brett, M.R., at p. 887, says: 'So that when the transfer has been executed and handed over to the transferee, it is then for the latter to pay the consideration money and to get the transfer registered. Now is there any difference made in respect of this by sect. 26 of the Companies Act, 1867? I think not. It was not, I think, intended by the Legislature that that enactment should alter or have any effect on the duty of the transferee, and that it is still his duty, as it was before that enactment, to get himself registered as a member of the company in respect of the shares which have been transferred to him, and that this sect. 26 of the Companies Act, 1867, was only for the protection of the transferor in case the transferee failed to perform his duty.'

There must therefore be a declaration in favour of the plaintiff that this action is properly constituted and that the plaintiff as transferee of the shares referred to in the statement of claim is entitled to have brought the action to have the respective rights of the parties determined.

The second question that has been raised is that, on the true construction of Article 21 of the Articles of Association, it was, and is, a condition precedent that before any member of the Company can transfer his shares to any person he must serve a notice upon the Company of his intention to do so, giving the name and address of the proposed transferee, and that no valid transfer can take place unless and until that notice has been served. Article 21 is in the following terms:

"Any member proposing to transfer any share shall give notice in writing of this intention so to do to the Directors, giving the name and address of the proposed transferee; and if the Directors are of opinion that the proposed transferee is not a desirable person to admit to membership, they may decline to register the transfer of any such share, and it shall be lawful for them, within three months from the receipt of such notice, to transfer any such share to such person as the Directors shall nominate, at such price as the person giving notice and the nomineee of the Directors may agree upon; and in default of agreement [61] at such price as the Directors may determine, and the Directors may cause the name of their nominee to be entered in the Register in respect of the share transferred by them, and the receipt of the Company shall be a full discharge to the nominee of the Directors, and after his name has been entered in the Register the validity of the transaction shall not be questioned by any person. The proceeds of any share transferred by the Directors under this Article shall be applied in or towards satisfaction of the debts, liabilities, or engagements (if any) to the Company of the member whose share is transferred, and the residue (if any) paid to such member, his executors, administrators, or assigns. . . ."

It seems to me that Article 21 must be construed reasonably and not oppressively, and I do not think that it was intended by the framers of the same that service of such a notice was to be a condition precedent to the execution by the holder of shares of an agreement to transfer or even to the execution of an actual transfer deed. A transfer is not legally complete until the transferee has been registered in the books of the Company, and it was not incorrect for the Article to refer to a person to whom shares had been transferred by deed but who had not yet [62] been registered as 'the proposed transferee'. The Directors are given the power, not 'to decline to permit the execution by the proposed transferor of a deed of transfer' but merely to 'decline to register the transfer of any such share'. This point was made clear by Eve J., in *In re Copal Varnish Co. Ltd.* [1917] 2 Ch. 349, where the provision in question was this: 'No share shall be transferred to any person who is not already a member of the company without the consent of the directors.' Even that clause was held not to amount to a condition precedent. Eve J. said: 'So long as prior to the completion of the transaction an opportunity is given to the directors sitting as a board to determine whether the proposed transferee is a person whom they are prepared to admit as a member of the company, the conditions imposed by the Article are, in my opinion, complied with, and the contract into which the vendor on becoming a shareholder entered with his co-shareholders is sufficiently discharged.' In a somewhat analogous case – namely that of the pre-emption clause in sect. 1 of the Land Law (Ireland) Act 1881 – the Vice-Chancellor and Bewley J. arrived at a similar result in the cases of *Fisher v. Coan* [1894] 1 I.R. 179, and *Meath v. Megan* [1897] 2 I.R. 39 at p. 48. I am, therefore, prepared to give a declaration that on the construction of Article 21 service upon the Company of the notice referred to in that Article was not a condition precedent to the execution of a transfer of the shares by the Hibernian Bank to the plaintiff.

The third argument that has been addressed to me by the defendants, on the construction of this Article, is that the power given therein to the Directors is absolute and unrestricted, and is not confined to the case of a transfer of shares to persons who are not already shareholders and, as such, members of the Company. I am asked by the defendants to hold that the word 'member-ship' should be read as meaning 'membership in respect of the shares which are proposed to be transferred'. The plaintiff, on the other hand, says that the Article should be read as it stands, and that, read in that way, its meaning and intention are perfectly plain. Whenever a deed of transfer is submitted to the Directors they are empowered to decline to register the transfer; but their power to do so is not unlimited. It only arises whenever they are of the opinion that the proposed transferee is not a desirable person to admit to membership. It seems to me that that clause [63] was intended to meet the case of a stranger proposing to come into the family, as it were. In such a case the Directors were given the power to determine whether such person was 'a desirable person', and their power to decide that question seems to be absolute and cannot be questioned, except by showing affirmatively that they are exercising their pow-ers capriciously or wantonly: *Ex parte Penney* (8 Ch. App. 446). As was pointed out by Eve J., in *In re Bede Shipping Co., Ltd.* [1917] 1 Ch. 123, the right of an owner of shares to get rid of them by transfer is absolute except in so far as it is restricted by contract inter socios, and 'it is to the Articles of Association that we must turn for the purpose of ascertaining the nature and the extent of the restrictions imposed'. The powers that have been conferred upon Direc-tors in this respect vary widely in their extent and operation. One of the com-monest forms of such restrictions, as Cozens Hardy M.R. pointed out in the same case (p. 132), was and is the power to restrict the transfer of shares except to persons who were already members of the company. That device has been adopted by company draftsmen in many different forms – that is, to place no restrictions upon the circulation of the shares amongst the members of the company, but to enable the heavy hand of the Directors to come down when a stranger seeks to enter into the charmed circle. This is the policy that is to be discerned in Articles 42 and 43 in the present case. Whenever the Directors with the sanction of the company decide to increase the capital of the Com-pany by the issue of new shares, all such new shares must, subject to any direction of the Company that sanctions the increase of capital 'be offered to the members in proportion to the existing shares held by them'; and if new shares are issued in the future the plaintiff will be entitled to his proportion of them as a matter of course, and the Directors cannot refuse to let him have them on the ground that he is not 'a desirable person'.

The case of *In re Dublin North City Milling Co.* [1909] 1 I.R. 179, which is relied upon by the defendants, is of no assistance in this case. The article in question there provided that the Directors 'may decline to register any transfer of shares . . . unless the transferee is approved of by the board'; and it was held that the Directors could decline to register a transfer of shares to a person who was already a member of the company. This was not a decision upon [64] the construction of an Article of Association. It was an ordinary case where the Directors had an unrestricted power to decline to permit the registration of any transfer of shares. The transferee sought to get behind the power conferred by the Article by contending that because he was already a member of the company, the action of the board could not possibly be *bona fide*. The argument of the transferee's counsel opened in this way: 'The refusal of the directors to register the transfer is not *bona fide*'; and Meredith M.R. decided that he could not come to such a conclusion of fact upon the mere ground that the transferee was already a member of the company.

I cannot accede to the argument of the defendants that a shareholder is a member of the Company in regard to the particular shares he holds. That is too narrow a view of the principles of the law as to the nature and constitution of a public company. The Act of 1862, under which this Company was constituted, provides (sect. 18) that upon the registration of the company, 'the subscribers of the Memorandum of Association, together with such other persons as may from time to time become members of the company, shall thereupon be a body corporate by the name contained in the Memorandum of Association, capable forthwith of exercising all the functions of an incorporated company'. Sect. 23 provides further that the subscribers 'and every other person who has agreed to become a member of a company under this Act, and whose name is entered on the register of members, shall be deemed to be a member of the company'. These provisions are continued with small verbal differences, by sect. 16, sub-sect. 2, and sect. 24 of the Act of 1908. It seems to me, therefore, that the word 'membership' in Article 21 can only mean membership of the corporate body of which the members in the aggregate consist.

I shall therefore declare that on the true construction of Article 21 the Directors had no power to refuse to register the transfer of shares by the Hibernian Bank to the plaintiff, he being at the time a shareholder and a member of the Company.

In re Hafner
[1943] I.R. 426

The company was a small family company and one of its articles of association was very similar to clause 3 of part II of Table A (supra). The plaintiff inherited some shares in the company but, without assigning any reasons, the directors refused to register him as a member. Among the facts that came out in evidence was that one director drew £7,000 per annum in remuneration and another director had a service contract providing for £3,000 per annum salary, the duration was 20 years, but if the company was wound up before that term expired, the director would become entitled to the equivalent of £1,500 per annum for the residue of the term.

BLACK J.: . . . [438] [W]hen discovery was obtained, it came to light that the company, or in reality, the three directors, who are the defendants in this action, had voted or agreed to pay various salaries and emoluments to one another, which, the plaintiff says, would swallow up the net profits, and thereby reduce the value of the 500 shares bequeathed to him to a cipher. He says that this procedure would amount to a fraudulent abuse of their fiduciary position by the defendants, and that the directors' refusal to register him in respect of these 500 shares was decided upon with the intention and for the purpose of facilitating them in making this fraudulent procedure more easily effective. That being his view, he seeks to have the refusal of registration overridden by order of the Court. Having made the discovery and formed the conclusion in question, the plaintiff sought leave of this Court to amend his statement of claim so as to raise the contentions mentioned. This leave was granted by me and my decision in that regard was upheld by the Supreme Court. The statement of claim has accordingly been amended, and a new ground is now put forward for requiring the defendants, as directors of the company, to register the transfer of the 500 shares to the plaintiff, namely, that in refusing such registration the directors, instead of exercising a *bona fide* discretion, acted with a view to compel the plaintiff to sell the said shares at an undervalue, and also with a view to preventing the plaintiff from questioning the payment of the impugned emoluments.

In dealing with this question, two Articles of Association are in question. These are as follows:

Article 6. 'The directors may, in their absolute and uncontrolled discretion and without assigning any reason, refuse to register any transfer of shares, and clause 20 of Table A shall be modified accordingly.'

Article 7. 'No member may transfer or dispose of his shares or any of them without first offering them to the directors of the company, who shall have the first option of purchasing same at a fair market price to be fixed, in [439] the event of dispute, by the auditors of the company at the expense of the vendor. On payment of the price so fixed, the registered owner shall forthwith transfer the shares in manner directed by the directors.'

Now it seems to me that unless the plaintiff was entitled as a matter of law to demand to be registered, he cannot compel the company to register him however fraudulent the directors' object in refusing registration might be. The statement of claim does not expressly allege that the plaintiff was entitled to be registered. But if I might paraphrase it freely, it alleges certain facts from which the plaintiff considers that his right *prima facie* to be registered must follow. Of course it is the pleader's business to plead facts and not law. What, then, are these facts? Freely paraphrased they are as follows:

(*a*) The late Frederick A. Hafner was the registered holder of the 500 shares in question.

(*b*) By his last will he bequeathed them to the plaintiff absolutely.

(*c*) The executors by a proper form of transfer transferred the said shares to the plaintiff.

(*d*) The plaintiff duly transmitted this transfer to the company for registration.

The plaintiff then alleges in substance that the directors' refusal to register him was fraudulent, and claims that he is therefore entitled to be registered. He plainly assumes that the defendants have refused to register him purporting to exercise the discretion given them by Art. 6. But the defendants have taken care not to admit either by their pleadings or by their evidence that they purported to act under Art. 6. They have not disclosed which of the Articles they purported to act under, and this information has not been elicited from them either by pleading or by cross-examination. The mystery had been well guarded. But their counsel have claimed for them that they were entitled to refuse registration because the requirement in Art. 7 was not, as they say, complied with.

I am thus obliged to deal with both Articles.

First, Article 6. It is well settled that under such an Article as this the directors may refuse to register a transfer. It is equally settled that the directors' power in this regard is a fiduciary one and must be exercised in the interest of the company as a whole. They must not exercise it arbitrarily, capriciously, or corruptly. They are not bound to assign their reasons, and the Court is not entitled to infer merely from their omission to do so that their reasons were not legitimate.

[440] Hedged round with the privilege of remaining mute and the *prima facie* presumption of rectitude, the astutely silent director who wishes to exercise this power illegitimately may well consider himself all but invulnerable. No need to speak and no unfavourable inference from reticence – that is the settled rule. Yet, like many another settled rule, I am persuaded that it is not proof against possible exceptions. The case of *Bell Brothers* (7 T.L.R. 689), was one illustration of this, and I have to consider whether the present case provides another.

In *Bell's* case, certain directors exercised an unrestricted power to refuse a transfer and also stood upon their privilege of declining to give any reasons. But it so happened that one of the directors, like Mr McGrath in this case, was executor of the will of the deceased owner of the shares in question. The shares were directed to be sold to raise money to provide for the widow's annuity. A Mr Hodgson purchased, and took out a summons for confirmation of the contract. The executor-director opposed; but the contract was confirmed and he was reluctantly obliged to execute the transfer as executor – just as Mr McGrath as executor executed the transfer of 500 shares to the plaintiff here, although it does not appear that he did it reluctantly. The director in *Bell's* case, then, as director, proceeded to join with his co-directors in refusing registration of the transfer he had himself executed as executor, precisely as Mr McGrath joined in refusing as director to register the very transfer he had himself executed as executor. So far the likeness of the two cases is remarkable. But it turned out in *Bell's* case that the director in question, when opposing the sale to Hodgson, had admitted that he wanted to have the shares sold to his father and co-director for the purpose of keeping all the company shares in the Bell family. Upon these facts Mr Justice Chitty put two and two together. He concluded that the admitted motive for opposing the sale to Hodgson was also likely to be a motive for refusing registration to Hodgson, and he held that a refusal actuated by such a motive would not be a legitimate exercise of the directors' discretion. If the learned judge had stopped there, it seems to me that the directors might still have defied interference by the Court; for proof that they had a motive which was illegitimate, would not negative the possibility that they might also have had another and sufficient motive which was not illegitimate, and I apprehend that if directors had a good [441] and adequate reason for refusing a transfer upon which they would have acted in any case, the fact that they had at the same time an ulterior and perhaps still stronger motive of an illegitimate character would not invalidate the exercise of their discretion. I think that in order to interfere the Court must not only firm that the directors had an invalid motive, but it must also find that they had no valid motive that might be itself sufficient. That is precisely what Mr Justice Chitty did. Yet this finding would have been impossible if the rule continued to apply that directors who do not state any reason for refusing a transfer must be presumed to have had valid reasons and that no unfavourable inference can be drawn from their silence. Once a reason which was invalid was proved to the satisfaction of the Court, the rule ceased to hold good, and the Court felt itself free to examine the possibility of other reasons that would not be invalid and even to comment upon and draw inferences from the directors' failure to state their reasons, although in *Bell's* case their solicitor presumed to suggest possible reasons for them which the Court rejected. They themselves gave no reasons.

Now in the present case it is very clearly alleged in the statement of claim that the defendant directors had an illegitimate purpose in refusing to register the plaintiff in respect of his 500 shares, and this alleged purpose is plainly specified. It is alleged that the object was to compel the plaintiff to sell the 500 shares at an under value and also to prevent him from questioning the acts of the defendants in voting themselves large emoluments, which, it is said, would have the effect of reducing, if not of extinguishing altogether, the dividends which otherwise the plaintiff would be entitled beneficially to receive, whether registered as a member or not. When the statement of claim refers to 'compelling' the plaintiff to sell, of course it means putting pressure upon him to do so by rendering it unprofitable for him to refuse to sell, such pressure as an average business man would think amounted to virtual compulsion. Similarly, when mention is made of 'preventing' the plaintiff from questioning the defendants' act, I interpret 'preventing' to mean 'making it more difficult' for the plaintiff to question those acts, and thereby tending to prevent him from doing so. I do not think the defendants could literally prevent him from questioning the emoluments concerned, but I do think that if he were deprived of the privilege of attending the [442] company's meetings, he would lose a valuable opportunity of questioning the acts of its directors; and, moreover, by not being a member of the company his remedy, while not in my opinion taken away, might well be rendered more difficult – a possibility made very obvious by the fact that Mr FitzGibbon and Mr Leonard seemed to take different views as to what that remedy would be.

In partial, but only partial, reply to all this it is said that, even if refusal of registration would virtually compel the plaintiff to sell the shares, it would not compel him to do so at an undervalue, since the price would be fixed by the auditor and would have to be the fair value on the assumption that the impugned emoluments, if excessive, were reduced to proper and legitimate amounts. I am disposed to agree with that view of the auditor's duty in fixing the fair value. But, even so, as I suggested during the arguments, the refusal to register the plaintiff might still virtually compel him to sell at an undervalue, because the directors might decline to exercise any right of pre-emption, and I think it is only when they exercise that right that they are bound to pay the price fixed by the auditor. If they waived that right and left the plaintiff free to sell his shares as best he could, I think the directors, like any outsider, would be free to buy at any price they could get the plaintiff to accept. Hence, if the directors declined to pre-empt as of right, refusal of registration would be calculated to put pressure upon the plaintiff to get rid of these shares, whether to the directors or to outside purchasers, at an unfair under-value, always assuming that the payment of the emoluments complained of would be illegitimate and would, therefore, illegitimately reduce the market value of the shares.

Were, then, the impugned emoluments justified as a reasonable commercial proposition? . . . [443] I feel no manner of doubt that the payment of these bloated emoluments would convert this flourishing company from a dividend-paying concern into a director-remunerating [444] enterprise, either paying no dividends at all or at best paying only such reduced dividends as would amount to a grave injustice to the plaintiff, who, after all, was the nephew of the men who made the business and had been left 500 shares in it. The payments of these sums would benefit Mr and Mrs Powderley to a substantial extent at the expense of the plaintiff, and for the reasons I have mentioned would be facilitated by the refusal to put the plaintiff on the register of members. I hold that it would be a natural, and I imagine an inevitable, consequence of that refusal that the payment of these indefensible emoluments would be facilitated, and that Mr and Mrs Powderley would be more easily enabled to reap unjustifiable benefits to a substantial extent at the expense of Mr Olhausen. Now, when parties take a decision calculated to bring them personal gain as its natural, if not inevitable, result, it is in accord with a well known legal principle to infer that they intended that decision to produce or facilitate that result, and that the facilitating of that result was at least a motive for taking the decision. This inference seems the more justifiable when one is not given, and cannot regard as apparent, any other reason that could justify such a decision on the part of the directors, who were bound to have regard only to the interests of the company as a whole. I am, therefore, forced to the conclusion that a desire to facilitate the payment of these emoluments was at least a motive actuating the decision of the defendants to refuse to register the plaintiff in respect of the 500 shares.

I consider such an exercise of their discretion so actuated would not be a *bona fide* discharge of their fiduciary duty, and that, if they acted under Art. 6, at least one illegitimate motive must be attributed to them. Once an illegitimate motive for such a decision is brought home to directors, I think the normal legal presumption that they acted legitimately must go by the board, and that I am set free to consider whether they should be given credit for having had other and better reasons, and, further, that I am free to comment – as Mr Justice Chitty did in *Bell's* case – upon their omission to state what any of their reasons were. I feel no longer bound to ignore their silence, or to refuse to draw any inference from it. It was not ignored in *Bell's* case and I cannot ignore it in this case. So far as I am aware, the judgment in *Bell's* case has never been dissented from in any particular. It has stood the [445] test of a good many years. While no reasons have been volunteered by the defendants, who stood firmly on their privilege of reticence, certain innuendos loomed up in the evidence, based on unconfirmed and not very precise rumours and also on a query made by the plaintiff regarding one of the Hafner formulae at a time when he was being paid at the rate of £1,000 a year as a kind of general supervisor of the business. It seems he also ventured to offer some critical opinion about the methods of the firm's pig buyer. Without further elucidation I could only regard these complaints about the plaintiff as trumpery reasons for refusing to register him as a shareholder, if, indeed, they were meant to do more than hint that something graver lurked in the background. Without special information I can think of only one plausible reason for this refusal, namely, that he was an important member of a competing firm. But this reason was not even suggested by the defendants' counsel, or by their solicitor, Mr Beatty, who gave evidence, as a like reason was insinuated by the directors' solicitor in Bell's Case. In that case, Mr Justice Chitty remarked that if the directors themselves had sworn it was the true reason, he might have accepted it, but that as they did not do so, he inferred that was not the true reason. I adopt the same attitude here. Perhaps it would have seemed daring to suggest such a reason after Mrs Powderley had gone out of her way to bring the plaintiff into the firm and to give him a supervising job at £1,000 a year.

On account of the considerations I have detailed, I consider that I am entitled, as a matter of law, and coerced, as a matter of fact, to conclude that if, and so far as, the defendants' refusal to register the plaintiff was based upon the discretion given them by Art. 6, it cannot be justified at all. But, as I have said, the defendants have taken care to fit their bow with two strings, and although one of them is sundered, there remains another tougher texture. Art. 7 has still to be reckoned with.

The judgment was appealed to the Supreme Court.

SULLIVAN C.J.: . . . [471] In seeking to establish that the action of the directors was not *bona fide* in exercise of the fiduciary power conferred upon them by Art. 6, the plaintiff was faced with the difficulty that under that Article the directors need not assign any reason for their refusal to register the transfer, and that the mere omission of the directors to state their reasons would not entitle the Court to infer that their reasons were not proper and legitimate.

And accordingly the plaintiff had to adduce evidence of relevant circumstances from which the Court could legitimately infer that the directors had acted improperly. From the evidence given at the hearing Black J. was satisfied that such an inference should be drawn, and he accordingly held as a fact that the refusal to register the transfer was not the result of a *bona fide* exercise by the directors of their discretion under Art. 6. The evidence was read to this Court and was discussed at length by counsel on both sides, and after full consideration we have come to the conclusion that the decision of the learned judge on that matter was right. Any difficulty that we have had in arriving at that conclusion was mainly attributable to the fact that, in respect of some incidental but material matters, inconsistent and contradictory evidence was given by the same witness. In such circumstances it was for the learned judge to decide which evidence he accepted, and, in the absence of any statement to the contrary by him, we think that we are entitled to assume, and should assume, that he accepted the evidence that would tend to support the conclusion at which he arrived on the main question, and we accordingly do so. . . . [474]

There can be little doubt that, if the transfer to the plaintiff had been registered, he would at the next meeting of shareholders have challenged the action of the directors in fixing such salaries, and there can be as little doubt that this was in the minds of the directors, when they decided to refuse the plaintiffs application. It may be, as Mr FitzGibbon contended, that the plaintiff, while not a member of the company, would be entitled to apply to the Court for a declaration that the resolutions authorising these salaries were void, and for an injunction to restrain the directors from paying them but even if that be so, the directors would realise that the plaintiff would be more likely to make such an application if he was a member.

We are satisfied that the learned judge was entitled to come to the conclusion, as an inference of fact, that a desire that the payment of these salaries should not be questioned by the plaintiff was a motive actuating the directors' refusal to register the transfer to the plaintiff, and, in the absence of any evidence that would indicate a different motive — and there was no such evidence beyond a general statement by each director that it was in the interest of the company that registration of the transfer should be refused – we think that conclusion is unassailable. That a refusal actuated by such a motive could not be supported as a decision arrived at by the directors *bona fide* in exercise of their power conferred upon them by Art. 6 is not denied.

It was further contended on behalf of the plaintiff that in refusing to register the transfer the directors had in view a further object, namely, to compel the plaintiff to sell his shares to the directors, or to some of them at an undervalue. In support of that contention it was said that the directors contemplated that when, by reason of the salaries payable to them, the plaintiff had been deprived of any reasonable prospect of receiving a dividend on his shares, he would be willing to sell them at almost any price, and that the directors, who would under Art. 7 have the first option of purchasing them, would then purchase them at an undervalue.

In answer to that argument counsel for the defendants pointed out that Art. 7 provides that on a sale to the directors under that Article the fair market price of the shares must, if the plaintiff so requires, be fixed by the auditors of the company, and they contended that in fixing the price the [475] auditors would have regard to such remuneration only as it would be reasonable to pay, and not to the remuneration that was in fact paid, to the directors.

The expert evidence on that matter was given by three chartered accountants: Mr Brock, who was examined on behalf of the plaintiff, and Mr Purtill and Mr Shortall, who were witnesses for the defendants. The evidence of Mr Purtill and of Mr Shortall would support the contention of the defendants' counsel, as would the evidence of Mr Brock on his examination-in-chief, with which his evidence on re-examination does not seem to be quite consistent.

We think that the weight of evidence on this point is in favour of the view expressed by Mr Purtill and Mr Shortall, and Black J., who had the advantage of seeing and hearing these witnesses, says that he was disposed to agree with that view.

We are, therefore, not satisfied that by refusing to register the transfer the directors could compel the plaintiff to sell his shares to them at an undervalue if they purchased the shares by virtue of their right of pre-emption under Art. 7, and there is nothing in the evidence that would suggest – and it would not, we think, be reasonable to suppose – that they ever contemplated the possibility of purchasing the shares otherwise than in exercise of that right.

We are, therefore, of opinion that, while it would be quite a reasonable inference from the evidence that the object that the directors had in view in refusing to register the transfer was to compel the plaintiff to sell his shares to them, it would not be reasonable to infer that their object was to compel him to sell the shares to them at an undervalue.

But as we are satisfied that the directors were actuated by one improper motive, the fact that we are not satisfied that they had a second improper motive is not material, as it would not affect the plaintiff's right to a declaration that the refusal of the directors was not *bona fide* in exercise of their discretion under Art. 6.

The relief, however, which the plaintiff seeks is a declaration that he is entitled to be registered as the holder of the 500 shares, and an order directing the company to register the transfer of these shares to him.

Black J. refused to make such a declaration or order on the ground that Art. 7 of the Articles of Association, when read in conjunction with section 29 of the Companies (Consolidation) Act, 1908, and with Art. 22 of Table A, applied to the transfer of these shares by the executors of the testator's will to the plaintiff, and that as, admittedly, these shares had not in the first instance been offered to the directors [476] as prescribed by Art. 7, the executors were not entitled to transfer the shares to the plaintiff, and the directors were therefore entitled to refuse to register the transfer.

Counsel for the plaintiff contend that in so holding the learned judge misdirected himself in law, and, in the alternative, that the directors, by their action in entertaining under Art. 6 the plaintiff's application to register the transfer, waived the right to refuse registration on the ground that the provision of Art. 7 had not been complied with. Both questions have been fully and ably argued before us.

The conclusion at which we have arrived on the latter question renders it unnecessary to finally determine the former. But in deference to the learned judge and to the arguments that were addressed to this Court, we think it right to say, that, as at present advised, we are of opinion that, for reasons which he states, he was right in holding that the provisions of Art. 7 applied to the transfer of the shares by the executors to the plaintiff.

In considering the question of waiver we must in any event assume the existence of the right, the waiver of which is in question, and accordingly we assume that these shares should in the first instance have been offered by the executors to the directors.

The law on the subject of waiver is reasonably clear and it is not in controversy in this case. It is sufficient to say that a person, who to his knowledge, is entitled to a right may waive it by conduct which is inconsistent with the continued existence of that right, and the fact that another person acts upon such waiver is sufficient consideration to make it effectual.

In the present case the directors could, in our opinion, waive their right to require that the shares should be first offered to them. They would, admittedly, do so if they registered the transfer to the plaintiff, and we think that they also do so if, instead of calling upon the plaintiff to offer the shares to them, they proceed to deal with and dispose of the application for registration under Art. 6 by refusing to register the transfer.

We are of opinion that the directors should consider and decide whether they will exercise their option to purchase the shares under Art. 7 before they proceed to consider the exercise of their discretionary power under Art. 6.

The Articles contemplate that when a member proposes to transfer his shares he will first offer them to the directors. On that being done two alternative courses are open to the directors: 1, they may decide to purchas the shares, and, if they do so, they are then bound to purchase them at [477] a price to be fixed in default of agreement by the auditors of the company, or 2, they may decline to purchase the shares. In either event the directors' rights under Art. 7 are at an end, but in the latter event their rights under Art. 6 would be exercisable when a transfer of the shares is submitted to them for registration.

Accordingly it seems to us that the fact that the directors have considered and disposed of an application to register a transfer under Art. 6, whether such application is granted or refused, indicates clearly that the directors have waived their rights under Art. 7, as those rights should have been exercised before the application was finally disposed of.

In the present case the directors, with the knowledge of their rights under Art. 7, considered and refused the plaintiffs application under Art. 6. They have by so doing waived their rights under Art. 7, and the plaintiff has acted upon that waiver by bringing this suit in which he challenges the validity of their action under Art. 6.

We are therefore of opinion that they are not entitled to rely on the fact that the shares were not offered to them in compliance with Art. 7 as a ground for their refusal to register the transfer of those shares to the plaintiff, and accordingly that the plaintiff is entitled to a declaration that he is entitled to be registered as the holder of the shares, and to an order directing the company to register the transfer to him.

Walsh v. Cassidy & Co. Ltd
[1951] Ir. Jur. Rep. 47

A private limited company's articles of association dealt with the transfer of shares, *inter alia*:

> "31 (a) No share shall . . . be transferred to a person who is not a member so long as any member or any person selected by the directors as one whom it is desirable in the interests of the company to admit to membership is willing to purchase the same at the fair value.

> (b) In order to ascertain whether any member or person selected as aforesaid is willing to purchase any share, the person proposing to transfer the share (hereinafter called 'the proposing transferor') shall give notice in writing (hereinafter called the 'transfer notice') to the company at its registered office that he desires to transfer the same. Such transfer notice shall specify the sum he fixes as the fair value of the share and shall constitute the company his agent for the sale of the share. . . .

(j) The directors may, in all or any circumstances, and at all or any time or times refuse to register any transfer of any share or shares without assigning any reason therefor and whether the share or shares which it is proposed to transfer be fully paid up or not. . . ."

"32 Whenever any member of the company who is employed by the company in any capacity ceases to be so employed by the company the directors may at any time thereafter resolve that such member do retire and thereafter he shall be deemed to have served the company with a transfer notice pursuant to Art. 31 hereof and to have specified thereon the amount paid up on his shares as the fair value and subsequent proceedings may be taken on that footing and in accordance with the clauses of Art. 31 hereof. Notice of the passing of any such resolution shall be given to the member affected thereby."

The plaintiff in the first action, while a director and member of the company, was dismissed from the office and thereupon served on the company a notice under Art. 31(b) for the purpose of enabling him to transfer his shares at a fair value fixed by him. The remaining directors subsequently passed a resolution pursuant to Art. 32 deeming the plaintiff to have served on the company a notice under Art. 31 specifying the amount paid up on his shares as their fair value. The plaintiff in the second action, while a director and member of the company, served the company a similar notice under Art. 31(b) and on the following day gave three months notice of his intention to leave the employment of the company. The remaining directors thereupon determined this plaintiff's employment, paying him three months salary in lieu of notice, and passed a resolution pursuant to Art. 32 similar in effect to that passed in relation to the first plaintiff. In each case the value which would attach to the shares by virtue of the resolutions was less than the value which would attach by virtue of the notice served by the member.

Separate actions were brought by the plaintiffs claiming, inter alia, declarations that the notices served by them under Art. 31(b) were valid and effective and that the resolutions passed pursuant to Art. 32 were *ultra vires.*

KINGSMILL MOORE J.: [51] The question in this case is one of construction of the articles of the defendant company, more particularly of articles 31 and 32, more particularly still of article 32. Fraud on the part of the directors is not pleaded and therefore cannot be suggested; and it was further conceded at a late stage that no issue as to lack of *bona fides* was before the Court. The facts common to the case of all parties are only of importance as raising in a net form the problem of construction. Certain further facts, alleged in affidavits filed on behalf of the defendants and not expressly contradicted by the plaintiffs would be vital if any question of *bona fides* were involved; but in the absence of this issue I am not at liberty to take them into account nor to make any assumption as to their truth or falsity. If true they would, certainly in the case of Mr Walsh, dispose of any suggestion that the defendant directors had acted in any way harshly. If untrue, but believed by the defendant directors to be true, they would justify a claim by them that they were acting in what they believed to be the best interests of the company. If false and known by the defendant directors to be false, but nevertheless put forward by the defendant directors as the reasons for their action, a case of fraud might be made out; but the plaintiffs have carefully refrained from putting forward any such case.

Article 31, with certain minor and chiefly verbal variations, and one important addition, follows the standard form for private companies to be found in successive editions of vol. 1 of *Palmer's Company Forms*. The important addition is to be found in the first sentence of paragraph (j) which give the directors an unqualified and uncontrolled power to refuse to register any transfer. It is not suggested that there is anything illegal in this power and counsel for the defendants assert that a power of this nature is, if not usual, yet certainly not exceptional in private companies formed to take over a family business and to preserve the family interest. It certainly indicated clearly the desire of the draftsmen and the adopters of the articles that the directors should have an ultimate and unfettered control over transfers. The second sentence of this paragraph is the usual *Palmer* form and it is suggested by Mr Lavery that there is such an inconsistency between the two sentences as to show that the articles were not framed as a logically connected whole but were the result of some casual work with scissors and paste. I am invited in the [52] light of this conclusion to hold that the whole of articles 31 and 32 are inconsistent with each other and so to refrain from approaching the construction of these articles with a desire so to interpret them as to give to them both the maximum effective validity.

It is quite true that the second sentence of article 31(j) is unnecessary if the first sentence is to be given its full meaning. Mr Wilson suggests that the second sentence, though not necessary, is put in as a reminder of what would be the practice in normal circumstances in the same way as articles often repeat unnecessarily what are statutory provisions in the Companies Acts. This may be so, though it seems more likely that the draftsmen after adopting the standard form considered that the nature of the company demanded something more universal and added the first paragraph. Be this as it may I think the apparent surplusage is not by itself sufficient ground to make me approach the construction of articles 31 and 32 with a disposition to find an inconsistency between them or to assume that article 32 is not to be given its face value.

Article 32 also follows in its essentials an established *Palmer* form. The contention for the plaintiffs was that a service of the requisite notice under article 31 altered irrevocably the previous position and set in motion a machinery which must grind out to the end. Once such a notice was served, it was said, article 32 was displaced and the directors, even if they were entitled ultimately to refuse to register a transfer under article 31, yet could not call to their aid the provisions of article 32. On this view the serving of a notice under article 31 ensured that the shareholder must at least receive the fair price of his shares if his shares were disposed of at all. For the defendants it was argued that article 32 meant what it said, no more and no less. If the shareholder who served the notice under article 31 happened also to be a servant of the company and subsequently ceased to be so employed the directors might at any time thereafter resolve that he do retire (a phrase which it was agreed meant 'cease to be a member') and thereupon he was to be deemed to have served a transfer notice specifying the amount actually paid up on his shares. The result would be that he would only recover for his shares at most the paid-up value even though this might be but a fraction of the market value.

There would seem to be no half way house between these two interpretations of the articles; at least none was suggested. Either interpretation might in certain circumstances result in apparent hardship or absurdity. If the defendants are right a person who had bought the shares at their full market value and who subsequently took some minor employment under the company (*e.g.* as a visiting dentist under a welfare scheme) could never vacate such employment without the risk of having his shares forcibly transferred from him at their paid-up value. If the plaintiffs are right a trusted employee who had been allotted shares, perhaps free, perhaps at an undervalue, can betray his trust, damage the company, serve a notice ensuring that he gets the full value of his shares, retire from his position and use his realised money to set up a rival business. If an employee is dismissed his rights depend on whether he can serve a notice on the company under article 31 before the directors take action under article 32.

Mr Lavery for the plaintiffs was faced with this obvious argument that article 32 was clear and unambiguous and that in the absence of ambiguity effect must be given to the plain meaning of its words, even if its operation might sometimes work hardship; and with the second argument that the articles must be construed as a whole so as to give the fullest practical effect to both articles 31 and 32, whereas his contention, if successful, might have the effect of nullifying for all practical purposes the provisions of article 32. To displace these he called attention, by way of general observation, to the fact that the shareholders between them were the real owners of all the assets [53] of the company, and urged that a court should avoid, if in any way possible, a construction which would enable the directors to alienate compulsorily the property of a shareholder 'at a gross undervalue'. This argument perhaps goes too far, for in a case where no notice has been served under article 31 there is no doubt that article 32 enables directors to alienate, and indeed to acquire for themselves, shares of a member at less than their real value.

But the position of a shareholder cannot be so simply stated. He is not a mere owner in common, subject to certain restrictions in the articles. His position was carefully laid down by Kenny J. in the case of *Attorney-General v. Jameson* [1904] 2 I.R. 644.

The property of the shareholder is really a bundle of contractual rights and obligations and among those obligations is the disadvantage of having to submit to the operation of article 32 if the shareholder finds himself in the position of an employee whose employment has terminated. It has long been decided that there is nothing illegal in provisions whereby compulsory retirement is enforced *Sidebottom v. Kershaw Leese Co.* [1920] 1 Ch. 154; *Phillips v. Manufactures' Securities Ltd.* (1917) 116 L.T. 290 is an authority that an article is valid even if it provides for compulsory expropriation at a gross undervalue, and that it may be operated to secure this result with a deliberate intention of punishing the member whose retirement has been enforced. Any person acquiring a share in Cassidy and Company, Limited, must be deemed to have known that in certain circumstances he might become liable to be expropriated on the terms of article 32. If on a fair reading of those terms they involve harshness he cannot subsequently ask the Court to endeavour to give them a more lenient interpretation or to find in their harshness a reason why they should not be invoked.

[54] Mr Lavery, I think, fully appreciated such considerations, and his main argument was that article 32 contained in its own words a clear indication that it was not meant to apply to any case where a member had already taken steps which, unless deliberately nullified by the directors, would result in his ceasing to be a member. The main – indeed the only object – of article 32 was, he argued, to enforce the retirement of a member. If that retirement was already in train this article was displaced and could not be operated. The provisions which fixed the price to be paid to a retiring member were only ancillary and if a member was in the way of retiring it was not contemplated that a resolution should be passed under article 32 merely for the purpose of bringing those auxiliary provisions into operation. He cited the case of *Robert Batcheller & Sons Ltd. v. Batcheller* [1945] 1 Ch. 169, which at first seemed very greatly in his favour. In that case Romer J. refused to apply an article on the ground that it only operated where the known circumstances of a particular case are such as sensibly and legitimately admit of its application. His view was that the circumstances in *Batcheller's* case did not warrant such a conclusion and he said 'To deem, however, that a thing happened when not only is it known that it did not happen, but it is positively known that precisely the opposite of it happened, is a conception which to my mind, if applied to a subject matter such as that of article 93, amounts to a complete absurdity'.

Mr Lavery points out that if article 32 is to be applied in the present case it will be necessary to deem that a notice had been served naming the amount paid up on the shares (namely £1) as their fair value, when not only has such notice not been served but a completely different notice naming £5 as their value has actually been served. *Batcheller's* case may be summarised as one in which – to borrow the terse phraseology of Mr Wilson – the Judge came to the conclusion that the article was only intended to come into operation on a hypothesis which on the particular facts had not come into existence. If I were of opinion that there was a lack of clarity in the wording of article 32 and that common sense led me irresistibly to the conclusion that it was never intended to apply where a notice had already been served under article 31, *Batcheller's* case would be an authority. I have not been able to reach this conclusion, despite the resemblences between this case and *Batcheller's* case which Mr Lavery pointed out. I would agree that the main object of article 32 as drafted and adopted was to provide a power of compulsory retirement. I do not agree that this was its sole object.

The practice of encouraging employees to take an interest in the business which employs them by allotting to them shares either free or at a value less than the market value is one which has increased very greatly in the last fifty years. It is natural that directors should desire to keep some control over such shares and not allow them to be retained as of right when employees leave the service. It is also natural that directors should desire to have some lever whereby employees maybe prevented from misconducting themselves while in employment and then, when they are dismissed or anticipate dismissal by retirement, enjoying the full fruits of shares allotted to them. I have said that I am not in any way basing my judgment on the truth of the allegations in Mr Cassidy's affidavit, but I am of opinion that the possibility of such conduct as is alleged is a matter normally present to the minds of commercial men and that it is natural to suppose that they desire to arm themselves against its occurrence by providing means of penalising it. It will be noted that article 32 is optional. In any case the directors may or may not avail themselves of the power it gives to them. The existence of such a power, arbitrary if you like, punitive if you like, may be a powerful weapon to secure diligence and loyalty among the employees and so be in the best interests of the company and the shareholders as a whole.

[551] would draw the conclusion that article 32 was deliberately framed, inserted and adopted to give the directors such a power. If it is exercised fraudulently it may be restrained. If exercised in the case of shares acquired at full value by a person who was not then an employee (as in the instance I suggested) it might perhaps be possible to argue, that this was a hypothesis not contemplated by the article and so to afford relief along the lines of *Batcheller's* case. But in the present case I find myself forced to decide against the contention of the plaintiffs, first because I find that the article read in its ordinary and grammatical sense is free from ambiguity, and secondly because, even if I should admit ambiguity, I have reached the conclusion that it was intended to confer power to take such action as was taken in the present case even if a prior notice had been served under article 31.

Note: In *Re New Cedos Ltd* [1994] 1 B.C.L.C. 797, where the directors purportedly refused to register a transfer of shares, relying on article 3 of part II of Table A, it transpired that there had been no retirements and re-elections under the rotation of directors provisions in the articles and, accordingly, there was no validly constituted board of directors Oliver J. held that, accordingly, the directors' veto had never been exercised.

In *Stothers v. William Stewart Holdings Ltd* [1994] 2 B.C.L.C. 266, where the directors refused to register the transmission of shares to the widow of the company's deceased chairman and chief executive, the Court of Appeal held that they were not entitled under the articles of association to do so. According to Peter Gibson L.J. at pp.272-273, the following general considerations apply to the construction of such articles:

(1)Shares, being personal property, are *prima facie* transferable; if the right of transfer is to be taken away it must be done by language of sufficient clarity in the articles.

(2)The articles must be construed together and given effect, so far as possible, to every provision; it is only if the express articles are inconsistent with the incorporated regulations of Table A that the former will override the latter.

(3)There is a distinction well recognised in company law between the transfer of shares and their transmission on death.

In *Popely v. Planarrive Ltd* [1997] 1 B.C.L.C. 8, concerning a family owned and managed company where there were bitter differences between family members, the directors refused to register a transfer of shares to another family member, relying on article 3 of Part II of Table A. Laddie J held that, in the circumstances, it had not been proved that the directors did not act bona fide in the interests of the company. Moreover, the mere fact that the intended shareholder had not been notified promptly of the directors' veto did not invalidate it where there was no delay in exercising the veto.

PREFERENCE SHARES

See *Company Law*, pp. 301–307.

In re Lafayette Ltd
[1950] I.R. 100

The company had preference and ordinary shares. A reorganisation being contemplated, questions arose as to 1, whether the preference shareholders were entitled on a winding up of the Company, to have any credit balance shown on the profit and loss account, together with all moneys placed in reserve funds, which represented undistributed profits, applied to pay off arrears of dividend; 2, whether, if such funds and moneys were insufficient to discharge all arrears, capital assets should be applied to discharge the outstanding arrears; 3, whether capital subscribed by preference shareholders was payable out of assets in priority to capital subscribed by the ordinary shareholders; 4, whether any surplus assets after such repayment of capital to both classes of shareholders, should be divided equally between both classes.

Article 10 provided:

> '10. The holders of the Preference Shares shall be entitled to receive out of the profits of the Company a cumulative preferential dividend for each year of £6 per cent. per annum on the amount for the time being paid on the Preference Shares held by them respectively, such dividend shall be cumulative, and arrears thereof shall be the first charge on the subsequent profits of the Company. The Preference Shares shall also have a preferential right in distribution of assets of the Company.'

Article 142 provided:

> '142. The Directors may, notwithstanding the provisions of Article 132, but shall not be obliged before recommending or declaring any dividend or bonus, or interest on capital, in respect of any class of shares, out of, or in respect of the earnings or profits of the Company for any yearly or other period, cause to be reserved, or retained and set aside out of such profits, such sums as they may think proper to form a reserve fund, and such reserve fund is to be regarded as allotted to meet contingencies, or for equalising dividends, or for repairing, improving and maintaining any of the property of the Company, or in payment or satisfaction of any moneys for the time being owing by the Company on mortgage or otherwise, and for such other purposes as the Directors, in their absolute discretion, may think conducive to the interests of the Company.'

Articles 11, 132, and 133 provided, respectively:

> (a) that surplus profits in each year, after payment of the dividend (and arrears) on the preference shares, should be applied to payment of dividend on the ordinary shares;
> (b) that, subject to the provisions of the articles, the net profits should be applied to payment of a dividend on the capital paid up, or credited as paid up, on the shares; (c) that an appropriate dividend might be declared in general meeting of the Company but such dividend should not be larger than that recommended by the directors.be applied to payment of a dividend on the capital paid up, or credited as paid up, on the shares;
> (c) that an appropriate dividend might be declared in general meeting of the Company but such dividend should not be larger than that recommended by the directors.

KINGSMILL MOORE J.: . . . [109] It has been admitted that the articles are not perfectly drafted or entirely consistent. The inconsistency may not be as great as at first appears. There was power in the articles to create new classes of shares (though such shares were not to affect 'the priority or privileges' of the existing preference shareholders without their consent), and the use of the words in arts. 132, 133 and 142, which are relied on by Mr FitzGibbon as clearly referring to more than one class of shares, and so, presumably, including the preference shares in their provisions, may be explained as being designed to apply to any future class of shares which might be created after the formation of the Company. Article 11, if anything, seems to tell against Mr FitzGibbon's contention. It deals with 'surplus profits', a very different thing from the 'net profits' referred to in art. 132. Surplus profits must mean 'surplus of net profits' after something has already been taken from them. What that something is, would be abundantly plain from the foregoing art. 10, even if it was not defined as being 'the surplus profit after payment of the said dividend on the preference shares and all arrears thereof'. Article 11 appears to me to deal only with such profits as would be applicable to pay dividends on the ordinary shares after satisfying all claims of preference shareholders to current dividend and arrears, and only such profits are to be subject to the powers given to the directors (including the power to create a reserve). It is significant that in art. 11 the permissory phrase, 'shall be applicable', is used, in contrast with the mandatory words, 'shall be entitled to receive', in art. 10.

The position of the words, 'subject to the powers hereafter given to the directors', is not very happy. This phrase would come in more properly either at the beginning of the clause or after the word, 'thereof, but it does not appear to me that this malposition can alter the meaning I have given to the article as a whole.

I have suggested a way in which the articles may be interpreted so as to avoid manifest inconsistency, but, if there is inconsistency between the articles, I hold that the general phraseology of arts. 132, 133, and 142 must yield to [110] the clear and specific wording of art. 10, and that the rights given to preference shareholders by that article cannot be diminished by the subsequent articles unless such articles make evident an intention to do so. I do not find any such intention. If the articles are in fact entirely inconsistent, not only must the general yield to the particular, but there is authority to show that the earlier article must prevail over the latter; *Forbes v. Git* [1922] 1 A.C. 256.

The interpretation which I have given does not, as has been suggested, stultify the power conferred on the directors to create a reserve fund. If in any year the preference dividends and any outstanding arrears have been paid, then the directors may set aside a sum to reserve, and this sum is not available to satisfy future preference dividends, for art. 10 expressly limits the rights of the preference shareholders to be paid their arrears out of 'subsequent profits of the Company'.

Mr FitzGibbon, if forced reluctantly to concede that my interpretations of the present articles, standing by themselves, was correct, or, at least, not plainly erroneous, would – and does – maintain that, nevertheless, the general principles of company law and the accepted manner of interpreting articles prevents me from giving effect to the claim of the preference shareholders to be paid arrears out of the reserve fund and any undistributed net business profits, and he has cited many authorities for his view. I shall examine them separately, with the general prefatory remark that they seem to me all to be decisions on the particular wording of particular, though, no doubt, commonly used, articles, and that, general principles are referred to in such cases merely as an aid to the interpretation of the particular articles. The articles in Lafayette Ltd. are different in form, and contain at least one provision which I have found nowhere else, viz., the provision that arrears are to be a 'first charge' on subsequent profits. This is a strong expression. A charge is a hypothec, and the thing charged cannot be released for purposes other than those of satisfying the charge, until that charge has been satisfied. It seems to me a mere begging of the question to say that the use of the words, 'first charge,' is equivalent to the use of the word, 'cumulative'. That is exactly what it is not. A charge earmarks the property which is subject to it for one particular purpose in priority to all others, and, if that purpose is one legally possible of being attained, then attained it must be. None of the cases cited by Mr FitzGibbon go so far as to lay down that there is anything illegal in providing that any particular sum is to be applied [111] in a winding up for the discharge of arrears of dividends. They do lay down that certain forms of articles are not sufficient to attain this end. Again, none of the cases cited lay down that articles may not give to preference shareholders an absolute right to be paid their fixed dividend and arrears out of profits without any previous declaration of dividend by the directors or the company. They do lay down that certain forms of articles require a dividend to be declared before it is presently payable.

I turn to the authorities. The first is *Bishop v. Smyrna and Cassaba Railway Co.* [1895] 2 Ch. 265, in which Kekewich J. decided that the provisions in the memorandum overrode inconsistent provisions in the articles, and that a sum of money standing to reserve account at the date of the commencement of liquidation was properly applicable to payment of arrears of dividend due at that date to the preference shareholders. Somewhat astonishingly the terms of the memorandum are nowhere given in the report but may be found in the judgment of Byrne J. in *In re Odessa Waterworks Co.* (printed in a note to *In re Crichton's Oil Company* [1901] 2 Ch. 184). From this it appears that the memorandum in the *Smyrna Railway* case provided that the preference shares should have a right 'to a dividend of 7 per cent. per annum upon the amount paid up by preference and priority over the ordinary shares' and 'It is, however, understood and agreed, that if in any year or years the dividend on the ordinary shares shall fall below 7 per cent., and that in subsequent years means shall exist of dividing larger profits than the above-mentioned first dividend of 7 per cent. per annum, the surplus profits shall be first of all applied to make up the deficiency borne by the ordinary shares in previous years. . . .' It will be seen that the rights of the preference shares were declared in terms less extensive than they are in the present case, but Kekewich J. found them sufficient to ensure payment of arrears on a winding up. He held that in a winding up, when the powers of the directors to recommend, and the company to declare, a dividend were at an end, the rights of the preference shareholders still remained and were enforceable. Their rights were conferred as a right independent of the declaration of a dividend. The judgment was, indeed, rested on the fact that the rights of the preference shareholders were conferred by the memorandum, and so not assailable by contradictory provisions in the articles. I think, however, that if, on a fair interpretation of the articles themselves, a conclusion is reached that they were intended to confer similar rights on the preference shareholders, the [112] same result must follow as if those rights were declared in the memorandum. The *Odessa Waterworks Co. Case* [1901] 2 Ch. 190 is of no assistance because the rights of the preference shareholders were considered by Byrne J., on the construction of the articles, to be absolutely dependent on the declaration of a dividend. There was no article, such as art. 10 in the present case, purporting to give particular rights to the preference shareholders.

In re Crichton's Oil Co. is, on the wording of the articles, nearer to the present case. Article 6 provided that the holders of the preference shares should be entitled to a cumulative preference dividend at the rate of £6 per cent. per annum. Article 103 gave the directors power to set aside a reserve fund out of profits. Article 108 provided that the profits available for dividends should be applicable first to the payment of a fixed cumulative preference dividend on the preference shares in the original capital. The company was wound up and, on the taking of the accounts, it was found that there had been a profit on the last year of trading sufficient to pay the last year's preference dividend and some of the arrears of previous years. Wright J. held that this sum was not available for dividend but must be applied to repayment of capital in the winding up. He was of opinion that the dividend was only payable out of profits made available for dividend and that, as the directors had not recommended a dividend and no dividend had been declared by the company, the claim of the preference shareholders must fail. The terms of art. 6 were somewhat similar to those of art. 10 of Lafayette Ltd., but they lack the essential provisions that arrears shall be the first charge on subsequent profits, words which, in my view, make any recommendation by directors or declaration by the Company unnecessary.

I respectfully accept the interpretation of the *Crichton's Oil Company* case which was given by Bennett J. in *Re W. Foster & Son, Ltd.* [1942] 1 All E.R. 314 and adopted by Wynn-Parry J. in *Re Catalinas Warehouses and Mole Co., Ltd.* [1947] 1 All E.R. 51 namely, that when once a company has passed a resolution for liquidation the provisions in the articles for declaration of dividends come to an end, and so, when a winding up has commenced, prima facie a dividend is no longer payable; but it seems to me that in Lafayette Ltd. the articles give the preference shareholders a right to their dividend, irrespective of any declaration, and, again without any declaration automatically charge arrears of preference dividend on any [113] future profits.

Bond v. Barrow Hoematite Steel Co. [1902] 1 Ch. 353 turned on a small point of construction. The articles contained provisions for declaration of a dividend by the directors, with the consent of the company; for payment of dividends out of business profits and creation of a reserve fund; and for power to increase capital by creation of new shares, which were, however, to be subject to the provisions of the original articles, save that they might be given priority over the old shares by the resolutions creating them. In pursuance of this power new preference 8 per cent. shares were created in the year 1872, and new 6 per cent. preference shares in the year, 1876. The resolutions creating the 6 per cent. shares contained the following words, 'in case in any year the net profits of the company shall not be sufficient for the payment in full of the dividends on such new preference shares, the net profits of any subsequent year shall . . . be applied in payment to the holders of the said new preference shares of the amount by which the dividends of any previous year or years may have fallen short of the fixed rate of £6 per cent.' It was argued that these words gave to the 6 per cent. preference shareholders an absolute right to their fixed dividends out of any year's profits before any sum was carried to reserve, applied to replace lost capital, or carried forward. Farwell J., with apparently some little doubt, rejected this contention, but only on the ground that, as the original articles had subjected any new shares to the provisions of such original articles, any preference dividend must be declared, and was subject to the powers given to the directors to create a reserve. It may be gathered from his judgment that, but for the express provision in the original articles, he would have upheld the contention of the preference shareholders.

The case which seems to me most in point, and, indeed, decisive, is a recent decision of our own Courts, viz., *In re The Imperial Hotel (Cork) Ltd*. [1950] I.R. 115. In a voluntary liquidation of the Company the liquidator, after discharging the claims of creditors who were not members and his own costs and repaying the capital of the preference shareholders, found himself with about £6,500 in hand. The ordinary shareholders claimed that this sum should be applied in repaying their capital. The preference shareholders argued that the arrears of the cumulative dividend – some £4,477 – should first be paid, and the President unhesitatingly accepted their argument.

Article 13 of the articles in the *Imperial Hotel* case was almost identical with the first sentence of art. 10 in the [114] present case, save that, instead of the words, 'such dividend shall be cumulative, and arrears thereof shall be the first charge on the subsequent profits of the Company,' there appeared the words, 'such dividend to be computed from the date of allotment and such holders to have the right to resort to the profits of subsequent years to make up the deficiency, if any, in preceding years.' Of the two phrases, the former, creating an actual first charge, seems to me the more emphatic in favour of the preference shareholders. The other articles in the *Imperial Hotel* case in regard to declaration of dividends, creation of a reserve fund, payment out of net profits, and application of surplus after paying preference dividends, are similar in effect to those in Lafayette Ltd., though their order and wording are not identical.

The learned President held that the profits of each financial year must first be applied to the payment of the cumulative preference dividend, including any outstanding arrears; that the right of the preference shareholders to receive their dividend was independent of any declaration of dividend by the Company in general meeting; and that the right of the directors to create a reserve fund out of profits was irreconcilable with, and must yield to, the right of the preference shareholders to receive their dividends and arrears thereof. With those findings and the reasoning on which they are based I respectfully agree, and, applying the reasoning of the President, I hold that the preference shareholders are entitled to be paid their arrears of dividend out of profits shown in the profit and loss account for subsequent years; that this right is one independent of any recommendation by the directors or declaration of dividend by the Company; that this right takes precedence over the power of the directors to set aside sums for a reserve fund, and that, if such reserve fund has been set aside, it is applicable to pay the arrears; that this right to be repaid arrears is a charge upon subsequent profits and on the reserve fund; and that, on a winding up, the reserve fund and any undistributed profits shown in the profit and loss account are applicable, after payment of creditors of the Company, to the discharge of such arrears.

Note: In *Re Bradford Investments Ltd* [1991] B.C.L.C. 225, one of the issues was whether the preference shareholders were entitled to vote at a general meeting of the company; under the articles of association, they could vote only if their dividends had been in arrears for more than six months, dividends being 'deemed payable' half-yearly on January 1 and July 1.

In re Cork Electric Supply Co. Ltd
[1932] I.R. 315

A company that ran trams and supplied the city with electricity had its undertaking nationalised under the Electricity Supply Act, 1927, and received substantial compensation. One question that then arose was whether, in a liquidation, any surplus remaining must be divided between the ordinary shareholders and the preference shareholders. The articles did not expressly indicate what was to become of the surplus.

KENNEDY C.J.: . . . [327] We cannot approach the question with the advantage of statutory guidance to the answer. Sect. 186 of the Companies (Consolidation) Act, 1908, leaves the matter as follows, as regards voluntary winding-up: '(i). The property of the Company shall be applied in satisfaction of its liabilities pari passu, and, subject thereto, shall, unless the Articles otherwise provide, be distributed among the members according to their rights and interests in the Company.' Sect. 170 provides that, in the case of a winding-up by the Court: 'The Court shall adjust the rights of the contributories among themselves, and distribute any surplus among the persons entitled thereto.' Hence a problem appears in every case in so far as specific provision is not made in the Articles of Association. A rule was, however, established by the decision of the House of Lords in England in the case of *In re The Bridgewater Navigation Co., Ltd., Birch v. Cropper* (14 App. Cas. 328), that, on the voluntary winding-up, the assets remaining after discharging all debts and liabilities and repaying to the ordinary and preference shareholders the capital paid on their shares, ought to be divided among all the shareholders (both preference and ordinary), not in proportion to the amounts paid on the shares, but in proportion to the shares held. The decision is very important for the elementary principles it affirmed (of which there is a tendency to lose sight in argument). Preference shareholders are holders of shares in the capital of a company in the same way as ordinary shareholders are holders of shares in its capital. Both classes of shareholders are equally members of the Company. Their respective positions are differentiated only to the extent to which the rights and privileges attaching to their respective shares are qualified contractually by the Memorandum and Articles of Association of the Company.

I turn, therefore, to the Memorandum and Articles of Association of the plaintiff Company to ascertain whether the right of the preference shareholders to participate in surplus assets on a winding-up of the Company has been [328] abrogated, cut down, or qualified in any way. There is no such specific provision, and we have to look for a limitation by implication. No. 10 of the Articles of Association (already quoted) is the basis of the argument on behalf of the ordinary shareholders. That Article confers on the preference shareholders two special privileges, viz.: (1) the right to a fixed dividend at the rate of £5 per cent. per annum out of the profits of each half-year, 'but to no further dividend,' and (2) the right in a winding-up to priority in payment of capital over the ordinary shares. The effect of the two amendments of the Article (already quoted) was to make the preferential dividend cumulative and to delete the words 'but to no further dividend.' We have been asked to hold with Johnston J. that the Article (as amended) is an exhaustive statement of the rights of the preference shareholders which excludes any other right or privilege and deprives (by implication) these shareholders of their right to participate in a distribution of surplus assets on a winding-up. We were referred to a series of decisions of judges of first instance in England on analogous questions, in which, though they were cases of construction arising on a variety of forms of Articles, a certain conflict of opinion appeared among the judges: *In re Espuela Land and Cattle Co.* [1909] 2 Ch. 187; *In re National Telephone Co.* [1914] 1 Ch. 75 5; *In re Fraser and Chalmers Ltd.* [1919] 2 Ch. 114; *Anglo French Music Co., Ltd., v. Nicoll* [1921] 1 Ch. 386; *Collaroy Co., Ltd.*

v. Giffard [1928] 1 Ch. 144. We have also been referred to *Will v. United Lankat Plantations Co., Ltd.* [1914] A.C. 11. Out of all these cases, after consideration, what we derive is only this, that the right to participate in a distribution of surplus assets on a winding-up will be taken from preference shareholders by a clause in the Articles of Association delimiting their rights exhaustively to the exclusion of any other rights, and that the question whether a particular clause does so delimit the rights attached to the preference shares exhaustively and exclusively is a question of the construction of the particular Articles of Association in each case, and that we cannot construe one set of Articles by the construction applied by some Court to another set of Articles of another Company (save, of course, as to any principle or rule of construction of general application authoritatively declared for the purpose of such construction).

[329] Upon the construction of the Articles of Association before us it is to be observed that, while as regards participation in profits, the words of exclusion 'but to no further dividend' were carefully inserted, no such limitation was added to the immediately following clause as to priority in payment of capital. Moreover, I can find no ground for cutting down the word 'shareholders' in Art. 114, or the words 'members of the Company for the time being' in Art. 115, to ordinary shareholders only, from which it follows that Art. 10 is not an exhaustive statement of the rights of the preference shareholders. In answer to another argument borrowed from a passage in the judgment of Astbury J. in *Collaroy Co., Ltd. v. Giffard*, I must say that there is not, so far as I know, any rule of law or construction requiring a Court of construction to find a logical consistency between the rights of preference shareholders while a company is a going concern and their rights on a winding-up. It is difficult to know what is meant precisely by 'logical consistency' in this connection, but, as I understand it, it is quite foreign to the great diversity of bargain which may lawfully be made in these business contracts.

In my opinion, therefore, the question in paragraph 3 of the claim on the summons should be answered in the affirmative – 'rateably.' I am also of opinion that an affirmative answer – '*pro rata*'– should be given.

FITZGIBBON J.: [331] In construing a document such as that with which we have to deal, decided cases are of little assistance, except in so far as they lay down principles of general application, or place a judicial interpretation upon a clause identical with that which is under consideration. The slightest [332] variation in the language employed may alter the effect of the clause, as, for instance, in the present case, reliance was placed upon the substitution of 'the' for 'a' in the phrases 'the right to be paid out of the profits,' and 'the right in a winding-up,' as indicative of an intention to limit the right of the preference shareholders to that which was expressed, rather than to define the preferential advantages which they were to enjoy in addition to their ordinary rights as members of the Company.

The House of Lords in *Birch v. Cropper* [1889] 14 App. Cas. 525, laid down as a principle of general application, that where the right of preference shareholders in a winding-up is not negatived or restricted by the Memorandum or Articles of the Company the surplus remaining after the payment off of the preference shares and the capital paid up on the ordinary shares is distributable amongst the shareholders of both classes in proportion to the shares held by them respectively. Lord Herschell says : 'When the whole of the capital has been returned both classes of shareholders are on the same footing, equally members and holding equal shares in the Company, and it appears to me that they ought to be treated as equally entitled to its property. It may be that the principle which I recommend your Lordships to adopt will not secure absolutely equal or equitable treatment in all cases, but I think that it will in general attain that end more nearly than any other which has been proposed.' I do not find that either Lord Macnaghten or Lord FitzGerald dissented from or qualified in any way the principle which Lord Herschell recommended them to adopt, and it appears to have received universal acceptation thenceforth at the hands of text writers, and what is more important, company draughtsmen. Bearing that principle in mind, I have read the Memorandum and Articles of Association, the latter as originally adopted, and then as amended by the successive resolutions increasing the capital of the Company, with a view to ascertaining whether there was any provision in them which conveyed to my mind an intention on the part of the Company to negative or restrict the right of the holders of the preference shares, in the event of a winding-up, to share in any surplus which might remain after the whole of the capital had been returned to the shareholders. In my opinion the provision in Art. 10 that the preference shareholders were to be repaid the amount contributed by them in priority to the ordinary shareholders does not by implication negative or restrict their right to share in a surplus, if any. It is a definition [333] of the amount of preferential treatment which they are to receive, not a deprivation or restriction of any other right to which they are, *prima facie*, entitled.

Having arrived at this interpretation without reference to decisions upon other and different Articles, I read all the cases to which we were referred in argument, and several others, in order to see whether there was any rule of law, recognised canon of construction, or binding decision, which precluded me from giving effect to that which appeared to me to be the natural interpretation of the Articles, because I think that if a particular article, clause, or expression has received a judicial interpretation, and has been subsequently adopted as a precedent in the formation of other Companies, it is better, in a doubtful question of construction, to adhere to previous decisions rather than upon a nice balance of opinion to disaffirm a construction in reliance upon which large amounts of capital may have been invested. The old reluctance of Courts – to which Lord Westbury and Lord Cranworth referred in *Young v. Robertson*, (4 Macq. H.L. 314, 337) – to disturb decisions upon which titles of land depended, seems to me, when we are called upon to construe commercial documents, to be no less applicable to 'decisions which, not being manifestly erroneous and mischievous, have stood for some time unchallenged, and from their nature and the effect which they may reasonably be supposed to have produced upon the conduct of a large portion of the community . . . in matters affecting rights of property, may fairly be treated as having passed into the category of established and recognised law': *Pugh v. Golden Valley Railway Co.* (15 Ch. D. 330).

I have not discovered any decision, or even any dictum, which can be regarded as having placed a definite interpretation upon the Article with which we are concerned, and accordingly I feel quite free to adopt the construction which commends itself to me. I think that little assistance can be derived from an elaborate discussion of cases such as that to be found in the judgment of Astbury J. in *Collaroy Co. v. Gifford*, where the point, as he says, 'must necessarily depend upon the exact language and context of the contract in each case.' He has, however, stated in that case one 'proposition' as of general application, which I am not at present prepared to accept. 'There ought to be a logical consistency between the preference shareholders' rights while the Company is a going concern [334] and their rights in a winding-up.' I do not see any reason for this. In every case the promoters of a company will consider the terms which are best calculated to induce the public to subscribe the capital required, and the conditions which should be attached to shares allotted to a vendor as part of the purchase consideration. An examination of the precedents in the different editions of Palmer's works and of other text-writers will show that there is an almost infinite variety of conditions attached to preference shares both as concerns dividends and capital, and that there is no 'logical consistency' required or observed. It is not unworthy of observation that Mr Palmer, in discussing the question 'whether the preference shares are to have any preference as regards return of capital in a winding-up or in relation to a reduction of capital,' after referring to *Birch v. Cropper* as deciding that in the absence of provisions negating or restricting their rights they will be entitled to share in the surplus after paying off the preference shares and the capital paid up on the ordinary shares, proceeds: 'But very commonly it is desired to negative the right of the preference shareholders to participate in such a surplus, and accordingly words are inserted to the effect that the holders shall *not* be entitled to participate any further in the profits or assets,' and he gives a form containing such negative words. In the present case the framers of the Articles appear to have recognised the necessity for or advisability of such negative words, as in the clause dealing with capital, which defines the preferential rights of the preference shares there is an express limitation of the preferential dividend 'to £5 per cent. per annum, *but to* no further dividend,' while no such restriction or negation is attached to the condition for repayment of the capital. The right of priority is conferred, but the right to participate in any possible surplus is not negatived.

In my opinion question No. 3 upon the summons should be answered in the affirmative.

Scottish Insurance Corp. Ltd. v. Wilsons & Clyde Coal Co. Ltd.
[1949] A.C. 462

The company's undertaking, coal mines, were nationalised and substantial compensation was paid. The company then proposed to repay its preference shareholders under the powers given in the equivalent of section 72 *et seq.* of the 1963 Act. Preference shareholders claimed that they should not be repaid because, firstly, they had a right to share in the surplus on the winding up and that repayment would deprive them of that right. The articles of association did not indicate expressly who was to participate in any surplus.

LORD SIMONDS: . . . [486] The first plea makes an assumption, *viz.*, that the articles give the preference stockholders the right in a winding up to share in surplus assets, which I for the moment accept but will later examine. Making that assumption, I yet see no validity in the plea. The company has at a stroke been deprived of the enterprise and undertaking which it has built up over many years: it is irrelevant for this purpose that the stroke is delivered by an Act of Parliament which [487] at the same time provides some compensation. Nor can it affect the rights of the parties that the only reason why there is money available for repayment of capital is that the company has no longer an undertaking to carry on. Year by year the 7 per cent. preference dividend has been paid; of the balance of the profits some part has been distributed to the ordinary stockholders, the rest has been conserved in the business. If I ask whether year by year the directors were content to recommend, the company in general meeting to vote, a dividend which has left a margin of resources, in order that the preference stockholders might in addition to repayment of their capital share also in surplus assets, I think that directors and company alike would give an emphatic negative. And they would, I think add that they have always had it in their power, and have it still, by making use of arts. 139 or 141, to see that what they had saved for themselves they do not share with others. I observe that the learned Lord President was of opinion that such a use of one or other of these articles would be an impropriety which would at least be open to challenge in a court of law, but learned counsel for the appellants candidly admitted that he could not support this view. Reading these articles as a whole with such familiarity with the topic as the years have brought, I would not hesitate to say, first, that the last thing a preference stockholder would expect to get (I do not speak here of the legal rights) would be a share of surplus assets, and that such a share would be a windfall beyond his reasonable expectations and, secondly, that he had at all times the knowledge, enforced in this case by the unusual reference in art. 139 to the payment off of the preference capital, that at least he ran the risk, if the company's circumstances admitted, of such a reduction as is now proposed being submitted for confirmation by the court. Whether a man lends money to a company at 7 per cent. or subscribes for its shares carrying a cumulative preferential dividend at that rate, I do not think that he can complain of unfairness if the company, being in a position lawfully to do so, proposes to pay him off. No doubt, if the company is content not to do so, he may get something that he can never have expected but so long as the company can lawfully repay him, whether it be months or years before a contemplated liquidation, I see no ground for the court refusing its confirmation. To combat the suggestion that, so far as any benefit to the preference stock- [488] holders is concerned, the position is substantially the same whether they are now repaid their capital or full use is made of arts. 139 and 141, it was urged that the incidence of income tax would be a sufficient deterrent of this alternative measure. I do not, however, consider that the court can properly have regard to such a consideration as this in determining what is fair between the parties. It might indeed be considered improper to do so if it drove the ordinary stockholders to a course less advantageous to themselves but no more advantageous to the preference stockholders.

It will be seen, my Lords, that, even making an assumption favourable to the appellants, I reject their first plea. But it is perhaps necessary, in case there should be a division of opinion which would make this a decisive issue, that I should shortly examine the assumption. It is clear from the authorities, and would be clear without them, that, subject to any relevant provision of the general law, the rights inter se of preference and ordinary shareholders must depend on the terms of the instrument which contains the bargain that they have made with the company and each other. This means, that there is a question of construction to be determined and undesirable though it may be that fine distinctions should be drawn in commercial documents such as articles of association of a company, your Lordships cannot decide that the articles here under review have a particular meaning, because to somewhat similar articles in such cases as *In re William Metcaffle & Sons Ltd.* [1933] Ch. 142, that meaning has been judicially attributed. Reading the relevant articles, as a whole, I come to the conclusion that arts. 159 and 160 are exhaustive of the rights of the preference stockholders in a winding up. The whole tenor of the articles, as I have already pointed out, is to leave the ordinary stockholders masters of the situation. If there are 'surplus assets' it is because the ordinary stockholders have contrived that it should be so, and, though this is not decisive, in determining what the parties meant by their bargain, it is of some weight that it should be in the power of one class so to act that there will or will not be surplus assets.

There is another somewhat general consideration which also, I think, deserves attention. If the contrary view of arts. 159 and 160 is the right one and the preference stockholders are entitled to a share in surplus assets, the question will still arise what those surplus assets are. For the profits [489] though undrawn, belong, subject to the payment of the preference dividend, to the ordinary stockholders and, in so far as surplus assets are attributable to undrawn profits, the preference stockholders have no right to them. This appears to follow from the decision of the Court of Appeal in *In re Bridgewater Naviga-tion Company* [1891] 2 Ch. 317, in which judgment of the House of Lords in *Birch v. Cropper* (14 App. Cas. 525) is worked out. This again is not decisive of the construction of particular articles, but I am unwilling to suppose that the parties intended a bargain which would involve an investigation of an artifi-cial and elaborate character into the nature and origin of surplus assets.

But, apart from those more general considerations, the words of the spe-cifically relevant articles, 'rank before the other shares . . . on the property of the company to the extent of repayment of the amounts called up and paid thereon', appear to me apt to define exhaustively the rights of the preference stockholders in a winding up. Similar words, in *Will v. United Lankat Planta-tions Co. Ltd.* [1914] A.C. 11, 'rank both as regards capital and dividend, in priority to the other shares', were held to define exhaustively the rights of preference shareholders to dividend, and I do not find in the speeches of Vis-count Haldane L.C. or Earl Loreburn in that case any suggestion that a differ-ent result would have followed if the dispute had been in regard to capital. I do not ignore that in the same case in the Court of Appeal [191212 Ch. 571, the distinction between dividend and capital was expressly made by both Cozens-Hardy M.R. and Farwell L.J., and that in *In re William Metcaffle & Sons Ltd.*, Romer L.J. reasserted it. But I share the difficulty, which Lord Keith has ex-pressed in this case, in reconciling the reasoning that lies behind the judg-ments in *Will's* case and *In re William Metcaffle & Sons Ltd.* respectively. In *Collaroy Co. Ltd. v. Giffard* [1928] Ch. 144, Astbury J., after reviewing the authorities, including his own earlier decision in *In re Fraser and Chalmers* [1919] 2 Ch. 114, said: 'But whether the considerations affecting them [sc. capital and dividend preference respectively] are "entirely different" is a ques-tion of some difficulty', and approved the proposition [490] there urged by the ordinary shareholders that a fixed return of capital to shareholders in a wind-ing up is just as artificial as a provision for a fixed dividend and that, if the latter is regarded as exhaustive, there is no prima facie reason why the former should not be similarly regarded. So also that learned judge was influenced by the consideration which appears to me to have much weight, that, if such an article as our art. 159 is regarded as a complete definition of the rights of the preference stockholders in a winding up, then there is a logical consistency between their rights before and after the company is put into liquidation. In effect I prefer the reasoning of Astbury J. in the case last cited to that of Eve J. and the Court of Appeal in *In re William Metcaffle & Sons Ltd.* Counsel for the appellants in the present case sought to draw a distinction between the right to repayment of capital and the right to some further share in surplus assets and pointed to the fact that arts. 159 and 160 said nothing about surplus assets. But this distinction is not in my opinion in the present context a valid one. Articles 159 and 160 are the first two in a number of articles headed 'Distribution of assets in winding up' and there is nothing in them to suggest a distinction between 'surplus assets' and 'property of the company', the expression in fact used in arts. 159 and 160, required for repayment of capital or distributable as surplus assets. Nor, I think, is the latter expression used throughout the articles: it is perhaps an expression which is better avoided.

Finally on this part of the case I ought to deal with an observation made by Lord Macnaghten in *Birch v. Cropper* upon which counsel for the appellants relied. 'They,' he said '[sc. the preference shareholders] must be treated as having all the rights of shareholders, except so far as they renounced these rights on their admission to the company.' But, in my opinion, Lord Macnaghten can have meant nothing more than that the rights of the parties depended on the bargain that they had made and that the terms of the bargain must be ascertained by a consideration of the articles of association and any other relevant document, a task which I have endeavoured in this case to discharge. I cannot think that Lord Macnaghten intended to introduce some new principle of construction and to lay down that preference shareholders are entitled to share in surplus assets unless they expressly and specifically renounce that right.

Note: Cf. *House of Fraser plc v. A.C.G.E. Investments Ltd* [1987] A.C. 387, *post*, p. 529 and *Re Northern Engineering Industries plc* [1994] 2 B.C.L.C. 704, noted *post*, p. 533.

PROPERTY RIGHTS IN SHARES

See *Company Law*, pp.308–315.

Table A articles 7, 8 (new), 11–14, 22–39

7. Except as required by law, no person shall be recognised by the company as holding any share upon any trust, and the company shall not be bound by or be compelled in any way to recognise (even when having notice thereof) any equitable, contingent, future or partial interest in any share or any interest in any fractional part of a share or (except only as by these regulations or by law otherwise provided) any other rights in respect of any share except an absolute right to the entirety thereof in the registered holder: this shall not preclude the company from requiring the members or a transferee of shares to furnish the company with information as to the beneficial ownership of any share when such information is reasonably required by the company.

8. Every person whose name is entered as a member in the register shall be entitled without payment to receive within 2 months after allotment or lodgement of a transfer (or within such other period as the conditions of issue shall provide) one certificate for all his shares or several certificates each for one or more of his shares upon payment of 12½ new pence for every certificate after the first or such less sum as the directors shall from time to time determine, so. however, that in respect of a share or shares held jointly by several persons the company shall not be bound to issue more than one certificate, and delivery of a certificate for a share to one of several joint holders shall be sufficient delivery to all such holders. Every certificate shall be under the seal or under the official seal kept by the company by virtue of section 3 of the Companies (Amendment) Act, 1977, and shall specify the shares to which it relates and the amount paid up thereon.

Lien

11. The company shall have a first and paramount lien on every share (not being a fully paid share) for all moneys (whether immediately payable or not) called or payable at a fixed time in respect of that share, and the company shall also have a first and paramount lien on all shares (other than fully paid shares) standing registered in the name of a single person for all moneys immediately payable by him or his estate to the company; but the directors may at any time declare any share to be wholly or in part exempt from the provisions of this regulation. The company's lien on a share shall extend to all dividends payable thereon.

12. The company may sell, in such manner as the directors think fit, any shares on which the company has a lien, but no sale shall be made unless a sum in respect of which the lien exists is immediately payable, nor until the expiration of 14 days after a notice in writing, stating and demanding payment of such part of the amount in respect of which the lien exists as is immediately payable, has been given to the registered holder for the time being of the share, or the person entitled thereto by reason of his death or bankruptcy.

13. To give effect to any such sale, the directors may authorise some person to transfer the shares sold to the purchaser thereof. The purchaser shall be registered as the holder of the shares comprised in any such transfer, and he shall not be bound to see to the application of the purchase money, nor shall his title to the shares be affected by any irregularity or invalidity in the proceedings in reference to the sale.

14. The proceeds of the sale shall be received by the company and applied in payment of such part of the amount in respect of which the lien exists as is immediately payable, and the residue, if any, shall (subject to a like lien for sums not immediately payable as existed upon the shares before the sale) be paid to the person entitled to the shares at the date of the sale.

Transfer of Shares

22. The instrument of transfer of any share shall he executed by or on behalf of the transferor and transferee, and the transferor shall be deemed to remain the holder of the share until the name of the transferee is entered in the register in respect thereof.

23. Subject to such of the restrictions of these regulations as may be applicable, any member may transfer all or any of his shares by instrument in writing in any usual or common form or any other form which the directors may approve.

24. The directors may decline to register the transfer of a share (not being a fully paid share) to a person of whom they do not approve, and they may also decline to register the transfer of a share on which the company has a lien. The directors may also decline to register any transfer of a share which, in their pinion, may imperil or prejudicially affect the status of the company in the State or which may imperil any tax concession or rebate to which the members of the company are entitled or which may involve the company in the payment of any additional stamp or other duties on any conveyance of any property made or to be made to the company.

25. The directors may also decline to recognise any instrument of transfer unless–

    (*a*) a fee of 2s. 6d. or such lesser sum as the directors may from time to time require, is paid to the company in respect thereof; and

    (*b*) the instrument of transfer is accompanied by the certificate of the shares to which it relates, and such other evidence as the directors may reasonably require to show the right of the transferor to make the transfer. and

    (*c*) the instrument of transfer is in respect of one class of share only.

26. If the directors refuse to register a transfer they shall, within 2 months after the date on which the transfer was lodged with the company, send to the transferee notice of the refusal.

27. The registration of transfers may be suspended at such times and for such periods, not exceeding in the whole 30 days in each year, as the directors may from time to time determine.

28. The company shall be entitled to charge a fee not exceeding 2s, 6d, on the registration of every probate, letters of administration, certificate of death or marriage, power of attorney, notice as to the stock or other instrument.

Transmission of Shares

29. In the case of the death of a member, the survivor or survivors, where the deceased was a joint holder, and the personal representatives of the deceased where he was a sole holder, shall be the only persons recognised by the company as having any title to his interest in the shares; but nothing herein contained shall release the estate of a deceased joint holder from any liability in respect of any share which had been jointly held by him with other persons.

30. Any person becoming entitled to a share in consequence of the death or bankruptcy of a member may, upon such evidence being produced as may from time to time properly be required by the directors and subject as hereinafter provided, elect either to be registered himself as holder of the share or to have some person nominated by him registered as the transferee thereof, but the directors shall, in either case, have the same right to decline or suspend registration as they would have had in the case of a transfer of the share by that member before his death or bankruptcy, as the case may be.

31. If the person so becoming entitled elects to be registered himself, he shall deliver or send to the company a notice in writing signed by him stating that he so elects. If he elects to have another person registered, he shall testify his election by executing to that person a transfer of the share. All the limitations, restrictions and provisions of these regulations relating to the right to transfer and the registration of transfers of shares shall be applicable to any such notice or transfer as aforesaid as if the death or bankruptcy of the member had not occurred and the notice or transfer were a transfer signed by that member.

32. A person becoming entitled to a share by reason of the death or bankruptcy of the holder shall be entitled to the same dividends and other advantages to which he would be entitled if he were the registered holder of the share, except that he shall not, before being registered as a member in respect of the share, be entitled in respect of it to exercise any right conferred by membership in relation to meetings of the company, so, however, that the directors, may at any time give notice requiring any such person to elect either to be registered himself or to transfer the share, and if the notice is not complied with within 90 days, the directors may thereupon withhold payment of all dividends, bonuses or other moneys payable in respect of the share until the requirements of the notice have been complied with.

Forfeiture of Shares

33. If a member fails to pay any call or instalment of a call on the day appointed for payment thereof, the directors may, at any time thereafter during such time as any part of the call or instalment remains unpaid, serve a notice on him requiring payment of so much of the call or instalment as is unpaid together with any interest which may have accrued.

34. The notice shall name a further day (not earlier than the expiration of 14 days from the date of service of the notice) on or before which the payment required by the notice is to be made, and shall state that in the event of non-payment at or before the time appointed the shares in respect of which the call was made will be liable to be forfeited.

35. If the requirements of any such notice as aforesaid are not complied with, any share in respect of which the notice has been given may at any time thereafter, before the payment required by the notice has been made, be forfeited by a resolution of the directors to that effect.

36. A forfeited share may be sold or otherwise disposed of on such terms and in such manner as the directors think fit, and at any time before a sale or disposition the forfeiture may be cancelled on such terms as the directors think fit.

37. A person whose shares have been forfeited shall cease to be a member in respect of the forfeited shares, but shall, notwithstanding, remain liable to pay to the company all moneys which, at the date of forfeiture, were payable by him to the company in respect of the shares, but his liability shall cease if and when the company shall have received payment in full of all such moneys in respect of the shares.

38. A statutory declaration that the declarant is a director or the secretary of the company, and that a share in the company has been duly forfeited on a date stated in the declaration, shall be conclusive evidence of the facts therein stated as against all persons claiming to be entitled to the share. The company may receive the consideration, if any, given for the share on any sale or disposition thereof and may execute a transfer of the share in favour of the person to whom the share is sold or disposed of and he shall thereupon be registered as the holder of the share, and shall not be bound to see to the application of the purchase money, if any, nor shall his title to the share be affected by any irregularity or invalidity in the proceedings in reference to the forfeiture, sale or disposal of the share.

39. The provisions of these regulations as to forfeiture shall apply in the case of non payment of any sum which, by the terms of issue of a share, becomes payable at a fixed time, whether on account of the nominal value of the share or by way of premium, as if the same had been payable by virtue of a call duly made and notified.

Companies Act 1963 Act, sections 123 and 124

Trusts not to be entered on register

123.—No notice of any trust, express, implied or constructive, shall be entered on the register or be receivable by the registrar.

Register to be evidence

124.—The register of members shall be prima facie evidence of any matters by this Act directed or authorised to be inserted therein.

Rearden v. Provincial Bank of Ireland
[1896] 1 I.R. 532

The assets of a trust included shares in the defendant bank and those shares were registered in the trustee's [Mr Barry's] name. The bank was fully aware of the trust's existence and terms. When the trustee failed to pay his own debts to the bank, it claimed a lien over the shares registered in his name, contending that it was entitled to do so in the light of what today is section 123 of the 1963 Act and article 7 of Table A.

PORTER M.R.: . . . [555] The bank say, here are certain shares in Barry's name. Whether he is the owner or not does not matter. By the effect of the Companies Act of 1862, section 30, and by virtue of our own articles of association, and neglecting the knowledge given to us that he is merely a trustee for another, we are entitled to hold the shares answerable for his debt. That is the way the question of law arises.

In the case of *The New London and Brazilian Bank v. Brocklebank* (21 Ch. D. 302), the articles of association were substantially the same as here. But in that case, there was no notice even alleged by the company of the absence of beneficial ownership on the part of the registered owners of the shares. The lien of the bank prevailed, and rightly; but the case has no authority or bearing on the point, when the clearest notice I have ever known (whatever the result of it may be) is proved. . . .

[562] Is it then the case that any notice 'if given to a Company would be absolutely inoperative to affect the Company with any trust? In my opinion

the case of *The Bradford Bank v. Briggs* (1889) 12 App. Cas. 29, shows that this is not so, and that for some purposes, at any rate, notice may bind the Company, not with specific trusts, but with knowledge that shares are held by one who has no interest in them which he can lawfully deal with for his own benefit.

That case came originally before Field, J. The articles of association of a Company provided that the Company should have a first and permanent lien and charge on every share of every person who was the holder for all debts due by him to the Company. A shareholder deposited the certificates of some shares belonging to him in the Company with his bankers as security for the balance due, or which should become due, on his current account, and the bank gave notice to the Company of the deposit, the certificates deposited stating that the shares were held subject to the articles of association of the Company. It was held in the House of Lords, reversing the decision of the Court of Appeal, which had in turn reversed the decision of Field J., that the Company could not, in respect of moneys which became due from the shareholder to the Company after notice of the deposit with the bank, claim priority over advances by the bank made after such notice, but that the principle of *Hopkinson v. Rolt* (9 H.L. Cas. 514) applied.

[563] On this question of notice there are two important distinctions to be noted between the case of the Bradford Bank and the present. In that case there was no clause in the articles of association similar to clause 8 in the present. The question of notice there turned upon the effect of section 30 of the Act. Again, the equity affecting the shares there was that they had been deposited with a bank to secure advances, not as here, where they were held by a trustee.

Bearing these two points in mind, it is necessary to see exactly what was decided in *The Bradford Bank v. Briggs*. It is to be observed that there were three transactions – first, a lien by the Company; secondly, a mortgage by equitable deposit of the certificates of the shares by the shareholder for advances made by the bank; and, thirdly, further advances by them after notice to the Company; and the contest was as to whether the Company were enabled, notwithstanding notice of the intervening security, to draw up their subsequent advances and tack them to the previous advances. . . .

[566] [I]n *Bradford Bank v. Briggs* the transaction of which the bank had notice was this – the legal and equitable owner of shares had pledged them by depositing the share certificates with his bankers. He remained the legal owner after the deposit; but in equity the bank were the real owners subject to being redeemed at the option of the shareholder. The position of the bank was not disputed, that is, it was not denied that they were equitable mortgagees. The contest was between their equitable rights and the claims of the defendant Company to a lien for advances to the shareholder after and with actual notice of the bank's equitable mortgage.

That such a transaction did for some purposes constitute the relation of trustee and *cestui que trust* between the bank and Easby could not I think be questioned. One person is legal owner. The other is the equitable owner (to the extent of his charge). If instead of a mortgage the transaction had been a sale, the certificates being deposited pending completion, it could not be doubted that the vendor would have held the legal tide as a trustee for the purchaser so soon as the price was paid; and a mortgage is only a conditional sale.

But though undoubtedly for some purposes a trust, the condition or state of facts in *Bradford Banking Co. v. Briggs*, did not amount to a trust within the meaning of section 30, of the Act of 1862. Why is this?

The judgments in the House of Lords seem to say that the notice was not notice of a trust, in the sense of being notice of such a character as to attach to the Company the character of trustee. Section 30 deprives it of this character. It is not, therefore, the case of an attempt to affect the Company with a trust. It is merely notice that the person with whom the Company deals, that is the registered shareholder, is not really the owner of the shares. It does not enable the Company to 'charge what they knew was one man's property with another man's debt if only that property consisted of shares in the Company.'

[567] [T]he real object of the Legislature in enacting section 30, and that of similar provisions embodied in articles of association, may supply the key to the whole matter. It cannot be doubted that the intention was to spare the Company the responsibility of attending to any trusts or equities whatever attached to their shares, so that they might safely and securely deal with the person who is registered owner, and with him alone, recognising no other person and no different right; freeing them, in short, from all embarrassing inquiries into conflicting claims as to shares, transfers, calls, dividends, right to vote, and the like; and enabling them to treat the registered shareholder as owner of the shares for all purposes, without regard to contract as between himself and third persons. But it could never have been the object of the Legislature to enable the Company, say a trading Company like the Provincial Bank, to ignore for their own purposes and interests the rights of other persons of which they have actual knowledge, so as, in the words of Lord Blackburn, 'to charge what they knew was one man's property with another man's debt.' There is no obligation upon a bank or other Company to lend money on its shares, and no reason why any special protection should be afforded them if they do: or why, if they choose to do so, they should be exempt from the rules of law and justice. . . . [568]

Sect. 30 provides 'No notice of any trust, expressed or implied or constructive, shall be entered on the register, or be receivable by the registrar, in case of Companies under this Act, and registered in England or Ireland,' and clause 8 of the articles of association provides, 'No person shall be recognised by the Company as holding any share upon any trust, and the Company shall not be *bound* by, or recognise, any equitable, future, or partial interest in any share , , , or any other right in respect of any share except an absolute right to the entirety thereof in the registered holder.' In both cases the language is, I think, intended for the protection of the Company; not to enable it to commit frauds, or knowingly take the benefit of them.

In the present case it is not sought (any more than in *Bradford Banking Co. v. Briggs*), to affect the bank with any particular trust, or with direct notice of any trust whatever. It is sought to show that no matter what trust or equity may have attached to the shares or to Barry, yet the bank had notice that Barry was not owner of the shares, and that they had this knowledge before they lent him the money in respect of which they claim to have a lien. I cannot see how in this point of view, the special facts of the present case render the reasoning in *Bradford Banking Co. v. Briggs* inapplicable.

But in the present case there is far more than mere notice to the Company of the rights of the plaintiff, or the absence of right and title in Barry. There is conduct on the part of the bank amounting to positive aquiescence in her position, or rather in the position that Barry had no property or right to the shares which he could use for his own benefit.

Casey v. Bentley
[1902] 1 I.R. 376

The plaintiff executed a transfer of shares to the defendant and was paid the purchase money. Under the company's regulations, the directors could refuse to register the defendant as a shareholder.

LORD ASHBOURNE C.: . . . [384] This case raises a novel and interesting question on the duty of registering a transfer of shares purchased on the Stock Exchange, and the question is, What is the position of buyer and seller when the directors of the Company, acting within their powers, refuse to register the transfer though the purchaser has paid his money? It appears that the plaintiff, Mrs Casey, was possessed of two shares in the Dublin and Glasgow Steam Packet Company, which is an unlimited Company, and being desirous of escaping from a Company with unlimited liability, she agreed on the 31st January, 1898, through her stockbroker, Mr Kelly, to sell her shares to the defendant. In pursuance of that agreement the transfer was signed by the plaintiff, and accepted, and the purchase money was paid. When the defendant sought to have his name placed on the list of shareholders, the directors of the Company refused to register the transfer, relying on their 15th Regulation, which prescribes: 'It shall be lawful for the directors to decline to register the transfer of shares to any person not approved of by the directors as transferee, and thereupon such a transfer shall be void, and the directors shall not be compellable to give any reason for such refusal.'

The defendant unquestionably acted with perfect good faith, and exhausted all the opportunities open to him of getting the transfer registered; on the other hand, it is not denied that the Company are within their rights in acting as they did in the matter. The dividends which have accrued since the sale of the shares have been regularly paid to Mrs Casey, and she has paid them over to the defendant, on his demand, but under protest.

Matters have stood thus for four years. The plaintiff desired to bring the question to an issue, and in order to elucidate her position she issued an equity civil bill in January, 1901, before the Recorder, [385] claiming specific performance of the agreement so far as the same remained unperformed, and asking that the defendant might be ordered to procure the shares to be registered in his own name or in that of some other person. When the matter came before the Recorder in February, 1901, it was found that that civil bill would not really present the case, and therefore an amendment was assumed to be necessary by all the parties. The civil bill was accordingly amended by the Court, a claim being added to the prayer for specific performance, asking for an indemnity and also for rescission of the contract. This amendment was made because the plaintiff, who was the vendor, finding that the original purchaser could not give her the relief she sought, thought that the best thing to do was to get rescission of the contract, and than seek for another purchaser, to whom the Company would not object. . . .

There is a clear distinction between the purchase of shares on the Stock Exchange and by private contract, and it is essential to keep this distinction clearly in view when reading the authorities, and when considering the comments in *Fry on Specific Performance* and *Lindley on Companies*.

There are many cases where purchasers have proceeded against vendors of shares on the Stock Exchange seeking for relief where the directors have refused to register the transfers, and thus complete their legal tide. But I have been unable to find any case, like the present, where the vendor, having been paid the purchase money and executed the transfer, and the purchaser having *bona fide* failed to obtain registration owing to a legitimate refusal on the part of the directors acting within the scope of their legal powers, is perfectly willing to remain equitable owner of the shares and let matters rest, but is nevertheless, sued by the vendor praying for the rescission of the contract, in consequence of the purchaser not having succeeded in getting the shares registered in his name, which he admittedly could not have done.

The general position is stated by Fry, L.J., in his work on Specific Performance, 1519:

"Where the constitution of the Company gives the directors a power to refuse to register transfers, the question arises whether the refusal on the part of the directors to register the purchaser relieves him from the obligation of performing the contract. This question must be answered [387] differently according to circumstances. Where the contract is not made on the Stock Exchange, but is made in the reference to the constitution of the Company or subject to its rules, and the constitution of the Company requires the vendor to do all that is essential to the transfer, the vendor is under an obligation to procure the assent of the directors, and if he fail so to do, the purchaser is relieved from the contract, and if he have already paid his purchase money in ignorance of this refusal he may recover it back. Where the contract is made on the Stock Exchange, and subject to its rules, it is clear that the refusal of the directors to register the transfer is immaterial, for, according to the construction put upon such a contract, it is performed on the vendor's part by the delivery of the transfer and certificates, and the vendee is entitled to the right which he thereby acquires to procure himself to be registered, if the directors so choose; he is not entitled to an absolute and unconditional right to registration. In a sale on the Stock Exchange it is no part of the vendor's duty, irrespective of express contract, to procure the registration of the transfer."

The position of the purchaser I take to be sufficiently clear from the cases cited by the learned writer . . . . [391]

It is thus abundantly clear on the authorities that the purchaser cannot rescind the contract because he cannot obtain registration. The effort is now made for the first time to turn the tables and say that the vendor is entitled to rescind the contract because the directors have refused the most urgent requests of the purchaser to be registered. There is no authority for this to be found in any case of transfer of shares on the Stock Exchange. . . .

In his judgment in *Stray v. Russell* (I E. & E. 888), Crompton, J., said (at p. 913) -'The fact of the payment being to be made on the handing over of the certificates and transfers, and the practice stated as to no prior consent being ever asked for, and as to no assent being ever refused, make it very probable that the vendee in such case bargains only for the delivery of the shares and transfers and takes the chance of getting himself or his nominee or subvendee accepted and registered. The plaintiff must be taken to have known of the clause in the deed as to the consent, and he may well have bought, taking the chance of procuring such acceptance or registration on himself. He seems to have bought the shares, certificates and transfers, on the agreement to pay for them on delivery of the documents. In *Wilkinson v. Lloyd* (7 QB. 27) the Court assumed that the consent to the assignment was a part of the vendor's tide, as in the case of sale of a lease; but whatever may have been the case of the purchase of the partnership shares in the mines (real [392] property to some extent), in that case on a sale between the parties not according to any course of business on the Stock Exchange, I can make no such assumption in the present case, where the sale was, according to the regulations of the Stock Exchange, which made the price payable on handing over the shares and transfers, and according to which it is at least probable that the vendee was to take upon himself the duty of getting the transfers completed and the shares registered, and where from the nature of the transaction, it seems to me very unlikely that the vendor should undertake for the acceptance of any particular name or person when he may have been entirely ignorant at the time of the contract of the name and responsibility of the intended transferee.'

It is said that it would be hard on the plaintiff to hold her bound to the shares she had sold and struggled to get rid of. But it was equally hard to hold the parties bound in the decided cases to which I have referred. If the plaintiff had been well advised she could have safeguarded her position and stipulated with her stockbroker that he was to stipulate for registration as a clear term in his Stock Exchange contract. In *Cruse v. Paine* (L.R. 6 Eq. 461) where the purchaser expressly guaranteed the registration of the shares, he was held liable to indemnify the seller. The sale note in that case had written across it the words 'registration guaranteed'. Lord Hatherley in his judgment expressly pointed out that the superadded provision of 'registration guaranteed' made the defendant liable to procure registration.

CHAPTER 10

Minority Shareholder Protection

Almost invariably, differences will arise between shareholders about their company's affairs. One of the fundamental principles of company law is majority rule; it is for the majority of shareholders with voting rights to decide most matters concerning the company. Certain fundamental matters should be resolved by super-majorities (usually either a special resolution or decision of three quarters in value of the shareholders). Consequently, the dissatisfied shareholder or shareholders who cannot persuade the majority to come around to their point of view will often have to choose between having their preferences ignored or selling out their shares. In companies whose shares are quoted on the Stock Exchange, the threat to dispose of a large block of shares may persuade the majority to make their peace with the minority. In private companies, on the other hand, restrictions in the articles of association on the transferability of shares may render a minority stake virtually unsaleable.

Judges have always been somewhat hesitant about adjudicating on inter-shareholder disputes. Many of the matters that give rise to conflict between shareholders concern essentially business judgments, such as hiring and firing employees, expanding or contracting particular lines of activity, paying dividends or placing profits in reserve. If such matters were readily reviewable by the courts, then the spectre of judges 'taking on the management of every playhouse and brewhouse' in the country would be realised. Lawyers do not possess any special competence in business matters, and legal procedures are far too expensive and cumbersome for resolving differences of policy between shareholders. There nevertheless are several grounds on which the courts will intervene on the minority shareholder's behalf. Many of the Companies Acts' provisions entitle individual members to bring suit in order to enforce the statutory requirements. A shareholder may bring suit alleging breach of the 'section 25 contract' that is contained in the memorandum and articles of association; or alleging unfair discrimination against a minority; or a derivative suit claiming that the majority defrauded the company; or a petition under section 205 of the 1963 Act, claiming 'oppression'; or the drastic step of petitioning to have the company wound up on 'just and equitable' grounds or on the grounds of 'oppression'.

ILLEGALITY

See *Company Law*, p. 324.

Cockburn v. Newbridge Sanitary Steam Laundry Co. Ltd.
[1915] 1 I.R. 237

The company had a contract to do certain work for the military authorities in the Curragh for £3,268 but payment was to be made to the defendant director, who handed over only £1,038 to the company.

O'BRIEN L.C.: [252] The principle of law applicable to cases of this kind are well settled and, indeed, as has been said, are elementary. The difficulty arises in applying well-settled principles to the particular facts of each case, and the only trouble in the present instance arises from the circumstance that the facts do not at once readily group themselves under any of the reported cases.

Thomas Llewellyn, one of the defendants, was a director of the Newbridge Sanitary Steam Laundry Co., Ltd., and acted, although not possibly legally qualified, as managing director. The business had been founded by the husband of Louisa Cockburn, the plaintiff, and on his death practically the entire management of the company was carried on by Llewellyn, and, as the Master of the Rolls accurately puts it, the plaintiff did not control the affairs of the company, never inquired into them, and was in fact a mere dummy; and I see no reason to form the conclusion, even if the question could affect the result, that she was in a way privy or party to the transaction which gives rise indirectly to the present claim.

Owing to the proximity of the large military establishments near Newbridge, the business carried on by the defendant company is large, and appears to have been very remunerative. In the years 1909, 1910 and 1911, contracts were entered into between the military authorities and the defendant Llewellyn in his own name, for washing to be done in connexion with the military hospital, and otherwise under circumstances which would make the War Office liable to pay large sums for laundry work.

It is not disputed that although Llewellyn's name only appeared in the contracts, he really entered into them on behalf of the company. The washing was done by the company, and the remuneration to be paid for the work done was earned by the company, and, prima facie, the whole of it should be payable to them. The amount admittedly received by Llewellyn from the War Department was £3268, and the amount which he paid into the coffers of the company was only £1038, leaving an extraordinarily large balance for which he refuses to account.

[253] The plaintiffs, who hold a large number of shares in the company, but not a preponderating amount, seek to make him account, or, more simply, to pay to the company the money which he has received, and which he refuses to pay.

The Master of the Rolls came to the only conclusion that a court could come to, that, as between Llewellyn and the company, there could be no answer to the action if the company had been the plaintiffs, but he was pressed by, and yielded to, the argument that in substance this was merely an attempt to enforce by a member of a company a claim against a director which the company might lawfully and reasonably refuse to enforce; that accordingly the question was one merely relating to the 'internal management' of the company, and therefore that a shareholder could not invoke the aid of the Court against the will of the company, and compel Llewellyn to account to the company.

There is no doubt that if this was merely a matter of 'internal management' the decision of the Court below could not be disturbed, and the sole question that we have to determine is whether on the peculiar facts of this case this is a question of merely 'internal management'.

The rule of law and of good sense laid down in *Foss v. Harbottle* (2 Hare 461) is indisputable, but it is subject to the exception that where the acts complained of are of a fraudulent character, or beyond the powers of the company, the action may be maintained by a shareholder suing on behalf of himself and the other shareholders, the company being made a defendant in the action. *Dominion Cotton Mills Co., Ltd. v. Amyot* [1912] A.C. 546, and *Burland v. Earle* [1902] A.C. 83, are recent cases where the rule had been considered and expounded, and its limitations defined.

Let us now return to the evidence. The defendant Llewellyn refuses to disclose what he did with the money, because he says [254] that the disclosure might criminate him. Mr Beck, the secretary of the company, says that it would be unwise to investigate Llewellyn's dealings, presumably because the criminality of some kind lying at the root would be laid bare. On being pressed, Llewellyn said that to give an account might incriminate him, because it would show that the differences in the amounts paid to the company and received by him had been disbursed in secret commissions, which of course would be a criminal offence. It is very hard to understand, even on the wildest scheme of bribery, that £2230 out of £3268 were paid in secret commissions, but it makes the case no better for Llewellyn that he claims the right of secrecy on this ground alone.

It has been argued most ingeniously by counsel for the company that there was a contract with Llewellyn, which it is suggested would be perfectly lawful, that he was to give the company whatever he thought right out of what he received. There is no evidence of such a contract having been made, even if it could lawfully be made; and the only question is whether, on the facts as we have now got them, it would be within the powers of the company to take up the attitude, 'We will not inquire.' If this company had entered into a contract with Llewellyn, giving him authority to commit a crime on behalf of himself and the company, such a contract would, of course, be absolutely illegal, and it requires no argument to see that it would be equally illegal to adopt such a contract either affirmatively or indirectly.

Illegality and ultra vires are not interchangeable terms, but it is difficult, if not impossible, to conceive a case in which a company can do an illegal act, the illegality arising from public policy, and act within its powers.

Dealing with a case not of this class, but of ultra vires unaffacted by criminality, Lord Cairns, says, in *Ashbury Railway Carriage & Iron Co. v. Riche* (L.R. 7 H.L. 653, at p. 672): 'But, my Lords, if the shareholders of this company could not *ab ante* have authorized a contract of this kind to be made, how could they subsequently sanction the contract after it had, in point of fact, been made . . . [255] It appears to me that it would be perfectly fatal to the whole scheme of legislation to which I have referred, if you were to hold that, in the first place, directors might do that which even the whole company could not do, and that then the shareholders finding out what had been done, could sanction, subsequently, what they could not antecedently have authorized.'

How much stronger is the position when the whole matter is tainted with criminality. The real agreement which it is suggested the directors did make in this case would have been an agreement, if made, so tainted with crime and so subversive of public policy as to be illegal in itself. It would, accordingly, have been quite beyond the powers of the company to have entered into it, nor could any memorandum or articles have given it power; it would be equally wrong for the company to ratify it, and it would be idle to give them an opportunity to vote on such a question, because the carrying of the resolution would be, in my judgment, nugatory as being illegal, and consequently wholly outside the powers of a company. To do a thing which would have for its main object either the commission of a crime, or the aiding or abetting of a crime, or the hushing up of a crime, could not be in any way within the powers of a company, and a matter of 'internal management' in which the Court should not interfere.

In this view of the case I do not find myself constrained by the difficulties which affected the Master of the Rolls. I do not go into the question of the sufficiency or insufficiency of the demand which was made for the plaintiff on the directors to summon a meeting of their company. In the view that I take of the case it would not be within the power of the company either to make, ratify or adopt a proceeding of the scandalous character sought to be cloaked over in the present case by such a resolution.

The appearance of the company, and the arguments of the counsel, are sufficient in my judgment to justify the Court in holding that the plaintiffs are entitled to direct relief in the present case, and that an account should be directed against the defendant Llewellyn in respect of the moneys which the company earned by these contracts, and which he either received or ought to have received.

HOLMES L.J.: . . . [258] The Master of the Rolls was satisfied that, on the facts before him, the company was entitled to enforce an account. When the director who manages the business of a company, like that of this steam laundry, admits that he has entered into many contracts on behalf of the company, that he has been paid the contract prices, and that he has not accounted therefor, he could have no answer to an action of account by the company; and O'Connor M.R. would have so held, if such an action had been brought by them; but the difficulty he feels is that the company not only refuse to assist the plaintiffs, but, being named as defendants, actively defended the suit on the well-known legal ground that the matter in controversy relates to the mode of managing the company's business. The company may have such a question settled by action; but, if it does not desire to do so, one or more shareholders cannot, by constituting themselves plaintiffs, do so. There is, however, one well-recognized exception to this rule. Where the question involves the investigation of misconduct or criminality on the part of the company and one or more of its officers, or something ultra vires the company itself, the arm of the law cannot be stayed by the rule of law to which I have referred.

O'Connor M.R. was of opinion that there was no evidence of this exception in the present case . . . On this point I have come to a different conclusion. The only evidence in favour of himself given by Mr Llewellyn is that he neither kept nor used any of the contract prices for himself. [But h]e declined to answer the simple question as to what he had done with the portion thereof which he had not paid over to or for the company. When asked the ground of his refusing to answer, he said that to do so would incriminate himself. The case has been tried in the Rolls and argued in this Court, in the shadow of this answer. Surely, without some explanation, it is a matter of certainty that what became of this money involves some criminality or misconduct by the managing director . . .

Note: A sequel to this case was *Re The Newbridge Sanitary Steam Laundry Ltd* [1917] 1 I.R. 617, and see post p. 494. Compare *O' Neill v. Ryan* [1993] I. L. R. M. 257, (post p. 458), where it was held that a minority shareholder does not have locus standi to sue the principal shareholder and others on the grounds that they were in breach of Articles 85 and 86 of the E. E. C. Treaty. *Quare* whether the position would be the same for claims of breach of the Competition Acts 1991–1996, which are criminal offences as well as actionable wrongs?

Breach of the Memorandum or Articles of Association

See *Company Law*, pp.325–329.

Companies Act 1963, section 25(1)

Effect of memorandum and articles

25.—(1) Subject to the provisions of this Act, the memorandum and articles shall, when registered, bind the company and the members thereof to the same extent as if they respectively had been signed and sealed by each member, and contained covenants by each member to observe all the provisions of the memorandum and of the articles.

Salmon v. Quin & Axtens Ltd.
[1909] 1 Ch. 311

The company's articles of association gave each of two named managing directors, who as well were the company's principal shareholders, what in effect was a veto over major property transactions envisaged by the company. Against the objections of the plaintiff, who was one of them, the board and then the members in general meeting resolved to enter into such a transaction. The plaintiff sought to enjoin the company from acting on that resolution.

FARWELL L.J.: . . . [318] The articles, by section 16 of the Act of 1862, are made equivalent to a deed of covenant signed by all the shareholders. The Act does not say with whom that covenant is entered into, and there have no doubt been varying statements by learned judges, some of them saying it is with the company, and with the shareholders. Stirling J. in *Wood v. Odessa Waterworks Co.* (1889) 42 Ch. D. 636 says: 'The articles of association constitute a contract not merely between the shareholders and the company but between each individual shareholder and every other.' I think that that is accurate subject to this observation, that it may well be that the Court would not enforce the covenant as between individual shareholders in most cases. Now the general power of the board to manage here is qualified by the stipulation which follows, that it is to be subject to the provisions of these articles. I therefore turn to article 80, and I find this provision to which these general powers of management are made subject: (His Lordship read the article.) In the present case Mr Salmon did so dissent according to the terms of that article, and therefore the veto therein provided came into operation. That was met by the company being called together by a requisition of seven shareholders and by passing general resolutions for the acquisition of this property and the letting of the vacant premises. It is said that those resolutions are of no effect, and I am of opinion that the contention is right. I base my opinion on the words of article 75, 'subject, nevertheless, to the provisions of any Acts of Parliament or of these articles,' which I read to be [320] 'subject, nevertheless, to article 80' and to such regulations (being not inconsistent with any such provisions of these articles) as may be prescribed by the company in general meeting.' That is to say, 'subject also to such regulations not inconsistent with article 80 as may be prescribed by the company in general meeting.' But these resolutions are absolutely inconsistent with article 80; in truth this is an attempt to alter the terms of the contract between the parties by a simple resolution instead of by a special resolution. The articles forming this contract, under which the business of the company shall be managed by the board, contain a most usual and proper requirement, because a business does require a head to look after it, and a head that shall not be interfered with unnecessarily. Then in order to oust the directors a special resolution would be required. The case is, in my view, entirely governed, if not by the decision, at any rate by the reasoning of the Lords Justices in *Automatic Self-Cleansing Filter Syndicate Co. v. Cuninghame* [1906] 2 Ch. 34 (ante p. 179) and *Gramophone and Typewriter, Ltd. v. Stanley* [1908] 2 K.B. 89. I will only refer to one passage in Buckley L.J.'s judgment in the latter case. He says: 'This Court decided not long since, in *Automatic Self-Cleansing Filter Syndicate Co. v. Cuninghame*, that even a resolution of a numerical majority at a general meeting of the company cannot impose its will upon the directors when the articles have confided to them the control of the company's affairs. The directors are not servants to obey directions given by the shareholders as individuals; they are not agents appointed by and bound to serve the shareholders as their principals. They are persons who may by the regulations be entrusted with the control of the business, and if so entrusted they can be dispossessed from that control only by the statutory majority which can alter the articles. Directors are not, I think, bound to comply with the directions even of all the corporators acting as individuals.' That appears to me to express the true view. Any other construction might, I think, be disastrous, because it might lead to an interference by a bare majority very inimical to the interests of the minority who had come into a company on the footing that the business should be managed by the board of directors.

Beattie v. E. & F. Beattie Ltd.
[1938] 1 Ch. 708

One provision in the company's articles of association was that whenever 'any . . . dispute shall arise between the members of the company, or between the company and any member or members,' it shall be referred to arbitration. The plaintiff shareholder sought to bring a derivative action against the company's chairman and managing director, who was also a shareholder, for breach of fiduciary duty. A central issue was whether the above clause obliged the plaintiff to have the matter resolved by arbitration.

SIR WILFRED GREENE M.R.: . . . [720] The appellant . . . seeks to find in the articles themselves a contract to which he is a party giving him the right to demand an arbitration in the present circumstances. . . . [His counsel] says – Here is a member, [and] here is an article which provides that a dispute between the company and a member shall be referred to arbitration. It covers, among other things, a dispute relating to an act or default of a director. And he says that what he is seeking in the present case to do is to enforce that right as a member under that article and not any right as a director; that he has a right, and all other members have a right, when they find the company disputing with a director, to insist on that dispute being referred to arbitration. [His counsel] says that the case must be treated as though the circumstance that the appellant happens to be a director is immaterial. He says that it is quite immaterial that the member who is demanding arbitration is himself the member attacked.

[721] In my judgment, that argument is based on an incorrect view both as to the effect of the article and as to the effect of section 20 of the Companies Act. The question as to the precise effect of section 20 has been the subject of considerable controversy in the past, and it may very well be that there will be considerable controversy about it in the future. But it appears to me that this much, at any rate, is good law: that the contractual force given to the articles of association by the section is limited to such provisions of the articles as apply to the relationship of the members in their capacity as members.

I do not think, in saying that, that I am in any way departing from or extending (and it certainly is not my intention to depart from or extend) certain observations of Astbury J. in the well-known case of *Hickman v. Kent or Romney Marsh Sheep-Breeders' Association* [19151] Ch. 88 1. In that case Astbury J. made a careful review of all the decisions, and he expressed his conclusions with regard to them in this way. He referred to *Eley v. Positive Life Assurance Co., Ltd.* (1876) 1 Ex. D. 21, and certain other cases, and pointed out that those decisions amounted to this: 'An outsider to whom rights purport to be given by the articles in his capacity as such outsider, whether he is or subsequently becomes a member, cannot sue on those articles treating them as contracts between himself and the company to enforce those rights. Those rights are not part of the general regulations of the company applicable alike to all shareholders and can only exist by virtue of some contract between such person and the company.' Then, again, he said: 'no right merely purporting to be given by an article to a person, whether a member or not, in a capacity other than that of a member, as, for instance, as solicitor, promoter, director, can be enforced against the company.'

With those two statements I respectfully agree. They are statements with regard to the true construction and operation of section 20, and they have the result in the present case of preventing that section from giving contractual force to the article as between the company and its directors as such.

[722] It is to be observed that the real matter which is here being litigated is a dispute between the company and the appellant in his capacity as a director, and when the appellant, relying on this clause, seeks to have that dispute referred to arbitration, it is that dispute and none other which he is seeking to have referred, and by seeking to have it referred he is not, in my judgment, seeking to enforce a right which is common to himself and all other members. He is seeking to enforce a quite different right. I will explain what I mean. Let me assume that this article on its true construction entitles any member of the company to say to the company, when it is in dispute with a director: 'You, the

company, are bound by your contract with me in the articles to refer this dispute to arbitration, and I call upon you so to do.' That is the right, and the only right in this respect, which is common to all the members, under this article. If that were the right which the appellant was seeking to exercise, there might be something to be said for that argument but, with all respect to the able argument of [his counsel] it appears to me that that is not at all the right which the appellant is seeking to enforce. He is not seeking to enforce a right to call on the company to arbitrate a dispute which is only accidentally a dispute with himself. He is asking, as a disputant, to have the dispute to which he is a party referred. That is sufficient to differentiate it from the right which is common to all the other members of the company under this article, which I have tried to define. That right is one which a member might find very great difficulty in enforcing in the Courts, because it concerns a matter relating to the internal management of the company, with which the Courts will not, in general, interfere.

But quite apart from that consideration, the two rights are, in my judgment, perfectly distinct and quite different – the general right of a member as a member and the right which the appellant as a party to the dispute is seeking to enforce. Indeed, [counsel] agrees that his argument really amounted to saying that the present application is in essence the same as proceedings brought by Mr Ernest Beattie, as a shareholder, to restrain the company from litigating and [723] to obtain a mandatory order on the company to go to arbitration. But that is a very different thing from what he is now seeking since his claim, as I have said, is to insist on a reference of his own dispute.

UNFAIR DISCRIMINATION

See *Company Law*, pp. 329–340.

Greenhalgh v. Arderne Cinemas Ltd.
[1951] 1 Ch. 286 (C.A.)

This case is part of a series of litigation between parties interested in the company in question. Under the company's articles of association, no shares could be transferred to outsiders until they were first offered to and refused by the existing shareholders; the directors were empowered to refuse to register any transfer of shares. Principally to enable a controlling shareholder to sell his shares to an outsider, the company resolved to alter these provisions by adding to them a clause whereby, with the approval of an ordinary resolution in general meeting, any member could transfer his shares to any named outsider. The plaintiff claimed that this resolution was unlawful.

EVERSHED M.R.: [290] The burden of the case is that the resolution was not passed bona fide and [291] in the interests of the company as a whole, and there are, as Mr Jennings has urged, two distinct approaches.

The first line of attack is this, and it is one to which, he complains, Roxburgh J., paid no regard: this is a special resolution, and, on authority, Mr Jennings says, the validity of a special resolution depends upon the fact that those who passed it did so in good faith and for the benefit of the company as a whole. The cases to which Mr Jennings referred are *Sidebottom v. Kershaw, Leese & Co. Ltd.* [1920] 1 Ch. 154, Peterson, J.'s decision in *Dafen Tinplate Co. Ltd. v. Llanelly Steel Co. (1907) Ltd.* [1920] 2 Ch. 24, and, finally, *Shuttleworth v. Cox Brothers & Co. (Maidenhead), Ltd.* [1927] 2 K.B. 9. Certain principles, I think, can be safely stated as emerging from those authorities. In the first place, I think it is now plain that 'bona fide for the benefit of the company as a whole' means not two things but one thing. It means that the shareholder must proceed upon what, in his honest opinion, is for the benefit of the company as a whole. The second thing is that the phrase, 'the company as a whole', does not (at any rate in such a case as the present) mean the company as a commercial entity, distinct from the corporators: it means the corporators as a general body. That is to say, the case may be taken of an individual hypothetical member and it may be asked whether what is proposed is, in the honest opinion of those who voted in its favour, for that person's benefit.

I think that the matter can, in practice, be more accurately and precisely stated by looking at the converse and by saying that a special resolution of this kind would be liable to be impeached if the effect of it were to discriminate between the majority shareholders and the minority shareholders, so as to give the former an advantage of which the latter were deprived. When the cases are examined in which the resolution has been successfully attacked, it is on that ground. It is therefore not necessary to require that persons voting for a special resolution should, so to speak, dissociate themselves altogether from their own prospects and consider whether what is thought to be for the benefit of the company as a going concern. If, as commonly happens, an outside person makes an offer to buy all the shares, prima facie, if the corporators think it a fair offer and vote in favour of the resolution, it is no ground for impeaching the resolution that they are considering their own position as individuals.

Accepting that, as I think he did, Mr Jennings said, in effect, that there are still grounds for impeaching this resolution: first, because it goes further than was necessary to give effect to the particular sale of the shares; and, secondly, because it prejudiced the plaintiff and minority shareholders in that it deprived them of the right which, under the subsisting articles, they would have of buying the shares of the majority if the latter desired to dispose of them.

What Mr Jennings objects to in the resolution is that if a resolution is passed altering the articles merely for the purpose of giving effect to a particular transaction, then it is quite sufficient (and it is usually done) to limit it to that transaction. But this resolution provides that anybody who wants at any time to sell his shares can now go direct to an outsider, provided that there is an ordinary resolution of the company approving the proposed transferee. Accordingly, if it is one of the majority who is selling, he will get the necessary resolution. This change in the articles, so to speak, franks the shares for holders of majority interests but makes it more difficult for a minority shareholder, because the majority will probably look with disfavour upon his choice. But, after all, this is merely a relaxation of the very stringent restrictions on transfer in the existing article, and it is to be borne in mind that the directors, as the articles stood, could always refuse to register a transfer. A minority shareholder, therefore, who produced an outsider was always liable to be met by the directors (who presumably act according to the majority view) saying, 'We are sorry, but we will not have this man in'.

Although I follow the point, and it might perhaps have been possible to do it the other way, I think that this case is very far removed from the type of case in which what is proposed, as in the *Dafen* case, is to give a majority the right to expropriate a minority shareholder, whether he wanted to sell or not, merely on the ground that the majority shareholders wanted the minority man's shares.

As to the second point, I felt at one time sympathy for the plaintiffs argument, because, after all, as the articles stood he could have said: 'Before you go selling to the purchaser you have to offer your shares to the existing shareholders, and that will enable me, if I feel so disposed, to buy, in effect, the whole of the shareholding of the Arderne company'. I think that the answer is that when a man comes into a company, he is not entitled to assume that the articles will always remain in a particular form; and that, so long as the proposed alteration does not unfairly discriminate in the way which I have indicated, it is not an objection, provided that the resolution is passed bona fide, that the right to tender for the majority holding of shares would be lost by the lifting of the restriction. I do not think that it can be said that that is such a discrimination as falls within the scope of the principle which I have stated.

[293] Mr Jennings further says that, if that is wrong, he falls back on his other point that the defendant Mallard acted in bad faith. He concealed, it is said, various matters; he confessed to feelings of envy and hatred against the plaintiff; he desired to do something to spite him, even if he cut off his own nose in the process. Following the judge's line of reasoning, it is said that the defendant Mallard did control all these other submissive persons who supported him, so that they are equally tainted with the defendant Mallard's bad faith. I agree with Mr Jennings that, if an ordinary shareholder chooses to give what Mr Jennings called 'carte blanche' to the promotor of a scheme and that promoter is then found to have been acting in bad faith, the persons who gave him carte blanche cannot then say that they exercised any independent judgment, and they would likewise be tainted with the evil of their leader.

Mr Jennings had, early in his argument, formulated his grounds for bad faith against the defendant Mallard at greater length, and I need not, I think, go through the several heads.

[His lordship considered certain specific criticisms of the defendant Mallard's conduct, and continued:] Mr Jennings says that all these various matters cast such doubt upon the transaction that the defendant Mallard must be taken to have been acting in bad faith. I think that he acted with grave indiscretion in some respects; but the judge has said that he was in no way guilty of deliberate dishonesty; and I cannot see where and how it can be suggested that he was grinding some particular axe of his own. He was getting 6s. a share; but he was getting no more and no less than anyone else would get who wished to sell; and I am unable and unwilling to put upon the actions of the defendant Mallard, because of his unfortunate secrecy and other conduct, so bad a complexion as to impute bad faith in the true sense of the term, of which, indeed, Roxburgh J., acquitted him.

In my opinion, in spite of all these complexities, this was, in substance, an offer by an outside man to buy the shares of this company at 6s. a share from anybody who was willing to sell them. As commonly happens, the defendant Mallard, as the managing director of the company, negotiated and had to proceed on the footing that he had with him sufficient support to make the negotiation a reality. That was the substance of what was suggested. It discriminated between no types of shareholder. Any who wanted to get out at that price could get out, and any who preferred to stay in could stay in.

Gambotto v. W.C.P. Ltd
[1994–1995] 182 C.L.R. 432 (1993)

A company passed a special resolution for the amendment of its articles of association, the effect of which was to enable a shareholder holding 90 per cent or more of the issued shares to acquire compulsorily shares held by minority shareholders for a stipulated price per share. The notice of meeting was accompanied by a valuation of shares prepared by a firm of accountants. The stipulated price exceeded the net asset value of a share as so valued. Two minority shareholders applied for a declaration that the amendment of the articles was invalid. The majority shareholders, who were related, held about 99.7 per cent of the issued capital. The shareholding of the company was such that the majority shareholders or companies associated with them could not have acquired the plaintiff shareholders' shares compulsorily under section 414 or section 701 of the *Corporations Law* (similar to section 204 of the 1963 Act). The plaintiffs conceded that the accountants' valuation was independent and fair. There would have been considerable tax advantages and administrative benefits for the company if it had become a wholly-owned subsidiary of the holding company of the majority shareholders. The majority shareholders did not vote upon the special resolution, which was passed upon the votes of minority shareholders other than the plaintiffs:

MASON C.J., BRENNAN, DEANE AND DAWSON JJ.: [437] This appeal raises an important question concerning the validity of an amendment to the articles of association of a company, the purpose of which is to enable the shareholder holding 90 per cent or more of the issued shares to acquire compulsorily shares held by minority shareholders. . .

[439] *Expropriation of minority shareholdings*
The fundamental issue in this case is whether, and if so in what circumstances, the taking of a power by majority shareholders by amendment to the articles to acquire compulsorily the shares of the minority shareholders will be held invalid on the basis that it is oppressive. The logical starting point for a consideration of this issue is *Allen v. Gold Reefs of West Africa Ltd.* [1900] 1 Ch. at p.671 (see post, p. 506), where Lindley M.R. stated that the power of the majority to alter the articles by special resolution "must be exercised, not on in the manner required by law, but also bona fide for the benefit of the company as a whole, and it must not be exceeded". The validity of the resolution altering the articles in that case was upheld by [440] Lindley M.R. and Romer L.J., who concurred in Lindley M.R.'s reasons. Vaughan Williams L.J. dissented on the ground that the resolution was not passed in good faith, "being really passed merely to defeat the existing rights of an individual shareholder".

Strictly speaking, *Allen v. Gold Reefs of West Affica Ltd.* did not involve an expropriation of shares. Rather, it concerned an alteration that gave a company a lien on fully paid shares to cover debts owed to it by the only shareholder who held such shares. Its importance for present purposes lies in the fact that the test outlined above has been used in subsequent cases in England to determine the validity of an amendment that purports to allow the majority to expropriate minority shareholdings. *Brown v. British Abrasive Wheel Co.* [1919] 1 Ch. 290 is an example of such a case. There, the proposed alteration provided that a member would be "bound upon the request in writing of the holders or holder of nine-tenths of the issued shares to sell and transfer his shares . . . to the nominee of such holders or holder". Astbury J., after noting that there was no allegation of mala fides on the majority's part, stated at pp. 295-296:

> "The question therefore is whether the enforcement of the proposed alteration on the minority is within the ordinary principles of justice and whether it is for the benefit of the company as a whole. I find it very difficult to follow how it can be just and equitable that a majority, on failing to purchase the shares of a minority by agreement, can take power to do so compulsorily.
>
> The defendants contend that it is for the benefit of the company as a whole because in default of further capital the company might have to go into liquidation . . . [The proposed alteration] is merely for the benefit of the majority. If passed, the majority may acquire all the shares and

provide further capital. That would be for the benefit of the company as then constituted. But the proposed alteration is not for the present benefit of this company."

Astbury J. seems to have regarded the statement of principle by Lindley M.R. in *Allen v. Gold Reefs of West Africa Ltd.* as requiring both good faith and a tendency to benefit the company as a whole.

In *Sidebottom v. Kershaw, Leese & Co. Ltd.* [1920] 1 Ch. 154 the English Court of Appeal upheld a proposed amendment that would empower the majority shareholders to expropriate the shares, at full value, of any shareholder who carried on business in direct competition with the company or was a director of another company [441] carrying on such a business. Lord Sterndale M.R. and Warrington L.J. rejected the view that Lord Lindley's statement of principle involved two distinct elements.

However, in *Dafen Tinplate Co. v. Llanelly Steel Co.* [1920] 2 Ch. 124 Peterson J. took a different view of the principle. There one of the proposed alterations empowered the defendant company in general meeting to determine that the shares of any member "be offered for sale by the Board to such person or persons as the Board shall think fit". Peterson J. held that the amendment was invalid, stating at pp. 141-142:

"It may be for the benefit of the majority of the shareholders to acquire the shares of the minority, but how can it be said to be for the benefit of the company that any shareholder, *against whom no charge of acting to the detriment of the company can be urged*, and who is in every respect a desirable member of the company, and for whose expropriation there is no reason except the will of the majority, should be forced to transfer his shares to the majority or to anyone else? The power of compulsory acquisition by the majority of shares which the owner does not desire to sell is not lightly to be assumed whenever it pleases the majority to do so." (Emphasis added.)

Subsequently, in *Shuttleworth v. Cox Brothers & Co. (Maidenhead) Ltd.* [1927] 1 K.B. 9, the English Court of Appeal rejected Peterson L's view of the principle, holding that it denoted one condition only, a condition expressed by Scrutton L.J. in these words, namely "that the shareholders must act honestly having regard to and endeavouring to act for the benefit of the company" (26).

The last English case of interest, *In re Bugle Press Ltd.* [1961] Ch. 270 (see post p. 562) involved an attempted expropriation of shares in reliance or the compulsory acquisition provisions contained in section 209 of the English Companies Act 1948. Lord Evershed M.R. noted that an expropriation without consent would appear to conflict with the fundamental legal principle that prima facie, if a person has a legal right which is an absolute right, then that person can deal with the right as he or she pleases. That consideration led his

Lordship to conclude that the relevant legislative provisions could not be used in such a [442] way so as to expropriate the shares of the minority, unless there was a good reason for the expropriation, at 287:

> "[F]or example, that the minority shareholder was in some way acting in a manner destructive or highly damaging to the interests of the company from some motives entirely of his own."

Harman L.J. stated that it was a "fundamental rule of company law" that majority shareholders could not expropriate a minority, unless the articles contained an expropriation provision from the outset: cf. *Phillips v. Manufacturers' Securities Ltd* (1917) 116 L.T. 290.

Peters' American Delicacy Co. Ltd. v. Heath (1939) 61 C.L.R. 475

In that case, this Court held that an alteration of the articles which discriminated against holders of partly-paid shares in favour of the majority shareholders did not constitute a fraud on the minority. In the course of his judgment, Latham C.J. (with whom McTiernan J. agreed) expressed the view that, although the power to alter articles must be exercised bona fide, the fact that an alteration prejudices or diminishes some (or all) of the rights of the shareholders is not in itself a ground for attacking the validity of an alteration). On the contrary, his Honour considered that such an alteration must be valid unless the party complaining can establish that the resolution was passed fraudulently or oppressively or was so extravagant that no reasonable person could believe that it was for the benefit of the company". His Honour noted that the criterion of the "benefit of the company as a corporation" could not be invoked as the sole solution to the problem where the amendment in question affected the relative rights of different classes of shareholders.

Dixon J. also considered that the amendment was valid, although his Honour arrived at that conclusion by a different route. Dixon J. declined to leave any analysis of this question to general notions of fairness and propriety, preferring instead to focus on the purpose of the proposed amendment. The steps in his Honour's reasoning may be summarised in this way. A share in a company is property consisting of proprietary rights as defined by the articles of [443] association. The power of alteration of the articles might be used by the majority shareholders for their own aggrandisement at the expense of the minority shareholders. It has seemed incredible that this could be so. But reliance on the doctrine that powers shall be exercised bona fide and for no extraneous purpose presents difficulties. The power of alteration is not a fiduciary power and the right to vote is an incident of property which may be exercised for the shareholder's personal advantage. *Prima facie*, rights dependent upon the articles are not enduring and indefeasible but arc liable to modification or destruction by special resolution. So, "if a resolution is regularly passed with the single aim of advancing the interests of a company considered as a corporate whole, it must fall within the scope of the statutory power to alter the articles and could never be condemned as mala fides".

His Honour went on to say [at pp. 511-512]:

> "The chief reason for denying an unlimited effect to widely expressed powers such as that of altering a company's articles is the fear or knowledge that an apparently regular exercise of the power may in truth be but a means of securing some personal or particular gain, whether pecuniary or otherwise, which does not fairly arise out of the subjects dealt with by the power and is outside and even inconsistent with the contemplated objects of the power. It is to exclude the purpose of securing such ulterior special and particular advantages that Lord Lindley used the phrase 'bona fide for the benefit of the company as a whole.'"

His Honour considered that "benefit as a whole" is a very general expression negativing purposes foreign to the company's affairs and that the "bona fide for the benefit of the company as a whole" test was "inappropriate, if not meaningless", where the amendment proposed to adjust the rights of conflicting interests. Although his Honour did not expressly state which test or tests might be applied in such circumstances, he upheld the resolution in question on the basis that it "Involved no oppression, no appropriation of an unjust or reprehensible nature and did not imply any purpose outside the scope of the power".

In conformity with the views expressed in *Peters*, the use of the expression "for the benefit of the company as a whole" is no longer [444] influential in the context of an alteration of the articles designed to effect or authorise the expropriation of a minority's shares. But the expression is still in vogue in the context of the exercise by directors of their powers, particularly the power to issue or allot shares.

Striking a balance

The foregoing analysis of the authorities reveals that the courts have struggled to strike a balance between the interests of the majority and the minority. On the one hand, the courts have recognised that the proprietary rights attaching to shares are subject to modification, even destruction, by a special resolution altering the articles and that the power to vote is exercisable by a shareholder to his or her own advantage. On the other hand, the courts have acknowledged that the power to alter the articles should not be exercised simply for the purpose of securing some personal gain which does not arise out of the contemplated objects of the power. The problem of stating a workable criterion arises, as Dixon J. said in *Peters* at p.507, "in attempting to discover and fasten upon some element the presence of which will always vitiate a resolution for the alteration of articles of association".

The test for determining whether an expropriation is valid
In the context of a special resolution altering the articles and giving rise to a conflict of interests and advantages, whether or not it involves an expropriation of shares, we would reject as inappropriate the "bona fide for the benefit of the company as a whole" test of Lindley M.R. in *Allen v. Gold Reefs of West Affica Ltd.* The application of the test in such a context has been criticised on grounds which, in our view, are unanswerable. It seems to us that, in such a case not involving an actual or effective expropriation of shares or of valuable proprietary rights attaching to shares, an alteration of the articles by special resolution regularly passed will he valid unless it is *ultra vires*, beyond any purpose contemplated by the articles or oppressive as that expression is understood in the law relating to corporations. Somewhat different considerations apply, however, in a case such as the present where what is involved is an alteration of the articles to allow an expropriation by the majority of [445] the shares, or of valuable proprietary rights attaching to the shares, of a minority. In such a case, the immediate purpose of the resolution is to confer upon the majority shareholder or shareholders power to acquire compulsorily the property of the minority shareholder or shareholders. Of itself, the conferral of such a power does not lie within the "contemplated objects of the power" to amend the articles.

The exercise of a power conferred by a company's constitution enabling the majority shareholders to expropriate the minority's shareholding for the purpose of aggrandising the majority is valid if and only to the extent that the relevant provisions of the company's constitution so provide. The inclusion of such a power in a company's constitution at its incorporation is one thing. But it is another thing when a company's constitution is sought to be amended by an alteration of articles of association so as to confer upon the majority power to expropriate the shares of a minority. Such a power could not be taken or exercised simply for the purpose of aggrandising the majority: *In re Bugle Press Ltd.* [1961] Ch., at pp. 286-287, 287-288. In our view, such a power can be taken only if (i) it is exercisable or a proper purpose and (ii) its exercise will not operate oppressively in relation to minority shareholders. In other words, an expropriation may be justified where it is reasonably apprehended that the continued shareholding of the minority is detrimental to the company, its undertaking or the conduct of its affairs – resulting in detriment to the interests of the existing shareholders generally – and expropriation is a reasonable means of eliminating or mitigating that detriment.

Accordingly, if it appears that the substantial purpose of the alteration is to secure the company from significant detriment or harm, the alteration would be valid if it is not oppressive to the minority shareholders. So, expropriation would be justified in the case of a shareholder who is competing with the company, as was the case in *Sidebottom v. Kershaw, Leese & Co.* [1920] 1 Ch. 154 so long as the terms of expropriation are not oppressive. Again, expropriation of a minority shareholder could be justified if it were necessary in order to ensure that the company could continue to comply with a regulatory regime governing the principal business which it carries on. To take a hypothetical example: if the conduct of a television station were the undertaking of a company and a renewal of a television licence under a statute depended upon the licensee's [446] entire share capital being held by Australian residents, the expropriation of foreign shareholders who are unwilling to sell their shares to Australian residents might be justified assuming it is fair in all the circumstances. But that is not to say that the majority can expropriate the minority merely in order to secure for themselves the benefit of a corporate structure that can derive some new commercial advantage by virtue of the expropriation.

Notwithstanding that a shareholder's membership of a company is subject to alterations of the articles which may affect the rights attaching to the shareholder's shares and the value of those shares, we do not consider that, in the case of an alteration to the articles authorising the expropriation of shares, it is a sufficient justification of an expropriation that the expropriation, being fair, will advance the interests of the company as a legal and commercial entity or those of the majority, albeit the great majority, of corporators. This approach does not attach sufficient weight to the proprietary nature of a share and, to the extent that English authority might appear to support such an approach, we do not agree with it. It is only right that exceptional circumstances should be required to justify an amendment to the articles authorising the compulsory expropriation by the majority of the minority's interests in a company. To allow expropriation where it would advance the interests of the company as a legal and commercial entity or those of the general body of corporators would, in our view, be tantamount to permitting expropriation by the majority for the purpose of some personal gain and thus be made for an improper purpose: *Brown v. British Abrasive Wheel Co.* [1919] 1 Ch., at pp. 295-296. It would open the way to circumventing the protection which the *Corporations Law* gives to minorities who resist compromises, amalgamations and reconstructions, schemes of arrangement and take-over offers.

As noted in the preceding paragraphs, an alteration to the company's articles permitting the expropriation of shares will not be valid simply because it was made for a proper purpose; it must also be fair in the circumstances. Fairness in this context has both procedural and substantive elements. The first element, that the process used to expropriate must be fair, requires the majority shareholders to disclose all relevant information leading up to the alteration: (*Re John Labatt Ltd.* (1959) 20 D.L.R. (2d) 159, at p.163) and it presumably requires the shares to be valued by an independent expert. Whether it also requires the majority shareholders to refrain from voting on the proposed amendment is a question that is best left open at this stage.

[447] The second element, that the terms of the expropriation itself must be fair, is largely concerned with the price offered for the shares. Thus, an expropriation at less than market value is prima facie unfair (*Nova Scotia Trust*

Co. v. Rudderham (1969) 1 N.S.R. (2d) 379 at p. 398; but cf. *Phillips v. Manufacturers' Securities Ltd.* (1917) 116 L.T. 290) and it would be unusual for a court to be satisfied that a price substantially above market value was not a fair value: *Re Sheldon; Re Whitcoulls Group Ltd.* (1987) 3 N.Z.C.L.C. 100 at 105. That said, it is important to emphasise that a shareholder's interest cannot be valued solely by the current market value of the shares: *Weinberger v. U.O.P. Inc.* (1983), 457 A. 2d 701. Whether the price offered is fair depends on a variety of factors, including assets, market value dividends and the nature of the corporation and its likely future (ibid. at p. 171).

Onus

The respondents' submissions, which are based heavily on *Peters*, are premised on the proposition that an alteration allowing an expropriation is prima facie valid. It is conceded that the suggested presumption of validity will be rebutted if the minority shareholder proves either that the alteration was made for an improper purpose or that it is oppressive to that particular shareholder. Nonetheless, the respondents' approach, which forces the minority shareholder to shoulder a heavy onus of proof, tilts the balance too far in favour of commercial expediency and falls to attach sufficient weight to the proprietary nature of a share. A share is liable to modification or destruction in appropriate circumstances (*Peters* (1939) 61 C.L.R. at p. 507, per Dixon J.), but is more than a capitalised dividend stream" (but cf. *Sanford v. Sanford Courier Service Pty. Ltd.* (1986) 10 A.C.L.R. 549 at p. 563; *Re Shoppers City Ltd. and M. Loeb Ltd.* [1969] 1 O.R. 449 at 454): it is a form of investment that confers proprietary rights on the investor. Accordingly, in the case of expropriation, we consider that the onus lies on those supporting expropriation to show that the power is validly exercised.

It is for the majority to prove that the alteration is valid because it was made for a proper purpose and is fair in all the circumstances. This approach ensures that the application of the relevant principle does not unduly favour the majority and it largely alleviates the sting of practical difficulties, such as poor access to information, that would otherwise confront minority shareholders.

[448] As the appellants did not contend that the expropriation was not fair in the sense explained above, the validity of art. 20A hinges on whether the respondents have proved that the amendment was not made for a proper purpose. The immediate purpose of the amendment was to allow the expropriation by the majority shareholder of the shares held by the minority, including the shares held by the appellants. There is no suggestion that the appellants' continued presence as members puts W.C.P.'s business activities at risk or that the appellants have in some way acted to W.C.P.'s detriment. Nor is there any suggestion that W.C.P. sought 100 per cent ownership in order to comply with a regulatory regime. All that is suggested is that taxation advantages and administrative benefits would flow to W.C.P. if minority shareholdings were ex-

propriated and W.C.P. were to become a wholly-owned subsidiary of I.E.L. In our view, however, that cannot by itself constitute a proper purpose for a resolution altering the articles to allow for the expropriation of a minority shareholder's shares. In that regard, it is not irrelevant to note that it is difficult to conceive of circumstances in which financial and administrative benefits would not be a consequence of the expropriation of minority shareholdings by a majority shareholder.

Accordingly, we would hold art. 20A invalid and ineffective on the basis that it was not made for a proper purpose.

Transferability of shares
Having reached this conclusion, it is strictly unnecessary for us to deal with the appellants' alternative argument based on section 180(3) of the *Corporations Law*. However, we shall indicate our conclusions on this issue.

Section 180(3) relevantly provides as follows:

> "A member of a company, unless either before or after the alteration is made the member agrees in writing to be bound by It, is not bound by an alteration of the constitution made after the date on whic6 the member became a member so far as the alteration:
>
> (c) increases, or imposes, restrictions on the right to transfer the shares held by the member at the date of the alteration."

The respondents submit that art. 20A does not impose any restriction on the right of the appellants to transfer their shares in W.C.P. because those shares would remain transferable without restriction even after an expropriation notice had been issued. There is considerable force in this submission. To give section 180(3)(c) a wider [449] interpretation could lead to the result that any amendment empowering the expropriation of shares would be invalid, notwithstanding that the amendment was made for a proper purpose and is fair in all the circumstances. Such a result would tilt the balance too far in favour of the minority. Accordingly, the appellants' argument on this point must fail.

FRAUD ON THE COMPANY

See *Company Law*, pp. 340–354.

Cook v. Deeks
[1916] 1 A.C. 554 (P.C.)

See *ante*, p. 280 for the background to this case. After several shareholders' meetings, resolutions were passed, with the aid of the defendants' votes, approving the sale of part of the plant of the company to the Dominion Construction Company, and a declaration was made that the company had no interest in the Shore Line contract, and that the directors were authorized to defend this action, which had in the meantime been instituted.

LORD BUCKMASTER L.C.: . . . [560] Two questions of law arise out of this long history of fact. The first is whether, apart altogether from the subsequent resolutions, the company would have been at liberty to claim from the three defendants the benefit of the contract which they had obtained from the Canadian Pacific Railway Company; and the second, which only arises if the first be answered in the affirmative, whether in such event the majority of the shareholders of the company constituted by the three defendants could ratify and approve of what was done and thereby release all claims against the directors. . . .

[563] There remains the more difficult consideration of whether this position can be made regular by resolutions of the company controlled by the votes of these three defendants. The Supreme Court of Canada have given this matter the most careful consideration, but their Lordships are unable to agree with the conclusion which they reached.

In their Lordships' opinion the Supreme Court has insufficiendy recognized the distinction between two classes of case and has applied the principles applicable to the case of a director selling to his company property which was in equity as well as at law his own, and which he could dispose of as he thought fit, to the case of a director dealing with property which, though his own at law, in equity belonged to his company. The cases of *North-West Transportation Co. v. Beatty* (1887) 12 App. Cas. 589 and *Burland v. Earle* [1902] A.C. 83 both belonged to the former class. In each, directors had sold to the company property in which the company had no interest at law or in equity. If the company claimed any interest by reason of the [564] transaction, it could only be by affirming the sale, in which case such sale, though initially voidable, would be validated by subsequent ratification. If the company refused to affirm the sale the transaction would be set aside and the parties restored to their former position, the directors getting the property and the company receiving back the purchase price. There would be no middle course. The company could not insist on retaining the property while paying less than the price agreed. This would be for the Court to make a new contract between the parties. It would be quite another thing if the director had originally acquired the property which he sold to his company under circumstances which made it in equity the property of the company. The distinction to which their Lordships have drawn attention is expressly recognized by Lord Davey in *Burland v. Earle* and is the foundation of the judgment in *North-West Transportation Co. v. Beatty* and is clearly explained in the case of *Jacobus Marler Estates v. Marler,* (1913) 85 LJ.P.C. 167n, a case which has not hitherto appeared in any of the well-known reports.

If, as their Lordships find on the facts, the contract in question was entered into under such circumstances that the directors could not retain the benefit of it for themselves, then it belonged in equity to the company and ought to have been dealt with as an asset of the company. Even supposing it be not ultra vires of a company to make a present to its directors, it appears quite certain that directors holding a majority of votes would not be permitted to make a present to themselves. This would be to allow a majority to oppress the minority. To such circumstances the cases of *North-West Transportation Co. v. Beatty* and *Burland v. Earle* have no application. In the same way, if directors have acquired for themselves property or rights which they must be regarded as holding on behalf of the company, a resolution that the rights of the company should be disregarded in the matter would amount to forfeiting the interest and property of the minority of shareholders in favour of the majority, and that by the votes of those who are interested in securing the property for themselves. Such use of voting power has never been sanctioned by the Courts, and, [565] indeed, was expressly disapproved in the case of *Menier v. Hooper's Telegraph Works* (1874) L.R. 9 Ch. 359.

If their Lordships took the view that, in the circumstances of this case, the directors had exercised a discretion or decided on a matter of policy (the view which appears to have been entertained by the Supreme Court) different results would ensue, but this is not a conclusion which their Lordships are able to accept. It follows that the defendants must account to the Toronto Company for the profits which they have made out of the transaction.

Daniels v. Daniels
[1978] Ch. 406

Minority shareholders sought to sue a director and controlling shareholder who had purchased property from the company for significantly less than its current value. The defendant applied to have the action struck out for not disclosing a reasonable cause of action.

TEMPLEMAN J.: . . . [408] The plaintiffs complaint appears from paragraphs 3 and 4 of the statement of claim. Paragraph 3 alleges that in October 1970 the company sold certain land in Warwickshire to the second defendant for £4,250 on the instructions and by the direction of the directors, who were the first and second defendants. Paragraph 4 alleges that the price of £4,250 paid to the company by the second defendant was less than the current value of the land at the time of the sale, as the first and second defendants well knew or ought to have known. The particulars of that allegation are first that the first and second defendants purported to adopt a probate value made on the death, which took place on 8 June 1969, of the father of the plaintiffs and the first defendant; secondly, that 'probate values being conservative in amount, are customarily less than the open market value obtainable as between a willing vendor and a willing purchaser'; thirdly, that in 1974 the land was sold by the second defendant for the sum of £120,000.

Putting it broadly, all the allegations will be denied by the defendants if the action proceeds. But it is common ground that for the purpose of this application I must proceed upon the basis that all the allegations in the statement of claim can be sustained.

Mr Richards, for the first two defendants who bring this application to strike out, says there is no cause of action shown because the statement of claim does not allege fraud, and in the absence of fraud, minority shareholders are unable to maintain a claim on behalf of the company against a majority. For that proposition he referred first of all to the principles set out in *Foss v. Harbottle* (1843) 2 Hare 461. That case established the general proposition that minority shareholders cannot maintain an action on behalf of the company, subject to certain exceptions. The exceptions are four in number, and only one of which is of possible application in the present case. The first exception is that a shareholder can sue in respect of some attack on his individual rights as a shareholder; secondly, he can sue if the company, for example, is purporting to do by ordinary resolution that which its own constitution requires to be done by special resolution; thirdly, if the company has done or proposes to do something which is ultra vires; and fourthly, if there is fraud and there is no other remedy. There must be a minority who are prevented from remedying the fraud or taking any proceedings because of the protection given to the fraudulent shareholders or directors by virtue of their majority.

[409] Mr Richards says, and it is conceded, that the statement of claim in its present form does not allege fraud. Mr Blackburne, for the plaintiffs, says of course he is not alleging fraud because the plaintiffs do not really know what happened: all they know is what is set out in the statement of claim. There has been a sale at an undervalue and the second defendant has made a substantial profit; therefore, fraud is not pleaded. But, says Mr Blackburne, when the authorities are considered, the rights of a minority are not limited to cases of fraud; they extend to any breach of duty. In the present case if the defendants sold at an undervalue then that was a breach of duty. As the plaintiffs cannot remedy the breach, save by a minority shareholders' action, they should be entitled to bring the action, *Foss v. Harbottle*, 2 Hare 461, was a case in which there was no oppression by a majority.

The next case in point of time, to which I was referred, was *Atwool v. Merryweather* (1867) L.R. 5 Eq. 464n. The exception of fraud in Foss v. Harbottle was emphasised, the reason being, according to Page Wood V.-C., at p.468:

"If I were to hold that no bill could be filed by shareholders to get rid of the transaction on the ground of the doctrine of *Foss v. Harbottle*, it would be simply impossible to set aside a fraud committed by a director under such circumstances, as the director obtaining so many shares by fraud would always be able to outvote everybody else. . . ."

[410] In *Menier v. Hooper's Telegraph Works* (1874) L.R. 9 Ch. App. 350, a minority shareholders' action was allowed where the majority intended to divide the assets of the company more or less between themselves to the exclusion of the minority. Mellish L.J. said, at p.354:

> "I am of the opinion that although it maybe quite true that the shareholders of a company may vote as they please, and for the purpose of their own interests, yet that the majority of shareholders cannot sell the assets of the company and keep the consideration, but must allow the minority to have their share of any consideration which may come to them. . . ."

[413] Then in 1956 there was a case on which Mr Richards very strongly relies and from which Mr Blackburne asked me to differ. In *Pavlides v. Jensen* [1956] Ch. 565, it was alleged that directors had been guilty of gross negligence in selling a valuable asset of the company at a price greatly below its true market value, and it was alleged that the directors knew or well ought to have known that it was below market value. Danckwerts J. struck out the statement of claim as disclosing no cause of action because no fraud was pleaded. The headnote says, at p. 566:

> " . . . since the sale of the asset in question was not beyond the powers of the company, and since there was no allegation of fraud on the part of the directors or appropriation of the assets of the company by the majority shareholders in fraud of the minority, the action did not fall within the admitted exceptions to the rule in *Foss v. Harbottle*. . . ."

Danckwerts J. said, at p. 576:

> "On the facts of the present case, the sale of the company's mine was not beyond the powers of the company, and it is not alleged to be ultra vires. There is no allegation of fraud on the part of the directors or appropriation of assets of the company by the majority shareholders in fraud of the minority. It was open to the company, on the resolution of the majority of the shareholders, to sell the mine at a price decided by the company in that manner, and it was open to the company by a vote of the majority to decide that, if the directors by their negligence or error of judgment had sold the company's mine at an undervalue, proceedings should not be taken by the company against the directors."

Mr Richards relies very stongly on this decision as showing that, whatever the exceptions to *Foss v. Harbottle* may be, mere gross negligence is not actionable, and he says all that is pleaded in the present case is gross negligence at the most. But in *Pavlides v. Jensen* no benefits accrued to the directors. Mr. Blackburne asks me to dissent from *Pavlides v. Jensen* but the decision seems to me at the moment to be in line with the authorities, in what is a restricted exception to the rule in *Foss v. Harbottle*.

In *Birch v. Sullivan* [1957] 1 W.L.R. 1247 the decision really went off on a point of pleading; moreover the judge was not satisfied that the dissenting shareholders could not put matters right by a meeting of the company. Finally I was referred to *Heyting v. Dupont* [1963] 1 W.L.R. 1192; [1964] 1 W.L.R. 843. But that was only an instance of the court refusing on its own initiative to hear an action begun by minority shareholders where the *Foss v. Harbottle* exceptions did not come into play.

The authorities which deal with simple fraud on the one hand and gross negligence on the other do not cover the situation which arises where, without fraud, the directors and majority shareholders are guilty [414] of a breach of duty which they owe to the company, and that breach of duty not only harms the company but benefits the directors. In that case it seems to me that different considerations apply. If minority shareholders can sue if there is fraud, I see no reason why they cannot sue where the action of the majority and the directors, though without fraud, confers some benefit on those directors and majority shareholders themselves. It would seem to me quite monstrous – particularly as fraud is so hard to plead and difficult to prove – if the confines of the exception to Foss v. Harbottle, were drawn so narrowly that directors could make a profit out of their negligence. Lord Hatherley L.C. in *Turquand v. Marshall*, L.R. 4 Ch. App. 376, 386, opined that shareholders must put up with foolish or unwise directors. Danckwerts J. in *Pavlides v. Jensen* accepted that the forbearance of shareholders extends to directors who are 'an amiable set of lunatics.' Examples, ancient and modern, abound. To put up with foolish directors is one thing; to put up with directors who are so foolish that they make a profit of £115,000 odd at the expense of the company is something entirely different. The principle which may be gleaned from *Alexander v. Automatic Telephone Co.* [1900] 2 Ch. 56 (directors benefiting themselves), from *Cook v. Deeks* (*ante*, p. 280) (directors diverting business in their own favour) and from dicta in *Pavlides v. Jensen* (directors appropriating assets of the company) is that a minority shareholder who has no other remedy may sue where directors use their powers, intentionally or unintentionally, fraudulently or negligently, in a manner which benefits themselves at the expense of the company. This principle is not contrary to *Turquand v. Marshall*, because in that case the powers of the directors were effectively wielded not by the director who benefited but by the majority of independent directors who were acting bona fide and did not benefit. I need not consider the wider proposition for which Mr Blackburne against some formidable opposition from the authorities contends that any breach of duty may be made the subject of a minority shareholder's action.

I am certainly not prepared to say at this stage of the game that the action brought by the plaintiffs in the present instance is bound to fail. What the result of the action will be I know not, but if the statement of claim is right, and the husband and wife who control 60 per cent. of the shares were responsible for a sale by the company to the wife at an undervalue, which they knew or ought to have known, then a remedy for the minoriity shareholders ought to lie.

Prudential Assurance Co. Ltd. v. Newman Industries Ltd. (No. 2)
[1981] 1 Ch. 257

This decision also forms part of protracted and complex litigation. A minority shareholder (Prudential Ltd.) contended that the company's *de facto* controllers had effectively defrauded the shareholders and the company, by arranging for the company to buy a business in which those controllers had a large financial interest. That shareholder commenced what is known as a derivitive claim against those effective controllers.

VINELOTT J.: . . . [304] The real issue in this action is whether; the derivative claim is barred by the rule commonly known as the rule in *Foss v. Harbottle* (1843) 2 Hare [305] 461. This rule was stated by Jenkins L.J. in *Edwards v. Halliwell* [1950] 2 All E.R. 1064, 1066-1067, in the following terms:

> "The rule in *Foss v. Harbottle*, 2 Hare 461, as I understand it, comes to no more than this. First, the proper plaintiff in an action in respect of a wrong alleged to be done to a company or association of persons is prima facie the company or the association of persons itself. Secondly, where the alleged wrong is a transaction which might be made binding on the company or association and on all its members by a simple majority of the members, no individual member of the company is allowed to maintain an action in respect of that matter for the simple reason that, if a mere majority of the members of the company or association is in favour of what has been done, then cadit quaestio. No wrong has been done to the company or association and there is nothing in respect of which anyone can sue. If, on the other hand, a simple majority of members of the company or association is against what has been done, then there is no valid reason why the company or association itself should not sue. In my judgment, it is implicit in the rule that the matter relied on as constituting the cause of action shall be a cause of action properly belonging to the general body of corporators or members of the company or association as opposed to a cause of action which some individual member can assert in his own right."

Jenkins L.J. went on to point out that the rule so formulated can have no application unless the members of the company can by ordinary resolution, passed in general meeting, validly resolve that no proceedings should be instituted to remedy the wrong to the company. Thus, the rule cannot apply (a) to cases where the minority seek to restrain the commission of an act which is ultra vires or illegal or to recover on behalf of the company property disposed of under an ultra vires or illegal transaction; (b) to cases where the minority seeks to have a resolution of the company in general meeting declared void upon the ground that the resolution was one which could only be passed by a special resolution; or (c) to cases where the wrong done to the company is also an infringement of the minority's own individual rights, whether as members or otherwise.

These three categories of cases are sometimes referred to as exceptions from the rule in *Foss v. Harbottle*. They are exceptions only in the sense that cases within these categories fall outside the ambit of the rule as formulated by Jenkins L.J. There is another exception which is an exception in a different sense, namely that it operates to exclude from the rule cases which would otherwise fall within its apparent scope. This exception, which I shall call simply 'the exception', is stated by Jenkins L.J. in these terms, at p. 1067:

> "It has been further pointed out that where what has been done amounts to what is generally called in these cases a fraud on the minority and the wrongdoers are themselves in control of the company, the rule is relaxed in favour of the aggrieved minority who are allowed to bring what is known as a minority shareholders' action on behalf of themselves and all others. The reason for this is that if they [306] were denied that right, their grievance could never reach the court because the wrongdoers themselves, being in control, would not allow the company to sue."

The exception is commonly stated in terms which require the plaintiff in a minority shareholders' action to establish two things. First, that the wrong to the company which it is sought to remedy was a wrong of a fraudulent character and, secondly, that the wrongdoers are in control of the company. I shall examine each of these two requirements in turn. . . .

[316] Th[e] authorities show that the exception applies not only where the allegation is that directors who control a company have improperly appropriated to themselves money, property or advantages which belong to the company or, in breach of their duty to the company, have diverted business to themselves which ought to have been given to the company, but more generally where it is alleged that directors though acting 'in the belief that they were doing nothing wrong' (*per* Lindley M.R. in *Alexander v. Automatic Telephone Co.* [1900] 2 Ch. 56, 65) are guilty of a breach of duty to the company, including their duty to exercise proper care, and as a result of that breach obtain some benefit. In the latter case it must be unnecessary to allege and prove that

the directors in breaking their duty to the company acted with a view to benefiting themselves at the expense of the company; for such an allegation would be an allegation of misappropriation of the company's property. On the other hand, the exception does not apply if all that is alleged is that directors who control a company are liable to the company for damages for negligence it not being shown that the transaction was one in which they were interested or that they have in fact obtained any benefit from it. It is not easy to see precisely where the line between these cases is to be drawn. For instance, is an action to be allowed to proceed if the allegation is that the controlling director is liable to the company for damages for negligence and that as a result of his negligence a benefit has been obtained by his wife or a friend or by a company in which he has a substantial shareholding? In *Pavlides v. Jensen* [1956] Ch. 565 would it have been enough if, in addition to the allegation of negligence, it had been alleged that Portland Tunnel had a substantial shareholding in the Cyprus company and therefore benefited indirectly? It is also not easy to see what principle underlies the distinction. Whether the claim is for property improperly withheld or for damages for negligence or breach of fiduciary duty and, in the latter case, whether those controlling the company have or have not obtained some benefit the reason for the exception is the same, namely that the claim is brought against persons whose interests conflict with the interest of the company. It may be said, in a perfectly intelligible sense, to be a fraud on the minority that those against whom the claim would be brought are in a position to procure, and, if the derivative claim is not brought, will procure, that the company's claim, however strong it may appear to be, will not be enforced. Mr Scott, very frankly, admitted that he could not put forward any valid [317] ground of distinction between a case where the claim by the company is of a proprietory nature and one where it is for damages only, nor between a claim for damages for negligence where the loss to the company is either not matched by any benefit to anybody or is not matched by a benefit to those in control. However, Mr Scott also conceded that the claim by Prudential is a claim founded on acts of a 'fraudulent character,' whatever meaning is attributed to those words. I have endeavoured to state the principle which underlies the first limb of the exception, because the second limb cannot be construed in isolation from it, but it is unnecessary for me to decide precisely where the boundary limiting the category of cases which permit of a minority shareholder's action is to be drawn and it would be wrong for me to attempt to do so.

The central issue in this case is whether a derivative action can be brought against defendants who do not have voting control of the company on whose behalf the derivative claim is brought and, if it can, in precisely what circumstances such claim will be allowed to proceed. . . .

[323] If the rule and the exception cannot be confined within the rigid formulation expressed in terms of voting control by the persons against whom relief is sought on behalf of the company, then the question whether a given

case falls within the exception can only be answered by reference to the principle which underlies the rule and the exception to it. Mr Scott submitted, I think rightly, that the principle which underlies the rule is that it would be wrong to allow a minority shareholder to bring proceedings joining the company as defendant and claiming against other defendants relief on behalf of the company for a wrong alleged to have been done to it if the majority of the members of the company take the view that it is not in the interests of the company that the proceedings should be pursued. Indeed, it would be so plainly wrong that it might be said that, in a broad sense, the court would have no jurisdiction to allow the wishes of the minority to override the wishes of the majority in that way. The principle which underlies the exception to the rule is that in ascertaining the view of the majority whether it is in the interests of the company that the claim be pursued, the court will disregard votes cast or capable of being cast by shareholders who have an interest which directly conflicts with the interest of the company. Those are general principles of substantive law and are not mere rules of procedure. But in any derivative action the plaintiff must allow in his statement of claim some ground which, if established at the trial, would bring the case within the exception and justify an order that the company recover damages or property from the other defendants.

O'Neill v. Ryan
[1993] I.L.R.M. 557

The plaintiff held 7.5 per cent of the shares in and was chief executive of the then privately owned company Ryanair Ltd., who following a dispute with the principal shareholder, Mr Ryan, was dismissed from office. He then sued, *inter alia*, Mr. Ryan and the company, claiming breach of contract and wrongful dismissal. In the same action he sued Mr. Ryan, Aer Lingus and its chief executive, G.P.A. Group and another air carrier, alleging breach of Articles 85 and 86 of the E.E.C. Treaty; he contended that those defendants' conduct caused damage to the company and thereby damaged him by reducing the value of his shareholding in the company. These defendants applied to have his claim struck out on the grounds that the pleadings did not disclose cause of action. The plaintiff had also brought a claim for 'oppression' under section 205 of the 1963 Act against the company and its principle shareholders, but those proceedings were settled on terms, *inter alia*, that the Ryans buy his shares in the company. By the time the appeal from Lynch J.'s judgment ([1990] 2 I.R.200) came on for hearing in the Supreme Court, his shares had been purchased in accordance with that settlement and he was no longer a shareholder in the company.

BLAYNEY J.: [566] The submissions on behalf of the plaintiff were made under two broad headings. It was submitted firstly, that the plaintiff's claim came within one of the exceptions to the rule in *Foss v. Harbottle* (1843) 2 Hare 461 and secondly, that if it did not, as the plaintiff had rights under directly applicable provisions of community law he must be entitled to a remedy under national law. I will deal with each of these separately having first expanded the actual submissions made.

As regards the first submission, it was accepted that the plaintiff did not come within any of the four exceptions to the rule in *Foss v. Harbottle* set out at paragraph 28.03 of the second edition of *Company Law in Ireland* by Keane J, but it was submitted that there was a fifth exception and he came within it. Such exception was where it was necessary to permit an exception 'in the interests of justice'. In my opinion, however, there is no need to consider whether such an exception exists as I am satisfied that for other reasons the plaintiff's claim to come within an exception to the rule in *Foss v. Harbottle* is untenable even if he [567] were still a shareholder in Ryanair.

The nature of the plaintiff's claim is such that it falls totally outside the rule and any possible exceptions to it. The rule is concerned with answering the question of who is the proper plaintiff to bring an action in respect of damage suffered by a company. It states that the proper plaintiff is the company itself (referring to *Prudential Assurance Co. Ltd. v. Newman Industries Ltd. (No. 2)* [1982] Ch. 204) (supra p. 455). . . . The exceptions made to the rule, which allow minority shareholders to bring a derivative or representative action, are made in order to ensure that a majority control of the company should not be able with impunity to act illegally or oppressively or in such a way as to commit a fraud on the minority. But where a derivative or representative action is permitted as an exception to the rule, the action is brought in respect of damage to the company. Instead of the company itself bringing the action in respect of such damage, the exceptions permit one or more minority shareholders to bring it. But the action is always brought in respect of damage to the company.

The plaintiff's claim here is not in respect of damage to the company. It does not purport to be a representative or derivative action. It is a claim in respect of alleged damage to his shareholding in the company. Because of this it is totally different from the type of claim with which the rule in *Foss v. Harbottle* is concerned. It cannot be an exception to the rule because it is not a claim in respect of damage to the company.

The cases cited by counsel for the plaintiff illustrating exceptions to the rule were all cases in which the plaintiffs were suing in respect of damage to the company (referring to *Cockburn v. Newbridge Sanitary Steam Laundry Co. Ltd.* [1915] 1 I.R. 237 (supra, p. 431) and *Russell v. Wakefield Waterworks Co.* (1872) LR 20 Eq 474). . . .

[568] Counsel cited a later passage in the judgment of Sir G. Jessel MR (in *Russell*) to support his submission that exceptions to the rule in *Foss v. Harbottle* would be allowed when necessary in the interest of justice. The passage in question, which occurs at p. 483, begins with the following sentence:

> "It remains to consider what are those exceptional cases in which, for
> the due attainment of justice, such a suit should be allowed."

This sentence, however, is preceded by the following sentence which makes it
clear that the types of case he was dealing with were cases concerned with
providing a remedy for an injury to a corporation and not for an injury to the
shareholding of a particular corporator. The preceding sentence is as follows:

> "If a case should arise of injury to a corporation by some of its members,
> for which no adequate remedy remained except that of a suit by indi-
> vidual corporators in their private characters, and asking in such charac-
> ter the protection of those rights to which in their corporate character
> they were entitled, I cannot but think that the principles so forcibly laid
> down by Lord Cottenharn in *Wallworth v. Holt* and other cases would
> apply, and the claims of justice would be found superior to any difficul-
> ties arising out of technical rules respecting the mode in which corpora-
> tions are required to sue."

It is clear from this and particularly from the last phrase 'respecting the mode
in which corporations are required to sue' that the exceptional cases which Sir
[569] G. Jessel MR had in mind were cases of injury to a corporation for
which it would be entitled to sue so that the remedy being given was a remedy
for such injury and not for an injury to the alleged rights of an individual
corporator which is what is in issue here.

Counsel further submitted that even though the damage was primarily to
Ryanair, the plaintiff nonetheless was entitled to sue, but he was unable to
point to any authority for this proposition. I am satisfied that there is none.
What was being submitted was that a shareholder in a company has a personal
action in respect of the reduction in value of his shareholding resulting from
damage to the company against the party who caused such damage. Such a
proposition was firmly rejected by the Court of Appeal in England in the *Prudential Assurance Co. Ltd* case to which I referred earlier (quoting from [1982]
Ch. at p. 224):

> "A personal action would subvert the rule in *Foss v. Harbottle* and that
> rule is [570] not merely a tiresome procedural obstacle placed in the
> path of a shareholder by a legalistic judiciary. The rule is the conse-
> quence of the fact that a corporation is a separate legal entity. Other
> consequences are limited liability and limited rights. The company is
> liable for its contracts and torts; the shareholder has no such liability.
> The company acquires causes of action for breaches of contract and for
> torts which damage the company. No cause of action vests in the share-
> holder. When the shareholder acquires a share he accepts the fact that
> the value of his investment follows the fortunes of the company and that

he can only exercise his influence over the fortunes of the company by the exercise of his voting rights in general meeting. The law confers on him the right to ensure that the company observes the limitations of its memorandum of association and the right to ensure that other shareholders observe the rule, imposed upon them by the articles of association."

In my opinion that is a correct statement of the law in regard to the status of a shareholder in a limited liability company. What is also a relevant consideration in addition to the matters referred to in the two passages cited is the consequences which would flow from giving shareholders in a company a personal action against a party causing damage to the company. It would enable a multiplicity of actions to be brought and deprive the company itself of the ability to control them. So it would be both harmful to companies and very much against the public interest in opening the door to irresponsible litigation. For these reasons also I am satisfied that a personal claim by a shareholder should not be permitted.

I am satisfied, accordingly, that even if the plaintiff were still a shareholder in Ryanair he would have no cause of action against the last four defendants. *A fortiori* he has none since he is no longer even a shareholder.

Note: Since the proceedings here were a motion by Aer Lingus and other air transport companies to have Mr. O'Neill's claim against them dismissed, it is very difficult to see what relevance *Foss v. Harbottle* could have to the matter, even if the plaintiff had never disposed of his 7.5% shareholding in the company. Consideration of *Foss* only arises where a shareholder sues those who he contends control his company, not when the defendants are complete outsiders. Only the company, Ryanair Ltd., and not its shareholder or managing director, could bring proceedings against Aer Lingus et al: *Breckland Group Holdings* case [1989] B.C.L.C. 100 (ante p. 182). Thus, there was no need for Blayney J. to expound at length on *Foss v. Harbottle* and the current status of that celebrated decision.

OPPRESSION AND DISREGARD OF INTERESTS

See *Company Law*, pp.354–363.

Companies Act 1963, section 205(1)

Remedy in cases of oppression

205.—(1) Any member of a company who complains that the affairs of the company are being conducted or that the powers the directors of the company are being exercised in a manner oppressive to him or any of the members (including himself), or in disregard of his or their interests as members, may apply to the court for an order under this section.

Note: There are a vast number of reported cases in the U.K. courts on the equivalent provisions of the Companies Act (presently section 459 of the 1985 Act) and in the space available it is not possible to provide even a vaguely representative sample of those decisions, most of which in any event turn on their own special facts. One recent decision perhaps best sums up the state of the law there.

Re BSB Holdings Ltd (No. 2)
[1996] 1 B.C.L.C. 155

This extract from Arden J.'s judgment is an excellent summary of the case law, in Britian. There was a dispute between shareholders in an satellite broadcasting business arising out of complex funding arrangements and its merger with News International.

ARDEN J.: [234] While the Companies Acts and company law generally observe a principle of majority rule, the law also seeks to protect the position of minority shareholders in a number of ways. For instance, minority shareholders are given the right to convene a general meeting (see section 366); to have resolutions proposed by them and a statement circulated in advance (see section 376); to require the company to investigate share interests (see section 214); and to require a private company which has elected not to hold an annual general meeting to do so (see section 366A). Resolutions of the company must be passed bona fide in the interests of the company (see *Allen Gold Reefs of West Africa* [1900] 1 Ch. 656; see post. p. 506). There is a general principle–

> "applicable to all authorities conferred on majorities of classes enabling them to bind minorities; namely, that the power must be exercised for the purpose of benefiting the class as a whole, and not merely individual members only. . ." (See *British America Nickel Corp Ltd. v. MJ O'Brien Ltd.* [1927] A.C. 369 at 371 *per* Viscount Haldane.)

Thus at a meeting of holders of a class of shares, the holders must vote bona fide in the interests of the general body of members of that class. If a resolution constitutes a fraud by the majority on the minority, a minority shareholder can bring derivative proceedings on behalf of the company under one of the exceptions to the rule in *Foss v. Harbottle* (1843) 2 Hare 461, 67 ER 189. A minority shareholder has a statutory right to apply to the court for cancellation of an alteration to the memorandum (see section 5); for cancellation of a resolution passed by a public company that it should be re-registered as a private company (see section 54); for cancellation of a variation of class rights which is unfairly prejudicial to holders of shares of that class (see section 127); for cancellation of a resolution approving the giving of financial assistance (see section 157); for an order calling a general meeting (see section 371); for an order for the appointment of inspectors to investigate the affairs of the company (see section 432); and for an order directing a company to remedy its default in making returns to the Registrar of Companies (see section 713). In the event of a take-over offer, a minority shareholder has a statutory right in certain circumstances to require the offeror to acquire his shares (see section 430A); he may also apply to the court for an order preventing the offeror from acquiring his shares or requiring him to do so on different terms from those contained in the take-over offer (see section 430C). The courts have adopted a rule that if a reduction of capital requiring the confirmation of the court under section 135 is in breach of share rights, the onus of proving that the reduction is fair shifts to the company making the application (see *Re Holders Investment Trust Ltd.* [1971] 1 W.L.R. 583 – see post p. 533). Where a scheme of arrangement under ss. 425 to 427 discriminates between members, separate meetings are required before the court will sanction the scheme (see *Re Hellenic & General Trust Ltd.* [1976] 1 W.L.R. 123 – see post p. 541).

Section 459 has to be viewed in the context of legislation and a field of law which provides extensive minority protection in specific areas. A section of [235] the same kind as section 459 has appeared in the Companies Act, since 1947. The mischief to which this kind of section is directed is to be found in paras 58 to a 60 of the *Report of the Committee on Company Law Amendment 1945* (Cmd 6659) (the Cohen committee).

"58. *Restrictions on transfer of shares.* – It has been represented to us that the provisions which are inserted in the articles of a private company for the restriction of the transfer of the shares have caused hardship especially where the legal representatives of minority shareholders have to raise money to pay estate duties. The directors of the company, who are usually the principal shareholders, sometimes exercise their power to refuse to register transfers to outsiders, with the result that executors, who must realise their testators' shares in order to pay estate duty, have to sell to the directors or persons approved by them at prices much lower that the values at which the shares are assessed by the Board of Inland Revenue in valuing the estate of the deceased for purpose of estate duty. This difficulty is not in law peculiar to private companies since there is no legal impediment to a public company having in its articles a provision subjecting transfer of shares to the approval of the directors though Stock Exchanges do not accept it where leave to deal is required. This restriction is valued as a means of keeping a family business under the control of the family and we see no sufficient reason for its removal, particularly if our suggestion in paragraph 60 is adopted.

59. *Excessive remuneration of directors.* – An other abuse which has been found to occur is that the directors absorb an undue proportion of the profits of the company in remuneration for their services so that little or nothing is left for distribution among the shareholders by way of dividend. This may happen where, for example, two persons trading in partnership form their business into a limited company and one partner dies, leaving his share to his widow who takes no active part in the business. At present the only remedy open to the minority shareholder is to commence an action to restrain the company from paying the remuneration on the ground that such payment is a fraud on the minority, since the Court would not make a winding-up order in view of the alternative remedy.

60. *Oppression of minorities.* – We have carefully examined suggestions intended to strengthen the minority shareholders of a private company in resisting oppression by the majority. The difficulties to which we have referred in the two preceding paragraphs are, in fact, only illustrations of a general problem. It is impossible to frame a recommendation to cover every case. We consider that a step in the right direction would be to enlarge the power of the Court to make a winding-up order by providing that the power shall be exercisable notwithstanding the existence of an alternative remedy. In many cases, however, the winding-up of the company will not benefit the minority shareholders, since the break-up value of the assets may be small, or the only available purchaser may be that very majority whose oppression has driven the minority to seek redress. We, therefore, suggest that the Court should have, in addition, the power to impose upon the parties to a dispute whatever settlement the Court considers just and equitable.

[236] This discretion must be unfettered, for it is impossible to lay down a general guide to the solution of what are essentially individual cases. We do not think that the Court can be expected in every case to find and a impose a solution; but our proposal will give the Court a jurisdiction which it at present lacks, and thereby at least empower it to impose a solution in those cases where one exists."

It appears that the Cohen committee accepted that there were circumstances in which directors could properly refuse to register a transfer of shares, but the remedy they were recommending is not excluded in those circumstances. Second, if that is right, the Cohen committee considered that there was a need for a remedy to be available even if directors acted in good faith towards the company.

In consequence of the Cohen committee's recommendation, a section which became section 210 of the Companies Act 1948 was introduced which provided a remedy where the company's affairs were conducted in an oppressive manner. . . .

By 1962, when the next Company Law Committee (the Jenkins committee) (Cmnd 1749) reported, section 210 had been successfully invoked in two cases: *Scottish Co-op Wholesale Society Ltd. v. Meyer* [1959] A.C. 324 (see post, p. 472) and *Re H R Harmer Ltd.* [1959] 1 W.L.R. 62. It was suggested to the Jenkins committee that the word .'oppressive' was too strong a word to be appropriate in all the cases in which relief ought to be given under the section. Lord Simonds, in *Scottish Co-op Wholesale Society Ltd.* had adopted the dictionary definition of 'oppressive' as 'burdensome, harsh and wrong'. However this left open the question whether the applicant had to show that the law had been broken or his rights infringed. In the opinion of the Jenkins committee (paras. 203-205 and 212):

"203 . . . if the section is to afford effective protection, it must extend to cases in which the acts complained of fall short of actual illegality.

204. In *Elder v. Elder and Watson Ltd.* 1952 S.C. 49, it was said by Lord Cooper (at p.55) with reference to the meaning of oppression in section 210 'the essence of the matter seems to be that the conduct complained of should at the lowest involve a visible departure from the standards of fair dealing, and a violation of the conditions of fair play on which every shareholder who entrusts his money to a company is entitled to rely'. This statement accords with our own view as to the intention underlying section 210 as originally framed, namely that it was meant to cover complaints not only to the effect that the affairs of the company were being conducted in a manner oppressive (in the narrower sense) to the members concerned but also to the effect that those affairs were being conducted in a manner unfairly prejudicial to the interests of those members. . .

[237] 205. As the Cohen Committee observed in paragraph 60 of their report, it is impossible to frame a recommendation to cover every case, and we do not propose to attempt to do so. But we may perhaps usefully mention as illustrative of the situations in which action under section 210 might be appropriate those in which directors appoint themselves to paid posts with the company at excessive rates of remuneration . . . Other possibilities are the issue of shares to directors and others on advantageous terms [The Jenkins committee then addressed the question of derivative actions, and other changes to section 210).

212. We recommend that:

> "(c) it should be made clear that section 210 extends to cases where
> the affairs of the company are being conducted in a manner unfairly
> prejudicial to the interests of some part of the members and riot
> merely in an oppressive" manner . . ."

The meaning of 'oppressive' was further considered by the Court of Appeal in
Re Jermyn Street Turkish Baths Ltd. [1971] 1 W.L.R. 1042. The Court of
Appeal held that to establish oppression, the applicant must show that he is
being constrained to submit to something which is unfair to him as a result of
an act or omission by the majority shareholders.

Principally to meet the criticisms made in the Jenkins committee, section
210 was superseded by section 75 of the Companies Act 1980, which became
section 459 of the Companies Act 1985. Certain further (but for present purposes immaterial) amendments were made by the Companies Act 1989 and
section 459 as set out above is as so amended.

The starting point must be the words of section 459 itself. I have set out the
material provisions. The words 'unfairly prejudicial' are wide and general and
the circumstances in which they apply cannot therefore be exhaustively categorised (see per Lord Wilberforce in *Ebrahimi v. Westbourne Galleries Ltd.*
[1973] A.C. 360 at 374 in the passage cited by Neill L.J. and set out below).

The leading authority on section 459 is now *Re Saul D. Harrison & Sons
plc* [1995] 1 B.C.L.C. 14. That case was an appeal against an order striking
out the application as disclosing no cause of action. The company was a small
manufacturing company. It secured a large capital sum on the compulsory
acquisition of its works. Despite poor trading results, it acquired new premises
and carried on business. The applicant held non-voting but dividend-bearing
shares. The applicant's case was summarised as follows by Hoffmann L.J. . . .

[238] Hoffmann L.J. accepts that the test of unfairness is objective, and
proceeds to examine the factors which the court takes into account in establishing whether conduct is unfair (at 17–18):

> "In deciding what is fair or unfair for the purposes of section 459, it is
> important to have in mind that fairness is being used in the context of a
> commercial relationship. The articles of association are just what their
> name implies: the contractual terms which govern the relationships of
> the shareholders with the company and each other. They determine the
> powers of the board and the company in general meeting and everyone
> who becomes a member of a company is taken to have agreed to them.
> Since keeping promises and honouring agreements is probably the most
> important element of commercial fairness, the starting point in any case
> under section 459 will be to ask whether the conduct of which the share-
> holder complains was in accordance with the articles of association. The
> answer to this question often turns on the fact that the powers which the
> shareholders have entrusted to the board are fiduciary powers, which

must be exercised for the benefit of the company as a whole. If the board act for some ulterior purpose, they step outside the terms of the bargain between the shareholders and the company."

In my summary, above, I have worked on the basis that what Hoffmann L.J. said above about the articles applies equally to any other contractual arrangement which governs the relationship between the shareholders.

Hoffmann L.J. then observes that a remedy may be under section 459 even though an applicant may not have been able to bring a derivative action under the exceptions to the rule in *Foss v. Harbottle* (1843) 2 Hare 461, cites with approval the decision of Harman J. in *Re a company (No 00370 of 1987), ex p Glossop* [1988] 1 W.L.R. 1068 where the court approached the question whether a consistent refusal by a board to recommend the payment of a dividend constituted unfairly prejudicial conduct by asking whether the board had abused its fiduciary powers.

Hoffmann L.J. then holds that section 459 does not entitle an applicant to relief for trivial or technical breaches of the articles. This is conduct which is [239] [239] unlawful but not unfair. The reference to infringement of the articles must in this context include breaches of other contractual arrangements governing a the shareholders' relationship and breaches of the directors' fiduciary duty. Hoffmann L.J. states (at 18):

> "Although one begins with the articles and the powers of the board, a finding that conduct was not in accordance with the articles does not necessarily mean that it was unfair, still less that the court will exercise its discretion to grant relief. There is often sound sense in the rule in *Foss v. Harbottle*. In choosing the term "unfairly prejudicial" the Jenkins Committee (para 204) equated it with Lord Cooper's understanding of "oppression" in *Elder v. Elder and Watson Ltd.* 1952 SC 49 at 55: "a visible departure from the standards of fair dealing, and a violation of the conditions of fair play on which every shareholder who entrusts his money to a company is entitled to rely." So trivial or technical infringements of the articles were not intended to give rise to petitions under section 459."

Hoffmann L.J. then deals with the narrow class of cases in which there are understandings between the parties which are not set out in the articles but which may give rise to understandings whose breach may be actionable under section 459 (at 19-20):

> "Not only may conduct be technically unlawful without being unfair: it can also be unfair without being unlawful. In a commercial context, this may at first seem surprising. How can it be unfair to act in accordance with what the parties have agreed? As a general rule, it is not. But there

are cases in which the letter of the articles does not fully reflect the understandings upon which the shareholders are associated. Lord Wilberforce drew attention to such cases in a celebrated passage of his judgment in *Ebrahimi v. Westbourne Galleries Ltd.* [1973] A.C. 360 at 379, which discusses what seems to me the identical concept of injustice or unfairness which can form the basis of a just and equitable winding up: "The words [just and equitable] are a recognition of the fact that a limited company is more than a mere legal entity, with a personality in law of its own: that there is room in company law for recognition of the fact that behind it, or amongst it, there are individuals, with rights, expectations and obligations inter se which are not necessarily submerged in the company structure. That structure is defined by the Companies Act 1948 and by the articles of association by which the shareholders agree to be bound. In most companies and in most contexts, this definition is sufficient and exhaustive, equally so whether the company is large or small. The "just and equitable" provision does not, as the respondents suggest, entitle one party to disregard the obligation he assumes by entering a company, nor the court to dispense him from it. It does, as equity always does, enable the court to subject the exercise of legal rights to equitable considerations; considerations, that is, of a personal character arising between one individual and another, which may make it unjust, or inequitable, to insist on legal rights or to exercise them in a particular [240] way." Thus the personal relationship between a shareholder and those who control the company may entitle him to say that it would in certain circumstances be unfair for them to exercise a power conferred by the a articles upon the board or the company in general meeting. I have in the past ventured to borrow from public law the term "legitimate expectation" to describe the correlative "right" in the shareholder to which such a relationship may give rise. It often arises out of a fundamental understanding between the shareholders which formed the basis of their association but was not put into contractual form, such as an assumption that each of the parties who has ventured his capital will also participate in the management of the company and receive the return on his investment in the form of salary rather than dividend. These relationships need not always take the form of implied agreements with the shareholder concerned; they could enure for the benefit of a third party such as a joint venturer's widow. But in *Ebrahimi v. Westbourne Galleries Ltd.* Lord Wilberforce went on to say: "It would be impossible, and wholly undesirable, to define the circumstances in which these considerations may arise. Certainly the fact that the company is a small one, or a private company, is not enough. There are very many of these where the association is a purely commercial one, of which it can safely be said that the basis of association is adequately and exhaustively laid down in the articles. The superimposition of equitable considerations requires something more . . ." Thus in the absence of "something more", there is no basis for a legitimate expectation that the board and the company in general meeting will not exercise whatever powers they are given by the articles of association."

Hoffmann L.J. held that in *Re Saul D Harrison & Sons plc* no legitimate expectation arose on the facts. Concluding discussion of section 459, Hoffmann L.J. said (at 20):

"Thus it seems to me that in this case one can be a good deal more precise than to ask in general terms, as [counsel for the appellant] suggested, whether a bystander would think that the board had been unfair. As there are no grounds for saying that it would be unfair for the board to act in accordance with the bargain between the petitioner and the company, the very minimum required to make out a case of unfairness is that the powers of management have been used for an unlawful purpose or the articles otherwise infringed . . ."

Neill L.J. held that the statutory ground for an order under section 459 should be construed against the background of section 210 of the Companies Act 1948, which he examined. He concluded that the scope of protection conferred by section 459 is intended to be more extensive than that provided by section 210. Neill L.J. continued (at 30):

"At this stage, however, the precise boundaries of the protection are unclear and they will have to be worked out on a case by case basis."

However, Neill L.J. then set out a number of guidelines as to the correct approach to section 459. From the context it seems clear that these guidelines are [241] not comprehensive. So far as material, the guidelines laid down by Neill L.J. are as follows (at 30-31):

"Nevertheless it seems to me that it is already possible to collect from the cases decided under the1948 Act and under the 1985 Act the following guidelines as to the correct approach to the concept of "unfairly prejudicial" in section 459. (1) The words "unfairly prejudicial" are general words and they should be applied flexibly to meet the circumstances of the particular case. I have in mind the warning which Lord Wilberforce gave in *Ebrahimi v. Westbourne Galleries Ltd.* [1973] A.C. 360 at 374 in relation to the words "just and equitable": "Illustrations may be used, but general words should remain general and not be reduced to the sum of particular instances." It is also relevant to bear in mind that whereas a winding-up order on just and equitable grounds will terminate the existence of the company a wider range of remedies is available under section 461. . . .

(2) On the other hand, as Hoffmann J. pointed out in *Re a company (No 007623 of 1986)* [1986] B.C.L.C. 362 at 367 in relation to a section 459 petition: ". . . the very width of the jurisdiction means that unless carefully controlled it can become a means of oppression." These words have been echoed in later cases."

I pause to note that, although it was not necessary for this point to be elaborated in *Re Saul D Harrison & Sons plc*, it is a consideration which I have borne well in mind. It is important that the legitimate and proper workings of business and the investment of capital should not be inhibited by for example unfounded threats of action under section 459. Neill L.J. continues (at 31):

"(3) The relevant conduct (of commission or omission) must relate to the affairs of the company of which the petitioner is a member: see Peter Gibson J. in *Re a company (No 005685 of 1988), ex p Scklwarcz (No 2)* ([1989] B.C.L.C. 427 at 437).

(4) The conduct must be both prejudicial(in the sense of causing prejudice or harm to the relevant interest) and also unfairly so: conduct may be unfair without being prejudicial or prejudicial without being unfair, and it is not sufficient if the conduct satisfies only one of these tests: see Peter Gibson J. ([1989] B.C.L.C. 427 at 437).

(5) In construing the word "unfairly" in this context it will be necessary to take account not only of the legal rights of the petitioner, but also consider whether there are any equitable considerations such as the petitioner's legitimate expectations to be weighed in the balance.

(6) For the purpose of determining the legal rights of the petitioner one turns to the memorandum and articles of the company because the articles constitute the contract between the company and the member in respect of his rights and liabilities as a shareholder. Furthermore, it is to be remembered that the management of a company is entrusted to the directors, who have to exercise their powers in the interests of the company as a whole.

[242] (7) In order to establish unfairness it is clearly not enough to show that some managerial decision may have prejudiced the petitioner's interest. A shareholder on joining a company will be deemed to have accepted the a risk that in the wider interest of the company decisions may be taken which will prejudice his own interests. Thus it may be necessary for the directors to take steps which are prejudicial to some of the members in order to secure the future prosperity of the company or even its survival: c.f. *Nicholas v. Soundcraft Electronics Ltd.* [1993] B.C.L.C. 360 at 372 per Ralph Gibson L.J."

Nicholas v. Soundcraft Electronics Ltd. concerned an allegation that the conduct of a majority shareholder responsible for the financial management of a company in withholding balances due to it was not unfairly prejudicial where the majority shareholder was acting to ensure its own survival. This was for the benefit of the company in question. It is far removed from the present facts but demonstrates that under section 459 conduct must be both prejudicial and unfair.

Neill L.J. continues (at 31):

> "(8) Though it is open to the court to find that serious mismanagement of a company's business constitutes conduct that is unfairly prejudicial to the interests of the shareholders the court will normally be very reluctant to accept that managerial decisions can amount to unfairly prejudicial conduct: see *Re Elgindata Ltd.* [1991] B.C.L.C. 959 at 993."

No suggestion of mismanagement in this sense has been alleged by LMS but I set out para (8) to make it clear that when I refer to the directors' fiduciary duty I am referring to the directors' duty to act bona fide in what they consider to be the interests of the company, and not to their duties of skill and care. Different considerations may apply to breaches of such duties.

> "(9) A shareholder can legitimately complain, however, if the directors exceed the powers vested in them or exercise their powers for some illegitimate or ulterior purpose.
>
> (10) Though in general members of a company have no legitimate expectations going beyond the legal rights conferred on them by the constitution of the company, additional legitimate expectations may be superimposed in certain circumstances. These may arise from agreements or understandings between the members or between the members and the directors. Thus I am satisfied that the concept of fairness in the phrase "unfairly prejudicial" is capable of introducing considerations similar to those explained by Lord Wilberforce in the *Westbourne Galleries* case [1973] A.C. 360 at 379) where he said that "just and equitable" provision in section 222(f) of the Companies Act 1948 enabled the court to subject the exercise of legal rights to equitable considerations . . ." (See at 31-32.)

The judgments do not separately consider the meaning of the words 'the interests of' any member in section 459. These words did not appear in section 210. However counsel have not suggested to me that these words have any relevance in this case and I thus express no view thereon. The third member of [243] the court, Watc L.J., concurred with the judgments of both Hoffmann L.J. and Neill L.J.

On the allegations made in *Re Saul D Harrison & Sons plc*, the order to strike out was unanimously upheld. Although the company had traded unsatisfactorily, the directors had made changes and considered that the business was viable and capable of expansion. The relocation of the company's premises had been conducted under professional advice. The company had newly-equipped and modern premises from which to expand. The directors' remuneration, even including that of the directors' wives, was not excessive. The Court of Appeal was satisfied that there was no basis for alleging that the company had conducted its affairs in an unfairly prejudicial manner.

Following *Re Saul D Harrison & Sons plc*, it is necessary to examine the ambit of a director's fiduciary duty as a matter of law. The duty is to act bona fide in what the director considers to be the interests of the company, and not for any collateral purpose (see *Re Smith and Fawcett Ltd.* [1942] Ch. 304). Two questions arise: First, when and how does the court ascertain whether a power has been exercised for a collateral purpose? Second, are the interests of the company to which the directors must have regard, in a case such as this, those, and only those, of the company as a separate legal entity? I consider each of these questions below.

However, in my judgment, it is not the effect of *Re Saul D Harrison & Sons plc* that a remedy under section 459 can he given only if the directors have acted in breach of duty or if the company has breached the terms of its articles or some other relevant agreement. These matters constitute in most cases the basis for deciding what conduct is unfair. But the words of the section are wide and general and, save where the circumstances are governed by the judgments in *Re Saul D Harrison & Sons plc*, the categories of unfair prejudice are not closed. The standards of corporate behaviour recognised through section 459 may in an appropriate case thus not be limited to those imposed by enactment or existing case law.

Scottish Co-Operative Wholesale Soc. v. Meyer
[1959] A.C. 324

The petitioners and the Scottish Co-Op. agreed to establish a company that would be run as a joint enterprise. The company was a subsidiary of the Co-Op.'s, and was very dependant on the Co-Op. for its raw materials (yarn). Five years later the Co-Op.'s stake in the company was increased to 70 per cent. Shortly afterwards it sought to buy out the petitioners' £1 shares at par even though those shares were then worth about £6 each; but they refused to sell out. From then on the company was allowed to run down; supplies of raw materials to the company were effectively cut off, and the majority directors, who were the Co-Op.'s nominees, did nothing to halt the company's decline. The petitioners sought to have the company wound up under the U.K. Act's equivalent of section 205 of the 1963 Act (section 210 of the 1948 Act).

VISCOUNT SIMONDS: . . . [339] It is common ground that at the date of presentation of the petition on July 13, 1953, it was just and equitable that the company should be wound up. It could hardly be denied that to wind up the company would unfairly prejudice the respondents. The only question is whether its affairs were being conducted in a manner oppressive to the respondents and, if so, whether the court ordained the appropriate remedy. . . .

It is, however, necessary, if section 210 is to be successfully invoked, to show, not only that there has been oppression of the minority shareholders of a company but also that it has been the affairs of the company which have been conducted in an oppressive manner, and it was to this point that a large part of the appellants' argument was directed. I must therefore state in broad outline the course of events which led to the presentation of the petition.

The last event that I mentioned was the failure of the society to acquire at par shares that were worth a far greater sum. This was at a time of the company's great prosperity which, subject to the ups and downs of the textile trade, might be expected to continue. It was, however, followed by a recession in the rayon trade, of which the dates of beginning and ending were a matter of dispute. Such dates cannot be precisely determined and are of no consequence. It is, however, to be noted that it was in the course of it that rayon control came to an end, so that neither the society nor the company any longer depended on the personality [340] of the respondents to get supplies of yam. It was also in the course of it that the respondent Meyer was anxious to visit Germany with a view to increasing the company's trade in that country but was prevented by his co-directors from doing so. This was undoubtedly the cause of much ill-feeling. . . .

An important consequence of the removal of cotton control was this. In or about June, 1951, a new department of the society had been formed called the merchant converting department. It was under the control of a Mr Wand, the manager of the drapery department, and its function was to convert loom state cloth by dyeing, printing and finishing into material for manufacture into garments. It therefore became possible upon the removal of cotton control and upon a revival of the rayon trade for the society to divert to their own converting department the product of their Falkland Mill. It was the fact, as they were well aware, that the company which had throughout been practically tied to them for the greater part of its supplies, would have great difficulty upon a revival of trade in getting them elsewhere. Deliberately they supplied the necessary material to the converting department but, in spite of Meyer's protests, declined to supply the company except at higher and non-competitive prices. An attempt to justify this discrimination was rightly regarded by their Lordships of the First Division as unsatisfactory. I have no doubt that at any rate by the end of 1952 it was the policy of the society by one means or another to destroy the company it had created, knowing that the minority shareholders alone would suffer in that process . . . . Robert Taylor, a director of the society and then chairman of the company, had an interview with [the petitioners] and told them frankly that the society was out to destroy the company, that they had no chance against such a powerful organisation, and that they should make their peace with the society by offering to sell their shares. . . .

At this time the three nominee directors of the company were aware (Taylor by his own confession) of the policy of the society. It is undeniable that persons so placed may find themselves in a difficulty. But in all the evidence I have not been able to find the least trace that they regarded themselves as owing any duty to the company of which they were directors. They were the nominees of the society and, if the society doomed the company to destruction, it was not for them to put out a saving hand. Rather, they were to join in that work, and, when a frank and prompt statement to their co-directors might have enabled them to retrieve its fortunes, they played their part by maintaining silence. That is how they conducted the affairs of the company, and it is impossible to suppose that that was not part of the deliberate policy of the society. As I have said, nominees of a parent company upon the board of a subsidiary company may be placed in a difficult and delicate position. It is, then, the more incumbent on the parent company to behave with scrupulous fairness to the minority shareholders and to avoid imposing upon their nominees the alternative of disregarding their instructions or betraying the interests of the minority. In the present case the society pursued a different course. It was ruthless and unscrupulous in design and it was effective in operation, and, as I have said, it was promoted by the action or inaction of the nominee directors. The company, which might have recovered [342] its former prosperity, had 'served its purpose.' It would conveniently be liquidated. I have omitted much which reflects no credit on the society and its officers, for I do not want to repeat what has already been said, or to anticipate what will fall from some of your Lordships. I will only mention the final fact that on August 24, 1953 (that is, after the presentation of the petition under section 210) Meyer and Lucas were given three months' notice of termination of their appointments as managing directors, and Mr Wand, the manager of the society's drapery department was appointed manager of the company.

My Lords, upon the facts, as I have outlined them and as they appear in greater detail in the judgments of their Lordships of the First Division, it appears to me incontrovertible that the society have behaved to the minority shareholders of the company in a manner which can justly be described as 'oppressive.' They had the majority power and they exercised their authority in a manner 'burdensome, harsh and wrongful' – I take the dictionary meaning of the word. But, it is said, let it be assumed that the society acted in an oppressive manner: yet they did not conduct the affairs of the company in an oppressive manner. My Lords, it may be that the acts of the society of which complaint is made could not be regarded as conduct of the affairs of the company if the society and the company were bodies wholly independent of each other, competitors in the rayon market, and using against each other such methods of trade warfare as custom permitted. But this is to pursue a false analogy.

It is not possible to separate the transactions of the society from those of the company. Every step taken by the latter was determined by the policy of the former. I will give an example of this. I observed that, in the course of the argument before the House, it was suggested that the company had only itself to blame if, through its neglect to get a contract with the society, it failed in a crisis to obtain from the Falkland Mill the supply of cloth that it needed. The short answer is that it was the policy of the society that the affairs of the company should be so conducted and the minority shareholders were content that it should be so. They relied – how unwisely the event proved – upon the good faith of the society, and, in any case, they were impotent to impose their own views. It is just because the society could not only use the ordinary and legitimate weapons of commercial warfare but could also control from within the operations of the company that it is illegitimate to regard the conduct of the company's affairs as a matter for which they had no responsibility. After much [343] consideration of this question, I do not think that my own views could be stated better than in the late Lord President Cooper's words on the first hearing of this case. 'In my view,' he said, 'the section warrants the court in looking at the business realities of a situation and does not confine them to a narrow legalistic view. The truth is that, whenever a subsidiary is formed as in this case with an independent minority of shareholders, the parent company must, if it is engaged in the same class of business, accept as a result of having formed such a subsidiary an obligation so to conduct what are in a sense its own affairs as to deal fairly with its subsidiary.' At the opposite pole to this standard may be put the conduct of a parent company which says: 'Our subsidiary company has served its purpose, which is our purpose. Therefore let it die,' and, having thus pronounced sentence, is able to enforce it and does enforce it not only by attack from without but also by support from within. If this section is inept to cover such a case, it will be a dead letter indeed. I have expressed myself strongly in this case because, on the contrary, it appears to me to be a glaring example of precisely the evil which Parliament intended to remedy.

Some criticism was made of the relief given by the order of the court. It was said that only that relief could be given which had as its object and presumably its effect the 'bringing to an end of the matters complained of' and that an order upon the society to purchase the respondents' shares in the company did not satisfy that condition. This argument is without substance. The matter complained of was the oppression of the minority shareholders by the society. They will no longer be oppressed and will cease to complain if the society purchase their shares.

Finally, it was said that the court had not properly exercised its discretion in fixing a price of £3.15s.0d. per share. I see no ground for interfering with this decision. Necessarily a price cannot be scientifically assessed, but I heard no argument, nor had any evidence called to my attention, which suggested that their Lordships had acted on any wrong principle or adopted a measure too generous to the respondents.

The following are the principal Irish cases on 'oppression'

In re Murph's Restaurants Ltd. (No. 2)
Gannon J., July 31, 1979 (HC)

The Company ran an extremely successful restaurant business which had grown very rapidly, and had three shareholders who were also its directors, BS., K. and M. The latter two were brothers and had worked full-time for the company since its foundation in 1972, whereas BS., the petitioner, in 1977 gave up a promising career in the computer business in order to work for the company full-time. No annual meetings were ever held, no annual accounts were prepared and board meetings were most informal. Dividends and directors fees as such were never paid. Instead, drawings were made by the directors against projected earnings; there was an informal arrangement by which each could take about £200 a month 'slush money' from cash, and on various occasions sums were transferred into accounts in building societies in the names of one or other of the directors. Special care was taken to ensure that each shared these disbursements equally. In 1977 they agreed to enter the property market and they bid, unsuccessfully, for a hotel. But in the following year K. and M. bought that property on their own behalf. In the meantime, BS. had gone to Cork to run the very successful branch there. In early 1979 K. and M. agreed that BS. should be removed from the board and be no longer employed by the company. While BS.'s management of the Cork branch was criticised by K. and M., it was the profits from it that, in the form of a loan from the company, financed K. and M.'s hotel purchase; and BS. did not agree with various aspects of the loan. [10.94]

GANNON J.: [19] In his petition Brian asks that the company be wound up under paragraphs (f) and (g) of section 213 of the Companies Act 1963. In reply Kevin and Murph on behalf of the company submit that Brian has been deprived of his directorship for good reason and as a shareholder can be afforded sufficient relief under section 205 of the Act, by allowing them to purchase his shares at a valuation. It is also submitted that it would not be in the best interests of the company to have it wound up because in the course of compulsorily winding up the assets of the company would not meet the liabilities and Brian could gain nothing from it, and because his interest as a shareholder has not been affected he is not entitled to an order under section 213. As to the matter of his removal from directorship I am satisfied from the evidence that the reasons advanced are neither good nor sufficient and are wholly inadequate to justify that action. But the evidence further discloses that the purported removal was irregular and ineffective in law. Furthermore it is clear from the evidence that in the conduct of the affairs of the company the directors did not exercise their [20] powers in a regular manner so far as the company is concerned, and the purported exclusion of Brian by Kevin and Murph in an irregular and arrogant manner is undoubtedly oppressive. As to the matter of what would be the best interests of the company and the consequences of an order for winding up evidence was given on behalf of the company by Mr. Kidney who is the accountant for the company. He was first engaged by the company about March, 1977. On instructions he prepared a draft balance sheet for the company as of the 3rd February, 1979 from information obtained from the books of the company and given to him by Kevin and Murph. He estimated the assets (including the presumed repayment of the £25,000 loan) to be £189,672 and the liabilities to be £185,829. He expressed the opinion that in a winding up of the company under Court order the apparent net balance could not be achieved because all assets would not realise the estimated values and consequently there would be no surplus or dividend for shareholders. He had not included monies in building societies' accounts and he was not aware of the 'siphoning off of funds'. From my observation and assessment of the evidence of Kevin and of Murph I believe they would not be as truthful and forthcoming when instructing the accountant as the Court would require them to be in order to be in a position to place reliance on the opinion of the accountant founded on [21] their information to him.

It is clear from the evidence that there is no form of order of the nature indicated in section 205(3) which could bring to an end the matters complained of by Brian in the proceedings or which could regulate the affairs of the company for the future. It appears to me that the circumstances in which by order under section 205 the Court may direct the purchase of the shares of a member by other members or by the company are circumstances in which the Court would do so 'with a view to bringing to an end the matters complained of' by the person applying to the Court. It is my opinion that in this case with the fundamental relationship between Brian, Kevin and Murph sundered that proceedings under section 205 would not in any circumstances be appropriate.

In the course of argument and submissions I was referred to the judgment of the House of Lords in England in *Re Westbourne Galleries Ltd* [1973] A.C. 360 in support of the claim of the petitioner Brian to have the company wound up on the grounds that such order would be just and equitable. It was relied upon also in answer to the contentions of the company, per Kevin and Murph, that Brian is not entitled to such an order on the grounds that there was no disregard of his interests [22] as a member, he had nothing to gain as a contributory, there was no lack of probity or unfair dealing on their part, that their conduct was based on their concern for the welfare of the company and to ensure the business would prosper, and that it would not be in the best interests of the company, its staff, customers or creditors that it be wound up.

The claim before the House of Lords was by one of three directors/shareholders of a limited company for an order to have the company wound up pursuant to section 222(f) of the English Companies Act 1948, the wording of which corresponds exactly with section 213 (f) of the Companies Act 1963. I find the opinions delivered in the course of this judgment in the House of Lords very helpful because of the statements of principle the application of which depends upon the facts under consideration. I have accordingly set out first the facts in the case before me from which it can be seen where they may be distinguishable from those in the case to which the House of Lords judgment relates. But that judgment reminds us that the principles of equity which are applicable in every Court of law are the same and should be given application in the like manner in cases affecting the commercial relations of companies, in which rules of law tend to be technical and rigid, as much as in cases of personal relations between private individuals.

[23] Having regard to the contentions advanced on behalf of Kevin and Murph I think it appropriate to quote the following passage from the report of the speech of Lord Wilberforce in *Re Westbourne Galleries Ltd.*:

"For some 50 years, following a pronouncement by Lord Cottenham L.C. in *Ex parte Spackman* (1849) 1 Mac. and G. 170, 174 in 1849, the words 'just and equitable' were interpreted so as only to include matters *ejusdem generis* as the preceding clauses of the section, but there is now ample authority for discarding this limitation. There are two other restrictive interpretations which I mention to reject. First, there has been a tendency to create categories or headings under which cases must be brought if the clause is to apply. This is wrong.

Illustrations may be used, but general words should remain general and not be reduced to the sum of particular instances. Secondly, it has been suggested, and urged upon us, that (assuming the petitioner is a shareholder and not a creditor) the words must be confined to such circumstances as affect him in his capacity as shareholder. I see no warrant for this either. No doubt, in order to present a petition, he must qualify as a shareholder, but I see no reason for preventing him from relying upon any [24] circumstances of justice or equity which affect him in his relations with the company, or, in a case such as the present, with the other shareholders.

One other signpost is significant. The same words 'just and equitable' appear in the Partnership Act 1892 section 25 as a ground for dissolution of a partnership and no doubt the considerations which they reflect formed part of the common law of partnership before its codification. The importance of this is to provide a bridge between cases under section 222(F) of the Act, of 1948 and the principles of equity developed in relation to partnerships."

Before proceeding further with consideration of the speech of Lord Wilberforce it would be helpful to refer at this stage to what was said by Lord Cross of

Chelsea in his speech:

> "In some of the reported cases in which winding up orders have been made those who opposed the petition have been held by the Court to have been guilty of a 'lack of probity' in their dealings with the petitioners."

He then cites two examples and then goes on the say 'but it is not a condition precedent to the making of an order under the subsection that the conduct of [25] those who oppose its making should have been unjust or inequitable. This was made clear as early as 1905 by Lord M'Laren in his judgment in *Symington v. Symington's Quarries Ltd.* (8 F. 121. 130). To the same effect is the judgment of Lord Cozens-Hardy M.R. in *Re Yenidje Tobacco Go. Ltd.* [1916] 2 Ch. 426, 431-432. It is sometimes said that the order in that case was made on the ground of deadlock. That is not so.' Having explained why he takes that view he goes on to say:

> "People do not become partners unless they have confidence in one another and it is of the essence of the relationship that mutual confidence is maintained. If neither has any longer confidence in the other so that they cannot work together in the way originally contemplated then the relationship should be ended – unless, indeed, the party who wishes to end it has been solely responsible for the situation which has arisen. The relationship between Mr Rothman and Mr Weinberg (the names of parties in the case under his then consideration) was not, of course, in form that of partners; they were equal shareholders in a limited company. But the Court considered that it would be unduly fettered by matters of form if it did not deal with the situation it would have dealt with it had the parties been partners in form as well as in substance."

[26] Turning again to the speech of Lord Wilberforce I draw attention to the nature of the submissions made to the Court in that case as summarised in the speech of Lord Wilberforce and the manner in which he expressed his opinion on these matters following examination of a number of cases dealing with the partnership features of companies. At page 379 he then says:

> "My Lords, in my opinion these authorities represent a sound and rational development of the law which should be endorsed. The foundation of it all lies in the words 'just and equitable' and if there is any respect in which some of the cases may be open to criticism, it is that the Courts may sometimes have been too timorous in giving them full force. The words are a recognition of the fact that a limited company is more than a mere legal entity, with a personality in law of its own; that there is room in company law for recognition of the fact that behind it, or amongst

it, there are individuals, with rights, expectations and obligations inter se submerged in the company structure. That structure is defined by the Companies Act and by the articles of association by which shareholders agree to be bound. In most companies and in most contexts, this definition is sufficient and [27] exhaustive, equally so whether the company is large or small. The 'just and equitable' provision does not, as the respondents. suggest, entitle one party to disregard the obligation he assumes by entering a company, nor the Court to dispense him from it. It does, as equity always does, enable the Court to subject the exercise of legal rights to equitable considerations; considerations, that is, of a personal character arising between one individual and another, which may make it unjust or inequitable, to insist on legal rights, or to exercise them in a particular way."

Lord Wilberforce then gives examples of circumstances in which relations of a special personal character may be essential to the members of a company with particular reference to mutual confidence. At page 380 he goes on to say:

"My Lords, this is an expulsion case, and I must briefly justify the application in such cases of the just and equitable clause. The question is, as always, whether it is equitable to allow one (or two) to make use of his legal rights to the prejudice of his associate(s). The law of companies recognises the right, in many ways, to remove a director from the board. Section 184 of the Companies Act 1948 confers this right upon the [28] company in general meeting whatever the articles may say. Some articles may prescribe other methods; for example, a governing director may have the power to remove (compare in *Re Wondoflex Textiles Pty. Ltd.* [1951] V.L.R. 458). And quite apart from removal powers, there are normally provisions for retirement of directors by rotation so that their reelection can be opposed and defeated by a majority, or even by a casting vote. In all these ways a particular director/member may find himself no longer a director, through removal, or non-reelection; this situation he must normally accept, unless he undertakes the burden of proving fraud or mala fides. The just and equitable provision nevertheless comes to his assistance if he can point to, and prove, some special underlying obligation of his fellow member(s) in good faith, or confidence, that so long as the business continues he shall be entitled to management participation, an obligation so basic that, if broken, the conclusion must be that the association must be dissolved. And the principles on which he may do so are those worked out by the Courts in partnership cases where there has been exclusion from management (see *Const v. Harris* (1824) Tur. and Rus. 496, 525) even where under the partnership agreement there is a power of expulsion (see *Blisset v. Daniel* (1853) 10 Hare 493; *Lindley on Partnership*, 13th Ed.(1971) pp 331, 595)."

[290] I make one final quotation from this speech which concludes as follows at page 381:

> "I must deal with one final point which was much relied on by the Court of Appeal. It was said that the removal was, according to the evidence of Mr Nazare, bona fide in the interests of the company; that Mr Ebrahimi had not shown the contrary; that he ought to do so or to demonstrate that no reasonable man could think that his removal was in the company's interest. This formula 'bona fide in the interests of the company' is one that is relevant in certain contexts of company law and I do not doubt that in many cases decisions have to be left to majorities or directors to take which the Courts must assume had this basis. It may on the other hand, become little more than an alibi for a refusal to consider the merits of the case, and in a situation such as this it seems to have little meaning other than 'in the interests of the majority'. Mr Nazar may well have persuaded himself, quite genuinely, that the company would be better off without Mr Ebrahimi, but if Mr Ebrahimi disputed this, or thought the same with reference to Mr Nazar what prevails is simply the majority view. To confine the application of the just and equitable clause to proved cases of mala fides would be to [30] negative the generality of the words. It is because I do not accept this that I feel myself obliged to differ from the Court of Appeal."

I accept the statements of principles given in the Lords' speeches in that case as the correct guidance for my consideration of the questions before me on this petition.

Reverting now to the facts: there is only one answer to the question, was Brian lawfully removed from the office of director of this company? Was this not a business in which all three engaged on the basis that all should participate in its direction and management? Was it an abuse of wrongfully or mistakenly arrogated power and a breach of the good faith 'which these three partners owed to each other to exclude him from all participation in the business of the company? To these questions there can be only an affirmative answer. Even if the intended resolution for his removal had been proposed in a regular manner, and even if the resolution had been considered at a regularly convened meeting what justification could have been offered to support it? The only matters of complaint of their nature were such that they probably could have been resolved by a temporary spell of personal attention by one of the other directors more experienced in that area of work. But the facts belie the complaints. The business at the Cork branch was exceeding [31] expectations and seemed likely to outstrip the business of the best branch in Dublin and provided support for private investment for the partners making the complaints. The action of Kevin and Murph on the 3rd February, 1979 was wholly unjustified as well as being irregular. But by that action, and in their evidence relating to it, they made it clear that they did not regard Brian as a partner but simply as an employee. Their refusal to recognise any status of equality amounted to a repudiation of their relationship on which the existence of the company was founded. By ceasing to be a director Brian would lose not director's fees for there were none, nor dividends on his shares for there were none, but his very livelihood consisting of an equal share of all capital and profits and active participation in direction and management of the company.

I am satisfied that the petitioner has made out a case for a winding up order, and has shown that proceedings under section 205 would not be appropriate. A liquidator will be appointed and notice of the presentation of the petition and the making of the winding up order will be advertised. The petitioner will have his costs of the hearing to be borne by Kevin and Murph and the company will bear such of its own costs as are not related to these of Kevin and Murph.

In re Greenore Trading Co. Ltd
[1980] I.L.R.M. 94

Between 1966 and 1975 the shareholders and directors of the company were Parge (the petitioner), Boyle and Vanlandeghem, each of whom owned 8,000 £1 shares. The petitioner was chairman, Boyle was its manager, and Vanlandeghem, who was also a cattle exporter, its major customer. The company's main business was providing a service to exporters of cattle. In 1975, when the company encountered difficulties, Vanlandeghem contributed £10,000 in return for the issue to him of 10,000 new shares. At this time the petitioner resigned as a director and Vanlandeghem became managing director. The issue of new shares was inconsistent with a resolution in existence since 1966 that no single shareholding should exceed 8,000 and was otherwise irregular.

In 1978 Boyle agreed to sell his shares to Vanlandeghem for £22,500, or alternatively for their par value of £8,000 together with a severance payment from the company of £14,500. He received a personal cheque from Vanlandeghem for £8,000 and a company cheque for £14,500. The petitioner alleged that Vanlandeghem was using his control of the company in a manner that was oppressive, and sought from the court various declarations on aspects of the company's affairs, including ones that the share transactions of 1975 and 1978 were invalid.

KEANE J.: [97] I shall consider first the general complaint that the affairs of the company have been conducted and his powers as a director exercised by Mr Vanlandeghem in [98] a manner which is oppressive to the petitioner and in disregard of his interests as a member of the company. The general complaint is essentially based on two allegations: first, that Mr Vanlandeghem abused his position as a director and shareholder to obtain preferential treatment for himself as a customer of the company and, secondly, that he induced other customers of the company not to trade with it in order to obtain for himself the exclusive benefit of the company's services. So far as the first allegation is concerned, it is common case that for a limited period, at least, Mr Vanlandeghem was, in fact, afforded preferential treatment so far as the rates of payment were concerned in respect of cattle exported by him through the port, but that this was with the express approval of his fellow directors and shareholders. It is also not in dispute that Mr Vanlandeghem's custom was of very great importance to the company: it might not, indeed, be overstating the position to say that it was of paramount importance, to such an extent that, when he withdrew his custom in the years 1973 and 1974, the company did virtually no business.

It would not be surprising to find preferential treatment being accorded to such a customer; and I doubt very much whether Mr Vanlandeghem in seeking it could be said to be acting oppressively towards his fellow shareholders. It was claimed that in the post-1975 period, he was charged an all-in figure per head in respect of cattle shipped by him through the port, in contrast to his competitors who had to pay extra in respect of weighing, lairage etc. I do not think that the evidence went so far as to establish that the company to any significant extent afforded Mr Vanlandeghem preferential treatment because of pressure brought to bear on them by him. If he was afforded such preferential treatment – and it is not in dispute that at one stage it was given to him with the full accord of his fellow shareholders and directors – it was simply the consequence of his dominant position as a customer and as such did not, in any way, reflect oppressive treatment by him of the petitioner or any disregard of his interests.

It was also alleged that Mr Vanlandeghem systematically discouraged other exporters of cattle from using the port of Greenore with a view to securing a monopoly of the cattle trade out of the port. Doubtless if it could be established in evidence that Mr Vanlendeghem acted in a manner which was so patently detrimental to the company's interests, this would constitute the sort of conduct envisaged by section 205. The evidence in support of this allegation was principally that of Mr Boyle; and it was strenuously disputed by Mr Vanlandeghem. I think that the significant feature of this conflict of evidence was that no attempt was made on behalf of the petitioner to call any of the persons who were alleged to have been actively discouraged by Mr Vanlandeghem from exporting their cattle through Greenore. In my opinion, the petitioner failed to discharge the onus of proof resting on him so far as this allegation was concerned.

The two transactions concerning the share capital of the company which were challenged must next be considered. So far as the issue of 10,000 additional shares to Mr Vanlandeghem at the meeting of 5 February, 1975, is concerned, it was submitted on behalf of the petitioner that it was invalid for the following reasons:

[99] "(1) Although the allotment involved an increase in the capital of the company, no notice was given of any intention to propose a special resolution to that effect, nor was any such resolution passed;

(2) the resolution of 14 January 1966 to the effect that the shareholding of individual members should not be increased beyond £8,000 was riot rescinded;

(3) although the meeting of 5 February 1975 was an extraordinary general meeting of the company and not a meeting of the directors, it purported to allot the shares to Mr Vanlandeghem, whereas this should have been done at a meeting of the directors alone."

I think that it is clear that each of these grounds of objection is well founded. It is also the case, however, that the issue of shares was made to Mr Vanlandeghem in order to given him some security in respect of the £10,000 which he was prepared to advance to the company in order to get it out of its serious financial problems. The money was made available by him when it became obvious that neither the petitioner nor Mr Boyle could nor would come to the rescue of the company. The petitioner was present at the commencement of the meeting on 20 January 1975, and was represented at the adjourned meeting on 5 February 1975 by his solicitor, Mr John Kieran, acting under a power of attorney. It was not seriously disputed that had Mr Vanlandeghem not been willing to advance the sum of £10,000 the company would have been in very serious financial trouble and might well have gone to the wall. The petitioner and Mr Boyle were obviously perfectly happy that Mr Vanlandeghem should come to the company's assistance and were willing that he should be secured by the issue of the debenture. It was only when the company's solicitors advised that it would be more in the interests of the company for Mr Vanlandeghem to be allotted the 10,000 shares that this course was adopted. It was not questioned by the petitioner until long afterwards. While the procedure adopted was technically not in conformity with the Companies Act 1963 and the terms of the earlier resolution, the petitioner, although not present at the meeting when the shares were allotted, by his conduct clearly indicated that he was satisfied that the additional shares should be allotted to Mr Vanlandeghem, provided he came to the aid of the company financially. This Mr Vanlandeghem did: but if the contention advanced on behalf of the petitioner is well founded it means that, should the company go into liquidation, Mr Vanlandeghem will have to prove for his £10,00 as an ordinary creditor and will be without any security whatsoever. This would be the result of his having foregone the debenture, which would have made him a secured creditor, and which was abandoned simply because the company's solicitor advised that it was against the company's interest. The company, and the petitioner, will accordingly have had the benefit of Mr Vanlandeghem's £10,000 while he will be deprived of all security in relation to it, although he had acted in the reasonable belief, which his fellow shareholders did nothing to dispel, that the transaction was not merely fully acceptable to them, but the only means available of saving the company.

It would seem to me entirely contrary to justice and to be singularly unfair and unreasonable that, in these circumstances, the petitioner could successfully assert that the issue of shares was invalid. I think, however, that in these circumstances the doctrine of estoppel in pais is applicable: because where a person has so conducted himself that another would, as a reasonable man, understand [100] that a certain representation of fact is intended to be acted on, and the other has acted on the representation and thereby altered his position to his prejudice, an estoppel arises against the party who made the representation, and he is not allowed to aver that the fact is otherwise than he represented it to be. This principle of law, which is to be found summarised in Halsbury's *Laws of England*, Fourth Edition, Volume 16, paragraph 1505, is fully applicable, in my view, to the resolution of 14 January 1966. The petitioner, by his conduct, having led Mr Vanlandeghem to believe that he was treating that resolution as of no effect, and thereby induced him to alter his position to his prejudice, cannot now aver that the resolution is binding on the company. Similarly, he cannot now aver that the necessary notice was not given of an intention to pass a special resolution or that no such special resolution was passed; nor can he aver that the meeting was a meeting of shareholders only and not of directors. It is, of course, clear that a party cannot set up an estoppel in the face of a statute; but that principle does not seem to me to be directly applicable to a case such as the present, where the transaction in issue was not prohibited by law and its recognition or enforcement by the court would violate no principle of public policy or social policy. (See *Re Stapleford Colliery Company, Barrow's Case*, (1880) 14 Ch. D. 432 at 441, *Bradshaw v. McMullan* [1920] 2 I.R. 47, 412, 490, and *Kok Hoong v. Leong Cheong Kweng Mines Ltd.* [1964] A.C. 991) In this case the petitioner is clearly estopped, in my opinion, from asserting the irregularity of a transaction which he tacitly approved of when it was being implemented, which does not offend against any principle of law and which was entirely for the benefit of the company.

Different considerations entirely apply to the transfer of Mr Boyle's shares to Mr Vanlandeghem. It is immaterial whether the real price paid for the shares was £22,500 or whether the sum of £14,500 represented compensation to Mr Boyle for quitting the company, as the respondent claim. If it was compensation of this nature, then the transaction was clearly unlawful having regard to the provisions of section 186 of the Companies Act 1963, since the proposed payment was not disclosed to the other member of the company (the petitioner) nor was it approved by the company in general meeting. Indeed, the illegality of the transaction, if this was its nature, was compounded by the fact that the sum paid in respect of compensation was not specified in the company's accounts, as required by section 191 of the Act. If, on the other hand, the sum of £14,500 did represent part of the consideration for the shares, the transaction was unlawful, since it was in violation of section 60 of the Act, which prohibits a company from giving financial assistance for the purchase of its shares. On any view, accordingly, this transaction was not merely irregular, but grossly irregular.

I am satisfied that this latter transaction constituted conduct of such a nature as to justify, and indeed require, the making of an order under section 205(3) of the Act. Prior to that transaction, Mr Vanlandeghem, as a result of the issue of 10,000 shares to him in 1975, was the holder of just over 50% of the issued share capital. Had the transfer of shares by Mr Boyle to him gone unchallenged, he would have become the owner of more than 75% of the company share capital. 'Oppressive' conduct for the purposes of the corresponding section 210 of the English [101] Companies Act 1948 has been defined as meaning the exercise of the company's authority 'in a manner burdensome, harsh and wrongful.' (See *Scottish C. W.S. Ltd. v. Meyer* [1959] A.C. 324 at p. 342 – see supra, p. 472.) The patent misapplication of the company's monies for the purpose of giving Mr Vanlandeghem a dominant position in its affairs seems to me to be properly described as 'burdensome, harsh and wrongful' quoad the petitioner. It cannot be equated to the allotment of shares in *Re Jermyn Street Turkish Baths Limited* [1971] 1 W.L.R. 1042 which was treated by the Court of Appeal as being one entered into in good faith for the benefit of the company. Nor can the actual misapplication of the funds be properly treated as an isolated act of oppression (which would not normally be sufficient to justify relief under the section: see *Re Westbourne Galleries* [1970] 1 W.L.R. 1378). As I have already noted, not merely were the company's monies purportedly applied towards an unlawful purpose, *i.e.* the payment of compensation to a director for loss of office without the sanction of a general meeting: the payment of that compensation was not separately dealt with in the company's accounts for the relevant year, as required by law.

It is true that the wording of the section envisages that the oppression complained of is operative at the time when the petition is launched. (See *Re Jermyn Street Turkish Baths Ltd.*) In this case the transfer of shares took place in March 1978. The accounts for the year were certified by the company's auditors on 9 June 1978. The petition was presented just over a year later on 15 June 1979, after protests had been made in correspondence on behalf of the petitioner at the manner in which the company's affairs were being conducted. The company had not merely failed to take any steps to deal with these gross irregularities in its affairs prior to the issuing of the petition; it had also wholly ignored letters written on behalf of the petitioner which clearly called for an answer. It seem to me that in these circumstances the oppressive conduct can properly be regarded as having continued up to the date of the issuing of the petition.

It is obvious that the present circumstances would justify an order being made for the winding up of the company under section 213(f) and (g). It is agreed, however, that such an order, in the present circumstances, would not be in the interests of the members; and, accordingly, the remedy for the oppressive conduct must be the alternative remedy provided by section 205. I think that the only effective method of bringing to an end the oppressive conduct of which the petitioner complains is an order for the purchase of his shares by Mr Vanlandeghem.

The shares, accordingly, must be purchased by Mr Vanlandeghem at a fair price; and it remains to consider what that price should be, in all the circumstances of the case. Having regard to the findings I have made, it is clear that the petitioner's shareholding must be valued on the assumption that the purported purchase of Mr Boyle's shares had not taken place. This would leave the petitioner owning 8,000 shares, Mr Vanlandeghem 18,000 and Mr Boyle 8,000 shares. I doubt very much whether a shareholder already in control of more than 50% of the share capital would, in the particular circumstances of this company, have paid more than their par value to acquire the shareholding of the petitioner. I do not think that the fact that Mr Boyle may have got £22,500 for his shareholding is of much assistance in determining the value of the petitioner's shareholding.

[102] In the first place, the purchaser was not willing to pay more than £8,000 for the shares from his own resources. In the second place, Mr Boyle was more conspicuously involved in the company's affairs – usually in contest with Mr Vanlandeghem – and, accordingly, had more of a nuisance value from the point of view of Mr Vanlandeghem than the petitioner. In the third place, there remains the possibility that some, at least, of the consideration was genuinely, if illegally, related to compensation for the loss of office rather than the purchase price of the shares themselves. Having regard to the uncertain financial future of the company I doubt very much whether, from the point of view of the majority shareholder, if would have been worth paying more than £8,000 for the Petitioner's shareholding,– nor do I think that somebody buying an interest in the company, who had not already any interest in it, would have been willing to pay more than that sum.

That, however, does not conclude the matter, since it is clear that, in prescribing the basis on which the price is to be calculated, the court can, in effect, provide compensation for whatever injury has been inflicted by the oppressors. (See *Scottish Co-operative Wholesale Society v. Meyer* [1959] A.C. 324, supra p. 472.) The accounts in the present case show that the company had been pursuing a conservative policy in relation to the payment of dividends in the years immediately preceding the wrongful purchase of Mr Boyle's shares; and this policy may well have been justified by the company's uncertain trading future. There seem to me, however, no reason why the petitioner should be deprived of the share to which he would have been entitled of the £14,500 wrongfully applied in the transaction regarding Mr Boyle's shares. It is immaterial whether that sum comes back to the company following these or other proceedings and is ultimately paid out by way of dividend or as a return on capital to the contributors, since the petitioner will derive no benefit from that once the shares have been purchased by Mr Vanlandeghem. It follows that he is entitled, in my view, to be paid a sum bearing the same proportion to that sum of £14,500 as his share-holding of £8,000 did to the total issued share capital of £34,000 prior to the unlawful transaction in relation to Mr Boyle's shares; and I will order that sum to be paid, in addition to the sum of £8,000 representing the par value of his shares.

In re Williams Group Tullamore Ltd
[1985] I.R. 613

Two brothers had run a business as a partnership. In 1966 they formed a company and held 133,540 shares of £1 each in it. When their children inherited those shares, confusion arose and the business suffered. It was then re-organised and the capital structure was changed into ordinary and preference shares, of which 133,540 in all were issued. The preference shares carried a right to a fixed 8% non-cumulative dividend and voting rights; so long as any preference shares were outstanding, the ordinary shares conferred no voting rights. The company prospered and the ordinary shareholders received very substantial dividends and fared much better than the preference shareholders.

Thereafter, the business prospered greatly. The board of directors decided that it would be fair to allow the preference shareholders to participate to the accrued profits earned from a particular part of the business. To this end a scheme was devised and passed in general meeting (which the ordinary shareholders were not entitled to attend) to allow the distribution of a sum of £267.000 between all the shareholders. A number of the ordinary shareholders objected, claiming that the action of the preference shareholders was oppressive and had been taken in disregard of their rights, and petitioned the High Court for relief under section 205 of the Act of 1963.

BARRINGTON J: [616] The founder members had run the business. in effect, as a partnership. They apparently worked very well together and there was no necessity to define the powers of either of them. There was no formal of managing director. A problem, however, came into existence when their children inherited their shares. Some of the children naturally had a greater interest in, and aptitude for, business than others. The result was some confusion which reflected adversely on the business. To counteract this Mr. Edmund Williams was invited, in 1965, to become the first managing director of the company and he has retained that post ever since.

A major reorganisation of the capital structure of the company took place in November. 1972. when the preference shares were created. . . .

These amendments to the memorandum and articles of association of the company were carried by agreement of all concerned and their object was to consolidate control of the company in the hands of those members of [617] the family who were most intimately concerned with its management. In time Mr. Edmund Williams came to own or control some 45% of the issued preference shares in the company. There can be no doubt that he acquired these shares fairly and by agreement. Neither can there be any doubt that under his stewardship the company has prospered and been exceedingly successful. By the capital reorganisation of 1972, the ordinary shareholders abandoned their right to receive notice of, or to attend, or to vote at general meetings of the company, so long as any preference share in the capital of the company remained issued and outstanding. Nevertheless the ordinary shareholders have received very substantial dividends over the years and have done very much better than the preference shareholders. No one questions but that, over the years, they have been very fairly treated.

The present dispute is confined to the proposed method of distributing a sum of £267,080 accrued profits earned from exporting Irish Mist Liqueur. The board of the company apparently took the view that, over the years, the ordinary shareholders had done extremely well – at times earning dividends of over 100% on their capital. By comparison the preference shareholders, who were stuck with their fixed interest of eight per cent, had done very poorly. Moreover, inflation had eaten away the value of their dividends. On this occasion, apparently, management thought it fair to rectify the balance. A memorandum circulated to members of the board for the purpose of explaining the proposed distribution put the matter as follows:

> "Those whose capital remained tied up have lost out by inflation and dividend pay-out. The board has considered that to be fair and equitable to the preference shareholders they should, on this occasion, be permitted to participate in the opportunity for bonus presenting itself on the sale of Irish Mist."

The proposed scheme was that each ordinary and each preference shareholder should receive one fully paid up penny share in the share capital of the company for each ordinary and for each preference share held by him. This would involve the issue of 267,080 new "A" shares. Each of these shares would then qualify for one single dividend of £1 each. The preference shareholders and the ordinary shareholders would each receive their usual dividends, but over and above this, each of them would also receive a dividend of £1 for each "A" share held by him. A number of the ordinary shareholders objected to the scheme. . . .

[618] It was this decision which gave rise to the present petition. The petitioners originally claimed that the creation and issue of the "A" shares of 1p each amounted to a variation or abrogation of the rights of the ordinary shareholders but Mr. O'Neill abandoned this point at the hearing and presented a

case solely as a case of oppression under section 205 of the Act. The resolutions passed on the 13th May, 1985, contemplated that the dividend of £1 payable on the 1p "A" shares should be paid before the 31st August. 1985. The petitioners obtained an injunction to restrain the payment out. Unfortunately the petition could not be heard before the date fixed for the payment out on the 31st August. 1985. The parties have arrived at a private arrangement to deal with this matter, the result of which is that I can regard the proposed payment out as an ongoing proposal which the petitioners claim is oppressive to them.

[619] The petition is presented under section 205 of the Companies Act 1963. Section 205 is clearly modelled on section 210 of the English Companies Act. 1948. There are, however, significant differences in the wording of the two sections. . . .

[620] The English section refers only to the affairs of the company whereas the Irish section refers to both the affairs of the company and the powers of the directors. More importantly the English section refers to the affairs of the company being conducted in an oppressive manner, while the Irish section refers to the affairs of the company being conducted in an oppressive manner or in disregard of the interests of some members. Moreover, the English section appears to suggest that the oppression should be of such a nature that it would. in normal circumstances, make it just and equitable to wind up the company. The Irish section contains no such precondition. Indeed. section 213 of the Irish Act, provides that the court may in certain circumstances dismiss a petition to wind up a company if it is of opinion that proceedings under section 205 of the Act would be more appropriate. The English section has now been amended by section 75 of the English Companies Act 1980, but the difference in wording between section 210 of the English Act, of 1948 and section 205 of the Irish Act means that authorities on section 210 of the English Act must be treated with some reserve when interpreting the Irish section.

If one regards "oppression" as a course of conduct which is "burdensome, harsh and wrongful" or as conduct which involves lack of probity or fair dealing towards some members of the company (see *Scottish Co-operative Wholesale Ltd. v. Meyer* [1959] A.C. 324 – see *supra*, p. 472; *In re Jermyn Street Turkish Baths Ltd* [1971] 1 W.L.R. 1042. and the judgment of Keane J. in *In re Greenore Trading Company Ltd* [1980] I.L.R.M. 94 – see supra p. 482) there is no history of such a course of conduct in the present company prior to the events giving rise to the present case. On the contrary, the ordinary shareholders appear to have been treated extremely well.

Moreover, in the present case, we are not dealing with a course of conduct but with an individual transaction. It appears however that an isolated transaction can give rise to relief under the Irish section. See the judgment of Kenny J., in *In re Westwinds Holding Company Ltd* (unreported, High Court, May 21, 1974). Besides, in the present case we are dealing with a transaction which is ongoing at the date of the hearing of this petition in the sense that it is one which will be implemented if the petitioners do not obtain the relief they are seeking. It is perhaps worth noting that the Irish section offers relief not only when the affairs of the company are being conducted in an oppressive manner but also (and alternatively) where they are being conducted in disregard of the interests of some member or members.

There can be no doubt that the preference shareholders in passing the resolutions of May 13, 1985, acted within their formal powers. There can be no doubt either that they acted honestly in the sense that they felt entitled to make the decision which they did make. Indeed, Mr. Thomas P. [621] Hardiman who is chairman of the company and who chaired the meeting of May 13, 1985, thought that the decision made was a fair one. Mr. Hardiman was in the unique position to form an unbiased opinion because not only is he a businessman of wide experience, and chairman of the company, but he holds no shares in the company and therefore has no special interest which would cause him to favour either the preference or the ordinary shareholders.

Mr. O'Neill, on behalf of the petitioners, quoted a passage from the judgment of Sir Raymond Evershed M.R. in *Greenhalgh v. Arderne Cinemas Ltd.* [1950] 2 All E.R. 1120 (see *ante*, p. 438) where Sir Raymond, having surveyed the English authorities continued (at p. 1126 of the report):

> "Certain things, I think, can be safely stated as emerging from those authorities. In the first place, it is now plain that "*bona fide* for the benefit of the company as a whole" means not two things but one thing. It means that the shareholder must proceed on what, in his honest opinion, is for the benefit of the company as a whole. Secondly, the phrase, "the company as a whole," does not (at any rate in such a case as the present) mean the company as a commercial entity as distinct from the corporators. It means the corporators as a general body."

There is no doubt that shareholders, voting at a general meeting of the company, are entitled to have regard to their own interests. The problem is the degree to which they are entitled to disregard the interests of other shareholders. The structure of the present company prior to the 13th May, 1985, contemplated that the share capital of the company should be divided between preference shareholders and ordinary shareholders. The preference shareholders were entitled to a fixed preferential dividend of eight per cent and to priority over the ordinary shareholders in the repayment of capital on a winding up of the company. This structure seems to contemplate that the ordinary shareholders would take the greater risks and would, in the event of the company being successful, reap the greater rewards.

The structure of the company was, however, peculiar in that the ordinary shares in the company's capital carried no voting rights as long as there were preference shares issued. This meant that at all times material to these proceedings the preference shareholders had control of the company. During this time two things have happened. The company has been hugely successful and the value of the preference shareholders' fixed dividends has been eroded by inflation. The result has been an unhappy one for the preference shareholders, but it is doubtful if it can properly be regarded as "unfair". Moreover, a large part of the preference shares are held by the managing director of the company. But the success of the company probably springs from his ability as managing director rather than from his status as a preference shareholder.

Mr. O'Neill has admitted that the formal rights of the ordinary [622] shareholders have not been affected by the resolutions of the 13th May, 1985. However, he maintains that the effect of the resolution is to make available to the preference shareholders, or more correctly those preference shareholders who receive the new "A" shares. a sum of £133,540 which would otherwise be available for distribution among the ordinary shareholders as dividends or on the winding up of the company. It is not an answer to this argument to say that this sum, if not distributed in dividends to the preference shareholders, need not necessarily be distributed to the ordinary shareholders. The board might put it to some other use such, for example, as to reduce the borrowings of the company. But it appears to me that it must follow that if these monies are paid out to the preference shareholders or to such of the preference shareholders as hold "A" shares they will not be available for distribution to the ordinary shareholders or for purposes of which the ordinary shareholders may approve. In that sense it appears to me that the payment out referred to is contrary to the interests of the ordinary shareholders.

It appears to me also that the resolutions of May 13, 1985, were carried in disregard of the interests of the ordinary shareholders. It appears to me that the implementation of these resolutions is an ongoing matter in the company and justifies the view that the affairs of the company are being conducted in disregard of the interests of the ordinary shareholders. I fully accept that the proposal put forward in the resolution of May 13, 1985, was put forward in good faith. Nevertheless, it appears to me that it is in objective disregard of the interests of the ordinary shareholders and that to persist in implementing it would, in the circumstances, be oppressive to the ordinary shareholders.

In these circumstances it appears to me that the petitioners have brought themselves within the section and that they are entitled to appropriate relief.

In re Clubman Shirts Ltd
[1983] I.L.R.M. 323

The petitioner owned or controlled about 20 per cent of the equity in the company, which had failed to hold annual general meetings or to present audited accounts or to file annual returns in a number of years. Its directors refused to give the petitioner information to which he was entitled under the Companies

Acts. They offered to buy his shares at a low figure and he alleged that this involved unfair pressure as they had not given him the information which they possessed and which was necessary to assess the value of the shares. In 1980, when the company was in grave financial difficulties and threatened with receivership and probably liquidation, the directors transferred the entire business undertaking and the assets of the company to another company in a deal which extricated the company from its financial liabilities but which did not involve any payment to shareholders. The petitioner was not given full details of this transaction at the time. He alleged that all this constituted oppression.

O'HANLON J.: [327] My conclusion is that the evidence tends to show a series of irregularities by the directors in complying with their obligations under the Companies Act, rather than a case of oppression in the sense of section 205 of the Act. I would not classify as oppression the attempts made from time to time to buy out the petitioner's shareholding in the company. In my opinion the directors were entitled to make any offer they thought fit, whether realistic or unrealistic, and to hedge their offers around with conditions if they thought fit to do so. The petitioner, on receipt of the offers never responded by saying that he was unable to assess the true value of his shares by reason of the wrongful withholding of information by the directors, coupled with a request for such information as he needed to safeguard his interests. Neither did he at any time sell, or consider selling, his shareholding or any part thereof, on the terms offered to him. Consequently any claim for relief under section 205 which is based on these transactions cannot succeed.

Similarly, I would not classify as oppressive conduct within the meaning of the Act, the omission to comply with the various provisions of the Act, referrable to the holding of general meetings and the furnishing of information, and copy documents. These were examples of negligence, carelessness, irregularity in the conduct of the affairs of the company, but the evidence does not suggest that these defaults or any of them formed part of a deliberate scheme to deprive the petitioner of his rights or to cause him loss or damage.

There remain the events of 1980 to which fuller reference has been made already. In this case the petitioner had genuine ground for complaint although I have some reservations about putting it into the category of oppressive conduct towards a minority. I feel the petitioner has made out a case for limited relief, [328] of a type which the majority shareholders appear to be willing to concede in his favour, and accordingly I would propose to make an order in his favour under section 205 of the Act directing the majority shareholders who are represented in these proceedings to buy out the petitioner's shareholding in the company at a valuation based on the true value of the shares as of July 31, 1980 – this being the time when he should, in my opinion, have been given a fuller opportunity of concurring or not concurring in the course of action embarked upon by the majority shareholders.

It seems unlikely that the parties will be able to agree on this valuation, and I propose to direct that in default of agreement it should be carried out by an accountant to be agreed upon by the parties; if they cannot agree on a suitable person to, carry out the valuation, I will appoint an accountant for the purpose. The case will be listed for mention in two weeks time, so that the appointment can be made. I do not propose to make any order at this stage about convening meetings or preparing accounts but it will be understood that whatever accountant is called upon to value the shares he must have his reasonable requirements met to enable him to carry out his task.

Note: The value to be put on the petitioner's shareholding was considered by O'Hanlon J. in *Re Clubman Shirts Ltd.* [1991] I.L.R.M. 43.

The section 205 proceedings involving the Irish Press group of newspapers established two important points of principle, *viz.*

In *Irish Press plc v. Ingersoll Irish Publications Ltd* [1994] 1 I.R. 177, the Supreme Court refused to direct, under section 205(7) of the 1963 Act, that the petition should be heard *in camera* and laid down restrictive guidelines for, when *in camera* hearings would be appropriate.

In *Irish Press plc v. Ingersoll Irish Publications Ltd* [1995] 2 I.R. 175, the Supreme Court held that section 205(3) did not empower the courts to award damages to petitioners who succeed, ' in establishing that they had been oppressed, although there might be some compensatory element in the price a court fixes for the purchase of an oppressed party's shares.

WINDING UP ON JUST AND EQUITABLE GROUNDS

See *Company Law*, pp. 363–368.

Companies Act 1963, section 213(f)

Circumstances in which a company may be wound up by the court

213.—A company may be wound up by the court if

(f) the court is of opinion that it is just and equitable that the company should be wound up;

In re Newbridge Steam Laundry Co.
[1917] 1 I.R. 67, 75

This case was the sequel to *Cockburn v. Newbridge Sanitary Steam Laundry Co. Ltd* [1915] 1 I.R. 237, ante p. 431. The managing director of a laundry company entered into contracts in his own name for work to be done by the company, the profits of which amounted to £3268, of which he accounted to the company for £1038 only. This he alleged was done with the consent of his co-directors. The capital of the company consisted of 2000 £1 shares, the majority of which were controlled by the managing director and a co-director who was a business partner of his. In an action brought by two shareholders against the company and him, to compel an account of the profits so received, an order was made that he should so account; but no payment was made or account rendered, and no steps were taken by the company to compel him to account. Subsequent to the action, a resolution of confidence in his management was passed by a majority of shareholders at a general meeting. The two shareholders then petitioned to have the company wound up on just and equitable grounds.

O'BRIEN L.C.: [87] I find as a fact that throughout, this ease the majority of the shareholders of the company have had no other intention than to shield Llewellyn (the managing director)l, and I repeat that a winding-up order affords the only means of enabling justice to be done to the petitioners. It is said that the Court is paralysed, and that there is no jurisdiction to make the order. I decline, however, to accede to the proposition that the words of sect. 129 of the Companies (Consolidation) Act 1908, to which I have already referred, are not sufficiently wide to enable justice to be done. Now, in the earlier cases in which the corresponding section of the Act, of 1862 was considered, there is no doubt that a somewhat restricted, not to say narrow, construction was placed on the words of the final sub-section, namely, that this "just and equitable" clause ought to he construed on the *ejusdem generis* principle, and having regard to the matters dealt with in the preceding sub-sections. In the judgment of Lord Cairns in *In re Suburban Hotel Co.* L.R. 2 Ch. App. 737, to which I referred at the commencement of my judgment, I find the following passage:

> "The next case referred to was the case of the *Anglo-Greek Steam Co.* L.R. 2 Eq. 1. The precise point there decided by the Master of the Rolls was, that the misconduct of the directors and of the managers of the company, though it might render them liable to [88] a suit, was not a ground upon which the Court would consider it just and equitable to wind tip the company. But his Lordship made these important observations. He said (L. R. 2 Eq. 5): 'There are five different rules laid down in sect. 79, and the four previous rules are these.' Then he enumerates the four previous rules which I have already mentioned. 'Then the fifth is – Whenever the Court is of opinion that it is just and equitable that the company should be wound up.' In that case Lord Cottenham laid down, and I have followed him, and all the other Courts, I think, have done the same, that these words are to be considered as referring to matters *ejusdem generis* with the four subject-matters previously stated in the four previous rules".

There is no doubt, therefore, that Lord Cairns in that judgment did adopt what I have termed the restricted construction of this clause, which is first to be found in the judgment of Lord Cottenham. I do not think, however, that this view particularly appealed to Lord Cairns. Later in his judgment he says:

> "At the same time I am of opinion that this principle would be satisfied if it were established that the company never had a proper foundation, and that it was a mere fraud, what is commonly called a bubble company. . . In that case the Court would consider that it came within the fifth rule."

And he adds:

> "It is not necessary now to decide it; but if it were shown to the Court that the whole substratum of the partnership, the whole of the business, which the company was incorporated to carry on, has become impossible, I apprehend that the Court might, either under the Act of Parliament, or on general principles, order the company to be wound up."

Lord Cairns, I think, hesitated to dissent from Lord Cottenham's decision, but he was clearly of opinion that a company might be wound up under this just and equitable clause', not only when it was a bubble company, or when the substratum of the company had disappeared, but also when the, general principles on which Courts of equity act required it. That he would be right in so thinking is shown by the decision of Vaughan Williams J., and of the Court of Appeal, affirming that decision, in *In re Thomas Edward Brinsmead & Son* [1897] 1 Ch. 45 at p. 406. There an order for the winding up of the company was made [89] although it was not a bubble company, and although, as distinctly stated by Vaughan Williams L.J., part of the substratum of the company remained. I apply to the present case the words there used by A. L. Smith L.J., on the hearing of the appeal: "Although the words 'just and equitable' have had a narrow construction put upon them, they have never been construed so narrowly as to exclude such a case as this. If ever there was a case in which it was just and equitable that a company should he wound up by the Court, I cannot doubt that that case is this case" (p. 420). For my part I have always felt the greatest difficulty in placing this limited construction on the final clause of sect. 129, because I fail to see what effective force is to be given to it if it is confined to cases coming within the proceeding clauses. In this view I am confirmed by modern authority. In Lord Justice Lindley's *Law of Companies* (6th ed. at p. 852) I find the following passage:– "At the same time, if it can be shown to the satisfaction of the Court that a company, although not insolvent, ought to be annihilated, the Court will order it to be wound up. Proof of inability to commence business after the lapse of a year, *or of continuing fraud*, will induce the Court to put an end even to a solvent company.' The statement of the law contained in the article in Lord Halsbury's *Laws of England*, vol. v, p.

397, dealing with "companies," which is edited by that eminent authority Lord Justice Swinfen Eady is explicit on this point. "The words as to its being 'just and equitable' to wind up are not to be read as being ejusdem generis with the preceding words of the enactment." The authorities cited for that proposition are – Re Amalgamated Syndicate [1897] 2 Ch. 600; Re Brinsmead & Sons [1897] 1 Ch. 400; Re Sailing Ship "Kentmere" Co. [1897] W.N. 58; and reference is also made to Re Suburban Hotel Co. 2 Ch. App. 737; and Re Langham Skating Rink Co. 5 Ch. D. 669. If that proposition, supervised as it has been by Lord Justice Swinfen Eady, is an accurate statement of the law, it disposes of the argument based upon Lord Cairns' judgment so strongly pressed upon us by the appellants, counsel. The matter is thus dealt with in the last edition of Lord Justice Buckley's work on the Companies Acts [90] (9th ed., 304-5-6): 'Sub-s. (vi), although thus worded in order to include all cases not before mentioned, should be interpreted in reference to matters *ejusdem generis* as those in the previous clauses; though the tendency of the Court is now to give a somewhat wider meaning under special circumstances, *e.g.* if a winding up will be the means of getting rid of a complete deadlock, or putting an end to a vicious career, or in winding up is desirable in order to enable a scheme of arrangement to be sanctioned." . . . "The 'just and equitable' clause gives the Court power to wind up a company in not coming under any of the first four heads, but there must be strong ground for exercising the power at the instance of a shareholder."

An instance of the tendency of the Court to give a wider meaning to the words of the section is to be found in *In re Amalgamated Syndicate* [1897] 2 Ch. 600 at p. 607, where Vaughan Williams L.J., after referring to the statement of the law on this question contained in the 7th edition of *Buckley on the Companies Acts*, said, "Without going into details, what I said during the argument, that the stringency of the general rule has been considerably relaxed of late." I think that the view of the learned Lord Justice when he made use of these words, although he does not implicitly so state, was that not only was the stringency of the rule relaxed, but that it had no foundation in point of law.

The later cases which have been cited, *In re Chic Ltd.* [1905] 2 Ch. 345; *In re Crigglestone Coal Co. Ltd.* [1906] 2 Ch. 327; and *In re Alfred Melson & Co. Ltd.* [1906] 1 Ch. 841, to my mind entirely support the view put forward by the respondents' counsel, but I shall not occupy public time by dealing with these in detail. I have arrived at the clear conclusion that the final clause of sect. 129 of Companies Act 1908, ought not to be construed in this restricted way, but that in all cases which cannot be brought under the preceding clauses, but where, having regard to the established principles of courts of equity, justice and equity require a company to be wound up, an order for its winding up ought to made (See *Inland Revenue Commissioners v. Muller & Co.'s Margarine, Ltd*).

That being my view of the law, the petitioners in the present case are entitled, in my judgment, to the relief claimed. If it be refused, the result will undoubtedly be, as I have already said, that all the steps hitherto taken to enforce an account by Llewellyn of the moneys received by him will prove abortive

PROCEDURAL MATTERS

In re Murph's Restaurants Ltd.
McWilliam J., April 5, 1979

Subsequent to this motion being decided, the petition was heard by Gannon J., who found that there had been oppression and ordered the company to be wound up (see supra p. 476.) The facts are stated in that judgment.

McWILLIAM J.: [2] The present motion is brought on behalf of the Company for an Order restraining the Petitioner from advertising the petition. . . .

[4] It has been urged on behalf of the company that the advertisement of the petition would greatly damage the Company, that the matters complained of by the Petitioner are such as could properly be dealt with under the provisions of section 205, that the petition is not presented in good faith, and that it is a case in which the Court would, under the provisions of paragraph (g) of section 213, dismiss a petition to wind up on the grounds that proceedings under section 205 would be more appropriate. I was referred to the case entitled *Re A Company* [1894] 2 Ch. 394 as authority for the proposition that I have jurisdiction to restrain the advertisement of the petition if it is not presented in good faith but for the purpose of putting pressure on the company.

For the Petitioner it is argued that his co-directors are trying to acquire his shares on unfavourable terms and that, if any of the matters complained of could be a ground for [5] winding up, this application should be refused. I was referred to the case of *Bryanston Finance Ltd. v. de Vries* [1976] 1 All E.R. 25. I was also referred to the case of *Mann v. Goldstein* [1968] All E.R. 769 in support of the proposition that pursuing a valid claim in a normal manner is not an abuse of the process of the court even though it is done with personal hostility and with some ulterior motive.

It occurs to me that some confusion may have been caused in the minds of both parties by the reference in the correspondence to paragraph (g) of section 213. This paragraph and section 205 apply only to members of a company as members. Apart from the allegations in paragraph 13 of the petition, which are not grounded on any facts, the petition is based on facts which prejudice the Petitioner in his capacity as director. Although there has been an offer to purchase the Petitioner's shares, this did not arise until the Petitioner had threatened to issue his petition to have the company wound up on the ground that he was being deprived of his rights as a director and there does not appear to have been a threat of any sort to the Petitioner's shareholding or [6] to his rights as a member.

On the other aspect of the case, it is perfectly clear that the directors are at loggerheads and that the Petitioner has been deprived of all his functions as director. This appears to be a case, similar to that of *Re Lundi Brothers Ltd.* [1965] 1 W.L.R. 1051, in which, in substance, a partnership exists between the three persons carrying on the business of the company together and that, prima facie, the Petitioner would have been entitled to a dissolution of the partnership if it were a partnership and not a company, and that, accordingly, he has a bona fide claim to have the Company wound up.

On the views I have taken that the petition is based on the Petitioner's office of director and as to the application of section 205 and paragraph (g) of section 213, it does not appear to me to be open to the Court to dismiss the petition on the grounds that proceedings under section 205 would be more appropriate.

Under these circumstances, I will refuse the application to restrain the Petitioner from advertising the petition, [7] although it may well be that the Petitioner should consider whether it is to his advantage to proceed with his petition or not.

I should add that I would be hesitant to restrain the advertisement of a petition if the circumstances were not such that I should also restrain any further proceedings on the petition, as was done in the Case of *Re A Company*.

Wallersteiner v. Moir (No. 2)
[1975] QB. 373

This decision is one of several that was made in a protracted and complicated case. A minority shareholder (Moir), in a derivative proceeding, contended that the appellant had been defrauding the company by various elaborate devices.

LORD DENNING M.R.: . . .

[390] *2. The Derivative Action*
It is a fundamental principle of our law that a company is a legal person, with its own corporate identity, separate and distinct from the directors or shareholders, and with its own property rights and interests to which alone it is entitled. If it is defrauded by a wrongdoer, the company itself is the one person to sue for the damage. Such is the rule in *Foss v. Harbottle* (1843) 2 Hare 46 1. The rule is easy enough to apply when the company is defrauded by outsiders. The company itself is the only person who can sue. Likewise, when it is defrauded by insiders of a minor kind, once again the company is the only person who can sue. But suppose it is defrauded by insiders who control its affairs – by directors who hold a majority of the shares -who then can sue for dam-

ages? Those directors are themselves the wrongdoers. If a board meeting is held, they will not authorise the proceedings to be taken by the company against themselves. If a general meeting is called, they will vote down any suggestion that the company should sue them themselves. Yet the company is the one person who is damnified. It is the one person who should sue. In one way or another some means must be found for the company to sue. Otherwise the law would fail in its purpose. Injustice would be done without redress. In *Foss v. Harbottle*, Sir James Wigram V.-C. saw the problem and suggested a solution. He thought that the company could sue 'in the name of some one whom the law has appointed to be its representative.' A suit could be brought by individual corporators in their private characters, and asking in such character the protection of those rights to which in their corporate character they were entitled. . . .

This suggestion found its fulfilment in the *Merryweather* case which came before Sir William Page Wood V.-C. on two occasions: see (1864) 2 Hem. & M. 254 (*sub nom. East Pant Du United Lead Mining Co. Ltd. v. Merryweather*) and L.R. 5 Eq. 464n. It was accepted there that the minority shareholders might file a bill asking leave to use the name of the company. If they showed reasonable ground for charging the directors with fraud, the court would appoint.the minority shareholders as representatives of the company to bring proceedings in the name of the company against the wrong-doing directors. By that means the company would sue in its own name for the wrong done to it. That would be, however, a circuitous course, as Lord Hatherley L.C. said himself, at any rate in cases where the fraud itself could be proved on the initial application.

To avoid the circuity, Lord Hatherley L.C. held that the minority shareholders themselves could bring an action in their own names (but in truth on behalf of the company) against the wrong-doing directors for the damage done by them to the company, provided always that it was impossible to get the company itself to sue them. He ordered the fraudulent directors in that case to repay the sums to the company, be it noted, with interest. His decision was emphatically approved by this court in *Menier v. Hooper's Telegraph* (1874) 9 Ch. App. 350 and *Mason v. Harris* (1879) 11 Ch. D. 97. The form of the action is always 'A.B. (a minority shareholder) on behalf of himself and all [391] other shareholders of the company' against the wrongdoing directors and the company. That form of action was said by Lord Davey to be a 'mere matter of procedure in order to give a remedy for a wrong which otherwise would escape redress': see *Burland v. Earle* [1902] A.C. 83, 93. Stripped of mere procedure, the principle is that, where the wrongdoers themselves control the company, an action can be brought on behalf of the company by the minority shareholders on the footing that they are its representatives to obtain redress on its behalf.

I am glad to find this principle well stated by Professor Gower in *Modern Company Law*, 3rd ed. (1969), p. 587, in words which I would gratefully adopt:

"Where such an action is allowed, the member is not really suing on his own behalf nor on behalf of the members generally, but on behalf of the company itself. Although . . . he will have to frame his action as a representative one on behalf of himself and all the members other than the wrongdoers, this gives a misleading impression of what really occurs. The plaintiff shareholder is not acting as a representative of the other shareholders, but as a representative of the company. . . . In the United States . . . this type of action has been given the distinctive name of a 'derivative action,' recognising that its true nature is that the individual member sues on behalf of the company to enforce rights derived from it."

As it happens in the present case the formula has been discarded. The counter-claim by Mr Moir was prepared by a careful, learned and skilful member of the bar, Mr William Stubbs. It is not headed 'on behalf of himself and all the other shareholders.' It is just headed 'M. J.G. Moir, plaintiff on counterclaim.' The two companies were made parties by being added to the counterclaim. The prayer is: 'Mr Moir counterclaims for' several declarations of wrongs done to the two companies and orders on Dr Wallersteiner to pay specified sums to the two companies, and that he do pay the costs of Mr Moir and the two companies. No objection has been taken to that form of proceeding. No suggestion has been made that it should be amended. Quite right. Let it stand as it is. It is in accord with principle. Mr Moir sues in his own name but in reality on behalf of the companies: just as an agent may contract in his own name but in reality on behalf of his principal.

3. Indemnity
Now that the principle is recognised, it has important consequences which have hitherto not been perceived. The first is that the minority shareholder, being an agent acting on behalf of the company, is entitled to be indemnified by the company against all costs and expenses reasonably incurred by him in the course of the agency. This indemnity does not arise out of a contract express or implied, but it arises on the plainest principles of equity. It is analogous to the indemnity to which a trustee is entitled from his cestui que trust who is sui juris: see *Hardoon v. Belilios* [1901] A.C. 118 and *Re Richardson, Ex parte Governors of St Thomas's Hospital* [1911] 2 K.B. 705. Seeing that, if the action succeeds, the whole benefit will go to the company, it is only just that the minority [392] shareholder should be indemnified against the costs he incurs on its behalf. If the action succeeds, the wrongdoing director will be ordered to pay the costs: but if they are not recovered from him, they should be paid by the company. And all the additional costs (over and above party and party costs) should be taxed on a common fund basis and paid by the company: see *Simpson and Miller v. British Industries Trust Ltd.* (1923) 39 T.L.R. 286. The solicitor will have a charge on the money recovered through his

instrumentality: see section 73 of the Solicitors Act 1974.

But what if the action fails? Assuming that the minority shareholder had reasonable grounds for bringing the action – that it was a reasonable and prudent course to take in the interests of the company – he should not himself be liable to pay the costs of the other side, but the company itself should be liable, because he was acting for it and not for himself. In addition, he should himself be indemnified by the company in respect of his own costs even if the action fails. It is a well known maxim of the law that he who would take the benefit of a venture if it succeeds ought also to bear the burden if it fails. *Qui sentit commodum sentire debet et onus.* This indemnity should extend to his own costs taxed on a common fund basis.

In order to be entitled to this indemnity, the minority shareholder soon after issuing his writ should apply for the sanction of the court in somewhat the same way as a trustee does: see *Re Beddoe, Downes v. Cottam* [1893] 1 Ch. 547, 557-558. In a derivative action, I would suggest this procedure: the minority shareholder should apply ex parte to the master for directions, supported by an opinion of counsel as to whether there is a reasonable case or not. The master may then, if he thinks fit, straightaway approve the continuance of the proceedings until close of pleadings, or until after discovery or until trial (rather as a legal aid committee does). The master need not, however, decide it ex parte. He can, if he thinks fit, require notice to be given to one or two of the other minority shareholders – as representatives of the rest – so as to see if there is any reasonable objection. (In this very case another minority shareholder took this very point in letters to us). But this preliminary application should be simple and inexpensive. It should not be allowed to escalate into a minor trial. The master should simply ask himself: is there a reasonable case for the minority shareholder to bring at the expense (eventually) of the company? If there is, let it go ahead. . . .

[393] *5. Contingency fee*
English law has never sanctioned an agreement by which a lawyer is remunerated on the basis of a 'contingency fee', that is that he gets paid the fee if he wins, but not if he loses. Such an agreement was illegal on the ground that it was the offence of champerty. In its origin champerty was a division of the proceeds (*campi partitio*). An agreement by which a lawyer, if he won, was to receive a share of the proceeds was pure champerty. Even if he was not to receive an actual share, but payment of a commission on a sum proportioned to the amount recovered – only if he won – it was also regarded as champerty: see *Re Attorneys and Solicitors Act 1870* [1875] 1 Ch. D. 573, 575, per Sir George Jessel M.R. and *Re A Solicitor, Ex parte Law Society* [1912] 1 K.B. 302. Even if the sum was not a proportion of the amount recovered, but a specific sum or advantage which was to be received if he won but not if he lost, that too, was unlawful: see *Pittman v. Prudential Deposit Bank Ltd.* (1896) 13 T.L.R. 110, per Lord Esher M.R. It mattered not whether the sum to be

received was to be his sole remuneration, or to be an added remuneration (above his normal fee), in any case it was unlawful if it was to be paid only if he won, and not if he lost.

CHAPTER 11

Fundamental Structural Changes

The system laid down in the Companies Acts for the governance of companies can be divided into four distinct tiers. The board, which ordinarily runs the business, is subject to the *de facto* control of a simple majority of the shareholders, who have the power to remove directors by an ordinary resolution. Most provisions of a company's regulations can be altered by special majorities of the members in that the articles of association can be changed by special resolution. Thirdly, certain vital or fundamental changes in the nature of companies cannot be made unless they are approved of by super-majorities of the members and either are not vetoed by or are endorsed by the court: notably, altering the objects clause, reducing or repaying capital, varying class rights, and making an arrangement under section 201 of the 1963 Act. In dealing with most of these matters, the Companies Acts override or modify any special voting rights and disabilities that may exist under the company's regulations, and wholly or partly enfranchise shareholders to the extent of their shares' nominal values. Thus, a section 201 arrangement must be approved by a majority representing 75 per cent in value of those members of each class affected by it who vote on the proposal. Somewhat similarly, the holders of not less than 15 per cent in nominal value of the company's issued share capital, or of any class of shares or debentures, may apply to the court to veto a change in the company's objects; and the holders of not less than 10 per cent of the issued shares of the class in question can apply to the court to have an agreed variation of class rights blocked. The Acts also empower the court, when approving some of these changes, to order appraisal for dissenting shareholders, *i.e.* order that their shares be bought out at an objectively determined price. The fourth tier in the statutory system of governance is provided for in section 28 of the 1963 Act, which permits matters to be 'entrenched' in the memorandum of association so that they can be altered only in some special way, or indeed be unalterable.

ALTERING THE MEMORANDUM AND ARTICLES OF ASSOCIATION

See *Company Law*, pp.370–373.

Companies Act 1963, sections 9, 11, 15, 27, 28

Restriction on alteration of memorandum

9.—A company may not alter the provisions contained in its memorandum except in the cases, in the mode and to the extent for which express provision is made in this Act.

Articles prescribing regulations for companies

11.—There may, in the case of a company limited by shares and in the case of a company limited by guarantee and not having a share capital, and there shall, in the case of a company limited by guarantee and having share capital or unlimited, be registered with the memorandum articles of association signed by the subscribers to the memorandum and prescribing regulations for the company.

Alteration of articles by special resolution

15.—(1) Subject to the provisions of this Act and to the conditions contained in its memorandum, a company may by special resolution alter or add to its article.

(2) Any alteration or addition so made in the articles shall, subject to the provisions of this Act, be as valid as if originally contained therein, and be subject in like manner to alteration by special resolution.

Alteration in memorandum or articles increasing liability to contribute to share capital not to bind existing members without consent

27.—(1) Subject to subsection (2), and notwithstanding anything in the memorandum or articles of a company, no member of the company shall be bound by an alteration made in the memorandum or articles after the date on which he became a member, if and so far as the alteration requires him to take or subscribe for more shares than the number held by him at the date on which the alteration is made, or in any way increases his liability as at that date to contribute to the share capital of, or otherwise to pay money to, the company.

(2) subsection (1) shall not apply in any case where the member agrees in writing, either before or after the alteration is made, to be bound thereby.

Power to alter provisions in memorandum which could have been contained in articles

28.—(1) Subject to subsection (2) and sections 27 and 295, any provision contained in a company's memorandum may, subject to the provisions of this section, be altered by the company by special resolution.

(2) If an application is made to the court for the alteration to be cancelled, it shall not have effect except in so far as it is confirmed by the court.

Table A, articles 44 and 45

44.—The company may from time to time by ordinary resolution increase the share capital by such sum, to be divided into shares of such amount, as the resolution shall prescribe.

45.—The company may by ordinary resolution–

(*a*) consolidate and divide all or any of its share capital into shares of larger amount than its existing shares;

(*b*) subdivide its existing shares, or any of them, into shares of smaller amount than is fixed by the memorandum of association subject, nevertheless, to section 68 (1) (d) of the Act;

(*c*) cancel any shares which, at the date of the passing of the resolution, have not been taken or agreed to be taken by any person.

Allen v. Gold Reefs of West Africa Ltd.
[1900] 1 Ch. 656

The company passed a special resolution to the effect that its articles of association shall be amended by giving the company a lien over the shares in the company held by any member who was indebted to the company. A Mr Z. was then indebted to the company and became bankrupt; it was anticipated that the company would reimburse itself through the lien that the altered articles of association would give it over Z's shares.

LINDLEY M.R.: [669] This is an appeal [which] raises several questions of great general interest relating to the power of limited companies to alter their articles, and especially to their power to alter their articles so as to affect shares standing in the names of deceased shareholders, and to the effect of an alteration duly made on vendors' fully paid-up shares issued before the alteration is made. . . . [670]

The facts above stated raise the following very important questions, namely, (1) Whether a limited company, registered [671] with articles conferring no lien on its fully paid-up shares, can by special resolution alter those articles by imposing a lien on such shares? (2) Whether, if it can, the lien so imposed can be made to apply to debts owing by fully paid-up shareholders to the company at the time of the alteration of the articles? (3) Whether, if it can, fully paid-up shares allotted to vendors of property to the company are in any different position from other fully paid-up shares issued by the company? (4) Whether, assuming the altered articles to be valid and to be binding on the general body of the holders of fully paid-up shares in the company, there are any special circumstances in this particular case to exclude the fully paid-up shares held by Zuccani from the operation of the altered articles?

The articles of a company prescribe the regulations binding on its members: Companies Act, 1862, section 14. They have the effect of a contract (see section 16); but the exact nature of this contract is even now very difficult to define. Be its nature what it may, the company is empowered by the statute to alter the regulations contained in its articles from time to time by special resolutions (ss. 50 and 51); and any regulation or article purporting to deprive the company of this power is invalid on the ground that it is contrary to the statute: *Walker v. London Tramways Co.* [1893] 2 Ch. 311.

The power thus conferred on companies to alter the regulations contained in their articles is limited only by the provisions contained in the statute and the conditions contained in the company's memorandum of association. Wide, however, as the language of section 50 is, the power conferred by it must, like all other powers, be exercised subject to those general principles of law and equity which are applicable to all powers conferred on majorities and enabling them to bind minorities. It must be exercised, not only in the manner required by law, but also bona fide for the benefit of the company as a whole, and it must not be exceeded. These conditions are always implied, and are seldom, if ever, expressed. But if they are complied with I can discover no ground for judically putting any other restrictions on the power conferred by the section than those [672] contained in it. How shares shall be transferred, and whether the company shall have any lien on them, are clearly matters of regulation properly prescribed by a company's articles of association. This is shewn by Table A in the schedule to the Companies Act, 1862, clauses 8, 9, 10. Speaking, therefore, generally, and without reference to any particular case, the section clearly authorizes a limited company, formed with articles which confer no hen on fully paid-up shares, and which allow them to be transferred without any fetter, to alter those articles by special resolution, and to impose a lien and restrictions on the registry of transfers of those shares by members indebted to the company.

But then comes the question whether this can be done so as to impose a lien or restriction in respect of a debt contracted before and existing at the time when the articles are altered. Again, speaking generally, I am of opinion that the articles can be so altered, and that, if they are altered bona fide for the benefit of the company, they will be valid and binding as altered on the existing holders of paid-up shares, whether such holders are indebted or not indebted to the company when the alteration is made. [673]

It was urged that a company's articles could not be altered retrospectively, and reliance was placed on Rigby L.J.'s observations in *James v. Buena Ventura*

Nitrate Grounds Syndicate [1896] 1 Ch. 466. The word 'retrospective' is, however, somewhat ambiguous, and the concurrence of Rigby L.J. in *Andrews v. Gas Meter Co.* [1897] 1 Ch. 361 shows that his observations in *James v. Buena Ventura Nitrate Grounds Syndicate* are no authority for saying that existing rights, founded and dependent on alterable articles, cannot be affected by their alteration. Such rights are in truth limited as to their duration by the duration of the articles which confer them.

Greenhalgh v. Arderne Cinemas Ltd
[1951] 1 Ch. 286

See *ante*, p. 438.

Gambotto v. W.C. P. Ltd
182 C.L.R. 432 [1993]

See *ante*, p. 441.

Cumbrian Newspapers Group Ltd v. Cumberland & Westmoreland Herald etc. Co.
[1987] Ch. 1

The main issue in this case was whether certain provisions in the company's articles of association gave the plaintiff 'class rights', which could not be altered without its consent; see *infra*, p. 516. It was also contended that the plaintiff had contracted with the company that it would not alter its articles in a way that would prejudice those entitlements of the plaintiff.

SCOTT J.: [22] The conclusion I have reached on the plaintiff's first point disposes of this action. However, the second point, the contractual point, has been fully argued. I think, therefore, that I should deal with it. The contractual point is based upon the allegation first, that in or about 1968 the plaintiff and the defendant entered into an agreement of which it [23] was a term that the plaintiff would have the rights conferred on it under articles 5, 7, 9 and 12 and, secondly, that it was an implied term of that agreement that those articles would not be altered or abrogated without the prior consent of the plaintiff. This point fails, in my judgment, on the facts.

There was, in my judgment, no agreement ever entered into between the plaintiff and the defendant, under which the defendant agreed that the plaintiff would have the rights in question. I have already set out the relevant history; I will not repeat it. The agreement evidenced or constituted by the second letter of 2 August 1968, was not an agreement between the plaintiff and the defendant. It was an agreement between the plaintiff and the directors of the defendant, as individuals. These directors did not agree that the plaintiff would have the rights in question. At most they agreed that a resolution for the adoption of the agreed articles would he put before a general meeting of the defendant. I have already stated my opinion that the adoption of those articles represented a condition precedent to the coming into effect of the rest of the agreed arrangement. There was no contractual obligation on the directors, let alone on the defendant, to ensure that the articles would be adopted. In these circumstances, the contention that there was an agreement between the plaintiff and the defendant that the plaintiff would have the rights in question is, in my judgment, unsustainable.

The implied term argument fails for the same reasons. There was no agreement between the plaintiff and the defendant that the articles would be adopted, so how could there be an implied term that the articles would not be changed? Moreover, as Mr. Howarth pointed out, the right to alter articles by special resolution is not a right of the company; it is a right of the members. A contract made by the company cannot deprive the members of that right. It is, of course, possible that a company might, nonetheless, contract that an article would not be altered, but it would be a strong thing to imply an agreement by a company to that effect. In *Allen v. Gold Reefs of West Africa Ltd.* [1900] 1 Ch. 656, 673 Sir Nathaniel Lindley M.R. said:

> "when dealing with contracts referring to revocable articles, and especially with contracts between a member of the company and the company respecting his shares. care must be taken not to assume that the contract involves as one of its terms an article which is not to be altered."

When, on 29 August 1968, the defendant issued to the plaintiff, and the plaintiff accepted, the 280 ordinary shares of £5 each. the plaintiff became a shareholder in the defendant with its new articles. The new articles had been adopted with a view to the issue of the shares. It may very well be the case, as Mr. Brisby submitted, that both parties thought the arrangement would be permanent, but that does not justify, in my judgment, saddling the defendant with an implied agreement that the articles would not he altered. The directors of the defendant were careful to keep the defendant free of any contractual commitment as to the content of its articles. It would be quite wrong, in my judgment, to imply the term contended for.

[24] I have had considerable argument as to what the consequences would have been had I concluded that the defendant ought to be saddled with the alleged implied term. I ought shortly to state my views on those arguments. First, it is, in my view, as I have already stated, well-established that a company cannot, by contract, deprive its members of their rights to alter the arti-

cles by special resolution: see *Punt v. Symons & Co. Ltd.* [1903] 2 Ch. 506. Second, if a company does contract that its articles will not be altered, nonetheless its members are entitled to requisition a meeting and pass a special resolution altering the articles. Third, if the articles are validly altered, the company cannot be prevented from acting on the altered articles, even though so to act may involve it in breach of its contract. The law is, in my view, correctly stated in an obiter passage from the judgment of Lord Porter in *Southern Foundries (1926) Ltd. Shirlaw* [1940] A.C. 701, 740:

> "The general principle therefore may, I think, be thus stated. A company cannot be precluded from altering its articles thereby giving itself power to act upon the provisions of the altered articles-but so to act may nevertheless be a breach of contract if it is contrary to a stipulation in a contract validly made before the alteration."

Mr. Brisby submitted that this dictum did not represent the law. In my view, it does. Fourth, where a company has contracted that its articles will not be altered. I can see no reason why it should not, in a suitable case, be injuncted from initiating the calling of a general meeting with a view to the alteration of the articles. But an injunction could not, in my view, be properly granted so as to prevent the company from discharging its statutory duties in respect of the convening of meetings: see, for example, section 368 of the Companies Act 1985.

In the event, however, the plaintiff's case, in my judgment, succeeds on the class rights point. I am prepared to make a declaration accordingly.

CHANGING THE NATURE OF THE BUSINESS

Companies Act 1963, section 10(1)

Way in which and extent to which objects of company may be altered

10.—(1) Subject to subsection (2), a company may, by special resolution, alter the provisions of its memorandum by abandoning, restricting, or amending any existing object or by adopting a new object and any alteration so made shall be as valid as if originally contained therein, and be subject to alteration in like manner.

In re Munster & Leinster Bank Ltd
[1907] 1 I.R. 237

The bank proposed to alter its objects clause so as to give itself power to act as trustees. Some shareholders applied to the court to veto this proposal.

PORTER M.R.: [247] So far as the proposed change relates to the undertaking and execution of the duties of treasurer there is no objection to the prayer of the petition. The opposition is confined to the proposed extension of the business of the bank to the business of trustee or executor. I am impressed by the fact that the seven gentlemen represented here today (who are shareholders, holding in all 398 shares) had full knowledge of the proposed alteration in the memorandum of association, and had due notice of the meetings of the company at which the special resolution was passed and confirmed, yet did not raise any objection, or take any exception, to the proposed alteration until the hearing of this petition. It appears . . . that the special resolution was passed without dissent, and was confirmed without opposition. If these seven gentlemen had even now come forward and opposed this petition, as shareholders, I should, perhaps, have given more weight to their objections, and to the argument offered on their behalf; but the learned counsel who nominally appeared for them did not seek to deny, but rather prided himself on the fact, that he represented, not individual shareholders, but the Incorporated Law Society of Ireland and the Southern Law Society. I have read the resolutions passed by these eminent bodies, on which the present opposition is based, and in accordance with which the petition of the bank is resisted today, and it is apparent that they were framed not really in the interests of shareholders, but in apprehension of the injury which might result to the solicitor profession from the proposed extension of the objects of the bank. The apprehension is that the new business would prove so attractive that other banks in Ireland would follow the lead of the Munster and Leinster Bank, and that the general body of solicitors would, under the circumstances suggested, suffer no inconsiderable injury. Mr Ronan and Mr O'Connor urge that the resolutions demonstrate that the extension of the business of the bank would prove beneficial to the shareholders. Why should there be apprehension of sustained and severe competition unless the real truth is that the Munster and Leinster Bank have discovered [248] something new, something likely to be advantageous to their shareholders, and profitable in one way or another? . . . I have the fact that, after the fullest notice, the shareholders at two meetings voted in favour of the enlargement of the bank's powers, and I have the fact that Mr Lillis, the general manager, and a director of the bank, states to the Court on oath his opinion that the proposed extension of the objects of the company is required to carry on certain businesses and classes of business which may conveniently and advantageously be combined with the business of the company. Mr Lillis is a business man, and, as manager of the bank, he should be, and, I think, he would be, the last person in the world to propose any change except in the interest of the bank and of its shareholders.

In support of the petition, I have positive statements, while, on the other side, I have nothing but vague apprehensions, vague fears; not so much that the bank or its shareholders may suffer, but that the general body of solicitors may suffer. Far be it from me to say that the eminent bodies whose duty it is to safeguard the interests of their profession were wrong in viewing the proposed new departure in banking business with some dislike; but I think that they have taken an exaggerated view of the situation, and apprehend misfortune which is not likely to occur. That this bank, or any other bank, would be able to carry out on a large scale the duties of executors or trustees, without the assistance of the general body of solicitors, is, to my mind, absolutely impossible. I am rather inclined to think that the proposed alteration, if carried into effect, would probably result in benefit to the solicitors' profession, as it certainly would result in benefit to the public in many respects. All these considerations are, however, beside the question. I am bound, as Mr Wilson says, to concentrate my attention on the bank and the shareholders, and taking all the circumstances of the case into consideration it appears to me that material advantage may accrue to the bank, not so much from the few cases in which they may receive remuneration for their services, as from the attraction to customers [249] arising from knowledge of the fact that they can rely upon the bank to act as their trustee or executor, in full confidence that property entrusted to the bank will be in safe custody; not liable to be lost or made away with by ignorance, negligence, or default.

I see good grounds for supposing that this knowledge and confidence may retain and attract customers, and thus ultimately result in benefit to the shareholders. At all events, so the great majority of the shareholders appear to think, and I see no reason why I should set the apprehension of the solicitors in opposition to the views of the shareholders. 1, therefore, exercise the discretion which I possess by confirming the resolution, with one alteration. I do not think it desirable that any question should be raised as to the power of the bank to accept trusts in cases where the trust estate or property is situate altogether outside the jurisdiction of this Court. Some words must be inserted limiting the extended powers to cases where at least some portion of the trust estate or some portion of the assets is within the jurisdiction of the High Court of Justice in Ireland. As regards change of name, I am of opinion that the cases cited by Mr Wilson are not such as to make it incumbent upon me to direct any alteration in the name of the bank.

VARIATION OF CLASS RIGHTS

See *Company Law*, pp. 373–378.

Companies Act 1963, section 78(1)

Rights of holders of special classes of shares

78.—(1) If, in the case of a company the share capital of which is divided into different classes of shares, provision is made by the memorandum or articles for authorising the variation of the rights attached to any class of shares in the company, subject to the consent of any specified proportion of the holders of the issued shares of that class or the sanction of a resolution passed at a separate meeting of the holders of those shares, and in pursuance of the said provision the rights attached to any such class of shares are at any time varied, the holders of not less in the aggregate than 10 per cent. of the issued shares of that class, being persons who did not consent to or vote in favour of the resolution for the variation, may apply to the court to have the variation cancelled and, where any such application is made, the variation shall not have effect unless and until it is confirmed by the court.

Companies Act 1983, section 38

Variation of rights attached to special classes of shares

38.—(1) This section shall have effect with respect to the variation of the rights attached to any class of shares in a company whose share capital is divided into shares of different classes.

(2) Where the rights are attached to a class of shares in the company otherwise than by the memorandum, and the articles of the company do not contain provision with respect to the variation of the rights, those rights may be varied if but only if—

(*a*) the holders of three-quarters in nominal value of the issued shares of that class consent in writing to the variation; or

(*b*) a special resolution passed at a separate general meeting of the holders of that class sanctions the variation;

and any requirement (howsoever imposed) in relation to the variation of those rights is complied with to the extent that it is not comprised in paragraphs (*a*) and (*b*).

(3) Where—

(*a*) the rights are attached to a class of shares in the company by the memorandum or otherwise;

(*b*) the memorandum or articles contain provision for the variation of those rights; and

(*c*) the variation of those rights is connected with the giving, variation, revocation or renewal of an authority for the purposes of section 20 or with a reduction of the company's share capital under section 72 of the Principal Act.

those rights shall not be varied unless—

(i) the condition mentioned in subsection (2)(*a*) or (*b*) is satisfied; and

(ii) any requirement of the memorandum or articles in relation to the variation of rights of that class is complied with to the extent that it is not comprised in the condition in subparagraph (i).

(4) Where the rights are attached to a class of shares in the company by the memorandum or otherwise and—

(a) where they are so attached by. the memorandum, the articles contain provision with respect to their variation which had been included in the articles at the time of the company's original incorporation; or

(b) where they, are so attached otherwise, the articles contain such provision (whenever first so included);

and in either case the variation is not connected as mentioned in subsection (3)(c), those rights may only be varied in accordance with that provision of the articles.

(5) Where the rights are attached to a class of shares in the company by the memorandum and the memorandum and articles do not contain provision with respect to the variation of the rights, those rights may be varied if all the members of the company agree to the variation.

(6) The provisions of sections 133 and 134 of the Principal Act and the provisions of the articles relating to general meetings shall so far as applicable, apply in relation to any meeting of shareholders required by this section or otherwise to take place in connection with the variation of the rights attached to a class of shares, and shall so apply with the necessary modifications and subject to the following provisions, namely—

(a) the necessary quorum at any such meeting other than an adjourned meeting shall be two persons holding or representing by proxy at least one-third in nominal value of the issued shares of the class in question and at an adjourned meeting one person holding shares of the class in question or his proxy;

(b) any holder of shares of the class in question present in person or by proxy may demand a poll.

(7) Any alteration of a provision contained in the articles of a company for the variation of the rights attached to a class of shares or the insertion of any such provision into the company's articles shall itself be treated as a variation of those rights.

(8) Section 78 of the Principal Act shall apply in relation to subsection (2) as it applies in relation to a provision of the memorandum or articles of a company, to the like effect.

(9) In this section and, except where the context otherwise requires, in any provision for the variation of the rights attached to a class of shares contained in the company's memorandum or articles references to the variation of those rights shall include references to their abrogation.

(10) and (11) – Omitted

Table A articles 3 and 4

3. If at any time the share capital is divided into different classes of shares, the rights attached to any class may, whether or not the company is being wound up, be varied or abrogated with the consent in writing of the holders of three-fourths of the issued shares of that class, or with the sanction of a special resolution passed at a separate general meeting of the holders of the shares of the class.

4. The rights conferred upon the holders of the shares of any class issued with preferred or other rights shall not, unless otherwise expressly provided by the terms of issue of the shares of that class, be deemed to be varied by the creation or issue of further shares ranking *pari passu* therewith.

White v. Bristol Aeroplane Co. Ltd
[1953] 1 Ch. 65

The company's capital was comprised of 600,000 £1 preference shares and 3,000,000 £1 ordinary shares. It was proposed to increase the capital by issuing 660,000 new £1 cumulative preference shares and 1,000,000 new £1 ordinary shares, and that the entirety of the new issue should be distributed among the present ordinary shareholders. The preference shareholders sought to block this proposal, claiming that it was an impermissible interference with their class rights. The company's articles of association contained the following class rights variation clause: 'Subject to the provisions of.. the Companies Act . . . all or any of the rights and privileges attached to any class of shares forming part of the capital for the time being of the company may be affected, modified, varied, dealt with, or abrogated in any manner with the sanction of an extraordinary resolution passed at a separate meeting of the members of that class. To any such separate meeting all the provisions of these articles as to general meetings shall . . . apply.'

LORD EVERSHED M.R.: . . . [73] [W]ill the effect of this proposed distribution, if carried out, be to 'affect' the rights of the preference stockholders? . .

[74] It is necessary, first, to note – although on this matter Mr Gray has not argued to the contrary – that what must be 'affected' are the rights of the preference stockholders. The question then is – and indeed, I have already posed it – are the rights which I have already summarised 'affected' by what is proposed? It is said in answer – and I think rightly said – No, they are not; they remain exactly as they were before; each one of the manifestations of the preference stockholders' privileges may be repeated without any change whatever after, as before, the proposed distribution. It is no doubt true that the enjoyment of, and the capacity to make effective, those rights is in a measure affected; for as I have already indicated, the existing preference stockholders will be in a less advantageous position on such occasions as entitle them to

register their votes, whether at general meetings of the company or at separate meetings of their own class. But there is to my mind a distinction, and a sensible distinction, between an affecting of the rights and an affecting of the enjoyment of the rights, or of the stockholders' capacity to turn them to account. . . .

[80] have no doubt, as I have already indicated, that upon a sufficient analysis what is here suggested will 'affect' the preference stockholders 'as a matter of business'; but we are concerned with the question whether the rights of the preference stockholders are 'affected', not as a matter of business, but according to the articles, that is, according to their meaning construed under the rules of construction and as a matter of law. I further think that having regard to the fact that the word 'affected' was in the article in the *Mackenzie* case [1916] 2 Ch. 450, it would be wrong for this court now to say that its presence in this set of articles – and I dare say it has appeared in many others before and since that case – has so restrictive an effect upon the ordinary shareholders in the company that separate meetings of preference stockholders and shareholders would have to be held whenever it could be shown that as a matter of business, upon a close analysis, that which was proposed would, or might, affect in some degree the value of the preference shares, or the way in which the rights conferred upon them by the regulations of the company were to be enjoyed.

Cumbrian Newspapers Group Ltd v. Cumberland & Westmoreland Herald etc. Co.
[1987] Ch. 1

The plaintiff and defendant, who were both publishers of newspapers, negotiated a transaction whereby the defendant would acquire *inter alia* one of the plaintiff's newspapers and the benefit of certain advertising arrangements; in return, the plaintiff would acquire, *inter alia*, 10 per cent of the defendant's share capital. The defendant duly issued the 10 per cent shareholding to the plaintiff and, as part of the agreement under which those shares were issued, amended its articles to grant to the plaintiff rights of pre-emption over other ordinary shares, rights in respect of unissued shares and the right to appoint a director. The purpose of such rights was to enable the plaintiff, in its capacity as shareholder, to be in a position to prevent a take-over of the defendant. After these arrangements had continued for several years, the directors of the defendant proposed to convene an extraordinary general meeting and to pass a special resolution to cancel the articles which gave such special rights to the plaintiff. The plaintiff sought (1) a declaration that the rights were class rights which could not be abrogated without its consent and (2) an injunction restraining the defendant from convening or holding the extraordinary general meeting.

SCOTT J.: . . . [12] I must, at this stage, set out more fully the contents of the articles in question. The defendant's articles adopt Table A. There are no relevant exclusions or variations. Under article 3, the share capital is declared to be £25,000, divided into 500 six per cent. preference shares of £5 [13] each, 2,000 unclassified shares of £5 each, and 2,500 ordinary shares of £5 each. This provision repeats a corresponding provision in the defendant's memorandum of association.

Article 4 sets out the special rights attached to the preference shares and provides under paragraph (d):

> "The said 2,000 unclassified shares shall subject to the provisions of article 5 be issued either as ordinary shares or with such preferred, deferred or other special rights or with such restrictions whether in regard to dividend, voting, return of capital or otherwise as the directors may from time to time determine subject to any special rights previously conferred on the holders of any existing shares or classes of shares."

Article 5 provides:

> "(a) Subject to any direction to the contrary by special resolution of the company and subject also to paragraph (b) of this article, no unissued shares in the capital of the company shall be issued to any person save (i) Cumberland Newspapers Ltd. (ii) a person who on 28 August 1968 was entered on the register of members of the company (iii) persons who at the time of such issue are in the full time employment of the company. (b) Subject to any direction to the contrary by special resolution of the company in general meeting, all unissued ordinary shares shall, before issue, be offered to such persons as at the date of the offer are registered as holders of ordinary shares in proportion, as nearly as the circumstances admit, to the amount of the existing shares to which they are entitled . . ."

This article 5 was obviously intended to give the plaintiff protection against its percentage of the issued share capital in the defendant being diluted by means of an issue of unissued ordinary shares. The protection is not, however, absolute. The provisions of the article are expressed to be "subject to any direction to the contrary by special resolution."

Article 7 provides:

> "The directors may in their absolute discretion and without assigning any reason therefor decline to register any transfer of any share whether or not it is a fully paid share not being a transfer to Cumberland Newspapers Ltd. under the provisions of article 9."

This article serves to ensure that if the plaintiff should exercise its right of pre-emption over any shares, the directors cannot decline to register the transfer. Article 8 authorises the transfer of shares (a) to other members, (b) to certain relatives of the transferor member, (c) to employees of the defendant and (d) to certain defined family trusts. Article 9 is the important pre-emption article. Except in the case of a transfer expressly authorised by article 8, article 9 imposes, in respect of all shares in the company, a restriction on the right to transfer unless, in accordance with a prescribed procedure, the shares are first offered to the plaintiff. Finally, article 12 provides:

> "If and so long as Cumberland Newspapers Ltd. shall be registered as the holder of not less than one tenth in nominal value of [14] the issued ordinary share capital of the company Cumberland Newspapers Ltd. shall be entitled from time to time to nominate one person to be a director of the company . . ."

The plaintiff contends that its rights under articles 5, 7, 9 and 12 are class rights that cannot validly be varied or abrogated without its consent.

Section 9(1) of the Companies Act 1985 (same as section 15 of the 1963 Act) provides:

> "Subject to the provisions of this Act, and to the conditions contained in its memorandum, a company may by special resolution alter its articles."

Section 125 of the Act of 1985 (similar to section 38 of the 1983 Act – supra, p. 513) is headed "Class Rights." Several of its subsections are relevant to the plaintiff's contention. Subsection (1) introduces the section. It reads:

> "This section is concerned with the variation of the rights attached to any class of shares in a company whose share capital is divided into shares of different classes."

I draw attention to the phrase "rights attached to any class of shares." It is a phrase which recurs in this section and is to be found also in article 4 of Table A. Section 125(2) deals with the case:

> "Where the rights are attached to a class of shares otherwise than by the company's memorandum, and the company's articles do not contain provision with respect to the variation of the rights . . ."

In such a case, the subsection permits the variation of the rights only if:

> "(a) the holders of three-quarters in nominal value of the issued shares of that class consent in writing to the variation; or (b) an extraordinary resolution passed at a separate general meeting of the holders of that class sanctions the variation; . . ."

Section 125(4) deals, inter alia, with the case where the rights are attached to a class of shares otherwise than by the memorandum, and where the articles do contain provision for their variation. In such a case, the subsection permits the variation of those rights in accordance with provision of the articles, but not otherwise.

Section 125 is, in my judgment, intended to provide a comprehensive code setting out the manner in which "rights attached to any class of shares" (whatever that phrase truly means) can be varied. I must decide, therefore, whether or not the plaintiff's rights under articles 5, 7, 9 and 12 are, for the purposes of section 125, rights attached to a class of shares. If they are, they can only be altered in the manner provided by the articles or, as the case might be, by the procedure described in subsection (2). But if they are not rights attached to a class of shares, section 125 has no application to them.

The articles adopted by the defendant on 29 August 1968 contained no special article dealing with the alteration, either of the articles generally, or of articles 5, 7, 9 and 12, in particular; Table A was, however, incorporated, and article 4 of Table A (art. 3 of the 1963 Act's Table A) contains provision for the variation or abrogation of class rights. The article provides:

[15] "If at any time the share capital is divided into different classes of shares, the rights attached to any class (unless otherwise provided by the terms of issue of the shares of that class) may, whether or not the company is being wound up, be varied with the consent in writing of the holders of three-fourths of the issued shares of that class, or with the sanction of an extraordinary resolution passed at a separate general meeting of the holders of the shares of the class."

The terms of this article underline the importance of the question whether or not the plaintiff's rights can properly be described as rights attached to any class of shares. If the rights can be so described, both section 125 and article 4 of Table A apply. The effect would be that articles 5, 7, 9 and 12 could not be altered without the plaintiff's consent. But if the rights cannot be so described, then neither section 125 nor article 4 of Table A apply. The articles could therefore, it is said, be varied or cancelled by special resolution under the statutory authority granted by section 9. In effect, the plaintiff could be deprived of the rights which it enjoys under articles 5, 7, 9 and 12 by the other members of the company who do not enjoy such rights. Moreover, that would have been the position at all times since the adoption of the articles in August 1968.

I turn to the critical question: are the plaintiff's rights under articles 5, 7, 9 and 12, rights attached to a class of shares?

Rights or benefits which may be contained in articles can be divided into three different categories. First, there are rights or benefits which are annexed to particular shares. Classic examples of rights of this character are dividend rights and rights to participate in surplus assets on a winding up. If articles provide that particular shares carry particular rights not enjoyed by the holders of other shares, it is easy to conclude that the rights are attached to a class of shares, for the purpose both of section 125 of the Act of 1985 and of article 4 of Table A. It is common ground that rights failing into this category are rights attached to a class of shares for those purposes. Mr. Howarth submitted at first that this category should be restricted to rights that were capable of being enjoyed by the holders for the time being of the shares in question. Such a restriction would exclude rights expressly attached to particular shares issued to some named individual, but expressed to determine upon transfer of the shares by the named individual. *Palmer's Company Precedents*, 17th ed. (1956), Pt. 1, p. 818, contains a form for the creation of a life governor's share in a company. Mr. Howarth accepted that the rights attached to a share in accordance with this precedent would be rights attached to a class of shares. He accepted, rightly in my judgment, that a provision for defeasance of rights on alienation of the share to which the rights were attached, would not of itself prevent the rights, pre-alienation, from being properly described as rights attached to a class of shares. The plaintiff's rights under articles 5, 7, 9 and 12 cannot, however, be brought within this first category. The rights were not attached to any particular shares. In articles 5, 7 and 9, there is no reference to any current shareholding held by the plaintiff. The rights conferred on the plaintiff under article 12 are dependent on the plaintiff [16] holding at least 10 per cent. of the issued ordinary shares in the defendant. But the rights are not attached to any particular shares. Any ordinary shares in the defendant, if sufficient in number and held by the plaintiff, would entitle the plaintiff to exercise the rights.

A second category of rights or benefits which may be contained in articles (although it may be that neither "rights" nor "benefits" is an apt description), would cover rights or benefits conferred on individuals not in the capacity of members or shareholders of the company but, for ulterior reasons, connected with the administration of the company's affairs or the conduct of its business. *Eley v. Positive Government Security Life Assurance Co. Ltd.* (1875) 1 Ex.D. 20, was a case where the articles of the defendant company had included a provision that the plaintiff should be the company solicitor. The plaintiff sought to enforce that provision as a contract between himself and the company. He failed. The reasons why he failed are not here relevant, and I cite the case only to draw attention to an article which, on its terms, conferred a benefit on an individual but not in the capacity of member or shareholder of the company. It is, perhaps, obvious that rights or benefits in this category cannot be class rights. They cannot be described as rights attached to a class of shares. The plaintiff in *Eley v. Positive Government Security Life Assurance Co. Ltd.* was not a shareholder at the time the articles were adopted. He became a shareholder some time thereafter. It is easy, therefore, to conclude that the article in question did not confer on him any right or benefit in his capacity as a member of the company. In a case where the individual had been issued with shares in the company at the same time and as part of the same broad arrangement under which the article in question had been adopted, the conclusion might not be so easy. But if, in all the circumstances, the right conclusion was still that the rights or benefits conferred by the article were not conferred on the beneficiary in the capacity of member or shareholder of the company, then the rights could not, in my view, be regarded as class rights. They would not be rights attached to any class of shares.

In paragraph 7 of the defence in the present case, it is pleaded that the plaintiff's rights under articles 5, 7, 9 and 12 "are privileges personal to the plaintiffs, whether or not they hold any shares in the defendant company." If this plea were well-founded, the rights would fall into this second category and would not be class rights. Mr. Howarth did not, however, persist in this plea. In my judgment he was right not to do so. The evidence in this case has clearly established that the adoption by the defendant of articles 5, 7, 9 and 12, was inextricably connected with the issue to the plaintiff, and the plaintiff's acceptance, of the 280 ordinary £5 shares in the defendant. The purpose of the rights and privileges conferred on the plaintiff by those articles, was to enable the plaintiff, in its capacity as shareholder in the defendant, to obstruct an attempted take-over of the defendant. In my judgment, the plaintiff's rights under those articles do not fall within this second category.

That leaves the third category. This category would cover rights or benefits that, although not attached to any particular shares, were nonetheless conferred on the beneficiary in the capacity of member or [17] shareholder of the company. The rights of the plaintiff under articles 5, 7, 9 and 12 fall, in my judgment, into this category. Other examples can be found in reported cases.

In *Bushell v. Faith* [1969] 2 Ch. 438, affirmed by the House of Lords [1970] A.C. 1099 (see *ante*, p. 165), articles of association included a provision that on a resolution at a general meeting for the removal of any director from office, any shares held by that director should carry the right to three votes. The purpose of this provision was to prevent directors being removed from office by a simple majority of the members of the company. The validity of the article was upheld by the Court of Appeal and by the House of Lords; the reasons do not, for present purposes, matter. But the rights conferred by the article in question fall, in my view, firmly in this third category. They were not attached to any particular shares. On the other hand, they were conferred on the director/beneficiaries in their capacity as shareholders. The article created, in effect, two classes of shareholders-namely, shareholders who were for the time being directors, on the one hand, and shareholders who were not for the time being directors, on the other hand.

The present case is, and *Bushell v. Faith* was, concerned with rights conferred by articles. The other side of the coin is demonstrated by *Rayfield v. Hands* [1960] Ch. 1. That case was concerned with obligations imposed on members by the articles. The articles of the company included an article entitling every member to sell his shares to the directors of the company at a fair valuation. In effect, the members enjoyed "put" options exercisable against the directors. Vaisey J. held that the obligations imposed by the article on the directors for the time being were enforceable against them. He held that the obligations were imposed on the directors in their capacity as members of the company. It follows from his judgment that, as in *Bushell v. Faith* [1970] A.C. 1099, there were in effect two classes of shareholders in the company. There were shareholders who were not for the time being directors, and shareholders who were for the time being directors: the former had rights against the latter which the latter did not enjoy against the former. The two classes were identifiable not by reference to their respective ownership of particular shares, but by reference to the office held by the latter. But the rights of the former, and the obligations of the latter, required their respective ownership of shares in the company. Accordingly, as a matter of classification, the rights in question fall, in my view, into the third category.

In the present case, the rights conferred on the plaintiff under articles 5, 7, 9 and 12 were, as I have held, conferred on the plaintiff as a member or shareholder of the defendant. The rights would not be enforceable by the plaintiff otherwise than as the owner of ordinary shares in the defendant. If the plaintiff were to divest itself of all its ordinary shares in the defendant, it would not then, in my view, be in a position to enforce the rights in the articles. But the rights were not attached to any particular share or shares. [18] Enforcement by the plaintiff of the rights granted under articles 5, 7 and 9, would require no more than ownership by the plaintiff of at least some shares in the defendant. Enforcement by the plaintiff of the rights granted under article 12, require the plaintiff to hold at least 10 per cent. of the issued shares in the defendant. But any shares would do. It follows, in my judgment, that the plaintiff's rights under the articles in question fall squarely within this third category.

The question for decision is whether rights in this third category are within the meaning of the phrase in section 125 of the Companies Act 1985 and in article 4 of Table A, rights attached to a class of shares. Mr. Howarth relied on the natural meaning of the language used. Article 4 is expressed to apply "If at any time the share capital is divided into different classes of shares." Section 125 is expressed, by subsection (1) to be dealing with companies "whose share capital is divided into shares of different classes." This language, submitted Mr. Howarth, coupled with the repeated references to the rights attached to any class of shares, shows that the legislature had in contemplation only the first category of rights. It intended to protect rights attached to particular shares; it withheld protection from rights which were not attached to particular shares.

Mr. Brisby, on the other hand, submitted that whenever rights were conferred by articles on individuals in their capacity as members or shareholders, the shares that they for the time being held, and by virtue of which they were for the time being entitled to the rights, constituted a class of shares for the purposes of section 125 and article 4 of Table A. For those purposes, the rights were, he submitted, attached to the shares for the time being held, This is a question on which there is, it seems, no authority. It is a question to which the language of section 125 of the Act of 1985 provides, in my view, no certain answer. I ought, therefore, I think, to try and discern the legislative purpose behind section 125 and take that purpose into account in construing the section.

The class rights, or alleged class rights, with which this case is concerned, are contained in the articles; that is common practice. Class rights may, however, as section 125 in terms recognises, be contained in the memorandum. It is, and always was, clear company law that in the absence of some statutory enabling provision, or unless the memorandum itself provides a procedure for variation, rights embodied in the memorandum cannot be altered: see *In re Welsbach Incandescent Gas Light Co. Ltd.* [1904] 1 Ch. 87. This principle is recognised by section 17 of the Companies Act 1985, formerly section 23 of the Act of 1948 (similar to section 28 of the 1963 Act). Subsection (1) provides a limited power for the alteration of provisions in a company's memorandum; but subsection (2) provides, inter alia, that the section "(b) . . . does not authorise any variation or abrogation of the special rights of any class of members." I draw attention to the phrase "rights of any class of members." In the case of a company limited by shares, the phrase "rights of any class of shareholders" can be substituted.

Section 125(5) provides:

> "If the rights are attached to a class of shares by the memorandum, and the memorandum and articles do not contain provision with respect to the variation of those rights, those rights may be varied if all the members of the company agree to the variation."

[19] Section 125(5), read in conjunction with section 17(2), suggests that in relation to a company limited by shares, the expressions, "rights of any class of members" and "rights .. . attached to a class of shares", have the same meaning. If that were not so, then third category rights would be within the expression "rights of any class of members" but excluded from the expression "rights . . . attached to a class of shares." That would, apparently, leave third category rights contained in a memorandum unalterable, even if all the members consented to the alteration, otherwise than by a scheme of arrangement approved by the court. This would be an anomalous state of affairs.

Class rights are, however, more usually to be found in articles than in memoranda of association. There seems to have been at one time the view that shareholders' rights, conferred by articles, could not be varied unless special provision had been made in the articles for their variation: see, for example, the cases cited in the argument of counsel for the appellant in *Andrews v. Gas Meter Co.* [1897] 1 Ch. 361, 364. This view was shown to be wrong by the decision of the Court of Appeal in *Andrews v. Gas Meter Co.* The practice of including in articles of association special provision for the variation of class rights on the lines now to be found in article 4 of Table A, is said by the author of Gower, *Modern Company Law*, 4th ed.(1979), pp. 563-564. to have predated that decision. It is consistent with this view of the history of article 4, that it is couched in an enabling form and not in a restrictive form. It enables class rights to be varied by the procedure prescribed. It is not expressed to restrict the variation of class rights otherwise than by the procedure prescribed. It may, however, fairly be said to be implicit in article 4 of Table A that rights attached to a class of shares cannot be varied at least by the members themselves, otherwise than by the procedure there laid down.

Section 125 of the Companies Act 1985, reproduces (with variations not here relevant) section 32 of the Companies Act 1980. Section 32 was, however, new. Previous statutory provision regarding the variation of class rights, had been contained in section 72 of the Companies Act 1948, which now forms part of section 127 of the Act of 1985 (resembles section 78 of the 1963 Act). Section 72 of the Act of 1948, like section 32 of the Act of 1980 and section 125 of the Act of 1985, was expressed to apply to a company whose share capital "is divided into different classes of shares," and to be dealing with "the variation of the rights attached to any class of shares." Section 72, therefore, leaves open the same question, namely, whether third category rights, as well as first category rights, were within its scope. Section 721(1) was expressed to apply only where:

> "provision is made by the memorandum or articles for authorising the variation of the rights . . . subject to the consent of . . . the holders. . . or the sanction of a resolution passed at a separate meeting. . . ."

The section gave the right to a dissentient minority of at least 15 per cent. to apply to the court, and gave the court a discretion whether or not to confirm the variation. Section 72 of the Act of 1948 did not, therefore, apply where neither the memorandum nor the articles [20] contained any variation of class rights provision. So, where the class rights were contained in the articles, section 72 only applied where the articles contained some such provision as article 4 of Table A.

It has been forcefully pointed out by Professor Gower that this distinction made little or no sense, except on the footing that, in the absence of some variation of rights provision contained in the articles, class rights could not be varied at all: see Gower, *Modern Company Law*, p. 564. If, in the absence of such an article, class rights contained in the articles could be altered by a special resolution passed at a general meeting, why was not a dissentient 15 per cent. minority given the same rights as those conferred by section 72 of the Act of 1948? Professor Gower's suggested answer was that it should be regarded as implicit in section 72 that if the memorandum or articles did not contain any provision for the alteration of class rights, then there could be no alteration of them save, of course, an alteration forming part of a scheme of arrangement approved by the court. This argument is unexceptional so far as class rights contained in the memorandum are concerned: see section 23 of the Act of 1948, now section 17 of the Act of 1985. But so far as class rights contained in the articles are concerned, the argument regards the statutory power to alter articles (section 10 of the Act of 1948, now section 9 of the Act of 1985) as limited by the implicit limitations of section 72 of the Act of 1948.

The particular point made by Professor Gower has been overtaken by a combination of section 125 and section 127 of the Companies Act 1985. Rights attached to a class of shares can, if contained in the articles, now be varied, even if no provision for variation is contained in the articles: see section 125(2). A dissentient minority is given the same protection whether or not provision is made in the articles for the variation of the rights: see section 127(2).

But if Mr. Howarth is right in contending that there can be class rights which are not rights attached to any class of shares, within the meaning of section 125, then, as it seems to me, Professor Gower's argument is still relevant. If the rights are contained in the memorandum there is no problem. They cannot be altered: see section 17 of the Act of 1985. If, on the other hand, the rights are contained in the articles, can they be altered by special resolution pursuant to the statutory power contained in section 9 of the Act of 1985, or is section 125 to be read as excluding, by implication, the statutory power to alter class rights that are not rights attached to any class of shares?

The statutory power to alter articles by special resolution is expressed to be "subject to the provisions of this Act." The question is whether section 72 in the Act of 1948, and sections 125 and 127 in the Act of 1985, provide any sufficient context to justify restricting the breadth of the statutory power granted by section 9. In my judgment they do not. Section 72 was enacted in order to provide a benefit to certain members of a company in certain circumstances. The reason why the benefit was not extended to cover certain other circumstances may well have been, as Professor Gower has suggested, that the legislature was proceeding on a mistaken assumption as to the law. But that would not, in my view, justify reading into the section a restriction on the power of a company [21] to alter its articles in circumstances not covered by the section. As Viscount Simonds remarked in *Kirkness v. John Hudson & Co. Ltd.* [1955] A.C. 696, 714, "the beliefs or assumptions of those who frame Acts of Parliament cannot make the law." If, as I conclude, section 72 of the Act of 1948 did not prevent the alteration, by special resolution, of articles containing class rights in cases where the articles contained no provision for the alteration, it must, a fortiori, be the case that sections 125 and 127 of the Act of 1985 do not do so.

In my judgment, if it is right, as the defendant contends, that third category rights are not rights attached to a class of shares, for the purposes of section 125, it must follow that articles containing such rights can be altered by special resolution pursuant to section 9 of the Act of 1985. This conclusion is, I think, relevant to the question whether the defendant's contention is right. It would, in my opinion, be surprising and unsatisfactory if class rights contained in articles were to be at the mercy of a special resolution majority at a general meeting, unless they were rights attached to particular shares. If the articles of a particular company grant special rights to a special class of members, it would be odd to find that members not in that class could cancel the rights simply by means of a special resolution.

A number of considerations lead me to the conclusion that the purpose of sections 125 and 127 of the Act of 1985, and of section 32 of the Act of 1980, was to deal comprehensively with the manner in which class rights in companies having a share capital could be varied or abrogated. They are these: first, chapter 11 of Part V of the Act (which includes sections 125 to 129) is headed "Class Rights." The side note to section 125 reads "Variation of class rights." The language seems to treat "class rights" as synonymous with "rights attached to any class of shares," at any rate so far as companies with a share capital are concerned. Second, the use in section 17(2)(b) of the Act of 1985 of the expression "rights of any class of members" in connection both with companies having a share capital and with companies having no share capital, underlines the point that the expression "rights attached to any class of shares" in section 125, must have been regarded by the legislature as synonymous with the former phrase, so far as companies with a share capital were concerned. Third, the evident intention of the legislature to protect rights attached to any class of shares against variation or abrogation by the mere alteration of articles, would, if coupled with an intention to provide no such protection against variation or abrogation of class rights of the third category, be anomalous and arbitrary. Fourth, if the variation or abrogation of third category rights are not dealt with by section 125, then the conclusion would seem to follow that if the rights were contained in the memorandum, the rights could not be varied or abrogated at all. The enabling provisions of section 125 of the Act of 1985 would obviously not apply, nor would the enabling provisions of section 17 of the Act of 1985. The terms of section 17, to my mind, strongly suggest a legislative belief that section 125 would deal with the variation or abrogation of any "special rights of any class of member" contained in the memorandum. Fifth, the combination of the considerations thirdly and fourthly above mentioned, [22] leads to a further point. What sense could there be in a result under which third category rights contained in articles were more freely alterable than rights attached to any class of shares contained therein, but under which third category rights contained in the memorandum were less freely alterable than rights attached to any class of shares contained in the memorandum? The distinction would not be merely anomalous; it would, to my mind, be perverse.

For these reasons I conclude that section 125 of the Act of 1985 was intended by the legislature to cater for the variation or abrogation of any special rights given by the memorandum or articles of a company to any class of members – that is to say, not only rights failing into the first category I have described, but also rights failing into the third category. I must, therefore, construe section 125 so as to give effect to that legislative intention if the language of the section so permits. In my judgment, it does.

Subsection (1) refers to "the rights attached to any class of shares in a company whose share capital is divided into shares of different classes." In my judgment, if specific rights are given to certain members in their capacity as members or shareholders, then those members become a class. The shares those members hold for the time being, and without which they would not be members of the class, would represent, in my view, a "class of shares" for the purpose of section 125. The class would include those shares the ownership of which for the time being entitled the members of the company to the rights in question. For the purposes of section 125, the share capital of a company is, in my judgment, divided into shares of different classes, if shareholders, qua shareholders, enjoy different rights.

This construction of section 125 has the consequence that shares may come into or go out of a particular class on acquisition or disposal of the shares by a particular individual. I do not see any conceptual difficulty in this. Mr. Howarth pointed out certain administrative difficulties that might follow, mainly regarding the details to be included in annual returns. These seem to me to be capable of administrative solution. I do not think they have any real weight on the question of construction of section 125.

In my judgment, a company which, by its articles, confers special rights on one or more of its members in the capacity of member or shareholder thereby constitutes the shares for the time being held by that member or members, a class of shares for the purposes of section 125. The rights are class rights. I have already expressed the opinion that the rights conferred on the plaintiff under articles 5, 7, 9 and 12, were conferred on the plaintiff as member or shareholder of the defendant. It follows that, in my judgment, the shares in the defendant for the time being held by the plaintiff constitute a class of shares for the purpose of variation or abrogation of those rights.

(An argument that the company had separately contracted not to impair those rights was rejected; see supra p. 508.)

Note: In *Harmon v. B.M.L.* [1994] 2 B.C.L.C. 674, where the share capital was divided into A shares and B shares, a provision in a shareholders' agreement whereby no shareholders' meeting would be quorate unless a B shareholder or his proxy was present was held to constitute a class right.

Contrast *Forsayth Oil & Gas N.L. v. Livia Pty. Ltd. (No. 2)* [1985] B.C.L.C. 378, where it was held that the existence of an option to take up shares in a company does not by itself fetter the company's exercise of the powers conferred on it by the articles in relation to its share capital. Short of fraud, the company may increase or reduce its capital and consolidate or subdivide its shares. Accordingly, where an option contract contained no provision for variation should the company be reconstructed, where no power was reserved to the company to alter option terms unilaterally and where no prior agreement of option-holders was sought to a novation, any reorganisation of the company's capital causing disadvantage to shareholders vis-à-vis option- holders was a misfortune brought by the shareholders to themselves.

CAPITAL REDUCTION AND REPAYMENT

See *Company Law*, pp. 381–389.

Companies Act 1963, section 72

Power of company to reduce its share capital

72.—(1) Except in so far as this Act expressly permits, it shall not be lawful for a company limited by shares or a company limited by guarantee and having a share capital to purchase any of its shares or to reduce its share capital in any way.

(2) Subject to confirmation by the court, a company limited by shares or a company limited by guarantee and having a share capital, may, if so authorised by its articles, by special resolution reduce its share capital in any way and, in particular, without prejudice to the generality of the foregoing power, may—

(*a*) extinguish or reduce the liability on any of its shares in respect of share capital not paid up; or

(*b*) either with or without extinguishing or reducing liability on any of its shares, cancel any paid up share capital which is lost or unrepresented by available assets; or

(*c*) either with or without extinguishing or reducing liability on any of its shares, pay off any paid up share capita which is in excess of the wants of the company;

and may, if and so far as is necessary, alter its memorandum by reducing the amount of its share capital and of its shares accordingly.

Companies Act 1983, sections 45–51(3)

See *ante*, pp. 345–6.

Table A article 46

46.—The company may by special resolution reduce its share capital, any capital redemption reserve fund or any share premium account in any manner and with and subject to any incident authorised, and consent required, by law.

House of Fraser plc v. A.C.G.E. Investments Ltd
[1987] 1 A.C. 387

At an extraordinary general meeting of the company a special resolution was passed reducing the company's capital by paying off and cancelling the cumulative preference shares. No class meetings of preference shareholders were held to approve or disapprove the reduction. The company presented a petition praying that the reduction of capital be confirmed. Answers to the petition were lodged by the registered owners of a number of the preference shares, who contended, inter alia, that the failure to hold class meeting of the preference shareholders was in contravention of their rights under the articles of association of the company, article 12 of which provided for such a meeting if the shares were "modified, commuted, affected or dealt with."

LORD KEITH OF KINKEL: [389] The matter arises in connection with a petition for confirmation of reduction of capital presented by House of Fraser. The reduction, which involves the paying off of the whole preference share capital of the company as being in excess of the wants of the company, was accomplished by special resolution passed at an extraordinary general meeting attended by ordinary shareholders only. No class meetings of preference shareholders were held to approve or disapprove the reduction. The appellants maintain that this failure was in contravention of their rights under the articles of association of the company, and that confirmation of the reduction of capital should therefore be refused.

At the material time the share capital of House of Fraser was £50m. divided into (i) 350,000 3.15 per cent. cumulative preference shares of £1 each, (ii) 42,639 3.85 per cent. cumulative preference shares of £1 each, (iii) 365,328 5.25 per cent. cumulative preference shares of £1 each, (iv) 985,752,975 ordinary shares of 1p each, (v) 153,679,045 deferred shares of 25p each, and (vi) 964,742 unclassified shares of £1 each. All the preference shares were issued and fully paid. 153,679,045 of each of the ordinary shares and the deferred shares were issued and fully paid. The remaining shares were unissued.

The appellants are holders of 97,953 of the 5.25 per cent. cumulative preference shares. All the issued ordinary and deferred shares are held by House of Fraser Holdings plc. It is to be observed that in the articles of association of House of Fraser the 3.15 per cent., 3.85 per cent. and 5.25 per cent. cumulative preference shares are referred to respectively as 4½ per cent., 5½ per cent.

and 7½ per cent. cumulative preference shares, and that the two latter classes are there referred to collectively as "the second preference shares." The reason for the difference in the stated rates of interest is to be found in paragraph 18 of Schedule 23 to the Finance Act 1972.

Article 4 of the company's articles of association provides that the 4½ per cent. preference shares and the second preference shares shall respectively carry certain rights and privileges, and be subject to certain restrictions and limitations. Those relating to the second preference shares are set out as follows. . . .

[391] It is to be observed that paragraph (A)(*e*) of the article, which is one of the provisions dealing with the rights of 4½ per cent. preference shareholders, and which corresponds roughly to paragraph (B)(*f*), provides that any resolution for the winding up of the company shall be deemed to be a resolution affecting the rights and privileges of the 4½ percent. preference shareholders. There is no similar provision in relation to the second preference shareholders.

Article 12, headed "Variation of Rights" provides:

> "If at any time the capital of the company is divided into different classes of shares, the special rights attached to any class may, subject to the provisions of the statutes, be modified, commuted, affected or dealt with by agreement between the company and any person purporting to contract on behalf of that class provided such agreement is ratified in writing by the holders of at least three-fourths in nominal value of the issued shares of the class or is confirmed by an extraordinary resolution passed at a separate general meeting of the holders of shares of that class and all provisions herein contained as to general meetings shall, *mutatis mutandis*, apply to every such meeting but so that the quorum thereof shall be members or corporation representatives holding or representing by proxy one-third of the nominal amount of the issued shares of that class, and that at any such meeting, immediately upon a declaration of the result of the show of hands, a poll may be demanded by the chairman or by at least three members or corporation representatives present in person or by proxy entitled to vote at the meeting and holding together not less than one-twentieth of the nominal amount of the issued shares of the class. Without prejudice to the rights of the holders of the 4½ per cent. preference shares and the second preference shares, the special rights conferred upon the holders of any shares or class of shares shall not, [392] unless otherwise expressly provided in the rights attaching to or the terms of issue of such shares, be deemed to be altered by the creation or issue of further shares ranking 'pari passu' therewith."

Article 14(13) provides that the company may by special resolution reduce its share capital in any manner authorised by the Companies Acts for the time being in force.

For the purposes of the proposed reduction of capital the company's auditors certified in terms of article 4(B)(*d*) that the average of the mean prices over the relevant period was 45p per share in the case of the 3.85 per cent. preference shares and 65p in the case of the 5.25 per cent. preference shares. The reduction of capital accordingly provided for the second preference shareholders to be repaid at par.

The argument for the appellants picked upon the words "commuted" and "affected" in article 12, it being maintained that these words were apt to describe the situation where the rights of the second preference shareholders under article 4(13) were converted into a right to receive payment of a capital sum. Reference was made to *White v. Bristol Aeroplane Co. Ltd.* [1953] Ch. 65 (see supra, p. 515). In that case the articles of association of the company provided that the rights of any class of shareholders might be "affected, modified, varied, dealt with, or abrogated" with the consent of a special resolution passed at a meeting of members of the class. The company proposed to increase its capital by the issue of further preference shares ranking pari passu with existing preference shares. The existing preference shareholders challenged the carrying out of the proposal without their consent signified at a separate class meeting. The Court of Appeal held that the proposed increase of capital did not "affect" the rights of the existing preference shareholders within the meaning of the relevant article. Lord Evershed M.R., at p. 74, expressed the opinion that the enjoyment of the rights of the preference shareholders would be affected by the increase of capital but drew a distinction between the affecting of the enjoyment of the rights and the affecting of the rights themselves. Counsel for the appellants criticised this distinction on the ground that it was excessively legalistic and gave insufficient weight to the importance from the business point of view of the practical consequences of a measure which affected the enjoyment of the rights of preference shareholders by diluting them. Attention was drawn to passages in a number of textbooks where similar criticism was made.

My Lords, in my opinion the only question at issue in this appeal is whether or not the proposed reduction of capital accords with the rights conferred upon the second preference shareholders by the articles of association, in particular article 4(B). In *In re Saltdean Estate Co. Ltd.* [1968] 1 W.L.R. 1844 the articles of association of the company required the consent of a class meeting to any proposal which was such as to "affect, modify, deal with or abrogate in any manner" the rights and privileges of that class of shareholders. The company proposed to reduce its share capital by paying off its preference shareholders, who opposed the reduction on the ground that no separate class meeting had been [393] held. Buckley J., a judge of unrivalled experience in company law, granted confirmation of the reduction. He said, at pp. 1849-1850:

"It has long been recognised that, at least in normal circumstances, where a company's capital is to be reduced by repaying paid up share capital, in the absence of agreement or the sanction of a class meeting to the contrary, that class of capital should first be repaid which would be returned first in a winding up of a company (see *In re Chatterley-Whitfield Collieries Ltd.* [1948] 2 All E.R. 593, 596 *per* Lord Greene M.R.). In the present case the preferred shareholders are entitled to prior repayment of capital in a winding up and, consequently, if the company has more paid-up capital than it needs and wishes to repay some part of it, the first class of capital to be repaid should prima facie be the preferred shares.

". . . it is said that the proposed cancellation of the preferred shares will constitute an abrogation of all the rights attached to those shares which cannot validly be effected without an extraordinary resolution of a class meeting of preferred shareholders under article 8 of the company's articles. In my judgment, that article has no application to a cancellation of shares on a reduction of capital which is in accord with the rights attached to the shares of the company. Unless this reduction can be shown to be unfair to the preferred shareholders on other grounds, it is in accordance with the right and liability to prior repayment of capital attached to their shares. The liability to prior repayment on a reduction of capital, corresponding to their right to prior return of capital in a winding up, is a liability of a kind of which Lord Greene M.R., in the passage I have referred to, said that anyone has only himself to blame if he does not know it. It is part of the bargain between the shareholders and forms an integral part of the definition or delimitation of the bundle of rights which make up a preferred share. Giving effect to it does not involve the variation or abrogation of any right attached to such a share."

I consider this to be an entirely correct statement of the law. Buckley J. does not address his mind to any special meaning which might fall to be attributed to the words "affect, modify, deal with" in juxtaposition with the word "abrogate." There was no need for him to do so. The proposed reduction of capital involved an extinction of the preferred shares in strict accordance with the contract embodied in the articles of association, to which the holders of the preferred shares were party. One of the rights attached to these shares was the right to a return of capital in priority to other shareholders where any capital was appropriately to be returned as being in excess of the company's needs. That right was not being affected, modified, dealt with or abrogated, but was being given effect to.

In the present case article 4(B)(c) refers specifically to a return of capital on a winding up or otherwise. The words "or otherwise" are plainly apt to apply to repayment of capital which is in excess of the needs of the company, which may be brought about by a reduction of capital such as is authorised by article 14(D). In such a reduction of [394] capital the second preference shareholders are entitled to priority of repayment after the 3.15 per cent. preference shares and before any other shareholders. The reduction of capital now proposed to be made gives effect to that right. This necessarily involves, of course, that all other rights attached to the shares will come to an end, but that is something to which the holders of the shares must be taken to have agreed as a necessary consequence of their right to prior repayment receiving effect. Upon no view of the matter can it be said that as a result any of the special rights attached to the shares has been "modified, commuted, affected or dealt with" within the meaning of article 12. These words all contemplate that after the relevant transaction the shareholders in question will continue to possess some rights, albeit of a different nature from those which they possessed before the transaction. The proposal for reduction of capital involves the complete cancellation of the shares. I respectfully agree with the passage in the opinion of the court below delivered by the Lord Justice-Clerk, 1987 S.L.T. 273, 278:

> "In our opinion the proposed cancellation of the preference shares would involve fulfilment or satisfaction of the contractual rights of the shareholders, and would not involve any variation of their rights. Variation of a right presupposes the existence of the right, the variation of the right, and the subsequent continued existence of the right as varied. A different situation obtains where a right is fulfilled and satisfied and thereafter ceases to exist."

Note: In view of the former Supreme Court's decision in *Re Cork Electric Supply Co.* [1932] I.R. 315 (ante p. 410), it is debatable whether a repayment preference shares constitutes a variation of those shareholders' class rights in Irish law.

In *Re Northern Engineering Industries p.l.c.* [1994] 2 B.C.L.C. 704, the court refused to sanction a proposed repayment of the entire preference share capital because the company's articles of association stipulated that the rights attached to any class of shares shall be deemed to be varied by 'the reduction of the capital paid up on those shares' and there was no resolution of the preference shareholders approving the proposal.

In re Holders Investment Trust Ltd
[1971] 2 All E.R. 289

The company's issued share capital comprised of ordinary shares and 5 per cent cumulative preference shares that were to be redeemed in 1971. In 1970 it was proposed that the 5 per cent preference shareholders should be repaid by being allotted 6 per cent unsecured loan stock 1985-1990 in the same nominal amounts. This proposal was approved by a special resolution of the company and also by a special resolution of the preference shareholders meeting separately. Of the latter, however, approximately 3 per cent did not vote; 7 per cent opposed the proposal; and the remaining 90 per cent who supported the proposal were trustees who also held over half of the ordinary shares. From the evidence it was clear that, in voting for the proposed capital repayment, the trustees were influenced solely by the benefit to the trust as a whole and were not concerned with the advantages to themselves *qua* preference shareholders.

MEGARRY J.: . . . [290] Put briefly, counsel for the opposing trustees' opposition to the confirmation of the reduction is twofold. First, he contends that the extraordinary resolution of the [291] preference shareholders was not valid and effectual because the supporting trustees did not exercise their votes in the way that they ought to have done, namely, in the interests of the preference shareholders as a whole. Instead, being owners of much ordinary stock and many shares as well, they voted in such a way as to benefit the totality of the stocks and shares that they held. Secondly, he contends that even if the extraordinary resolution was valid, the terms on which the reduction of capital is to be effected are not fair, in particular in that the increase in the rate of interest from 5% to 6% is not an adequate recompense for having the right of repayment or redemption postponed from 31 July 1971, until at earliest 31 October 1985, and at latest some unspecified date in 1990. I may say at the outset that it is common ground that the proposed reduction is not in accordance with the class rights of the preference shareholders. . . .

Counsel for the company put before me four propositions based on the authorities. Discarding what does not apply in this case, and putting the matter shortly, I think that three relevant propositions emerge. First, a reduction of capital which is not in accordance with the class rights is nevertheless regular if it is effectually sanctioned in accordance with the regulations of the company. Second, there is an effectual sanction to the modification of class rights if those holding a sufficient majority of the shares of that class vote in favour of the modification in the bona fide belief that they are acting in the interests of the general body of members of that class. Third, the burden of proof depends on whether or not there is any such sanction. If there is, the court will confirm the reduction unless the opposition proves that it is unfair; if there is not, the court will confirm the reduction only if it is proved to be fair. These propositions were based on *Carruth v. Imperial Chemical Industries Ltd.* [1937] A.C. 707, when read in conjunction with *British America Nickel Corpn Ltd. v. M.J. O'Brien Ltd.* [1927] A.C. 369, and *Shuttleworth v. Cox Bros & Co. (Maidenhead) Ltd.* [1927] 2 K.B. 9. Whatever may be said about the formulation of the propositions, their substance was, I think, common ground between the parties. Accordingly, I must first consider the validity of the class resolution.

In the *British America* case, Viscount Haldane, in speaking for a strong Board of the judicial Committee, referred to 'a general principle, which is applicable to all authorities conferred on majorities of classes enabling them to bind minorities; namely, that the power given must be exercised for the purpose of benefiting the class as a whole, and not merely individual members only. . . .' The matter may, I think, be put in the way in which Scrutton L.J. put it in the Shuttleworth case, where the question was the benefit of the company rather than of a particular class of members. Adapting his language . . . I have to see whether the majority was honestly endeavouring to decide and act to the benefit of the class as a whole, rather than with a view to the interests of some of the class and against that of others. . . .

[292] I pause here to point the obvious. Without guidance from those skilled in these matters, many members of a class may fail to realise what they should bear in mind when deciding how to vote at a class meeting. The beneficial owner of shares may well concentrate on his own personal interests: even though he regards the proposal per se as one to be rejected, collateral matters affecting other interests of his may lead him to vote in favour of the resolution. Trustees, too, are under a fiduciary duty to do the best they properly can for their beneficiaries. A proposal which, in isolation, is contrary to the interests of those owning the shares affected may nevertheless be beneficial to the beneficiaries by reason of the improved prospects that the proposal will confer on other shares in the company which the trustees hold on the same trusts: and that, in essence, is what is in issue here. . . .

[His Lordship referred to correspondence between the 'supporting trustees' and their professional advisers, and continued:] [294] That exchange of letters seems to me to make it perfectly clear that the advice sought, the advice given, and the advice acted upon, was all on the basis of what was for the benefit of the trusts as a whole, having regard to their large holdings of the equity capital. From the point of view of equity, and disregarding company law, this is a perfectly proper basis; but that is not the question before me. I have to determine whether the supporting trustees voted for the reduction in the bona fide belief that they were acting in the interests of the general body of members of that class. From first to last I can see no evidence that the trustees ever applied their minds to what under company law was the right question, or that they ever had the bona fide belief that is requisite for an effectual sanction of the reduction. Accordingly, in my judgment there has been no effectual sanction for the modification of class rights. It may be observed that I have said nothing as to the burden of proof on this issue whether the sanction to the modification of class rights has been validly given, and I propose to continue to say nothing. However that burden lies, in my judgment there was no effectual sanction. The result is therefore that on the issue of fairness the burden of proof devolves on those supporting the reduction to prove that it is fair. Unless this burden is discharged, confirmation of the reduction will be refused.

[His Lordship considered the evidence and ruled that the reduction had not been shown to be fair to the preference shareholders. Accordingly, he refused to confirm the reduction.]

SCHEMES OF ARRANGEMENT AND RECONSTRUCTION

See *Company Law*, pp. 389–394.

Companies Act 1963, section 201(1), (3)

Compromise between company and its members or creditors

201.—(1) Where a compromise or arrangement is proposed between a company and its creditors or any class of them or between the company and its members or any class of them, the court may, on the application of the company or of any creditor or member of the company, or, in the case of a company being wound up, of the liquidator, order a meeting of the creditors or class of creditors, or of the members of the company, or class of members, as the case may be, to be summoned in such manner as the court directs.

(3) If a majority in number representing three-fourths in value of the creditors or class of creditors or members or class of members, as the case may be, present and voting either in person or proxy at the meeting, vote in favour of a resolution agreeing any compromise or arrangement, the compromise or arrangement shall, if sanctioned by the court, be binding on all the creditors or the class of creditors, or on the members or class of members, as the case may be, and also on the company or, in the of a company in the course of being wound up,on the liquidator and contributories of the company.

In re John Power & Son Ltd
[1934] I.R. 412

The company was established in 1921 with a capital of 400,000 £1 ordinary shares and 400,000 £1 preference shares carrying an 8 per cent per annum cumulative preferential dividend. After ten years of continuously falling profits, the directors concluded that there was no prospect of the company ever earning enough to meet the preference dividend every year and at the same time provide for depreciation. The directors, therefore, proposed to reduce the ordinary shares' nominal value to 50p per share, and that each preference share to be exchanged for a redeemable loan of £1 at 5 per cent per annum interest. This proposal was approved by a special resolution of the company, and by large majorities of the ordinary shareholders and the preference shareholders meeting separately.

FITZGIBBON J.: . . . [423] It seems to have been contended in the Court of first instance, and the appellants certainly adumbrated a similar contention here, that where a proposal for a reduction of capital under sect. 46, and a scheme of arrangement under sect. 120, have been approved by majorities considerably in excess of those prescribed by the Companies Act, the Court is practically bound, in the absence of bad faith, or unless there is some statement or omission likely to mislead the shareholders, to give its confirmation or sanction, as the case may be, to the proposed reduction or scheme. In my opinion the duty of the Court is not confined to these considerations. Until 1908 the power of the Court to bind a minority by the vote of a majority was limited to creditors and to cases of winding-up, but sect. 120 extended the power in the case of a compromise or scheme of arrangement, in the same words, to the 'members or any class of them', and the decisions under the earlier Acts have always been treated, and in my opinion necessarily so, as authorities to be followed in exercising the extended powers conferred by sect. 120 of [424] the Act of 1908, in cases where no winding-up was in progress.

The rule was stated by the Court of Appeal in England in *Re Alabama, New Orleans, Texas and Pacific Junction Railway Co.* [1891] 1 Ch. 213, by a Court consisting of Lindley, Bowen and Fry LL.JJ., and I take the following passage from the judgment of Lindley L.J.: 'What the Court has to do is to see, first of all, that the provisions of that statute [the Joint Stock Companies Arrangement Act 870, which corresponds, with the addition of the provisions as to 'members', with sect. 120 of the Companies Act 1908] have been complied with; and, secondly, that the majority have been acting *bona fide*. The Court also has to see that the minority is not being overridden by a majority having interests of its own clashing with those of the minority whom they seek to coerce. *Further than that*, the Court has to look at the scheme, and see whether it is one as to which persons acting honestly, and viewing the scheme laid before them in the interests of those whom they represent, take a view which can be reasonably taken by business men, The Court must look at the scheme, and see whether the Act, has been complied with, whether the majority are acting *bona fide*, and whether they are coercing the minority in order to promote interests adverse to those of the class they purport to represent; *and then* see whether the scheme is a reasonable one, *or* whether there is *any reasonable objection* to it, *or such an objection* to it as that *any reasonable man* might say that he could not approve of it.' That decision came up for consideration two years later in the very important case of *Re English, Scottish, and Australian Chartered Bank* [1893] 3 Ch. 385, when Sir Horace Davey *arguendo* in support of the scheme contended that the passage I have cited meant no more than that the Court should see 'whether the majority are acting *bona fide*'. Vaughan Williams J. – a great authority not only on Company Law but especially on the law and practice in bankruptcy, where similar principles in the case of creditors were of daily application – corrected him, and pointed out in a luminous judgment, in which they are set forth as clearly and concisely as in any judgment I have read, the principles and considerations which should govern a Court in dealing with such a scheme, and he put his interpretation upon the words of Lindley L.J. An appeal was taken from this decision.

which was affirmed in the Court of Appeal, where Lindley L.J. expressly reaffirmed all that [425] he had said in the *Alabama Case* [1891] 1 Ch. 213, and Lopes and A. L. Smith LL.JJ. agreed that the law had been most clearly stated there. The House of Lords, in *British and Amercian Trustee and Finance Corp. v. Couper* [1894] A.C. 399, and in *Poole v. National Bank of China Ltd.* [1907] A.C. 229, affirmed the right of a majority to bind a minority both on the question whether there should be a reduction of capital, and on the mode by which that reduction should be carried out, provided always that it was fair and equitable as between the different classes of shareholders, and in the latter case Lord Macnaghten deprecated 'a growing tendency to narrow and restrict the power conferred by the Act of 1867 on companies limited by shares'.

Having dealt with the principles which I think should govern the Court, I now come to the objections which have been urged in this particular case against the proposals of the Company.

I confess that I find great difficulty in ascertaining the ground upon which the learned judge based his rejection of the proposals.

He says that 'if a simple proposal, under sects. 46 and 120 of the Companies Act 1908, had been brought forward for the conversion, to put it shortly, of the 400,000 preference shares into 400,000 £1 5 per cent. Debenture Stock' (I think his '£1' has been misplaced) 'and if all requisite formalities had been observed, and if the statutory majority had been obtained, I should have had no difficulty whatever in giving the required sanction. Under existing circumstances I consider that the £5 Debenture Stock may quite reasonably be regarded as a more attractive investment than the 8 per cent. Cumulative Preference.' He then points out that this 'simple proposal' is complicated by an additional proposal that half the ordinary capital should be cancelled by the reduction of the £1 shares to 10s. shares, and adds: 'It is obvious that this addition to the scheme cannot prejudice the preference shareholders.' No wonder he says 'That being so, it may well be asked "Is not that all the more reason for sanctioning the scheme?" The scheme has the unanimous approval of the ordinary shareholders, and opposition only comes from a comparatively small number of preference shareholders. If, then, the Court would readily have sanctioned the simple scheme for conversion, should it not all the more readily give its sanction when the scheme is only complicated by being indissolubly bound up with [426] a cancellation of half of the ordinary share capital which must make the scheme more attractive to the preference shareholders.' He then proceeds to point out what he calls 'the fallacy in this argument'. 'No doubt,' he says, 'if the preference shareholders had approved by the required majority of a simple scheme for the conversion of the preference shares into 5 per cent. Debenture Stock the Court would have sanctioned the scheme at once. Further, if the preference shareholders would have so approved they would, of course, also approve of the scheme with the addition of the provision for the cancellation of half the ordinary capital. But there is no use stressing the attractiveness of the simple scheme for conversion when the preference shareholders were not given an opportunity for voting on that, but were only presented with the complex scheme, as one integral whole, recommended to them mainly on the ground that a reduction of capital was necessary.' What does this mean but that a man, presumably reasonable, would approve of the substitution of 5 per cent. Debenture Stock for 8 per cent. Cumulative Preference Shares as, 'under existing circumstances a more attractive investment', and would 'of course, also approve of the scheme with the addition of the provision for the cancellation of a half of the ordinary capital', as 'it is obvious that this addition to the scheme cannot prejudice the preference shareholders,' while the same reasonable man would be justified in rejecting either or both of the proposals because they were propounded simultaneously? The learned judge appears to think that there is something improper or unfair in propounding a composite scheme involving the reduction of capital under sect. 120, or in making the one conditional or dependent upon the other. The contrary was expressly decided in *Re Hoare* [1910] W. N. 87, not long after the passing of the Act. In that case it is true there was no opposition, but in Re Odham's Press, Ltd. [1925] W.N. 10, to which my brother Hanna referred during the argument, the question was argued, and Eve J. decided against the objection. The procedure has become so common that the precedent books contain examples of the necessary and usual forms. The learned judge then appears to regard the statement in the Directors' circular that 'the earning capacity of the Company is not equal to the strain of providing the cumulative [427] preference dividend (requiring an annual sum of £32,000, less income tax) if proper provision for depreciation, reserves, etc., is to be made in the future' as 'a direct threat to the preference shareholders that if they do not accept the integral scheme, or, to adopt Mr Overend's simile, if they do no swallow the physic the doctor has prescribed in a prescription that cannot be changed or tampered with, the Directors must resort, at least as a matter of prudence, to the annual profits to make good as far as possible all the depreciation in the fixed assets.' I am unable to regard a simple statement of essential facts as 'a direct threat', and I confess, that if the Directors had not drawn the attention of the shareholders to the fact that for several years nothing had been set aside for depreciation, and had allowed the shareholders to cast their votes under the false impression that, as the respondents' circular stated, 'the Company is able not only to pay the preference dividends in full but to carry forward very large credit balances', they would have laid themselves open to a far stronger charge of misleading the shareholders than any that has been suggested. I do not know whence the proposition was derived that the preference shareholders must 'swallow the physic the doctor has prescribed in a prescription that cannot be changed or tampered with'. The resolution proposed 'a scheme to be framed in accordance with the terms following:' of which No. 4 was: 'The Company may assent to any modification or condition which the Court may think fit to approve or impose.' No condition or modification was suggested by the opponents of the scheme, either in the Court below, in response to the express invitation of the judge (who stated that he had 'jurisdiction to intervene in an appropriate manner, either by refusing sanction *or by imposing appropriate conditions*'), or here; their demand was to stand upon their original rights, no matter how ruinous such a course might be to the Company and their fellow preference shareholders who had approved the scheme by a vast majority, and this is a matter upon which reliance was placed by Lord Loreburn C. (at p. 236) and Lord Macnaghten (at p. 239) when dismissing the appeal of the dissentient shareholders in *Poole v. National Bank of China.*

It might be supposed from some passages in the judgment of the learned judge that he thought it possible that some shareholders had been misled by the Directors' circular. It is certain that the three shareholders who opposed the scheme were not misled, and the concluding paragraph of [428] the learned judge's opinion seems to me to demonstrate that he did not believe that anyone not before the Court could have been under any misconception, because he says: 'Now that the position has been fully investigated, the "objectors" – (who had not been misled) – might consent to withdraw their objections and if *they* so consented, I would be satisfied that the circular would only leave matters where they stand, and accordingly would allow the scheme to go through.' He could not allow the scheme to go through, if he believed that shareholders not before the Court had been, or might have been, misled into supporting, or into refraining from opposing it, and the action of the three opponents, who *ex concessis* had not been misled, in withdrawing their opposition, based upon totally different grounds, ought not to be allowed to prejudice the ignorant absentees. This passage shows that the learned judge had disregarded the suggestion, if it was ever made by counsel for the opponents, that the circular had inadvertendy misled anyone. He says 'Personally I think it unlikely that any preference shareholder would desire to withdraw his approval of the scheme if he were sent a further circular,' an expression of opinion with which I entirely agree, and agreeing also, as I do, 'that the circular would only leave matters where they stand,'I 'accordingly would allow the scheme to go through.'

I can find nothing misleading in the circular, and the proposals seem to me quite intelligible to any person of ordinary intelligence. The only omission which has occurred to me is one which was not stressed, or even mentioned during the argument, of a statement as to the probable market value of the new Debenture Stock, but as any expression of opinion on this point would be purely speculative, and might be challenged as misleading, I am satisfied that it was properly omitted, and that it was not unfair to leave the shareholders to form their own estimates of the merits of the exchange which the learned judge considered might 'reasonably be regarded as a more attractive investment'.

That the substitution of debentures for shares is not per se an objection to the sanctioning of a scheme was settled by the decisions in *Re Nixon's Navigation Co.* [1897] 1 Ch. 872, and *Re Thomas De la Rue & Co.* [1911] 2 Ch.

361, which dispose of the objection by the respondents that the scheme would alter their position from that of shareholders to that of [429] creditors.

The *bona fides* of the Directors is conceded; it has been stated without challenge or contradiction that the required majority of preference shareholders was obtained without reckoning the votes of any preference shareholders who were also holders of ordinary shares; there is, in my opinion, nothing by way of statement or omission in connection with the circular which could have the effect of misleading even a less then ordinarily intelligent shareholder; and there is nothing about the proposed scheme which appears to me intrinsically unfair or inequitable.

Finally, no suggestion of any modification of the proposal has been put forward by the three dissentients, and in these circumstances I am of opinion that the proposed reduction of capital should be confirmed, and that the scheme of arrangement should be sanctioned by the Court.

In re Hellenic & General Trust Ltd
[1976] 1 W.L.R. 123

A company which carried on business as an investment trust applied for the sanction of the court to a scheme of arrangement. Those shares were held as to 53.01 per cent by another company ('MIT') which was a wholly owned subsidiary of a bank ('Hambros'), and as to 13.95 per cent by the National Bank of Greece SA ('NW'). By the proposed arrangement the ordinary shares of the company were to be cancelled and new ordinary shares were to be issued to Hambros, with the result that the company would become a wholly owned subsidiary of Hambros. The former shareholders of the company were to be compensated in cash for the loss of their shares. The offer price was 48p per share which was said to represent the true net asset value of the shares. On that basis it was between 20 and 25 per cent more than the shareholders would have been able to obtain elsewhere. However, if the scheme went through, NBG would become liable to a very substantial capital gains tax in Greece. At the meeting of all the ordinary shareholders summoned by the court, 91 per cent of the shareholders by value attending and voting, MIT voted in favour of the arrangement and NBC voted against it. A resolution in favour of the proposal was carried by the requisite majority of three-fourths in value of the class present and voting, but without the votes of MIT the resolution would not have been carried against the opposition of NBG. NBG opposed the company's petition for the sanction of the court.

TEMPLEMAN J.: [125] The first objection goes to jurisdiction, and the other three concern the discretion of the court in sanctioning an arrangement and the proper principles for the exercise of that discretion.

The first objection put forward is that the necessary agreement by the appropriate class of members has not been obtained. The shareholders who were summoned to the meeting consisted, it is submitted, of two classes. First there were the outside shareholders, that is to say the shareholders other than M.I.T.: and secondly M.I.T., a subsidiary of Hambros. M.I.T. were a separate class and should have been excluded from the meeting of outside shareholders. Although section 206 provides that the court may order meetings, it is the responsibility of the petitioners to see that the class meetings are properly constituted, and if they fail then the necessary agreement is not obtained and the court has no jurisdiction to sanction the arrangement. Thus in *In re United Provident Assurance Company Ltd.* [1910] 2 Ch. 477 the court held that the holders of partly paid shares formed a different class from holders of fully paid shares. The objection was taken that there should have been separate meetings of the two classes, and Swinfen Eady J. upheld the objection, saying, at p. 481: " . . . the objection that there have not been proper class meetings is fatal, and I cannot sanction the scheme."

Similarly Eve J. issued a practice direction, *Practice Note* [1934] W.N. 142, in which he reminded the profession, in dealing with the predecessor of section 206, that the responsibility for determining what creditors are to be summoned to any meeting as constituting a class rests with the petitioner, and if the meetings are incorrectly convened or constituted, or an objection is taken to the presence of any particular creditors as having interests competing with the others, the objection must be taken on the hearing of the petition for sanction and the petitioner must take the risk of having the petition dismissed. That direction applies equally to meetings of shareholders.

The question therefore is whether M.I.T., a wholly owned subsidiary of Hambros, formed part of the same class as the other ordinary shareholders. What is an appropriate class must depend upon the circumstances but some general principles are to be found in the authorities. In *Sovereign Life* [126] *Assurance Co. v. Dodd* [1892] 2 Q.B. 573, the Court of Appeal held that for the purposes of an arrangement affecting the policyholders of an assurance company the holders of policies which had matured were creditors and were a different class from policyholders whose policies had not matured. Lord Esher M.R. said, at p. 580:

> " . . . they must be divided into different classes . . . because the creditors composing the different classes have different interests; and, therefore, if we find a different state of facts existing among different creditors which may differently affect their minds and their judgment, they must be divided into different classes."

Bowen L.J. said, at p. 583:

> "It seems plain that we must give such a meaning to the term 'class' as will prevent the section being so worked as to result in confiscation and injustice, and that it must be confined to those persons whose rights are

not so dissimilar as to make it impossible for them to consult together with a view to their common interest."

Vendors consulting together with a view to their common interest in an offer made by a purchaser would look askance at the presence among them of a wholly owned subsidiary of the purchaser.

In the present case on analysis Hambros are acquiring the outside shares for 48p. So far as the M.I.T. shares are concerned it does not matter very much to Hambros whether they are acquired or not. If the shares are acquired a sum of money moves from parent to wholly owned subsidiary and shares move from the subsidiary to the parent. The overall financial position of the parent and the subsidiary remain the same. The shares and the money could remain or be moved to suit Hambros before or after the arrangement. From the point of M.I.T., provided M.I.T. is solvent, the directors of M.I.T. do not have to question whether the price is exactly right. Before and after the arrangement the directors of the parent and the subsidiary could have been made the same persons with the same outlook and the same judgment. Mr. Heyman, on behalf of the petitioners, submitted that since the parent and subsidiary were separate corporations with separate directors, and since M.I.T. were ordinary share-holders in the company, it followed that M.I.T. had the same interests as the other shareholders. The directors of M.I.T. were under a duty to consider whether the arrangement was beneficial to the whole class of ordinary share-holders, and they were capable of forming an independent and unbiased judg-ment, irrespective of the interests of the parent company. This seems to me to be unreal. Hambros are purchasers making an offer. When the vendors meet to discuss and vote whether or not to accept the offer, it is incongruous that the loudest voice in theory and the most significant vote in practice should come from the wholly owned subsidiary of the purchaser. No one can be both a vendor and a purchaser and in my judgment, for the purpose of the class meet-ings in the present case, M.I.T. were in the camp of the purchaser. Of course this does not mean that M.I.T. should not have considered at a separate class meeting whether to accept the arrangement. But their consideration will be different from the considerations given to the matter by the other sharehold-ers. Only M.I.T. could say, within limits, that what was good for Hambros must be good for M.I.T.

Mr. Heyman submitted that difficulties will arise in practice if every sub-sidiary or associated company may constitute a separate class. So far as a wholly owned subsidiary is concerned there is no difficulty at all, and in [127] most cases it will be sufficient to judge the class composition by reference to the shareholding. In most cases if the parent controls 50 per cent. or the more of the shares of the subsidiary company it can be assumed that they have a community of interest for the purposes of section 206, and in most cases a different interest from that of other shareholders. Mr. Heyman rellied on *Harold Holdsworth & Co. (Wakefield) Ltd. v. Caddies* [1955] 1 W.L.R. 352. But this only decided that the managing director of a group of companies could be obliged to devote his attention to one subsidiary, and Lord Morton of Henryton said, at p. 363:

> "It is true that each company in the group is in law a separate entity, the business whereof is to be carried on by its own directors and managing director, if any; but there is no doubt that the defenders, by taking any necessary formal steps, could make any arrangements they pleased in regard to the management of the business They owned all the issued capital and the directors were their nominees."

Since that case was directed to management I do not think it is of any great assistance to either party in this case, but it certainly is of no assistance to Mr. Heyman.

Accordingly I uphold the first objection, which is fatal to the arrangement. But in view of the careful arguments put forward by both sides I will consider the other objections which are raised by Mr. Wright and which are material if the class meeting in the present case, contrary to my view, was properly constituted.

The second objection is founded on the analysis of the arrangement as an offer by Hambros to acquire the ordinary shares for 48p. Section 209 (similar to section 204 of the 1963 Act) provides safeguards for minority shareholders in the event of a takeover bid and in a proper case provides machinery for a small minority of shareholders to be obliged to accept a takeover against their wishes. Thus section 209 provides that where a scheme or contract involving the transfer of shares in a company to another company has been approved by the holders of not less than nine-tenths in value of the shares whose transfer is involved (other than shares already held at the date of the offer by, or a nominee for, the transferee company or its subsidiary), the transferee company may give notice to any dissenting shareholder, and then, unless on an application made by the dissenting holder the court thinks fit to order otherwise, shall be entitled and bound to acquire those shares on the terms of the takeover bid. If the present arrangement had been carried out under section 209, M.I.T. as a subsidiary of Hambros would have been expressly forbidden to join in any approval for the purposes of section 209, and in any event the objectors could not have been obliged to sell because they hold 10 per cent. of the ordinary shares of the company.

The fact that an arrangement under section 206 produces a result which is the same as a takeover under section 209 is not necessarily fatal. It is not always so unfair as to preclude the court from exercising its discretion in favour of the scheme. Thus in *In re National Bank Ltd.* [1966] 1 W.L.R. 819 (see *post*, p. 565). where a similar objection was taken, Plowman J. considered the argument that the scheme in that case ought to be treated as a section 209 case needing a 90 per cent. majority. . . .

[128] Accepting that, the present proposals nevertheless seem to me to place the petitioners in an inescapable dilemma. They cannot succeed under section 209 because of the express provisions of that section and the size of the shareholding of the objectors. They can only succeed under section 206 by using the votes of their own subsidiary company, M.I.T., to secure the necessary majority. In these circumstances I agree with Mr. Wright that the court should not in the exercise of its discretion authorise the acquisition of the shares of the objectors, the National Bank of Greece, against the wishes of the bank. The petitioners cannot succeed at all under section 209 and in my judgment they cannot fairly succeed under section 206.

Earlier authority appears to support that proposition. In *In re General Motor Cab Co. Ltd.* [1913] 1 Ch. 377, a company proposed to sell its assets and undertaking to a new company to be formed for that purpose and to compel shareholders to accept shares in the new company instead of their shares in the old company. The creditors were to be taken over by the new company. There was no provision for preserving the rights of dissentient shareholders. It was held by the Court of Appeal that the scheme was not a compromise or arrangement which could be sanctioned. That was admittedly a very strong case where the court came to the conclusion that what was being asked was not a compromise or arrangement at all, but it is significant that the court approached the application on the basis of it being something which if it had been a takeover bid would have required the rights of dissentient shareholders to be preserved.

Similarly in *In re Anglo-Continental Supply Co. Ltd.* [1922] 2 Ch. 723, the reconstruction of an existing company by winding up and sale of its entire undertaking and assets for shares in a new foreign company outside the scope of a reconstruction under the Companies (Consolidation) Act 1908 was effected as an arrangement under section 120 of that Act, the predecessor of the present section 206. But that was only done on terms that the rights of the dissentient minority were preserved in the same way as they would have been under a reconstruction.

Finally in *In re Bugle Press Ltd.* [1961] Ch. 270 (see post, p. 562), where two majority shareholders formed a new company and propounded an arrangement simply for the purpose of enabling them to get the requisite majority under section 209, the court refused to have any truck with the proposals put forward. . . .

Whereas in *Bugle Press* the motives of the applicants for the scheme were not particularly praiseworthy I hasten to say that in the present case the motives of the petitioners are entirely different, as will appear when I come to consider the details of the scheme. The petitioners are anxious that the ordinary shareholders should be offered the full net asset value of their shares which exceed the value of those shares on the open market. They are persisting with the scheme because they do not consider that it is fair to those shareholders who wish to accept the scheme that they should be frustrated by the opposition of the objectors.

But the decision in *In re Bugle Press Ltd.* fortifies me in thinking that where one has what is in effect a section 209 scheme then, putting it at its lowest, there must be a very high standard of proof on the part of the petitioner to justify obtaining by section 206 what could not be obtained by section 209. especially when there is the added element that section 206 itself works with the help of a wholly owned subsidiary of the petitioners.

The third alternative objection raised by Mr. Wright is that the arrangement is unfair to all the ordinary shareholders. I am satisfied that it is more than fair. The shares of the company are listed on the Stock Exchange and in common with other investment trust companies normally stand between 20 per cent. and 25 per cent. below the net asset value of the company's assets. Thus the offer price of 48p, if it represents the true net asset value of the shares, is 20 per cent. to 25 per cent. more than the shareholders can now obtain elsewhere. The assets of the company consist largely of cash and Stock Exchange investments, so that the ordinary shareholders, if they receive 48p, instead of their existing shares, can follow the same outline of investment and will have roughly 48p to invest instead of a share worth on the Stock Exchange 36p. There has been independent advice provided to shareholders and I am quite satisfied that the offer is extremely fair.

On behalf of the objectors several reasons were advanced why it could be said that the scheme was unfair to all the ordinary shareholders, but I do not find any of those reasons convincing. It was said that the scheme would involve the ordinary shareholders in a disposal for the purposes of United Kingdom capital gains tax and that would not apply to Hambros and M.I.T. On the other hand I was told that in fact the effect will be disadvantageous to Hambros and M.T.T. in that losses will not be allowed to be carried forward. The imposition of capital gains tax is a fate which we must all suffer. It was said that the offer was made at a time when assets value had declined drastically, that there was a belief that share prices in general would go up, that the offer was made at a time when sterling was low, and, although this may sound rather strange at the moment, it was said to be unwise [130] to sell until sterling had recovered. Finally it was said that the real value of the investments can only be maintained by holding shares in investment trusts with a substantial portfolio of overseas investments.

Whatever the future of sterling and whatever the future of Stock Exchange investments, since the holding of this particular company consists almost entirely of cash and Stock Exchange investments anyone who holds at the moment a share in the company is relying simply on the present management. I have heard no argument that the objectors prefer the management of Hambros Ltd. to their own or any other form of management. If a shareholder receives 48p he can back his fancy as regards the future of Stock Exchange investments, the future value of cash and the future value of sterling. He can even, by taking a list of the company's investments, slavishly follow the exact pattern of their investments. The claim that there is some peculiar advantage in holding shares in the present company because of its portfolio of overseas investments, was based on a misunderstanding. In fact the overseas investments of this company do not amount to more than 9 per cent., and there are other substantial investment trusts which have a far higher proportion of overseas investments if a shareholder thinks that is a good thing. Accordingly I am quite satisfied that the scheme is fair or more than fair to the ordinary shareholders is a class.

Mr. Heyman says, that being so, I ought to ignore the earlier indications of unfairness, namely, the effect of the section 209 machinery, and the exploitation of the section 206 machinery; and it may be that in some extraordinary case that would be true. But I cannot bring myself to believe that it would be right to exercise a discretion in favour of the petitioners in the present case. It may be that there is some advantage in hanging on. At any rate the objectors were entitled to say that they purchased more than 10 per cent., they could not be expropriated under section 209, and they object to expropriation, albeit it is said in the best interest of other shareholders, under section 206. That leaves the final objection; why if the scheme is beneficial is it not acceptable to the objectors? In the first place they themselves seem to hold the opinion that there is some advantage in retaining their present shareholding. They voice some misgivings as to whether the petitioners themselves are not doing rather better out of the arrangement than appears to be the case. But substantially the objectors' view is coloured by the fact that they will, as the evidence states, although I am not given details, become liable to a swingeing capital gains tax in Greece. Mr. Heyman says the tax must be ignored because in considering their votes at a meeting under section 206 each shareholder must put himself in the impossible position of deciding what is in the best interests of the class. That appears from the judgment of Megarry J. in *In re Holders Investment Trust Ltd.* [1971] 1 W.L.R. 583 (see supra, p. 533), and in particular the passage at p. 586 where Megarry J. refers to a general principle that a power conferred on a majority of a class to bind minorities, must be exercised for the purpose of benefiting the class as a whole and not merely individual members only. Similarly in *In re Grierson, Oldham & Adams Ltd.* [1968] Ch. 17, under section 209 it was held the test was one of fairness to the body of shareholders and not to individuals and the burden was on the applicants to prove unfairness and not merely that the scheme was open to criticism. Although [131] under section 206 the onus is the other way round it is submitted that the test of fairness is exactly the same.

In a good many cases so it would be, but in the present case it seems to me that the individual loss which the objectors will suffer from the scheme is one which should be borne in mind. When one adds together the three objections of Mr. Wright, first of all that it is really a scheme by Hambros to purchase the outside shareholding, secondly, that under section 209 the scheme could not have been carried out against the wishes of the objectors, and thirdly, that it could not have been carried out under section 206 save with the votes of M.I.T., the wholly owned subsidiary of Hambros, it seems to me that it is unfair to deprive the objectors of shares which they were entitled to assume were safe from compulsory purchase and with the effect of putting on the objectors a swingeing fiscal impost which, if the matter had proceeded under section 209, they could have avoided simply and quite properly by refusing to join in approving the scheme under that section.

Accordingly in the result, both as a matter of jurisdiction and as a matter of discretion, I am not prepared to make any order approving this scheme.

Note: In *British & Commonwealth Holdings p.l.c. v. Barclays Bank p.l.c.* [1996] 1 W.L.R. 1, the court, approved a scheme of arrangement whereby *inter alia* the defendant company and one C. entered into an option agreement under which the company was to issue redeemable preference shares in substitution for ordinary shares. The company failed to redeem them and, in an action for damages for breach of that arrangement, it was contended that it contravened the equivalents of section 219(2) of the 1990 Act and section 60 of the 1963 Act. It was held that the plaintiff s claim did not involve breach of those sections and that, in any event, since the covenants in question had been sanctioned by the court, their validity could not be challenged by the company.

CHAPTER 12

Take-Overs and Mergers

By take-overs and mergers is meant where one company (or exceptionally an individual) acquires control of another company or where both companies amalgamate. There are no general definitions for these terms in the Companies Acts. Such transactions can be brought about in significantly different ways. For instance, one company may simply sell its entire undertaking to another – either for cash or for securities in that other company. Section 260 of the 1963 Act provides a convenient mechanism where it is sought to sell the undertaking for shares in the acquiring company and then distribute those securities to the seller's own shareholders. The procedure under section 201 of the 1963 Act for arrangements can be used in order to take over or merge with another company. But the most common method today is where one company simply acquires most or all of the shares in another company, so that the latter becomes a subsidiary of the former.

AUTHORITY

Automatic Self-Cleansing Filter Syndicate Co. Ltd. v. Cuninghame
[1906] 2 Ch. 34

See *ante*, p. 179.

FINANCING

In re M.J. Cummins Ltd
[1939] I.R. 60

See *post*, p. 574.

Belmont Finance Corp. v. Williams Furniture Ltd (No. 2)
[1980] 1 All E.R. 393

See *ante*, pp. 351 and 357.

Bank of Ireland v. Rockfield Ltd.
[1979] I.R. 21

See *ante*, p. 359.

In re Wellington Publishing Co. Ltd.
[1973] 1 N.Z.L.R. 133

A company borrowed approximately $NZ 3 million in order to finance the take-over of another company. When the take-over was completed, the acquired company's assets were revalued and were shown to be worth far more than their stated value. In anticipation of the profit that would be made on those properties if ever realised, a dividend of approximately $NZ 3 million was paid, which the successful bidder then used to pay off the overdraft. It was contended that these transactions contravened the New Zealand near-equivalent of section 60 of the 1963 Act.

QUILLIAM J.: . . . [136] Section 62 of the Companies Act 1955, so far as is material for the present purpose, is as follows:

> "(1) Subject as provided in this section, it shall not be lawful for a company to give, whether directly or indirectly, and whether by means of a loan, guarantee, the provision of security or otherwise, any financial assistance for the purpose of or in connection with a purchase or subscription made or to be made by any person of or for any shares in the company."

This case resolves itself into the question of whether the declaration and payment of a dividend by Blundell Brothers Limited is the giving to the Wellington Company of 'financial assistance'.

There is no doubt that the words of section 62 are intended to have a wide application. This does not mean that they are to have unlimited application. Nor does it mean that they are to be given any strained or unnatural interpretation. The purpose of the section would seem to be the protection of minority shareholders and creditors. If, therefore, a transaction in question is likely to detract from that protection then the words of the section may the more readily be regarded as extending to embrace that transaction.

I think the first approach should be to look at the words of the section and see whether, giving those words their normal and popular meanings, they appear to extend to the declaration and payment of a dividend. I find it very difficult to say that this is the case. It is necessary first to eliminate the words 'loan, guarantee, the provision of security'. By no process of reasoning can those words be regarded as including a dividend. There remain the words 'or otherwise' which undoubtedly have the widest application and will presumably include transactions of any kind. Any transaction which is being considered, however, must be of a kind which gives 'any financial assistance for the purpose of or in connection with a purchase' of shares. The expression 'financial assistance' is an indefinite one and it is beyond normal experience to regard that expression as applying to the payment of a dividend. The payment of a dividend is part of the normal functions of a company, and indeed, in the final analysis, is probably as much the reason for the company's existence as is the earning of profits the reason for an individual trader being in business. To be more precise, a dividend must be regarded as first and foremost a return on an investment. In the customary usage of words the payment by a company of a dividend to a shareholder is not to be regarded as giving financial assistance to that shareholder.

I think it is beyond doubt that the payment of a dividend is not something which will ordinarily be regarded as the giving of financial assistance. It is necessary therefore to inquire whether there is anything in the decided cases or the substance of the transaction itself which would [137] require the payment of a dividend to be treated as falling Within a special category so as to bring it under section 62. . . .

[140] It is, I think, clear that the Court may go beyond the form of a transaction in a case such as this and look at the substance of it. It was suggested by Mr Blank that once this is done the payment of the dividend must be regarded as giving financial assistance to the Wellington Company for the purchase of the shares. As I understand Mr Blank's argument it was that assistance would arise principally in two ways. First, it would enable the Wellington Company to purchase on a cheaper basis than if it had to adopt an alternative method. It is true that the evidence was that the use of dividend money to make the payment would save the Wellington Company from adopting more expensive methods of financing and would also free it from the limitations upon its activities which would result from the need to raise a substantial loan liability. It may be that a situation such as that could in appropriate circumstances amount to financial assistance as contemplated in *Dey's* case [1966] V.R. 464, but I do not think any such conclusion is to be reached here. All that the Wellington Company proposes is to use money to which it as a shareholder would be entitled. It does not amount to any disadvantage to Blundell Brothers Limited which would be applying revenue reserves which would properly be the subject of a dividend. The second matter raised by Mr Blank was that the dividend proposed would be non-taxable in the hands of the Wellington Company by virtue of the provisions of section 86c(1) of the Land and Income Tax Act of 1954, whereas if the dividend had been paid to the former shareholders (at least as private individuals) it would have been taxable (s. 81(1)(f). This meant that the Wellington Company by being relieved from a liability for tax, would be able to pay more for the shares than would otherwise be the case. Here again there may be circumstances in which this could be the case but I can see

no basis upon which it could be a relevant situation in the present circumstances. The proposed method of payment forms no part of the offer made by the Wellington Company. Before the offer was made the Wellington Company was already aware that doubt had been expressed as to the validity of what it proposed and [141] in fact the present originating summons had been issued before the offer was sent to shareholders. I can, therefore, see no basis upon which it could be said that the declaration of a dividend could have had any bearing on the amount offered for the shares. There is certainly nothing in the evidence to suggest that the price offered has been influenced by the company's belief that it may be able to use the dividend payment.

Finally, I should say a word about the effect of the payment of the dividend on the financial structure of the two companies. It was common ground that the Wellington Company's proposed treatment of the dividend payment in its accounts was correct. That treatment involved deducting the amount of the dividend from the cost of acquisition of the shares so that the balance sheet would then record the net cost of acquisition. So far as Blundell Brothers Limited is concerned a notional balance sheet of its position after payment of the dividend shows that it would then have assets totalling $5,690,478 and term and current liabilities of $2,546,652. If the purpose of section 62 is the protection of minority shareholders and creditors, there would appear to be no detriment involved. There are in this case no minority shareholders because all the shareholders have accepted the offer. Existing creditors are amply protected by the substantial excess of assets over liabilities. It was suggested by Mr Blank that future creditors should also be taken into account. On principle I think this is incorrect. It would be unrealistic to say that a company should never make a financial move which might involve an inability to meet the demands of creditors who may at some indefinite time appear and who of course may never appear at all, unless of course it were to do so at a time when it had no reasonable margin of assets over liabilities.

In summary, the position is that the proposal involves the declaration of a dividend by Blundell Brothers Limited out of money which is in every respect a proper subject for a dividend. What is intended is that the Wellington Company will apply the money to which it is entitled in this way towards the purchase of the shares. I consider this to be a normal application by it of funds to which it is entitled and I cannot regard this upon the facts of the present case as constituting 'financial assistance' within the meaning of section 62.

Securities Trust Ltd. v. Associated Properties Ltd.
McWilliam J., November 19, 1980

Associated and Estates were two companies which carried on business in conjunction for a number of years; the directors and managers of both companies were the same. When Estates commenced its operation to acquire shares in

Associated, the plaintiff owned shares of each denomination in Associated. A special resolution was then passed by Associated under the powers conferred by section 204 of the 1963 Act, 'That the making of an interest-free loan of £1,800,000 by the Company to Estates Development Limited which shall be repayable on demand to assist the Estates to purchase ordinary, ordinary A and preference shares in the capital of the Company be and is hereby approved.' The validity of this resolution was challenged.

McWILLIAM J.: [6] In the summons herein the plaintiff claims that the special resolution of 15th August 1979 was unlawful as being in contravention of Section 60, subsection (1) of the Act of 1963 and in contravention of Article 5 of the articles of association of Associated. In argument it was also claimed that there had been a breach of faith in calling the general meeting of 21st August 1979 to pass the resolution altering the memorandum and articles after the loan had been made, and also in concealing in the offer document that the resources available to pay for the shares were the resources of Associated itself . . .

[9] Article 5 of the articles of association of Associated provided as follows: 'None of the funds of the Company shall be employed in the purchase of, or lent on, shares of the Company.'

On the facts as they have been put before me, I have difficulty in accepting the accuracy of the statement at paragraph (a) under the heading 'General' in Appendix IV in the letter of offer. It may be assumed, in the absence of compelling evidence to the contrary, that, in a transaction involving the borrowing of a sum in the nature of two million pounds, the parties organising the transaction had worked out the method of completing it before embarking on the transaction. As the directors of the two companies were the same, nothing in the nature of a written agreement between the two boards was required.

I do not know what is the reason for the provisions of section 204 of the 1963 Act or why is should be thought desirable that minority shareholders may be compulsorily bought out, but I am of opinion that, on a compulsory [19] purchase of this nature, the people whose shares are being compulsorily purchased are entitled to be given full particulars of the transactions, its purpose, the method of carrying it out and its consequences. The purpose of the transaction and its consequences have not yet been disclosed and the method of carrying it out was not disclosed to the persons concerned.

I have not been addressed on the duty of directors towards their own members or their positions as agents or otherwise *vis-à-vis* the shareholders on such a transaction but, although a director is not a trustee of the shareholders, directors are to some extent in a fiduciary position and I am of opinion that, on a transaction such as this, the shareholders are entitled to be given reasonably full particulars by their directors about the matters I have just mentioned. Certainly, in the offer documents in this case there was no indication that the money for the purchase of the shares was to be provided by Associated itself.

As a result of the procedures adopted, the plaintiffs ordinary shares had been compulsorily acquired before the [11] meeting of 15th August 1979, at which, if the plaintiff had then held its ordinary shares, it would have been able, under the provisions of subsection (7) of section 60, to have prevented the transaction being carried out in the way in which it was carried out. In itself this is not a matter of great importance but it may help to explain the procedures adopted by the directors.

However this may be, I am of opinion that the special resolution of 15th August 1979 was one which came within the provisions of subsection (2) of section 60 of the 1963 Act so as to avoid the prohibition contained in subsection (1) and would have been effective to authorise the loan had such a resolution been within the power of the company under its memorandum and articles of association.

I am also of opinion, however, that Associated had no power under its memorandum and articles of association to advance money by way of loan or otherwise for the purchase of its own shares. Lending money was not one of the objects in the memorandum and Article 7 stated unequivocally that none of the funds of the company could be employed for [12] the purchase of shares in the company. Section 25 of the 1963 Act provided that the articles and memorandum bind the company and the members. Accordingly, at the time of the resolution of 15th August 1979, Associated had no power to pass the resolution making the interest free loan of £1,800,000 to Estates. This circumstance was brought to the attention of the company and its directors at the meeting but the resolution was passed notwithstanding.

The subsequent proceedings by Association to rectify the position were also unsatisfactory. The general meeting of 21st August to alter the memorandum and articles of association was effective for that purpose but, in my opinion, this would not retrospectively validate the resolution of 15th August. There should have been a new resolution after there was authority to pass it. Again, this is not in itself a matter of great importance but it is a matter which I should take into consideration with regard to the attitude of the directors in conducting the transaction.

I am not impressed by the procedures of repaying the [13] earlier loan and making new loans which are alleged to have taken place immediately after the resolutions of 21st August had been passed. I am sure that the necessary book entries were made but what was required at that stage was a new resolution authorising the loan.

One of the matters mentioned in the arguments on behalf of the plaintiff was that the bank had been left in an invidious position by the statements of the directors. This may be so, but the bank issued the letter of offer under its own name and recommended the offer and advanced the money for the purchase of the shares and was completely identified with the transaction, although I accept it acted in accordance with current practice in such matters.

PROFITEERING

Regal (Hastings) Ltd v. Gulliver
[1967] 2 A.C 134n

See *ante*, p. 281.

Percival v. Wright
[1902] 2 Ch. 421

See *ante*, p. 293.

Coleman v. Myers
[1977] 2 N.Z.L.R. 225

(*From headnote*) The first and second respondents, a son and his father, were managing director and chairman of an old established private company in which many of the shareholders, individually or through trusts, were relatives. They were also directors of a wine and spirit company in which the family company owned a half share, the book value of which was about $NZ5 million. It also owned properties, including the Strand-Coburg block, and had about $NZI.8 million in cash. The first respondent, who had only a small shareholding in the family company, evolved a plan whereby he would acquire all the shares at a price of $4.80 each and would pay for them entirely out of the company's assets, by using the cash and selling Strand-Coburg and other properties, leaving him sole owner of the company with remaining interests (principally the share in the wine and spirit company) worth some millions. The major shareholders included certain family trusts of which the second respondent was a trustee. As a result of approaches by both respondents, the shares of these trusts were secured at $4.80; before the subsequent take-over offer they had consequently been transferred to the second respondent's trust. As opposition from a minority was feared, the first respondent formed a new company (the third respondent) of which he was sole owner. This enabled a take-over offer to be made to all the then shareholders in the name of an offeror which, not already holding any shares, could expect to obtain acceptance from holders of nine-tenths of the shares for which offers were made, so making available the compulsory acquisition provisions of the Companies Act 1955, section 208 (cf. section 204 of the 1963 Act). The new company made such an offer. In their statutory statement under the Companies Amendment Act 1963 the first and second respondents, as directors of the offeree company, recommended shareholders to accept.

The appellants, who were minority shareholders, reluctantly accepted when served with notice that the offeror had acquired nine-tenths. The first respondent successfully carried out his plan, selling Strand-Coburg at much above book value soon after the take-over and using the proceeds of $3.5 million and the $1.8 million cash to pay for the shares. He made these resources available to himself by temporary loans from the company, followed by capital dividends. When they learnt these facts the appellants brought action, claiming fraud, breach of fiduciary duty, negligence and breach of the Companies Act 1955, section 62. They alleged that the first respondent's plan and the magnitude of his potential gain had not been disclosed to shareholders; and that he had represented that he intended to keep Strand-Coburg, whereas in fact he had engaged property consultants to sell it and had himself been negotiating for its sale and had advice as to its true value; and that he had also represented that the cash was committed to the wine and spirit company, whereas in fact it was available for capital dividends. They gave evidence of these representations; the documentary evidence included a letter in which the first respondent indicated that because of doubts as to legality he had been advised to keep the method of financing to himself. The appellants claimed rescission and alternatively damages. The respondents gave no evidence themselves but called expert witnesses. In the Supreme Court the action was dismissed. The plaintiffs appealed.

Held, allowing the appeal and awarding damages, 1. The respondent directors owed fiduciary duties to the shareholders, the circumstances from which their duties arose being the family character of the company; the position of father and son in the family and in the company; their high degree of inside knowledge; and the way in which they went about the take-over and the persuasion of shareholders. They were therefore obliged not to make to shareholders statements on matters material to the proposed dealing which were either deliberately or carelessly misleading, and to disclose material matters as to which they knew or had reason to believe that the shareholder whom they were trying to persuade to sell was inadequately informed. On the take-over bid, asset-backing was a material factor. On the facts breach of fiduciary duty and causation were established.

2. Per Woodhouse and Cooke JJ. The respondent directors, being admittedly under a duty of care in recommending shareholders to accept the take-over offer, were also in breach of that duty, in that the circumstances, including the knowledge of the directors as to asset-backing and the plan, the recommendation to sell at $4.80 was not made with reasonable care for the interests of shareholders.

3. Per Woodhouse and Casey JJ. As to fraud, which allegation was pursued on appeal against the first respondent only, although an appellate court will hesitate to differ from the trial judge on questions of fact upon the uncontradicted oral evidence of the appellants and the documentary evidence fraudulent misrepresentations by the first respondent had been established.

DEFENCES

Kinsella v. Alliance & Dublin Gas Consumers Co. Ltd
Barron J., October 5, 1982 (HC)

See *ante*, p. 168.

Howard Smith Ltd v. Ampol Petroleum Ltd.
[1974] A.C. 821

See *ante*, p. 273.

Clark v. Workman
[1920] 1 I.R. 107

Consideration was being given to reconstructing a company owned by two families, the Workmans and the Clarks. Negotiations began with a U.K. consortium with a view to the company being taken and after protracted discussions, the consortium offered to buy the company's shares. By this stage, the directors and shareholders were deeply divided about the company's future. At a board meeting which was attended by all eight directors, resolutions dealing with the transfer of a controlling interest in the company were passed with the casting vote of the chairman, the defendant. He had been elected to the chair in 1881, and since then he had acted as chairman without objection from any director (on this point, see ante, p. 195).

ROSS J.: [111] Prior to [this] meeting there had been no less than five attempts to deal with the matter, either by reconstruction or by the sale of all or portion of the shares of the company. No unfriendly attempt had been made to prevent Sir George Clark from purchasing. Everybody was willing to accept his offer until he withdrew it, on discovering that it had been made in error. But all this could not get rid of the fiduciary obligations incumbent on every director when he attended that all-important meeting on 26th November. They were bound to consider the interests of all the shareholders, unfettered by any undertaking or promise to any intending purchaser. They were bound to consider all offers, by whomsoever made, and they were bound to weigh and consider the desirability of admitting the persons or companies who proposed to come into their concern. If they failed in any of these matters, they disabled themselves from performing their duty to the shareholders, and nothing that they did would in the eye of the law be held to have been done in good faith.

The notice of motion now before me is for an interlocutory injunction until the hearing of the action or until further order restraining the defendant directors in respect of three matters: First, from approving of or voting in favour of a resolution approving of any sale or sales or transfers of shares of the company, submitted under Article 139 of the Company's Articles of Association, to any person or persons or body corporate without complying with the provisions of the said Article 139(2).

[112] The second matter in respect of which an injunction is required I pass over, as it is not pressed for, the present.

The third is that the defendant company and the named defendants be restrained from acting on the resolution of the directors passed at a meeting of the directors on 26th November, 1919, which resolution purports to have been carried by the casting vote of the defendant, Frank Workman.

I have granted an application of the plaintiffs that they be at liberty to amend the writ of summons by a statement that they are suing on behalf of themselves and other shareholders of the company associated with them.

There is no real controversy, as I have said, as to the facts, but there is much as to the proper inferences to be derived from these facts. There is no real controversy between the parties as to the legal principles, but there is much as to the application of these principles to the facts of the case.

We must first consider what is the position of a shareholder in this and similar companies. He does not hold his property simply at the mercy of the majority. His rights are carefully guarded, and his chief protection consists in the articles of association. Now, what do the articles of association amount to in point of law? They constitute a contract between every shareholder and all the others, and between the company itself and all the shareholders. It is a contract of the most sacred character, and it is on the faith of it that each shareholder advances his money (section 14 of the Companies Act 1908): *Wood v. Odessa Waterworks* (42 Ch. D. 636); see judgment of Farwell L.J. in *Salmon v. Quin* [1910] 1 Ch. 311 (*ante*, p. 435). Can this contract be altered or varied?

It can only be varied by a special resolution. A special resolution is defined by sect. 69 of the Act of 1908. It must first be passed as an extraordinary resolution, which requires a three-fourths majority of the shareholders at a general meeting, with notice of the extraordinary resolution. It must then be confirmed by a majority at a general meeting, held not earlier than fourteen days or later than a month after the first meeting, and there must be due notice of the special resolution.

It is therefore a matter of no small difficulty to alter the articles of association. In this case they cannot be altered, because [113] the plaintiffs contol only 55 per cent of the share capital, while the defendants control 45 per cent.

Again, the company is what is known as a private company. This means, according to sect. 121 of the Companies Act, a company that by its articles – (a) restricts the right to transfer its shares; (b) limits the number of its members to fifty; (c) prohibits any invitation to the public to subscribe for debentures or shares.

On 16th April, 1908, this company passed resolutions forming itself into a statutory private company. This was carried into effect by articles 138-142. By article 138 the directors can refuse to sanction (inter alia) a transfer to any transferee not approved by them. They need give no reason for refusal, and their decision is final. Article 139 provides the formal procedure which must be gone through in effecting a transfer of shares. Shareholders must give notice in writing, to be left at the office of the company, of their desire to sell. The directors have then a month to look about for a desirable purchaser. If they find a purchaser within a month, the shareholder is obliged to sell to him. If they do not, the shareholder may after a month sell to a person found by himself, but even then the directors may refuse to register the transfer.

What is the intent and meaning of these provisions? There must be bona fides. There must be no indirect motives. The directors are to act strictly as trustees in the matter of the transfers: *Bennett's Case* (5 De G.M. & G.)

In all cases bona fides is the test of the valid exercise of powers by trustees. An opportunity for deliberation in the full light of the facts and circumstances is impliedly required. I must say that I think it is hardly within the spirit of the articles that shareholders holding 55 per cent. of the shares should be allowed to declare their desire to sell at 12.30, and that at 2.30 the chairman, who had previously refused to give any information, should disclose the names of the proposed transferees. We are not to forget the magnitude and importance of the proposed operation. It is a strong proposition to assert that a majority is to overbear and stifle a minority when the intention is to do such a serious thing as to give a controlling interest in one company to [114] another company that is engaged in the same line of business, and that may be to some extent a rival company. Article 70 prohibits a person engaged in similar business from being a director of this company, and excludes a director of a similar company.

When the test of bona fides comes to be applied, all these matters and the surrounding circumstances call for the most careful attention. I refer in this connexion to the weighty observations of Lord Lindley when Master of the Rolls in *Allen v. Gold Reefs Co. of West Africa* [1900] 1 Ch. 656 (*ante*, p. 506). Even the statutory powers of altering articles of association by a special resolution must be exercised subject to those general principles of law and equity which are applicable to all powers enabling majorities to bind minorities. They 'must be exercised', says the learned Master of the Rolls, 'not only in the manner required by law, but also bona fide for the benefit of the company as a whole, and must not be exceeded. These conditions are always implied, and are seldom if ever expressed.' These observations refer to the exercise of powers by shareholders. They apply with augmented force when the powers are being exercised by directors.

There is one other matter of law affecting the case, and it is this: the powers given to directors are powers delegated to the directors by the company, and when once given the company cannot interfere in the subject-matter of the delegation unless by special resolution: *Automatic Self-Cleansing Filter Co. v. Cuninghame* [1906] 2 Ch. 34 (*ante*, p. 179).

I have stated the principles of law applicable to this case, and I now proceed to apply them. The first question that arises is whether Frank Workman was lawfully chairman of the meeting of directors on the 26th November. Since he was not, (see *ante*, p. 195) everything that was done was ultra vires and wholly inoperative. . . .

[115] But it is contended that this is an irregularity that can be cured by acquiescence. The office of chairman becomes important in connexion with the power to give a casting vote. The question of a casting vote never became material, so far as we know, until the meeting of the 26h November, 1919. I am therefore of opinion that Mr Frank Workman was not legally chairman at that meeting, and that the whole of the resolutions which were carried by his casting vote are inoperative, and of no effect. This decision is of merely transient importance, inasmuch as by Article 82 the number of directors may by a resolution at a general meeting be increased, provided the total number shall not exceed ten. [116] Consequently a nominee of the defendants can be elected by the majority which the defendants possess.

I now proceed to examine the more important questions, whether the matter was one of internal management, with which the Court cannot interfere, and whether the defendant directors were acting bona fide, with a view to the interests of the company as a whole. It has been pointed out by the Solicitor-General that they were not altogether abandoning the company. They are retaining twenty-five shares each, which is the amount that would qualify them to be elected directors. But when we come to figures, the importance of their remaining is comparatively small. In value they are selling £1,562,037 and retaining £7,783. Whence it appears that those directors who remain are more vitally interested in the success of the company than those who are departing.

The Solicitor-General and Mr Whitaker contended that the Court has no jurisdiction to interfere in a question of internal management. That proposition cannot be disputed. The Court has no right to say how much is to be distributed in dividends or how much is to be added to the reserve account; what contracts for material are to be accepted, what remuneration is to be paid to their employees and such like. All these things must be dealt with by the directors, and no Court can interfere so long as they are acting within their powers.

But what was the nature of the contemplated operation as distinguished from its expediency? On the question of its expediency I am not called on to express any opinion whatever. I do not presume, with my limited knowledge of this particular kind of business, to express an opinion, on which these most eminent men of business hold divided views. Great combinations of business establishments, banks, and railways are now deemed expedient by many. On the other hand, it was no doubt present to the minds of the plaintiffs that the fine quality of their work might be watered down by the introduction of these

English firms. The owners of the great shipping lines, who had found it a true economy to get the best work and the best material, might no longer resort to the company if it ceased to produce ships of the highest quality, as in the past. Which was right and which [117] was wrong I am not called on to decide. But I am obliged to decide whether it was a question of mere management or otherwise, and I am distinctly of the opinion that it was not. It was not a mere matter of the sale of shares. We must look at the contemplated results of the manifest intentions of the parties. It was a matter involving a complete transformation of the company– a fundamental alteration of policy from a policy of isolation to a policy of co-operation with a great syndicate in England, about which very little is known in this country. This operation could in no sense be held to be mere management. Furthermore, if it turns out that there was a breach of trust, that could never be a matter of internal management.

I must now consider the action of the defendant directors, their motives and intentions, and ascertain whether what they proposed and supported was, in the circumstances, inconsistent with a right performance of their fiduciary duty to the company. In the recent Scotch case of *Hindle and John Cotton Ltd.* (1919) 56 Sc.L.R. 625, Lord Finlay said: 'Where the question is one of abuse of powers, the state of mind of those who acted, and the motive in which they acted, are all important, and you may go into the question of what their intention was, collecting from the surrounding circumstances all the materials, which genuinely throw light upon that question of the state of mind of the directors, so as to show whether they were honestly acting in discharge of their powers in the interests of the company, or were acting from some by-motive, possibly of personal advantage, or for any other reason.'

I now refer to two uncontradicted statements in the affidavits. Par. 14 of R. W. Smith's affidavit: 'In my presence Frank Workman stated that he had promised the chairman of the Northumberland Shipbuilding Company, Ltd., that he would use his best endeavours to get the controlling interest in the defendant company into the hands of the chairman of the Northumberland Company, and that he would not attempt to get any better offer from anyone else.' We must take it that this represented the motives and intentions of Mr Frank Workman and those associated with him. By acting thus he had fettered himself by a promise to the [118] English syndicate, and had disqualified himself from acting bona fide in the interests of the company he was leaving. Again, take the affidavit of Sir George Clark, par. 10: 'I consider the offer of Robert Clark more beneficial to the shareholders who desire to sell than the offer of the Northumberland Shipbuilding Company or the Doxford Company, and I believe the defendant directors refused to consider it because they had entered into an agreement with the Northumberland Shipbuilding Company and the Doxford Company to force the sale of the control of the defendant company to them, even at the expense of the shareholders of the defendant company.' Sir George Clark swears that he believes the defendant directors are acting in the interest of the English syndicate, and not in the interest of the defendant company or its shareholders, and he states his belief that if the control is transferred to the syndicate the liquid assets of this company may be used for the purpose of buying debentures in the Northumberland Shipbuilding Company instead of for the benefit of the defendant company. Although this is not quite a statement as to facts, it is declared to be the belief of Sir George Clark. It was a challenge that required some answer, and no answer has been given. I desire it to be known that although I hold the defendants' action to have been wrongful and inconsistent with their duty as trustees, I do not in any way impute to them dishonourable conduct or anything in the nature of fraud. What they have done is analogous to cases we are all familiar with, where the donee of a power executes it in pursuance of an arrangement or bargain which he thinks erroneously he is entitled to make.

If I am right in my view of the law on the evidence, I am bound to make the two-fold order applied for, so as to prevent anything final being done to the prejudice of the plaintiffs before the trial of the action. When it does come to be tried it is quite possible that after discovery and interrogatories the case may assume a different complexion.

REMOVING DISSIDENTS

Re Bugle Press Ltd
[1961] Ch. 270

The company had 10,000 issued £1 shares, two members holding 4,500 shares each and the third member holding the remaining 1,000 shares. After differences arose between the first two members and the third 'minority' shareholder, the first two established another company, which then launched a take-over bid for Bugle Press Ltd. The bid was accepted by the first two members; and with 90 per cent of the shares in its hands, the bidder than sought to 'take out' the third shareholder under the U.K. near-equivalent to section 204 of the 1963 Act.

LORD EVERSHED M.R.: . . . [283] Mr Instone, in opening the appeal, put his case broadly as follows. First, he said: this case is within the four corners of the section upon the ordinary construction of its language; secondly, it follows that the onus must be upon the dissident shareholder to show that an order should be made otherwise than as the section envisages; and that argument, I interpolate, depends upon the language of the section which I have already read -'the transferee company shall, unless on an application made by the dissenting shareholder . . . the court thinks fit to order otherwise, be entitled and bound to acquire,' etc. Thirdly, Mr Instone conceded that he cannot in this case rely upon the mere fact that 90 per cent of the shareholders in this company did accept or were prepared to accept this offer, but, says he, since there was an independent valuation of the interest in the company held by the minority shareholder, he fails to discharge the onus which the section puts upon him. . . . [285] He freely accepts that the mechanism of the section has here been invoked by means of the incorporation of this holding company, Jackson & Shaw (Holdings) Ltd., especially for the purpose, and in order to enable the two persons, Shaw and Jackson, to expropriate the shares of their minority colleague, Treby. He says that although that is undoubtedly true, nevertheless, in the result, the case does fall within the strict language of the section and falling within it the consequences must follow. If that argument is right it would enable by a device of this kind the 90 per cent majority of the shareholders always to get rid of a minority shareholder whom they did not happen to like. And that, as a matter of principle, would appear to be contrary to a fundamental principle of our law that prima facie, if a man has a legal right which is an absolute right, then he can do with it or not do with it what he will. . . .

[286] Nevertheless, when regard is had to the opening words and to the parenthesis, it seems to me plain that what the section is directed to is a case where there is a scheme or contract for the acquisition of a company, its amalgamation, re-organisation or the like, and where the offeror is independent of the shareholders in the transferor company or at least independent of that part or fraction of them from which the 90 per cent is to be derived. Even, therefore, though the present case does fall strictly within the terms of section 209, the fact that the offeror, the transferee company, is for all practical purposes entirely equivalent to the nine-tenths of the shareholders who have accepted the offer, makes it in my judgment a case in which, for the purposes of exercising the court's discretion the circumstances are special – a case, therefore, of a kind contemplated by Maugham J. to which his general rule would not be applicable. It is no doubt true to say that it is still for the minority shareholder to establish that the discretion should be exercised in the way he seeks. That, I think, agreeing with Mr Instone, follows from the language of the section which uses the formula which I have already more than once read 'unless on an application made by the dissenting shareholder the court thinks fit to order otherwise'. But if the minority shareholder does show, as he shows here, that the offeror and the 90 per cent of the transferor company's shareholders are the same, then as it seems to me he has, prima facie, shown that the court ought otherwise to order, since if it should not so [287] do the result would be, as Mr Instone concedes, that the section has been used not for the purpose of any scheme of contract properly so called or contemplated by the section but for the quite different purpose of enabling majority shareholders to expropriate or evict the minority; and that, as it seems to me, is something for the purposes of which, prima facie, the court ought not to allow the section to be invoked – unless at any rate it were shown that there was some good reason in the interests of the company for so doing, for example, that the minority shareholder was in some way acting in a manner destructive or highly damaging to the interests of the company from some motives entirely of his own.

McCormick v. Cameo Investments Ltd.
McWilliam J., October 27, 1978

The defendant owned shares in the Central Hotel Ltd., which managed the hotel of that name in Exchequer Street, Dublin, until it closed in 1973. Subsequently, an offer was made by the defendant's parent company, Charterhouse (Ireland) Ltd. It bought out all the other shareholders and thereby acquired more than 90 per cent of the share capital. The plaintiffs then brought proceedings for a declaration that, notwithstanding, the defendant shall not be permitted to acquire his shares under the 1983 Act in a section 204 procedure. What particularly concerned them was that they wanted more information about an £800,000 loan the defendant had made to Central Hotel Ltd.

McWILLIAM J.: [5] The object of a multiplicity of associated companies is to save tax, to conceal the operations of the effective owners, to conceal the actual ownership of property, to conceal the control of businesses, and, by means of the foregoing to increase the profits of the enterprise with particular regard to the interests of the people in effective control.

Such arrangements are (though some may think unfortunately) perfectly lawful under the provisions of the [6] Companies Act and it has to be borne in mind that a series of transactions designed primarily to benefit the people and the company in effective control may also be to the advantage of the people and companies associated in subsidiary capacities. I emphasise this aspect of the matter because the applicants' case is, essentially, that the scheme is not fair to them, and they claim that the circumstances of the loan of £800,000 have not been adequately explained and that this makes it impossible for them to form an accurate opinion about the scheme and confirms their view that they are incurring a substantial loss under it.

I consider it unsatisfactory that they and I do not understand the full implications of the scheme and that a full and simple statement elucidating the ramifications of the group or groups of companies involved and the purpose and effect of this scheme has not been made, but I am only concerned with the scheme as it stands and the provisions of the statute enabling it to be put through and, the statutory provisions being complied with, the onus is on the applicants [7] to establish that it is unfair to them. *Re Hoare & Co. Ltd.* (150 L.T. 374) *Grierson, Oldham & Adams Ltd.* [1966] 1 Ch. 17. . . .

[8] [T]he applicants say that, in the present state of the property and commercial world, this is a most unsatisfactory time for them to sell their shares and that they will become much more valuable in the future. This is denied by the accountants for the respondent and by a director of the Ulster Investment Bank Limited who was brought in an independent advisory capacity before the scheme was submitted to the shareholders. His view was that the offer was a good one and that it is unlikely that the value of the shares will go above the price being offered although it is possible that it could do so.

The applicants further allege that there was oppression in that they were being expropriated by a company which has a majority shareholding. I was referred to the case of *Re Bugle Press* [1961] 1 Ch. 270 (*supra*, p. 562) although it is not suggested that the position here is as clear as it was in that case. Not only is the position not so clear but it seems to me that there is very little resemblance between the two cases, the main difference being that here there were several active and fairly substantial shareholders [9] well-informed in business matters who have accepted the scheme, to whose views I should pay the greatest attention. See *Grierson, Oldham & Adams Ltd.*, and *Re Bugle Press Ltd.*

The applicants also allege that there was oppression in that the loan of £800,000 being payable on demand should have been called in by the Transferor Company (Central Hotel Ltd) and suggest that it was due to the controlling interest of the respondent that it was not called in and no interest was paid in respect of it during the past three years. As this policy was not queried by the applicants at general meetings or otherwise until the scheme was propounded, I cannot accept that there is any evidence of oppression in this regard. It is not oppression for the directors to make an unsatisfactory decision in the conduct of the business of a company.

Finally, it is alleged that the scheme is, in effect, a breach of the provisions of section 60 of the Act in that the respondent owed the Transferor Company a great [10] deal more than is being paid for the shares and, therefore, it was the money of the Transferor Company which was being used to purchase its own shares. There is something to be said for this view of the scheme but I have the sworn testimony of Mr Crowley that he and another person were putting up the money by way of advance to the respondent for the purchase of the shares and that the respondent had not the money either to repay the loan or purchase the shares. I have no information as to the terms of this advance to the respondent but Mr Crowley stated that he and the other person were the main shareholders in the respondent, and they obviously thought it was to their advantage to make the advance. I am not satisfied that he is correct in saying that their major motivation was to see that the shareholders of the Transferor Company should receive the full price for their shares, but this does not alter the fact that the money for the purchase has been financed by another loan. Accordingly I hold that there has not been any breach of the provisions of section 60.

In re National Bank Ltd
[1966] 1 All E.R. 1006

The National Bank, which had many branches in Ireland, also had branches in England, was registered as a company there and its head office was in London. An elaborate scheme of arrangement was devised to enable the Bank of

Ireland to take over National's Irish business and assets, and to enable a Scottish bank to take over its English business and assets. In brief, National's Irish affairs were to be transferred to a new Irish company, N.B.I., in return for shares in it; and those shares would then be sold to the Bank of Ireland in return for cash and renounceable loan stock, which would be distributed pro rata to National's shareholders once the scheme was approved by a special resolution. This was a scheme of arrangement under the U.K. equivalent of section 201 of the 1963 Act. At a meeting convened to consider the scheme, 90 per cent of those attending (61 per cent of the voting shares) supported it.

PLOWMAN J.: . . . [1008] [I]f the scheme is sanctioned, the Irish business of National Bank will be vested in N.B.I., which will become a wholly-owned subsidiary of the Bank of Ireland, while the remaining business of National Bank, that is to say, the other third of its business and its membership of the Committee of London Clearing Banks, will continue to belong to National Bank, which will become a wholly owned subsidiary of the Scottish Bank. Subject to this it will be a case of 'business as usual'.

The opposition to this petition comes in at sub-para. (d) and (e) of para. 4 of that circular, which I have just read and need not read again, and it is based on two propositions. In the first place, it is submitted that the court will not approve a scheme under section 206 of the Companies Act, 1948 (cf. section 201 of the 1963 Act) if the explanatory statement under section 207 does not fully and fairly disclose all material facts, and that circular which I have just read and need not read again, and its based on is then said that the circular to which I have been referring does not give this information. The second proposition is this, that where an arrangement under section 206 is in essence a scheme or contract for the purchase by an outsider of all the issued shares of the company the court should not approve the arrangement unless both (i) the petitioner proves on full disclosure that the price is fair and (ii) the arrangement is approved by the ninety per cent majority referred to in section 209 (it is 80 per cent in section 204 of the 1963 Act). It is said that this arrangement is one of that section 209 character and has not been approved by the appropriate majority. I should perhaps add this, that no part of the opposition's case here casts any reflection whatever on the bona fides of anybody propounding the scheme.

As regards the first proposition the case put forward by National Bank is this. It agrees that full disclosure of the value of the assets and the amount of liabilities has not been made, but says that it is putting forward this arrangement on the basis that a full disclosure of those matters shall be deliberately withheld, and it submits that nevertheless the scheme is a fair one which the court should sanction. This attitude arises from the fact that National Bank is a bank and subject to the special statutory provisions of Part 3 of Sch. 8 to the Companies Act, 1948. Those provisions exempt banks from disclosing in their accounts certain information (which I will call 'exempt information') which

ordinary trading companies are required by Part 1 of that schedule to disclose.
. . .

[1011] I should perhaps also refer to an affidavit which was sworn by Mr Carroll, the Governor of the Bank of Ireland, in which he says this:

> "All the banks which were parties to the negotiations and which will be concerned in carrying the scheme into effect agreed and proceeded on the basis that none of the banks would be required to disclose any information which under the exemptions in Sch. 8 to the Companies Act, 1948, and the corresponding provision in Ireland, it would not be required to disclose in its accounts. As far as the Irish Bank is concerned this was a vital requirement. It was for the foregoing reason and in order to protect the interests of all parties concerned that Messrs. Cooper Brothers & Co. were instructed to make an investigation of [National Bank] and they have stated that an aggregate consideration of 56s. 6d. in respect of each share of [National Bank] is fair and reasonable."

Mr Macdonald, the chairman of the Scottish Bank, swore an affidavit to the same effect as that of Mr Carroll. Mr Rait also gave evidence before me as to the reason why the disclosure of exempt information might prejudice the bank and its shareholders and he explained that if competitors have a greater knowledge of your business than you have of theirs you are at a disadvantage.

It was for reasons such as these that National Bank has put forward an arrangement which preserves inviolate exempt information but at the same time, within that framework attempts to produce a scheme which will appeal to an ordinary intelligent man as a fair commercial proposition.

[1012] Counsel for National Bank, in regard to the question of fairness, points out that independent accountants of eminence in their profession were instructed to make a detailed investigation and all relevant information, including the exempt information, was made available to them. They say in their report that the compensation offered was fair and reasonable. Secondly, two other firms of eminent accountants, namely, the joint auditors, are of the same opinion as Cooper Brothers & Co., and the board of National Bank unanimously recommended the acceptance of the proposals.

Reference was also made to the substantial profit which on current values the shareholders are able to see. In October last the Stock Exchange quotation for National Bank shares was a shilling or two under £2. In January of this year it had risen to 56s. 6d. A comparison was also made of the income position. On last year's dividend of sixteen per cent a holder of one hundred 10s. shares received £8 gross. If the arrangement is sanctioned he will get £100 of seven per cent loan stock producing £7 gross and £182 10s. in cash, which on a five per cent basis would produce £9 2s. 6d. gross, making a total of £16 2s. 6d. as compared with £8. All these matters are prayed in aid of the submission that within its self-imposed limits the scheme is a fair one.

The question, however, which I have to consider is whether the deliberate omission to disclose exempt information is fatal to the arrangement despite the weight of the evidence that the compensation is fair and despite the evidence that the disclosure of exempt information might result in damage to all the shareholders. In my judgment the answer to that question is No.

The principles on which the court acts in an application under section 206 are well settled and are stated in *Buckley On The Companies Acts* (13th Edn.) p. 409 as follows:

> "In exercising its power of sanction the court will see, first, that the provisions of the statute have been complied with [I interpolate there that no question arises with regard to that matter]; secondly, that the class was fairly represented by those who attended the meeting and that the statutory majority are acting bona fide and are not coercing the minority in order to promote interests adverse to those of the class whom they purport to represent [nothing arises on that] and thirdly, that the arrangement is such as an intelligent and honest man, a member of the class concerned and acting in respect of his interest, might reasonably approve."

I comment there that in fact very nearly four thousand shareholders did approve. Then the passage goes on:

> "The court does not sit merely to see that the majority are acting bona fide and thereupon to register the decision of the meeting; but at the same time the court will be slow to differ from the meeting unless, either the class has not been properly consulted, or the meeting has not considered the matter with a view to the interests of the class which it is empowered to bind, or some blot is found in the scheme."

It is against the background of those principles that the opposition to this scheme has to be considered.

Section 206 and section 207 say nothing about disclosure either of valuations or of profits or of assets or of liabilities. By section 206 the court is given the widest possible discretion to approve any sort of arrangement between a company and its shareholders. It seems to me that to say that full disclosure must be made of all material facts begs the question of the nature of the scheme which is being propounded. The extent of the disclosure required must depend on the nature of the scheme. Here the scheme is one which is based on the withholding of exempt information. If the evidence satisfies me (as it does) that the scheme is fair I see no reason why I should not sanction it.

As regards counsel for the opposing shareholders' second objection, namely, that the scheme really ought to be treated as a section 209 case needing a ninety per cent [1013] majority, I cannot accede to that proposition. In the first place, it seems to me to involve imposing a limitation or qualification either on the generality of the word 'arrangement' in section 203 or else on the discretion of the court under that section. The legislature has not seen fit to impose any such limitation in terms, and I see no reason for implying any. Moreover, the two sections . . . involve quite different considerations and different approaches. Under section 206 an arrangement can only be sanctioned if the question of its fairness has first of all been submitted to the court. Under section 209, on the other hand, the matter may never come to the court at all. If it does come to the court then the onus is cast on the dissenting minority to demonstrate the unfairness of the scheme. There are, therefore, good reasons for requiring a smaller majority in favour of a scheme under section 206 than the majority which is required under section 209 if the minority is to be expropriated.

CHAPTER 13

Transactions with Outsiders

The vast majority of companies are formed with a view to their doing business with persons other than their principal shareholders or directors, *i.e.* with 'outsiders'. A major problem, therefore, is when or in what circumstances contracts and engagements with outsiders which are purported to be entered into by or on behalf of a company are legally binding on it. Since companies by their very nature can act only through individuals, or agents, it must first be established that the person negotiating the transaction in question is authorised by the company to do so. Secondly, persons apparently authorised to act for the company in a particular way in fact may not have authority to do so. The transaction in question may even be *ultra vires*, or the company's regulations may place other restrictions on the agent's power to act. Subject to what is said below, since companies' memoranda and articles of association are public documents, outsiders dealing with companies are deemed to know the contents of such documents; accordingly, they are deemed to have 'constructive notice' of companies' objects and any other restrictions that those documents impose on company agents' authority. In the past, companies would not be bound by contracts made on their behalf but contrary to such restrictions. Nor would companies be held to contracts made for them before they were incorporated. Nor could companies ratify either *ultra vires* or pre-incorporation contracts. Doing business with companies. therefore, presented special risks in that undertakings entered into with them could transpire not to be legally binding on them.

These very questions were the subject of the E.C. First Directive on Company Law. According to the central part of the Directive's preamble:

> Whereas the basic documents of the company should be disclosed in order that third parties may be able to ascertain their contents and other information concerning the company, especially particulars of the persons who are authorised to bind the company; Whereas the protection of third parties must be ensured by provisions which restrict to the greatest possible extent the grounds on which obligations entered into in the name of the company are not valid; . . .

FORMALITIES

See *Company Law*, pp. 423–424.

Companies Act 1963, sections 38–39

Form of contracts

38.—(1) Contracts on behalf of a company may be made as follows:

(*a*) a contract which if made between private persons would be by law required to be in writing and to be under seal, may be made on behalf of the company in writing under the common seal of the company;

(*b*) a contract which if made between private persons would be by law required to be in writing, signed by the parties to be charged therewith, may be made on behalf of the company in writing, signed by any person acting under its authority, express or implied;

(*c*) a contract which if made between private persons would by law be valid although made by parol only, and not reduced into writing may be made by parol on behalf of the company by any person acting under its authority, express or implied.

(2) A contract made according to this section shall bind the company and its successors and all other parties thereto.

(3) A contract made according to this section may be varied or discharged in the same manner in which it is authorised by this section to be made.

Bills of exchange and promissory notes

39.—A bill of exchange or promissory note shall be deemed to have been made, accepted or endorsed on behalf of a company, if made, accepted or endorsed in the name of or by or on behalf or on account of, the company by any person acting under its authority.

PRE-INCORPORATION AGREEMENTS

See *Company Law*, pp.425–427.

Companies Act 1963, section 37

Contracts, Deeds and Powers of Attorney

Pre-incorporation contracts

37.—(1) Any contract or other transaction purporting to be entered into by a company prior to its formation or by any person on behalf of the company prior to its formation may be ratified by the company after its formation and thereupon the company shall become bound by it and entitled to the benefit thereof as if it had been in existence at the date of such contract or other transaction and had been a party thereto.

(2) Prior to ratification by the company the person or persons who purported to act in the name or on behalf of the company shall in the absence of express agreement to the contrary be personally bound by the contract or other transaction and entitled to the benefit thereof.

HKN Investment OY v. Incotrade PVT Ltd
[1993] 3 I.R. 157

There was a dispute about the ownership of money in bank accounts that was obtained through a fraud, which was carried out by several individuals through the first named defendant, the company. Some of the transactions that were part of this fraud involved contracts purportedly with that company, but which had been made prior to its incorporation. The company had since been put into liquidation and one of the issues was whether the company or its liquidator could ratify those contracts, thereby rendering them enforceable by the company.

COSTELLO J.: [159] I propose now to consider the law in relation to pre-incorporation contracts. In so doing, however, it is to be borne in mind that this case concerns the beneficial ownership of monies paid under pre-incorporation contracts and not the enforceability of such contracts.

(i) At common law
It is well established that because a company before incorporation has no capacity to contract it follows that nobody can contract on behalf of an unincorporated company. This means that a pre-incorporation contract could not, at common law, be ratified by the company after incorporation (but it could, of course, enter into a new contract after incorporation to put into effect the terms of the pre-incorporation contract). A pre-incorporation contract which is purported to be made on behalf of a company which does not exist is in fact a nullity (see Palmer *"Company Law'* 1987 Ed. para. 20.02 and *Newborne v. Sensolid (Great Britain) Ltd* [1954] 1 Q.B. 45).

(ii) Statute
The rigours of, and possible injustices flowing from, the strict common law rules were modified by statute. Section 37 of the Companies Act 1963 ("the Act of 1963") provides:–

"Any contract or other transaction purporting to be entered into by a company prior to its formation or by any person on behalf of the company prior to its formation may be ratified by the company after its formation and thereupon the company shall become bound by it and entitled to the benefit thereof as if it had been in existence [160] at the date of such contract or other transaction and have been a party thereto."

In this case a question of fact arises as to whether or not the first defendant ratified any of the pre-incorporation contracts which were made prior to its incorporation.

I do not think that any formal meeting to ratify must be shown to have taken place before this section can be applied. Each case must depend on its own facts, but it seems to me that ratification can in certain circumstances occur informally, for example, in a one man company where, after incorporation, the controlling shareholder implements the contract without the benefit of a formal board meeting. However, in this case no evidence of any sort has been produced to permit the court to infer a post-incorporation ratification of any of the pre-incorporation contracts and I do not think that I can infer such ratification from the mere acceptance by the principal shareholder of sums paid by way of commission.

It has been urged on behalf of the liquidator of the first defendant that he can now ratify the pre-incorporation contracts under section 37 of the Act of 1963. In principle, I can see no reason why this could not be done – the first defendant remains in existence after an order has been made to wind it up (or, in the case of voluntary liquidations when the resolutions required by the Act of 1963 have been passed) and what has to be ascertained is whether the liquidator has any statutory powers to ratify conferred by the Act of 1963. Certainly, no express powers are to be found but section 231(2)(i) empowers liquidators "to do all such other things as may be necessary for winding-up the affairs of the company and for distributing its assets". As section 37 of the Act of 1963 confers a statutory right on a company to obtain the benefits of pre-incorporation contracts and as this statutory right may properly be regarded as an asset conferred on companies by the section, it seems to me that the powers conferred by section 231(2)(i) includes a power to ratify pre-incorporation contracts as by this means assets could be obtained for distribution to the first defendant's creditors which otherwise would not be available.

But can the liquidator properly ratify these particular contracts? They contained provisions that (a) the first defendant would render certain services, and (b) that if it did not do so within 30 days the commission would be repayable. This means that the act of ratification would be in respect of a contract under which the other party is entitled to a return of the money paid under it at the date of ratification, and in respect of which the first defendant had undertaken obligations which [161] it had failed to fulfil and which the liquidator could not fulfil after ratification. But I do not think that the pre-ratification breach of a term of a contract which can be brought into existence under the section means that the contract cannot be ratified. Ratification brings into existence an agreement which would otherwise be a nullity, and it creates contractual rights and obligations on the basis that it had always had a legal existence. Ratification in this case will mean that as a matter of law the preincorporation contracts will have existed from their date of execution – it will not affect the rights of either party arising from the manner in which the contract has or has not been performed since then. I will therefore declare that the liquidator is entitled to ratify the pre-incorporation contracts entered into on behalf of the first defendant prior to its incorporation.

Ratification, however, will not determine the issue that arises on this motion – namely, the beneficial ownership of the monies in the accounts to which I have referred. To determine that issue it is necessary to refer to and apply the principles of equity which, it seems to me, will apply whether the contracts are ratified or not.

CAPACITY AND *ULTRA VIRES* ENGAGEMENTS

See *Company Law*, pp. 427–433.

In re M.J. Cummins Ltd
[1939] I.R. 60

The shareholders decided that the company's business should be sold to Mr Cummins for £3,000. He did not possess that money but a scheme was made with the bank whereby the bank would advance money to the company, which would then put him into sufficient funds to acquire the company's entire share capital.

JOHNSTON J.: . . . [64] The exercise by the company of its borrowing powers was, as I have indicated, clearly an act *ultra vires* the powers of the company, and it is contended on behalf of the liquidator that the bank, at the time when they advanced this sum were well aware that company was exceeding its powers and that no valid debt was thereby incurred which – so far, at any rate, as the innocent trade creditors of the company are concerned – can be relied upon by the bank.

Now, there are certain propositions of the law which have been advanced on behalf of the bank with which I entirely agree. For instance, it is the law that while a proposed lender in his dealings with a public company must be presumed to have notice of the provisions of its memorandum and articles of association, he is not called upon in the case of a company which has a general power of borrowing, to make any inquiries as to the purpose of the loan in order to make sure that that purpose is within the powers of the company. That proposition is very conveniently illustrated in the case of *In re David Payne &* *[65] Co., Ltd.* [1904] 2 Ch. 608, where it was further decided that knowledge on the part of the lender that the money was intended to be misapplied will avoid the loan. In the same case it was held that knowledge, on the part of a director of the lenders, of the *ultra vires* purpose for which the loan is being got will not be imputed to the lending company if the person having such knowledge has a personal interest in the transaction. That principle, however, does not apply to the present case.

The main question in the case, therefore, is whether the bank had knowledge of the wrongful purpose for which this money was being raised; and, having analysed all the circumstances connected with the loan, I am satisfied that not only had the bank the fullest knowledge of that purpose, but the local Agent of the bank in Mullingar . . . was the person who arranged the ingenious plan by which the loan was carried through; so that, so far as the bank's participation in the affair is concerned, the case goes far beyond the question of mere knowledge. In saying so much I do not wish it to be thought that I am imputing to the bank blame of any kind. I think that the mistake took place through a failure, to appreciate the limitations that must be read into Article 3 (o) of the memorandum of association and the realities as to the purpose of the loan . . . .

[69] [T]he matter that the liquidator has brought before me . . . involves only a question as between the claims of a number of ordinary trading creditors and the claim of the bank founded upon an *ultra vires* transaction of the company of which they had notice; but, out of courtesy to the learned counsel for the bank, I think that I should say a word or two as to a number of extraneous matters.

First of all, it is almost unnecessary to say that a company cannot ratify an act of its own or an act of its directors which is outside and beyond the constitutional powers of the company. If such a thing were possible it would mean an end for ever of the salutary principle [70] of *ultra vires*. There are cases in which the *ultra vires* acts of directors have been held to be ratified by the conduct of the company; but those were cases in which the acts, if done by the company, would have been *intra vires*. In the case of *The Ashbury Railway Carriage & Iron Co. v. Riche* (L.R. 7 H.L. 653), Lord Cairns said: 'It would be perfectly fatal to the whole scheme of legislation . . . if you were to hold that, in the first place, directors might do that which even the whole company could not do, and that then, the shareholders finding out what had been done, could sanction subsequently what they could not antecedently have authorised,' and Lord Hatherly laid down a proposition which is very pertinent in the present case; 'I think that the Legislature had in view the object of protecting outside dealers and contractors with this limited company from the funds of the company being applied . . . for any other object whatsoever than those specified in the memorandum of association.' Similarly Lord Macnaghten in the case of *Trevor v. Whitworth* (12 A.C. 409), quoting Cotton L.J., said that no part of the capital of a company 'can be returned to a member so as to take away from the fund to which the creditors have a right to look as that out of which they are to be paid.' This matter has been very neatly summed up in the following proposition which I take from Mr Howard A. Street's excellent text-book on *Ultra vires*. The learned author says: 'No act which is *ultra vires* of the corporation itself can be validated by ratification or acquiescence, or otherwise than by statute.'

The learned counsel for the bank then discussed at length the law as to subrogation and tracing orders, and endeavoured by some such means to place the bank's claim on an equality with the debts of the ordinary trading creditors. There is here a confusion of thought which must be set right. When an *ultra vires* act is committed by a borrowing company, on the one hand, and by a lending company, on the other, no debt, common law, equitable or otherwise, is thereby created in favour of the latter as against the former. The theory of the law is that the whole transaction is null and void and can give rise to no legal rights or claims whatever. In dealing with a limited company, which must act strictly within its constitution, a contracting party must watch his step; and in regard to this liability there is no difference between a family company and a great trading corporation. As was said by that master of clear-thinking and lucid exposition – Lord Macnaghten – in *Trevor* [71] *v. Whitworth*, 'a family company . . . does not limit its trading to the family circle. If it takes the benefit of the Act, it is bound by the Act as much as any other company. It can have no special privilege or immunity.' In the *Ashbury* case, Lord Cairns quotes with approval the following words of Blackburn J., in all their useful harshness, as to the effect of an *ultra vires* transaction: 'I do not entertain any doubt that if, on the true construction of a statute creating a corporation it appears to be the intention of the Legislature, expressed or implied, that the corporation shall not enter into a particular contract, every Court, whether of law or equity, is bound to treat a contract entered into contrary to the enactment as illegal, and therefore wholly void.'

It frequently happened, however, that corporations, found themselves with surplus assets in their hands, after the ordinary creditors had been paid in full, and the anxious question then arose whether the shareholders of the company were to be allowed to make a profit for themselves by means of the money which had been wrongly or mistakenly advanced by their partner in the *ultra vires* transaction. That question was discussed at great length in the great case of *Sinclair v. Brougham* [1914] A.C. 398 (the celebrated *Birkbeck Bank* case), in which a building society had opened a bank and had taken huge sums, amounting to millions of pounds, from depositors. In the liquidation of the company, after the ordinary creditors had been paid in full, a large surplus remained in the hands of the liquidators, and the question arose whether that sum should be paid to certain classes of members of the building society – that is, whether the surplus in its entirety was assets of the society – or should be paid back in whole or in part to the depositors (the lenders). The problem before the House was how to work out 'the higher equity that no one has a right to keep either property or the proceeds of property which does not belong to him,' without trenching upon the principle of *ultra vires*. The anxious search of the Law Lords, set out in fifty pages of the Law Reports, for a formula which would on the one hand, be based upon sound principles of equity, and, on the other would not be a mere good-natured gesture, is the most remarkable illustration of which I am aware of the meticulous care with which that House approaches the task of reconciling what is called 'abstract justice' with the strict rule of law. In the result, it was pointed out [72] that that reconcilement could be effected either through the principle of subrogation (the principle, as Lord Dunedin explained, that if the lender could show that the borrowed moneys had been expended in paying the just debts of the borrower, the lender would be entitled *pro tanto* to the benefit of the relief that the borrower had thereby gained), or through the principle that the money that was lent was not a debt, but was trust money that the lender might follow by means of a tracing order.

But these considerations have no applicability to the present case. Neither principle could possibly be brought into operation in a contest between the genuine creditors of a company and a person who had lent money to the company under an arrangement that was 'illegal and therefore wholly void.' In the *Birkbeck Bank* case, the ordinary creditors had been paid in full, and their right to that treatment was not controverted. Lord Dunedin (at p. 437) says that the trade creditors were, in his judgment, 'rightly paid, under the circumstances of the actual case, and had they not been, they would stand, after expenses of the liquidation, as first in the ranking. For, in a question with shareholders, we are told that they were debts of a character which the directors had a power to make. And in a question with the depositors [the lenders] they were incurred in a business, illegally carried on no doubt, as for the society, but yet one which the depositors had been willing that the directors should carry on.' That is exactly the question that arises in the present case, and it seems to me that this proposition of Lord Dunedin determines it. Lord Sumner seems to express the same view in a passage at p. 459, and the implications that are to be drawn from a passage in Lord Haldane's judgment at p. 414 are to the same effect.

The case of *Re National Permanent Benefit Building Society* (1869) L.R. 5 Ch. 309, seems to me to afford further authority – if such is needed – for the conclusion at which I have arrived. The case decides that if the bank had applied for the winding up of M.J. Cummins Ltd., claiming to be creditors by virtue of the loan that had been made, the Court would have been obliged to refuse the order. In that case a lender who had advanced an *ultra vires* loan was held to be unable to get a winding up order, and Romilly M.R. who had made such an order, was reversed. Giffard L.J. held that there was no debt, either legal or equitable owing to the petitioners and that therefore they could not ask for the [73] winding-up of the company. He said that if the lenders had any rights founded in equity, either against the property of this company, which was pledged to them, or against the persons to whom the money was lent, 'they can only be asserted by filing a bill and taking a very different proceeding from that which has been taken here.' In other words, he held that there could be no controversy between the *ultra vires* lenders and the creditors of the society, but that the former persons might establish rights as against the persons to whom the money was lent or against the property to which it could be traced.

The last case to which I need refer is that of the *Bank of Ireland v. Cogry Flax-Spinning Co. Ltd* [1900] 1 I.R. 219, in which Porter M.R., in the course of the winding-up of a one-man company, found that certain debentures which had been issued to a supposedly secured creditor were 'issued without authority and without consideration' and that 'they do not bind the assets as against the creditors.'

In this judgment I have said nothing as to the collateral security which the bank insisted upon getting not only from Mr Cummins but from Mr T.J. Dowdall as well – the guarantee for the whole debt from Cummins, the promissory note from the two of them and the guarantee for £500 from Dowdall; but it might be said that all this suggests at least a certain amount of misgiving in the mind of the bank as to the entire regularity of the transaction with M.J. Cummins Ltd. It is satisfactory to know, however, that the taking of this wise precaution on the part of the bank may have useful consequences in regard to the balance owing to them.

Rolled Steel Products (Holdings) Ltd. v. British Steel Corp.
[1986] Ch. 246

See *ante*, p. 110.

Companies Act 1963, section 8(1)

Modification of the *ultra vires* rule

8.—(1) Any act or thing done by a company which if the company had been empowered to do the same would have been lawfully and effectively done, shall, notwithstanding that the company had no power to do such act or thing, be effective in favour of any person relying on such act or thing who is not shown to have been actually aware, at the time when he so relied thereon, that such act or thing was not within the powers of the company, but any director or officer of the company who was responsible for the doing by the company of such act or thing shall be liable to the company for any loss or damage suffered by the company in consequence thereof.

European Communities (Companies) Regulations 1973, S.I. No. 163 of 1973, regulation 6

Organs authorised to bind company

6. (1) In favour of a person dealing with a company in good faith, any transaction entered into by any organ of the company, being its board of directors or any person registered under these regulations as a person authorised to bind the company, shall be deemed to be within the capacity of the company and any limitation of the powers of that board or person, whether imposed by the memorandum or articles of association or otherwise, may not be relied upon as against any person so dealing with the company.

(2) Any such person shall be presumed to have acted in good faith unless the contrary is proved.

(3) For the purpose of this Regulation, the registration of a person authorised to bind the company shall be effected by delivering to the registrar of companies a notice giving the name and description of the person concerned.

Northern Bank Finance Corp. Ltd v. Quinn
[1979] I.L.R.M. 221

The first defendant's unlimited company guaranteed a loan to him from a bank. Keane J. held (*ante*, p. 127) that the guarantee was outside the company's objects and, further, that the company could not retrospectively extend its objects to encompass that guarantee. Section 8(1) of the 1963 Act then called for consideration.

KEANE J.: . . . [228] I think that the probabilities are that Mr O'Connell (the bank's solicitor) did read the objects clause of the memorandum; it would be surprising if he did not, since it was furnished to him so that he could satisfy himself as to the existence in law of the company and its power to enter into the proposed transaction. It may well be that, as is not uncommon with busy practitioners when dealing with [228] matters of this nature, his eye travelled reasonably rapidly over a number of the clauses. But I think that the probabilities are that he did read the memorandum and came to the conclusion that the execution of the guarantee and the mortgage was within the powers of the company. Had he come to any other conclusion, I have not the slightest doubt but that he would have advised his principals not to close the transaction until the necessary amendment had been effected to the memorandum. It follows that Mr O'Connell was aware of the contents of the objects clause of the memorandum, but must have mistakenly believed that they empowered the company to execute the guarantee and mortgage. It would not have been in accordance with his normal practice to dispense with reading the memorandum and I have no reason to suppose that he departed from his normal practice on this occasion. It is, of course, inconceivable that he appreciated the lack of vires but simply did not do anything about it.

The question accordingly arises as to whether, in these circumstances, the bank were 'actually aware', within the meaning of section 8 (1) of the lack of *vires*. Mr O'Neill SC submitted that the language of section 8(1) clearly demonstrated that the onus of establishing actual knowledge within the meaning of the section is on the person who asserts that such knowledge existed and that, accordingly, the onus was on the company, to establish that the bank were 'actually aware' of the lack of vires. This may very well be so, but I do not think it is material to the issue which has to be resolved in the present case. There is no conflict as to the facts in the present case; Mr O'Connell was the only witness on this issue and he was called by the bank. The only question that arises is as to whether, having regard to that evidence and the inferences, which, in my view, necessarily follow from it, the bank can be said to have been 'actually aware' of the lack of *vires*.

Mr O'Neill SC submitted that actual, as distinguished from constructive, notice of the lack of vires was essential if a third party was to lose the protection of section 8 (1). I accept that this is so: altogether apart from authority, the language used would suggest that what the legislature had in mind was actual and not constructive notice. Moreover, to interpret the section in any other way would be to frustrate its manifest object. While there is no authority of which counsel were aware or which I have been able to discover on the section, the mischief which it was designed to avoid is clear. Prior to the enactment of the section, all persons dealing with a company were deemed to have notice of the contents of the company's public documents, including its memorandum and articles. If a transaction was *ultra vires*, the other party to it, speaking generally, had no rights at all. The manifest injustice and inconvenience which followed from this rule is amply illustrated by the decision in *Re John Beauforte Ltd.* [1953] Ch. 131, which was referred to in the argument.

But if constructive notice can still be relied on in answer to a party claiming the protection of this section, the protection in question would be, to a significant extent, eroded. It is clear, moreover, that the doctrine of constructive notice should not normally be applied to purely commercial transactions, such as the advancing of money. (See the observations of Mr Justice Kenny delivering the judgment of the Supreme Court in *Bank of Ireland Finance Ltd. v. Rockfield Ltd.* [1979] I.R. 2 1, *ante*, p. 359).

But while I am satisfied that the doctrine of constructive notice does not apply [229] to the sub-section under consideration, this does not dispose of the matter. The Bank, because of the knowledge of their Agent, Mr O'Connell, which must be imputed to them, were aware of the objects of the company. There were no further *facts* of which they could be put on notice. But they failed to draw the appropriate inference from those facts, *i.e.* that the transaction was *ultra vires*. Mr O'Neill submits that, even accepting this to be so, this is not the actual knowledge which the section contemplates.

A great number of transactions are entered into every day by companies, public and private, without any of the parties looking at the memorandum in order to see whether the transaction in question is in fact authorised by the memorandum. I think it probable that, on the occasions when the memorandum is looked at before a transaction is entered into, it is normally because the company's solicitor or a solicitor for a third party wishes to satisfy himself that the proposed transaction is *intra vires* the memorandum. I think it is clear that the section was designed to ensure that, in the first category of cases, persons who had entered into transactions in good faith with the company without ever reading the memorandum and accordingly with no actual knowledge that the transaction was *ultra vires* were not to suffer. I can see no reason in logic or justice why the legislature should have intended to afford the same protection to persons who had actually read the memorandum and simply failed to appreciate the lack of vires. The maxim *ignorantia juris haud neminem excusat* may not be of universal application, but this is certainly one situation where it seems fair that it should apply.

This is best illustrated by an example. The directors of a public company decide to invest the bulk of the company's resources in a disastrous property speculation as a result of which the company suffers enormous losses. The company in fact had no power to enter into any such transaction, but the Vendors' dolicitors, although furnished with the memorandum and articles, failed to appreciate this. If the submission advanced on behalf of the bank in this case is well founded, it would mean that, in such circumstances, the innocent shareholders would be the victims rather than the Vendors. There seems no reason why the consequences of the vendors' failure to appreciate the lack of vires should be visited on the heads of the blameless shareholders. I do not overlook the fact that the sub-section gives the company a remedy against any director or officer of the company who is responsible for the *ultra vires* act; but such a remedy may not necessarily enable the innocent shareholder to recoup all his losses.

It is interesting in this context to note that in the United Kingdom the Jenkins Committee recommended that even actual knowledge of the contents of the memorandum should not deprive a third party of his right to enforce a contract if he honestly and reasonably failed to appreciate that they precluded the company or its officers from entering into the contract. (See Cmnd. 1749, paras, 35–42). Writing in the early days of the operation of our Act, Mr Alexis Fitzgerald said of section 8:

> "The draughtsmen wisely reject the advice of the *Jenkins Committee*, which would have given contractual rights even to third parties with actual knowledge, where such a third party could prove he honestly and reasonably failed to appreciate the effect of the lack of power. Acceptance of this recommendation would have created uncertain and there-

fore bad law." (See 'A Consideration of the Companies Act 1948, the Companies Act (Northern Ireland) 1960, and Companies' Act 1963', *The Irish Jurist* Volume One (New Series) Part One at p. 16)

[230] In England, the *ultra vires* rule was modified by section 9 (1) of the European Communities Act 1972, and while the language of the section is different from that of section 8 of our 1963 Act, the requirement being that the third party should have acted in good faith, it is interesting to note that the editors of the 22nd edition of *Palmer's Company Law* take the view that it would not protect the third party in circumstances such as the present. (See Volume One, p. 97).

I am satisfied that, where a party is shown to have been actually aware of the contents of the memorandum but failed to appreciate that the company were not empowered thereby to enter into the transaction in issue, section 8(1) has no application. It follows that, in the present case, the bank cannot successfully rely on section 8 (1). . . .

Finally, Mr O'Neill SC submitted that the company were estopped at this stage from contesting the validity of the guarantee. He concedes that the doctrine of estoppel could not enable the company validly to perform an act which was *ultra vires*; but submits that as the company had been empowered since the 18th May, 1974, to enter into the transaction, they cannot now be heard to say that it is *ultra vires*. In particular, he relies on a letter written by the company to the Bank on 31 December 1976, in which they said

[231] As you are aware, this company has guaranteed the borrowings from the corporation of Mr Fursey Quinn.

Please let us have details, in confidence, of the guaranteed borrowings in relation to the amount outstanding including interest, the amount and timing of repayments made and interest paid to date.

Mr O'Neill SC points out that the bank had power at any time to call in the amount of the loan; and that, following the receipt of this letter, they acted to their detriment by failing to call it in.

The ingredients of estoppel in pais are set out in volume 16 of Halsbury's *Laws of England*, 4th edition, para. 1505 as follows:

"Where a person has by words or conduct made to another a clear and unequivocal representation of fact, either with knowledge of its falsehood or with the intention that it should be acted upon, or has so conducted himself that another would, as a reasonable man, understand that a certain representation of fact was intended to be acted on, and that [*sic*] the other has acted on the representation and thereby altered his position to his prejudice, an estoppel arises against the party who made the representation, and he is not allowed to aver that the fact is otherwise than he represented it to be."

Can it reasonably be said that, in the present case, the bank acted on the representation contained in the letter of 31 December – if representation it were – and thereby altered their position to their prejudice? There is no reason to suppose that at the date this letter was written the bank entertained the slightest doubts as to the validity of the guarantee or mortgage. Had they entertained any such doubts, they would have immediately required the re-execution of the guarantee and the mortgage before allowing any further interest to accumulate. There is nothing to suggest that this letter had any effect on the attitude of the bank towards calling in the loan. I do not think that it could be said that they in any way altered their position to their prejudice as a result of any representation that may have been contained in this letter. I think it is also clear that the mere fact that the company sent to the bank its memorandum and articles of association at the time of its application for a loan could not in any sense be said to constitute a representation which was subsequently acted on to their detriment by the bank. Their action in so doing was not a representation that the company had the power in question; it was no more than an invitation to the bank to satisfy themselves that the transaction was *intra vires* and there is no reason to suppose that any request to alter the memorandum would not have been immediately complied with. I am accordingly satisfied that this submission also fails.

In these circumstances, I am satisfied that the execution of the guarantee was *ultra vires* and that the bank cannot successfully rely on any of the grounds advanced by counsel. It is, I think, accepted that the mortgage is in turn dependent for its validity upon the guarantee; the company could not validly execute a mortgage in order to secure an obligation which they had no power to accept in the first place. This is, in any event, made clear by sub-paragraph (f) to which reference has already been made. The claim of the bank against the company will accordingly be dismissed.

Note: Because the company here was an unlimited company, S.I. No. 163 of 1973, which applies only to limited companies, could not arise; in any event this S.I. is most unlikely to have affected the outcome.

Re Frederick Inns Ltd
[1994] 1 I.L.R.M. 387

Under pressure from the Revenue Commissioners, several companies paid off the tax liabilities of other companies in the same group of companies. The Supreme Court held that those payments were outside the company's objects and *ultra vires*. The question then was whether those payments were validated by section 8(1) of the 1963 Act or by regulation 6 of the 1973 S.I. and, if not, whether any or all of the money paid was recoverable.

BLAYNEY J.: [394] It was then submitted that even if the payments were *ultra vires*, they were nonetheless validated in favour of the Revenue Commissioners by either section 8 of the Companies Act 1963 or article 6 of the European Communities (Companies) Regulations 1973. In my opinion neither of these provisions had this effect. I start with article 6. . . .

I think it is clear that none of the companies had any person registered under the regulations as a person authorised to bind the company, so if the Revenue Commissioners are to get the benefit of the article they would need to show that the payment to them was a transaction entered into by the board of directors of each of the companies. There is no evidence of this in any of the affidavits filed [395] by either side. The payment appears to have been agreed to be made as a result of informal meetings between accountants acting on behalf of the companies and Mr Patrick Burke acting on behalf of the Revenue Commissioners. In these circumstances it seems to me that the Revenue Commissioners cannot rely on article 6 as validating the payment.

They are confined then to relying on section 8 of the Companies Act 1963. . . .

It seems clear that the Revenue Commissioners cannot be shown to have been actually aware that the payment was not within the powers of the four companies. Mr Burke seems generally to have been of the belief that he was dealing with a group of companies and that the payment was being made by some of the companies within the group on behalf of the entire group. I consider, accordingly, that the Revenue Commissioners would be entitled to rely on the section if they could show that the payment by the four companies, if they had been empowered to make it, 'would have been lawfully and effectively done.' The view I take is that the facts here are such that the Revenue Commissioners could not establish this.

At the time the payments were made, all four companies were insolvent and were known by the Revenue Commissioners to be insolvent. Frederick Inns Ltd, The Rendezvous Ltd and The Graduate Ltd had each sold their licensed premises and had ceased to trade. In addition, a section 214 demand had been served on each of the companies and had not been complied with. The position of each of the companies was, accordingly, that all that was required to wind it up was that a petition should be presented. And the moment that had been done, it is clear that the relevant payments could not have been made as the company would have ceased to be the beneficial owner of its assets. In *Ayerst v. C. & K. (Construction) Ltd* [1974] 1 All E.R. 676 Templeman J. cited in his judgment at p. 684 the following passage from the judgment of James L.J. in *In re Oriental Inland Steam Co.* (1874) 9 Ch. App. 557 at p. 559 setting out the effect of a winding-up order:

> "The English Act of Parliament has enacted that in the case of a winding-up the assets of the company so wound up are to be collected and applied in discharge [396] of its liabilities [there is a similar provision in section 235 of the Companies Act 1963]. That makes the property of the

company clearly trust property. It is property affected by the Act of Parliament with an obligation to be dealt with by the proper officer in a particular way. Then it has ceased to be beneficially the property of the company; and, being so, it has ceased to be liable to be seized by the execution creditors of the company."

It is clear from this that as soon as a winding-up order has been made (*Note*: wrong – it is from the time the petition is presented, provided a winding-up order is made) the company ceases to be the beneficial owner of its assets, with the result that the directors no longer have power to dispose of them. Where, as here, a company's situation was such that any creditor could have caused it to be wound up on the ground of insolvency, I consider that it can equally well be said that the company had ceased to be the beneficial owner of its assets with the result that the directors would have had no power to use the company's assets to discharge the liabilities of other companies. Once the company clearly had to be wound up and its assets applied *pro tanto* in discharge of its liabilities, the directors had a duty to the creditors to preserve the assets to enable this to be done, or at least not to dissipate them.

This conclusion is supported by the decision of the Court of Appeal in New South Wales in *Kinsela v. Russell Kinsela Property Ltd (in liquidation)* [1986] 4 NSWLR 722. The essential facts of the case were summarised as follows by Street C.J. in his judgment at p. 727:

"This insolvent company, in a state of imminent and foreseen collapse, entered into a transaction which plainly had the effect, and was intended to have the effect, of placing its assets beyond the immediate reach of its creditors; it did this by means of a lease of its business premises entered into with the intention that two of its directors, as lessees, would use those premises for the purpose of continuing to conduct a business of the nature of that which the family of the directors and all of the shareholders had carried on for many years; the lease was executed on behalf of the company by the two directors who were to be lessees with the unanimous approval of all the shareholders of the company; it may be added, for what it is worth, that the terms of the lease were, to say the least, commercially questionable."

He went on to say at p. 728 of his judgment:

"Where, as here, a question arises regarding the extent to which a company is bound by a transaction entered into by it there are two separate questions, namely, is the transaction within the power or capacity of the company and, secondly, if it is, has that power been validly exercised so as to bind the company?"

He held that the transaction was within the power of the company but that it had not been validly exercised:

> [397] "The lease was not *ultra vires* and void as exceeding the capacity of the company. It was, however, entered into by the directors (albeit with unanimous approval of all of the shareholders) in breach of their duty to the company in that it directly prejudiced the creditors of the company. It was accordingly a voidable transaction and, no third party rights having intervened, the company on the initiation of the liquidator is entitled to the aid of the court to void it."

At p. 730 of his judgment he outlined as follows the principle on the basis of which he came to this conclusion:

> "In a solvent company the proprietary interests of the shareholders entitle them as a general body to be regarded as the company when questions of the duty of directors arise. If, as a general body, they authorise or ratify a particular action of the directors, there can be no challenge to the validity of what the directors have done. But where a company is insolvent the interests of the creditors intrude. They become prospectively entitled, through the mechanism of liquidation, to displace the power of the shareholders and directors to deal with the company's assets. It is in a practical sense their assets and not the shareholders' assets that, through the medium of the company, are under the management of the directors pending either liquidation, return to solvency, or the imposition of some alternative administration."

I would respectfully adopt and follow this statement of the law and when it is applied to the facts here I think it is clear that it could not be held that the payments by the four companies were 'lawfully and effectively done'. At the time the payments were made, the four companies were under the management of their directors pending imminent liquidation. Because of the insolvency of the companies the shareholders no longer had any interest. The only parties with an interest were the creditors. The payments made could not have been lawful because they were made in total disregard of their interests. And since the payments were not lawfully made, the Revenue Commissioners cannot rely on section 8 of the Companies Act 1963 to remedy the fact that the payments were *ultra vires*. So this submission also fails.

I would accordingly uphold the finding of the learned trial judge that the payments made by the four companies in reduction of the amounts owing by the other six companies were *ultra vires* and therefore void.

Note: Blayney J.'s approach to the phrase 'lawfully and effectively done' in section 8(1) here does not seem right. Section 8(1), in paraphrase, says that a transaction will not be treated as *ultra vires* and void unless the party seeking to enforce it was actually aware that it was beyond a company's objects. Since Blayney J. concluded that the Revenue were not so actually aware, then section 8(1) put an end to the question of *ultra vires* in the sense envisaged in the *Rolled Steel* case. But it does not follow that *intra vires* transactions always bind the company; companies are not so bound where the other party knows or should know that the company's agents are exceeding their authority in concluding the contract or in making the payment or whatever. For an excellent critique of aspects this case, see Fealy, 'The Role of Equity in the Winding Up of a Company' [1995] *D.U.L.J.* 18.

Re P.M.P.A. Garages Ltd (No. 2)
[1992] 1 I.R. 332

The P.M.P.A. group of companies collapsed and were heavily insolvent. One company in the group was an industrial and provident society, which to an extent acted as banker to the group. It made substantial loans to group companies on foot of guarantees they purported to give. In *Re P.M.P.A. Garage (Longmile) Ltd.* [992] 1 I.R. 315 Murphy J. held that those guarantees were not *ultra vires* but that, nonetheless, the loans in respect of which they had been given were *ultra vires* the society, being in contravention of provisions of the Industrial and Provident Societies Act 1893. The question then was whether, being *ultra vires*, could the society recover any of the money it had lent?

MURPHY J.: [335] As this judgment is supplemental to and must be read with the judgment delivered by me herein on 4 March last ([1992] 1 I.R. 315) it is unnecessary for me to repeat the history of the matter or to explain the abbreviations which I have adopted. Suffice it to say that I have already held that the purported lending by the P.M.P.S. to different companies within the P.M.P.A group of sums totalling approximately £3,000,000 was *ultra vires* the P.M.P.S. I have also decided that the granting of a series of guarantees and in particular the guarantee dated the 31st December, 1982, by the various companies within the P.M.P.A group was intra vires and that the guarantees in general, and that dated the 31st December, 1982, in particular, were validly and effectively executed by each of the companies purporting to be bound thereby. Insofar as one may be entitled to view the transaction from two separate standpoints it can be said that the purported lending was *ultra vires* the lender and as such it was void though not illegal. Viewed from the standpoint of the borrowers the transaction was valid, binding and [336] effective. As a matter of objective reality substantial sums were received by the companies within the P.M.P.A group and, as I understand it, significant repayments made from time to time but leaving a sum in excess of £3,000,000 due by the group at the date of the commencement of the liquidation of the debtor companies. What are the rights of the parties in these circumstances?

There are four possible solutions, namely,

(1) *That the purported lending being* ultra vires *was void and unenforceable.*

As the lender could not enforce the repayment of the debt "the borrowers" would be entitled to retain it for their own benefit. Counsel for the P.M.P.A. companies did not attempt to make this argument. The monstrous injustice which would flow from the acceptance of such an audacious proposition would certainly render it unattractive to any court seeking to achieve justice in accordance with law. However, counsel's concession in this respect is not entirely altruistic or even tactical: all of the decided cases appear to be in agreement on the proposition that where a transaction is successfully impunged on the grounds that it is *ultra vires* one or other of the parties to it, that is, the party who has delivered property or monies to the other of them, would be entitled to recover such property or monies from the donee whether the deficiency in capacity is that of the donor or the donee. The authorities differ, at least to some extent, as to the nature of the action in which the assets may be so recovered.

(2) *That the lender or donor, that is to say the P.M.P.S. in the present case, is entitled to recover from the individual companies within the P.M.P.A. group so much of the monies as were made available to them respectively in an action in rem on the basis that the monies made available were never validly lent or advanced by the P.M.P.S. and remained its property at all times.*

Again it is accepted, and properly so, by counsel on behalf of the P.M.P.A group of companies that this remedy is available to the P.M.P.S. and that it carries with it the right to follow the monies provided by the donor in the hands of the donee into any other assets into which they can be traced. This was in fact the solution approved by the House of Lords in *Sinclair v. Brougham* [1914] A.C. 398 where their Lordships had to consider problems which by coincidence bear an extraordinary resemblance to the facts of the present case with the crucial distinction that in *Sinclair v. Brougham* it was the borrowing which was *ultra vires* whereas in the instant case it is the lending which was incompetent. The [337] dilemma facing the House of Lords was that the Birbeck Permanent Benefit Building Society had borrowed *ultra vires* (by means of taking deposits) sums totalling over £10 million; and to permit the building society to retain that sum for the benefit of the shareholders (who in one sense were ultimately responsible for the wrongdoing) to the detriment of those who provided the monies would have been a cruel injustice. Nevertheless the court necessarily recognised that the monies could not be recovered on the basis of an action for debt. The position was explained by Viscount Haidane L.C., at p. 414, in the following terms:

"If it be outside the power of a statutory society to enter into the relation

of debtor and creditor in a particular transaction, the only possible remedy for the person who has paid the money would on principle appear to
be one *in rem* and not *in personam*, a claim to follow and recover specifically any money which could be earmarked as never having ceased
to be his property. To hold that a remedy will lie *in personam* against a
statutory society, which by hypothesis cannot in the case in question
have become a debtor or entered into any contract for repayment, is to
strike at the root of the doctrine of *ultra vires* as established in the jurisprudence of this country. That doctrine belongs to substantive law and is
the outcome of statute, and cannot be made different by any choice of
form in procedure."

The Lord Chancellor went on then to conclude, at p. 415, as follows:-

"I think it excludes from the law of England any claim *in personam*
based even on the circumstance that the defendant has been improperly
enriched at the expense of the plaintiff by a transaction which is *ultra
vires*."

Not only did the House of Lords eliminate the prospect of recovering monies
from a person by whom they had been borrowed *ultra vires* by means of a
personal action based on the promise to repay but their Lordships likewise
rejected the contention that such monies could be recovered on the basis of a
quasi contract based on the principle of unjust enrichment and a promise implied by law to repay. This proposition was dealt with by the Lord Chancellor,
at p. 417 of the report, in the following terms:

"My Lords, notwithstanding the wide scope of the remedy so described,
I think that it must be taken to have been given only, as I have already
said, where the law could consistently impute to the [338] defendant at
least the fiction of a promise. And it appears to me that as a matter of
principle the law of England cannot now, consistently with the interpretation which the courts have placed on the statutes which determine the
capacity of statutory societies, impute the fiction of such a promise where
it would have been *ultra vires* to give it. The fiction becomes, in other
words, inapplicable where substantive law, as distinguished from that of
procedure, makes the defendant incapable of undertaking contractual
liability. For to impute a fictitious promise is simply to presume the existence of a state of facts, and the presumption can give rise to no higher
right than would result if the facts were actual."

Having eliminated those methods of recovering monies from a borrower for
whom the transaction was *ultra vires* the court was left with either a remedy in
rem or none at all. Again the nature of that remedy was dealt with by the Lord
Chancellor, at p. 418, in the following terms:

"It follows that the depositors in the present case will not succeed unless they are able to trace their money into the hands of the society or its agents as actually existing assets. The question is whether they are able to establish enough to succeed upon this footing. Their claim cannot be *in personam* and must be *in rem*, a claim to follow and recover property with which, in equity at all events, they had never really parted."

(3) *That the monies should be refunded on the basis that it would be unjust and inequitable for the recipients to retain the same.*

In one sense it might be said that this solution is in conflict with the decision in *Sinclair v. Brougham* [1914] A.C. 398 inasmuch as it does involve recognising the availability of an action other than an action *in rem*. One reason advanced for entertaining this distinction is the evolution which has taken place in the law relating to quasi-contract. It was pointed out that Henchy J., delivering the judgment of the Supreme Court in *East Cork Foods v. O'Dwyer Steel* [1978] I.R. 103, had recognised that quasi-contract was no longer grounded on an imputed promise to pay. He explained the history and development of the matter, at pp. 110 and 111, in the following terms:

"So far, I have been dealing with the matter on the footing that the second defendant would be entitled, if its claim were resisted, to recover back the £20,000 in an action for money had and received. The basis of such a claim is quasi-contract. It is usually dealt with in the books on contract. The plaintiff succeeds in this type of action because, it is said, the law imputes to the debtor a promise to pay [339] the debt. The historical reason for this fiction was to enable the claim to be brought as a form of *indebitatus assumpsit*. It was a pleader's stratagem. In most cases, however, it is in the teeth of the facts to impute to the debtor a promise to pay. So long as the forms of action governed the course of litigation, it was necessary for the courts to go along with this transparent fiction. Nowadays, however, when the forms of action have long since been buried, the concept of implied contract is an unreal and outdated rationale for the action for money had and received. Judges in modern times generally prefer to look at the reality of the situation rather than engage in the pretence that the defendant has promised to pay the debt.

In the present case, while the second defendant (if it were necessary for it to do so) could recover the £20,000 in an action for money had and received, it would be an affront to truth and reality to say that the basis of that cause of action is an implied promise to repay the money. The real reason why the courts would uphold the claim is because it would be unjust and inequitable to allow the first defendant to keep the money. To refuse the claim would mean that the first defendant would be unjustly enriched."

The significance of this development is that by eliminating the need for an express or imputed promise to pay as an ingredient of the action for money had and received it overcomes the problem faced by the House of Lords in *Sinclair v. Brougham* [1914] AC. 398. If it is not necessary to infer some hypothetical or fictitious promise to pay then there is no impediment in availing of that remedy against a corporate body to recover monies received by it as a result of a transaction which was outside its corporate powers.

Moreover it must be recognised that even if no development had taken place in the law relating to quasi-contract, the issue in the instant case would be radically different from that which arose in *Sinclair v. Brougham* [1914] AC. 398 because there would not appear to be any real or theoretical difficulty in imputing an intention to the P.M.P.A group of companies to repay the monies received by them as they, unlike the Birbeck Permanent Benefit Building Society, did have power to borrow and to repay monies. This indeed is one respect at least in which different consequences flow depending upon whether one examines the transaction from the point of view of an *ultra vires* lending or an *ultra vires* borrowing.

Again, however, there is no serious difference of opinion between the parties as to the right of the P.M.P.S. to recover on a quasi-contractual [340] basis particularly on the basis of the more enlightened view of that cause of action. Moreover it is not seriously disputed that the P.M.P.S. would be entitled to interest, though not necessarily at the rate agreed between the parties, to compensate it for the loss of its assets over a period of years. Under this heading the substantial difference between the parties is whether liability on foot of the guarantee would extend to monies recoverable on an action which was not either an action *in rem* nor the repayment of a loan or advance made and repayable in accordance with the terms of a contract made between the parties. I will postpone for the time being this aspect of the matter.

(4) *That the individual companies in the P.M.P.A. group are bound by their respective promises to repay the monies received by them and in respect of which they furnished promissory notes and that all of the companies who joined in the guarantee are likewise committed by the express promise therein contained to repay the monies which counsel on behalf of the P.M.P.S. says are properly described as "sums of money advanced" within the meaning of the guarantee.*

This proposition which is the ideal solution from the standpoint of the P.M.P.S. is in fact supported by the decision of the Court of Appeal in England in *Re Coltman* (1881) 19 Ch. D. 64. In that case the trustees of a friendly society lent (or purported to lend) out of the surplus funds of the society a sum of £300 to a borrower on the security of a joint and several promissory note made by the borrower and two other persons as his sureties. One of the sureties died and the trustees of the society claimed against his estate on foot of the note. In the High Court Fry J. held that the loan on a personal security to a person who was not a member of the society was forbidden by the Friendly

Societies Act 1875, and that accordingly the transaction was illegal. He therefore rejected the proof for the debt in the surety's estate. On appeal the decision was reversed. It seems clear that the Court of Appeal – and indeed the
argument between counsel before them – focused essentially on whether the
transaction was illegal or merely unauthorised. The Court of Appeal, having
concluded, unlike the High Court, that the transaction was not illegal, had no
difficulty in deciding that the unauthorised lending could be recovered from
the surety on foot of the promissory note. This conclusion is expressed very
firmly in the decision of Brett L.J., at pp. 70-71, in the following terms:

> "The only objection to this loan is that it was made without authority.
> But it does not seem to me that the borrower can set up as a defence to an
> action that the person who lent him the money, and to whom he has
> made a promise to repay that money, [341] had no authority to lend it to
> him. That is an objection which it is not for him to take. The contract is,
> 'if you will lend me so much money I will pay you that money back on
> demand'. The consideration is the handing over the money. That is not
> illegal. The promise to pay back money which you have borrowed is not
> illegal. The money was not borrowed for any illegal purpose, in order to
> do any illegal or immoral thing, and I cannot see that there is anything
> illegal in the contract. The only objection is, that those who made the
> contract with the debtor had no authority to make it, and that is an objec-
> tion which he cannot take."

It is said that the decision, albeit the unanimous decision, in *Re Coltman* (1881)
19 Ch. D. 64 is not convincing. Indeed it does seem that the Court of Appeal
did not have a full argument available to it and perhaps it is appropriate to
recognise that the decision which dominates all of these cases, namely, *Ashbury
Railway Carriage and Iron Company v. Richie* (1875) L.R. 7 H.L. 653 was
comparatively recent when *Re Coltman* was decided and perhaps had not received the attention and analysis which was subsequently devoted to it. Certainly the court seemed to see the issue very much as one between illegality on
which the High Court had founded its judgment or *ultra vires* which was the
finding of the Court of Appeal.

Similar and additional issues came before Mocatta J. in *Bell Houses Ltd. v.
City Wall Properties Ltd.* [1966] 1 Q.B. 207 and he held first that, notwithstanding the decision in *Re Coltman* (1881) 19 Ch. D. 64, the plea of *ultra
vires* was available as a defence and, secondly, that there was no ground in
principle for distinguishing between executory and executed contracts. Mocatta
J. cited the passage from the decision of Brett L.J., quoted above, and having
dealt with other matters, in particular the decision of a Divisional Court in
Brougham v. Dwyer (1913) 108 LT. 504, he went on to say, at p. 223:-

> "In my judgment, *Re Coltman* (1881) 19 Ch.D. 64, properly regarded, is

a case, like *Brougham v. Dwyer* (1913) 108 L.T. 504, where the lender of money, although acting *ultra vires* in making the loan, was entitled to recover on the basis of money had and received. I do not think the *dicta* of Brett L.J. are relevant on the first point I have to decide."

I find it difficult to comprehend that conclusion. Brett L.J. had expessly stated, as Mocatta J. recognised, that "the only objection is, that those who made the contract with the debtor had no authority to make [342] it, and that is an objection which he cannot take". I cannot see how one could escape the relevance of that dictum. In addition to disregarding, as I would see it, the *dicta* of Brett L.J., Mocatta J. rejected the views expressed to the same effect by Professor Gower in his book, *Modern Company Law*, 2nd ed., at pp. 90–91, and supported by the views expressed in Street on *The Doctrine of Ultra vires*. Whilst I would be slow to disregard those learned authors I am even more reluctant to accept the conclusion of Mocatta J. that *Re Coltman* (1881) 19 Ch. D. 64 "properly regarded, is a case like *Brougham v. Dwyer* (1913) 108 L.T. 504 where the lender of money although acting *ultra vires* in making the loan was entitled to recover on the basis of money had and received". The undoubted facts of *Re Coltman* (1881) 19 Ch. D. 64 were that the particular person sued (or more correctly his estate) was a mere surety who had not in fact received any part of the monies advanced.

As to the second issue the learned High Court judge referred to an article by Mr. M.P. Furmston (see (1961) 24 M.L.R. 715) and cited a passage at p. 719 in which the author referred to the legal position in America as being:-

"[Once] the contract has been properly performed, the law lets it alone and any property rights acquired by either party thereunder will be protected, and most jurisdictions will give some relief either in contract or in quasi-contract where the contract has been partly performed."

The learned judge then went on, at p. 225, to summarise the argument based on that article in the following terms:

"[If] the defendant has had the benefit of money, goods or services under a contract made by a company *ultra vires*, the company can notwithstanding sue in respect thereof and the fact that the contract was made *ultra vires* is irrelevant."

That argument was rejected at pp. 225-226 in the following terms:

"In my judgment, there is no ground in principle for distinguishing between executory and executed contracts in the manner contended for by Mr. Dunn. If the plaintiff company that has made an *ultra vires* contract has to rely upon the terms of that contract in order to succeed in its

> action, it must in my judgment fail, since the contract was void *ab initio* and the defendant is entitled to raise the point. I need not repeat my reasoning on the first point, which is equally applicable here."

It may be that there has been some misunderstanding as to the possible relevance of a distinction between executory and executed [343] contracts relating to transactions which are *ultra vires* one of the parties thereto. It would seem to me that there would be an important distinction to make between the two classifications. Where a contract is wholly executory in the basic sense that it consists in outstanding mutual promises by each party to the other then clearly no court of law could compel or even permit one of the parties to implement his promise if by doing so it would exceed its statutory powers. On the other hand where the party with limited capacity has already implemented in full the promise made by him and the outstanding promise by the other party remains to be implemented the court is not similarly embarrassed. For this reason it seems to me that there is in fact a distinction to be drawn both between executory and executed contracts and also as between cases in which it is the lending rather than the borrowing which is impeached on the grounds of want of authority.

However, it was not as I understand it any absence of a distinction between executory and executed contracts which concerned Mocatta J. He might well have been prepared to accept that such a distinction did exist. His concern was – and the argument on behalf of the P.M.P.A. group of companies in the present case is – that the actions which were interpreted as constituting performance were in fact a nullity. In the instant case it has been forcefully argued that, notwithstanding appearances to the contrary or the actual intentions of the parties, no monies were ever "advanced" by the P.M.P.S. to the P.M.P.A. companies. A repayable advance or loan – and it seems to me that the terms are interchangeable – entails the donor divesting himself of the ownership of the monies advanced in consideration of a promise for their repayment. I believe that Mocatta J. was saying, as counsel on behalf of the P.M.P.A is arguing, that such a divesting was impossible as a matter of law.

The decision of Mocatta J. in *Bell Houses Ltd. v. City Wall Properties Ltd.* [1966] 1 Q.B. 207 was reversed on appeal. However, the decision of the Court of Appeal was to the effect that the particular disputed contract was *intra vires* the plaintiff company so that the views expressed by the High Court judge, and quoted above, did not require to be reviewed. However, I do think it is worth quoting the comments of Salmon L.J. at pp. 693-694 as follows:

> "Having regard to the view I have formed on this part of the case, it is unnecessary to consider the interesting, important and difficult question which would arise were the contract *ultra vires*, namely, whether, the plaintiff company having fully performed its [344] part under the contract and the defendants having obtained all the benefits under the con-

tract, the defendants could successfully take the point that the contract was *ultra vires* the plaintiff company and so avoid payment. It seems strange that third parties could take advantage of a doctrine, manifestly for the protection of the shareholders, in order to deprive the company of money which in justice should be paid to it by the third parties."

However, having made those observations and having referred to certain other authorities dealing with the purpose and effect of the doctrine of *ultra vires*, he expressly stated that he was expressing no opinion on the point and was leaving it to be decided in a case where it properly arose and was fully argued.

If it is regrettable that we do not have the decision of the Court of Appeal in England on the relevant judgment of Mocatta J. It is perhaps equally unfortunate that we do not have Mocatta J.'s views on the decision of the Australian courts in *Re K.L. Tractors Ltd.* (1961-62) 106 C.L.R. 318. In that case a company which had bought from the Commonwealth of Australia certain machinery manufactured by the Commonwealth became insolvent. The Commonwealth filed a claim for debt representing the purchase price of the machinery. Other creditors moved to strike out the claim on the ground that it was beyond the power of the Commonwealth to engage in the business of manufacturing machinery and therefore the debt which it was asserting was the product of an *ultra vires* act and could not be enforced by the vendor. What I believe would be recognised as a very distinguished Australian court unanimously held that the buyer ought not to be permitted to plead the *ultra vires* conduct of the Commonwealth in manufacturing the machinery. This was very solid judicial support for the estoppel-type argument. That judgment cannot be explained away as Mocatta J. sought to do in relation to *Re Coltman* (1881) 19 Ch.D. 64 on the basis that it was an action for money had and received. The claim was for debt arising out of a transaction which was outside the constitutional capacity of the vendor. On the other hand it is proper to recognise that the Australian court was placed in the dilemma that if the proof of debt was not admitted it would have resulted in the unjust enrichment of the buyer. Hopefully the foregoing represents a balanced analysis of the law on this troublesome topic when it came to be considered by the Appellate Division of the Alberta Supreme Court in *Breckenridge Speedway Ltd. v. the Queen (in the right of Alberta)* (1967) 64 D.L.R. 2d. 488.

[345] Like the Australian case, the Canadian one concerned a transaction which it was alleged was *ultra vires* because of the unconstitutionality of certain legislation. . . .

[346] The judgments in the *Breckenridge* case rely heavily on the decisions in *Re KL. Tractors Ltd.* and *In re Coltman* (1881) 19 Ch. D. 64 among others. Indeed the decision in the latter case appears to be strongly supported by the decision of the Supreme Court of Canada in *Rolland v. La Caisse d'Economie Notre-Dame de Quebec* [1895] 24 S.C.R. 405. . . .

[348] These delicately balanced arguments which are based on conflicting

persuasive authorities place me in considerable difficulty. I recognise the force of the simple cogent proposition that a body corporate cannot enforce a contract which it never had the capacity to make. It is demonstrated with equal clarity that all judicial authorities have set their face against any party who seeks to prevent the recovery from him of goods or monies which he has retained under an *ultra vires* transaction. The precise grounds on which such claims have been defeated have varied over the century during which the debate has spasmodically taken place but the result has been the same. No court would permit the manifest injustice which such a contention would involve. Ms. Finlay S.C. has summarised this by saying the courts have had difficulty in reconciling the intuitive desire for restitution with the strict observance of the doctrine of *ultra vires*. It is not permissible to deduce or infer the legal rights of citizens by reference to some broad principle of justice or fair play. Less still would any such principle justify ignoring or overriding a [349] principle of law based on statutory or judicial authority. There is no inconsistency between the proper application of the *ultra vires* doctrine and the recovery by means of an action *in rem* or on a quasi-contractual basis of monies or goods in the hands of the party receiving the same in consequence of the transaction. The problem which must be faced is whether there is any other basis on which such goods or monies can be recovered. It seems to me that the alternative basis is something akin to an estoppel. The venerable Canadian case of *Rolland v. La Caisse d'Economie Notre-Dame de Quebec* [1895] 24 S.C.R. 405 expressly so found in the following terms:

> "A borrower cannot be allowed to cheat his lender, under the pretext that the lender had no power to loan. Such a plea does not lie in his mouth; he is estopped from relying on it."

After quoting certain French maxims Taschereau J. went on to say as follows:

> "The proposition laid down in Randolf, Vol. 1, para. 333, that one who borrows money from a corporation cannot in his own defence question his power to lend' is based on principles which must necessarily prevail throughout all the civilised world."

I have already noticed that Brett L.J. in *Re Coltman* (1881) 19 Ch. D. 64 dealing with the position of a person borrowing from a lender who had no authority to make loans expressed his conclusion in the single sentence:

> "That is an objection which it is not for him to take."

The same words were used by Mann J. and in the same context in *City of Camberwell v. Cooper* [1930] V.L.R. 289. There are differences of opinion as to whether the restriction imposed on the borrower is properly described as an estoppel but it seems to me that the overwhelming body of judicial opinion is to the effect that the borrower is precluded from taking the point that the transaction was *ultra vires* where this would result in an injustice. In most cases the injustice envisaged is where the competent party would retain for his own benefit the fruits of the *ultra vires* transaction. However, the significance of the Australian case is that there the competent party no longer had the property derived from the incompetent party and that justice could only be achieved by allowing the invalid transaction to be implemented. In the present case the particular P.M.P.A. companies named in the title hereof do not have in their possession any monies or assets derived from the P.M.P.A. nor are they themselves indebted to the society on foot of any promissory note. Furthermore counsel on behalf of the companies [350] aforesaid concedes the right of the society to recover all monies in fact advanced to the individual companies within the group insofar as the same is now in their possession. To this extent the more obvious injustice is avoided. However that is a somewhat superficial view of the entire transaction. What the facts of the case proved beyond debate was that the accounts of the society would not have been certified at any time after the year 1977 unless either the auditors were satisfied as to the creditworthiness of the individual borrowers or else the successive guarantees were put in place. If the auditors' certificate was not forthcoming clearly the society could not have survived it. Its continued existence and its opportunity to take the substantial sums of money by way of deposit from members of the public turned essentially upon the existence of these guarantees. In those circumstances it seems to me that it would be unconscionable to allow the borrowing companies or the guaranteeing companies to rely on any want of authority of the society to lend money in the manner in which it did even though the absence of such authority has been established to the satisfaction of this court. I see no difficulty in reconciling the propositions that a particular state of facts or law may exist but that a party may in particular circumstances be precluded from relying on them.

In the circumstances it seems to me that the society must be admitted as a creditor of each of the companies concerned on foot of the guarantee. I appreciate that further questions may arise as to the precise amounts due on foot of the guarantee particularly in relation to the question of interest but they can be dealt with separately when the precise issues have been identified.

AGENCY AND UNAUTHORISED TRANSACTIONS

Table A article 81

81. The directors may from time to time and at any time by power of attorney appoint any company, firm or person or body of persons, whether nominated directly or indirectly by the directors, to be the attorney or attorneys of the company for such purposes and with such powers, authorities and discretions (not exceeding those vested in or exercisable by the directors under these regulations) and for such period and subject to such conditions as they may think fit, and any such power of attorney may contain such provisions for the protection of persons dealing with any such attorney as the directors may think fit, and may also authorise any such attorney to delegate all or any of the powers, authorities and discretions vested in him.

See *Company Law*, pp.433–447.

Mahony v. East Holyford Mining Co.
(1875) L.R. 7 H.L. 869

A group of fraudsters formed a company, ostensibly to work a mine, and by a prospectus induced members of the public to invest in the company. But instead of spending those funds on developing the mine, the fraudsters withdrew the money from the company's bank account for their own use. They misled the company's bank into believing that they were authorised to draw cheques on the company's behalf. When what transpired was discovered, the question arose who should bear the loss – either the investors or the bank.

LORD HATHERLEY: . . . [393] It is a point of very great importance that those who are concerned in joint stock companies and those who deal with them should be aware of what is essential to the due performance of their duties, both as customers or dealers with the company, and as persons forming the company, and dealing with the outside world respectively. On the one hand, it is settled by a series of decisions, of which *Ernest v. Nicholls* (1857) 6 H.L.C. 401, is one and *Royal British Bank v. Turquand* (1856) E. & B. 327, a later one, that those who deal with joint stock companies are bound to take notice of that which I call the external position of the company. Every joint stock company has its memorandum and articles of association; every joint stock company, or nearly every one, I imagine (unless it adopts the form provided by the statute, and that comes to the same thing) has its partnership deed under which it acts. Those articles of association and that partnership deed are open to all who are minded to have any dealings whatsoever with the company, and those who so deal with them must be affected with notice of all that is contained in those two documents.

After that, the company entering upon its business and dealing [894] with persons external to it, is supposed on its part to have all those powers and authorities which, by its articles of association and by its deed, it appears to possess; and all that the directors do with reference to what I may call the indoor management of their own concern, is a thing known to them and known to them only; subject to this observation, that no person dealing with them has a right to suppose that anything has been or can be done that is not permitted by the articles of association or by the deeds.

This being the case, a banker dealing with a company must be taken to be acquainted with the manner which, under the articles of association, the moneys of the company may be drawn out of his bank for the purposes of the company. [I]n this case, the bankers were informed that cheques might be drawn upon the bank by three directors of the company. And the bankers must also be taken to have had knowledge, from the articles, of the duties of the directors, and the mode in which the directors were to be appointed. But, after that, when there are persons conducting the affairs of the company in a manner which appears to be perfectly consonant with the articles of association, then those so dealing with them, externally, are not to be affected by any irregularities which may take place in the internal management of the company. They are entitled to presume that that of which only they can have knowledge, namely, the external acts, are rightly done, when those external acts purport to be performed in the mode in which they ought to be performed. For instance, when a cheque is signed by three directors, they are entitled to assume that those directors are persons properly appointed for the purpose of performing that function, and have properly performed the [895] function for which they have been appointed. Of course, the case is open to any observation arising from gross negligence or fraud. I pass that by as not entering into the consideration of the question at the present time. Outside persons when they find that there is an act done by a company, will, of course, be bound in the exercise of ordinary care and precaution to know whether or not that company is actually carrying on and transacting business, or whether it is a company which has been stopped and wound up, and which has parted with its assets, and the like. All those ordinary inquiries which mercantile men would, in the course of their business make, I apprehend, would have to be made on the part of the persons dealing with the company. . . .

[897] Now if the question came to be which of two innocent parties (as it is said) was to suffer loss, I apprehend, my Lords, that in point of law what must be considered in cases of that kind is this: which of the two parties was bound to do, or to avoid, any act by which the loss has been sustained. I think there can be no doubt that in this case the shareholders of the company were the persons who were bound to see that nobody usurped or assumed the office of director unduly; that is to say, without that office having been properly conferred upon him. The shareholders of the company were persons some of whom had, though others perhaps had not, received the prospectus originally, when they did receive it they must have seen those persons named in the first or in the second prospectus issued after the incorporation had taken place. At all [898] events the shareholders knew that if the company was to be carried on at all there must be some acting body, and as the subject matter of the prospectus to which they were invited to contribute was a mine, which was to be set at work, immediately, they must have known that if it was to be immediately set

at work, there must be expenditure, and they must have known the expenditure would necessarily go on from time to time upon the ordinary business of the company, independently of that special work which they were undertaking amongst themselves to execute. Now whose business was it to see that that was all properly done? It was the business of the shareholders to see that it was done, and properly done, and if they allowed this duty to be assumed by persons who had no tide to it, in their office at *12 Grafton Street*, the place where the office of the company was described in the prospectus as being – if they allowed persons who were not entitled to do it to carry on all the business of the company there – to act as directors and as secretary there; especially if they allowed them to perform the most important business of drawing cheques (for they must have known their own deed, which says that that can only be done by a draft of three directors, and they must have known that money must be had for the purposes of the company), if there is a fault on the one side or the other, it is on the side of those who allowed all these transactions to take place, when they were not conducted by persons legitimately appointed on the part of the company.

On the other hand, on the part of the bankers, I see no possible mode by which they might have pursued their inquiries in the manner contended for at the Bar without requiring all the minute-books of the company to be produced to them, and without conducting a detailed investigation into all the transactions of the company as to the appointment of directors and the like – a duty they were not called upon to perform, and a duty which, if it was objected to, they could not have insisted upon performing. I apprehend, my Lords, that the bankers having done all that was strictly their duty to do – having made themselves acquainted with the articles of the company, and having seen the offices of the company, with persons there affecting to perform all the duties of directors according to those articles, and having seen those who [899] had the power of appointing them continually present there, witnessing their performance – there can be no doubt that in this state of circumstances the bankers are not in any default whatsoever, and that the cheques must be taken, as between them and the company, to have been properly drawn, and the shareholders must be held liable to the loss.

Freeman & Lockyer v. Buckhurst Park Properties (Mangal) Ltd
[1964] 2 QB. 480

K. a property developer, and H. formed the defendant company to purchase and resell a large estate. K. personally agreed to pay the running expenses and to be reimbursed out of the proceeds of the resale. K. and H. and a nominee of each were appointed directors of the company. The articles of association contained power to appoint a managing director but none was appointed. K. instructed the plaintiffs, a firm of architects, to apply for planning permission to develop the estate and do certain other work in that connection. The plaintiffs executed the work and claimed their fees, the amount of which was not in dispute, from the company. The county court judge held that, although K. was never appointed managing director, he had acted as such to the knowledge of the board of directors of the defendant company and he gave judgment for the plaintiffs. The defendant company appealed.

DIPLOCK LJ.: . . . [502] It is necessary at the outset to distinguish between an 'actual' authority of an agent on the one hand, and an 'apparent' or 'ostensible' authority on the other. Actual authority and apparent authority are quite independent of one another. Generally they co-exist and coincide, but either may exist without the other and their respective scopes may be different. As I shall endeavour to show, it is upon the apparent authority of the agent that the contractor normally relies in the ordinary course of business when entering into contracts.

An 'actual' authority is a legal relationship between principal and agent created by a consensual agreement to which they alone are parties. Its scope is to be ascertained by applying ordinary principles of construction of contracts, including any proper implications from the express words used, the usages of the trade, or the course of business between the parties. To this agreement the contractor is a stranger; he may be totally ignorant of the existence of any authority on the part of the agent. Nevertheless, if the agent does enter into a contract pursuant to the [503] 'actual' authority, it does create contractual rights and liabilities between the principal and the contractor. It may be that this rule relating to 'undisclosed principals,' which is peculiar to English law, can be rationalised as avoiding circuity of action, for the principal could in equity compel the agent to lend his name in an action to enforce the contract against the contractor, and would at common law be liable to indemnify the agent in respect of the performance of the obligations assumed by the agent under the contract.

An 'apparent' or 'ostensible' authority, on the other hand, is a legal relationship between the principal and the contractor created by a representation, made by the principal to the contractor, intended to be and in fact acted upon by the contractor, that the agent has authority to enter on behalf of the principal into a contract of a kind within the scope of the 'apparent' authority, so as to render the principal liable to perform any obligations imposed upon him by such contract. To the relationship so created the agent is a stranger. He need not be (although he generally is) aware of the existence of the representation but he must not purport to make the agreement as principal himself. The representation, when acted upon by the contractor by entering into a contract with the agent, operates as an estoppel, preventing the principal from asserting that he is not bound by the contract. It is irrelevant whether the agent had actual authority to enter into the contract.

In ordinary business dealings the contractor at the time of entering into the contract can in the nature of things hardly ever rely on the 'actual' authority of the agent. His information as to the authority must be derived either from the principal or from the agent or from both, for they alone know what the agent's actual authority is. All that the contractor can know is what they tell him, which may or may not be true. In the ultimate analysis he relies either upon the representation of the principal, that is, apparent authority, or upon the representation of the agent, that is, warranty of authority.

The representation which creates 'apparent' authority may take a variety of forms of which the commonest is representation by conduct, that is, by permitting the agent to act in some way in the conduct of the principal's business with other persons. By doing so the principal represents to anyone who becomes aware that the agent is so acting that the agent has authority to enter on behalf of the principal into contracts with other persons of the [504] kind which an agent so acting in the conduct of his principal's business has usually 'actual' authority to enter into.

In applying the law as I have endeavoured to summarise it to the case where the principal is not a natural person, but a fictitious person, namely, a corporation, two further factors arising from the legal characteristics of a corporation have to be borne in mind. The first is that the capacity of a corporation is limited by its constitution, that is, in the case of a company incorporated under the Companies Act, by its memorandum and articles of association; the second is that a corporation cannot do any act, and that includes making a representation, except through its agent.

Under the doctrine of *ultra vires* the limitation of the capacity of a corporation by its constitution to do any acts is absolute. This affects the rules as to the 'apparent' authority of an agent of a corporation in two ways. First, no representation can operate to estop the corporation from denying the authority of the agent to do on behalf of the corporation an act which the corporation is not permitted by its constitution to do itself. Secondly, since the conferring of actual authority upon an agent is itself an act of the corporation, the capacity to do which is regulated by its constitution, the corporation cannot be estopped from denying that it has conferred upon a particular agent authority to do acts which by its constitution, it is incapable of delegating to that particular agent.

To recognise that these are direct consequences of the doctrine of *ultra vires* is, I think, preferable to saying that a contractor who enters into a contract with a corporation has constructive notice of its constitution, for the expression 'constructive notice' tends to disguise that constructive notice is not a positive, but a negative doctrine, like that of estoppel of which it forms a part. It operates to prevent the contractor from saying that he did not know that the constitution of the corporation rendered a particular act or a particular delegation of authority *ultra vires* the corporation. It does not entitle him to say that he relied upon some unusual provision in the constitution of the corporation if he did not in fact so rely.

The second characteristic of a corporation, namely, that unlike a natural person it can only make a representation through an agent, has the consequence that in order to create an estoppel between the corporation and the contractor, the representation as to the authority of the agent which creates his 'apparent' authority must be made by some person or persons who have [505] 'actual' authority from the corporation to make the representation. Such 'actual' authority may be conferred by the constitution of the corporation itself, as, for example, in the case of a company, upon the board of directors, or it may be conferred by those who under its constitution have the powers of management upon some other person to whom the constitution permits them to delegate authority to make representations of this kind. It follows that where the agent upon whose 'apparent' authority the contractor relies has no 'actual' authority from the corporation to enter into a particular kind of contract with the contractor on behalf of the corporation, the contractor cannot rely upon the agent's own representation as to his actual authority. He can rely only upon a representation by a person or persons who have actual authority to manage or conduct that part of the business of the corporation to which the contract relates.

The commonest form of representation by a principal creating an 'apparent' authority of an agent is by conduct, namely, by permitting the agent to act in the management or conduct to the principal's business. Thus, if in the case of a company the board of directors who have 'actual' authority under the memorandum and articles of association to manage the company's business permit the agent to act in the management or conduct of the company's business, they thereby represent to all persons dealing with such agent that he has authority to enter on behalf of the corporation into contracts of a kind which an agent authorised to do acts of the kind which he is in fact permitted to do usually enters into in the ordinary course of such business. The making of such a representation is itself an act of management of the company's business. Prima facie it falls within the 'actual' authority of the board of directors, and unless the memorandum or articles of the company either make such a contract *ultra vires* the company or prohibit the delegation of such authority to the agent, the company is estopped from denying to anyone who has entered into a contract with the agent in reliance upon such 'apparent' authority that the agent had authority to contract on behalf of the company.

If the foregoing analysis of the relevant law is correct, it can be summarised by stating four conditions which must be fulfilled to entitle a contractor to enforce against a company a contract entered into on behalf of the company by an agent who had no actual authority to do so. It must be shown:

[506] (1) that a representation that the agent had authority to enter on behalf of the company into a contract of the kind sought to be enforced was made to the contractor;

(2) that such representation was made by a person or persons who had 'actual' authority to manage the business of the company either gener-

ally or in respect of those matters to which the contract relates;

(3) that he (the contractor) was induced by such representation to enter into the contract, that is, that he in fact relied upon it; and

(4) that under its memorandum or articles of association the company was not deprived of the capacity either to enter into a contract of the kind sought to be enforced or to delegate authority to enter into a contract of that kind to the agent.

The confusion which, I venture to think, has sometimes crept into cases is in my view due to a failure to distinguish between these four separate conditions, and in particular to keep steadfastly in mind (a) that the only 'actual' authority which is relevant is that of the persons making the representation relied upon, and (b) that the memorandum and articles of association of the company are always relevant (whether they are in fact known to the contractor or not) to the questions (i) whether condition (2) is fulfilled, and (ii) whether condition (4) is fulfilled, and (but only if they are in fact known to the contractor) may be relevant (iii) as part of the representation on which the contractor relied.

In each of the relevant cases the representation relied upon as creating the 'apparent' authority of the agent was by conduct in permitting the agent to act in the management and conduct of part of the business of the company. Except in *Mahony v. East Holyford Mining Co. Ltd.* (1875) L.R. 7 H.L. 869 (*supra*, p. 598), it was the conduct of the board of directors in so permitting the agent to act that was relied upon. As they had, in each case, by the articles of association of the company full 'actual' authority to manage its business, they had 'actual' authority to make representations in connection with the management of its business, including representations as to who were agents authorised to enter into contracts on the company's behalf . . . [507] In *Mahony*'s case no board of directors or secretary had in fact been appointed, and it was the conduct of those who, under the constitution of the company, were entitled to appoint them which was relied upon as a representation that certain persons were directors and secretary. Since they had 'actual' authority to appoint these officers, they had 'actual' authority to make representations as to who the officers were. In both these cases the constitution of the company, whether it had been seen by the contractor or not, was relevant in order to determine whether the persons whose representations by conduct were relied upon as creating the 'apparent' authority of the agent had 'actual' authority to make the representations on behalf of the company. In *Mahony*'s case, if the persons in question were not persons who would normally be supposed to have such authority by someone who did not in fact know the constitution of the company, it may well be that the contractor would not succeed in proving condition (3), namely, that he relied upon the representations made by those persons, unless he proved that he did in fact know the constitution of the company. . . .

[509] In the present case the findings of fact by the county court judge are sufficient to satisfy the four conditions, and thus to establish that Kapoor had

'apparent' authority to enter into contracts on behalf of the company for their services in connection with the sale of the company's property, including the obtaining of development permission with respect to its use. The judge found that the board knew that Kapoor had throughout been acting as managing director in employing agents and taking other steps to find a purchaser. They permitted him to do so, and by such conduct represented that he had authority to enter into contracts of a kind which a managing director or an executive director responsible for finding a purchaser would in the normal course be authorised to enter into on behalf of the company. Condition (1) was thus fulfilled. The articles of association conferred full powers of management on the board. Condition (2) was thus fulfilled. The plaintiffs, finding Kapoor acting in relation to the company's property as he was authorised by the [510] board to act, were induced to believe that he was authorised by the company to enter into contracts on behalf of the company for their services in connection with the sale of the company's property, including the obtaining of development permission with respect to its use. Condition (3) was thus fulfilled. The articles of association, which contained powers for the board to delegate any of the functions of management to a managing director or to a single director, did not deprive the company of capacity to delegate authority to Kapoor, a director, to enter into contracts of that kind on behalf of the company. Condition (4) was thus fulfilled.

Cox v. Dublin City Distillery (No.2)
[1915] 1 I.R. 345

The company's regulations fixed the quorum of directors at two and provided that no director should vote on any matter in which he was personally interested. At a series of board meetings, the directors resolved to issue debentures to themselves as security for advances made by themselves to the company. At the same time, debentures were also issued to outsiders.

BARTON J.: . . . [353] I am of opinion that the three resolutions of the 12th and 16th May, 1903, and 20th January, 1904, were invalid. Article 94 of the company's articles of association provides that no director shall vote in respect of any contract or matter in which he is individually interested, otherwise than as a member of the company. Article 109 fixes the quorum, [354] until otherwise determined, at two. At the meeting of the 12th May, 1903, three directors were present, Kennedy, Doherty, and Howes, who resolved to issue £4,000 debentures to a trustee, whom I treat as an outsider, in trust for Kennedy and Doherty by way of security for advances. The case is quite indistinguishable in principle from *In re Greymouth Point Elizabeth Railway & Coal Co.* [1904] 1 Ch. 32. By the resolution of the 16th May, five directors, Doherty, Kennedy, Churton, Trower, and Howes, resolved to issue £1,150 debentures to the same trustee in trust for themselves in various proportions by way of security for advances. This resolution cannot, in my opinion, be split up, and is equally bad. By the resolution of the 20th January, 1904, three directors, Kennedy, Doherty, and Howes, resolved to issue thirty-seven debentures to the same trustee in trust for those making advances for a new yeast-plant by way of security, and proceeded to sign, seal, and issue debentures to themselves and other directors. The resolution was a nullity, and the two other directors cannot be regarded as outsiders who took without notice of the board's minutes.

Next I come to the case of debentures issued to non-directors. Four debentures were issued to the same trustee on May 16th, 1903, in trust for Adam S. Findlater; one debenture was issued on May 12th, 1903, and four on 20th January, 1904, to the same trustee, for William Findlater. One of these gentlemen had been a director some years previously; the other was a trustee for the second debenture holders; but they were not directors in 1903 and 1904; and, *qua* the board of directors, I hold them to be outsiders, to whom notice of the board's minutes cannot be attributed. In such a case the onus lies, in my opinion, upon the party impeaching the debentures to show that a person who is prima facie an outside holder of a debenture, which is good on its face, had actual or constructive notice of the irregularity: *County of Gloucester Bank v. Rudry Merthyr Colliery Co.* [1895] 1 Ch. 629. Accordingly, I hold that, although these resolutions were invalid, the ten debentures issued to a trustee for the Messrs. Adam and William Findlater are valid and binding.

Rolled Steel Products (Holdings) Ltd v. British Steel Corporation
[1986] 2 Ch. 246

Another company owned a substantial sum of money to the plaintiff's (British Steel) predecessor in title (Colvilles), which was guaranteed by one S., its controlling shareholder. S. was also a director of and major shareholder in the defendant company (Rolled Steel). The plaintiff doubted S.'s financial ability to honour his guarantee and persuaded him to have his guarantee substituted with one from the company. At a board meeting of its directors, including S., they resolved to grant that guarantee and one was executed in due course. But S. made no formal declaration that he had a financial interest in that transaction. The argument that the guarantee was *ultra vires* was rejected (see *ante*, p. 110).

SLADE LJ.: [282] Mr Shenkman unquestionably had a personal interest in the proposed guarantee and debenture which fell for consideration at the board meeting of the plaintiff on 22 January 1969. Under article 17 of the plaintiff's articles of association he was entitled to vote as a director in regard to these transactions and to be counted in the quorum of two directors required by article 18(a), notwithstanding his personal interest, if, but only if he declared his interest "in manner provided by section 199 of the [Companies Act 1948]." The manner provided by that section is this. Under section 199(1) the director has to declare "the nature of his interest at a meeting of the directors of the company." Section 199(2), so far as material, provides:

> "In the case of a proposed contract the declaration required by this section to be made by a director shall be made at the meeting of the directors at which the question of entering into the contract is first taken into consideration . . ."

The judge, as I have said, accepted the evidence of Mr. Shenkman that there had been no meeting of the board of the plaintiff before 22 January 1969 at which the desirability of the plaintiff giving a guarantee had been considered; and that he had made no declaration of his personal interest at the board meeting of 22 January 1969. . . .

[283] The possible relevance of the rule in *Royal British Bank v. Turquand*, 6 E. & B. 327 in the present context is obvious. The following statement of the rule, taken from *Halsbury's Laws of England*, 2nd ed., vol. V (1932), p. 423, was approved by the House of Lords in *Morris v. Kanssen* [1946] A.C. 459 (see *per* Lord Simonds at p. 474):

> "persons contracting with a company and dealing in good faith may assume that acts within its constitution and powers have been properly and duly performed and are not bound to inquire whether acts of internal management have been regular."

Lord Simonds later pointed out the rationale of the rule, at p. 475: "The wheels of business will not go smoothly round unless it may be assumed that that is in order which appears to be in order."

However, section 9(1) of the European Communities Act 1972 apart, persons dealing with a company registered under the Companies Acts must be taken not only to have read both the memorandum and articles of a company but to have understood them according to their proper meaning: See *Palmer's Company Law*, 23rd ed. (1982), vol. 1, para. 28-02 and the cases there cited.

Colvilles and British Steel Corporation, therefore, must be taken to have known that, under the articles of the plaintiff, a quorum of two was required for the transaction of the business of its directors and of the provisions of those articles relating to the declaration of a personal interest. They were well aware of the personal interest of Mr. Shenkman in the transactions proposed on 22 January 1969.

The signed minutes of the board meeting of that day, a copy which was subsequently supplied to Colvilles' solicitors (and indeed had been drafted by them), made no mention whatever of any declaration of a personal interest by

Mr. Shenkman. Since Colvilles and its legal advisers [284] must be taken to have had knowledge of the relevant provisions of the plaintiff's articles, they must also be taken to have known that the resolution could not have been validly passed *unless* Mr. Shenkman had duly declared his personal interest at that board meeting or a previous board meeting.

If, therefore, the defendants are to be allowed both to take and succeed on the *Turquand's* case point, this must mean that, in the circumstances subsisting in late January 1969, they were as a matter of law entitled to assume (contrary to the fact and without further inquiry) that Mr. Shenkman had duly declared his personal interest either at the board meeting of 22 January 1969 or at some previous board meeting of the plaintiff.

This contention might well have been unanswerable if the rule in *Turquand's* case, 6 E. & B. 327 were an absolute and unqualified rule of law, applicable in all circumstances. But, as the statement of the rule quoted above indicates, it is not. It is a rule which only applies in favour of persons dealing with the company in good faith. If such persons have notice of the relevant irregularity, they cannot rely on the rule.

Thus, in *Transvaal Lands Co. v. New Belgium (Transvaal) Land and Development Co.* [1914] 2 Ch. 488 the plaintiff company's articles, while enabling a director to be interested as a member of another company with which the plaintiff company was contracting, required that the director should disclose the nature of his interest and should not vote in respect of any contract in respect of which he was concerned. The provisions of this article were not observed when a contract was entered into by the directors of the plaintiff company when they resolved to enter into a contract with the defendant company, which had full notice of this irregularity. The Court of Appeal held that the plaintiff company had the right to rescind the contract.

Furthermore, even if persons contracting with a company do not have actual knowledge that an irregularity has occurred, they will be precluded from relying on the rule if the circumstances were such as to put them on inquiry which they failed duly to make. As Lord Simonds in *Morris v. Kanssen* [1946] A.C. 459 pointed out, at p. 475:

> "But the maxim has its proper limits. . . . It is a rule designed for the protection of those who are entitled to assume, just because they cannot know, that the person with whom they deal has the authority which he claims. This is clearly shown by the fact that the rule cannot be invoked if the condition is no longer satisfied, that is, if he who would invoke it is put upon his inquiry. He cannot presume in his own favour that things are rightly done if inquiry that he ought to make would tell him that they were wrongly done."

Mr. Heyman submitted that Lord Simonds's observation was confined to the particular facts of the case before him where the party seeking to take advantage of the rule was a director of the company and therefore under a duty to see that its transactions were effected in a regular manner: see p. 476. I do not, however, read Lord Simonds's statement of principle as confined in this manner. The decision of this court in A.[285]L. *Underwood Ltd v. Bank of Liverpool* [1924] 1 K.B. 775, which was cited in *Morris v. Kanssen* [1946] A.C. 459, in my opinion, illustrates that the very nature of a proposed transaction may put a person upon inquiry as to the authority of the directors of a company to effect it, even if he has no special relationship with the company. Whether in any given case the person dealing with the company is put on inquiry must depend on all the particular circumstances.

CHAPTER 14

Creditors and Debentures

While shareholder-protection is the dominant concern of company law, a major secondary theme is protecting those who give credit to companies. Because the debtor is the corporation itself and not its shareholders, and since the vast majority of companies possess limited liability, it is inevitable that there are special rules for companies' debts.

DIRECTORS' DUTIES TO CREDITORS

See *Company Law*, pp.492–493.

In Re Frederick Inns Ltd
[1994]1 I.L.R.M. 387 at pp.396–397

See *ante*, p. 583.

Note: See the critique of the Supreme Court's reasoning on several of the issues that arose in this case by Michael Fealy, 'The Role of Equity in the Winding Up of a Company' [1995] *D.U.L.J.* 18 at 21–23 on the question of directors' duties to creditors. Contrast the attitude of the Supreme Court in *Sweeney v. Duggan* [1997] 2 I.R. 531 (see *ante*, p. 87), where it was held that the managing director (and principal shareholder) of a 'one person' company, which at the time was in a financially precarious state and engaged in a quite dangerous business (quarrying), owed no duty of care to its employees, one of whom was seriously injured at the workplace and was never compensated.

Where a company is wound up, the Companies Acts give the liquidator a number of rights of action against errant directors and others who were involved in the management of the company, *inter alia*:

(i) sections 297 and 297A of the 1963 Act on 'fraudulent' and 'reckless trading'; see this author's *The Law of Company Insolvency* (1993), pp.258–267;

(ii) sections 202–204 of the 1990 Act on the duty to keep proper books of account;

(iii) section 298 of the 1963 Act, the 'misfeasance' procedure, which strictly is not a new right of action, but a speedy and convenient mechanism for bringing certain claims against present and former officers of the company.

FIXED AND FLOATING CHARGES

See *Company Law*, pp.493–512.
See too W.J. Gough, *Company Charges* (2nd ed. 1996).

Welch v. Bowmaker (Ireland) Ltd
[1980] I.R. 251

This case concerned a debenture which gave a composite charge. There was an undesignated charge on the company's 'undertaking and all its property and assets, present and future . . . for the time being'; at the same time, there was a specific charge over three identified properties the company owned. But the company also owned a fourth property, which was not expressly referred to in the debenture. The question was whether that property was also subject to a fixed charge. If yes, the first defendant (Bowmaker (Ireland)) got priority; if no, the second defendant (Bank of Ireland), with which the title deeds to the property in question had been deposited by way of security, got priority.

HENCHY J.: . . . [254] The complicating condition in the debenture is the first; it is in the following terms:
This debenture is to rank as a second charge on the property within mentioned and such charge is to be as regards the company's lands and premises for the time being and all its uncalled capital a specific charge and as regards all other the property and assets of the company a floating security but so that the company is not to be at liberty to create any mortgage or charge on its property for the time being in priority to or pari passu with this debenture.
Read literally and on its own, this condition is in conflict with the charging provision which I have already quoted. The charging provision makes only the properties specified in the schedule subject to a specific charge: an else (including Ivy Lawn) is subject only to a floating charge. If the first condition is to be given prevailing force, it would make 'the company's lands and premises for the time being' (thus including Ivy Lawn) subject to a specific charge.
Relying on the first condition, counsel for Bowmaker contend that, with regard to the Ivy Lawn property, the bank's equitable mortgage must yield priority to the rights of Bowmaker as holders of a specific charge under the debenture. On the other hand counsel for the bank contend that it is the charging provision that is definitive of Bowmaker's rights; they claim that Bowmaker had only a floating charge over Ivy Lawn so that, when the bank became equi-

table mortgagees on deposit of the tide deeds without (as is conceded) any actual notice of the prohibition in the debenture of the creation of a mortgage in priority to the debenture, the bank acquired rights over Ivy Lawn as mortgagees in priority to the rights of Bowmaker under the debenture.

In the High Court the judge, in an unreserved judgment, held with Bowmaker. He felt constrained to rule that the condition in the debenture gave Bowmaker a specific charge over Ivy Lawn. For my part, with the benefit of a fuller argument and after more mature consideration, I reach the opposite conclusion. I consider that the primary and dominant words and expressions delineating the extent of the powers and interests vested in Bowmaker by the debenture are to be found in the charging provision rather than in its attendant condition.

The relevant rule of interpretation is that encapsulated in the maxim [255] *generalia specialibus non derogant*. In plain English, when you find a particular situation dealt with in special terms, and later in the same document you find general words used which could be said to encompass and deal differently with that particular situation, the general words will not, in the absence of an indication of a definite intention to do so, be held to undermine or abrogate the effect of the special words which were used to deal with the particular situation. This is but a commonsense way of giving effect to the true or primary intention of the draftsman, for the general words will usually have been used in inadvertence of the fact that the particular situation has already been specially dealt with.

In this debenture the charging provision limits the creation of a specific charge to the properties specially marked out with particularity in the schedule. If given its full literal meaning the subsequent condition, which provides that the charge created by the debenture is to be a specific charge 'as regards the company's lands and premises for the time being', would have such a generality of application as to make nonsense of the clear distinction that is drawn in the charging provision between the properties marked out for a specific charge and the company's other properties. In such a case, in order to effectuate the draftsman's true intention, it is the special rather than the general words that must prevail. Those special words show that the primary and transcendent intention was that the Ivy Lawn property, since it was not included in the schedule, was not to be subject to a specific charge. Therefore, I would hold that the debenture gave Bowmaker only a floating charge over it.

The words in the condition referring to 'the company's lands and premises for the time being' should be construed as if they read 'the company's lands and premises for the time being *as specified in the schedule herein*', in that way the charging provision and the condition are brought into harmony.

I am fortified in this conclusion as to the extent of the specific charge by the fact that, when particulars of the charge created by the debenture were lodged with the registrar of companies for registration, the 'short particulars of the property' charged were given (over the signature of Bowmaker's solicitor) as 'the company's undertaking and all its property and assets present and future including its uncalled capital for the time being, goodwill and as a specific charge the following premises. . .'. The words after 'the following premises' described the properties specified in the schedule to the debenture. It would seem that Bowmaker did not consider (or intend anyone [256] consulting the statutory register of charges to consider) that the debenture had created a specific charge over the Ivy Lawn property. Bowmaker represented to the registrar of companies, and to the public at large, that the charge over the Ivy Lawn property created by the debenture was only a floating charge. In my view, that was a correct representation of the effect of the debenture.

Counsel for Bowmaker has argued that, even if that be so, the bank should be fixed with constructive notice of the provision in the debenture precluding the company from creating a mortgage (such as the bank got) which would have priority over the debenture. Since such a prohibition is more or less common form in modern debentures, there would be much to be said for applying the doctrine of constructive notice to such a situation were it not that it is settled law that there is no duty on the bank in a situation such as this to seek out the precise terms of the debenture: *Re Standard Rotary Machine Co.* (1906) 95 L.T. 829, *Wilson v. Kelland* [1910] 2 Ch. 306, and *G. & T. Earle Ltd v. Hemsworth R.D.C.* (1928) 140 L.T. 69. Actual or express notice of the prohibition must be shown before the subsequent mortgagee can be said to be deprived of priority.

Whatever attractions there may be in the proposition that priority should be deemed lost because a duty to inquire further was called for but ignored, and that such inquiry would have shown that the company was debarred from entering into a mortgage which would have priority over the debenture, the fact remains that it would be unfair to single out the bank for condemnatory treatment because of their failure to ascertain the full terms of the debenture when what they did was in accord with judicially approved practice and when such a precipitate change in the law would undermine the intended validity of many other such transactions. If the proposed extension of the doctrine of constructive notice is to be made, the necessary change in the law would need to be made prospectively and, therefore, more properly by statute.

I would allow the appeal and rule that the debenture did not give Bowmaker a specific charge over the Ivy Lawn property and that the bank's equitable mortgage over that property ranks in priority to Bowmaker's rights as the owners of a floating charge over that property under the debenture.

Note: A similar instance is *Re Armagh Shoes Ltd* [1982] N.I. 59.

In re Keenan Bros. Ltd
[1985] I.L.R.M. 641

This case concerns whether and, if so, in what circumstances a fixed charge can be given over a company's debtors or receivables. Ordinarily, book debts and the like are subject to floating charges. If the charge here was a fixed charge, then the Bank ranked before all the statutorily preferred creditors (on those preferences, see this author's *The Law of Company Insolvency* (1993) chapter 25).

The company created a charge in favour of Allied Irish Banks Ltd and a debenture in favour of Allied Irish Investment Bank Ltd The charge, which was stated to be a first fixed charge, was in respect of all the book debts and other debts of the company, present and future. The debenture charged by way of first fixed charge the present and future book debts of the company and all rights and powers in respect thereof. Clause 2 of the deed of charge provided that the company was obliged to pay into a designated account with the bank 'all moneys which it may receive in respect of the book debts and other debts hereby charged' and that it could not without the bank's prior consent make any withdrawals from the account. Clause 7(1) of the debenture was in similar terms. Clause 7(3) of the debenture provided that the company '[s]hall not without the consent in writing of the bank carry on its business other than in the ordinary and normal course'. In August 1983, the company entered into an agreement supplemental to the deed of charge. This provided for the opening of a 'Book Debts Receivable Account', withdrawals from which were to be in the joint names of the company and the bank. It also provided that the bank might, at the company's request, make sums available for the company's working account where required for carrying on its business; and that the account would be closed on the happening of any event making the money secured immediately repayable, when the bank could appoint a manager over the book debts charged. The account envisaged by the August 1983 agreement was opened in October 1983. A liquidator was appointed to the company in November 1983, and he applied to the High Court for directions as to whether the charge and debenture created fixed or floating charges on the monies in that account.

Keane J. held that the intention to be inferred from the instruments as a whole was that a floating charge had been created. The banks appealed.

McCARTHY J.: [420] The banks appealed against the decision of the High Court which held that the charges which had been created by the instruments of 3 May and 5 May 1983 were floating charges rather than fixed charges over the present and future book debts of the company. The result of that decision is that monies due to the Revenue have priority over the claims of the banks on foot of the instruments of May 1983; the claim by the banks is in respect of advances made between May 1983 and November 1983 when the company went into liquidation. It is unnecessary to detail the sequence of events or to recite the provisions of the instruments all of which are set out in detail in the elaborate judgment of Keane J. The underlying basis was that the company, in May 1983, was in serious financial difficulties and the banks, if they could secure the advances, were prepared to lend financial assistance. Because of the Companies Act 1963, a floating charge would not secure the required priority, but a fixed charge would. In *Siebe Gorman & Co. Ltd v. Barclays Bank Ltd* [1979] 2 Lloyd's Rep. 142, Slade J. had given a judicial blessing in England to a claim by way of fixed charge on book [421] debts where this was purported to be created by an instrument with marked similarities to those the subject of this appeal; during the course of the hearing, we were informed that they were, in fact, modelled on those in *Siebe Gorman*, although it was emphasised that monies received in respect of the book debts in the instant case were paid into a special account and not, as in *Siebe Gorman*, into the ordinary account of the mortgagor.

In *Re Armagh Shoes Ltd* [1982] N.I. 59, Hutton J. in the High Court of Northern Ireland identified an apparent divergence of judicial view and legal precedent in a series of decisions; *Tailby v. Official Receiver* (1888) 13 App. Cas. 523; *Re Yorkshire Woolcombers Association Ltd* [1903] 2 Ch. 284; *National Provincial Bank of England v. United Electric Theatres Ltd* [1916] 1 Ch. 132; *Stave Falls Lumber Co. Ltd v. Westminster Trust Co. Ltd* [1940] 4 WWR 382; *Evans v. Rival Granite Quarries Ltd* [1910] 2 KB 979; *Evans, Coleman & Evans Ltd v. RA. Nelson Construction Ltd* (1958) 16 MR 123 and the *Siebe Gorman* case.

It may well be that there are factual differences in the several cases but I think it desirable to identify some common ground so as to isolate the underlying principle and thereby resolve the two legal issues raised in this appeal, that is, (a) can a fixed charge be validly created in respect of future book debts? and (b) did the relevant instruments in this case do so?

Clearly, the parties wanted to secure the bank's advances in priority to all other claims, wanted to achieve this by a fixed charge whilst enabling the company to avail of advances from the bank covered, so to speak, by amounts received by the company in discharge of book debts and lodged to the special account; and wanted to achieve this result by using the *Siebe Gorman* scheme. It is not suggested that mere terminology itself – such as using the expression 'fixed charge' – achieves the purpose; one must look, not within the narrow confines of such term, not to the declared intention of the parties alone, but to the effect of the instructions whereby they purported to carry out that intention; did they achieve what they intended, or was the intention defeated by the ancillary requirements?

I turn, firstly, to the second issue, to determine the nature of the charge created by the instruments. In his judgment, Keane J. refers to the development of the floating charge in contrast to the fixed or specific charge:

"I think that one has to bear in mind at the outset that this form of charge made its first appearance in England as a by-product of the joint stock companies which began to flourish after the enactment of the joint Stock Companies Act 1844. In order to borrow money, such companies offered as security not merely their fixed assets, but also, assets which were regulary turned over in the course of business such as the companies' stock in trade. It was obviously cumbersome and impractical to charge such assets specifically with the repayment of advances, since it would mean the constant execution and release of securities as the assets were disposed of and replaced. Hence the concept developed of a charge which did not attach to any specific assets of the company, remained dormant until the mortgagee intervened and in the interim did not prevent the mortgagor from using the assets in question in the ordinary course of his business."

[422] It appears that what is now called a 'floating charge' on all property (the 'undertaking' – of a company) was first recognised in *Re Panama, New Zealand & Australian Royal Mail Co.* (1870) LR 5 Ch. App. 318, where it was held that the word 'undertaking' meant all the property present and future of the company, and that the charge thereon was effective and was to operate by way of floating security. In *Re Yorkshire Woolcombers Association Ltd* [1903] 2 Ch. 284; *sub nom. Illingworth v. Houldsworth* [1904] A.C. 355, there are a number of judicial analyses, if not definitions, of the term 'floating charge', or of the distinction between a floating charge and a specific or fixed charge. Citations from these judgments are to be found in the *Armagh Shoes* case and in the judgment of Keane J. in the instant appeal. I am content to cite the relevant extract from the speech, of enviable brevity, of Lord Macnaghten, [1904] AC 355, at p. 358:

"I should have thought there was not much difficulty in defining what a floating charge is in contrast to what is called a specific charge. A specific charge, I think, is one that *without more* [emphasis added] fastens on ascertained and definite property or property capable of being ascertained and defined; a floating charge, on the other hand, is ambulatory and shifting in its nature, hovering over and so to speak floating with the property which it is intended to affect until some event occurs or some act is done which causes it to settle and fasten on the subject of the charge within its reach and grasp."

I do not overlook the fact that Lord Macnaghten expressly agreed with the judgment of Farwell J. in the court of first instance.

I emphasise the phrase 'without more' because it seems to me to be the badge that identifies the specific charge. The other side of the coin, when one looks at the characteristics of a floating charge is that, before what is called crystalisation of the floating charge, the company has power to create legal mortgages and equitable charges in priority to the floating charge: see *Re Florence Land and Public Works Co.* (1879) 10 Ch. D. 530; *Re Colonial Trusts Corp.* (1880) 15 Ch. D. 465, and *Wheatley v. Silkstone & Haigh Moor Coal Co.* (1885) 29 Ch. D. 715, where North J. said:

> "but it (the equitable charge by deposit of title deeds) is not intended to prevent and has not the effect of in any way preventing the carrying on of the business in all or any of the ways in which it is carried on in the ordinary course; and, inasmuch as I find that in the ordinary course of business and for the purpose of the business this mortgage was made, it is a good mortgage upon and a good charge upon the property comprised in it, and is not subject to the claim created by the debentures."

The breadth of the company's powers in this regard may be limited by the terms of the floating charge, but such a qualification is strictly construed [423] and a legal mortgagee without notice would be entitled to his priority: see *Coveney v. Persse* [1910] 1 I.R. 194 (see *infra*, p. 629).

The learned trial judge laid particular emphasis on two clauses of the charging instruments. Clause 3(ii) of the charge dated 3 May 1983 in favour of Allied Irish Banks Ltd provides:

> "The company shall pay into an account with the bank designated for that purpose all monies which it may receive in respect of the book debts and other debts hereby charged and shall not, without the prior consent of the bank in writing, make any withdrawals or direct any payment from the said account."

Clause 7(1) of the instrument of 5 May 1983 with Allied Irish Investment Bank Ltd provides that the company:

> "shall not without the consent in writing of the bank carry on its business other than in the ordinary and normal course."

Clause 7(1) contains a provision to the same effect as that quoted from the instrument of 3 May, in respect of which Keane J. commented: 'it is patent that the parties intended the company to carry on its business so far as these assets were concerned. . . to collect the book debts, lodge them to its bank account and use them in the business in the ordinary way'. Mr Cooke S.C., for the banks, contends that this was a misconstruction of that clause, that its purpose was to give the bank a degree of control over exceptional transactions, but was far from directing the company to carry on its normal business, rather to trade subject to the express terms of the debenture with a provision for a cash flow set up by the bank in which the inflow of cash would go direct to the bank. In my view, this is the correct construction of that clause. As to the earlier quoted clause (in respect of the bank account) Keane J. said:

"Subject to the possible necessity to give notice in the case of the existing debts, the effect of the deeds was to vest the debts in the banks the moment they came into existence and to give the banks the right to collect them (on giving notice to the debtors); and the company, at the date of the execution of the deeds, ceased to have any interest in the debts whatever. If this, indeed, is what the parties intended, it is not easy to understand why it was thought necessary to provide that: (and he quotes Clause 3 (ii) of the first instrument). On this view of the transactions, the company had no business collecting any debts once the securities had been executed. If the charge in each case was intended to be a specific or fixed charge, such a provision was wholly unnecessary and indeed virtually meaningless."

In my view, it is because it was described as a specific or fixed charge [424] and was intended to be such that the requirement of a special bank account was necessary; if it were a floating charge, payment into such an account would be entirely inappropriate and, indeed, would conflict with the ambulatory nature of the floating charge to which Lord Macnaghten refers. In *Re Yorkshire Woolcombers Association Ltd* [1903] 2 Ch. 284 at p. 295, Romer L.J. postulated three characteristics of a floating charge, the third being that 'if you find that by the charge it is contemplated that, until some future step is taken by or on behalf of those interested in the charge, the company may carry on its business in the ordinary way as far as concerns the particular class of assets I am dealing with'. Mr Cooke S.C. has argued that this latter characteristic is essential to a floating charge and that the banking provision in the instruments here negatives such a characteristic; I would uphold this view. I have sought to identify from the speech of Lord Macnaghten the badge of a specific or fixed charge; that of the floating charge seems to me to be the absence of immediate effect or possible ultimate effect – in short, it may never happen; if the advances made or the debts incurred are repaid or discharged, then the cloud is dispersed never to return in that exact form. Towards the end of his judgment, Keane J. said:

"What the banks have sought to do in the present instance is to create a hybrid form of charge which incorporates all the advantages of a floating charge with none of the statutory limitations on its operation. The borrower continues to use the assets in the course of his business to his own benefit, and to the benefit of the lender who continues to earn interest on his loan in the knowledge that he can at any time realise his security if his prospects of ultimate repayment appear in peril. At the same time, he is protected from the consequences that would normally ensue for a lender who offers money on the security of the floating charge within 12 months of a winding up or in circumstances where the preferential creditors are owed substantial sums."

The charge, whatever it nature, for its validity had to be registered under the Companies Act 1963 and its existence would have been known to anyone upon casual enquiry – its existence as what was described as a fixed charge. Whilst acknowledging that the charge is somewhat hybrid in form because of the concession in respect of the collection of debts and lodgment to a special account, I do not recognise in it the ordinary characteristics of a floating charge – that it may crystalise on the happening of some future event. If the borrower, the company, is driven to such financial straits that it is prepared to effect an immediate charge upon its book debts, the existence of which charge is, in effect, published to the commercial and financial world, I do not accept that an elaborate system set up to enable the company to benefit by the collection of such debts detracts from its qualifying as a specific or fixed charge.

The remaining question, as raised by the Revenue Commissioners, is whether or not it is possible in law to create a fixed charge on future book [425] debts. There appears to be ample authority in England in support of this contention going back to the *Tailby* case (1888) 13 App. Cas. 523, and asserted in Canada in the *Evans, Coleman & Evans* case (1958) 16 DLR 123. I am content to adopt the observations of Davey J.A. at p. 127 of the latter report and hold that there is no legal bar to there being a fixed charge on future book debts. To echo Lord Watson in the *Tailby* case, at p. 536:

> "I cannot understand upon what principle an assignment of all legacies which may be bequeathed by any person to the assignor is to stand good, and effect is to be denied to a general assignment of all future book debts. As Cotton L.J. said in *Re Clarke* (1887) 36 Ch. D. 348, at p. 353: 'Vagueness comes to nothing if the property is definite at the time when the court comes to enforce the contract'. A future book debt is quite as capable of being identified as a legacy, and in this case the identity of the debt, with the subjects assigned, is not a matter of dispute."

Each book debt is a separate entity; granted, that even though it was assigned to the banks, it may be altered in whole or in part by, for example, a contra-account. That may go to the amount payable but it does not affect the transaction; there is no logic in seeking to distinguish between an accepted validity of a floating charge on future book debts and an alleged invalidity in a fixed charge on such debts.

In my judgment, the instruments executed between the company and the banks did effect what they were intended to effect and constituted fixed charges on all the book debts, present and future, of the company. I would allow the appeal accordingly.

In re Wogan's (Drogheda) Ltd
[1993] 1 I.R. 157

This case also concerns the circumstances in which a fixed charge can be given over a company's book debts. Unlike in the *Keenan Bros.* case (*supra*, 614) and in the *Siebe Gorman* case [1979] 2 Lloyd's Rep. 142 referred to there, the chargee bank was not one of the clearing banks. If the charge here were a floating charge, not alone would the financial viability of the company (then in examinership under the Companies (Amendment) Act 1990) have been more attractive but the entire charge may have been invalid under section 288 of the 1963 Act. Under Clause 5(b) of the charge, the company agreed not to deal in any way with its book debts, other than to realise them in the ordinary course of business; further, if so directed by the chargee, it would pay all those receivables into a designated bank account and would not then be free to withdraw them. At the relevant time the company was trading and realising its book debts in the normal way; unlike in *Keenan Bros.*, no special bank account had been designated by the chargee. For this reason, Denham J. held that it was a floating charge. The bank appealed.

FINLAY C.J.: [166] On behalf of the respondent it was submitted that the fundamental principle which is applicable to the construction of this debenture, which is a contract between the parties, is that which is common to the construction of all contracts, namely, that the intention of the parties is to be interpreted as evidenced by the terms of the contract itself, and that evidence of the conduct of the parties subsequent to entering into the contract is inadmissible to aid in its construction. It was, therefore, submitted that the learned trial judge in the court below erred in having regard to the evidence at all that a specified account pursuant to the clauses contained in the debenture had not been designated. Secondly, it was submitted in the alternative that it was incorrect in law to construe the decision of this Court in *In re Keenan Bros. Ltd* [1985] I.R. 401 (*supra*, p. 614) to be to the effect that in interpreting the terms of a debenture it was necessary that there should be evidence of the actual designation of a bank account into which book debts were to be paid, to be monitored and controlled by the lender, in order for the charge created by such debenture to be held in law a fixed charge, but that all that was necessary [167] was that the terms of the debenture itself, including a term with regard to the designation of accounts into which book debts were to be paid, as distinct from the actual designation of the accounts, should exist and that in those circumstances a fixed charge arose.

On behalf of the applicant it was urged that the interpretation of the decision of this Court in *In re Keenan Bros. Ltd* [1985] I.R. 401 arrived at by the learned trial judge was correct, and that it was necessary to inquire as to whether there was a specified or designated account into which book debts were to be paid.

In the alternative, it was submitted that, even if the debenture were to be construed and interpreted on its terms only, the provisions of clause 5(b) of the debenture providing for a designated banking account must be construed as a term imposing an obligation to lodge the monies received in respect of book debts and other debts or securities into such account, which was entirely conditional upon the specification or designation of the account concerned, and the condition or restriction arising from such provision did not operate and was not an element in the construction of the debenture until such designation had occurred. Without such provision, having regard to the decision in *Keenan's* case, it was argued, a floating charge only would be created by the debenture.

The relevant clauses of the debenture
At clause 4(d) the debenture provides as follows:

"The company as beneficial owner hereby assigns to and charges to and in favour of the lender by way of first fixed charge:

(iv) All book debts and other debts, revenues and claims both present and future (including choses in action which may give rise to a debt, revenue or claim and the proceeds of any insurance or similar claim) due or owing or which may become due or owing to or purchased or otherwise acquired by the company and the proceeds of payment or realisation of the same and the full benefit of all rights and remedies relating thereto" etc.

Clause 5(a) provides as follows:

"This debenture is one for securing the payment or repayment of all monies due or to become due by the company to the lender. The company shall not be at liberty without the prior consent of the [168] lender which may be granted or withheld at its absolute discretion to create or permit to subsist any mortgage charge or lien on or affecting any part of the charged properties and assets for the time being in priority to or pari passu with or puisne to the security created by this debenture."

Clause 5(b) provides as follows:

"The company shall not be entitled to deal with its book debts or other debts or securities for money as described in clause 4(d)(iv) hereof otherwise than by getting in and realising the same in the ordinary and proper course of business (and so that for this purpose the realisation of debts by means of block discounting, invoice discounting, sale, factoring or the like shall not be regarded as dealing in the ordinary proper course of business). The company hereby covenants to pay into such banking account or accounts as may be designated for such purpose by the lender, and whether with the lender or with any other banking institution designated by the lender, all monies which it may receive in respect of book debts and other debts or securities and not without the prior consent of the lender in writing withdraw or deal with such monies or to assign or purport to assign the same in favour of any other person and if called upon to do so by the lender to execute a legal assignment of such book debts and other debts and securities to the lender."

The only other clause specifically referred to in the submissions, though the general powers of the lender were relevant and referred to, was clause 8(a), which reads as follows:

"If the lender shall by notice in writing make a demand on the company as provided for in clause 8(a) hereof then the floating charge created by clause 4(e) hereof shall immediately on service of such notice on the company become crystallised and be a specific fixed charge on

(ii) all book debts and other debts and securities then due to the company (to the extent that the same are not already subject to the specific fixed charge created by clause 4(d)(iv) hereof)."

The decision
In his decision in the High Court in *In re Keenan Bros. Ltd* [1985] I.R. 401 Keane J. at the conclusion of his judgment, at p. 415, stated as follows:–

[169] "I should also add that in arriving at this conclusion I have had no regard to events which took place since the deed and debenture were executed. I have preferred to adopt the approach taken by Hutton J. in *In re Armagh Shoes Ltd* [1982] N.I. 59, which clearly accords with legal principle and with the decision of the House of Lords in *Whitworth Street Estates Ltd v. Miller* [1970] AC. 583, of rejecting the subsequent conduct of the parties as an admissible guide to the construction of a contract."

In the judgments of the members of this Court in *Keenan's* case, whilst Walsh J. deals in a limited way with the events which occurred and with the movements of money subsequent to the execution of the debenture, he appears to do so only for examination of the question as to how the operation of the fixed charge, which he agreed occurred under the debentures in that case, would affect the various accounts and monies. In none of the judgments, however, is there to be found any expression of dissent from the conclusion reached by Keane J. that the subsequent conduct of the parties was not a relevant evidential factor for the purpose of construing the debentures concerned, and in the detailed construction of the debenture concerned, the judgment of McCarthy J. in particular, appears clearly to me to be confined to the terms of the debentures.

In *Whitworth Street Estates Ltd v. Miller* [1970] AC. 583 in the speech of Lord Reid, at p. 603, it is stated as follows:

> "It has been assumed in the course of this case that it is proper, in determining what was the proper law, to have regard to actings of the parties after their contract had been made. Of course the actings of the parties (including any words which they used) may be sufficient to show that they made a new contract. If they made no agreement originally as to the proper law, such actings may show that they made an agreement about that at a later stage. Or if they did make such an agreement originally such actings may show that they later agreed to alter it. But with regard to actings of the parties between the date of the original contract and the date of Mr. Underwood's appointment, I did not understand it to be argued that they were sufficient to establish any new contract, and I think they clearly were not. As I understood him, counsel sought to use those actings to show that there was an agreement when the original contract was made that the proper law of that contract was to be the law of England. I must say that I had thought that it is now well settled that it is not legitimate to use as an aid in the construction of [170] the contract anything which the parties said or did after it was made. Otherwise one might have the result that a contract meant one thing the day it was signed, but by reason of subsequent events meant something different a month or a year later."

This view was concurred in by Lord Hodson, Viscount Dilhorne and Lord Wilberforce.

It is a principle which, in my view, must be adhered to in our law and the mischief created by departing from it would be in many instances considerable.

I therefore conclude that if the decision in the High Court is to be supported it cannot be supported upon the basis that it was correct to admit evidence of the failure to designate the account as evidence to assist in the interpretation of the contract. It could only be supported if clause 5 (b) of the contract is to be construed as providing, in effect, for a later agreement to be entered into between the parties by the designation by the respondent of a banking account into which the book debts proceeds are to be paid or, to put the matter in another way, if it can be construed as a clause which is conditional only and which can only become effective as between the parties if and when an account is designated, thus leading to the absence from the debenture of a characteristic which is essential to its interpretation as creating a fixed charge. I am not satisfied that the debenture can be so construed. It seems to me that the provisions of clauses 5(a) and 5 (b) of it, coupled with and, to an extent, supported by the express provision at clause 4 of a fixed charge over book debts and the subsequent reference to the specific fixed charge so created in clause 8, give to this debenture the precise characteristics which are set out in the judgment of McCarthy J. in *In re Keenan Bros. Ltd* [1985] I.R. 401 which render these charges to constitute in law what they are expressed to constitute, namely, fixed charges.

It would appear to me to be inconsistent with the terms of this deed and with the prohibition on construing it in accordance with the subsequent conduct of the parties to arrive at any other conclusion. If a lender, having availed of a debenture in these terms, as a concession delays the designation of a bank account or suspends for some period the operation of direct control over the bank account into which the proceeds of book debts are paid, thus permitting the company issuing the debenture to carry on trading in a more normal fashion than strict compliance with the terms of a fixed charge would permit, there does not appear to be any principle of law or of justice which would deprive [171] such a lender of the rights agreed by the debtor company of a fixed charge over the assets, whereas, a lender with a more draconian approach to the rights which were granted to it by a debenture would be in a more advantageous position.

Note: The core test of whether a charge is a floating charge is whether, at the time, the company is legally free to use up the charged assets in the course of its business. For such time as the bank above did not designate a special account, the company was entirely free under Clause 5(b) to consume its receivables in the course of its business, which might suggest that it was a floating charge; that once a special account is so designated, the charge would then crystalise into a fixed charge. The correctness of this decision has been questioned by Fealy, 'Fixed Charge Over Book Debts: A Loosening of the Reins' [1993] *I.L.T.* 133. In England, the Court of Appeal came to a similar conclusion as in *Wogan's* but by entirely different and less unconvincing reasoning, in *In re New Bullas Trading Ltd* [1994] 1 B.C.L.C. 485. But a differently constituted Court of Appeal disreguarded *New Bullas*, in *Royal Trust Bank v. National Westminister Bank* [1996] 1 B.C.L.C 682. English insolvency lawyers have been largely critical of the reasoning of *New Bullas*, e.g. Goode, 'Charges Over Book Debts: A Missed Opportunity' (1994) 110 *LQR* 592. Indeed in *Re Holdair (infra)* the Supreme Court almost performed a *volte face*.

In re Holidair Ltd
[1994] 1 I.R. 416

One of the main issues here also was whether the charge given over the company's book debts was indeed a fixed charge, as it purported to be, or only a floating charge. If it were a floating charge, an examiner who had been appointed under the Companies (Amendment) Act 1990, would have far greater freedom of action than if it were a fixed charge, in that it would be easier for him to raise funds in order to finance the company while it was in examinership. The charge closely resembled that in *Wogan's* case but the chargee here was a clearing bank (A.I.B.). Relying on *Wogan's* case, Costello P. held that it was a fixed charge. The examiner appealed.

BLAYNEY J.: [444] The provisions in the mortgage debenture in regard to the book debts are as follows:

"3.01 MORTGAGES AND FIXED CHARGES
Each of the companies as beneficial owner and to the intent that the mortgages and charges contained in this clause shall be a continuing security for the payment and discharge of the secured debt and all monies and liabilities hereby covenanted to be paid and discharged by it, hereby . . .

F: Charges by way of first fixed charge in favour of the trustee on behalf of the banks all book debts and other debts present now and from time to time due or owing to such company, together with all rights and powers of recovery in respect thereof . . .

3.08 BOOK DEBTS
With reference to the book debts and any other debts hereby charged the companies shall pay into such accounts with the banks or any of them as the trustee may from time to time select all monies which they may receive in respect of such debts and shall not without the prior consent in writing of the trustee sell, factor, discount or otherwise charge, assign or [445] dispose of the same in favour of any other person or purport so to do and the companies shall if called upon so to do by the trustee from time to time execute legal assignments of such book debts and other debts to the trustee in such form as the trustee shall require and at the companies' own expense."

Mr. Cooke submitted that because the charge was described as a fixed charge it should be accepted as such unless there were other indications in the debenture inconsistent with this construction. I would reject this submission for the same reasons that a similar submission was rejected by Keane J. in *In re Keenan*

Brothers Ltd [1985] I.R. 401. Keane J. said in his judgment at p. 410:

> "I take the view that where the intention of the parties, inferred from the instrument read as a whole, is to create a floating rather than a fixed security, this intention should not be treated as displaced by the fact that the parties have, for whatever reason, chosen to give the charge thus created an inapposite description." . . .

The normal characteristics of a floating charge were set out as follows in the well known passage from the judgment of Romer L.J. in the Court of Appeal in the case of *In re Yorkshire Woolcombers'Association Ltd* [1903] 2 Ch. 284 at p. 295:

> "I certainly do not intend to attempt to give an exact definition of the term 'floating charge', nor am I prepared to say that there will not be a floating charge within the meaning of the Act, which does [446] not contain all the three characteristics that I am about to mention but I certainly think that if a charge has the three characteristics that I am about to mention it is a floating charge.
>
> (1) If it is a charge on a class of assets of the company present and future;
> (2) if that class is one which, in the ordinary course of the business of the company, would be changing from time to time; and
> (3) if you find that by the charge it is contemplated that, until some future step is taken by or on behalf of those interested in the charge, the company may carry on its business in the ordinary way as far as concerns the particular class of assets I am dealing with."

It is quite clear that book debts have the first two characteristics. They are a class of assets of the companies present and future and in the ordinary course of the business of the companies they would be changing from time to time. The sole issue is whether the provisions in the debenture permitted the companies to carry on their business in the ordinary way in so far as concerned their book debts. In my opinion it did. The only provision in the debenture which might be relied upon as possibly preventing the companies from carrying on their business in the normal way using their book debts is clause 3.08, which I have already cited, and in my opinion it does not have this effect.

It should be noted firstly that the prohibition in the second part of the clause is a prohibition relating to the book debts and not monies received in respect of such debts. The phraseology used – "shall not without the prior consent in writing of the trustee sell, factor, discount or otherwise charge, assign or dispose of the same" is appropriate only to refer to book debts and not to cash received in respect of such debts. And this is clearly the sense in which this prohibition was understood by the banks. In the letter of January

31, 1994, from A.I.B. Capital Markets plc to the directors of Holidair Ltd this term of the debenture is referred to as follows:

"The company shall not, without the prior consent of the trustee, sell, factor, discount or otherwise charge, assign or dispose of such debts."

The sole question then is whether the first part of the clause prevented the companies from using the proceeds of their book debts in their ordinary day to day business. The relevant provision is that "the companies shall pay into such accounts with the banks or any of them [447] as the trustee may from time to time select all monies which they may receive in respect of such debts". What meaning is to be given to the phrase "such accounts with the banks or any of them as the trustee may from time to time select"? It seems to me that it must mean such accounts of one or other of the five companies who granted the mortgage debenture as the trustee may from time to time select. In other words, the trustee was being given a discretion to determine into what account, with what bank, the monies were to be paid. In the letter of January 31, 1994, to which I have already referred, the banks' attempt to put a different construction on this clause when they state that the trustee directs "that all book debts be lodged to accounts in the name of the trustee, relating to the appropriate company, at AIB Bank, 5/6, O'Connell Street, Clonmel". Such a construction would be wholly inconsistent with clause 8.12 of the mortgage debenture which provides as follows:

"To carry on business in proper and efficient manner: Each of the companies shall carry on and conduct and procure that any subsidiary of the companies shall carry on and conduct its business in a proper and efficient manner and not make any substantial alterations in the nature of its business."

If, from the date of the debenture, it would have been open to the trustee to direct that the proceeds of the book debts should immediately be paid to him, it would have been quite impossible for the companies to carry on business in the manner in which they were obliged to do so under clause 8.12.

I am satisfied, accordingly, that the correct construction of the clause is that the trustee had a discretion to determine into what company account, with what bank, the proceeds of book debts should be paid from time to time. But there is no restriction in the clause on the companies drawing the monies out of these accounts. Accordingly, there is nothing in it to prevent the companies from using the proceeds of the book debts in the normal way for the purpose of carrying on their business. By reason of this the charge has also the third characteristic referred to by Romer L.J. in his judgment in *In re Yorkshire Woolcombers' Association Ltd* [1903] 2 Ch. 284 and is accordingly a floating charge and not a fixed charge.

The two recent Irish cases in which a charge on book debts was held to be a fixed charge are both distinguishable by reason of the particular terms of the debenture in each case. In *In re Keenan Brothers Ltd* [1985] I.R. 401 (*supra*, p. 614) the debenture contained a clause as follows:

[448] "The company at all times during the continuance of this security:

7.1 shall pay all monies received by it from time to time in respect of book debts into an account with Allied Irish Banks Limited at 36, Tullow Street, Carlow, designated for that purpose and shall not without the prior consent of the bank in writing make any withdrawal from the said account nor direct any payment to be made from the said account."

The effect of this was that there was a complete prohibition on the company using the proceeds of the book debts: a prohibition which does not exist in the present case.

In *In re Wogan's (Drogheda) Ltd* [1993] 1 I.R. 157 (*supra*, p. 614) the debenture contained a very similar restriction which was as follows:

"The company hereby covenants to pay into such banking account or accounts as may be designated for such purpose by the lender, and whether with the lender or with any other banking institution, designated by the lender, all monies which it may receive in respect of book debts and other debts or securities and not without the prior consent of the lender in writing to withdraw or deal with such monies or to assign or purport to assign the same in favour of any other person and if called upon to do so by the lender to execute a legal assignment of such book debts and other debts and securities to the lender."

The existence of that clause in the debenture clearly distinguishes that case from the present.

For these reasons I am satisfied that the charge created by the debenture is a floating charge, and not a fixed charge, and accordingly that it is necessary to deal with the submission made on behalf of the companies and the examiner that, while the floating charge would have crystallised on the appointment of the receivers, it would have become decrystallised, that is to say, it would have resumed its character of a floating charge on the appointment of the examiner. In my opinion this submission is well-founded.

Once the examiner was appointed, the receivers could no longer act (s. 5, sub-s. 2 (b) of the Act of 1990). It would accordingly have been pointless to keep the book debts frozen. The receivers would have had no right to collect them. Apart from this, since the purpose of the Act of 1990 as emphasised by the Chief Justice in his judgment, is the protection of the company and consequently of its shareholders, workforce and creditors, it would be wholly inconsistent with that purpose [449] that the companies would be deprived of the use of their book debts particularly as it appears that they are absolutely essential for their survival during the period of protection. Furthermore, it is no injustice to the debenture holders who appointed the receivers since the companies are continuing to trade and so continuing to create new book debts to replace those that may be paid and the proceeds of which may be used by the companies. Finally, it seems to me that if the receivers were to insist upon the charge on the book debts remaining crystallised, they would be in breach of section 5, sub-s. 2 (d) of the Act of 1990, which provides that:

> "Where any claim against the company is secured by a charge on the whole or any part of the property, effects or income of the company, no action may be taken to realise the whole or any part of such security, except with the consent of the examiner."

For these reasons I would hold that on the appointment of the examiner the charge on the book debts ceased to be crystallised and became again a floating charge.

I would accordingly allow the appeal of the companies and the examiner against the decision of the High Court in regard to the nature of the charge on the book debts.

Note: One of the peculiar features of *Keenan*, *Wogans* and *Holdair* is that in all of them the trial judges were overruled on appeal and, further, the five-judge Supreme Court was always unanimous. The basis for Blayney J. distinguishing *Wogan's* is most unconvincing. The clause in the debenture in *Wogan's*, referred to above, is virtually identical to clause 3.08 in *Holdair* except that the former contained the stipulation 'shall not . . . withdraw or deal with such monies or assign . . . the same'. There was no need in *Holdair* for the bank to include a similar express stipulation because the debtors were to be lodged to an account with it, over which it had control and could veto any withdrawals so long as the company was indebted to it. By contrast, the bank in *Wogan's* was not a clearing bank, which meant that debtors' cheques had to be paid into an account elsewhere, which it did not directly control and therefore required an express provision to that effect.

Coveney v. Persse
[1910] I.R. 194

Debentures which grant floating charges usually contain restrictive or 'negative pledge' clauses, placing certain constraints on the chargeor's freedom to deal with the assets in question in the ordinary course of its business. In the present instance, a floating charge granted over stocks of whiskey contained the following proviso: 'the company shall not be at liberty to create any mortgage or charge ranking in priority to or *pari passu* with the debentures or these presents.' At one time the company purported to sell whiskey, subject to an undertaking to repurchase it. But on taking legal advice that this arrangement could very well contravene the above prohibition, a new arrangement was entered into with purchasers. All references in their agreements to pledges and redemptions were taken out and it was made clear that the whiskey was to be the purchasers' property, but the company still would have an option to repurchase it after four years. One the questions was whether this arrangement contravened the above 'negative pledge' clause.

PALLES C.B.: [214] I now come to the transactions which took place after March, 1906, when the plaintiff had admittedly received a copy of the debentures. As to these, I have, in the first place, to say that I see no reason to come to the conclusion that these transactions were not, in honesty and reality, such as the documents present them to be. The plaintiff had been in the habit of advancing money on transactions which the law considered pledges. He became aware of the debentures which prohibited such pledges. He was, doubtless, advised that if there were a change in the nature of the transaction, if a sale were substituted for a pledge, the transaction would be valid; and I hold, not that the form only of the transaction was changed, its substance remaining the same – but that the substauce was changed, that the real transaction was that which was represented by the documents. I see no more reason to impute any fraud or any difference between the real transaction and the document than there was in the *Yorkshire Railway Wagon Co. v. Maclure* 21 Ch. D. 309, and upon the construction of those documents I hold that the real transactions were sales, not loans: *Goodman v. Grierson* 2 Ba. & B. 274–9; *Williams v. Owen* 5 Myl. & Cr. 303. The parties must have expressly bargained that the Company should not be entitled to the right to redeem which was given by the former documents. The money was advanced upon the faith of the abandonment of that right. The presence or absence of reciprocal rights is the, determining element in ascertaining whether the document evidences a sale or a pledge. It is too much to ask us to hold that in an honest commercial transaction, in which the parties were at arms' length, the stipulation upon which, to their knowledge, the validity of the transaction depended is to be abrogated with the view of avoiding the transaction.

In re Brightlife Ltd
[1987] 1 Ch. 200

One of the issues here was whether a purported fixed charge on book debts was indeed a fixed charge; Hoffman J. held it was not, distinguishing, *inter alia*, *Re Keenan Bros. (supra)*. The other question was whether the floating charge could be converted or 'crystallised' into a fixed charge by the chargee serving a notice to that effect on the company. Clause 3B of the debenture stated that the chargee 'may at any time by notice to Brightlife convert the floating charge into a specific charge as regards any assets specified in the notice which (the chargee) shall consider to be in danger of being seized or sold under any form of distress or execution levied or threatened or to be otherwise in jeopardy and may appoint a receiver thereof.' If this stipulation enabled the chargee, by serving such notice, to crystallise the charge, then the chargee ranked in priority to the several statutorily preferred creditors.

HOFFMANN J.: [210] I come next to the alternative submission for Norandex, namely that the floating charge was converted into a fixed charge before the resolution for winding up. The relevant facts are as follows. On 4 December 1984 Brightlife sent out notices of a creditors' meeting to be held on 20 December 1984 pursuant to section 293 of the Companies Act 1948. Norandex sent Brightlife four separate notices dated 10 December. The first was a demand for payment of £221,658. The second was a notice pursuant to clause 3(B):

> "of the conversion with immediate effect of the floating charge created [by the debenture] into a specific charge over all the assets of Brightlife Ltd the subject of the said floating charge."

The third was a demand pursuant to clause 13 for the execution forthwith of "a legal assignment of all book and other debts currently due to Brightlife Ltd, specifying full details of the said debts therein." The fourth concerned the contractual arrangements between the parties and is now irrelevant. The four notices were served not later than 13 December. Brightlife did not execute the legal assignment required by the third notice, and on 20 December the winding up resolution was passed.

Mr. Sheldon relies upon the notice under clause 3(B) as having crystallised the floating charge over all the assets before the winding up. [211] Alternatively, he relies upon the notice under clause 13 as having done so in respect of the book debts. The uninitiated might ask why it is important to ascertain whether the floating charge crystallised on 13 December. After all, if it did not, there can be no doubt that it would have done so when the winding up resolution was passed on 20 December. The importance of the dates lies in the construction given to what is now section 614(2)(b) of the Companies Act 1985 (same as section 285(7)(b) of the 1963 Act) by Bennett J. in *In re Griffin Hotel Co. Ltd* [1941] Ch. 129. He decided in that case that the priority given by the statute to preferential debts applied only if there was a charge still floating at the moment of the winding up and gave the preferential creditors priority in property which at that moment was comprised in the floating charge.

It follows that if the debenture holder can manage to crystallise his floating charge before the moment of winding up, section 614(2)(b) gives the preferential creditors no priority. On the other hand, in the usual case of crystallisation before winding up, namely by appointment of a receiver, they may still be entitled to priority under another section of the Companies Act 1985. This is section 196 (same as section 98 of the 1963 Act), which applies:

> "where either a receiver is appointed on behalf of the holders of any debentures of a company secured by a floating charge, or possession is taken by or on behalf of those debenture-holders of any property comprised in or subject to the charge."

In such a case, subsection (2) provides:

> "If the company is not at the time in course of being wound up, the . . . [preferential debts] . . . shall be paid out of assets coming to the hands of the receiver or other person taking possession, in priority to any claims for principal or interest in respect of the debentures."

Both section 614(2)(b) and section 196 originate in the Preferential Payments in Bankruptcy Amendment Act 1897. One imagines that they were intended to ensure that in all cases preferential debts had priority over the holder of a charge originally created as a floating charge. It would be difficult to think of any reason for making distinctions according to the moment at which the charge crystallised or the event which brought this about. But *In re Griffin Hotel Co. Ltd*, [1941] Ch. 129 revealed a defect in the drafting. It meant, for example, that if the floating charge crystallised before winding up, but otherwise than by the appointment of a receiver, the preferential debts would have no priority under either section. For example, if crystallisation occurred simply because the company ceased to carry on business before it was wound up, as in *In re Woodroffes (Musical Instruments) Ltd* [1986] Ch. 366, the preferential debts would have no priority. One could construct other examples of cases which would slip through the net. Mr. Sheldon submits that this is such a case. He says that the notices under clauses 3(B) and 13 caused crystallisation of the floating charge over all or part of the assets before the winding up but without the appointment of a receiver.

Since *In re Griffin Hotel Co. Ltd* [1941] Ch. 129 Parliament has made many amendments to the Companies Acts but until very recently [212] no attempt was made to reverse the effect of the decision. The Insolvency Act 1985 has now done so by defining a "floating charge" as "a charge which, as created, was a floating charge" (see section 108(3) and compare paragraph 15 of Schedule 6) but the Act had not been passed at the time of these transactions. *In re Griffin Hotel Co. Ltd* has also been followed by Vinelott J. in *In re Christonette International Ltd* [1982] 1 W.L.R. 1245. Mr. Mummery therefore conceded for the purpose of the hearing before me that the commissioners would have no priority in respect of any assets over which the floating charge had crystallised before the resolution for winding up. But he reserved the point for a higher court.

The argument Mr. Mummery actually advanced before me was far more radical. He said that the events of crystallisation were fixed by law and not by the agreement of the parties. Those events were (1) winding up, (2) appointment of a receiver, and (3) ceasing to carry on business. These three events and only these three would cause crystallisation notwithstanding any agreement to the contrary. Their common features were that in each case the business of the company would cease, or at any rate cease to be conducted by the directors.

Mr. Mummery referred to a number of cases in support of this submission. First, there were cases in which it was held that crystallisation had taken place on one or other of the three events notwithstanding the absence of an express provision to that effect. For example, in *In re Crompton & Co. Ltd* [1914] 1 Ch. 954, Warrington J. held that a floating charge crystallised on a winding up for the purposes of reconstruction notwithstanding that event being excluded from a clause containing the events of default which made the loan immediately repayable. At p. 964 Warrington J. described winding up as an event "which by law independently of stipulation would make the debenture realisable." It must be observed that Warrington J. said "independently of stipulation" and not "notwithstanding any stipulation to the contrary." In a later passage he said, at p. 965: "the parties . . . have not provided as a matter of bargaining that, notwithstanding the general law, the other events shall not crystallise the security."

In my judgment, when Warrington J. said that crystallisation on winding up was a matter of general law, he meant only that such a consequence was an implied term of a floating charge in the sense described by Lord Tucker in *Lister v. Romford Ice and Cold Storage Co. Ltd* [1957] A.C. 555, when he said, at p. 594:

> "Some contractual terms may be implied by general rules of law. These general rules, some of which are now statutory, for example, Sale of Goods Act, Bills of Exchange Act, etc., derive in the main from the common law by which they have become attached in the course of time to certain classes of contractual relationships, for example, landlord and tenant, innkeeper and guest, contracts of guarantee and contracts of personal service."

The existence of such rules of law by which terms are implied in a floating charge is not inconsistent with the transaction being wholly [213] consensual and the implied terms liable to exclusion by contrary agreement.

Secondly, Mr. Mummery relied upon a number of cases in which courts have rejected a submission that an event of default, not being one of his three, has caused an automatic crystallisation. The most famous of these is the decision of the House of Lords in *Governments Stock and Other Securities Investment Co. Ltd v. Manila Railway Co. Ltd* [1897] A.C. 81. Mr. Mummery said that these cases showed that such events could not as a matter of law cause crystallisation.

In my view, however, the speeches in the *Manila Railway* case make it clear that the House of Lords regarded the question as being one of construction alone. They give rise to a plain inference that a sufficiently explicit provision for automatic crystallisation on default would have been given effect. It is true that the commercial inconvenience of automatic crystallisation gives rise to a strong presumption that it was not intended by the parties. Very clear language will be required. But that does not mean that it is excluded by a rule of law.

The nearest any judge in this country has come to asserting such a rule of law is in *Edward Nelson & Co. Ltd v. Faber & Co.* [1903] 2 K.B. 367, where Joyce L, after citing various judicial descriptions of the standard characteristics of a floating charge, said, at p. 376:

> "It follows, I think, from these and other cases that such a debenture as this in the present case does not cease to be a floating security . . . until the company has been wound up, or stops business, or a receiver has been appointed at the instance of the debenture-holders. . . ."

Taken by itself, that remark may appear to lend support to Mr. Mummery's tripartite rule of law. But I think that a fair reading of the whole judgment shows that Joyee J. also accepted that his enumeration was subject to contrary agreement.

Thirdly, Mr, Mummery cited several authoritative statements of the standard characteristics of a floating charge, particularly those of Lord Macnaghten in the *Manila Railway* case (1897) A.C. 81 and *Illingworth v. Houldsworth* [1904] A.C. 355, 358, and Romer L.J. in the latter case in the Court of Appeal, *In re Yorkshire Woolcombers Association Ltd* [1903] 2 Ch. 284, 295. For example, in the *Manila Railway* case [1897] A.C. 81, 86, Lord Macnaghten said that it was of the essence of a floating charge that it remained dormant "until the undertaking charged ceases to be a going concern, or until the person in whose favour the charge is created intervenes." Mr. Mummery said that this formulation appeared to rule out automatic crystallisation without any act on the part of the debenture-holder. To this Mr. Sheldon replied that he was not asserting automatic crystallisation: both of the notices upon which he relied were acts of intervention by the party entitled to the charge.

There is force in this answer but in my judgment there is a more fundamental objection to the use Mr. Mummery seeks to make of the authorities. In *Illingworth v. Houldsworth* [1904] A.C. 355, 358, Lord Macnaghten was at pains to point out that he had not attempted in the *Manila Railway* case [1897]

A.C. 81, to propound a "definition" of a [214] floating charge. He had only offered a "description." In making this distinction, it seems to me that what Lord Macnaghten had in mind was that a floating charge, like many other legal concepts, was not susceptible of being defined by the enumeration of an exhaustive set of necessary and sufficient conditions. All that can be done is to enumerate its standard characteristics. It does not follow that the absence of one or more of those features or the presence of others will prevent the charge from being categorised as "floating." There are bound to be penumbral cases in which it may be difficult to say whether the degree of deviation from the standard case is enough to make it inappropriate to use such a term. But the rights and duties which the law may or may not categorise as a floating charge are wholly derived from the agreement of the parties, supplemented by the terms implied by law. It seems to me fallacious to argue that once the parties have agreed on some terms which are thought sufficient to identify the transaction as a floating charge, they are then precluded from agreeing to any other terms which are not present in the standard case.

Fourthly, Mr. Mummery said that the courts should take a lead from Parliament, which in the Preferential Payments in Bankruptcy Amendment Act 1897 and subsequent company legislation apparently assumed that it need provide for only two possible events of crystallisation, namely the appointment of a receiver and a winding up. Even on Mr. Mummery's own submission this means that Parliament failed to consider his third event, cessation of business. It is true that *In re Woodroffes (Musical Instruments) Ltd* [1986] Ch. 366, was the first case in which a court expressly decided that cessation of business had crystallised a floating charge. But, as Nourse J. pointed out, this had been generally assumed for about a century. Furthermore, if Parliament is to provide any guidance, it is of some interest that section 7(1)(iv) of the Agricultural Credits Act 1928 creates a statutory floating charge which can be crystallised without appointment of a receiver or winding up by a notice not dissimilar from that given under clause 3(B) in this case. I therefore do not think that I can draw any inferences about the nature of a floating charge from the way in which it has been treated in legislation.

Fifthly, Mr. Mummery said that public policy required restrictions upon what the parties could stipulate as crystallising events. A winding up or the appointment of a receiver would have to be noted on the register. But a notice under clause 3(13) need not be registered and a provision for automatic crystallisation might take effect without the knowledge of either the company or the debenture-holder. The result might be prejudicial to third parties who gave credit to the company. Considerations of this kind impressed Berger J. in the Canadian case of *Reg. in right of British Columbia v. Consolidated Churchill Copper Corporation Ltd* [1978] 5 W.W.R 652 where the concept of "self-generating crystallisation" was rejected.

I do not think that it is open to the courts to restrict the contractual freedom of parties to a floating charge on such grounds. The floating charge was in vented by Victorian lawyers to enable manufacturing and trading companies to raise loan capital on debentures. It could offer the [215] security of a charge over the whole of the company's undertaking without inhibiting its ability to trade. But the mirror image of these advantages was the potential prejudice to the general body of creditors, who might know nothing of the floating charge but find that all the company's assets, including the very goods which they had just delivered on credit, had been swept up by the debenture-holder. The public interest requires a balancing of the advantages to the economy of facilitating the borrowing of money against the possibility of injustice to unsecured creditors. These arguments for and against the floating charge are matters for Parliament rather than the courts and have been the subject of public debate in and out of Parliament for more than a century.

Parliament has responded, first, by restricting the rights of the holder of a floating charge and secondly, by requiring public notice of the existence and enforcement of the charge. For example, priority was given to preferential debts in 1897 and the Companies Act 1907 invalidated floating charges created within three months before the commencement of the winding up. This period has since been extended and is now one year. The registration of floating and other charges was introduced by the Companies Act 1900. The Companies Act 1907 required registration of the appointment of a receiver and the Companies Act 1927 required notice of such appointment to be given on the company's letters and invoices.

These limited and pragmatic interventions by the legislature make it in my judgment wholly inappropriate for the courts to impose additional restrictive rules on grounds of public policy. It is certainly not for a judge of first instance to proclaim a new head of public policy which no appellate court has even hinted at before. I would therefore respectfully prefer the decision of the New Zealand Supreme Court in *In re Manurewa Transport Ltd* [1971] N.Z.L.R. 909, recognising the validity of a provision for automatic crystallisation, to the contrary dicta in the Canadian case I have cited. For present purposes, however, it is not necessary to decide any questions about automatic crystallisation. The notices under clauses 3(B) and 13 constitute intervention by the debenture-holder and there is in my judgment no conceptual reason why they should not crystallise the floating charge if the terms of the charge upon their true construction have this effect.

Mr. Mummery's last submission was that the actual notice under clause 3(B) was ineffective because the assets over which the charge was to be crystallised were not "specified in the notice." The notice said that it was to apply to "all the assets of Brightlife Ltd the subject of the said floating charge." In my judgment that is sufficient specification. It is not necessary to list each separate asset. Although my decision that the notice under clause 3(B) crystallised the charge makes it unnecessary for me to decide whether the notice under clause 13 did so in respect of the book debts, I will add for the sake of completeness that in my judgment it did. The company's obligation to execute an assignment removed that freedom to deal with the debts which made the charge float.

REGISTRATION OF CHARGES

Welch v. Bowmaker (Ireland) Ltd
[1980] I.R. 251

See *supra*, p. 611.

RECEIVERS

Airlines Airspares Ltd v. Handley Page Ltd
[1970] 1 Ch. 193

This case concerns what is often referred to as a 'hive down' arranged by receivers. The plaintiffs were the assignees of the benefit of an agreement of 1966 between K. Ltd and K. of the first part and the first defendants of the other part, under which the first defendants agreed, inter alia, to pay to K. Ltd and K. a commission of £500 in respect of every aircraft of a type known as 'Jetstream' sold by the first defendants. Subsequently, the first defendants issued a debenture to the bank; and later the bank, under the power contained in the debenture, appointed a receiver who was accorded the usual wide powers conferred on a mortgagee. In order to carry out his duties in the most effective manner, the receiver caused the first defendants to create a subsidiary company, A. Ltd, to which they assigned such parts of their undertaking as represented an economically viable business, namely, their business connected with the 'Jetstream' aircraft. The receiver then entered into negotiations for the sale of the shares of A. Ltd, and notified K. and the plaintiffs that he could no longer comply with the agreement of 1966. The plaintiffs sought an injunction to restrain the sale of the shares and a declaration that they were entitled to the agreed commission.

GRAHAM J.: . . . [196] Mr Lightman's argument is as follows: The first defendants are under an obligation, which is derived from an implied term of the contract and from general equitable principles, not to frustrate or put it out of their power to implement the agreement which the first defendants have entered into with the plaintiffs. In support of this proposition, he relies on [197] *Southern Foundries (1926) Ltd v. Shirlaw* [1940] A.C. 701; see, in particular, pp. 716, 717. Secondly, if it is said against the plaintiffs that the undertaking has already been transferred and that it is now too late and nothing can be done about it, that argument is unsound. It is unsound because in such circumstances the subsidiary will be treated by the court as the alter ego of the parent and the plaintiffs can obtain relief in respect of their contract against the parent and its subsidiary or either of them. Aircraft is at present admittedly a wholly owned subsidiary of the first defendants, and, as long as it remains so, the court can and will enforce the agreement against it. In this connection, he relies upon *Jones v. Lipman* [1962] 1 W.L.R. 832 (*ante*, p. 76).

Thirdly, the defendants could only succeed if they could show that the receiver and manager appointed by a debenture holder is in a better position that the company, in that he can legitimately avoid a contractual obligation such as the present. Mr Lightman concedes that the receiver cannot be compelled to perform such a contract, but he contends that the receiver cannot legitimately frustrate the contract by a transfer to a subsidiary such as has been effected here. The onus is on the defendants to show that the receiver is in a better position than the company [the first defendants] and that the defendants can lawfully do what they have done. They have cited no authority which justifies such a contention. On the contrary, *In re Botibol, decd.* [1947] 1 All E.R. 26 is against it, and it may properly be said here that the receiver has, by his actions, rendered himself liable in tort by inducing the first defendants to commit a breach of contract. There is, it is said, a clear distinction between declining to perform a contract, which the receiver is entitled to do, and frustrating the contract by his own act, which he is not entitled to do.

Mr Lindsay, on the other hand, argues that the plaintiffs' contentions are misconceived. First, says Mr Lindsay, this case is entirely different from *Jones v. Lipman*. That was a case of specific performance of a contract to sell land where the first defendant had purported to frustrate the whole transaction by selling the land in question after the date of his contract with the plaintiffs to a company, the second defendant, which he had acquired purely for the purpose in question. The court held the whole transaction was a sham, that a decree of specific performance would be made against the first defendant, and that, as he controlled the second defendant, he was in a position to cause the contract to be completed. Here, says Mr Lindsay, there is no question of a sham transaction and the receiver is doing his best to realise the best price for those of the first defendants' assets which remain and are saleable, a course which is in the best interests of all the creditors, secured and unsecured.

Further, if, as in *Jones v. Lipman*, the contract is of such a nature that specific performance is a normal remedy, a plaintiff could expect to obtain it both against a parent and a subsidiary company, but if, as in the present case, breach of the contract normally only leads to damages – and it is accepted here that the receiver cannot be compelled to perform the contract – then the case of *Jones v. Lipman* cannot have relevance.

[198] Secondly, the defendants say that the plaintiffs are really trying, by their action, to get themselves placed in a preferential position over all other unsecured creditors, of which there are a large number. Yet, when the position is fairly examined, it will be seen that the plaintiffs are in no different position

from any other unsecured creditor, in that they have an ordinary trading contract with the first defendants which the receiver can either adopt or decline. There is no evidence that the option granted by clause 2 of the agreement has been adopted by the plaintiffs and all the plaintiffs stand to receive under that agreement is £500 per aircraft sold. It would not be equitable for the receiver to prefer the plaintiffs to other unsecured creditors, and it is in the best interests of all such creditors that he should be able to sell that part of the first defendants' business which will constitute a viable unit in the way which will secure the highest price. If, in so doing, he does decline to take over the plaintiffs' contract, he may, of course, render the first defendants liable in damages and may also, to some extent, at any rate, damage their reputation as a trustworthy company which can be expected to honour its contracts. This, however, the defendants say, he is entitled to do, so long as the realisation of the net assets of the company [the first defendants] to the best advantage is not impaired. There may be cases where declining to adopt a contract of the company would so seriously impair the goodwill of the company that such realisation would be adversely affected, but that is not the case here. There is no evidence that it would so impair such realisation, nor that it would seriously damage the prospects of the first defendants' trading successfully in the future if they ever do so, and in fact the only goodwill of any real value, namely, that connected with the design, manufacture and prospects of sale of the 'Jetstream', has been transferred to Aircraft. It is not suggested that the first defendants themselves are likely to do any active trading in the future.

Thirdly, it is said that to merit the grant of an injunction, the acts complained of must threaten an invasion of the plaintiffs' legal rights and the relief asked for must relate to those rights. Here, the relief asked for relates to the transfer of shares in Aircraft, and if that be so the plaintiffs must show that they have some legal rights in respect of the shares in question, and no such right has been shown. This argument seems to me to beg the real question the answer to which, in my judgment, determines the issue in this case. The question may be stated as follows: is a receiver and manager, appointed by debenture holders, in a stronger position, from the legal point of view, than the company itself, in respect of contracts between unsecured creditors and the company? Assuming that the company, on the authority of *Southern Foundries (1926) Ltd v. Shirlaw*, cannot put it out of its own power to perform contracts it has entered into, can a receiver in effect do so on its behalf if, at the same time, he has made it clear that he is not going to adopt the contract anyway, and if, as is, in my judgment, the case here, the repudiation of the contract will not adversely affect the realisation of the assets or seriously affect the trading prospects of the company in question, if it is able to trade in the future?

[199] Counsel, when I asked them, were not able to produce any authority which gave a direct answer to this question, but there is a helpful passage dealing generally with 'current contracts' in *Buckley on the Companies Acts,*

13th ed. (1957), p. 244. This passage, to my mind, makes it clear that, in the author's view, the answer to the question I have posed above must be 'yes'. It seems to me that it is common sense that it should be so, since otherwise almost any unsecured creditor would be able to improve his position and prevent the receiver from carrying out, or at any rate carrying out as sensibly and as equitably as possible, the purpose for which he was appointed. I therefore hold that the receiver, within the limitations which I have stated above, is in a better position than the company, qua current contracts, and that, in the present case, the receiver, in doing what he has done and is purporting to do, in connection with the transfer of Aircraft's shares, is not doing anything which the plaintiffs are entitled to prevent by this motion.

In re Ardmore Studios (Ireland) Ltd
[1965] I.R. 1

The net issue was whether a collective agreement that existed between the company and a trade union was binding on the receiver and manager appointed over the company' assets.

McLOUGHLIN J.: . . . [38] (referring to section 316(2) of the 1963 Act) This subsection is similar to section 369(2) of the English Companies Act 1948, as to the effect of which I have been referred to *Palmer's Company Precedents* (16th ed., 1952, Part 3), at p. 19: 'It is usual to provide that the receiver shall be the agent of the company so as to prevent him being held to be the agent of the debenture holders or being personally liable on contracts entered into by him. Section 369 (2), however, now provides that he is to be personally liable to the same extent as if he had been appointed by the Court, on any contract entered into by him in the performance of his functions, "except in so far as the contract otherwise provides."'

Now as of the date of his appointment, the 1st October, 1963, the receiver went into possession of the mortgaged property and took over the management of the business of the Company in exercise of the powers of the lender under the deed of mortgage delegated to him by the deed of appointment, and advertised the mortgaged property for sale.

In the course of the argument I have been referred to many cases as to the effect of the appointment of a receiver for debenture holders but I do not find it necessary to refer to all of them. I obtained most assistance in dealing with this branch of the case from those which I shall now refer to and I shall quote from the reports.

Re B. Johnson & Co. (Builders) [1955] 1 Ch. 634, is not directly in point on the issue whether or not the receiver is bound or not by the alleged seniority list agreement, but many of the views expressed by the distinguished judges who constituted the Court of Appeal in the case are certainly helpful. At page

644 Evershed M.R., after stating some of the powers given to the receiver under the debenture, which are similar to those in this case, continued:

"The situation of someone appointed by a mortgagee or a debenture holder to be a receiver and manager – as it is said, 'out of Court' – is familiar. It has long been recognised and established that receivers and managers so appointed are, by the effect of the statute law, or the terms of the debenture, or both, treated, while in possession of the [39] company's assets and exercising the various powers conferred upon them, as agents of the company, in order that they may be able to deal effectively with third parties. But, in such a case as the present at any rate, it is quite plain that a person appointed as receiver and manager is concerned, not for the benefit of the company but for the benefit of the mortgagee bank, to realise the security; that is the whole purpose of his appointment; and the powers which are conferred upon him, and which I have to some extent recited, are . . . really ancillary to the main purpose of the appointment, which is the realisation by the mortgagee of the security (in this case, as commonly) by the sale of the assets.

All that is perhaps elementary; but it bears upon what I shall have to say as regards the charges made against the receiver; for it appears to me inevitable to negative the proposition that a person appointed, as Mr. Aizlewood was appointed, owes some duty to the company to carry on the business of the company and to preserve its goodwill."

Jenkins L.J., in the course of his judgment, says (for the sake of brevity I begin the quotation in the middle of a paragraph, at p. 661):

". . . whereas a receiver and manager for debenture holders is a person appointed by the debenture holders to whom the company has given powers of management pursuant to the contract of loan constituted by the debenture, and, as a condition of obtaining the loan, to enable him to preserve and realise the assets comprised in the security for the benefit of the debenture holders. The company gets the loan on terms that the lenders shall be entitled, for the purpose of making their security effective, to appoint a receiver with powers of sale and of management pending sale, and with full discretion as to the exercise and mode of exercising those powers. The primary duty of the receiver is to the debenture holders and not to the company."

Finally, Parker L.J., at p. 664, says:

"What, however, in my judgment, is decisive of the case is that any work of management done by a receiver is not done as manager of the company. The powers of management are ancillary to his position as receiver, and, in exercising those powers, he is not acting as manager of the company but as manager of the whole or part of the property of the company."

This case, of course, is not an authority binding on me, but the views expressed in it are very persuasive and deserving of respectful consideration.

Another up-to-date English case, *Robbie & Co. v. Witney Warehouse Co.* [1963] 3 All E.R. 613, is not directly in point, but, in effect, seems to support the contention that a receiver appointed by [40] debenture holders is not bound by a contract made by the company before his appointment.

During the course of the argument I was referred to many other English cases – no Irish cases were cited to me on this branch of the case – but I did not get much assistance from them, many of them being liquidation and winding up cases and cases where the receiver was appointed by the Court and subject to control as an officer of the Court.

The defendants' argument put most reliance on the clause in the debenture deed that the receiver is made the agent of the Company, but it should be pointed out that this does not make him the servant of the Company; the same clause – number 14 (c) of the debenture deed – also provides that the receiver shall in the exercise of the powers authorities and discretions conform to the directions from time to time given by the debenture holder. As agent for the Company, the Company is made fully responsible for his acts, but it is not a corollary to this that he is bound by all Company contracts and agreements entered into by the Company before the date of his appointment.

The mortgaged property of which the receiver entered into possession as defined by the deed includes also the property charged and assigned, i.e., all the undertaking and assets, machinery, book debts and goodwill; the argument of the defendants amounts to this: that he also took over, by operation of law, the obligations of the Company under the alleged agreement by the Company to employ the Union's electricians on the production of films in the studio. In as much as I find that it was the Union's insistence on this agreement that gave rise to the circumstances leading to the debenture holders putting in a receiver over all the Company's property and assets, this would seem to lead to an absurdity.

I have no hesitation in holding that there is no legal basis for their contention that the agreement as to the seniority list, even if it existed as an agreement on the date of the appointment of the receiver, became binding on him.

Index

(headings refer to subject headings in the chapters)